T0293677

Private Capital

Private Capital

The Complete Guide to Private Markets Investing

Stefan W. Hepp

WILEY

Registered Office(s)
John Wiley & Sons Ltd, The Atrium, Southern Gate, Chichester, West Sussex, PO19 8SQ, UK

John Wiley & Sons, Inc., 111 River Street, Hoboken, NJ 07030, USA

Editorial Office
The Atrium, Southern Gate, Chichester, West Sussex, PO19 8SQ, UK

For details of our global editorial offices, customer services, and more information about Wiley products visit us at www.wiley.com.

Library of Congress Cataloging-in-Publication Data is Available:
ISBN 9781394217694 (Cloth)
ISBN 9781394217700 (ePDF)
ISBN 9781394217717 (ePUB)

Cover Design: Wiley
Cover Image: © Digital Art/Getty Images
Author Photo: © ChicagoBooth Review/Josh Stunkel

Set in 11/14 AvenirLTStd by Straive, Chennai, India
SKY10063541_122923

In memory of
Dr. theol. Frank Jehle.

Contents

Abbreviations   *ix*

        Introduction   1

Part I   **The Beginning**   **9**

Chapter 1 Funding Private Enterprise   11

Chapter 2 Enterprise Financing in the USA from WWII
          to the 1960s   67

Chapter 3 How Silicon Valley Came to Be   77

Chapter 4 US Private Equity During the 1960s and 1970s   111

Part II   **Booms and Busts**   **157**

Chapter 5 Private Equity During the 1980s   159

Chapter 6 The 1990s: Dotcom Boom and Bust   193

Chapter 7 A Private Markets Boom Between Two Crises   261

Part III   **Becoming Indispensable**   **355**

Chapter 8   The GFC and the Surge of Private Markets   357

Chapter 9   Responding to Shifting Dynamics:
Intermediaries, VC, and Growth Financing   435

Chapter 10   Buyouts, Private Debt, and Real Assets
During the Post-GFC Boom   517

References   607

Acknowledgments   671

About the Author   675

Index   677

Abbreviations

AC alternating current

ACRS accelerated cost recovery system

AGM annual general meeting

AI artificial intelligence

AM arithmetic mean

ARD American Research & Development Corporation

APRR Autoroutes Paris-Rhine-Rhône

ARPA Advanced Research Projects Agency

AuM assets under management

BA British Airways

BATS Baidu, Alibaba, and Tencent

BREP Blackstone Real Estate Partners

BRIC Brazil, Russia, India, and China

BTS Bureau of Transportation Statistics

CAD computer-aided design

CalPERS California Public Employees Retirement System

CAPA Centre for Aviation

CAPAM Capital Asset Pricing Model

CDLI Cliffwater Direct Lending Index

CDO collateralized debt obligation

CFA chartered financial accountant

CLO collateralized loan obligation

CMBS commercial mortgage-backed security

CPI consumer price inflation

CPPIB Canada Pension Plan Investment Board

CPU central processing unit

CRV Charles River Ventures

CSRC China Securities Regulatory Commission

DARPA Defense Advanced Research Projects Agency

DC direct current

DC defined contribution

DDR&D Directorate of Defense Research & Development

DEC Digital Equipment Corporation

DPI distributions to paid-in

DST Digital Sky Technologies

E&P exploration and development

EBIT earnings before interest and taxes

EBITDA earnings before interest and taxes, depreciation, and amortization

ECB European Central Bank

EDA electronic design automation

EFH Energy Futures Holdings

EFSF European Financial Stability Facility

EIA (US) Energy Information Agency

EIB European Investment Bank

EIOPA European Insurance and Occupational Pensions Authority

EOP Equity Office Properties

EPS earnings per share

ERISA Employee Retirement Income Security Act

ERTA Economic Recovery Tax Act

ESG environment, social, and governance

ESM European Stability Mechanism

ETF exchange-traded fund

EU European Union

FAANG Facebook, Amazon, Apple, Netflix, and Google

FCFE free cash flow to equity

FDIC Federal Deposit Insurance Corporation

FED Federal Reserve Board

FIRREA Financial Institutions Reform, Recovery, and Enforcement Act

FoFs fund of funds

FOMC Federal Open Market Committee

FSLIC Federal Savings and Loan Insurance Corporation

FTC Federal Trade Commission

GAAP generally accepted accounting principles

GDP gross domestic product

GE General Electric

GenAI generative AI

GFC Global Financial Crisis (2008)

GP general partner

HCC Homebrew Computer Club

HNI high-net-worth individual

IASB International Accounting Standards Board

IC integrated circuit

ICT information and communication technology

IFSWF International Forum of Sovereign Wealth Funds

ILPA Institutional Limited Partner Association

IMF International Monetary Fund

I/O input/output

IPO initial public offering

IRR internal rate of return

IS infrastructure

ISSB International Sustainability Standards Board

ITT International Telephone and Telegraph Company

ITU International Telecommunication Union

KfW Kreditanstalt für Wiederaufbau

KKR Kohlberg Kravis Roberts

KP Kleiner Perkins

KPCB Kleiner Perkins Caufield & Byers

KYC know your client

LBO leveraged buyout

LCOE levelized cost of electricity

LCY London City Airport

LLC limited liability company

LLM large language model

LNG liquified natural gas

LP limited partner

LPA limited partnership agreement

LPE listed private equity

LTV loan-to-value

M&A mergers and acquisitions

MAC material-adverse-change

MBI management buy-in

MBO management buyout

MBS mortgage-backed securities

MENA Middle East and North Africa

MIT Massachusetts Institute of Technology

MOIC multiple on invested capital

MOSFETs metal-oxide-semiconductor field-effect transistors

MSCI Morgan Stanley Capital International

MSREF Morgan Stanley Real Estate Fund

NASA National Aeronautics and Space Administration

NASDAQ National Association of Securities Dealers Automated
   Quotations

NAV net asset value

NBC National Broadcasting Corporation

NBER National Bureau of Economic Research

NLP natural language processing

NR natural resources

NRDC National Resources Defense Council

NVCA National Venture Capital Association

NYMEX New York Mercantile Exchange

NYSE New York Stock Exchange

OCS Offices of the Chief Scientist

OMERS Ontario Municipal Employees Retirement System

ONR Office of Naval Research

OS operating system

OSRD Office of Scientific Research and Development

OTPP Ontario Teachers' Pension Plan

PC personal computer

PCG Pacific Corporate Group

PD private debt

PE private equity

P/E price earnings ratio

PIK payment in kind

PME Public Market Equivalent

PPF private pension funds

PRI Principles of Responsible Investing

PRISA Prudential Property Investment Separate Account

QIA Qatar Investment Authority

QIC Queensland Investment Corporation

R&D research and development

RCA Radio Corporation of America

REIT real estate investment trust

RePowerEU European program to reduce CO_2 emissions

RMB renminbi

ROI return on investment

S&L savings and loans

SaaS software as a service

SAFE State Administration of Foreign Exchange

SAMR State Administration for Market Regulation

SASB Sustainability Accounting Standards Board

SBDA Small Business Investment Act

SBIC small business investment company

SDS Scientific Data Systems

SEC Securities and Exchange Commission

SFA (Japanese) Financial Services Agency

SFDR (EU) Sustainable Finance Disclosure Regulation

SIFI systemically important financial institution

SMA separate managed account

SMI Semiconductor Manufacturing International

SOEs state-owned enterprises

SOFR secured overnight financing rate

SOX Sarbanes-Oxley Act

SPAC special purpose acquisition company

SPC State Planning Commission

SPV special purpose vehicle

STAR segment of the Shanghai Stock Exchange for tech stocks

SWFs sovereign wealth funds

TCJA Tax Cuts and Jobs Act

TPG Texas Pacific Group

TRA United States Tax Reform Act

TVPI total value to paid-in

TXU Energy Future Holdings Corporation

UN PRI/UNRIP UN Principles of Responsible Investment

USPTO United States Patent and Trademark Office

VC venture capital/venture capitalist

VPN virtual private network

WACC weighted average cost of capital

WaMu Washington Mutual Insurance Company

WTI West Texas Intermediate

WTO World Trade Organization

WWI World War I

WWII World War II

Introduction

You can't really understand what is going on now unless you understand what came before.

—*Steve Jobs*[1]

Throughout history, private capital has been crucial for funding ventures, infrastructure, and risky endeavors. While stock markets gained in significance, they did not replace direct private investments. *Private Capital* takes readers on a journey exploring the drivers of capital accumulation, the interplay between private and public investing in entrepreneurial endeavours that enabled the rise of Western economies and shaped modern capitalism. Drawing from the author's three decades of investment experience in private markets, the book investigates how investors' approaches to this asset class have evolved. It also delves into how the institutionalization of financial capital, involving the separation of ownership and management of financial resources, has shaped the private markets industry.

Moreover, the book integrates new findings from a wide range of scholarly studies on the evolution of capital markets and entrepreneurial finance. These findings provide a foundation for the narrative that charts the advancement of modern private market investment from a niche sector to a large financial industry dominated by mega-firms with assets worth hundreds of billions of dollars.

---

[1] Intel (2012).

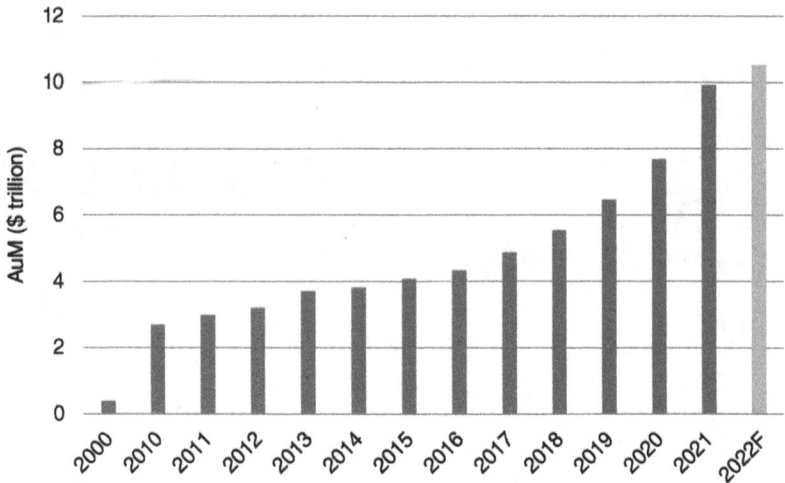

Figure 0.1 Private markets' alternative assets under management and forecast, 2010–2022.
Source: Preqin data platform, Sept. 2021.
Note: 2021 is annualized, 2022 are Preqin's forecast figures.

Private market investing increased 25-fold over the new millennium, surpassing $10 trillion in assets under management (AuM) in 2021 (Figure 0.1).[2] This book aims to tell the story of this distinct form of investing. Its intended audience includes investment professionals, investors, and students who are exploring this asset class, presented in a format that offers ease of understanding and includes technical explanations where they add value.

Private equity is the most widely recognized type of private market investment and its influence is far-reaching. The media often covers transactions carried out by buyout firms or venture capitalists. Private equity investments involve providing capital to startups or mature enterprises that require funding for growth or improvement, with the ultimate goal of exiting and generating profits after a few years. According to an American Investment Council (2021) study,[3] private equity-owned firms employed 11.7 million Americans in 2020 and generated approximately 6.5% of total GDP. The "big tech" successes in Silicon Valley have a significant

---

[2] Preqin estimate as of September 2022.
[3] American Investment Council (2021).

impact on our daily lives. Companies such as Facebook, Apple, Alphabet, Amazon, and others have transformed the way we interact with technology. Private equity's investments extend beyond technology to include sectors such as healthcare, media, aerospace, satellites, and telecommunications, among others. While private equity's growth has increased its public profile, it has also created controversy and found detractors.

Private markets encompass more than just buyouts and venture capital. For example, an infrastructure fund may own a local toll road or airport, while a natural resource manager's investment may be your energy supplier. Your landlord may be a private real estate fund, and your life insurance premium could be funding private debt. Private markets have expanded over time to include investment strategies, such as growth equity, real estate, credit, infrastructure, natural resources, and, more recently, impact and environmental, social, and governance (ESG) investments. Despite the broad range of investment strategies that comprise private market investing, most of the literature on the subject is focused on private equity. This book intends to fill the void by offering an objective perspective as the first compendium that provides an in-depth overview of the full spectrum of private markets investing. Following a chronological timeline to chart the history of private capital investing (Figure 0.2), the growth and complexity of the private markets' asset class are explored.

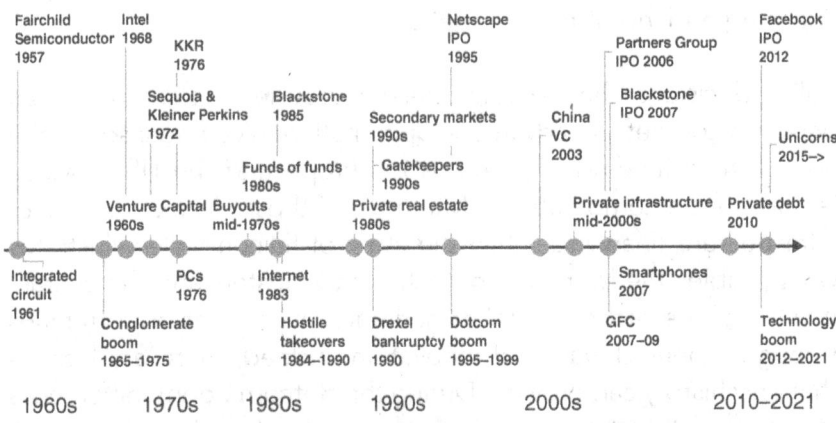

Figure 0.2   A timeline of the evolution of the private markets industry.

This book will focus on the industry as a whole and the reasons behind its emergence in its current form. It consciously avoids focusing on the colorful personalities and personal histories of founders and deal-makers, which often attract media attention. The private market industry's evolution has not occurred in isolation; it has been influenced by economic, legal, and regulatory shifts, alongside the increasing institutionalization of capital markets since World War II. The requirement of substantial minimum subscriptions, often exceeding $10 million, underscores that this is not an asset class tailored for small-scale investors but primarily aimed at large institutional investors.

To invest in the asset class, one needs to understand the economic and legal developments that provided opportunities for deal-making and value creation during different cycles. An in-depth analysis of the development of different types of private markets investments provides valuable insights into the conceptual issues faced by investors in this asset class.

The broader economic perspective of this book serves to explain why a kind of investment centered on the temporary ownership of companies and other assets, the prominent use of leverage, and the alignment of managerial incentives continue to prosper while being criticized by many detractors as obsolete or broken. Taking a historical perspective underscores the dynamics propelling innovation and organizational transformation. The analysis is focused on the structural and institutional changes that introduced new financing and investment models.

Policy decisions that enable these investments to flourish can bestow a competitive advantage upon nations. A comparison of the approach to funding of railroads in Europe and the US provides lessons of the comparative advantages of those distinct models of infrastructure financing, while the story of Silicon Valley illustrates what enables the formation of technology clusters and the characteristics of the technology that generate investment opportunities through repeated waves of innovation. Indeed, there are lessons that only history can provide. During the dotcom boom, differences in investment patterns go a long way to explain the relative lack of success of the European venture capital industry compared to their US peers. A closer look at the factors that enable a successful venture ecosystem also helps to understand the direction venture capital in China is taking and what its "state-guided" model means for investors.

Knowledge of the asset class is vital for professionals who work in the financial sector, regardless of whether they work for traditional investors in the asset class, such as pension funds, endowments, or sovereign wealth funds, or are banks and asset managers who are increasingly adding private markets to their investment offerings. It is also required by the large number of investment professionals that private markets managers employ globally and the many business school graduates who—for years—made firms specializing in private market investments their most sought-after employers.

The book also addresses the need to better understand the role of different types of intermediaries in private markets. By providing a comprehensive guide to service providers and their respective roles, as well as describing the different access routes used by investors to gain exposure, the book is a valuable resource for professionals in the field.

Investors need to understand the different risk/return profiles of private market investment strategies. Frequently, asset classes are categorized based on similar risk/return characteristics. This is not the case for private markets. The risk-reward profile of venture capital is significantly different from infrastructure or private debt. One must inquire about the typical characteristics of the asset class and ask whether a venture capital and buyouts-based investment model has been successfully applied to those asset types. To answer these questions, it is necessary to examine the industry's track record and deal-making in greater detail.

The book reviews the empirical evidence of the private market industry's track record by using a wealth of data that is typically not publicly accessible. Indeed, one of the challenges in writing this book was ensuring that the data used throughout was reasonably consistent. There is no single accredited data source equivalent to stock market indices or official fund performance data. Instead, what passes as industry data is collected by a multitude of providers using diverse data sources. In recent years, the availability of better private market data has significantly contributed to our understanding of this asset class's characteristics. This book high-lights academic research and quantitative studies that have been instrumental. Notably, deal-level data has not only improved our understanding of successful strategies in private market investing but has also provided fresh insights into the concept of diversifica-tion and portfolio construction.

Readers will gain an understanding of the challenges that must be addressed to make private markets investing accessible to individ-ual investors. But the lessons learned from studying the facts relat-ing to private markets investing are equally important for financial practitioners who seek to emulate large institutional investors in their efforts to make private markets investing available to indi-vidual investors.

These insights are combined with a practitioner's view and the experience gained over many years of investing in the asset class that provides context and highlights relevant lessons for those investing in the asset class or dealing with private market firms.

THE STRUCTURE OF THE BOOK

Part I, The Beginning, describes the early forms of funding avail-able for commercial endeavors and the formation of the modern corporation. What follows is a description of the motivation behind attempts to raise venture capital from institutional investors after WWII and the reasons why limited partnerships became the domi-nant investment vehicle for private equity. Then we take a closer look at the role of the silicon microchip in ushering in the digital revolution that transformed our lives and the interplay between technology, government, academic institutions, and venture capi-tal to create the technology cluster that became known as Silicon Valley. Understanding these drivers helps investors to gauge the opportunity set that technology offers before and after it is com-moditized and when venture capital has most of its impact.

Part II, Booms and Busts, describes the emergence of buyout firms and why buyouts differ from other merger and acquisition

(M&A) strategies. We explore the conglomerate boom that led to hostile takeovers and the beginning of private market globalization in the 1980s. The hostile takeovers of the 1980s, the telecom and dotcom boom and bust of the 1990s, and their impact on investors and the private markets industry are all discussed. Subsequently, the book delves into the industry's evolution and its performance history throughout the initial decade of the new millennium, ultimately culminating in the Great Financial Crisis (GFC).

Part III, Becoming Indispensable, traces the growth of private markets since the Great Financial Crisis (GFC) and its emergence as a core institutional asset class across a wide range of strategies. The rise of infrastructure or private debt strategies, the emergence of mega-firms doing mega-deals, and the industry's response to the GFC are vital topics. The new millennium's second decade witnessed unprecedented growth and profound structural change. Late-stage venture deals and the unicorn phenomenon—startups worth $1 billion or more—increasing institutional direct investments, non-traditional investors, special purpose acquisition companies (SPACs), semi-liquid and permanent capital structures are all manifestations of that transformation.

Additionally, the book explores contemporary shifts that have redefined the landscape of the private markets. As it progresses, it examines the terminology, distinct legal and economic aspects, and the analytical concepts that define the asset class and are essential knowledge for anybody who works or invests in that space. By examining the characteristics of diverse entities, such as major pension funds and sovereign wealth funds, the book demonstrates how the private market industry has been shaped by major providers of capital—large institutions, which now play dual roles as both clients and competitors. Understanding this symbiotic relationship is crucial for anticipating the future evolution of the private markets industry.

PART I

The Beginning

Chapter 1

Funding Private Enterprise

Obtaining financing for dangerous endeavors has always been tricky. Then and now, it required refusing to accept no for an answer. Vasco Da Gama's successful voyage to India in 1497–1498 began a new era of maritime trade and exploration, but it was met at first with rejection from Portuguese King John II in 1495 due to concerns about the expedition's feasibility and cost. It was not until 1497, after King Manuel I ascended to the throne, that da Gama finally received the necessary funding and resources for his voyage.

Christopher Columbus, an Italian, lobbied European rulers for nearly a decade to find funding for his mission to seek a western sea passage to Asia. In Portugal, England, and France, the answer was "No." Finally, King Ferdinand and Queen Isabella of Spain consented to support him, allowing him to set sail in 1492.

Ferdinand Magellan was rebuffed in his native Portugal before finding support for his proposed expedition to find a western

Figure 1.1 Portuguese explorer Ferdinand Magellan's fleet of five ships—the *San Antonio*, the *Trinidad*, the *Concepción*, the *Nao Victoria*, and the *Santiago*—after their departure from Spain on September 20, 1519.
Source: Science History Images/Alamy Stock Photo.

route to the Moluccas (Spice Islands) from King Charles I of Spain, and his fleet departed Spain in 1516 (Figure 1.1).

In addition to their shared goal of discovering a sea route to Asia, the Portuguese and the Spanish were driven by a strong desire to obtain gold. However, their paths to success diverged significantly. The Spanish achieved their objectives primarily by looting native gold artifacts in the New World and later through gold and silver mining. Unlike the Spanish experience in the Americas, where the conquest of empires like the Aztecs and Incas led to the extraction of vast amounts of precious metals, Africa's west coast did not possess similar wealth regarding precious metals. This made it less enticing for outright conquest. Portugal also lacked the manpower and resources for large-scale conquests on the scale seen in the Americas. The Portuguese pursued a trade-based approach, engaging with African merchants to acquire these valuable commodities. Ship captains assumed a crucial role as business agents, transcending their traditional role as mere transportation providers. They exercised agency in determining the most advantageous locations and prices for exchanging goods for gold. Furthermore, ship captains allocated a portion of their cargo to cover expenses related to supplies and ship repairs, ensuring the smooth progression of their trade ventures.

1.1 FUNDING MARITIME VENTURES

The voyages of Vasco Da Gama, Christopher Columbus, and Ferdinand Magellan marked the beginning of an important trans-formation, noted by some scholars as the beginning of the Great Divergence—the growing gap in economic performance between Europe and other parts of the world after Columbus's discovery of the New World.[1] The significance of their journeys, however, did not become apparent until much later, which is a perfect example of Denis Gabor's dictum that "the future cannot be predicted, it can only be discovered."[2]

Sea journeys are risky, as ships can get lost at sea or raided by pirates, and cargo can perish or get diverted by the crew. In addition, maritime trade is capital-intensive as the ship and the cargo must be paid for in advance. Long-distance trading was an arbitrage based on the price disparity between two distant market-places. Demand and supply were ignorant of each other and brought into touch by intermediaries who knew little about the worth of a shipment to a buyer. An understanding of how those voyages were financed is thus of critical importance for understanding the evolution of risky enterprises' financing.

The earliest overseas mercantile ventures emanating from Spain and Portugal drew on Mediterranean precedents established by Italian city-states. There, merchants sent their ships out onto the Adriatic, the Black Sea, and the eastern Mediterranean with the hope of

---

[1] The Great Divergence is a term coined by the late American political scientist Samuel P. Huntington. Many scholars attribute it to the technology-led industriali-zation from the late eighteenth century onwards. Acemoglu et al. (2005) provide compelling data that suggest that this process started much earlier than is often assumed. This has important implications for our understanding of capital formation and the financing of industrial enterprises after the mid-eighteenth century.
[2] Denis Gabor won the Nobel Prize for Physics in 1971, and the quote is taken from his book, *Inventing the Future* (Gabor, 1964).

accessing established markets in the Levant and further east. The earliest instrument used for funding maritime trade, the "sea loan," secured capital for seafaring commercial voyages through advances of goods or credit to purchase the cargo from producers and local merchants, who would be reimbursed with interest at the close of the expedition.[3] This form of financing required, however, that there was sufficient certainty about the terms of exchange for the goods carried and an acceptance of the risk of loss by the creditors, which makes the arrangement unsuitable for the exploration of new markets.

By the twelfth century, this practice was eclipsed by the Commenda, a medieval form of partnership that opened early transoceanic trading opportunities to a diverse group of traders, colonists, and mariners, creating a decentralized mercantile trade that diffused profits among many stakeholders.[4] The Commenda distinguished between "stationary" partners who remained in port and "traveling" (managing) partners who organized the voyage. Both parties would contribute to the cargo by supplying goods or sometimes finance. Because the traveling partner did not assume liability for the home port-based partner's capital in case of accident or other forms of loss, the arrangement was premised on the stationary party's contributing equity to a particular voyage organized by a traveling partner.[5] After the voyage's completion, the profits were split, with 25% of the profit attributable to the stationary party's goods going to the traveling party, i.e., shipowner, captain, and crew. Such partnerships could include multiple investors who owned different types of cargo or even fractions thereof. The fractional ownership further enabled individuals to invest small amounts in a single commercial expedition. Beyond the Italian city-states of Venice, Genoa, and Pisa, the Commenda contract became central to long-distance overland and seaborne trades.[6] The practice of offering captain and crew a commission as an incentive to act in the best interest of their investors became a feature of maritime trade that survived the ages: Nantucket whalers,

---

[3] The sea loan originated in ancient Rome (Constable, 1994).
[4] For instance, Genovese merchants labeled this commercial mechanism *societas marls*, while their Venetian counterparts branded it *colleganza*, and the practice perhaps originated with the Islamic qiriid contract used by Arabian caravan traders (Hicks, 2017).
[5] Harris (2009).
[6] Hicks (2017).

for example, could keep up to 20% of the cargo. According to some sources, this is where the term "carried interest" comes from.[7]

1.2   PRIVATE CAPITAL AND THE SUGAR BOOM

The Portuguese crown used an arrangement similar to the Commenda for its African trade. From the fifteenth century until the end of the sixteenth century, the Portuguese were the only Europeans trading on the Gold Coast (present-day Ghana) along the Gulf of Guinea. There they obtained gold, ivory, and a commodity which would consistently gain in importance—African slaves—after sugar production started in São Tomé. The slave trade saw rapid growth once Brazil eclipsed São Tomé, becoming the foremost sugar producer in the early seventeenth century. What was termed the "slave plantation complex"[8] fed a sugar boom that lasted well into the nineteenth century and was controlled by Portugal for almost 150 years.

The importance of sugar cannot be understated. H. W. French (2021) estimated that Brazil's sugar crop accounted for 40% of Portugal's total revenue in 1620. In 1660, Barbados's sugar production was worth more than the combined exports of all of Spain's New World colonies. The sugar produced in Saint-Domingue, a French colony in modern-day Haiti, accounted for 15% of the overall French economic growth during 1716–1787.[9] By some estimates, sugar was the most important overseas commodity that accounted for a third of Europe's entire economy during the sixteenth to the eighteenth centuries.[10] Maritime trade was the critical element that tied commerce between Europe, Africa, and the sugar-growing colonies in a transatlantic pattern that became famous as the triangular trade.[11]

---

[7] Nicholas and Akins (2012).
[8] The term is used by Burnard (2017), who describes the development of large scale British colonial sugar, rice, and tobacco plantations. The slave trade enabled the sugar plantation economy. It propelled the massive, forced transportation of millions of captive Africans to the Americas after the center of sugar production shifted to Brazil and later to the Caribbean.
[9] French (2021).
[10] Whipps (2008).
[11] Phyllis (1995).

Recent research illustrates the link between maritime trade and capital formation. Mary E. Hicks of the University of Chicago records an episode that sheds some light on the financing arrangements of the seaborne trade during the eighteenth century:

> In 1767, the slaving vessel Nossa Senhora left Salvador da Bahia bound for the West African coast and was sized by Dutch pirates. The owner sought restitution from the Dutch government, revealing that the cargo belonged to 35 investors including two Catholic brotherhoods.[12]

The ship's numerous investors illustrate the existence of economic arrangements that constituted an early form of private equity that provided opportunities for many, and access to investment opportunities was thus different from the highly concentrated land ownership of the nobility that characterized feudal societies.

The sugar boom also increased intra-European trade as the northern Europeans sold the Portuguese the goods in demand in Africa. The wealth created in the plantation economies, which were largely monocultures, increased the demand for traded goods, which led to an expansion in manufacturing in Northern Europe. In the seventeenth century, the sugar-growing Caribbean islands would become important export markets for Britain's American colonies, too, providing food, horses, timber, and other natural resources.

The quest to control the sugar trade also increased competition among a broadening array of European powers.[13] New actors that challenged the Portuguese arrived in the sixteenth century when the Dutch increasingly took over Portuguese possessions. Still, they, in turn, faced competition almost from the outset from a rising England and later France. In their attempts to gain control of the transatlantic trade, the Dutch and the English eschewed royal monopolies—probably a reflection of their parliamentary systems, which gave opponents of royal monopolies lobbying powers to ensure the business opportunity was more widely available. Furthermore, the latecomers challenged Portugal's monopoly by

---

[12] Hicks (2017).
[13] The description of the importance and impact of the sugar trade is based on French (2021).

encroaching on what the Portuguese crown deemed its sphere of influence, often leading to armed conflicts. Outsourcing this task to a private company provided deniability for the Dutch and English governments, as it could have been perceived as an act of war if their navies were directly involved. From the sixteenth century onwards, chartered trade companies received concessions to exploit trading opportunities in specific regions and raised risk capital from a broader public. Chartered companies derived the principles of their organization from the medieval merchant guilds. An early example is the Company of Merchant Adventurers of London, founded in 1407. It was a corporation of merchants, each of whom traded on his own account and was personally liable. There was no pooling of capital.

The Muscovy Company, founded in London in 1553, to trade with Russia, is regarded by some sources to be the first European company to issue equity-type participations in the sixteenth century. It lasted until 1917.[14]

French economist Thomas Piketty observed that the share of financial wealth (including businesses and other resources) in total wealth (including additionally housing and land) increased steadily and roughly doubled overall in Britain between 1700 and 1850. The trend in France was similar. This period coincides with those countries' control of the sugar trade as well as the unfolding First Industrial Revolution. One can assume that this part of national wealth was much wider spread than the ownership of land and housing, increasing the number of potential investors and thus allowing those countries to finance more significant undertakings.[15] As ownership of financial capital expanded beyond the traditional aristocracy, a financing approach that could reach a wider audience of potential investors was required.

As the French historian Fernand Braudel shows, it was mainly merchants, who coordinated trade, who formed financial capital, not producers. Evidence from plantation economies in South America and the West Indies reveals that Portugal (and later France for

---

[14] Morgan and Thomas (1971).
[15] Piketty (2014).

Saint-Domingue, modern-day Haiti, and England for Barbados) provided loans for sugar mills (equipment), which would not have been necessary if producers had maintained a large financial surplus on their production.[16]

1.3 THE JOINT-STOCK CORPORATION

The Dutch East India Company (VOC) (1602–1733) was granted a 21-year monopoly of trade with Asia. It is sometimes considered the first multinational corporation in the world (Figure 1.2). The VOC pioneered features that later became textbook characteristics of modern corporations: permanent capital, legal personhood, separation of ownership and management, limited liability for shareholders and directors, and tradable shares. Those features were not the result of some enlightened corporate design

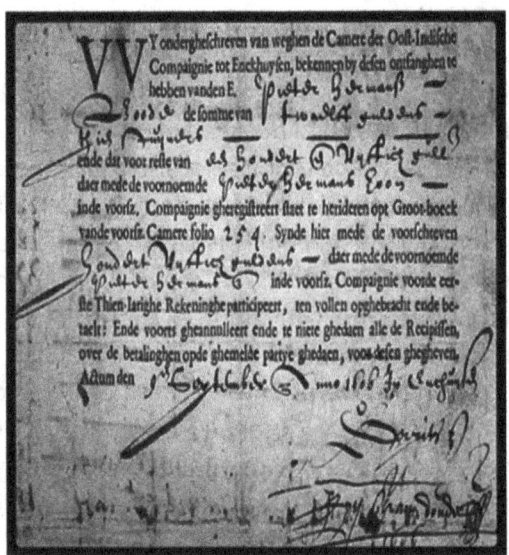

Figure 1.2   Stock certificate of the Dutch East India Company (VOC), issued in 1606.
Source: Exploring Markets / Flickr / Public Domain.

---

[16] Braudel (1992). While some sugar plantation pioneers got wealthy, they seemed to have mostly re-invested in the expansion of their sugar plantations and not provided financial capital for other ventures. For example, Sir James Drax (c. 1609–1662), an English planter in Barbados invested his profits in more slaves and land to expand his plantations, while the sugar mills were financed with loans from London. (French, 2021).

fit for establishing a multinational trading business or reflecting early corporate law that provided a generally accepted framework. Instead, it reflected tinkering by the VOC directors to amend the company charter to address issues as they arose. Over time, it became clear that the VOC required permanent capital to finance infrastructure (harbors, fortifications, warehouses, shipyards, etc.).

The financing needs of a trading corporation were thus different from the single voyage financing model established for maritime trade. As Gelderbom, de Jong, and Jonker (2013) show, the directors remedied the flaws of the initial set-up of the VOC in a process of piecemeal engineering, creating both stopgaps and more lasting solutions which by the early 1620s had hardened into the corporate form we know today. Therefore, that emergent form of a joint-stock corporation owed more to a sequence of actions to relieve the friction between the company's governance, specific operational demands, and the available finance options than to the logic of any legal system or specific regulations that provided a framework for such corporate activities.[17] Other trading companies, such as the British East India Company, could draw on that experience. While it is often claimed that the British East India Company was the first to issue stock, the company conducted separate voyages, separately subscribed until 1612, and used temporary joint stocks until 1657, when the company raised permanent common equity.[18]

Some of those joint-stock companies were chartered and thus provided limited liability,[19] while others were incorporated without a charter. Historical records suggest that new share offerings were often oversubscribed, trading volumes were significant, despite the lack of rules and organized trading. Stock trades were isolated bilateral agreements between buyer and seller. Despite these imperfections, investing in stock appeared to be increasingly popular, and shareholders numerous. The British East India Company, for example, had about 500 investors in 1688, increasing to more

---

[17] Gelderbom, de Jong, and Jonker (2013).
[18] *Encyclopaedia Britannica* (2023a).
[19] A chartered company is an association with investors or shareholders that is incorporated and granted rights (often exclusive rights) by royal charter (or similar instrument of government) and the charter could provide for limited liability of directors and stockholders.

than 1,000 investors in 1692.[20] Those observations support the view that investable capital was abundant, risk capital for new ventures was available, and participation in stock investing increased over time. For investors, a key attraction of investing in the shares of these trading companies appeared to have been high dividends that provided a steady source of revenue in the absence of a market for longer-term government or corporate debt. The East India Company paid dividends of 25% and the Royal Africa Company paid 10.5% during that period.[21]

The English "Patent Boom," 1692–1695: The First Tech IPO Bubble

In a study of joint-stock investments during the seventeenth century, British historian K. G. Davies observes that many joint-stock companies focused on trading opportunities or patents. Between 1689 and 1695, the number of joint-stock companies in England increased from 11 to about a hundred, almost entirely focused on domestic ventures that aimed to exploit new inventions rather than overseas trade.[22] It was also the period when "stock jobbers," professional intermediaries who would buy and sell securities and act as market makers, emerged.[23] Estimates put the total number of investors at the time at 4,000–5,000, a number that would decline significantly after the end of the boom. Despite the significant increase in the number of joint-stock companies after 1692, trading still was heavily concentrated in about eight companies, which formed the core of the stock market in the early 1690s.[24]

Patents were yet to be established as the regular or standard recourse for inventors at the time. Would-be patentees were likely to be discouraged by the investment of time and money, so many inventions were never patented. Some industries were less likely than others to value patenting because patentees faced opposition from vested interests. Powerful guilds supervised the practice of their craft/trade in a specific territory, limiting both competition and the scope for inventions. Because a patent was similar to a business license to operate

---

[20] Davies (1952), Murphy (2009).
[21] Murphy (2009).
[22] Davies (1952).
[23] Murphy (2009).
[24] Ibid.

outside the purview of guilds, it was more likely to be granted for an innovation pertaining to a trade, manufacturing, or business that was not governed by guilds. Since patent applications often lacked detail and there was no systematic record of existing patents, the government had considerable leeway to open businesses to competition.

Given this context, the increase in patenting in the early 1700s was not due to an innovation boom but rather to the Crown's growing demand for military supplies because of the Nine Years' War (1688–1697) between France and the European coalition that included England. War also erected a protective wall around several English sectors by prohibiting French imports and obstructing external commerce, limiting international trade investments. In 1693–1695, inventions with immediate significance to the army and navy accounted for one-fifth of all patents. Military demand substantially increased prices and generated what appeared to be a stable market for all types of technologies that promised to cater to the needs of the military. Another stimulus to enterprise was deregulation in the form of the legislation of 1689 and 1693 that withdrew the Crown's claims to mines of base ores which contained any silver or gold, thereby removing the control exercised by the Mines Royal and the Mineral and Battery Work companies.[25]

An abundance of capital fostered a speculative frenzy, and entrepreneurs recognized the publicity value of a patent, feeding on the misperception that a patent was a form of royal guarantee or at least a validation of a project.[26] But contemporary observers noted that the plausible business case of many enterprises was a secondary concern to the potential gains from a rise in share prices for many who joined the ranks of share owners.[27]

[25] Heton (1707). *Some Account of Mines, and the Advantages of them to This Kingdom*, preface, and pp. 18–21, 33–35, cited in Macleod (1986).
[26] Macleod (1986).
[27] Murphy (2009). The Patent Boom likely commenced in 1697 when William Phips (1651-1695), an American colonialist who had successfully raised capital for numerous wreck-diving expeditions, returned to England with a substantial hoard of silver, resulting in a remarkable profit for his investors. This event sparked the funding of several companies based on patents associated with new diving apparatuses. (New England Historical Society, 2014). However, this initial wave was soon eclipsed by the impact of the Nine Years' War (1689–1697) that began in 1689. The focus shifted to patents related to innovations in metallurgy, armament, and mining, crucial to the war effort and benefiting from the increased procurement needs of the British Navy.

This was an early example of a bubble involving companies that were floated on the basis of ideas rather than an established business and the bubble in patent stocks provided an opportunity for promoters eager to adopt any plausible-sounding scheme or exploit any plausible-looking idea.[28] When the bubble burst, many investors lost their money. The famous author Daniel Defoe—known to modern audiences for such novels as *Robinson Crusoe*—was forced into bankruptcy and later said: "I could give a very diverting history of a patent-monger, whose cully [i.e., dupe] was nobody but myself."[29] But the ready availability of risk capital was also credited to advancing the English copper, brass, glass-making, and paper production industries. Even Defoe stated that these frauds were "no reason why invention upon honest foundations, and to a fair purpose, should not be encouraged."[30] From mid-1697 to late 1700, there were few new joint-stock companies as disillusionment with projects and patents set in. Even well-managed and technically competent companies suffered from the general loss of confidence.[31]

Thus, the mid-1690s London stock market boom was a response to a war economy and the chance to explore sectors outside of the guild system through new inventions and patent-based companies. War reduced trade-related investment opportunities, making equity and debt financing abundant. The lack of such conventional investment opportunities facilitated the funding of increasingly implausible ventures.[32] Even so, the boom produced a few successful companies, and several English industries appeared to have benefited from the influx of capital.[33] The episode illustrates the growing significance of stock trading

---

[28] Ibid.

[29] Davies (1952), Akst (2019).

[30] Defoe (1697).

[31] Macleod (1986).

[32] The list includes projects to reclaim land, a new process to heat liquors and the Africa Company, which wanted to exploit a monopoly trading concession for Africa—ignoring the fact that the part of Africa targeted for commerce was at the time controlled by the Dutch.

[33] Macleod (1986).

since the early seventeenth century and the pattern of a financial bubble that finances investments in all sorts of new ventures followed predictably by a crash that would repeat itself throughout history. In the sixteenth century, investors were attracted to joint-stock companies by the prospect of high dividends generated by monopoly profits on trade with the New World and, later, by quick capital gains on companies proposing to capitalize on innovations protected by patents. The state played a role in this by providing concessions, patent registrations, and armament demand. Once the initial euphoria over the possibility of instant wealth subsided, patents lost their credibility and ceased to add prestige to a scheme or reassure investors and customers. This made it difficult to raise capital to commercialize innovations in the following decades, but, as the subsequent events demonstrate; after the crash is before the boom.

Fueled by Leverage: The South Sea and Mississippi Bubbles

Around 20 years after the 1690s boom, stocks surged again, driven by the potential for profits from newly created overseas trading monopolies. Governments somehow believed that granting overseas trade monopolies, which were popular among investors, could be a conduit to reduce public debt. However, they soon discovered that this new funding method carried systemic risks and could threaten the economy. While the events described as follows have been extensively written about and have become infamous as some of the most significant stock bubbles in history, narratives frequently give the impression that they occurred as isolated events when, in fact, they were part of a process of increasing stock trading activity that has gained traction with ebbs and flows since the turn of the previous century.

In France, the Compagnie d'Occident was founded in 1717 and was granted exclusive rights to develop the sizable French territory in the Mississippi River valley of North America. By 1719, the renamed Compagnie des Indes ("Company of the Indies") operated on a charter that gave it monopoly over France's colonial trade and merged with the Banque Générale, a bank with authority to issue notes. One objective of the merger was to retire France's public debt by selling shares of the company to the public in exchange for state-issued debt. The company doubled as an issuer of currency and provided loans to investors to buy its shares or accepted government loans as payment. This allowed shareholders to buy shares on margin. Wild speculation ensued, resulting in a 36-fold surge in the share price and a widespread stock market boom throughout Europe. The term "millionaire" was coined to designate a newly wealthy stock market speculator.

The British joint-stock South Sea Company was granted a monopoly to supply "South Seas" and South American islands with African slaves to raise capital. Expecting a repeat of the success of the East India Company, which provided England with a flourishing business with India, investors were eager buyers of shares of the South Sea Company when it was established in 1711. The British government granted the company the monopoly in exchange for assuming a significant portion of Britain's national debt. The company's monopoly never yielded a considerable profit. However, the value of stock increased 10-fold in 1720 as the company expanded its trading in government debt and circulated false claims about its overseas business.[34] In a recent article, Braggion et al describe how the Bank of England allowed shareholders to borrow money by collateralizing their shares and 20% of new share issuance were bought on margin.[35] As Charles Mackay (1841) observed, the stock frenzy caused numerous schemes to be launched and lists 86 companies established in England alone in 1720.

But when the share prices of the Compagnie des Indes and the South Seas Company collapsed later that year in 1720, it triggered a general stock market crash in Britain, France, and other nations, later dubbed the Mississippi and South Sea bubble (Figure 1.3).[36] The share price crash in France and England devastated investors and the significant use of leverage in both bubbles contributed to the depth of the financial crisis and subsequent contraction of the real economy.[37]

---

[34] Paul (2011).
[35] Braggion, Frehen, and Jerphanion (2020).
[36] *Encyclopaedia Britannica* (2022b).
[37] Janeway (2018).

Figure 1.3 Emblematical print on the South Sea Scheme, by William Hogarth (1721).
Source: William Hogarth / https://www.historic-uk.com/HistoryUK/HistoryofEngland/
South-Sea-Bubble. / last accessed July 19, 2023.

Subsequent discoveries of fraud and manipulations tarnished it. Share trading still had no standard rules, required a physical exchange of stock certificates, and directors could manipulate share registers. Reliable accounting and limited liability were rare. But companies raised capital despite those challenges.[38]

Funding Enterprises During the First Industrial Revolution

The First Industrial Revolution was the transition to new manufacturing processes in Great Britain, continental Europe, and the United States, that occurred during the period from around 1760 to about 1820–1840. This transition included going from hand production methods to machines; iron production processes; the increasing use of water power and steam power; and the rise of

---

[38] Munn (2022).

the mechanized factory system.[39] Section 1.3 showed that private wealth creation beyond the Crown and landed aristocrats can be traced back to the sixteenth century. In its wake, partnerships and joint-stock companies emerged that could be used to raise equity from a broader set of investors, a common practice before the Industrial Revolution. As sugar production increased in the British possessions in the West Indies, the number of refineries in London shot up from 5 in 1615 to 75 in 1700. In 1733, the first cotton mill was established in Britain. In 1836, there were 318 cotton mills in Bradford alone.[40]

Evidence shows that risk capital was available to seize new opportunities throughout the centuries leading to the Industrial Revolution. W. H. Janeway cites the double wave of Britain's canal mania, first in the 1770s and later during the 1790s, as evidence of the growing maturity of capital markets that allowed the financing of capital-intensive ventures and infrastructure.[41]

But the industries that became dominant during the First Industrial Revolution, like mining, steel, pottery, and textiles, rarely resorted to fundraising from the public and thus provided few opportunities for stock investors and limited scope for wealthy individuals to become partners in a business unless they chose to be actively involved.

One of the reasons that explains the lack of outside financing required was that the industries that marked the beginning of the Industrial Revolution, particularly the textile industry, were surprisingly capital-light. As H. Heaton put it:

> The textile industry was the land of opportunity for the energetic and ambitious man with little capital. "Go textile, young man!" would have been a good bit of . . . advice to those whose courage was great but whose purse was light.[42]

---

[39] Landes (1969).
[40] Heaton (1937).
[41] Janeway (2018).
[42] Heaton (1937), p. 2.

During the initial stages of transitioning to the factory system, the financial burden appeared relatively light, and this was not solely due to the modest fixed capital requirements. Established merchant houses played a significant role in investing in the early generations of factories. Evidence supports the hypothesis that these merchants experienced little difficulty shifting from working to fixed capital investment required to establish industrial production.[43]

Another factor was that the industries in the early stages of the First Industrial Revolution often continued long-standing businesses that had already operated profitably during the sugar boom. Josiah Wedgwood was at least the fifth generation of potters and had a history of trading his goods overseas. The builder of one of Yorkshire's early large factories was the eleventh generation of clothmakers. In each generation, the business conscripted as many members of the family as it needed. Some ran the mill or warehouse; others were sent to New York, Lisbon, or Rio de Janeiro and traveled around the British Isles to buy wool or sell their product.[44] Their businesses were neither startups nor did they operate in new industries in search of new markets. Instead, many of those firms were incumbents who had the means to invest in new technologies that allowed them to transition from workshop to factory, using their own resources to meet growing demand in their core markets. The typical pattern of funding new enterprises well into the twentieth century was friends and family money and partnering with wealthy individuals.

This was the case of Thomas Bentley and Josiah Wedgwood, or the partnership between Matthew Boulton with Scottish engineer James Watt that resulted in 1775 in the commercial production of the Watt steam engine.

In addition to the hereditary merchants and producers who were incumbents in their sectors, another type of entrepreneur emerged during the Industrial Revolution: the inventors/industrialists. Richard Arkwright (1732–1792) and James Watt (1736–1819) set a precedent

---

[43] Chapman (1970).
[44] Ibid.

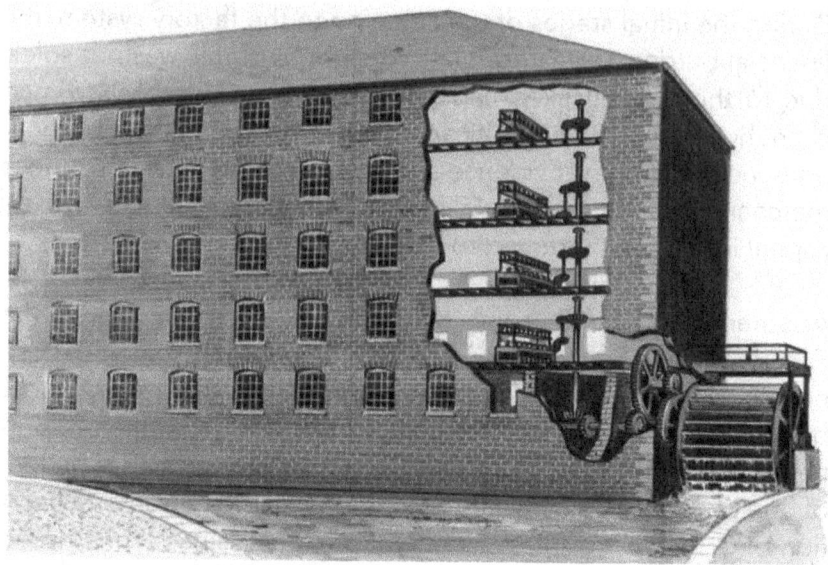

Figure 1.4 Water-powered textile mill supplied from a stream or dam, the water wheel is linked to a mechanical system of gears and shafts. Running at a steady, uniform speed, it drives the long rows of machinery on the floors above.
Source: https://www.locallocalhistory.co.uk/brit-land/power/page06.htm (public domain).

for transformative nineteenth-century inventors such as Morse, Siemens, and Edison by pioneering revolutionary technologies and engineering concepts and building successful companies centered on their ground-breaking inventions. Arkwright's most renowned invention, the water frame, revolutionized cotton spinning with its water-wheel-powered spinning frame, ultimately propelling the adoption of the modern factory system (Figure 1.4).[45]

The water frame gained significant demand among textile manufacturers.[46] Arkwright earned substantial income from selling licenses and allowing others to utilize his patented technology. Armed with a combination of personal savings, loans from investors and financial partners, and profits from his inventions, Arkwright successfully established and operated multiple textile factories, and became one of the wealthiest individuals of his time.

---

[45] Ashton (1964).
[46] Hills (1979).

1.4   ORGANIZATION OF STOCK MARKETS

Throughout the eighteenth and nineteenth centuries, stocks re-mained volatile. The South Sea and Mississippi bubbles of the 1720s were followed by another four panics in Britain (and three in the USA) during the eighteenth century and at least seven pan-ics between 1800 and 1900 in the USA. Often, those events were linked to credit contraction or bank failures.[47]

By the early nineteenth century, trading had moved from coffee houses to specialized exchanges in London, Amsterdam, and New York. For example, the New York Stock Exchange traces its origins to the Buttonwood Agreement signed by 24 stockbrokers on May 17, 1792. After reorganizing in 1817, it became the world's first regulated exchange.[48] A marketplace with defined trading practices, commissions, and published prices significantly broad-ened the appeal of share ownership to a broader public. Investors with different investment horizons could participate in the stock market as trading volumes and liquidity increased.

Likewise, the invention of the telegraph in 1832 and the first tel-egraphic ticker tape in 1867[49] allowed information about trades and prices to be transmitted over long distances, enabling more widespread and faster investing (Figure 1.5).[50] The establishment of the transatlantic telegraph cable connections between the USA and Europe during the second half of the nineteenth cen-tury played a decisive role in cross-border investing. The New York Stock Exchange (NYSE) used the cable connections to transmit stock prices to London and allowed European investors to buy shares in the USA. For example, initial investments in US railroads (see Section 1.5) were substantially financed by foreign (British) investors.[51]

---

[47] Scott (2022).
[48] *The Economist* (1999b).
[49] The ticker tape was created by American inventor Edward Calahan in 1867 and a later improvement was patented by Thomas Edison in 1871.
[50] Day (2019).
[51] Drummond (2003).

**Figure 1.5   (a) Trading floor of the New York Stock Exchange, 1889;
(b) Ticker-tape machine.**
Sources: (a) Granger - Historical Picture Archive / Alamy Stock Photo;
(b) Thomas Edison Papers, Rutgers University.

It is easy to forget that until the end of the nineteenth century, the USA had a relatively small (but rising) stock of investable capital. Immigrants did not arrive with industrial equipment or lots of money. In 1840, Alexis de Tocqueville noted, "the number of large fortunes [in the USA] is quite small and capital is still scarce."[52] The telegraph and the ticker tape were thus crucial for US enterprises to gain access to much-needed foreign capital, particularly from the UK.

Accounting Rules and Audits

But in the nineteenth century, existing information systems were still ineffective at tracking what was going on in a company's operations and finances. How could investors (shareholders) be sure their money was being put to good use if they weren't actively involved in the company's operations? It was difficult to determine how much profit a company made, let alone if it made any profit, without a comprehensive information system and a foundation of recognized accounting rules and independent audits, which came later. Neither were claims and statements provided by companies that offered shares to the public subject to any independent verification. Therefore, it was easier for investors to invest in bonds and loans and claim repayment at the agreed-upon date, regardless

---

[52] Quoted in Piketty (2014), p. 152.

of the company's financial situation. If a company's assets proved insufficient to repay the debt, creditors could turn to shareholders to satisfy their claims.[53]

Audits were required by law in England as early as 1845 to protect shareholders from "improper actions by promoters and directors."[54] However, there was no organized profession of accountants or auditors, no uniform auditing standards or rules, no established training or other qualifications for auditors, and no professional status for auditors.

The enactment of the Federal Securities Acts of 1933 and 1934 in the United States changed all that as they required all companies to have their financial statements audited by an independent Certified Public Accountant. The introduction of generally accepted accounting principles (GAAP) and auditing standards facilitated equity investing, brought consistency and transparency to financial statements and formed the basis for stock research and credit ratings. John Moody founded Moody's in 1909 to produce manuals of statistics related to stocks and bonds and bond ratings.[55]

Limited Liability

Early equity investors could face lack of limited liability when it wasn't established by charter or bylaws. This led to shares with different liability risks for investors. Anyone who owned company stock could be liable for all debts owed. Investing in equity was risky because you needed to know the owner, monitor the business, and make sure the company did not make commitments it could not meet with its assets in bankruptcy. To assess the degree of liability as an equity investor, you must also understand a government charter or a company's bylaws. Many investors probably didn't fully understand these issues and were exposed to unknown risks.

In response to the frequent booms and busts, governments attempted to discourage speculation. In England, for instance, the Bubble Act of 1719 prohibited the formation of joint-stock

---

[53] Colin (2016).
[54] Quoted in Levey (2020).
[55] White (2010).

companies unless authorized by royal charter. The Act was not strictly enforced and did little to prevent subsequent booms and busts, which culminated in the Panic of 1825, resulting in the closure of numerous banks, and ultimately led to the repeal of the Bubble Act. This paved the way for freedom of incorporation in England, resulting in the passage of the Companies Registration and Regulation Act of 1844, which also drew the first legislative distinction between a joint-stock company and an ordinary partnership. Banks, mining companies, and railroads were increasingly incorporated as joint-stock companies.[56]

However, limited liability did not become a universal right until 1855 and still had to be granted by the charter. The simple partnership, or in some cases and later, the "private company" or "close corporation," remained the predominant form of the standard commercial organization well into the twentieth century, with unlimited liability generally prevailing. John Coles, a prominent British businessman, advocated that the limited partnership would foster the alliance of "science and ability with capital" in an argument that echoes modern venture capital.[57] The Companies Act of 1862 permitted incorporators to design a corporation's liability regime in its Articles of Association. It allowed the formation of companies with limited liability in the modern sense and companies with liability for unpaid-up capital and reserve liability with varying percentages of paid-up capital and multipliers. The liability model was selected at the level of the individual corporation.[58] Given the frequency with which shares were moved, one may assume that stock investors were not always aware of a company's liability regime, which did not seem to impede the growing popularity of stock investments throughout time.

Trust Companies, which became popular as "quasi holdings" of corporations, limited liability more effectively because a third party has a direct right against the trustee but not the beneficiary, i.e., the holder of a trust certificate. Trusts, like UK chartered joint-stock companies, are created by charter and offer more personal liability protection than non-chartered businesses.[59]

---

[56] Hunt (1935).
[57] Chaplin (2016).
[58] Harris (2020).
[59] Symmonds (1931).

New York State limited manufacturing company liability in 1811. Its popularity and the flow of capital to jurisdictions with limited liability prompted most American states to follow suit. Britain, the world's largest economy at the time, followed 30 years later with its limited liability statute in 1854, but most corporations had not yet converged to modern limited liability.[60] The USA had state-level limited liability, and bankruptcy courts might interpret company liability regimes. California had unlimited liability until 1931.[61] It took well into the twentieth century for shareholders' limited liability to become universal in all industries. Public corporations with many shareholders thus existed before the emergence of modern limited liability and shareholders were often (unknowingly) liable to provide additional funds in the event of a bankruptcy.

While accounting rules and auditing requirements are considered today essential for the functioning and trustworthiness of stock markets, their introduction followed the growth and maturity of stock markets rather than enabling them. In the UK, the Limited Partnerships Act 1907 and the US 1916 Uniform Limited Partnership Act officially recognized limited partnerships. Delaware was one of the last states to implement it in 1973, but its provisions made it the preferred jurisdiction for US Limited Partnerships as it provided solid protections for general partners to limit their ostensibly infinite liability. Investment banking was the last significant industry to adopt the contemporary liability model. Before 1970, the New York Stock Exchange required investment banks to be established as partnerships with participants who could be held personally liable for debts.[62]

Voting Rights

The best evidence of corporate voting rights before the adoption of general incorporation statutes in the mid-1800s can be found

---

[60] *The Economist* (1999b). English chartered companies enjoyed complete limited liability under common law as a corporate privilege. But there were numerous companies that falsely claimed to be chartered and, as noted by K. G. Davis, formal limited liability was tempered by the authority exercised by many companies—unless explicitly disclaimed—to issue calls on shareholders that went beyond their liability on unpaid stock (Davies, 1952).
[61] Harris (2020).
[62] Ibid.

in individual corporate charters granted by legislatures. While one share equaled one vote was the most prevalent provision, many charters sought to limit the influence of larger shareholders, with the most extreme, but not uncommon, example being one vote per shareholder regardless of the number of shares held.

At the end of the nineteenth century, in the United States, most companies had adopted the one-share, one-vote system. Most preferred shares had voting rights equal to those of the common shares, which is not the case now. In the first two decades of the twentieth century, many issuers adopted dual-class governance structures, reversing the trend and seeking to maintain control of insiders.

Two twentieth-century departures from the one-share, one-vote standard occurred. One idea eliminated preferred stock voting rights. Notably, preferred share voting rights were increasingly conditioned on certain circumstances (such as non-payment of dividends). Now standard, this was controversial then. Common stock without voting rights is more current. After World War I, many corporations issued two types of common stock: one with one vote per share and one without (but sometimes with greater dividend rights). By offering the former to insiders and the latter to the public, the promoters could raise significant funds without relinquishing control.[63]

1.5 RISK CAPITAL DURING THE SECOND INDUSTRIAL REVOLUTION

The Second Industrial Revolution, was a phase of rapid scientific discovery, standardization, mass production, and industrialization from the late nineteenth century into the early twentieth century. It was driven by the commercial development, first, of team power and then of electricity. The manifestations of this process were the building of railroads, large-scale iron and steel production, widespread use of

[63]ProfBrainbridge.com (2017). The twenty-first century saw a return of super-voting shares for founders and insiders, in particular, in the technology sector. These developments will be discussed later.

machinery in manufacturing, greatly increased use of steam power, widespread use of the telegraph, use of petroleum and the beginning of electrification.[64] The technologies that drove the Second Industrial Revolution fit the description of general-purpose-technologies that allow ongoing technical improvement, enabling innovation in sectors where the technology is applied. The latter aspect of spillover and feedback results in innovation that can be sustained over an extended period and comes with big leaps in productivity.[65]

It was also the time when modern organizational techniques for operating large-scale corporations were developed. The high rate of technological advancement spawned new markets and a new sort of serial entrepreneur who capitalized on the opportunities presented by technological innovation. After 1870, the rapid expansion of rail and telegraph networks facilitated the unprecedented movement of people and ideas. Consequently, a new wave of globalization and the integration of continental markets led to the establishment of organizations of previously unheard-of scale and scope.

The railroads also serve as an example of the two modes of organizing and funding the construction of networks. The model adopted by the USA and Britain, was based on a reliance on private capital and competing ventures. In contrast, state planning and investment in pursuit of economic development and national security, were the route taken by Germany and France. Both approaches "delivered" and came with their specific drawbacks and benefits. One can argue that the lasting differences between "Anglo-Saxon capitalism" and "Rhine capitalism" (often also referred to as the "European" model)—in this context, referring to the tolerance of monopolies and managed competition—can trace their origins in the differing experiences related to the establishment of railroads.[66]

---

[64] Richmond Vale Academy (2022).

[65] Janeway (2018).

[66] The study of comparative institutional advantage related to the different models of capitalism has gained considerable attention from economists since the work of the Chicago School of Economics, which led to the Anglo-Saxon capitalist model of the 1970s. For a quick reference of its main characteristics, see MBN (2023).

Establishing organized stock exchanges and employing the telegraph to broadcast stock values and connect capital markets across continents paved the way for funding the Second Industrial Revolution's rising capital needs, particularly in infrastructure and asset-intensive industries. Driven by a strong trend toward industry-wide consolidation, an active mergers and acquisitions (M&A) market arose. Growing awareness of the evolving relationship between corporate power and society prompted a backlash in the form of the anti-monopoly movement and legislation meant to prevent monopolies.[67]

Nineteenth-Century Railroad Mania in the UK and the USA

Then and now, the emergence of new technology and the prospect of significant returns sparked public interest in holding shares, creating a boom that allowed firms to exploit the possibilities of new technologies to raise massive sums of cash. Starting in Britain, railroads were a transformative technology, and the public was eager to buy shares in newly founded railroad companies in 1838–1839, which started the first railroad boom. Despite numerous failures of railroad companies some, such as the London and South Western or the Liverpool and Manchester, and a few others were successful. This success triggered the "Railway Mania" from 1846 to 1848.[68] Companies had to seek Parliament's approval for the proposed route, which could have been used to ensure an orderly expansion of the railroad network. The British government, however, promoted an almost "laissez-faire" system of non-regulation in the railroads. In 1846 alone, at the height of Britain's railroad boom, Parliament approved the establishment of 263 new railroad companies with 9,500 miles of lines (15,300 km).[69]

The surge in the number and the rising valuation of railroad stocks resulted from rampant speculation as not all railroads were profitable. One-third of approved railroads were never built for various

---

[67] Janeway (2018).
[68] Ibid.
[69] Casson (2009), other sources such as (Odlyzko, 2010) claim that 12,000 miles were approved by Parliament.

reasons, including poor financial planning and outright fraud.[70] As the boom turned into bust, investors lost most of their capital.[71] English railroad chronicler C. Wolmar wrote: "in the end the boom was based on little more than optimism feeding on itself."[72]

In the United States, one could observe the same pattern of boom-and-bust cycles. The railroad boom began in the late 1830s and 1840s, and until the bust in 1857 railroad companies raised $700 million in the stock markets. Capital on this scale could no longer be raised from domestic investors and New York emerged as the financial center through which capital from Europe flowed into US railroad projects. After the Civil War, a second wave of US railway construction ensued, which was driven by a quest for scale of competing networks and, according to the US Department of Transportation, the total route mileage of railroads in the USA grew from 52,914 miles in 1870 to 166,703 miles in 1890.[73] Vast but often redundant or competing newly founded rail operators created national networks, and gigantic stations were built (Figure 1.6). This development took place in lockstep with the expansion of

(a)   (b)

Figure 1.6   (a) East Texas Railroad. (b) Grand Central Depot, New York City, 1871. The structure was later replaced by the first Grand Central Station in 1900.
Sources: (a) The History Center. (b) John Belle / Wikimedia Commons / Public Domain.

---

[70] Morgan (1940).
[71] Odlyzko (2010).
[72] Quoted in (McCullough, 2018a) whose reference is the work of British journalist Christian Wolmar. His book, *Fire and Steam: A New History of the Railways in Britain*, chronicles the British Railway Mania (Wolmar, 2008).
[73] US Department of Transportation's Bureau of Transportation Statistics (BTS), various years.

steel making, which experienced rapid technological progress that increased the quality and lowered steel production costs. The over-investment in railroads resulted in fierce price wars.[74] The US railroad boom ended in 1894. It was the result of overbuilt rail lines, as well as poor railroad financing; these began a series of bank failures starting in 1893, which then led to railroad failures. What became known as the (stock market) Panic of 1893 caused the largest economic depression in US history until that time. But the tracks were laid, and railroads became a major industry, stimulating other heavy industries such as iron and steel production.[75] Consolidation of the rail industry (see the section "Railroads and Steel: The Trust Boom" on p. 49) led to the formation of larger companies with more efficient operations, leading to further expansion of the railroad network to 254,037 miles in 1916 and the freight tons transported by US railroads increased from 435.6 billion ton-miles in 1890 to 1,161.6 billion ton-miles in 1916.[76] The industry had come of age.

The private funding of railroads was, however, not the only model used to expand a national railroad network. The French Second Empire under Napoleon III used an early form of public-to-private partnerships to accomplish the goal. The state built most of the railway system and invited private companies to operate the lines under leases of up to 99 years. They were publicly owned but privately operated. The state guaranteed the dividends of the railway operating companies, and in exchange took two-thirds of any greater profits.[77] In Germany, railroad construction was carried out by the individual autonomous states and sometimes by private companies operating on a concession. Following the unification of Germany in 1871, Otto von Bismarck pressed for the development of a state railway system, and local state and private railroad companies were amalgamated. By 1880, Germany had 9,400 locomotives, each annually pulling 43,000 passengers or 30,000 tons of freight, and the total length of the railroad network exceeded that of France and Britain in 1880.[78]

---

[74] Stilo (2022).
[75] Gross (2022), *National Geographic* (2022).
[76] US Department of Transportation's Bureau of Transportation Statistics (BTS), various years.
[77] Blanchard (1969).
[78] Mitchell (2000).

The Transformation of the Innovation System

During the nineteenth century, while railroads were the dominating industry for equity financing, a faster pace of innovation was observed in many other fields. Individual inventors, some with engineering backgrounds and others wholly self-taught, were responsible for this advancement. Doing research to patent an invention became a business, and obtaining a patent was the impetus for many firms to launch. In the USA, patents were considered so significant that Article 1 of the United States Constitution gave Congress the right to award them. The United States Patent and Trademark Office (USPTO) was already founded in 1790. A broad network of specialized middlemen emerged that simplified patent sales and licensing and reduced transaction costs for licenses in national and international marketplaces.[79] For the inventors/entrepreneurs of that age, the inventions that stood at the beginning of their business ventures were just a starting point: they would incorporate R&D into the fabric of their companies and start corporate research that would, over time, become the primary driver of innovation. The following are some of the era's most prominent investors/entrepreneurs. However, it is important to note that they represent only the tip of the iceberg.[80]

Samuel Morse, a painter and art teacher, invented the Morse Code and the telegraph.[81] He secured financial support from Congress in 1843 for the first US telegraph line. Morse and investors established the Magnetic Telegraph Co., which built the first transatlantic cable. Legal disputes over his patent were resolved by a 1854 US Supreme Court decision, affirming his patent rights.[82,83]

Thomas Alva Edison started as a newspaper salesperson before securing patents in power generation, light bulbs, communication,

---

[79] Lamoreaux, Sokoloff, and Suttisphisal (2013).

[80] Degner (2009), for example, shows that, from 1877 to 1900, two-thirds, and, from 1901 to 1932, between 40 and 55% of all valuable German patents granted to domestic firms were held by only 30 most innovative firms, whereas about 266,000 firms with more than five workers existed in Germany in 1930.

[81] Bellis (2009).

[82] Carleton (2022).

[83] Western Union Company, founded in 1851, consolidated the disparate industry using his patent. By completing a transcontinental line in 1861, it had obtained a near monopoly on the US telegraph business (*Encyclopaedia Britannica*, 2023a).

recording, and films. He founded the first industrial research lab, using patent funds for innovation. With over a thousand patents, he established multiple enterprises.[84]

George Westinghouse invented an air-compressed train brake in 1869, leading to his first company. With 330 patents, he founded 59 businesses, including Westinghouse Electric, and pioneered corporate R&D centers.[85]

Werner von Siemens, a Prussian army officer, innovated an electric sea mine and the pointer telegraph. He founded the "Telegraphen-Bauanstalt von Siemens & Halske" in 1847, which expanded rapidly into power generation, transmission, electric street cars, and elevators.[86] The company also expanded quickly abroad, establishing Siemens Brothers in London in 1858.[87]

Alexander Graham Bell, a key figure in the telephone's development, patented it as an "apparatus for telegraphically transferring vocal or other sounds." He conducted vocal sound transmission experiments and received a patent for the phone's design in 1876 while staying at a boarding home. The American Bell Company was founded in 1877 and later merged with the American Bell Telephone Company in 1880, forming AT&T. Bell Laboratories became one of the most consequential corporate research labs in the USA (Figure 1.7).[88]

Patents played a key role as a source of value creation either through licensing or as a basis to start a company to harness the commercial value of an invention. The electrical industry showed competitors' willingness to pool or license patents. This was the case between Westinghouse Electric and Thomson-Houston. Westinghouse also

---

[84] Baldwin (1995).
[85] Westinghouse (2023).
[86] Siemens Historical Institute (2018).
[87] Siemens Brothers is also an example of private wealth's role in financing venture-like enterprises. J. P. Morgan held a stake in Siemens Brothers (and also in Edison's company) and, in 1901, tried to finance the electrification of the London Underground and surface rail lines as well as the building of a new Hammersmith-City Tube line to generate business for his portfolio companies (Janeway, 2018).
[88] Matthews (1999), pp. 19–21.

Figure 1.7   John Bardeen (1908–1991), William Shockley (1910–1989), and Walter
H. Brattain (1902–1987) (left to right) shown at Bell Telephone Laboratories in
1948 with an apparatus used in the early investigations which led to the invention of
the transistor. These men won the Nobel Prize in Physics in 1956 for the invention
of the transistor.
Source: Grimm (1999). Science History Images/Alamy Stock Photo HRKNYX License
IY03691339.

imported generators from Siemens to build its first alternating current (AC) power stations. In 1883, Emil Rathenau acquired the rights
to manufacture products based on Edison's patents and founded
Deutsche Edison-Gesellschaft für angewandte Elektricität in Berlin.
Propelled by acquisitions, licensing agreements, and cooperation,
AEG had become the largest commercial company in the world
by 1907.[89]

---

[89] There was a difference between Siemens & Halske, which focused on internal R&D and took a lot of technology risk, and AEG, which worked on the basis
of "if you can buy it, don't invent it" by acquiring licenses and was much more
aggressive in expanding as it was taking less technology risk. When this competition threatened to undermine both firms, their bankers nudged them into a
"truce" where Siemens would focus on equipment manufacturing. In contrast,
AEG would focus on power generation and distribution. While this agreement
was short-lived, it showed a tolerance of monopolies as the German government
saw no reason to intervene and there was no public debate about monopolies
(Kocka, 1972).

The automotive industry experienced patent controversies in its early years.[90] Most notable were two long, drawn-out court cases in Britain and the United States, where a promoter sought to gain control of the new industry by filing comprehensive patents. In Britain, the court rejected the claim in 1901, five years after the patent application. In the USA, there was a legal battle between Ford and the Association of Licensed Automobile Manufacturers over the Selden patent, which the association claimed as a basic patent on gasoline-powered cars. In 1911, the courts held the patent "valid but not infringed" by Ford. The main consequence of the decision was the formation of the predecessor of the Alliance of Automobile Manufacturers to supervise an agreement for cross-licensing patents, which was ratified in 1915.[91]

The automobile industry started as a cottage industry, with early inventors focused on engines and almost all producers were assemblers who put together components and parts that different firms manufactured. Carl Benz developed the first four-wheel car

Figure 1.8   Benz & Co. Rheinische Gasmotoren-Fabrik during the 1890s.
Source: https://www.mercedes-benz.com/en/innovation/milestones/corporate-history/ / last accessed July 19, 2023.

---

[90] Mader (2001).
[91] G. B. Selden filed for a patent on May 8, 1879. His application included not only the engine but its use in a four-wheeled car. He then filed a series of amendments to his application which stretched out the legal process resulting in a delay of 16 years before the patent was granted on November 5, 1895. Despite never having gone into production with a working model of an automobile, he had a credible claim to have patented an automobile in 1895.

powered by an internal-combustion engine, patented in 1886. The model Victoria went into serial production in 1894 (Figure 1.8).[92] Gottlieb Wilhelm Daimler and Wilhelm Maybach developed in parallel the four-stroke engine. Henry Ford launched the Ford Motor Company in 1903 with $28,000 in cash from 12 investors, most notably John and Horace Dodge (who would later establish their own car company). Within a decade, the company led the world in expanding and refining the assembly line concept, and Ford soon brought much of the part production in-house. This started a trend toward vertical integration, a dominant M&A theme during the 1920s.[93]

Lehmann-Hasemeyer and Streb studied IPOs on the German stock market over the period of 1877 to 1913. The authors looked at the companies with the most valuable patents and identified a sample of 911 firms, of which 137 firms went public, and 774 stayed private. The patenting activities of both groups of firms were similar. In the later 1880s, however, the patenting activities of listed and private firms began to diverge. On the eve of World War I, listed firms filed, on average, about 3x as many new valuable patents as private ones. The authors demonstrate that, around 1900, German firms used about 90% of their new equity capital for internal investment (including R&D). Corporate research led to a concentration of innovations as during 1877–1900 two-thirds of all patents were obtained by just 30 companies.[94]

This marked a shift toward corporate R&D that was also observable in the USA. The inventor-led firms continued to invent and used their additional financial resources to push innovation further and faster than comparable private firms. The stock market thus enabled the accelerating pace of innovation.

Not only was R&D becoming more concentrated, but the benefits of innovation were also skewed toward a few early adopters. As Janeway describes, those who wanted to use electricity had to

---

[92] Mercedes-Benz Group (2023). The origins of the Mercedes-Benz Group trace back to the Agreement of Mutual Interest signed in 1924 between Benz & Cie. (established in 1883 by Carl Benz) and Daimler Motoren Gesellschaft (founded in 1890 by Gottlieb Daimler and Wilhelm Maybach).
[93] History.com (2020).
[94] Lehmann-Hasemeyer and Streb (2016).

purchase their generators because the grid was still being built. The Ford Motor Company could afford it, but smaller businesses had to wait until they could connect to the grid. This took place during the 1930s and in its wake the United States experienced the most rapid growth in manufacturing productivity in its history.[95]

On the eve of WWI, important new industries were created and began to make their market as adoption progressed and sectors that used these new technologies underwent transformation and started their own cycle of innovation. The powerful and large companies that had emerged were the result of relentless consolidation in each of their industries that had largely been accomplished. The joint-stock company became the most common form of incorporation for private and public firms. The trend toward large enterprises resulted in capital requirements that vastly exceeded private networks and rarely could be accumulated by retained earnings. Liquidity also favored large-cap stocks as trading volumes, and the number of stock market participants, increased. As banks and stockbrokers institutionalized financial intermediation, size became a factor in their share underwriting decisions, which created the risk for startups trying to raise smaller amounts of capital in public markets of being squeezed out.

Public Markets and the Financing of Innovation: A Tale of Two Industries

As the railroad industry matured, a new industry emerged: electrical utilities. The impact of electricity proved to be even more transformative than the railroad, revolutionizing industry, transportation, communication, and entertainment. Comparing the adoption and development rates of railways and electricity can help us understand the innovation economy in an age of increasingly maturing stock markets and provide valuable lessons for investors. Although electricity can be considered a general-purpose technology, the growth of the US electrical utility industry was slower than

---

[95] Janeway (2018).

that of the railroad companies. The first centralized electric power plant in the United States was built in 1882 in New York City, but it took much longer for electrical utilities to consolidate, compared to the railroad industry.[96] By 1890, there were more than 200 central power stations in the country, and that number increased to around 7,000 in the mid-1920s, with approximately 6,000 utilities still in operation during the 1930s.[97,98]

In the 1890s, the initial customers of early electrical utilities in the USA were primarily wealthy individuals, large businesses, in particular, manufacturing plants, which required large amounts of power for their operations. Electrical utilities were first established in urban areas where the concentration of customers was higher, and there was a greater demand for electricity. Electrical utilities also served streetcar and transit companies, which were rapidly expanding in the late nineteenth century. These companies relied on electricity to power their electric streetcars and trolley buses, which replaced the earlier horse-drawn carriages and cable cars.[99] Electricity was still expensive and distribution localized due to the limitations of technology at the time.

The ability to transmit electrical power over long distances was restricted by the technology available. The adoption of AC/DC hybrid systems helped to overcome some of these limitations. These hybrid systems use alternating current (AC) for high-voltage transmission over long distances and direct current (DC) for local distribution and powering equipment that requires steady DC voltage. Westinghouse played a significant role in the adoption of AC/DC hybrid systems, but the technology faced resistance, causing a "Current War" between Thomas Edison, who promoted DC electrical power distribution, and George Westinghouse, who promoted AC.[100] The AC technology only became established after

---

[96] Bradley (2011), pp. 18–19.
[97] Isser (2015).
[98] Hughes (1983), p. 70.
[99] Ibid., pp. 72–76.
[100] Silverstein (2018).

General Electric (GE) was formed in 1892 by merging T. A. Edison's Edison General Electric Company with the Thomson-Houston Electric Company, which later became a major player in the AC industry.[101]

As electric utilities increasingly adopted alternating current (AC) and developed AC transformers to transmit high-voltage electricity over long distances, AC became the dominant form of electricity used by utilities in the early twentieth century. The absence of a centralized planning process to balance supply and demand, along with the fact that many utilities were being independently built and operated, resulted in significant overcapacity for power generation in the United States during this period. One might expect that once the technology gave the industry the ability to transmit electricity over longer distances, consolidation would result in improved use of idle capacity. However, unlike the railroad industry which experienced rapid consolidation in response to overcapacity and price wars, the number of electrical utilities continued to increase.[102] The slower pace of consolidation of electrical utilities compared to railways can be attributed to several factors. During its early years, the electricity industry encountered unique technological risks and challenges—such as long-distance power transmission—that were absent in the railroad industry. Furthermore, the nature of the electricity industry, which revolved around intangible assets like patents and intellectual property, posed additional hurdles for consolidation and mergers. In addition, the electricity power generation and distribution were subject to significant state-level regulation, which made it more challenging to coordinate mergers and acquisitions on a national level and increased the cost of expanding networks.[103] This was further compounded by antitrust legislation that emerged after the consolidation of the railroad industry, making it harder for companies to merge and consolidate, as any significant changes in ownership or control required government approval. Unlike the railroad industry, which faced relatively few regulatory obstacles early on and was significantly concentrated by the time the new legislation was

---

[101] Schmalensee (1990).
[102] White (2011).
[103] Isser (2015), p. 70.

POWER HOUSE—HIGHLAND PARK PLANT. FORD MOTOR CO.   610

Figure 1.9 Photographic postcard depicting the powerhouse at the Ford Plant in Highland Park in 1920. Five smoke stocks have a "FORD" sign across them, and two water towers are in the background.
Source: F. H. Mill, Dearborn, MI. Detroit Historical Society Catalog # 1945.101.001.

actively enforced, the younger sector of electrical utilities was still a cottage industry. The industry was also perceived as a cottage industry, often with weak balance sheets and a lack of profitability. This discouraged investors and large potential corporate customers alike. Henry Ford, for example, built his first power station to generate electricity for his factories in 1913 (Figure 1.9).[104]

In order to understand the different evolution of railroads compared to electrical utilities, one must look at their access to the stock market. The railroad industry had tangible assets and a clear user case. In the eyes of its contemporaries, its potential seemed vast and the European example of rapid growth of railway traffic justified this view. It was also hard to imagine that this new mode of transport would ever become obsolete. In contrast, electricity faced skepticism from consumers, who did not immediately see its benefits and businesses that regarded it as expensive. It took time for people to recognize the practical applications of electric power

---

[104] Watts (2005).

in their homes and businesses and those applications became only available after the grid had expanded sufficiently to justify their development and production. Building an electrical grid was also recognized to be a more expensive undertaking than building a railroad network. This proved to be correct, as estimates for the total investment in electrical power generation facilities and the grid in the United States until 1929 range from $25 billion to $38 billion compared to some estimates that put the capital spent on constructing and expanding railroads at around $10 billion.[105] While there are no precise numbers and the investment cycles did not run in parallel as capital spending by electrical utilities took off only after WWI, the capital invested in electrical power generation and distribution appears higher than the capital invested in railroads.

But for the period until 1916, estimates from the Edison Electric Institute suggest that only a fraction of that amount—$3 billion—was invested.[106] During the decade that followed, an estimated $22–36 billion were invested—more capital than during all the US railway booms combined and between 25–30% of that amount was raised through the stock market.[107]

While the railroads were the dominant sector of the stock market at the end of the nineteenth century, the electrical utilities raised little capital on the stock market. Railroads were seen as a safer investment for shareholders in the early days because the benefits of their larger networks providing more and longer connections were intuitively obvious. Investors believed that while there were high financial risks associated with building railroads, demand risk was less of a concern. On the other hand, the benefits of power generation and distribution were not as easily understood by consumers and investors, since the technology was too new and still evolving and the uncertainty about the demand for electricity was

---

[105] Donaldson and Hornbeck (2013) estimate the cost of building railroads in the USA between 1839 and 1896 to be approximately $11 billion. Walton and Rockoff (2017) estimate the cost of building US railroads between 1830 and 1900 to be approximately $9 billion (in nominal dollars).
[106] Aitken (1985), Edison Electric Institute (1953).
[107] David (1990).

high. It was not until the 1920s and 1930s, after the electrical utilities had become established as stable businesses, that stock market investors embraced them. As of 1900, only 2.2% of US households had access to electricity, a number that increased to 35% by 1920 and to 68% by the end of the 1930s. During the 1920s and 1930s, electric washing machines and other household appliances became more common in the USA as more homes were electrified and more people gained access to electricity. However, it was not until after World War II, during the 1950s and 1960s, that electric dishwashers and other appliances became truly widespread and affordable for most households.[108]

Prior to World War I, utilities faced limitations in raising significant capital from stock markets, which led to a more localized and project-based approach. This approach resulted in a slower roll-out of the electrical industry, which prevented the efficiency gains that would have been achievable through economies of scale. As a result, the electrical industry took twice as long as the railroad industry to mature. This highlights the fact that public markets were more willing to fund business models with low technology and demand risks, while ventures with high technology and demand risks had to rely on private capital during their early stages, despite the establishment of public markets. Furthermore, this underscores the enduring and possibly increasing role of growth equity financing in shortening the time it takes for new technologies and the industries built around them to scale up.

Railroads and Steel: The Trust Boom

The end of the nineteenth century saw the first great wave of mergers in US history. Pummeled by a deep economic recession that started in 1892, a third of the US railway tracks went into receivership. Between 1894 and 1898, over 40,000 miles of track were sold or lost due to bankruptcy. The restructuring of the industry by investment bankers led by J. P. Morgan of Morgan & Co. and J. Schiff of Kuhn, Loeb & Co. heralded the first great wave of mergers in American history.[109] The creation of a trust would facilitate the exchange of

---

[108] Klein (2008).
[109] Janeway (2018).

stocks in individual companies for trust certificates, and the trust served as a holding company.[110] Shareholders were eager to change their railway stocks into trust certificates as it was a way to avoid potential additional "reserve" liability for capital that was not fully paid-in.[111] Trust companies thus became a catalyst for consolidation in various industries.[112] By 1901, these corporate behemoths dominated the railroad industry and sugar, steel, and coal. Frequently, trusts were formed by combining family-owned or closely held businesses, and the bankers acted as impartial arbitrators and appraisers of a company's fair value. They also received a share of the trust stock as payment and thus built a portfolio of trust holdings that gave them substantial influence over large parts of the economy. The railroads' overbuilding and duplication of services diminished their profitability. J. P. Morgan convened a meeting on his yacht *Corsair* of key railroad executives in 1885 to reduce economically damaging competition. J. P. Morgan persuaded them to end destructive rate wars and other policies by threatening to restrict their access to investment capital. Then, in 1886, he reorganized the Philadelphia & Reading Railroad, followed by the Chesapeake & Ohio Railroad in 1888. In reorganizing railroads, J. P. Morgan stabilized their finances overall. In the 1880s, Morgan's control expanded westward; he negotiated to finance the Great Northern and Northern Pacific railroads.[113] The acquirers often took possession of railroad tracks and rolling stock below replacement value, which resulted in lower capital amortization rates and reduced the operating cost in an industry where fixed capital expenditure is the primary cost driver.[114]

Hostile Takeovers

The consolidation of the entire industry did not unfold uncontested. For example, in 1901, the investment bank Kuhn Loeb & Co.,

---

[110] Chernow (1991).

[111] Ibid., Harris (2020).

[112] Neal (1971).

[113] Chernow (1991).

[114] Freightwaves (2021). In addition, it should be noted that the resulting losses from failed railway investments were substantially borne by foreign investors as a large part of the inward foreign capital had gone into railroads (Sylla, Tilly, and Tortella, 1999).

Union Pacific Railroad owner Edward H. Harriman, and the Rockefellers attempted a hostile takeover of the Northern Pacific Railroad, which was controlled by J. P. Morgan. Its stock price increased from approximately $70 to over $1,000. This resulted in a massive short squeeze that threatened to ruin thousands of investors and turned into a stock market crash as investors sold other shares to raise liquidity. When Morgan maintained control, short sellers were permitted to cover their short positions at $150 per share, preventing the collapse of several Wall Street firms.[115]

Mergers and Acquisitions Creating Billion-Dollar Companies
Trust companies were used to undertake horizontal mergers and create market dominant firms in many industries.

John D. Rockefeller and others founded Standard Oil as a partnership in Ohio in 1863; the company was incorporated in Ohio in 1870. Through aggressive acquisitions, Standard Oil gradually seized control of numerous oil companies and controlled 88% of the nation's refined oil flows by 1890. By 1904, Standard Oil's share of the nation's oil production reached 91% and 85% of its final sales.[116] By the time trading in Standard Oil shares, including all its subsidiaries, ceased in August 1912, the shares had reached 1100, giving the company a market capitalization of $1.1 billion.[117]

US Steel was another J. P. Morgan creation that used the trust company to consolidate an industry. In 1901, 11 steel companies, including his own Federal Steel and Andrew Carnegie's steel company, merged to form US Steel. It was to become the first company in history to reach a billion dollars and control more than half of the US steel production.[118]

---

[115] Chernow (1991).
[116] *Encyclopaedia Britannica* (2023b).
[117] Taylor (2017).
[118] Chernow (1991).

The General Electric Company (GE) was also formed on the initiative of J. P. Morgan, who organized a merger between the Edison General Electric Company, where he held a stake and Thomson-Houston Electric in 1892. This merger ended the "Current War" and paved the way for long-distance transmission of electricity and the creation of large utilities. In 1896, GE was one of the original 12 companies listed on the newly formed Dow Jones Industrial Average.[119] GE founded the Radio Corporation of America (RCA) in 1919, after purchasing the Marconi Wireless Telegraph Company of America. GE's president Owen D. Young helped to establish America's lead in the burgeoning technology of radio, making RCA the largest radio company in the world and, in 1926, RCA co-founded the National Broadcasting Company (NBC).[120]

AT&T dates back to the invention of the telephone. The Bell Telephone Company was established in 1877 by Alexander Graham Bell, who obtained the first US patent for the telephone, and his father-in-law also established American Telephone and Telegraph Company in 1885, which acquired the Bell Telephone Company and became the primary telephone company in the United States.[121] The company acquired its main competitor in 1881. It had bought a controlling interest in the Western Electric Company and after J. P. Morgan had gained control of AT&T, by 1907, the company systematically bought up smaller competitors until it agreed to the Kingsbury Commitment of 1913 with the US government to avoid antitrust action. The agreement forbade AT&T from acquiring any more independent phone companies without the approval of the Interstate Commerce Commission, which was created in 1887 with the original purpose to regulate the railroads.[122]

The economic significance of the great railroad booms has been debated among economists. Against the loss taken by many shareholders, there may be spillover effects for the industry and the economy: the impact on the marginal cost of transporting

---

[119] Ibid.
[120] Doenecke (2000). Quasi-monopolies could be found in many industries.
[121] Brooks (1976).
[122] Satkowiak (2013).

commodities, which may have been lower than those faced by railroads in Germany and France as the consolidation of railroads often involved acquiring rail lines and rolling stock below replacement cost. This may have further reduced the cost of transportation and thus accelerated the interlacing of local and regional markets. In the early 1900s, more than 60% of the US stock market consisted of railway companies and seven entities controlled two-thirds of the rail mileage. But over time, other industries proved to be more lasting creators of value for shareholders.

The early twentieth century saw a period of uninterrupted and rapid economic development, lasting until 1914, when World War I began in Europe, or until 1917 when the United States entered the war. This period became the age of the large corporation. As markets grew, the equity requirements for many businesses compelled them to tap the stock market, and as a result, the number of IPOs increased. The market for industrial securities, both by capitalization and volume of trading on the New York Stock Exchange, expanded massively. Increasingly widespread participation in stock investing was thus both a necessity and a consequence of the growing capitalization of joint-stock companies.

As early as 1917, the US stock market would be dominated by steel, oil, motor, and retailers such as Sears and F. W. Woolworth.[123,124] The IPOs of retailers also marked a gradual departure from the asset-rich companies that had dominated most of the stock market activity during the nineteenth century. In the early twentieth century, Henry Goldman (Figure 1.10) found a way to underwrite securities for companies like Sears and Woolworth that had few hard assets—traditionally a key to valuation and underwriting. He convinced investors of a new approach to valuation, not based simply on assets owned but on a company's ability to generate income and, ultimately, its earnings and goodwill. The use of the price-earnings ratio as a key metric would become common industry practice.

---

[123] *Forbes Magazine*, September 15, 1967.
[124] AT&T's desire to maintain its telecommunications monopoly and avoid antitrust actions required a delicate balance. By investing in research and development through Bell Labs and portraying itself as a responsible, innovative company, AT&T aimed to maintain the support of regulators and policymakers.

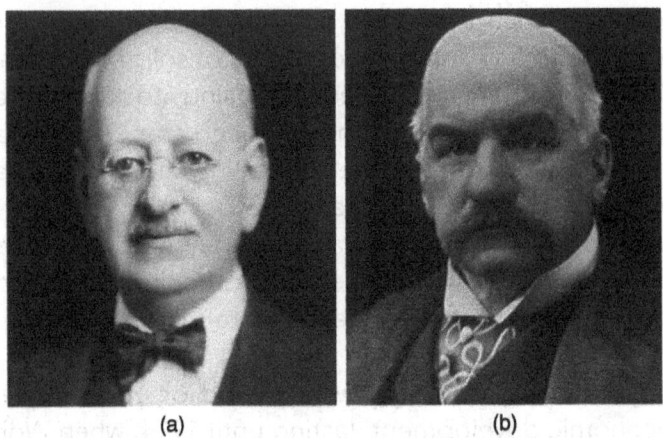

(a)   (b)

Figure 1.10 **(a) Henry Goldman (September 21, 1857–April 4, 1937) was an American banker and son of Marcus Goldman, who founded Goldman Sachs in 1869. He pioneered equity raising for consumer goods and other "asset-light" firms and invented the concept of earnings-based valuations and the price-earnings-ratio. (b) J. P. Morgan (April 17, 1837–March 19, 1913) was an American financier and investment banker who invested in everything from Thomas Edison's electric company to railroads and steel companies.**
Sources: Goldman Sachs and JohnPierpontMorgan / Wikimedia Commons / Public Domain.

A Regulatory Backlash

The use of trusts for consolidating industries and the M&A strategies employed in that context anticipated the methods buyout firms would later adopt, including the use of acquisition vehicles. However, what truly set these trusts apart was their exclusive focus on single industries and their relentless pursuit of market dominance. This distinction generated far more controversy than even the modern-day private equity industry, which is no stranger to controversies, has ever encountered.

The M&A boom of the 1880s created a backlash, as both the power of banks like Morgan and the growing public hostility toward monopolies increased (Figure 1.11). Banks like Morgan & Co. acted not only as organizers and financiers of the trusts but also exercised an outsized influence over their governance. As an example, Charles Costner, a partner of Morgan & Co., reportedly held 59 board seats in 1884.[125] This caused some states in the USA to enact anti-monopoly laws and led to the passage by the US Congress of the Sherman Antitrust Act in 1890, followed by the Clayton Act of 1914.[126]

---

[125] Carosso (1987).
[126] Bedier (2018).

Figure 1.11   The Bosses of the Senate. J. Ottmann Lith. Co. after Joseph Keppler Puck. January 23,1889.
Source: US Senate Collection / Wikimedia Commons / Public Domain.

Further attempts to reduce the power of the trust companies resulted in the Clayton Act of 1914 and that same year, Congress also created the Federal Trade Commission (FTC) to regulate monopolies, eliminate unfair competition, and prevent the use of unfair or deceptive business practices.

These initiatives aimed to restrict mergers and acquisitions of organizations that could substantially lessen competition or create a monopoly and focused on horizontal mergers in the same industry that aimed to create dominant market positions.[127]

Private and Public Equity Until WWII

The stock market Panic of 1907 set in motion a severe economic contraction swiftly followed by another (milder) contraction in 1910 and production and real incomes declined during this period and

---

[127] Railways would subsequently continue to be in the crosshairs of antitrust enforcement. In 1913, the Supreme Court ordered Union Pacific Railroad to divest itself of all Southern Pacific stock (acquired in 1901), and Congress enacted additional laws, giving increased regulatory powers to the Interstate Commerce Commission (ICC). After a brief period of nationalized management during WWI until 1920, the ICC continued to regulate the railroad industry (United States, 1906).

were not reversed until the start of WWI increased demand.[128] After the war, severe hyperinflation in Europe took place and the lack of demand from war-ravaged Europe reduced trade flows. Real exports from Canada and the USA to Germany—among the world's largest trade flows in 1913—collapsed from $4.6 billion in that year to zero in 1918. This reflected a broader erosion in the European share of world exports. In 1910, Europe commanded a 60% share of world exports, trailed by North America at 15%. In 1920, the respective figures were 39.4% and 33.8%.[129] Compared to Europe, the post-war recession in the USA was brief.

Still, the year 1920 had one of the highest inflation rates in American history;[130] production, however, did not fall as much as might be expected from the deflation with GNP estimates ranging from −2.5% to −7%.[131] In 1923, the US economy made a strong recovery but the popular characterization of the 1920s as a period of vigorous, vital economic growth paints too rosy a picture. GNP per capita grew 2.7% per year[132] between 1920 and 1929, which was about in line with its trend since the 1870s.[133]

In the 1920s, the US economy experienced a recovery and growth, driven by the adoption of inventions from previous decades. The widespread use of these inventions, such as electric motors, Aluminium, and synthetic materials, contributed to the growth of the manufacturing sector and the automobile industry. This led to the emergence of new consumer goods and marketing techniques, including catalog shopping and department stores. While this period of change brought increased living standards, mass mobility, and new forms of communication and entertainment, it also led to winners and losers. Some regions of the US experienced significant deindustrialization, as employment in industries such as cotton manufacturing and textiles declined. Other regions benefited from creating and expanding entirely new sectors, such as automobiles, radios, and other consumer durables, while mechanization

---

[128] NBER (2023).
[129] Jacks (2018).
[130] Minneapolis FED (2023).
[131] Jacks (2018).
[132] Smiley (2023).
[133] VisualizingEconomics (2023).

and migration to the cities changed the face of rural America. In the late 1920s, millions of people were employed in industries that did not even exist at the close of the last war—radio, air conditioning, rayon, and other synthetic fibers, and plastics are examples of the products of these industries.[134] By 1929, railways had disappeared from the list of the largest US companies, which was led by Standard Oil, GM, and Ford Motor Company, and included numerous oil firms, retail chains, electrical firms, and steel producers.[135]

During the war, financial dominance had crossed the Atlantic from London to New York. After WWI, the NYSE became the world's largest stock market overtaking London. This marked the beginning of the global pre-eminence of the US capital market.

The Roaring Twenties roared loudest and longest on the NYSE. Share prices rose to unprecedented heights. The Dow Jones Industrial Average increased six-fold from 63 in August 1921 to 381 in September 1929. After prices peaked, economist Irving Fisher proclaimed, "stock prices have reached what looks like a permanently high plateau."[136] The growth of retail investors in the stock markets drove the boom. A new sector of brokerage houses, radio broadcasting of stock prices and market news, new investment vehicles such as investment trusts, and (to a lesser extent) mutual funds helped to popularize stock investing.[137] The American people purchased stocks in record numbers. Stocks were purchased on a monthly basis, through investment clubs, and on margin. Nothing like the popular infatuation with stock investing that the United States experienced in the 1920s can be found in previous periods of its history.[138] But what drove retail investors to stocks? Inflation is one explanation. Annual inflation was over 12% from 1914 to 1920, compared to less than 1% in the previous 50 years until 1920. The loss of purchasing power was unprecedented, except for the 1860s.[139] Traditional savings investments had lost purchasing value, prompting investors

---

[134] Hsu and Kenney (2005).
[135] *Forbes Magazine*, September 15, 1967.
[136] Richardson et al. (2023).
[137] Shiller (2021).
[138] Domitrovic (2020).
[139] Official Inflation Data (2023).

to seek alternatives. The stock market promised income through dividends and inflation protection in the form of capital gains.

After 1920, interest rates that had climbed during the war started to decrease and debt became cheaper and more widely available. From the early 1920s to the end of 1927, interest rates declined, even though corporations, real estate owners, and state and local governments were large net borrowers. There was a large volume of savings, but part of the explanation for the downward drift in rates may have been the mix of public policy actions adopted. The federal government was operating at a surplus and retiring debt, and there was a rapid expansion of bank credit and money during much of this period.[140] Many brokerage firms introduced leveraged funds called "investment trusts" or offered margin accounts that enabled ordinary people to purchase corporate equities with borrowed funds. Purchasers put down a fraction of the price, typically 10%, and borrowed the rest. The stocks that they bought served as collateral for the loan. Borrowed money poured into equity markets, and stock prices soared. Commercial banks continued to loan money to speculators, and other lenders invested increasing sums in loans to brokers.[141]

The M&A market was thriving. Probably due to antitrust legislation, specifically the Clayton Act of 1914, the emphasis shifted to vertical mergers, i.e., manufacturers focused on vertical integration, with a desire to control their supply chains and distribution channels, rather than merging with competitors to increase market share. The Ford Motor Company, for example, owned steel factories, railroads, and automotive assembly lines. Utility holding companies were all the rage.

As a frontrunner to corporate raiders, holding firms would issue enormous amounts of debt to acquire smaller operating companies and then utilize their dividends to repay bondholders. The Alleghany Corporation, a holding company founded by the Van Sweringen brothers to develop a real estate and railway empire, was a notorious example. Their holding firm acquired control of other holding companies and used their acquisitions as collateral

---

[140] Luttrel (1965).
[141] Chernow (1991).

Figure 1.12   Westinghouse Electric Company factory, Pittsburgh.
Source: Science History Images / Alamy Stock Photo.

for new debt to finance additional acquisitions. In the words of the *New York Times*, it was "the holding company device pushed to its uttermost limits." By 1929, their holdings were valued at $3 billion.[142] The stock market boom was not driven by a particular sector or excitement about a new technology—it was broad-based, fueled by leverage, and reflected the simple belief that stocks go up and everybody can get rich.

But there were certainly new sectors that investors could choose from and get excited about: The automobile industry experienced significant growth during the 1920s, led by companies such as Ford, General Motors, and Chrysler.

The invention of radio and other electronic devices led to the growth of companies such as RCA, Westinghouse, and General Electric (Figure 1.12). These companies benefited from the increased demand for consumer electronics and the growing access to the electricity grid. Electricity had finally reached the consumer and many smaller electrical utilities went public during the stock

---

[142] McQuaig and Neil (2013).

market boom of the 1920s. The number of publicly traded utilities increased from about 300 in 1920 to over 1,000 in 1929. When the market crashed in 1929, it had a significant impact on the electric utility industry and resulted in accelerated consolidation.[143]

The aviation industry also saw significant growth during the 1920s, with the establishment of companies such as Boeing, Douglas Aircraft, and Lockheed.

The financial industry itself experienced significant growth during the 1920s, with the creation of investment trusts and the increasing popularity of buying stocks on margin.

This epic boom ended in a cataclysmic bust. On Black Monday, October 28, 1929, the Dow declined nearly 13%. On the following day, Black Tuesday, the market dropped nearly 12%. By mid-November, the Dow had lost almost half of its value (Figure 1.13). The slide continued through till the summer of 1932, when the Dow closed at 41.22, its lowest value of the twentieth century, 89% below its peak.

What followed was the Great Depression, which created high unemployment and a mass failure of businesses. As a result, manufacturing became even more skewed toward larger industrial units as smaller firms and factories failed in disproportionate numbers. In the financial sector, the story was similar, as 2,000 investment firms and 7,000 banks, the vast majority being smaller local firms, failed.[144] The financial sector difficulties severely impacted smaller firms' ability to secure long-term loans and contributed to a high rate of bankruptcies.[145] The worst years of the Great Depression were 1932 and 1933. Around 300,000 companies went out of business. Hundreds of thousands of families could not pay their mortgages and were evicted from their homes. Millions of people migrated away from the Dust Bowl region in the Midwest.[146] The Great Depression was the greatest recession in American history, lasting nearly ten years until the onset of World War II. Scholars

---

[143] David (1990), p. 87.
[144] Chernow (1991).
[145] Hsu and Kenney (2005).
[146] Duignan (2023).

Figure 1.13 **Crowds panic in the Wall Street district of Manhattan due to the heavy trading on the stock market in New York City on October 24, 1929.**
Source: Associated Press / Wikimedia Commons / Public Domain.

continue to argue about the elements that created it and contributed to its length, as well as the fiscal and monetary responses or lack thereof that contributed to its severity or hindered an earlier turnaround.[147] The stock market crash and the Great Depression that followed, demonstrated again that credit-fueled asset price inflation has the potential to cause a great financial crisis, followed by a recession. In contrast, speculative excess in equity markets—the tech mania—tends to leave relatively little wreckage behind.

Was the System of Financing Entrepreneurial Ventures Broken?

From a historical perspective, the ability of entrepreneurs to raise capital and the expansion of capital markets to connect capital

---

[147] St. Louis FED provides a series of articles and podcasts that investigate the causes of the Great Depression and the debate about policy responses (St. Louis FED, 2023).

owners and users had reached a high point. Private finance has long played a role in providing seed and venture capital for riskier ventures. As discussed in previous sections of this book, the tale of funding overseas ventures and the early patent boom in Britain do not imply a shortage of risk capital provided by major and minor capital owners. As the pace of invention quickened and new markets emerged, so did the potential to raise equity and engage an ever-increasing number of investors. Wealthy aristocrats, merchants, and, later, industrialists would offer seed capital for new businesses, and they were frequently joined by smaller investors when given the opportunity. There was no indication that this would change substantially during or after the Great Depression. On the contrary, wealthy industrialists and bankers used their personal relationships to invest. For example, Laurance Rockefeller, the fourth son of John D. Rockefeller Jr., led a carve-out of Eastern Airlines from GM and supplied seed funding to James McDonnell, who went on to found McDonnell Aircraft Corporation.[148] In doing this, he walked in the footsteps of magnates like J. P. Morgan, who provided capital to T. A. Edison or W. v. Siemens. After the war, he founded Rockefeller Brothers, Inc. (later Venrock), setting an example for other large family trusts such as the Whitney's, who founded J. H. Whitney & Company, and the Philipps, who founded Bessemer Securities, which became early examples of "modern" private equity. Those new family-funded firms used professional management teams that took charge of undertaking private equity transactions.[149]

The stock market evolved to the point where multinational industry behemoths' vast capital needs could be met. However, there is also a long history of companies raising smaller amounts of capital based on an idea or patent, and there was no reason why the British patent boom couldn't repeat itself.

Finally, the M&A markets had matured. Carve-outs, hostile takeovers, and industry consolidation via acquisitions or mergers to establish

---

[148] Ivashina and Lerner (2019).
[149] See Colin (2016) for a good description of the beginnings of private equity (PE) in the USA.

market leaders were all commonplace. Bankers would orchestrate the takeover and restructuring of underperforming or distressed companies and occasionally seek to consolidate entire industries. The magnitude and frequency of such transactions left no doubt that there was no scarcity of "private equity" in the market.

There was also no evidence that Schumpeterian creative destruction was being hampered or that the creation of large corporations reduced the pace of innovation. Anti-monopoly legislation's implementation and enforcement were designed to allay those concerns. Still, there has been and continues to be debate over whether technology manias are a rational way for investors to deploy capital. The answer may well be related to the assumed investment horizon. Concepts in finance and economics like stochastic dominance examine, for example, whether investors' initial enthusiasm and speculation yield sustainable, positive returns and are used to analyze how investors with different time horizons may perceive their opportunity sets differently.[150]

So, accepting that booms and busts are a natural part of the system of organizing resource (capital) allocation and looking back in time from the vantage point of the early 1930s, one could argue that the system of funding entrepreneurial ventures had evolved to the point where it was fit for purpose at the time.[151]

---

[150] The dominance of one data set over another in terms of the value of the outcomes is referred to as stochastic dominance. For example, participants in an initial public offering (IPO) may believe that their expected return on the next hot issue is positive based on previous data and a very short investment horizon, even if they are aware or believe that a bubble generates overall losses to investors over the entire cycle. Similarly, survivors who become dominant firms in their industry due to post-bubble consolidation may be able to generate value (a quasi-monopolistic rent) that compensates investors with a long investment horizon for the risk of trying to pick a winner.

[151] Market dominance was not limited to the core industries that drove the Industrial Revolution, such as railroads, steel, and electrical engineering. In 1895, the Eastman Kodak Company produced 90% of the world's film and maintained this near-monopoly market position for decades; one rationale suggested for its escape from antitrust action was that its break-up would have benefited the German industry, particularly AGFA. This exemplifies the relationship between global competitiveness and the ability to scale through a dominant position in the vast US home market (Hover, 2018).

A Changing Institutional Environment

During the decade that followed the stock market crash, there was a growing concern that the system of financing innovation that had sustained the rise of the USA to pre-eminence as a global economic power might be substantially broken. The following developments gave rise to such concern.

In 1933, the Glass-Steagall Banking Act fundamentally changed the operation of banks by forcing them to sever their commercial bank function of taking deposits and making loans from investment banking activities and the ownership of sizable equity positions in industrial firms.[152] This discouraged Wall Street firms like Morgan & Co. from restructuring, acquiring, and consolidating industries. They risked their capital to get shares or trust certificates, not just for the fees.

As many smaller investors lost their life savings during the crash, there were also calls for better investor protection that led in 1934 to the creation of the Securities and Exchange Commission (SEC) to curtail securities abuses and require greater disclosure for firms wishing to offer stock to the public.[153] This increased the hurdle for smaller firms or startups with no business record to raise equity on the stock market.

The trend toward larger firms, partly brought about by consolidation in many industries, started well before the Great Depression. Those large firms had the resources to conduct significant in-house R&D. But the growing role of corporate R&D raised concerns about large corporations' conflicts of interest. It is credible that those firms would focus on R&D that improves their products and processes or allows them to enter new markets. Still, it is less plausible that they would be interested in innovation that could disrupt their core market or reduce their profitability.

A progressive income tax made riskier investments less appealing. Higher taxation and the Great Crash's wealth reduction cast doubts on wealthy investors' willingness to fund entrepreneurs or startup firms developing new technology or commercializing innovations.

---

[152] Chernow (1991).
[153] Wikipedia (2022c).

The combination of many banking failures and the pivotal role of the stock market as a source of equity funding increased concerns that smaller companies would find their funding sources squeezed. Such firms had no access to the stock market and faced a lending squeeze.

With access to more sectors and companies due to stock market growth, the idea of pooling resources and spreading risk gained traction. Pooled investment vehicles were boosting this trend. By 1929, 19 open-ended mutual funds faced 700 closed-end investment trusts. After the 1929 stock market crash, highly leveraged closed-end funds collapsed while many open-ended funds survived.[154] Investment trusts took large leveraged positions in companies and participated in restructurings, mergers, and asset sales, but mutual funds did not. The Investment Company Act of 1940 regulated the mutual fund industry. It stipulated limited ownership stakes, making investing meaningfully in smaller firms and startups impossible and restricting capital for takeovers, mergers, and acquisitions.[155] The open-ended nature of those funds also steered them toward larger capitalization stocks that could be liquidated quickly to meet redemptions.[156] As diversified stock market investing gained traction, the concern was that startup and growth financing for unlisted firms would be crowded out.

The Federal Employees Retirement Act of 1920 established a comprehensive pension scheme for US public servants a year earlier. After 1920, an increasing number of state and local employees and all federal employees had occupational pensions. The Internal Revenue Act of 1921 exempted employee pension fund contributions

---

[154] McWinney (2022).

[155] Wikipedia (2022c). Fewer than a dozen funds—most notably, the Vanguard Wellington fund, launched in July 1929 and the Pioneer fund, launched in February 1928, have survived since the great crash of 1929. The first US mutual fund—the Massachusetts Investors Trust, founded in July 1924, is also still in existence (Barron's, 2017).

[156] The first modern mutual fund was launched in the USA in 1924, and Fidelity, still among the largest mutual fund managers in the world, was founded in 1946. The expectation that those funds would become significant holders of corporate equity proved prescient. In 2020, the Federal Reserve estimates that about 15% of US stocks were held by the mutual fund industry.

from corporate income taxes, promoting occupational pension schemes. Private sector pension coverage was initially small, with 15% of private workers enrolled in corporate pension plans in 1940. But the trend was clear: over time, enrollment would increase, and pension funds, especially public funds, would become significant pools of capital. With more savings in collective savings schemes, it was unclear if the public would continue to invest in IPOs to fund future technology waves.[157]

The rise of mutual funds and pension schemes, as well as life insurance firms, meant that an ever more significant portion of financial capital was in the hands of institutional investors. Investors were compelled to take a rather passive approach as shareholders and focused on investing in the market. Many observers believed this trend was set to continue. These institutions need to deal in size and thus prefer large cap stocks, causing fears that the capital markets were heading in a direction detrimental to the financing of innovation and entrepreneurship. As many jobs were lost during the Great Depression, another challenge was how employment could be created in promising industries to replace the jobs lost. Those topics were debated but did not result in significant action as WWII started, and the USA moved toward a war economy. But these concerns would resurface after the war and lead to developments that enabled private market investing in its modern form.

---

[157] The following decades would reveal the impact of those trends, and in 1960 about half of the US workforce was enrolled in a corporate pension plan; by 1991, pension funds would own 40% of US corporate stocks (Phipps, 2021).

Chapter 2

Enterprise Financing in the USA from WWII to the 1960s

Until World War II (WWII), the principal sources of private capital were wealthy entrepreneurial families, and the influence of private market investment firms linked to those families has continued to this day both in the USA and abroad. Examples include Vulcan Capital, Paul Allen's family office and Jeff Bezos's investment group, Bezos Expedition.[1] Mark Zuckerberg and Priscilla Chan invest through ICONIQ Capital and the Chan Zuckerberg Initiative.[2] They are part of a long line of entrepreneurs who turned into angel investors or engaged in private equity deals that stretches back at least to Bill Hewlett and David Packard. Outside the USA,

---

[1] Jeff Bezos invested in Google before it went public, Uber and Airbnb's Series B, and Twitter. These are just a few examples of Bezos's angel investments, and there may be others that are not publicly known.
[2] Krupp (2020).

the Fleming family office of the relatives of banking pioneer Robert Fleming and James Bond creator Ian Fleming (today Stonehage Fleming), private markets firm Bregal established by the Brennink-meijers (C&A fashion group), L Chatterton backed by LVMH owner Bernard Arnault, or Feri Trust that belongs to the German Quant family (BMW) are examples.

This isn't new, but a continuation of past patterns. Funding ventures via friends, family, partners, and stocks provided risk capital for the Industrial Revolutions, trade, and plantations. So, why a new startup financing form?

The American Research & Development Corporation's (ARD) sponsors thought that Depression-era reforms in the stock market and banking disrupted capital flow to new firms. Some people, especially in New England, were worried that mutual funds and investment trusts were diverting capital to safer investments, leaving less for riskier ones. This concern was not limited to just businesspeople and academics. Merrill Griswold, then president of a large investment trust, Massachusetts Investment Trust, believed that Americans investing in trusts managed by professionals were limiting capital available for new firms. Startup financing was seen as important for creating new industries and fostering innovation, which could lead to economic growth through creative destruction.[3]

2.1 RAISING PUBLIC EQUITY FOR STARTUP FINANCING

The first self-proclaimed venture capital firm in the USA was the American Research & Development Corporation (ARD), founded in 1946 by the Harvard Business School Professor Georges Doriot (Figure 2.1).[4]

---

[3] Hsu and Kenney (2005).
[4] ARD gets narrowly beaten by the Industrial and Commercial Finance Corporation that was established by the Bank of England and some UK banks in 1945, which later became 3i Group Plc, a listed private equity company still in existence (Merlin-Jones, 2010).

Figure 2.1 Georges Doriot (second right, seated) with project teams, 1963.
Source: HBS Archives Photograph Collection.

The problem, expressed by Ralph Flanders (1945),[5] was that large incumbent firms were willing—to use Clayton Christensen's terminology—to invest in sustaining technologies relevant to their existing business but not interested in pursuing disruptive technologies that would upend their market position or business model.[6] This bias required a market solution to the problem of how to fund innovations that fall outside existing corporate boundaries.

The founders and promoters of ARD aimed to provide a market solution to the problem of how to fund innovations that fall outside existing corporate boundaries. They envisioned venture capital as a mechanism for recycling a portion of the collective savings entrusted to institutional investors, such as investment trusts and mutual funds, into innovative new firms. In contrast to venture capital firms formed contemporaneously by wealthy families, ARD was the only non-family venture capital firm, meaning it had to raise

---

[5] Flanders (1945).
[6] The concept of sustaining and disruptive innovation goes back to Clayton Christensen and is further discussed in Box 3.3, "Disruptive Innovation" in Chapter 3 (Christensen, 1997).

capital from outside sources. As investment trusts and mutual funds invest in publicly traded stocks, the investment vehicle was required to be a publicly traded company to meet their investment criteria. ARD was viewed as a means of encouraging these diversified institutional funds to allocate at least a portion of their capital to ensure that these growing capital pools could provide expansion and venture capital. ARD was structured as a closed-end investment fund listed on the New York Stock Exchange to attract a small portion of the mutual funds' capital.[7] The earliest US venture capital fund was thus a listed private equity vehicle.

ARD was founded on the premise that there was a need for a new financial institution to make early-stage investments. However, until the early 1960s, it made a relatively small number of such investments, which nevertheless proved significant. In 1947, ARD made its first investment in the High Voltage Engineering Company. Several MIT professors established the company to develop X-ray technology for cancer treatment. In 1955, when High Voltage went public, the initial $200,000 investment was worth $1,800,000.[8] In 1957, ARD established the standard venture capital model with its highly successful investment in Digital Equipment Corporation (DEC). ARD contributed $70,000 to acquire a 77% stake in DEC. Over the subsequent 14 years, the value of the investment in DEC rose to $355 million. During its 26-year existence, ARD's investment in Digital contributed to nearly half of its revenue. During the 1980s and 1990s, venture capital's concept of the "home run" was synonymous with DEC, and the term spread throughout the industry.

The aim of ARD was to demonstrate attractive returns in order to entice additional institutions to provide capital. Even though some initial early-stage investments generated high returns, over time, this agenda focused it on generating income and may have prompted ARD to pivot its investments toward existing companies with lower risk that could generate dividends, interest, or management fees quickly.[9] However, the most likely explanation for the decline in R&D-based investments was the heightened competition for deals in the venture capital marketplace after 1960.

---

[7] Hsu and Kenney (2005).
[8] Ibid.
[9] Gompers (1994).

Competition came from both a federal initiative in 1958 to fund new ventures, small business investment corporations (SBICs), and, later, from an alternative private form of organizing startup financing—the venture capital limited partnership.[10]

The fact that ARD was a closed-end investment fund was problematic in three significant ways: first, the structure of the investment fund compelled ARD's management to generate a steady cash flow.[11] Second, it impeded the provision of competitive compensation to ARD's investment professionals, reducing their incentives and ultimately leading to their resignations.[12] Third, closed-end investment funds frequently trade at a discount to their net asset value. The share price performance thus lagged below the NAV performance and investors that needed to sell their shares could not realize the full value generated by the underlying investments.[13] As recorded by D. H. Hsu, ARD traded mostly at a discount to the value of its assets, which at the end of 1968, was 29.9% to its net asset value.[14]

2.2   SMALL BUSINESS INVESTMENT CORPORATIONS (SBICS)

The passage of the Small Business Investment Act (SBDA) in 1958 authorized the creation of Small Business Investment Corporations (SBICs) to provide funding to small firms. The bull stock market from 1959 through the beginning of 1962 was receptive to both

---

[10] Hsu and Kenney (2005).

[11] To achieve this, ARD invested part of its money in debt instruments issued by the portfolio companies to be able to pay dividends and would charge management fees to portfolio companies. The partial debt financing and the management fee charged to portfolio companies were not attractive to startups. Those features became a competitive disadvantage compared to other forms of venture capital funds that emerged over time.

[12] As a closed-end investment company, ARD was subject to regulation by the US Securities and Exchange Commission (SEC) under the Investment Company Act of 1940. It prevented employees of the investment company from taking equity stakes or receiving options in either the investment company or portfolio companies. As a result ARD lost staff. For example, Joseph Powell, Doriot's first assistant, left ARD and formed Boston Capital Corporation (a SBIC), in 1960.

[13] The discount to net asset value (NAV) would become a feature of listed PE companies and reduces relative performance compared to the broader stock market. This is exacerbated by the cash holdings resulting from asset disposals kept for future investments.

[14] Hsu and Kenney (2005).

the SBICs raising public capital and initial public stock offerings of electronics firms. SBICs were able to make several companies public during the boom. The initiative resulted in the creation of several hundred SBICs in less than four years. Many of these were formed expressly to invest in startups. By the mid-1960s, 700 SBICs controlled most of the risk capital invested in the United States.[15]

SBIC licensees received a significant subsidy and could receive up to 200% leverage in the form of senior and subordinated loans at favorable interest rates. An applicant organization needed at least $150,000 in paid-in capital to get an SBIC license and to receive the maximum 200% leverage in the form of 15-year loans and 20-year subordinated debentures with a 5% interest rate. SBICs offered specific tax incentives for investors, such as the deduction of a portion of dividends from the company's taxable income. This exclusion effectively decreased the tax burden on dividends received by investors.[16] SBICs did therefore benefit from a government subsidy and tax advantages that were not available to ARD.[17] These firms were direct competitors to ARD. But loans had to be serviced and forced SBICs to invest in startups that paid dividends, which is anathema to fast-growing firms.

The recession after the first oil embargo of 1973–1974 hit young firms particularly hard. IPO activity dropped to one-tenth its previous level and many SBIC-backed firms began losing money. SBIC-backed companies, which were often financed with a mix of equity and debt, could not meet interest obligations. At the same time, SBICs themselves were highly leveraged and could not meet their interest and principal repayment schedules. Many were forced to liquidate. By 1978, only 250 SBICs were still active.[18]

Despite their flaws, SBICs and ARD helped catalyze many of the VC firms created in the early 1960s.

> In 1962 Franklin "Pitch" Johnson thought the new law made the US
> "see that there was a problem and that [venture investing] was a way

---

[15] Gompers (1994).

[16] Hsu and Kenney (2005).

[17] Weinman (1974).

[18] Quoted from Gompers (1994). He shows that, in 1988, SBICs accounted for just 7% of venture capital financing.

*to do something . . . it formed the seed of the idea." Bill Draper also
saw the SBDA as a catalyst: "[Without it] I never would have gotten
into venture capital . . . it made the difference between not being able
to do it, not having the money."*[19]

Many believe SBICs filled a void from 1958 to the early 1970s, by
which point the partnership-based venture firms took off.[20]

ARD suffered from organizational design flaws, primarily because
it could not provide adequate compensation to its investment professionals, which put them at a disadvantage compared to SBICs.
But both types of investment vehicles relied on income and thus
the ability of their portfolio companies to pay dividends, which
steered them away from fast-growing companies that focused
on growth rather than net earnings. Doriot ultimately distributed
ARD's DEC stock and sold the company to Textron, an industrial
conglomerate, in 1991. The fact that he kept DEC stocks for more
than 30 years shows that Doriot saw ARD as a supplier of permanent capital rather than the temporary ownership that investing
through limited partnerships implies. The SBICs were constrained
in the amount of capital they could raise and showed the perils
of in-fund leverage. Substantial losses followed initial successes
once the economic environment became more challenging. ARD
and the SBICs were thus part of an evolution that made venture
capital a significant constituent of the US innovation system. But as
long as public venture capital firms are double-taxed on corporate
profits, tax-transparent limited partnerships are the more attractive investment vehicle. Limited partnerships aligned investment
managers (GPs) and their (tax-exempt) investors.

2.3 EARLY VC PARTNERSHIPS

Draper, Gaither, and Anderson, the first venture capital company
in Silicon Valley, was founded in September 1959 by two military
generals and the former chair of RAND. Many aspects of the modern venture capital firm may be traced back to Draper, Gaither, and

---

[19] Quoted from Feld (2014).
[20] Ibid.

Anderson, who combined the practices of famous family investors with the technology- and university-centered approaches pioneered by Georges Doriot at the Boston-based ARD.[21]

Some of the founders of venture firms were former members of the ARD team or students in Doriot's class at Harvard. Greylock Partners was founded in 1965 in Cambridge, Massachusetts, by Bill Elfers and Dan Gregory, who had both worked at ARD.

Other firms that can trace their origin to ARD were Boston-based Charles River Ventures (CRV), which was founded in 1970 by a group of venture capitalists, including Charles Waite, George Putnam III, and Ted Dintersmith. The firm is now known as CRV and has invested in companies such as Twitter, Zendesk, and HubSpot.

Matrix Partners was founded in 1977 by Paul Ferri, who previously worked at Venrock Associates and Greylock Partners. TA Associates was founded in Boston in 1968 by Peter Brooke with the backing of his former firm, Tucker, Anthony & RL Day, an investment bank, and broker. Warburg Pincus (1966), a New York-based firm, raised its first venture capital and growth fund in 1971, and Patricof & Co., the predecessor of Apax Partners, was founded in 1969. These firms formed the core of East Coast venture capital. While ARD and the early venture capital firms in Boston and New York focused on the East Coast, the new technology firms established in California and the opportunity they presented was noticed, leading to the formation of local VC firms:

Pitch Johnson and his friend, Bill Draper (the son of William Draper, the founder of Draper, Anderson) decided to co-found Draper and Johnson Investment Company in 1962, followed by Sutter Hill Ventures (1965), a venture capital company in Palo Alto. Bill's son, Tim, founded Draper Fisher Jurvetson in 1985, who later rebranded to Draper Associates (Figure 2.2).[22]

Arthur Rock, who is often considered one of the pioneers of the venture capital industry, co-founded several venture capital firms

[21] Berlin (2008b).
[22] Schubarth (2012).

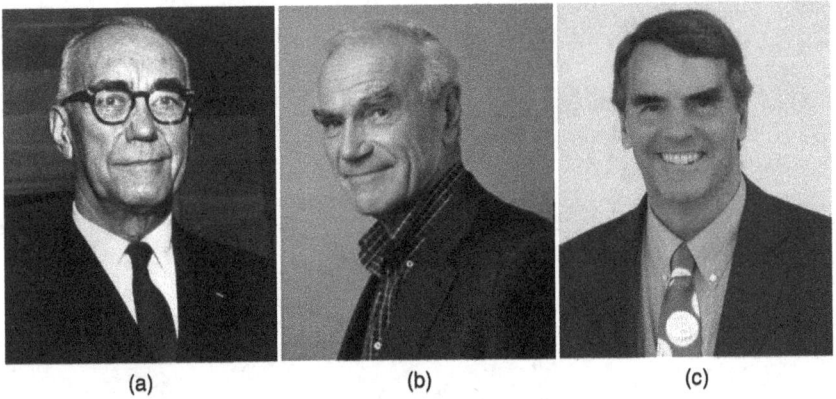

(a)   (b)   (c)

Figure 2.2 Three generations of venture capitalists in the Valley: (a) William Draper II of Draper, Gaither and Anderson; (b) his son, Bill Draper, who worked at a venture firm founded by his father in 1959 before setting up his own firm, Draper & Johnson. Subsequently, in 1965, Draper founded Sutter Hill Ventures, which remains one of the top venture capital firms. (c) Bill's son, Tim Draper, founder of Draper Fisher Jurvetson (DFJ) in 1985.
Sources: (a) Truman Library / Wikimedia Commons / Public Domain; (b) IMDb Inc.; (c) Web Summit / Flickr / CC BY-2.0.

throughout his career. His first venture capital firm was called Davis & Rock, which he founded in 1961 with his business partner, Tommy Davis (see Chapter 3). Mayfield Fund was founded in 1969 by Tommy Davis and Tully Friedman, Tom Davis was a successful entrepreneur and had founded several companies before starting Mayfield Fund. He co-founded Scientific Data Systems (SDS), a pioneering computer company that spun-out of Fairchild Semiconductors. Mayfield Fund is a Silicon Valley-based venture capital firm. The creation of the ARD and SBICs was an early attempt to address the funding gap faced by small businesses, but the emergence of Silicon Valley and subsequent technology clusters demonstrated that a self-sustaining ecosystem of innovation could be created with the right mix of factors. Understanding the factors that enabled Silicon Valley is critical for understanding the VC industry and the opportunities it targets because it provides insights into the types of companies and technologies that are most likely to succeed, and the key ingredients that are necessary to create successful technology clusters are examined in Chapter 3.

Chapter 3

How Silicon Valley Came to Be

People have heard about Silicon Valley for so long and often think it is a name on the map. Santa Clara Valley became known as Silicon Valley, a name that originated from the high concentration of silicon chip manufacturers and technology companies that emerged in the area during the development of the semiconductor industry. It has played a significant role in driving the digital revolution by incubating and nurturing groundbreaking technologies, supporting innovative startups, and shaping the global tech landscape, symbolizing technological progress and innovation worldwide. Figure 3.1 gives an overview of the story's different parts covered in this chapter. Logos are retrieved from the webpages of the organizations.

The background of this development is not well known. In this chapter we explore why silicon microchips were so disruptive, the role of government in assisting that technology's success, the role of research and education in forming an industrial cluster, and when venture capital started to play a significant role in

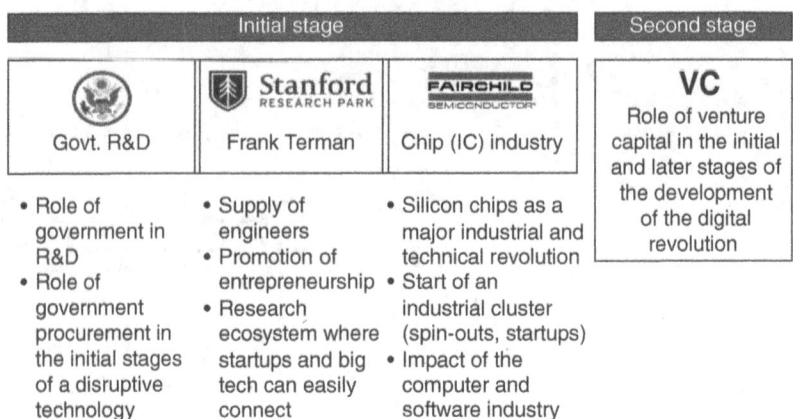

Figure 3.1   Overview of the drivers of the Silicon Valley technology cluster.

funding startups that drove the digital revolution. We investigate the general-purpose technology of silicon microchips and discuss essential concepts related to the disruptive nature of that technological revolution and its impact on the formation of technology clusters, such as Silicon Valley. This is important for understanding the opportunities that the digital transformation—sometimes called the Third Industrial Revolution—created for the venture capital industry and its investors.

3.1   THE GOVERNMENT'S CRITICAL ROLE

In entrepreneurship, the government often plays a supportive role. Since the 1980s, the prevailing view has been that the government should focus on economic liberalization policies, such as privatization and deregulation, to promote the private sector's role in society and the economy. Neoliberalism, which emerged in response to the state's increasing involvement in society and the economy, emphasizes that the private sector is the engine of innovation and economic prosperity. This view holds that the government should not attempt to pick winners or support national champions. Despite the government's role in the technological revolution that brought about the Information Age, scholarly debates have largely focused on the role of technology companies, entrepreneurship, and venture capital. The following sections provide a more balanced assessment of the various forces that contributed to these developments, which is critical to understanding them from an investor's perspective.

A "Non-military" Defense R&D Model During WWII

When Japan attacked Pearl Harbor in 1941, the USA found itself at war with both Japan and Germany, which it had hoped to avoid. Both Axis countries were known for their scientific and technological advances (Figure 3.2). To gain an advantage, the F. D. Roosevelt administration appointed Vannevar Bush (Figure 3.3) to chair the Office of Scientific Research and Development (OSRD) and recruit top researchers. Bush proposed providing public funding to the best universities instead of forcing researchers to join the military, a plan that President Roosevelt approved.[1] The OSRD gave money to more than 321 industrial companies and more than 142 academic institutions and other non-profit groups.

Figure 3.2 German V2 missile launcher.
Source: Weebly / http://sturgiswesthistory.weebly.com/world-war-ii.html / last accessed July 19, 2023.

---

[1] Stewart (1948).

Figure 3.3   Vannevar Bush, chairman of the OSRD who promoted research in US universities to aid the war effort rather than enlisting scientists in the military.
Source: worldpress.com.

Most public funding went to the East Coast, particularly institutions that had already conducted research. One of these was Harvard University's Radio Research Laboratory, led by Frederick Terman, a former MIT student of Vannevar Bush, who later joined Stanford University's engineering faculty.[2]

The Cold War and America's Sputnik Moment

Following the end of World War II, federal R&D spending increased further as the USA entered an arms race with the Soviet Union, particularly in the area of ballistic missiles. Sputnik 1 was launched into orbit by the Soviet Union in 1957 (Figure 3.4).

After the "Sputnik moment" created fear in the USA of falling behind the Soviet Union, President Dwight D. Eisenhower responded by creating two publicly funded institutions: the Defense Advanced Research Projects Agency (DARPA) and the National Aeronautics and Space Administration (NASA), and significantly increasing

---

[2] Zachary (1997).

(a)   (b)

Figure 3.4 (a) Sputnik, the first satellite in space. (b): Like early rockets developed in the USA, the Russian R7 rocket used for the launch was based on the German V2 design developed during WWII.

Sources: (a) http://nssdc.gsfc.nasa.gov/database/ MasterCatalog?sc=1957-001B.
(b) https://www.nbcnews.com/id/wbna21134276 (copyright Novosti Press).

spending on university science programs. Originally known as the Advanced Research Projects Agency (ARPA), DARPA was established on February 7, 1958, with a mission to collaborate with academia, industry, and government partners to conduct research and development projects that would push the boundaries of technology and science, often beyond immediate US military needs. In doing so, it is part of a vision that Bush, the first chairman of the Office of Scientific Research and Development (OSRD), once called "Science—the endless frontier."[3] DARPA differs from other major US research funding agencies in that it operates on a smaller budget ($3.5 billion in 2021). Its roughly 100 program managers, hired for 3-to 5-year stints from academia or business, have considerable discretion over what they finance and actively interact with the researchers they are funding.

The Economist has called DARPA the agency "that shaped the modern world." The article continued to point out that "Moderna's Covid-19 vaccine sits alongside weather satellites, GPS, drones, stealth technology, voice interfaces, the personal computer and the internet are on the list of innovations for which DARPA can claim at least partial credit." Its track record of success has inspired governments worldwide to launch similar research and development

---

[3] Bush (1945).

agencies.[4] DARPA has traditionally used an open research model, partnering with non-defense-focused entities instead of relying on the secrecy typically associated with military research. It operates independently, free from any specific government R&D agenda, and is not required to "pick winners." This approach has facilitated the development of research communities in diverse fields, enabling the rigorous development of ideas, which industry can then refine and manufacture, resulting in both economic and defense benefits.

DARPA's early investments centered on advancing integrated circuit technology.[5] These R&D commitments helped overcome early barriers to the transistor-scaling trends that Gordon Moore (see Box 3.2 for Moore's Law) articulated.

The National Aeronautics and Space Administration (NASA) was created in 1958 with a civilian focus on promoting peaceful space science (Figure 3.5). NASA led most US space exploration efforts, including the Apollo Moon landing missions, the Skylab space station, the Space Shuttle, and the Pathfinder Mars mission. During the 1960s, the US government spent heavily on research and development, with more than half going to the space program, which had strong military connections. This bias toward defense and space-related spending continued until the end of the 1960s. In 1973, NASA reported that the total cost of Project Apollo was $25.4 billion, equivalent to about $158 billion in 2020 dollars.[6]

Figure 3.5   NASA logo.
Source: www.nasa.gov.

R&D spending wasn't funneled only through DARPA and NASA; the Department of Defense also provided major funding,

---

[4] *The Economist* (2021c).
[5] For a detailed overview of the scope of technology investments, see (DARPA, 2018).
[6] Usselmann (2013).

increasing its R&D budget by 20% p.a. in the 1960s. Since 1946, the Office of Naval Research (ONR) and other defense groups have funded university research. While non-federal R&D funding rose 75% from 1953–1960, federal R&D investment under Eisenhower increased 178%, with federal funding for industrial R&D peaking at 59% in 1959 and remaining above 54% until 1967.[7]

Did other countries experience similar R&D developments as the United States? In the western world, the USA was the clear leader in R&D efforts in terms of scale and magnitude. After WWII, the economies of Europe and Japan were devastated and focused on rebuilding basic infrastructure. Many scientists left these countries for the USA where they saw more opportunities. However, the US approach to technology funding, particularly through DARPA, has generated interest from other countries. Several countries have established agencies modeled after DARPA, with varying degrees of success over time, likely due to the technology boom and the dominant role of US companies in that sector (see Box 3.4 Israel's Silicon Wadi).[8,9]

After Eldon C. Hall (Figure 3.6), who was lead hardware designer for the Apollo Guidance Computer at MIT's Instrumentation Laboratory, convinced NASA that integrated circuits (ICs) were the technology to use, NASA became an early client of the fledgling integrated microchip industry, NASA assisted with chip development, manufacturing, and testing. Its procurement accelerated chip development to the point where it could be used for various commercial purposes.[10]

---

[7] Ibid.

[8] Moonshot, Japan's initiative, was launched in 2018. Germany founded the Federal Agency for Disruptive Innovation (SPRIN-D) in 2019. The United Kingdom announced the development of an Advanced Research and Invention Agency (ARIA) in February 2022, with a budget of $1.1 billion over four years (*The Economist*, 2022b).

[9] In 2021, the USA copied its own blueprint by launching the Advanced Project Agency for Health (ARPA-H), to focus on ambitious biomedical research (*The Economist*, 2022h).

[10] Tomayko (1988). While MIT tested the chips, Raytheon was chosen to build the computers. Raytheon's production division for the Apollo computer went from 800 to 2,000 employees in a year to handle the production and was working closely with Fairchild to improve production and quality control of the chips.

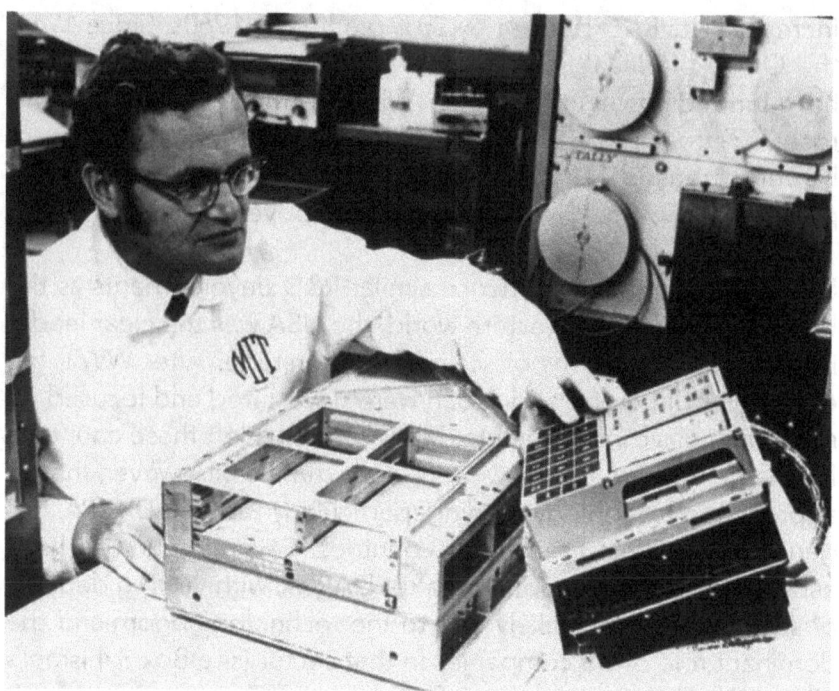

Figure 3.6 Eldon C. Hall with an Apollo guidance computer.
Source: CHM, Mountain View, CA. C. Stark Draper Laboratory CC By 4.0.

3.2   FREDERICK TERMAN'S VISION

After the war, Frederick Terman (Figure 3.7) returned to Stanford and served as Provost from 1955 to 1965. During his tenure, Terman greatly expanded the science, statistics, and engineering departments in order to win more research grants from the Department of Defense. In 1951, he spearheaded the creation of Stanford Industrial Park (now Stanford Research Park).

Frederick Terman played a significant role in the development of Silicon Valley as we know it today. He was not only an educator but also an entrepreneur who believed in the importance of commercializing scientific research. Even before the war, he encouraged his students to form their own companies and personally invested in some of them, resulting in firms such as Litton Industries or Hewlett-Packard.[11] Terman's influence on Stanford University and

---

[11] Stewart (2004).

(a)   (b)

Figure 3.7   (a) Frederick Terman, Dean of the School of Engineering from 1944 to 1958 and Provost at Stanford University from 1955 to 1965. (b) The ground breaking ceremony at the new Eastman Kodak plant in Stanford Industrial Park in 1953.
Sources: (a) https://en.wikipedia.org/wiki/Frederick_Terman. (b) https://www.paloaltohistory.org/stanford-research-park.php.

its engineering department cannot be overstated. His efforts to attract research funding and promote entrepreneurship paved the way for the creation of a vibrant technology cluster that would later become known as Silicon Valley.

Environments, such as the Rad Lab, the Manhattan Project, and the Aberdeen Proving Grounds demonstrated how innovation could develop spectacularly when scientists from universities interacted with industrial scientists and engineers on projects aimed at concrete ends.[12] Stanford Industrial Park was one of Terman's most significant contributions to the development of Silicon Valley. His initial focus was (in contrast to what is frequently written) to attract established companies with large research departments. Companies such as Varian Associates, Hewlett-Packard, Eastman Kodak, General Electric, and Lockheed Corporation (Lockheed Martin) were early movers that established a presence in Stanford Industrial Park.[13]

---

[12] Allen (1991).
[13] Sandelin (2004).

Terman also created an environment that fostered innovation and entrepreneurship. By providing office space and facilitating interaction between startups and established companies and through spillovers, such as patents, partnership agreements, and university spin-offs, the valley became a magnet for tech entrepreneurs.[14] This incubator attracted many promising startups, including Facebook, which relocated to Menlo Park soon after its foundation and subsequently took offices in Stanford Industrial Park.[15] The announcement played tribute to the cluster of high tech talent and innovation that Silicon Valley had become by that time, "The motivation behind the move was the need to scale the organization while taking into account employee preferences to be located together as much as possible."[16]

Previously, other promising startups had moved to the valley. The first personal computer—the Altair—was created in New Mexico, but moved to Sunnyvale, CA, and the first browser was developed by Marc Andreessen in Illinois before its headquarters was moved to Mountain View, CA.

The appeal of Stanford Industrial Park and Silicon Valley more broadly as a place to locate was not limited to domestic startups alone. Luxembourg-founded Skype moved its headquarters to San Francisco. Subsequently, it relocated to Stanford Industrial Park in 2010, and the park is the forerunner of similar efforts, such as the Polsky Center at the University of Chicago.[17]

The expansion of Stanford's engineering departments followed by UC Berkeley also played a crucial role in the formation of the Silicon Valley ecosystem. The availability of highly educated personnel was a critical factor in the emergence of new venture enterprises, and Stanford's engineering departments provided the necessary manpower.

---

[14] Lécuyer (2006), Ubeda et al. (2019).
[15] Amusingly, its webpage points to its 261 days of sunshine as one of its credentials.
[16] Penell (2008).
[17] The move of Skype there was reported in the *Stanford Daily* in 2010. The University of Chicago Booth's business proposal competition—the New Venture Challenge—was co-founded by Steven Kaplan and by 2019 had generated over a hundred firms, including GrubHub and Braintree/Venmo, that have raised about $600 million and created more than $4 billion in value.

In summary, Terman's contributions to the development of Silicon Valley were manifold. He envisioned Stanford as an institution that actively promotes collaboration between academia and industry, bridging the gap between theoretical research and practical applications.

His efforts to attract research funding, promote entrepreneurship, and expand Stanford's engineering departments were critical in creating an environment that fostered innovation and entrepreneurship.

3.3 DISRUPTIVE TECHNOLOGIES AND SPINOUTS

Personal Motivations: Shockley's Move to Silicon Valley

Formally announced by Bell Laboratories on June 30, 1948, the press release heralded the development with the following words—"known as the transistor, the device works on an entirely new principle, and may have far-reaching significance in electronics and electrical communication . . . it's essential simplicity, however, indicates the possibility of widespread use, with resultant mass-production economics."[18]

Eight years later, in 1956, the discovery team, i.e., William Shockley, Walter Brattain, and John Bardeen, shared the Nobel Prize in Physics in recognition of the importance of their invention. During that year, Shockley left Bell and founded his own company—Shockley Semiconductor Labs, funded by Beckman Instruments. The Shockley Semiconductor Laboratory opened for business in a small commercial lot in nearby Mountain View, and Shockley chose the location because he wanted to be closer to his elderly mother, who lived in Mountain View.[19] It was the first company to make transistors out of silicon and not germanium. Initially, he tried to hire more of his former colleagues from Bell Labs, but they were reluctant to leave the East Coast and he had to assemble a team

---

[18] Bell Laboratories (1948).
[19] *New York Times* (2008).

of young scientists and engineers, some from other parts of Bell Laboratories.[20]

The Traitorous Eight: Defection from Shockley

While Shockley was a recruiter, he reportedly was less effective as a manager. A core group of Shockley employees, later known as the "traitorous eight," became unhappy with his company management. Looking for funding for their project, they received help from New York–based investment banker Arthur Rock who connected them with Fairchild Camera and Instruments, an Eastern US company. The result was a joint venture for a new company.[21]

In 1957, Robert Noyce, Julius Blank, Victor Grinich, Jean Hoerni, Eugene Kleiner, Jay Last, Gordon Moore, and Sheldon Roberts departed Shockley's operation, and they started the Fairchild Semiconductors division with plans to make silicon transistors (Figure 3.8).

Figure 3.8   The Fairchild founders in 1960. Rear row from left: Victor Grinich, Gordon Moore, Julius Blank, Eugene Kleiner. Front row: Jay Last, Jean Hoerni, Sheldon Roberts, and Robert Noyce.
Source: © Wayne Miller/Magnum Photos.

---

[20] PBS (1999).
[21] Berlin, (2001).

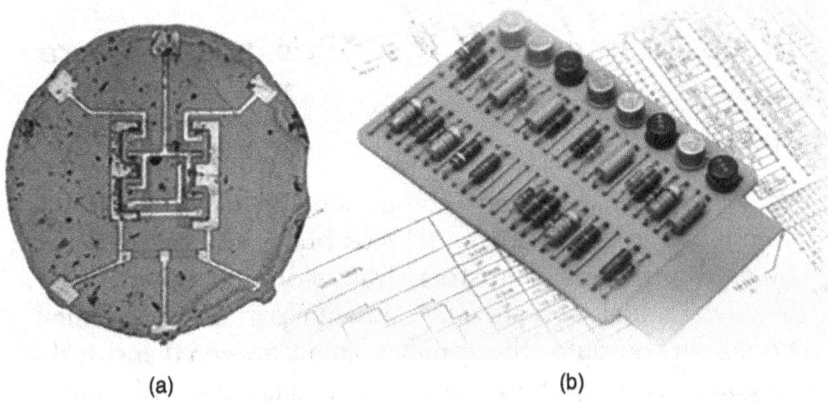

(a)   (b)

**Figure 3.9   (a) Fairchild's first integrated circuit had four transistors,1960.
(b) IBM Standard discrete diode-transistor logic printed modular system cards
developed by IBM in the late 1950s, which were used throughout IBM's second-
generation computers and represented the standard before integrated circuits
were widely adopted.**
Sources: (a) CHM, Mountain View, CA. (b) Arnold. Reinhold. https://en.wikipedia.org/
wiki/Standard_Modular_System#/media/File:SMScard.jpg. CC 2.0.

Fairchild Semiconductor's 1958 2N697 silicon transistor was a
breakthrough success, rapidly adopted by major clients such as
IBM and Autonetics for use in the B-70 bomber computer and the
Minuteman missile guidance system. The company experienced
rapid growth, expanding from 12 to 12,000 employees and earning $130 million annually.[22] Robert Noyce and Jack Kilby inde-
pendently developed the concept of the integrated circuit (IC),
which Jay Last brought to fruition with the first commercially available monolithic IC, the "micrologic" RTL line, in 1961 (Figure 3.9).
However, early microchips were expensive, unreliable, and slower
than traditional technology. Gordon Moore's Law (Box 3.2) predicted exponential computing power growth at constant prices,
but multiple cycles of innovation were required to address these
early flaws and generate widespread interest in microchip technology (Box 3.1).[23,24]

[22] Lojek (2007).
[23] Norman (2011).
[24] Hall (1996).

Box 3.1   Transistors, ICs, CPUs, and Software

Transistors

Vacuum tubes were early components in digital electronic computers in the 1930s and 1940s but were later replaced by semiconductor transistors. Transistors amplify or switch electrical signals and are a fundamental part of modern electronics. In computer chips, they switch between 0 and 1, the language of computing. Electronic circuits consist of components like resistors, capacitors, inductors, diodes, and transistors connected by conductive wires (Figure 3.10). Integrated circuits (ICs) have components and connections on a single substrate, usually silicon.

Integrated Circuits (ICs)

Large numbers of tiny MOSFETs (metal-oxide-semiconductor field-effect transistors) are integrated in a small chip. This results in circuits that are orders of magnitude smaller, faster, and less expensive than those constructed of discrete electronic components (Figure 3.10b). The ICs' mass production

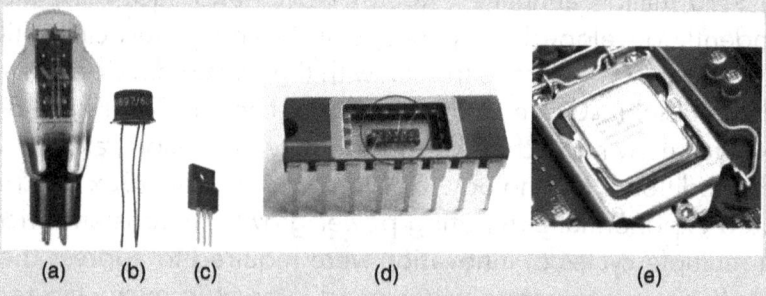

(a)   (b)   (c)   (d)   (e)

Figure 3.10   (a) Thyratron vacuum tube, 1950s. (b) Fairchild MOSFET transistor, 1962. (c) Fairchild MOSFET transistor FDPF5N50UT, first released on January 1, 2011. (d) Microchip. (e) Intel Core CPU i5 11400F.

Sources: (a) Western Electric; (b) Computer History Museum, Mountain View, CA; (c) https://fr.rs-online; (d) scienceforfun.com, wikipedia.com, Photo 21156413; (e) Digital Foundry.

capability, reliability, and building-block approach to integrated circuit design led—over time—to the rapid adoption of standardized ICs in place of designs using discrete transistors.

Central Processing Unit (CPU)

A central processing unit (CPU), also called a central processor, main processor, or just a microprocessor is the electronic circuitry that executes instructions comprising a computer program. The CPU performs basic arithmetic, logic, controlling, and input/output (I/O) operations specified by the instructions in the program (Figure 3.10 e).

Operating System

An operating system (OS) is the system software that manages computer hardware and software resources and provides common services for computer programs. The operating system manages the CPU. When software is opened, the OS finds it and loads it into memory (RAM). The CPU can then be instructed to execute the program. The operating system will manage the sharing of processor time.

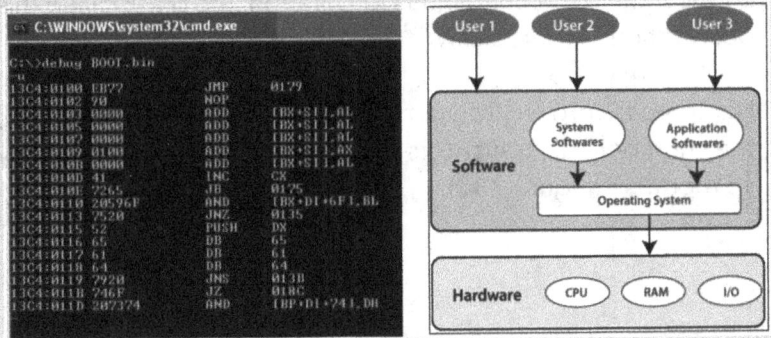

Figure 3.11 Unix operating system screenshot and illustration.
Source: Neowin.com.

Box 3.2   Moore's Law

Figure 3.12   Electronic Magazine cover, April 19, 1965.
Source: Catalog Number 102770822, Computer History Museum, Mountain View, CA (CC). "Intel Free Press / Wikimedia Commons / CC BY-SA 2.0" CC BY-SA.

On April 19, 1965, while director of the Research and Development Laboratory at Fairchild Semiconductors in Palo Alto, California, physical chemist Gordon Moore published an article "Cramming More Components onto Integrated Circuits" in *Electronics Magazine*[25] (Figure 3.12). In this article, Moore observed that for simple circuits, the cost per component is nearly inversely proportional to the number of components. The number of transistors that could be placed on an integrated circuit at constant cost per component doubled approximately every two years.

Moore predicted that this trend would continue at least well into the 1970s. In 1970, after Moore had left Fairchild Semiconductors to co-found Intel Corporation, the press called this observation "Moore's Law."[26]

His forecast proved to be rather accurate: from 1961–2011, the number of transistors doubled approximately every 18 months[27] (Figure 3.13).

---

[25] Moore (1965).
[26] Brock (2006).
[27] Moore (1975).

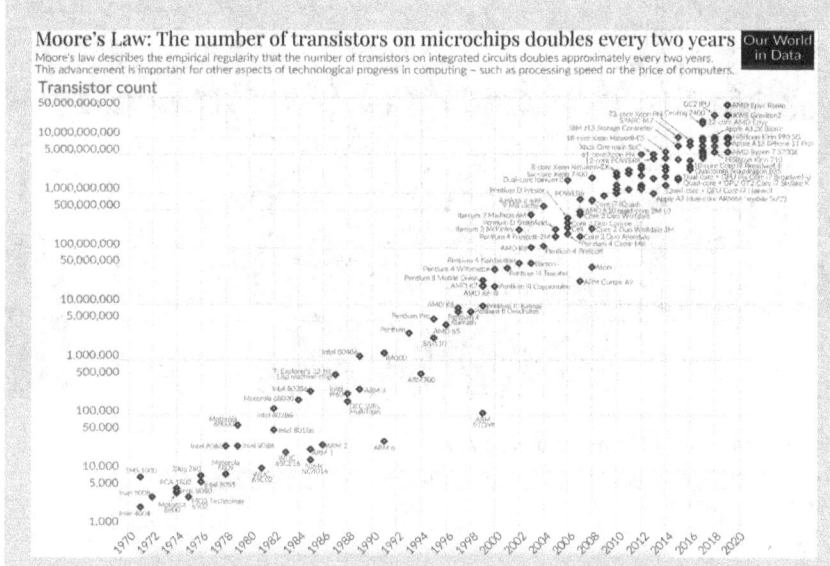

Figure 3.13   Moore's Law: The number of transistors on microchips doubles every two years.

Source: Roser and Ritchie (2020). Retrieved from: https://ourworldindata.org/uploads/2020/11/. Transistor-Count-over-time.png.

IBM Goes Its Own Way

The rapid adoption of computing is evident in the popularity of the IBM 1401 (Figure 3.14). Introduced in 1959, over 12,000 of these systems were sold before IBM retired the line in 1971. Users found them so valuable that they continually increased their workloads, eventually pushing the system to its limits. Once users reached their system's capacity, they faced unattractive options: moving to larger systems with costly software rewrites and staff training, implementing competitors' systems, or adding more 1401 units with duplicative costs. Customers sought upgradable and compatible systems.

The mainframe computer industry, which could have been a potential customer for bulk microchip purchases, did not embrace the new technology. Crucially, IBM had reservations about the

Figure 3.14   IBM 1401 mainframe, 1959.
Source: Michael Fraley, CC BY 2.0 https://creativecommons.org/licenses/by/2.0,
Wikimedia Commons.

readiness of the monolithic integrated circuit technology, also
known as the microchip, primarily due to concerns regarding its
scalability and the ability to maintain production quality. As a result,
IBM chose an alternative approach, referred to as a "hybrid" solution, which involved using ceramic chips with discrete transistors
glued on, a technology they named Solid Logic Technology (SLT).
While SLT offered improved speed and reliability compared to earlier packaging methods, IBM soon discovered that the expected
scalability of production remained a significant challenge due to
the complexity introduced by the analog circuitry during manufacturing and testing.[28]

After the announcement of the IBM System/360 (S/360) in April
1964, globally customers ordered over 100,000 systems in the
first month. This was a remarkable figure when compared to the
approximately 20,000 computers of any type installed in Western
Europe, the United States, and Japan combined that year. By 1969,

---

[28] Elliott (2010). The story of IBM and the System/360 is also told in Cortada (2019)
and the data on industry growth and IBM sales numbers during the 1960s is
quoted from there.

IBM had a market share of over two-thirds in the USA and became the world's biggest computer company.[29]

The surge in orders for S/360 systems in 1965 created production challenges, resulting in a decline in the quality of electronic components that caused severe production delays. However, IBM successfully addressed these issues, and in 1966, they exceeded the previous year's production volume by over 100%, effectively meeting the high demand for S/360 systems.[30]

The triumph of the IBM System/360 underscores the substantial and expanding market opportunities for computers that provide businesses with cost-effective entry options, while affording customers the flexibility to scale up as needed. As Cortada highlighted, IBM's S/360 significantly increased the overall demand for computing. Throughout the latter part of the 1960s, the sector consistently experienced double-digit annual growth. To meet the demand for more compact yet higher-capacity computers that offered interoperability, i.e., the ability of software and hardware from different sources (initially from the same manufacturer) to work together without having to be altered to do so, denser packaging of electronic components, more processing power, memory, standard interfaces and protocols, and (massively) scalable production had to be achieved. These developments faced obstacles due to the limitations of the technology that was reliant on analog circuitry. The surging demand for computing capacity ultimately paved the way for the ascendancy of monolithic integrated circuits, or microchips, which, despite their own design and manufacturing challenges, held the promise of driving rapid progress in packaging density, circuit performance, and production scalability. The IBM System/360 also moved computing power closer to the users

---

[29] Monegro (2018). The dominance of IBM caused a regulatory backlash. In 1969, the US government launched an antitrust case against IBM and alleged that it attempted to monopolize the business computer market. The case went on for 13 years but was withdrawn in 1982. In its wake came IBM's decision to split its software and hardware businesses, which had the dual effect of fostering the growth of an autonomous software industry and promoting the establishment of standards that enhanced the compatibility of computers produced by various manufacturers.
[30] IBM (2022).

as the machines were small enough to be installed in offices rather than the computer facilities that large mainframes required. Its success showed that users wanted the proximity and flexibility that the system offered and thus marked the beginning of a trajectory that would lead to personal computing in the following decade.

NASA as a Catalyst

A technology's potential does not ordain its success. At the time the first Fairchild chip was launched, any electronics firm could wire together transistors to produce the same circuits for much less. In addition, the chips were unreliable. A buyer had to have a severe space constraint to justify purchasing ICs.

Fairchild initially reacted in a typical way for incumbents. It put the new technology on the backburner due to a lack of customer demand and fear of losing existing customers. But the US space program had a space constraint for their in-flight computers, and the IC was the solution. From 1963 onwards, after the Apollo program was launched and two years after Fairchild decided not to spend further resources on ICs, it revisited the development and manufacturing of ICs. NASA chose those chips for that generation's most important national technology effort. This proves the point that Clayton Christensen (see Box 3.3) made in an article in the *Harvard Business Review*, i.e., that "it takes time to determine whether an innovator's business model is disruptive and will succeed."[31] Both NASA and the Air Force worked with Fairchild Semiconductors to ensure that the chips were reliable. Whereas Fairchild designed the ICs for the onboard computers of the Apollo spacecraft, most of them were produced by Raytheon and Philco Ford.[32] In 1963 and 1964, the US government bought 85% of all ICs produced in the USA. However, inside the government, only NASA and the Air Force's Minuteman missile, a relatively small project compared with the Apollo computers, were using the chips.[33]

---

[31] Christensen (1997).
[32] See Ceruzzi (2003) for a description of the production of the flight guidance computer and NASA's procurement. Fishman (2019) documents the prices paid for the different batches ordered.
[33] Ibid.

Box 3.3   Disruptive Innovation

Disruptive innovation, a term coined by Clayton Christensen in his book, *The Innovator's Dilemma*, published in 1997, describes a process by which a product or service takes root initially in simple applications at the low-margin end of a market or in emerging new markets ("new-market footholds," i.e., disrupters create a market where none existed) that value the advantages of a product while being less sensitive to the underperformance of the product in areas that are important to customers in established large markets[34] (Figure 3.15).

| (a) | (b) |

Figure 3.15   (a) Definition of disruptive innovation. (b) Clayton Christensen.
Source: World Economic Forum / Wikimedia Commans / CC-BY SA 2.0.

Incumbents focusing on improving products for demanding customers often exceed some needs and ignore others. Breakthroughs improving good products are not disruptive but sustainable.

Disruptive innovations are not technologies that make good products better; instead, they make products and services more accessible and affordable, thereby increasing the

(continued)

---

[34] Christensen, Raynor, and McDonald (2015), Christensen (1997).

addressable market. Entrants that prove disruptive begin by successfully targeting those overlooked segments, gaining a foothold by delivering more suitable functionality—frequently at a lower price. Incumbents chasing higher profitability in more demanding areas tend not to respond vigorously. Entrants then move upmarket, delivering on the performance attributes that incumbents' mainstream customers require while preserving the performance aspects that drove their early success. When mainstream customers start adopting the entrants' offerings in volume, disruption occurs.[35] Disruptive innovation creates significant opportunities for venture capitalists because it often involves the creation of new markets or the disruption of existing ones (Figure 3.16). Venture capitalists are typically looking for investments with high growth potential, and disruptive innovations can provide just that.

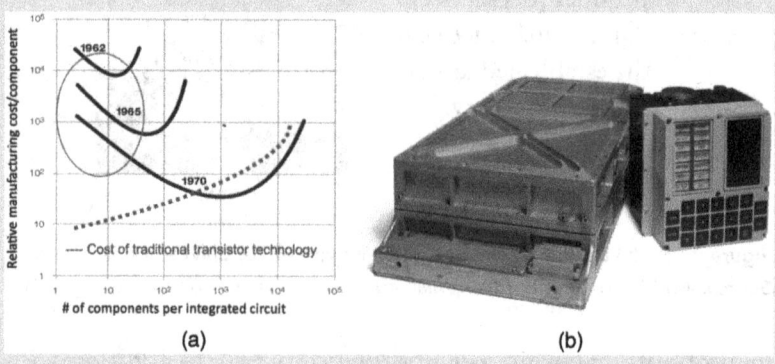

(a)   (b)

Figure 3.16   (a) Cost curve for existing technology. (b) Apollo computer.
Sources: (a) Zaman (2022). (b) Computer Historical Museum, Mountain View, CA.
Note: The display in (a) shows an illustrative cost curve for existing technology that is not part of the original diagram (henristosch / Wikimedia Commans / Public Domain).

On behalf of NASA, Massachusetts Institute of Technology (MIT) bought so many of the early chips that it drove the price down dramatically: prices declined from $1,000 a chip in that first order to $15 a chip in 1963 when MIT ordered 3,000. By 1969, those basic

---

[35] Larson (2016).

chips cost $1.58 each, except they had significantly more capability and reliability than the 1963 version. This way, NASA and the Pentagon prepared the ground for the non-military IC market. It took several rounds of development before the technology overcame its limitations and production could be scaled to become a viable alternative to existing technology on cost and performance. Integrated circuits became cheaper and more potent than competing solutions at a faster rate of technical progress. When reliability improved and mass manufacturing began, integrated circuits first beat traditional techniques on production cost and then on computing power. Over time integrated circuits managed to narrow the processing speed disadvantage as mainframes were gaining in speed by only 14% each year while microchips were increasing in speed by as much as 70% annually.[36] NASA's and other government agencies' demand for ICs, even at high prices, helped get the economies of scale up and costs down. NASA also provided a technological endorsement effect by supporting ICs, signaling to the market that they were convinced by this technology, which is a robust case for other market participants to adopt it.[37]

1969 was also the year of the first moon landing. NASA mission control used the IBM 360s computer while Apollo used two guidance computers that used Fairchild's Micrologic ICs.[38] The progress in chip technology that this represented led to another landmark event in 1969, which would only be recognized over time: Intel designed the first microprocessor, the 4004, released in 1972.[39] Microprocessors consolidated (nearly) all processing functions onto a single integrated circuit with multiple purposes. It would upend the world of mainframe manufacturers during the decade that followed.

In the end, mainframe manufacturers switched to ICs based on silicon as the performance attributes exceeded those of

---

[36] *New York Times* (1989).
[37] Paik and Woo (2017).
[38] CHM (2022a).
[39] A microprocessor is an integrated circuit, but not all integrated circuits are microprocessors. Unlike other integrated circuits, a microprocessor functions as a computing brain. It is able to process logical and arithmetic instructions that are programmed into it.

traditional solutions. But that was an afterthought for the chip manufacturers as the market for desktop PCs and later portable devices became much more significant.

The development of CPUs using microchips allowed for decentralized computer power and thus led to the desktop PC (during the 1970s) and the laptop computer during the 1980s. Thus began the shift from mechanical and analog electronic technology to digital electronics that continues today.[40]

Microchips turned out to be a general-purpose technology that would be widely adopted and diffused. In 1991, Mark Weiser's *Scientific American* article, "The Computer for the 21st Century" stated that "the most profound technologies are those that disappear. They weave themselves into the fabric of everyday life until they are indistinguishable from it."[41] The enormous advances in the density of chips and their declining cost powered this ubiquitous use.

3.4   THE "FAIRCHILDREN"

In 1961, Fairchild Semiconductors did not believe in the potential of Jay Last's work and decided not to spend further resources on the development of integrated chips.[42] Fairchild was concentrating on its discrete component business (mostly transistors) at the time, and its management believed that making integrated circuits (ICs) would make it lose customers.

On January 31, 1961, Jay Last, Jean Hoerni, Sheldon Roberts, and (briefly) Gene Kleiner of the "traitorous eight" resigned from Fairchild Semiconductors to create Amelco Corporation as a division of Teledyne where Arthur Rock was an investor.[43] As was the case

---

[40] Schoenherr (2004).
[41] Weiser (1991).
[42] Lojek (2007).
[43] Ibid.

with Shockley's company and Fairchild, the capital for the new company was provided by a corporate partner—Teledyne, a "platform company" formed with venture capital (supplied by Arthur Rock)— who formed a joint venture with the defecting team. Amelco is thus an early example of a spin-out involving venture capital, which was somewhat atypical for the early 1960s as capital usually came from a corporate partner and personal investments of the management team were mostly funded with the help of friends and family, including former colleagues. While still at Fairchild, Eugene Kleiner, for example, had encouraged a lab technician to start his own company, Electroglas, to build specialized manufacturing equipment, heralding the birth of a supporting ecosystem of specialty and service companies. Because of the variety of opportunities presented by this new technology, company defections were embraced rather than stigmatized. Job hopping became the norm, information was freely exchanged, and the culture promoted risk-taking, entrepreneurial experimentation, and collective learning.[44]

Numerous other spin-offs, known as "Fairchildren," followed as employees left to pursue opportunities that the new technology promised. Those companies produced chips and technologies that enabled new communications, computing, and consumer products and, in turn, spun off further companies to exploit them.[45]

Founded by Gordon Moore and Robert Noyce and joined by Andy Grove in 1968, Intel Corporation was the most influential and flourishing of the first generation of Fairchildren. Intel became the biggest chip maker by revenue in 1992 and held that position until 2018. In 2011, Intel enjoyed the largest market share in the overall worldwide PC microprocessor market (73%) and the mobile PC microprocessor (80%).[46] A pioneer in memory chips and microprocessors, the company is today the world's largest IC vendor with an enterprise value of nearly $200 billion and annual revenue of $55 billion. Intel also employed a successful strategy (as an incumbent)

---

[44] Klepper (2010), Wadhawa (2009).
[45] CHM (2022c).
[46] McGrath (2011).

to compete against market entrants by offering cheaper chips that would compromise on performance but allowed Intel to grow sales due to an expanded market share and the acquisition of new customers.

The Intel 4004 chips, launched in 1972, had 2250 transistors and cost $400 in today's money. Fast forward, an Apple A14 Bionic chip made in 2021 has 15 billion transistors and costs about $150. Had the price per transistor not changed, an Apple chip would cost $2.5 billion in constant prices per transistor.[47]

Intel built on the Fairchild management approach that emphasized meritocracy and openness over hierarchy derived from the Hewlett-Packard approach of "management by walking around." Open communication and accessibility encouraged direct employee interaction within a "flat" corporate structure. This came with a casual style that has become associated with the Valley. Soft factors are difficult to quantify, but even a casual visitor to the Valley will notice that things aren't the same here as they are back home.

Another legacy from Fairchild that became a model for these newly formed technology companies was stock options. Robert Noyce later said:

> People sharing profits naturally wanted to concentrate on already profitable products rather than plunge into avant-garde research that would not pay off in the short run even if it were successful. But people with stock options lived for research breakthroughs. The news would immediately send a semiconductor company's stock up, regardless of profits.[48]

Stock options became a tool to incentivize employees to join a startup working on untested technology rather than continuing with a firm that operated in an established market with proven technology and revenue.

---

[47] It also would take the Apollo flight computer 681 days to do the work your iPhone can do in less than one second.
[48] Wolfe (1983).

3.5   THE SILICON VALLEY INDUSTRIAL CLUSTER

Silicon Valley has become one of the world's best-known industrial clusters, and it is the benchmark among high-tech clusters. Centered on Stanford University and sprawling along a 30-mile corridor from San Francisco to San Jose, the Valley is home to the headquarters of many of the world's largest high-tech corporations, including more than 30 businesses in the Fortune 1000 as well as thousands of promising startups.[49] Silicon Valley as a cluster eclipsed others, such as Route 128 in Boston, dubbed "America's Technology Highway." Even in the 1980s, Silicon Valley and the Boston Corridor along Route 128 appeared very similar, with a mix of large and small tech firms, world-class universities, venture capital, and military funding. Route 128, in some ways, was more promising due to its long industrial history and proximity to many high-quality educational institutions (Harvard, Yale, Brown, MIT, Tufts, Amherst) and the Bell Laboratories and other large corporate research centers.

The very reasons why Shockley found it difficult to convince his colleagues at Bell to join him in his company would have informed observers' opinion on the prospects of the two clusters back then. But Route 128 was dominated by large, vertically integrated minicomputer manufacturers like DEC, Wang, Prime, and Data General. Technology, skill, and know-how resided with large corporations, and exchanging know-how and ideas between those organizations was limited. The differences were evident on many levels: venture capitalists in Silicon Valley had deep roots in local networks; educational institutions and research labs in the West Coast partnered with local startups as well as more established firms, whereas those in the East Coast only worked with the largest corporations.

Fairchild triggered a succession of new companies being formed as the new technology provided so many opportunities that they

---

[49] Athanasia (2022).

Table 3.1　Spinoffs of semiconductor producers

Firm	Years (through 1986)	# Spinoffs
Silicon Valley producers		
Fairchild	1957–1986	24
National	1967–1986	9
Intel	1968–1986	6
Signetics	1961–1975	5
Intersil	1967–1981	4
Synertek	1973–1985	4
Semi Processes	1975–1985	4
AMI	1966–1986	3
AMCC	1979–1986	3
Seeq	1981–1986	3
Amelco	1961–1986	2
Micro Power	1971–1986	2
Raytheon/Rheem	1961–1986	1
Siliconix	1963–1986	1
Avantek	1965–1986	1
AMD	1969–1986	1
Exar	1971–1986	1
Cal-tex	1971–1975	1
Nitron	1972–1985	1
Zilog	1974–1986	1
Supertex	1976–1986	1
Exel	1983–1986	1
Non-Silicon Valley producers		
General Instrument	1960–1986	4
Texas Instruments	1952–1986	3
Motorola	1958–1986	2
Mostek	1969–1985	2
RCA	1950–1986	1

Source: Klepper (2010).

often could not be pursued within existing firms. This pattern of the serial entrepreneur is characteristic of Silicon Valley. Successful entrepreneurs went on to recycle their wealth into new startups, often supporting former employees in their endeavors. Such angel investing became more significant in the decades that followed. The following (incomplete) list of spin-outs during the 1960s and 1970s illustrates the point (Table 3.1). As a result, the number of spin-outs generated in Silicon Valley firms is incomparable.

The basic building block of the Digital Revolution that followed is the metal-oxide-semiconductor field-effect transistor (MOSFET, or

MOS transistor. It is the basis of every commercial microprocessor, memory chip, and telecommunication circuit.[50]

How Important Are Clusters, and Can They Be Created?

The dominance of Silicon Valley as a hub for high-growth tech start-ups spans decades, but advances in technology have allowed start-ups to operate from anywhere with internet access. In 2021, Silicon Valley had the highest concentration of unicorns (220)—startups valued at $1 billion or more—in the world. But unicorns were also found in 45 countries outside the USA. Some cities, such as Beijing, London, and Tel Aviv, are mature startup hubs with global ambitions. Others, such as Bengaluru, Singapore, and São Paulo, are in the early stages of becoming a hub. According to data from *The Economist*, in each of the top 10 countries by number of unicorns 40% or more are concentrated in the country's leading startup hub.[51]

Drivers of Successful Tech and Innovation Clusters

1. **General-purpose technologies:** These technologies typically have a wide range of applications and lead to rapid progress and growth. They often come with a fast rate of technological progress as this drives the scope of applications.

2. **High-impact patents and disruptive technologies:** Research by economist Tarek Hassan has shown that these types of innovations tend to cluster together in certain geographic locations, which he refers to as "innovation hotspots."[52]

3. **Access to talent and research infrastructure:** Jobs, attracting highly qualified talent, related to high-impact technologies cluster in the areas where they have been originally invented for decades. Silicon Valley is well known for its proximity to prestigious universities such as Stanford and the University of California, Berkeley.

---

[50] Laws (2018).

[51] *The Economist* (2022g), Immigrant populations are also significant in European centers like Berlin, London, and Paris, each containing ten or more unicorns.

[52] Presentation at the George J. Stigler Center, University of Chicago Booth Graduate School of Business: "Economic Analysis Using Text," presented by Tarek Hassan, March 24, 2023. Silicon Valley and the Bay Area continued to represent 25% of all high-impact patents since 2010 (Hassan et al., 2023).

4. **People and ideas:** Silicon Valley's meritocratic openness made it a magnet for skilled immigrants, and they founded many of the most valuable IT businesses in the USA.[53]

5. **The federal government:** Contracts and grants provide funding and support. Silicon Valley received government contracts in its early years, and recent examples include SpaceX and Tesla.[54]

6. **Innovation and mobility:** The interplay of job hopping, spin-outs, and California's non-compete policy has fostered the development and diffusion of high-impact technologies in Silicon Valley.[55]

7. **Access to capital and support:** Angel investors and venture capitalists, who understand the ecosystem are vital. Empirical evidence shows that VCs select more innovative companies and then assist them with the commercialization process. It has been demonstrated that venture-backed enterprises are more innovative and file more influential patents than companies that receive no venture capital.[56]

In 1971, journalist Don Hoefler wrote an article entitled "Silicon Valley USA."[57] The name stuck. The Fairchildren turned the Santa Clara Valley into Silicon Valley. An Endeavor Insight (2014) looked at 130 Bay Area tech companies trading on the NASDAQ or the NXSE and found that, "70% of these firms can be traced directly back to the founders and employees of Fairchild. These 92 public companies . . . are now worth about $2.1 trillion—more than the annual GDP of Canada, India, or Spain."[58] Other countries have tried to recreate the Silicon Valley effect (Box 3.4).

---

[53] Wadhawa (2009).
[54] An analysis by Grid, an internet news platform, found that Tesla and SpaceX have received over $7 billion in government contracts alone, in addition to billions more in tax breaks, loans, and other subsidies. Tesla has sold at least $6 billion worth of government-backed electric vehicle credits in recent years (Severns, 2022).
[55] Wadhawa (2009).
[56] Howell et al. (2020) use US patent data over the 1976–2017 period to document that venture capital-backed firms were between 2- and 4x as likely to have filed patents that were in the top percentiles of influence (as measured by citations, originality, generality, and closeness to science). Kortum and Lerner (2000) find that a rise in venture capital causes higher rates of patenting.
[57] Hoeffler (1971).
[58] Morris and Penido (2014).

Box 3.4 Israel's Silicon Wadi

The DDR&D—Directorate of Defense Research & Development—established by Israel's first Prime Minister and Defense Minister, David Ben-Gurion, in 1953, is another successful example. The unit is tasked with two main functions. First, to initiate and conduct research, advance development projects, and promote the technology and building blocks for future systems. Second, they are responsible for managing the progress of these projects and bringing them to their full operational capabilities. Like DARPA, the DDR&D cooperates with academic institutions and high-tech companies. Government procurement is used to bring innovative technology to a level that becomes operational and diffusion viable. Both civilians and military personnel operate DDR&D.[59]

The Six-Day War and the subsequent French embargo generated new priorities for Israel with implications for R&D and high-tech industries. The Ministerial Offices of the Chief Scientist (OCS) was created, and the R&D Industrial Fund was established. This program was, and to some extent continues to be, the backbone of that country's R&D/innovation/technology strategy as far as the business sector is concerned. It supports the R&D of individual companies whose objective is the creation of new or improved products (or processes) directed to the export market. The OCS became the almost exclusive agency in charge of innovation and technology, which was a significant factor in developing a civilian high-tech industry.[60]

The share of this new high-tech sector in total manufacturing exports increased from 6% to 24% between 1968 and 1983. Despite the fact that R&D performed in industry increased considerably, the share of military R&D in total national R&D was about 40% in the 1970s and rose to 65% in 1981.

(continued)

---

[59] Israel Ministry of Defense (2021).
[60] Avnimelech and Teubal (2006), pp. 172–192.

DDR&D also became an efficient incubator of young researchers in many technological fields and seemed to have played a crucial contributory role in the emergence of the "Silicon Wadi" period of Israel's high-tech development during the 1990s. Numerous entrepreneurs and engineers in the private technology sector previously worked in the military industries or performed military R&D.[61]

The example of the successful implementation of a government-led research effort is relevant as it made the Israeli high-tech sector an important destination for European and US venture capital. Startups that originated from Israel also relocated to Silicon Valley as they aimed for an IPO in the USA and to gain scale in the larger US market. In 2014, more than 50,000 Israelis lived and worked around Palo Alto. Because it lacks a built-in domestic market, it has constantly looked outward for everything from venture funding to customers to sales teams, even as its main tech team stayed back in Israel.[62]

Israel's high-tech clusters also applied the concept of Frederick Terman's Stanford Industrial Park by encouraging large (foreign) tech companies to establish a presence. As of October 2021, out of 402 multinational companies with an innovation presence in Israel, 96 are California headquartered. While the list of Silicon Valley companies in Israel is long, several—Applied Materials, KLA Corporation, IBM (which has a major research laboratory in San Jose), Oracle, Cisco, Salesforce, and Intel—stand out as examples of the role that Israel plays in the global R&D and business strategy of multinational companies (Figure 3.17). Intel, with 14,000 employees, is both Israel's largest technology company and its most significant private employer.[63] This facilitated both cooperation and an M&A and broadened the scope of exit channels.

---

[61] Ibid.
[62] Randolph (2021).
[63] Randolph (2021).

Figure 3.17   Matam High-Tech Park in Haifa.
Source: Zvi Roger—Haifa Municipality—The Spokesperson, Publicity and Advertising Division. Zvi Roger / Wikimedia Commans / CC-BY 3.0.

If one adds the exchange of faculty between US and Israeli universities and research institutions, the close integration of the two hubs becomes apparent. The scale and depth of the Bay Area presence in Israel have produced a unique dynamic with a two-way flow of people and ideas.

As the tech sector presented significant opportunities, a local venture capital industry began to emerge, and local firms such as Pitango, Jerusalem Global Ventures, and Peregrine Ventures were joined by international firms like Index Ventures, Battery, Accel Partners, and Apax Partners. As of 2021, approximately 205 Israeli venture capital firms, 70 foreign firms, and 60 corporate venture capital entities were operating in Israel. This landscape highlights the diverse and dynamic nature of the venture capital industry within the Israeli ecosystem.[64]

Israel is both an example of the successful implementation of the combination of government research funding and procurement, private research and venture capital, and the integration of the venture ecosystem with Silicon Valley.

---

[64] Shamay (2020).

Some governments fund startups or give subsidies to venture capital rather than focusing on research and procurement. Josh Lerner of Harvard Business School reported that the failure rate for both US initiatives and initiatives abroad is very high.[65] Instead, successful clusters represent a flywheel driven by the factors described earlier. While venture capital plays a vital role as an enabler of spin-outs and financier of startups that continue the dynamics of innovation and high-impact patents, it does not "create" a cluster. It has little impact if the other elements mutually reinforcing the formation of a technology "hotspot" are missing.

---

[65] For a discussion of the success of public initiatives to support startups of VC, see Lerner (1999, 2022). However, with the Biden administration's declaration in October 2023 designating 31 communities nationwide as Regional Tech Hubs, it raises questions about whether that lesson has been completely embraced domestically. The White House (2023).

Chapter 4

US Private Equity During the 1960s and 1970s

4.1 THE RISE OF MODERN VENTURE CAPITAL

In 1957, when the "traitorous eight" left Shockley Semiconductor, Arthur Rock, an investment banker from New York–based Hayden Stone was the one who helped them find a place to go: he convinced Sherman Fairchild to partner with the former Shockley employees and start Fairchild Semiconductor. Rock, even with no technical background, understood that this new technology had transformative potential and, as a result, numerous investment opportunities would emerge. Teledyne Corporation, founded by Henry Singleton, was the company that aligned with Arthur Rock's investment thesis. Arthur Rock made a significant investment in Teledyne in 1961 soon after the company's founding by Henry Singleton. Rock found the financing and became a member of the executive committee. The use of a corporation as an acquisition vehicle must have seemed natural for Arthur Rock, who was a former student of Doriot.[1] Under Henry Singleton's leadership, Teledyne increasingly pursued the acquisitions of more established and revenue-generating targets that aligned with its strategic direction. At the same time, Arthur Rock shifted toward early-stage venture investments (Figure 4.1). This strategic decision was driven by Rock's desire to concentrate on nurturing and supporting young, innovative companies in their early growth stages.

To fund further investments, Arthur Rock and Thomas J. Davis— who had made corporate venture investments for Watkins-Johnson Company in Palo Alto—formed the venture capital firm Davis & Rock. They raised $3.5 million from 25 limited partners (no institutions among them). The partnership had a seven-year fund life, 20% carried interest, and 6% of the capital was provided by the general partners. Davis & Rock was in business from 1961 to 1968. This was the first venture capital limited partnership, and Arthur Rock is credited with coining the term. The fund's return amounted to 22.6x of invested capital, generating interest in this new style of venture capital investing.

(a)   (b)   (c)

Figure 4.1 Early VCs (a) Don Valentine, founder of Sequoia Capital; (b) Arthur Rock, one of the first venture capitalists; (c) Tom Perkins, co-founder of Kleiner Perkins.
Sources: (a) Courtesy of Arthur Rock; (b) Courtesy of Arthur Rock; (c) San Francisco Chronicle / Hearst Newspapers / Getty Images.

---

[1]Biography (2022).

Following the dissolution of Davis & Rock in 1968, Arthur Rock formed a new partnership and hired Dick Kramlich, who would in 1978 establish his own firm, New Enterprise Associates (NEA), probably the first late-stage and growth financing firm. Rock co-founded Intel and served as the first chairman. Later he bought 640,000 shares of Apple Computer for 9 cents a share and became a director of the company.[2] Davis went on to found Mayfield Partners in Menlo Park, California. Founded in 1969, it is one of Silicon Valley's oldest venture capital firms and is still going strong.

Kleiner Perkins Caufield & Byers, Menlo Park, CA, was founded in 1972 by Eugene Kleiner (Fairchild), Tom Perkins (HP), and Frank J. Caufield and Brook Byers (Stanford). Kleiner Perkins raised $8.4 million for their first fund in 1972, and by 1984 their 14 investments showed a combined profit of $209 million. Some 95% of the gain came from just two investments (Tandem and Genentech). Six investments lost money.

Don Valentine founded Sequoia Capital in 1972. Sequoia raised $5 million from institutions, such as the Ford Foundation, Yale University, Vanderbilt, and eventually Harvard University after a year and a half of trying. Valentine previously worked for Fairchild and was the marketing director at National Semiconductor. Like other early venture capitalists in Silicon Valley, he brought years of industry experience to the companies he backed. When Steve Jobs and Stephen Wozniak sought his help in 1976, Valentine recognized that the two engineers needed a competent manager. In addition to supplying capital, he brought in additional startup financing by syndicating the investment with other venture capitalists. The syndication of deals became a standard feature of US venture capital. By 1980 after the IPO of Apple, the fund showed an internal rate of return (IRR) of 60%.

In Europe, Multinational Management Group was founded in London in 1972 by Sir Ronald Cohen and Maurice Tchénio.[3] In

---

[2] HBS (1997).

[3] The firm would merge in 1977 with Patricof & Co., which in 1991 became Apax Partners. Over time, the firm focused increasingly on buyouts where it is still a major player today.

1973, with the number of new venture capital firms increasing, leading venture capitalists formed the National Venture Capital Association (NVCA). The NVCA was to serve as the industry trade group for the venture capital industry. But the 1970s also proved to be a difficult time to start an investment business. A recession caused by inflation and the 1972–1973 OPEC oil embargo roiled the financial markets. It caused a reduction of new capital committed to venture capital funds by more than 90% between 1969 and 1974. Even after that stagflation and a second oil price shock in 1979, the economic environment remained challenging for the entire decade.[4]

Though venture capital limited partnerships initially attracted capital from family offices and wealthy individuals, fundraising momentum only accelerated when they began to attract institutional capital from endowments and pension funds. In this case, the investors' long-term strategies and tax-exempt status matched the capabilities of limited partnerships. While the proponents of ARD and the SBICs correctly anticipated the need to respond to the rise of institutional investors to secure startup financing, mutual funds were not a significant source of venture capital. The supporters of ARD recognized the need for long-term capital (and did secure some funds from university endowments), but they focused on the wrong institutions, i.e., mutual funds.[5]

An initial obstacle for the industry was that the Employee Retirement Income Security Act of 1974 (ERISA) was interpreted as forbidding pension fund investments in venture capital. Thus, a potentially significant source of capital seemed to be excluded from VC financing just when the industry was gaining traction with some early successes and IPOs.[6] Endowments led by Harvard and Yale started investing in venture capital during the mid-1970s[7] and only after 1978 the Department of Labor clarified the interpretation of the "prudent man rule," did pension funds become a significant source of capital commitments. More than 20 years after the start

---

[4] *The Economist* (2022h).

[5] Hsu and Kenney (2005).

[6] Frost Brown Todd (2020).

[7] Yale University started investing in venture capital about ten years before David Swensen—who is often credited with starting the venture portfolio from scratch—after he became CIO.

of developments that gave rise to Silicon Valley, the venture capital industry was still in its infancy. 1978 was the first significant fundraising year for the venture capital industry when, according to J. Lerner of Harvard, $424 million[8] was raised for new venture capital funds followed by $1 billion in 1979. But even in those banner years, funds were still mainly raised from private investors (32%) while tax-exempt investors, i.e., pension funds and endowments accounted for a quarter of all commitments. In the mid-1990s, tax-exempt investors would provide about 60% of new commitments to US venture capital funds.[9,10]

However, the success of the initial funds of Arthur Rock, Kleiner Perkins, and Sequoia was the primary reason that indirect venture capital investing gained traction. This success drew investors' attention to the fledgling VC industry and increased the amount of capital flowing into it. Between 1978 and 1982, the average annual capital raised was $940 million, up from $42 million per year between 1973 and 1977.

Before the late 1970s, venture capital firms operated in a scarce capital environment and took time to evaluate deals and address technology risks before investing. The industry changed as more money flowed in, resulting in an increase of venture capital firms and a faster, more competitive deal-making process in the late 1970s.

The Venture Capital Playbook

Apart from using the limited partnership as an investment vehicle, the early venture capitalists created a wealth of insights regarding the structuring of deals, the role of VCs and their value-add

---

[8] There is considerable uncertainty as other sources put the fundraising in 1978 at more than $700 million or as low as $216 million. But the increase was certainly significant compared to the previous years when the industry raised less than $100 million annually. In 1978, Warburg Pincus raised what was the first $100 million fund.

[9] Kortum and Lerner (2000). Steve Jobs made it onto a *Time Magazine* cover in February 1982 and Arthur Rock followed in January 1984, which indicates that VC only rose to public prominence during the early 1980s.

[10] Berlin (1988).

in portfolio companies, different approaches to risk-taking, or the valuation of startups, to name a few that are worthwhile exploring.

From the start, the power of the network and informal contracts, as well as referrals from founders of previous portfolio companies, proved critical in sourcing deals.[11] Those deals would frequently come in the early days of venture capital when entrepreneurs left established companies because headquarters refused to commit the funds required to turn inventions into commercial solutions. As time passed, deals and entrepreneurs could be found in garages and college dorms tinkering with inventions, much like the nineteenth-century inventors/entrepreneurs.

Quantitative investment metrics such as a P/E ratio or discounted cash flow analysis could not be used to value deals. Spreadsheets, once available, never played a significant role in VC investment decisions. PitchBook with financial projections and business plans were mainly an expression of aspiration rather than reliable financial information. To close a deal, VCs had to consider the risks that a startup and its backers faced. W. J. Janeway, a highly successful venture capitalist, provided a summary in his book, *Doing Capitalism in the Innovation Economy*:

1. **Technology risk:** When I plug it in, will it light up?

2. **Market risk:** Who will pay to buy it if it does work? [Will there be competition?]

3. **Financing risk:** Will the capital be there to fund the venture to positive cash flow?

4. **Business risk:** Will the team be able to manage the startup and its transition to a sustainable business?[12]

Quite often, the answers to the first two questions were "we don't know" and "we hope so" to the third. VCs recognized their ignorance, and deals varied, depending on the level of technology and market risk. High technology risk can create a moat for a

---

[11] Kaplan et al. (2016).
[12] Janeway (2018).

new business by making its technological breakthrough challenging to replicate or make patentable. Low technology risk implies that competition is likely, and the critical questions revolve around identifying and gaining access to the most promising market segment. Technologists frequently dismiss these questions. As the audience for technology shifted from centralized IT departments to business units or even consumers, identifying the most promising target market and the most effective channels became critical to success.

Most venture capitalists tend to agree that their key focus—and maybe their most important skill—is the evaluation of founders and the selection of people. J. Davis once answered the question of what makes venture capital deals successful, with "back the right people."[13]

Marketing, distribution, and pricing are critical for startup success but often underestimated by founders who rely on hiring a salesperson. Sequoia Capital emphasizes the importance of these aspects in their *Guide to Business Plans* and encourages founders to carefully consider their pricing strategy. In conclusion, founders must prioritize marketing, distribution, and pricing decisions as much as they do technology.[14] These are crucial aspects of a startup's success, and the founder team must take full responsibility for their execution.

Next came the question of deal structuring. In the early days, startup deals were structured to preserve control by the founders and their early VC backers. Initially, VCs had the upper hand reflecting the scarcity of capital. In the early days of venture capital, the structuring of deals, including share options and employee participation, played a crucial role in enabling startups to attract and retain top talent. However, many founders lacked experience with these complex financial instruments, making it necessary for venture capitalists to step in and provide guidance.

---

[13] Quoted from ibid., p. 47.
[14] Sequoia (2023). Sequoia Capital first published their *Guide to Business Plans* in the early 2000s. The guide has since been updated and revised several times to reflect changes in the startup and venture capital landscape.

By structuring deals that included equity options for employees, VCs helped startups to build strong teams and incentivize their employees to work toward the company's success. Davis & Rock also established an investment playbook that other firms would follow, and which reflected the favorable environment for VCs in the late 1960s and early 1970s:[15]

- 45% of the shares go to the founder.
- 45% goes to the VC.
- 10% goes to additional manager hires.

Management shares of founders would often be voting-restricted to give the VC a majority, and VCs would also control the board. When capital became more abundant in the late 1970s, the share of VCs in a Series A would decline to around 30%.[16] An essential contribution of VCs was to structure incentives and stock option plans. In the 1960s and early 1970s, stock options were hardly known, and founders often had no financial background. It fell to the VC to structure the equity incentives for team members and, later, the entire workforce in what became known as "Silicon Valley Socialism."[17] But equity was also a powerful and necessary element to lure high-quality managers from established firms into startups. The tendency to "hire big guns early on" and thus the need to make room for attractive incentives at the outset of a deal were paramount. The design of incentive structures as well as the recruitment of additional talent into a startup are two standard elements where VCs add value.

While the first generation of VCs often had a financial background or hailed from investment banks, the second generation of Californian VCs were more often engineers and had worked in startups. This had several implications. It turned out that this translated into a different risk appetite: While East Coast VCs would try to play it safe and avoid losses, West Coast VCs would swing

---

[15] Mallaby (2022).
[16] Ibid.
[17] Lecuyer (2007).

to the fences. Tom Perkins said, "If it is not 10-times different, it is not different."[18] The experience with their early funds where one or two deals made the funds' returns most certainly played a role. So, while East Coast VCs aimed for 5x returns and tried to avoid losses, Silicon Valley aimed for "fund makers" and looked for companies that could up-end existing markets or create entirely new ones. Early experience had shown them that venture capital was most successful when it pioneered new markets or business models.

This had implications for the sector focus of their investments: that Staples, frozen yogurt store chain TCBY, and Federal Express all have received venture capital illustrates that VCs targeted a variety of sectors. But for almost 40 years since 1980 the information & communications sector (ICT) has received between 50–75% of capital invested, followed by the biomedical/biotech sector, which received 13–29% of capital during that period.[19] In Silicon Valley, it was the focus on "home runs" and the consecutive waves of disruptions and the emergence of new markets resulting from the digital revolution that coalesced to this narrow sector focus. Consequently, Silicon Valley VCs sought investments in high-risk technology companies and biotechnology (Genentech). Over time the focus on technology investments would become almost universal, as VCs everywhere embraced it.[20]

To skew the odds of investing in "improbable" startups in their favor, VCs adopted a staged investment process and multiple funding rounds and cooperated with each other. While firms doing multiple capital raises is nothing new, venture capital elevated this

---

[18] Mallaby (2022), pp. 106, 206.

[19] NVCA (2022). J. Lerner and R. Nanda from Harvard University used the example of Charles River Ventures (formed in 1970), which invested its first fund in 18 companies. Only eight of the 18 first portfolio businesses were in the communications, computer technology, or healthcare industries. In 2019, almost 90% of portfolio firms were related to information technology, including social networks, consumer applications, and software and services. The authors also use NVCA data to demonstrate that this narrower focus is consistent with other early venture capital firms. Furthermore, investments in biopharmaceuticals and medical devices accounted for approximately 15–20% of total investments, which have increasingly been contributed by VCs specializing in that area over time (Lerner and Nanda, 2020).

[20] Mallaby (2022).

to a concept that is integral to the investment strategy.[21] By raising capital for later rounds at least in part from other VCs, they allowed each other into their more successful deals, which increased the cap-weighted odds of achieving superior returns. If there are no enthusiastic buyers for the next tranche of a startup's equity, the VCs shut it down. This amounts to a "peer review" of investments held that is based on other opportunities in other portfolios. It can, however, also create conflicts of interests as investors in different rounds pay different valuations and their funds are in different stages of their life. To mitigate this, VCs prefer to work with VCs they know well, which is another aspect of the mix of cooperation and competition that characterizes the industry.

While VCs had learned from ARD's experience that they must monitor and assist their portfolio companies and, when necessary, actively participate in their management, the early VCs mostly took a monitoring role that focused on milestones and spending.[22] In comparison, VCs with an entrepreneurial/operational background also became more hands on. Eugene Kleiner, Tom Perkins, and Don Valentine led the way; they wrote business plans, mentored founders, and incubated startups in-house. They also backed firms with no credible or incomplete management teams, which became a distinguishing feature of West Coast VCs.[23]

It was quickly appreciated that aiming for outsized returns creates a dependence on the state of the IPO market, and with it came the risk, as J. M. Keynes put it, of an inducement on the part of VCs to back companies that the market likes.[24] In the words of W. H. Janeway,

---

[21] Da Rin et al. (2013) cite various studies that have shown that a staged financing, control rights, and the active role of VCs on the boards of portfolio companies add value for investors. In a staged investment procedure, the capital of a funding round (usually the Seed round and sometimes Series A) is paid in installments subject to agreed milestones rather than in full. This gives the venture capitalist negotiating power and helps them to de-risk investments. Multiple investment rounds represent the greater capital requirements of a go-to-market and operational scale-up. The sequential structure of both techniques raises the founders' funding risk and gives VCs additional leverage. But as a funding strategy it may be unworkable if acquisitions are part of the strategy from the start, as this demands more capital up front.

[22] In a 1989 survey, venture capitalists cited management failure as the main reason their investments performed poorly (Gorman and Sahlman, 1989).

[23] Mallaby (2022).

"The most potent enabler of risk-taking at the frontier of innovation is the possibility of winning even when the company fails."[25]

As the market got more crowded and more VCs became established, another lesson was learned, i.e., the importance of reputation.[26] As venture capitalists build a track record, i.e., doing highly successful deals, they build a reputation, which has been shown to provide a competitive advantage in deal flow, talent recruitment, and fundraising.[27] It did, however, also bring with it added pressure to stay in the game. If you do not invest, you may miss out on a star performer, and your reputation will suffer. Increasing fund sizes, as well as the need to earn or justify your reputation in each round of investing, compelled the investment managers (referred to as "GPs" due to their role as General Partners in the limited partnerships that funded the investments) to invest because sitting on the sidelines was no longer an option.

Later, it was established that persistence is also evident in the success rate of serial entrepreneurs.[28] The Intel investment by Arthur Rock, who previously backed the Fairchild Semiconductors founders, demonstrates an early willingness for VCs and entrepreneurs to renew successful collaboration. J. Zhang showed that previously venture-backed entrepreneurs could obtain additional capital quickly and on favorable terms. This "trust effect" became critical after the pendulum shifted toward founders and VCs' control over their deals dwindled due to declining Series A stakes and the inability to defer a portion of founders' voting rights.[29]

Lastly, VCs were temporary owners and had to manage an exit. Often, based on their own experience of selling too early and underestimating the power of exponential growth, they frequently cautioned founders to accept offers to acquire their company, organized a competitive bidding, or simply waited. They

[24] Keynes (1976 [1936]), p. 237.
[25] Janeway (2018), p. 237.
[26] Mallaby (2022).
[27] Achleitner (2018), Hsu (2004).
[28] Gompers et al. (2010).
[29] Zhang (2007).

understood that if you act too early on your most promising invest-ment, the impact on the entire fund could be massive.[30]

But as Paul Gompers would later identify, holding on to invest-ments is a quality that comes over time. He observed that less-established venture capital (VC) firms are more likely to sell their investments earlier than established firms. According to Gompers, this behavior is driven by several factors, including the desire to build a reputation, pressure to deliver returns to investors, and a lack of experience in managing and growing companies over the long term. He notes that this trend can have negative conse-quences for both the VC firm and the companies it invests in, as it can result in missed opportunities for value creation and a lack of commitment to the long-term success of the companies.[31] So, the competition for investors' dollars that came with the growing role of commingled funds (partnerships) in venture financing also came with some incentives that create potential conflicts of inter-ests between VCs and the founders of their portfolio companies.

The PC Revolution

In retrospect, information technology and, to a lesser extent, bio-technology[32] were the sectors where returns would be found and where most of the VC investments would be concentrated. J. Lerner cites a Sand Hill Econometrics study that looked at venture-backed deals from December 1991 to September 2019 and discovered an annualized gross return of 24% for software, far higher than invest-ments in hardware (17%), healthcare (13%), or cleantech (2%).[33]

---

[30]Vinod Khosla, one of the most successful venture capitalists in Silicon Valley, provides an example: he received an offer for Cerent from Cisco in December 1997 for $700 million, followed by a second offer in April 1998 for $700 million. He convinced the founders to wait, and in August 1999, Cisco came back with an offer for $7 billion, which was accepted. Quoted from (Mallaby, 2022), p. 10.
[31]Gompers (1994). This finding has been supported by Fried and Hisrich (1995), who looked at 14 case studies of VC-backed firms and Cumming and MacIntosh (2003), who studied exits from 112 portfolio companies by 13 venture capitalists in the USA and 134 portfolio companies by 22 venture capitalists in Canada.
[32]Biotech startups pose challenges for venture capital limited partnerships due to their long time to positive cash flow and high technological risk, while the cash flows from an investment are fairly predictable once scientific and regulatory milestones are reached. This illustrates that investors are willing to back compa-nies that have high technology, but low market risk, and biotech investments have found a supportive IPO market (Janeway, 2018).
[33]Lerner (2020).

The small number of firms receiving venture money reflects venture capital's narrowing emphasis. In the USA, 0.1–1% of startups receive venture funding, accounting for 2–3% of equity capital.[34]

The first computing generation occurred from 1942 to 1955 with the mainframe computer, a machine that used vacuum tube technology to make electronic digital computers. When transistors replaced the vacuum tube (1955–1964), it was categorized as the second computing generation. The transistor allowed computers to become smaller, faster, cheaper, more energy-efficient, and more reliable than their first-generation predecessors. Though the transistor still generated a great deal of heat that subjected the computer to damage, it was a vast improvement over the vacuum tube. Minicomputers (1964–1975) heralded the third computing generation (Figure 4.2).

Figure 4.2 **PDP-9 minicomputer. The PDP-9 minicomputer, which was two meters wide and about 75cm deep, was approximately twice the speed of its predecessor, the PDP-7. It was built using discrete transistors and weighed about 750 pounds (340 kg).**
Source: PDP-9, Sistema Bibliotecario di Ateneo - Università di Pisa.

---

[34] Da Rin et al. (2013).

In 1960, Digital Equipment introduced the first minicomputer. It was the first commercial computer equipped with a keyboard and monitor. Integrated circuits were used, which were smaller in size, more reliable, and used less energy than previous generations.

The history of the personal computer as a mass-market consumer electronic device effectively began in 1977 with the introduction of microcomputers. However, some mainframe and minicomputers had been applied as single-user systems much earlier.

A personal computer is intended for individual interactive use, as opposed to a mainframe computer where the end user's requests are filtered through operating staff or a time-sharing system in which many users share one large processor.

After the Intel 4004 was introduced in 1972, microprocessor costs dropped rapidly, and early home computer kits arrived, and were of interest primarily to hobbyists and technicians (Figure 4.3).

Figure 4.3 *Popular Electronics* **cover, 1/1970.**
Source: Ziff Davis / Wikimedia Commons / Public Domain.

The Altair 8800 sold well despite its limited initial memory size (a few hundred bytes) and a lack of available software. The first Microsoft product was a 4-kilobyte paper tape BASIC interpreter, allowing users to develop programs in a higher-level language.[35]

Many such hobbyists met and traded notes at the Homebrew Computer Club (HCC) meetings in Silicon Valley. Although the HCC was relatively short-lived, its influence on the development of the modern PC was enormous. Steve Wozniak (known as "Woz"), a regular visitor to the Homebrew Computer Club meetings, designed the single-board Apple I computer and first demonstrated it there. With specifications in hand and an order for 100 machines at $500 each from the Byte Shop, Woz and his friend Steve Jobs founded Apple Computer (Figure 4.4).[36]

Figure 4.4   Steve Jobs and Steve Wozniak in 1977.
Source: YouTube (screenshot) 60 Minutes Archive, https://www.youtube.com/watch?v=c-JkrlVhs_0. Getty Image License # 2093424091

---

[35] Davis (1975).
[36] Schuyten (1978); Evans (2020). The Homebrew Computer Club was just one example of a cultural movement that focused on the intellectual challenge of creatively overcoming and circumventing programming limitations—sometimes also referred to as "hacker culture"—and led to the open-source movement. Torvalds's Linux operating system was given away for free in 1991 (Mallaby, 2022).

By 1976, several firms were racing to introduce the first successful personal computers. Three machines, the Apple II, PET 2001, and TRS-80, were all released in 1977 (Figure 4.5).[37]

The development of CPUs based on microchips led to desktop PCs during the late 1970s and laptop computers during the 1980s. The decreasing cost of microchips enabled computers as a mass-market product and fostered an independent software industry. In the 1950s and 1960s, computer operating software and compilers were delivered as a part of hardware purchases without separate fees. At the time, hardware manufacturers generally distributed source code, with the software providing the ability to fix bugs or add new functions.

In the *United States vs. IBM* antitrust suit in 1969, the US government charged that bundled software was anticompetitive. While some software continued to come at no cost in the late 1970s and early 1980s, computer vendors and software-only companies began charging for software licenses and imposing legal restrictions on new software developments, now seen as assets, through copyrights, trademarks, and leasing contracts.[38] Microsoft signed

Figure 4.5 **The three computers whose makers *Byte Magazine* referred to as the "1977 Trinity": the Commodore PET 2001; the Apple II; and the Tandy/Radio Shack TRS-80.**
Source: Tim Colegrove / Wikimedia Commans / CC-BY-SA 4.0.

---

[37] *Byte Magazine* (1978).
[38] In 1976, Bill Gates wrote an article entitled "Open Letter to Hobbyists," in which he expressed his dismay at the widespread sharing of Microsoft's product Altair BASIC without paying its licensing fee (Gates, 1976).

the IBM PC contract in 1980, making MS-DOS the standard operating system. Microsoft became the dominant PC operating system thanks to this agreement. A single software firm would dominate operating systems and client/server software as a hardware firm dominated mainframes.[39] After a rocky start, Microsoft and IBM forged ahead to become the enterprise standard for computer technology. Apple debuted the Macintosh in 1984, and Microsoft released Windows 1.0 the following year. Around the same time, large firms like Oracle and SAP began to make an impact, highlighting the potential of databases to make a difference in enterprises. In the late 1980s, developers realized the importance of APIs (Advanced Programming Interfaces), which enabled software developers to build additional solutions on top of the foundation already in place. This pleased vendors since it made their solutions more customizable, adding significant value to their products and making them more appealing to a broader set of users.[40]

Impact of Modern Venture Capital on Startup Financing

The ARD and SBICs were established to address concerns about a risk capital shortage due to the introduction of commingled investment funds and institutional investors crowding out private investments. Despite fears, private investors remained important for startup financing until the 1970s. The listed investment vehicles paved the way for the use of commingled capital pools to fund startups and educated early venture capitalists. Corporate R&D's shift was feared to impede disruptive innovation, but while many disruptive ideas began in research labs and weren't exploited, it doesn't mean they were suppressed as many of those ideas were only commercialized years later.[41]

---

[39] In the 1990s, the US Department of Justice sued Microsoft for trying to monopolize the personal computer market. The focus had now shifted from a hardware monopoly (IBM) to a software monopoly (Microsoft). Microsoft lost the case but was able to overturn the break-up order on appeal in 2001.
[40] Tricostar (2023).
[41] For example, Xerox's Palo Alto Research Center (PARC) recognized the computer as "an idea whose time had come" and produced a prototype. Still, Xerox worried that the computerized "paperless office" would harm its core photocopying business. Example and citation from (Mallaby, 2022), p. 82.

But there is also evidence that suggests that promising ideas may have been sidetracked within these incumbent organizations, creating an opportunity for entrepreneurial employees to establish new business models based on emerging technologies. By leaving their current positions and starting their own ventures, these individuals might be able to bring these ideas to fruition and drive innovation in their respective industries. According to Bhidé, 71% of all founders had reproduced or modified an idea encountered during their previous employment.[42] There are numerous examples of such "spin-outs" from the early stages of the semiconductor revolution. Gompers et al. find that venture capital has played a vital role as a facilitator for such entrepreneurs, with 30–42% of all VC-backed founders coming from public corporations.[43]

By recognizing the potential of these new business models and investing in them early on, VCs have played a key role in driving innovation and supporting the growth of the startup ecosystem. However, the time constraints of venture capital limited partnerships can limit the scope of these investments. Typically, VCs have a ten-year window to raise, invest, and pay back their funds which incentivizes them to seek out startups that can be quickly commercialized and have the potential for a fast return on investment. They focus on startups that can resolve any uncertainty regarding their viability and market demand quickly, making technology companies, particularly software and service businesses, a natural fit.

Venture capital played no significant role in financing the early semiconductor revolution and the diffusion of mainframe computing in the 1960s; even later, when VCs did deals like Intel, Apple, and Oracle, several successful tech companies founded in the 1970s did not start with early round VC financing (see Figure 4.6) and only received venture capital in later rounds, if at all.

---

[42] Bhidé (1994), citation in Da Rin et al. (2013).
[43] Gompers et al. (2005).

FAIRCHILD SEMICONDUCTOR, SAN JOSE, CA (1957)
Founders: Fairchild corporation and Jean Hoerni, E.
Kleiner, Jay Last, Sheldon Roberts, et al.. No early
venture rounds recorded.

AMELCO SEMICONDUCTOR, MOUNTAIN VIEW, CA
(1961) Founders: Jean Hoerni, E. Kleiner, Jay Last,
Sheldon Roberts (all from Fairchild and Shockley).
No early venture rounds recorded.

APPLIED MATERIALS TECHNOLOGY, SANTA CLARA,
CA (1967)
With funding from Robert Noyce and others. No
early venture rounds recorded.

ADVANCED MICRO DEVICES, SUNNYVALE, CA (1969)
Founders: F. Botte, J. Carey, J. Giles, J. Gifford. J.
Sanders, et al. (all from Fairchild). No early venture
rounds recorded.

SAP SE, WALLDORF, GERMANY (1972)
Founders: D. Hopp, H. Plattner, K. Tschira, C.
Wellenreuter, H.-T. Hector et al. (all from IBM)
No early venture rounds recorded.

ORACLE, SANTA CLARA, CA (1977)
Founders: L. Ellison, B. Miner, E. Oates, B. Scott.
Oracle entered the Fairchild diaspora through
investments by Sequoia Capital and the acquisition of
Sun Microsystems in 2009.

NATIONAL SEMICONDUCTOR, DANBURY,
CT (1963) Founders: Dr. Bernard J. No early
venture rounds recorded.

GENERAL MICROELECTRONICS, SANTA
CLARA, CA (1963) Founders: H. Bobb, J.
Ferguson, R. Norman (all from Fairchild).
No early venture rounds recorded.

NATIONAL SEMICONDUCTOR, SANTA CLARA,
CA (Restart 1967) Founders: D. Valentine
(Fairchild, Founder Sequoia), P. Lamond, E.
Kvamme. No early venture rounds recorded.

INTEL CORPORATION, MOUNTAIN VIEW,
CA (1968) Founders R. Noyce, G. Moore, (all
from Fairchild) and Arthur Rock. Funding: A.
Rock.

APPLE COMPUTER, LOS ALTOS, CA, (1976)
Founders: S. Jobs, R. Wayne, S. Wozniak.
Chairman: Mike Markkula (Fairchild/intel)
Funding from Sequoia Capital and A. Rock.

MICROSOFT, SEATTLE, WA, (1975)
Founders: B. Gates and P. Allen.
No early venture rounds recorded.

Figure 4.6   Some prominent early startups during the 1960s and 1970s (most are somehow related to Fairchild Semiconductors, also referred to as the Fairchildren).

Sources: Wikipedia.org., Crunchbase.com, logos downloaded from commons .wikimedia.org.

4.2   BUYOUTS DURING THE 1970S

The US Economy During the 1970s

When people think of the US economy in the 1970s, a few things come to mind:

- high oil prices
- inflation
- unemployment
- recession
- weak stock market.

The 1950s and 1960s were benign economic periods with brief downturns, generally low inflation, and mostly positive GDP growth and interest rates. The growing welfare state, the Vietnam War, and increased spending on research and development were all part of a fiscal expansion that supported growth. But in 1968, inflation started creeping up. In 1969, when Richard Nixon became president, a recession began. The budget expanded as he continued to fund the Vietnam War and increased social welfare spending. When the dollar came under increased pressure in 1971, the USA faced a balance-of-payments crisis. Nixon suspended the dollar's convertibility into gold, causing a significant devaluation.[44] He also introduced wage and price controls and trade restrictions.[45] While these measures provided short-term relief, they bottled up adjustments that would later fuel double-digit inflation.[46]

Then came the 1973 oil crisis, a quadrupling of oil prices by OPEC, coupled with the 1973–1974 stock market crash, which led to a stagflation recession in the United States that lasted until 1975. Inflation peaked at 12% in 1974 and came down somewhat after that. But it went up again in 1979–1980 as a result of the second oil crisis when the Iranian revolution reduced world oil production by about 10%.[47]

---

[44] Solomon (1982).
[45] On August 15, 1971, President Nixon issued Proclamation 4074, in which he declared a national emergency and imposed a 10% supplemental duty on all dutiable articles imported into the United States (CRS, 2022).
[46] Congressional Budget Office (1977).
[47] TIME (1979).

Table 4.1 Economic and stock market indicators for 1950–1980 (%)

Time	S&P 500/w div. reinvested, nom. return	S&P 55/w div. reinvested, real return	CPI inflation avg. p.a.	GDP growth (real), avg. p.a.	10y Treasury bond yields (end of period)
1951-1960	16.0	14.3	1.7	4.5	4.1
1961-1970	8.1	5.0	3.1	4.7	6.5
1971-1980	8.4	0.3	8.1	3.2	12.4

Source: Inflationdata.com; S&P calculator (dqjdj.com).

West Texas Intermediate (WTI) crude oil reached $125 per barrel in April 1980. Twenty-eight years passed before oil reached that price again. Thus, the 1970s' economy differed from the 1950s and 1960s, which saw a robust economy, rising disposable incomes, low or moderate inflation, and an annual stock market return (S&P 500/w dividends reinvested) of about 13%.

The decade ended with a P/E ratio of 7.4, the third lowest in 100 years, and the S&P 500 index was barely positive (see Table 4.1). The 1970s were a lost decade for stockholders. The stock market's poor performance was partly a result of a conglomerate boom during the previous decade and their poor performance.

The Legacy of the Conglomerates Boom

In the early 20th century, concerns over the dominance of banking institutions in the economy and the growing power of trusts prompted a series of anti-monopoly measures and regulations, which had unintended consequences. The Celler-Kefauver Act of 1950 closed a loophole in the Clayton Act of 1914 that had allowed firms to engage in horizontal mergers as long as the buyer purchased a target's assets rather than its shares. Managers targeted firms in unrelated industries to avoid falling foul of antitrust laws as a result of M&A transactions involving firms in the same or related industries. During 1968, more than 4,400 M&A transactions closed with an estimated $43 billion transaction value—a record.[48]

---

[48] For an analysis of the factors that caused the conglomerate boom, see Jacoby (1970; Kaufman and Englander 1993).

In parallel with these regulatory changes, the age of computing brought about a profound shift in how businesses operated. It emphasized process optimization, hierarchical data structures, and efficient information processing. This shift in business practices, often called scientific management, was also reflected in a shift of MBA programs away from the "vocational" style education toward a more theoretical approach, which in the 1960s attracted more students to business programs. By 1975, MBAs were more popular than other traditionally high-earning degrees in law and medicine. With it came a recognition of recognition of management as a skilled profession. Managers were viewed as a distinct group of experts trained in management theory, which led to operations research and system-oriented management that viewed the corporation as a dynamic system and management's role as an agent that provides administrative structure and managerial coordination to accomplish the efficient allocation of resources and the optimization of processes.[49]

Managers were regarded as "generalists" who could apply their skills and knowledge to any industry and corporate setting. Those who knew how to apply management techniques to process the data for resource allocation and translate goals into measurable key performance indicators (KPIs) could manage any business. If you can measure it, you can manage it.[50]

---

[49] In the following, the author would like to name just a few important contributors that provided ideas and the intellectual framework for management as a science and the resulting management theory that gained prominence after WWII: E. Mayo, M. Parker Follett, C. Barnard, M. Weber, and C. Argyris imported theories from sociology and psychology to apply to management (McGrath, 2014), while the view of the corporation as a system that can be optimized using mathematical concepts such as probability and optimization as well as process design was derived from cybernetics that stresses causality and feedback can be traced back to H. Fayol (Fayol, 1949), A. P. Sloane (Sloane, 1964), A. D. Chandler (Chandler, 1962), and S. Beer (Beer, 1959).

[50] This is an adaptation of a quote attributed to Peter Drucker's famous quote "if you cannot measure it, you cannot manage it" (but some sources claim that he never said it) (Zak, 2013).

Centralized management was essential to harvest those advantages as the center had all the information.[51] It was only in the 1990s when an understanding of value networks as being specific to industries and market (segments) led to an appreciation that the very task of management—efficient resource allocation—reflects those value systems and the processes that have evolved to reflect them.[52]

The confluence of these factors—anti-trust legislation and the adoption of scientific management principles—laid the foundation for a prevailing belief that large organizations, with their ample resources, could improve the performance of any enterprise they acquired. By doing unrelated acquisitions, companies could not only stay clear of anti-trust regulations but also create shareholder value by diversifying their exposure to different product/market cycles.

However, plugging acquired firms that operate in different market/product settings into the management structure of the acquiring company may not be conducive to good outcomes.

But that was a lesson essentially still waiting to be learned. At the time, it was a common belief that a trained manager could

---

[51] The fact that the Soviet Union was seen as a strategic competitor and threat, and its centralized economy with its five-year plans and concentration of decision-making were still seen as an alternative model that might be able to perform even better than the "invisible hand" of capitalism, added to the worldview that centralized decision-making using big data (at the time) and scientific management methods were state-of-the-art and favored the large corporation.

[52] C. Christensen provides an organizational capabilities framework that is very useful for understanding the issues faced by corporations that acquired unrelated businesses in his book *The Innovators' Dilemma*. It is important to appreciate that value destruction within conglomerates is not a result of "bad" management. Good managers can make wrong decisions relating to non-core businesses by acting entirely rationally within the framework and value system of the parent company (Christensen, 1997). T. Levitt developed the concept of interdependence of producers and customers in the 1970s and 1980s, implying that corporate processes and value chains reflect the product/customer segment they focus on. It is easy to appreciate that a tobacco company that acquires food businesses does face some integration challenges (Levitt, 1983).

manage anything and that larger organizations could marshal more resources, including systems, to gather management information and afford higher qualified experts with superior managerial skills compared to smaller organizations. H. Geneen, CEO of International Telephone and Telegraph Company (ITT), a major conglomerate firm in the 1960s, stated:

> In picking and choosing what companies to acquire . . . with our expertise in management and our access to greater financial resources did something to that particular company . . . In instances, we kept the same management and introduced the company's management to the ITT system of business plans, detailed budgets, strict financial controls . . .[53]

In 1967, ITT was a global corporation with 150 companies and 204,000 employees, responsible for major developments such as the Moscow-Washington hotline. Business mergers were occurring at a record rate of 150 per month, with over 70% being conglomerate-style due to antitrust regulations. This trend was exemplified by American Tobacco's pursuit of apparel manufacturer Kayser-Roth Corp. Although H. Geneen and his colleagues did not favor the term "conglomerate," this style of merger appeared to be a successful strategy for US businesses.[54]

Hubbard and Palia looked at 392 conglomerates that undertook at least one acquisition in an unrelated industry, including 53 firms with multiple acquisitions during 1963–1970 and found that, unlike in the 1980s, the stock market was rewarding diversifying acquisitions during the 1960s.[55] Lopez confirms this. He refers to an analysis by James Litinsky of JHL Capital Group. Using data from the Chicago Booth Center for Research into Securities Prices, he created an index of conglomerates from the 1960s and charted their outperformance versus the S&P 500 from 1966–1969 (Figure 4.7). The author also pointed out that the 1960s saw the

---

[53] See Hubbard and Palia (1999).
[54] TIME (1967).
[55] Hubbard and Palia (1999).

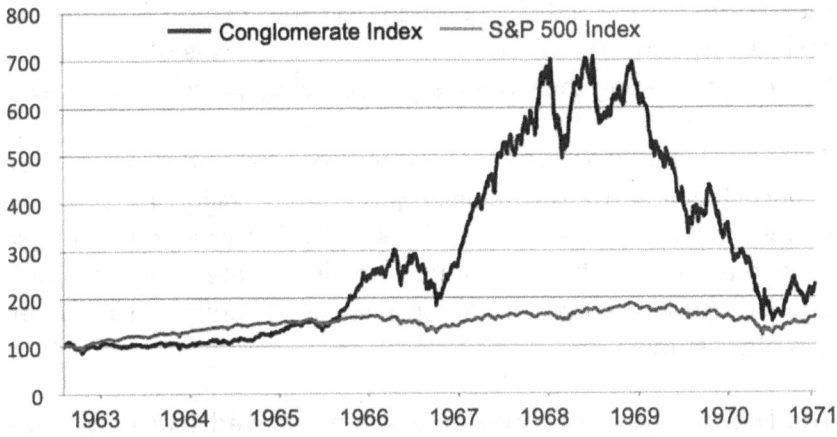

Figure 4.7   Conglomerate index vs. S&P 500 index.
Source: Chicago Booth Center for research into security prices, JHL Capital Research.

strongest increase in corporate leverage since the 1950s and until the 1990s.[56]

The belief of corporate CEOs that large organizations could acquire businesses somewhat or entirely unrelated to their core business and bring superior organizational skills to bear to create value was thus endorsed by investors. In addition, such a diversification strategy could reduce a firm's exposure to demand or product cycles and reduce the volatility of its earnings—resulting in higher valuations.

However, the difficulty of managing a diverse set of unrelated businesses resulted in bloated corporate structures with multi-tiered management structures. That means more overhead, more approval layers, and slower responses—but also more prospects for promotion. Such organizations found it difficult to adjust during times of economic crisis.[57]

The initial outperformance of conglomerates versus the broader stock market was reversed in 1970. Many of those firms struggled during the 1970s when recession and high-interest rates reduced

---

[56] Lopez (2015).
[57] Hamel (2011).

their ability to service the acquisition debt they carried. To conserve cash, investment spending in non-core divisions was often slashed, further accelerating the value destruction of acquired subsidiaries.

As a result, these acquired divisions and subsidiaries used to be financially viable before their acquisition but failed as part of a conglomerate. According to a Federal Trade Commission report, more than 40% of all acquisitions made in the late 1960s and early 1970s destroyed value. This finding has been confirmed in numerous other studies.[58],[59]

The line managers of those units often believed that they could substantially improve performance if they could regain their independence. Unsurprisingly, their "plan" often involved just returning to how things were done (successfully) before the acquisition. Long-suffering shareholders recognized the necessity for action. However, even large investors found their influence constrained, as regulatory measures designed to diminish the sway of major corporate entities also placed limitations on investors seeking significant or controlling stakes in companies. Consequently, the landscape of corporate ownership and control shifted in favor of management, which enjoyed added protection due to anti-trust legislation and restrictions on mergers and acquisitions, meant to prevent monopolistic practices but inadvertently safeguarding incumbent firms and their leadership. This scenario paved the way for new players who could surmount these obstacles and capitalize on opportunities from acquiring companies, divesting underperforming subsidiaries, or purchasing subsidiaries from conglomerates.

Another opportunity was present with family-owned firms that faced succession issues but were too small to go public and their owners

---

[58] Other estimates quoted in (Kaufman and Englander, 1993) put the rate of disposals much higher. Starting in 1970, the number of conglomerate divestitures increased dramatically, accounting for 53% of all transactions by 1977 according to the authors.
[59] FTC report cited in (Ravenscraft and Scherer, 1986). Research shows most mergers fail—destroying shareholder value and costing companies billions of dollars. Over the decades, multiple studies have shown that most mergers and acquisitions fail to generate the anticipated synergies—and many destroy value instead of creating it (Fernandes, 2020). Porter (1987) puts divestitures at >50%.

were unwilling to sell to competitors. The latter point is less compelling than it sounds, as the temporary ownership offered by a leveraged buyout (LBO) firm usually merely delays the sale to a strategic buyer by a few years. Instead, the lack of strategic buyers during the recessions and weak equity markets during the 1970s created opportunities for buyout firms. The acquisition of owner-managed mid-sized businesses became a staple of future buyout activity. Often, incumbent management would partner with a financial investor to submit a bid for "their" company that was in the process of being sold. Such management buyout (MBO)—sometimes also called a management buy-in (MBI)—transactions clearly added to the exit strategies available to owners of companies and had the advantage for the financial investor of acting in partnership with insiders. It also illustrates LBO firms' role in providing equity in times of low demand for equity and the resulting low valuations.

4.3 THE ESTABLISHMENT OF EARLY BUYOUT FIRMS AND THE LBO MODEL

During the 1960s and 1970s, Warren Buffett (Berkshire Hathaway) and Victor Posner (DWG Corporation), among others, popularized the use of publicly traded holding companies as investment vehicles to acquire portfolios of investments in corporate assets. These investment vehicles would employ several of the same strategies and target the same types of companies as more conventional leveraged buyouts. They could be viewed in many ways as a precursor to later private equity firms and sometimes would compete with them for deals. Posner is frequently credited with coining the term "leveraged buyout" (LBO).[60]

When Lewis Cullman acquired Orkin Exterminating Company in 1964, it was one of the first significant leveraged buyout transactions.[61] However, the business now known as private equity was established by a group of corporate bankers, Jerome Kohlberg Jr,

---

[60] Trehan (2006).
[61] Kirk (2005); Cullman also founded the Incubation Fund in the early 1960s, which invested in companies that were starting up or had just gone public.

Figure 4.8   Left to right: Jerome Kohlberg (left KKR in 1987), Henry Kravis and George Roberts.
Source: Kohlberg Foundation, KKR - reprinted with permission.

Henry Kravis, and George R. Roberts, all of whom had previously worked together at Bear Stearns (Figure 4.8).

At Bear Stearns, Kohlberg, Kravis, and Roberts executed "bootstrap" acquisitions by acquiring shares in a target company and using those shares as collateral to secure loans for additional share purchases. They targeted family-owned businesses struggling with succession issues and corporate divestitures. Their acquisition strategy relied heavily on leverage and Kohlberg collaborated with management to identify a company's potential value and develop business plans to realize that value. Their ideal targets were industrial companies with robust cash flow to manage high debt payments associated with a leveraged buyout. The ability to make a cash sweep, which allowed optional prepayment of debt with surplus cash and the tax benefit of interest deductibility from corporate earnings, was also crucial.[62] Following their successful use in venture capital, Kohlberg gave stock incentives to the acquired company's management to ensure alignment of interest with the owners.

In 1976, Kohlberg, Kravis, and Roberts failed to convince Bear Stearns to partner with them as a principal investor instead of just arranging transactions. This resulted in their departure and the founding of Kohlberg Kravis Roberts (KKR).

---

[62] Kaufman and Englander (1993).

On September 2, 1976, an article appeared in *The Wall Street Journal*, which mentioned a firm that had just completed a $25.6 million takeover of a company called A. J. Industries Inc. It was the *Journal's* first mention of KKR. The firm completed its first buyout of NYSE listed manufacturer A. J. Industries, for $26 million. For this deal, KKR raised capital from a small group of investors including the Hillman Company and First Chicago Bank.[63] In the mid-1970s, the law required a target company's board to respond to a cash offer for shares within eight days.[64] This put a lot of time pressure on a target company that wanted to block a deal while it made it impossible to do a drawn-out bootstrap acquisition if management did not agree. While corporate raiders could use their holding companies to raise capital and pledge assets as collateral for debt, KKR did not have that option. KKR needed to raise a pool of capital to be competitive, and the firm developed close ties with its investors, much as traditional investment banks had cultivated relations with their principal customers (issuers).

KKR targeted pension funds as investors and used limited partnerships as investment vehicles. The terms and conditions, including management fees and carried interest, mirrored those that were already established in the venture capital industry.[65] The fund life restrictions that came with limited partnerships also meant that ownership of portfolio companies would be temporary.

By 1978, with the revision of the ERISA regulations, the nascent KKR was successful in raising its first institutional fund with over $30 million of investor commitments, which was the first significant buyout fund raised.

KKR purchased Houdaille Industries for $380 million, a year after closing their first institutional fund. The company produced machine tools, industrial pipes, and car parts, with KKR liquidating some loss-making operations and repositioning the company through value-added acquisitions. However, the company defaulted on its debt and was liquidated in 1987 due to foreign competition, another

---

[63] *The Wall Street Journal*, September 2, 1976.
[64] Ellis (2008).
[65] But unlike the venture capital industry, buyout firms would also charge a transaction fee, which in the case of Forstmann Little was typically 1% of the purchase price.

recession, and re-leveraging.[66] But it was a landmark deal due to its size, high leverage, divestitures, and acquisitions, which were all characteristic of the buyout deals that would follow.

To leverage the equity provided by its investment funds to acquire companies, KKR relied on large commercial banks for senior bank debt, secured by the firm's assets. Insurance companies supplemented these funds by supplying subordinated debt. Until the mid-1980s, insurance companies were able to impose strict conditions on subordinated debt because of the lack of alternative sources.

Apart from KKR, there were several other buyout firms established during the 1970s:

- Thomas H. Lee, 1974
- Cinven, a European buyout firm, 1974
- Forstmann, Little & Company, 1978
- Clayton, Dubilier & Rice, 1978
- Welsh, Carson, Anderson & Stowe, 1979
- Candover, a European buyout firm, 1980.

KKR is widely regarded as the first buyout firm, and that claim seems correct if one uses the focus on leveraged buyouts and investments through limited partnerships as criteria. Some of the other early firms apparently sought capital on a deal-by-deal basis instead of raising a fund. Clayton Dubilier Rice, for example, did their first buyout in 1979 (Kux Manufacturing Company) but raised their first fund ($46 million) in 1984. In the same year, Thomas H. Lee closed their first fund at $66 million.[67]

This shows the difficulty of raising capital and finding targets in the late 1970s. After ERISA's "prudent man rule" was revised, institutional investors were slow to embrace leveraged buyouts. Early deals resulted in high exit multiples in the early 1980s, making headlines for the industry. For example, Forstmann, Little and Company made its first acquisition, the $420-million purchase of Kincaid Furniture Co.,

---

[66] Holl (1989).
[67] Kester and Luehrman (1995).

based in Hudson, NC, in 1980, which led to the public sale of stock 3½ years later at 10x its initial equity investment.[68] But LBO firms could not compete in M&A by seeking equity "deal-by-deal" as it was too slow. Committed-capital funds were needed and KKR was the first buyout firm in the 1970s that was able to raise institutional capital through limited partnerships and dominated fundraising well into the 1980s.

The enduring implications for deal structuring resulted from the LBO firms investing their capital, which was committed to limited partnerships, in individual deals rather than using holding companies as acquisition vehicles. This approach had the following characteristics:

- Leverage is assumed by the acquired companies on their balance sheet and not on a fund level.
- Each deal is stand-alone, i.e., there is no cross-financing between portfolio companies or pledging of assets of existing companies to collateralize new acquisition debt.
- Ownership is strictly temporary due to the limited life of a partnership.
- The investment professionals will usually give a (small) percentage of the capital invested alongside their clients (limited partners) out of their own pockets, providing some alignment of interest.
- The gains of the investment will typically be shared 80/20 between investors and investment managers, which is an outsized gain relative to their (much smaller) investment in the deals.
- The performance incentive is central to all private markets investing, as private market investment managers act like owners; not passive investors, as is the case with active public securities managers.

Early buyouts targeted low-volatility, low-valuation businesses. Value creation was mainly done through financial engineering, i.e., applying leverage and benefiting from the interest tax shield, as interest payments are deductible before taxes. LBO firms with Wall Street connections had an advantage in obtaining and structuring debt packages, especially compared to strategic buyers, which

---

[68] Vise (1986).

were mid-sized companies that usually had only regional bank relationships. Access to debt financing during bear markets and recessions, when traditional lenders retreat, was and still is essential for closing deals at low valuations.[69]

Governance, allowing management to become substantial shareholders and increasing senior management's compensation from equity ownership, was also important from the start. Owners and managers are focused on the company's exit within a few years, which increases time horizon alignment. In the 1980s, public company CEOs held very little equity and equity incentives such as stock options were hardly used in executive compensation packages.[70] The award of substantial share packages to management, sometimes tied to a requirement to invest a substantial portion of their personal wealth in a deal, was thus a powerful innovation that gave LBO firms an edge compared to strategic buyers.

High leverage is also often cited in the literature as a disciplining factor that forces management to avoid wasteful spending. This is reinforced by a significant equity stake held by management, which makes it "their money."[71] Wall Street investment banks supported LBO firms. While it's often said that bulge bracket Wall Street firms avoided hostile takeovers to avoid alienating their best clients, the reality was more nuanced. The hostile takeover bid of Canadian firm International Nickel for ESB, a leading US manufacturer of large storage batteries, was the first hostile takeover advised by Morgan Stanley, probably the most prestigious US investment bank at the time, and marked the beginning of major investment banks' involvement in takeovers.[72]

So, as the 1970s ended, some of the major levers for value creation would be in place that provided the basis for the growing role of LBOs that was to follow during the next decade.

---

[69] This has been examined by Ivashina and Kovner (2011), who investigated advantages that flow from LBO firms' relationships with major banks and found that this often resulted in debt financing at lower rates compared to strategic buyers. Kaplan and Stein (1993) studied the impact of the high-yield bond market, which is an extension of the debt financing options that LBO firms could use, and the authors found that this enabled them to pay higher valuations.

[70] Jensen and Murphy (1990).

[71] Jensen (1989).

[72] Ellis (2008).

4.4   LIMITED PARTNERSHIPS

Since the 1960s, venture capital firms have established limited partnerships to hold investments, with investment professionals serving as general partners and investors contributing capital as passive limited partners.

The limited partnership's prominence as an investment vehicle is a central element of most private market investment strategies. Since the late 1960s, when it was first used in venture capital, it has been adopted by early buyout firms and has become the standard investment vehicle. It came with jargon and a concept of performance measurement that even investment professionals may find occasionally perplexing. As not all readers may be familiar with private market jargon or its underlying concepts, the following brief introduction explains some of the most common terms associated with private market investments.

A limited partnership is a legal structure with a limited life span, whereas a general partner (GP) has full operational control, makes investment decisions, and, in principle, has unlimited liability. In contrast, limited partners (LPs) are passive investors and do not participate in the management of the partnership and are only liable for the amount of their investment. Limited partners (LPs) make capital subscriptions (commitments). But committed capital is usually not invested immediately. Instead, it is called by the general partner—over time and at its discretion. Paid-in capital (plus gains) is distributed back to LPs once an investment is exited. The resulting cash flow pattern is illustrated in Figure 4.9.

Given that cash flows are spread out over time, it is a standard return on investment (ROI) metric that is unhelpful to evaluate performance (see cash flow profile in Figure 4.8). Instead, private market investors use the internal rate of return (IRR), a time- and money-weighted performance metric that cannot be directly compared to ROI.

The example in Table 4.2 compares a $15 mutual fund investment to a $15 private markets fund commitment where both investments achieve the same absolute gain of $30. However, the private equity investment's internal rate of return (IRR) is significantly higher than the mutual fund's return due to the impact of the time- and

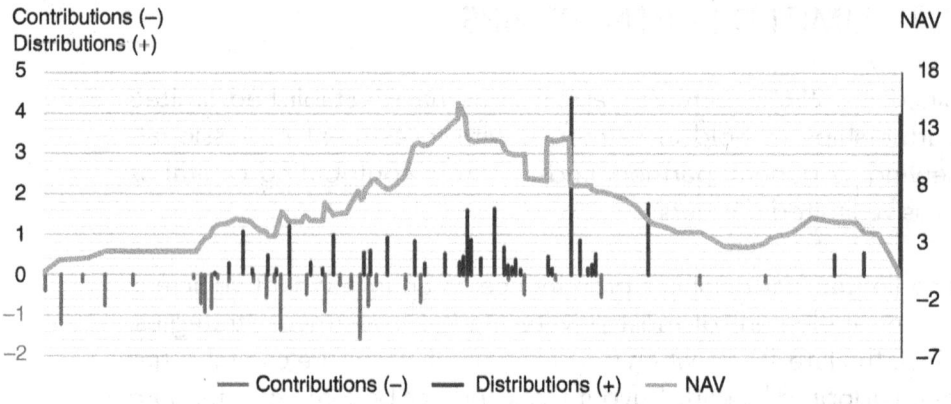

Figure 4.9   Cash flow profile of a $15 million commitment in a private equity fund, in $M.
Note: Figure 4.9 displays the cash flow profile of a $15 million commitment (subscription) in a private equity fund (partnership) over the period 4/2001–12/2010. Contributions (–) reflect paid-in capital and distributions (+) return of capital and gain to investors (left horizontal axis). The NAV development is shown on the right vertical axis. It starts and ends at zero as limited partnerships are self-liquidating, i.e., they distribute all paid-in capital and gains and unwind thereafter.

Table 4.2   Comparison of return on investment (ROI) and internal rate of return (IRR)

Date	Mutual fund investment and NAV	Mutual fund annual return (ROI)	Private equity fund cash flow and IRR	
31.12.15	$15		-$5	Capital is called in installments, i.e., not fully paid-in upfront.
31.12.16	$20	33.3%	-$5	
31.12.17	$27	35.0%	-$5	
31.12.18	$24	-11.1%	$10	
31.12.19	$37	54.2%	$15	Investments are repaid over time and capital is returned.
31.12.20	$45	21.6%	$20	
Total return		24.6%	40.5%	
Total gain	$30		$30	

Initial investment mutual fund = subscription PE partnership = $15

Both investments are done with the same amounts and generate the same gain. But the performance numbers are very different.

money-weighting of cash flows that follows from using the IRR. The mutual fund investment is paid in full and held until December 31, 2020, while the private markets fund commitment is called in three installments and returns the capital in several installments during the holding period. The example illustrates that the IRR is not an accurate measure of wealth creation. Comparing IRRs with ROIs

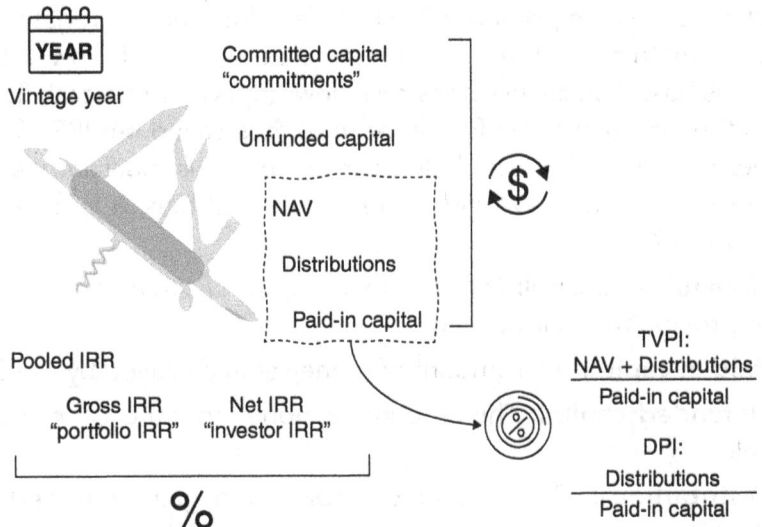

Figure 4.10 A "Swiss Army Knife" for common private market terms used by investors.
Source: Swiss Army Knife, Shutterstock #13690882 and #1688243668.

can be confusing and misleading as a performance measure. The IRR is very sensitive to the timing of cash flows and thus may indicate vastly different performance numbers, even when the absolute gains are similar.

Public and private markets investments not only differ in the measure of performance used but also in the way "assets under management" (AuM) numbers are calculated. Public market asset managers would calculate the AuM as the sum of their funds' net asset values (NAVs). In private markets, AuM is not just the NAV of the funds managed but additionally includes unfunded commitments, i.e., capital that has been committed by LPs but has not yet been invested. This portion of AuM is known as "dry powder," and its value is not trivial; estimated at around $3 trillion by the end of 2021.[73]

Figure 4.10 provides an overview of the most common private market terms:

- **Vintage year:** The year a limited partnership started operations.
- **IRR:** The time- and money-weighted performance of a private market funds or investment. A term often found in performance

---

[73] Preqin (2022b).

overviews is the pooled IRR, which calculates an aggregate IRR by combining cash flows to create a portfolio cash flow. If the IRR is based on an investor's cash flows (thus ignoring cash flows to the GP, such as performance fees), it is called net IRR. If the performance of the underlying investments is measured without considering any fund-related costs and fees, it is called a gross IRR.

- **Committed capital:** The number of capital LPs that have agreed to provide to a partnership.
- **Paid-in capital:** The amount of money already called by the GP.
- **Unfunded capital:** The amount of money that the GP can still call.
- **Distributions:** The amount of capital and gains returned to the LP.
- **Total value to paid-in (TVPI):** A measure of total gain, including the NAV of unrealized investments, compared to the capital contributed.
- **Distribution to paid-in (DPI):** A measure of the capital returned relative to the capital contributed.

Private markets occupy a parallel world to traditional investment performance concerning their performance metrics and cash flow patterns. As a result, investors are faced with conceptual issues when trying to integrate those two worlds in an asset allocation framework or even when comparing results of different asset classes.

The limited partnership came with features that resulted in a significant competitive advantage versus listed investment companies, such as ARD or Business Development Companies: First, all profits could be directly passed on to investors without taxing, while investors in listed investment companies could not offset losses against profits from other investments, and the companies were subject to corporate taxes. Second, the general partners not only received a management fee that covered their salaries and expenses, but they also received a share of the capital gains.

In addition, other structural features made limited partnerships more attractive to venture capitalists: The limited partners had little ability to affect the policies of the general partners. They were mandated to stay entirely out of the management process, thus freeing the general partners from interference. A partnership had a limited life. Usually, ten years after its establishment, it was liquidated, and the funds were invested only once. All returns were immediately distributed to the investors, so the partnership was self-liquidating. As the limited partnership was not traded on an exchange, it did not face the issue that the share price would trade at a discount to NAV, which is characteristic of listed investment companies.[74]

The compensation structure, which is still in use today, also evolved, with limited partners paying a 1–2% annual management fee and a carried interest typically representing 20% of the partnership's profits.

While the Delaware Uniform Limited Partnership Act was only adopted in 1973, it contained a few provisions to limit the unlimited liability of the general partner that made Delaware an attractive jurisdiction in which to organize limited partnerships. It quickly established itself as the preferred jurisdiction for organizing domestic US private equity partnerships.[75]

During the 1980s, more than 80% of all venture capital funds were organized as limited partnerships. Investing through limited partnerships has some features that set it apart from investing through mutual fund structures (Box 4.1). The use of limited partnerships as the predominant investment vehicle would impact how private market investments are made. The fund and investment period restrictions would compel managers to concentrate on medium-term results, thereby creating time pressure to achieve results. Investors also expected their capital to be invested, which obligated the industry to continue searching for investment opportunities when others would not. This included using unfunded capital commitments—the dry powder—to support exciting portfolio investments. Private markets are no strangers to overpaying

---

[74] Hsu and Kenney (2005).
[75] Kessler (1979).

during bull markets, but they also use these periods of exuberant valuations for exits. This resulted in time diversification that reduced the private markets' vulnerability to valuation cycles. The temporary ownership also necessitated an early focus on an exit strategy and viable exit routes. Individual transactions would not be cross-subsidized, as is common within conglomerates. Instead, they stood alone, their successes and failures evident. This focused the minds of deal partners accountable for these transactions and their management teams. The co-investments of GPs and carried interest led to an alignment with management teams to achieve the best possible outcome over a given time frame.

Limited partnerships are most suitable for investment strategies that involve the gradual deployment of capital. This is particularly beneficial for accommodating the time needed to source and execute deals and for making staged equity investments in the underlying assets. In contrast, income-oriented investment strategies are often evergreen or open-ended investment vehicles.

However, the adoption of the limited partnership structure, along with a fee arrangement comprising a management fee and what eventually became a standardized carried interest, occurred gradually. According to information provided by Warburg Pincus, one of the oldest private equity firms that has been involved in private equity investments since 1966, their initial fund, EMW Ventures (1971), still operated as a corporation, with distributions directed toward Class A (institutional) and B (primarily internal Warburg Pincus shareholders) units. Profits generated over the preference on the A units disproportionately benefited the B units, resulting in an ultimate profit split of approximately 65% for the fund manager and its executives and 35% for external investors. It wasn't until around 1985 that Warburg Pincus Associates, L.P. (1980) transitioned from Warburg Pincus Capital Corporation, established in 1981, marking the first time a Warburg Pincus fund paid carried interest as a formalized concept.

Boxes 4.2 and 4.3 show cash flows and IRR and the fee structure and waterfall of limited partnerships.

Box 4.1   Limited Partnerships: Characteristics

The limited partnership has become the preferred investment structure for private market investments. Limited partnership structures exist in many jurisdictions. The most important ones for private market investing are Delaware, the UK, Luxembourg, and offshore locations like the Cayman and the British Virgin Islands. Limited partnership structures may differ in some detail but share broad characteristics that set private market investing apart from other asset classes.

There are two types of partners: The **General Partner (GP)** has management control and the right to use partnership property. **Limited Partners (LPs)** are like shareholders in a corporation, i.e., they have limited liability, no management authority, and are not liable for the partnership's debts (Figure 4.11). The private equity firm that set up the partnership owns or has a stake in the GP. A management agreement lets the manager do the

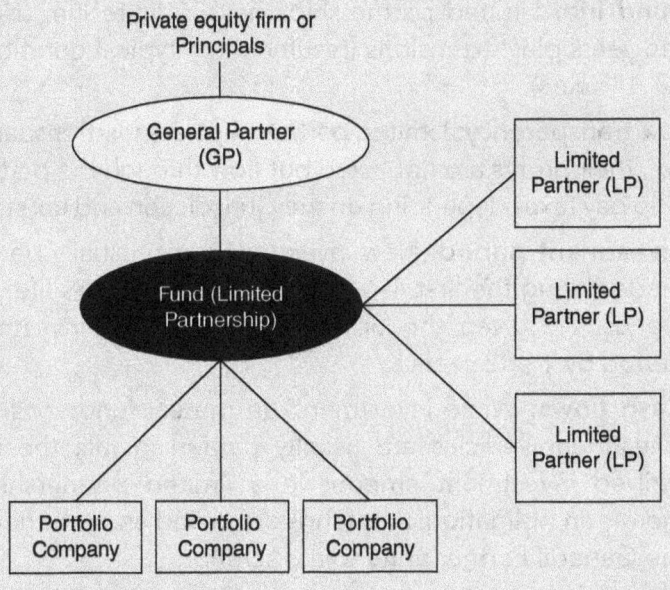

Figure 4.11   Limited partnership overview.

(continued)

Table 4.3   IRR formula and calculation

$$NPV = \sum_{n=0}^{N} \frac{C_n}{(1+r)^n}$$

NPV = Net Present Value

N = total number of periods

n = non-negative integer

C_n = cash flow

r = internal rate of return

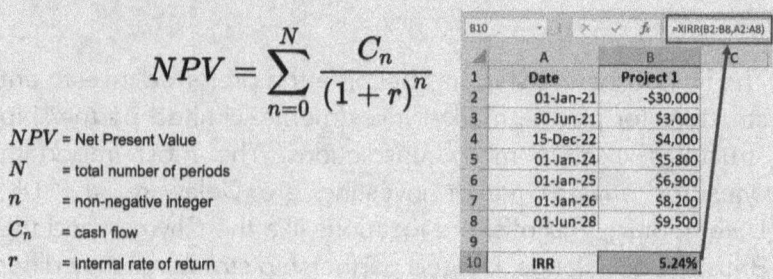

	A	B
	Date	Project 1
1	Date	Project 1
2	01-Jan-21	-$30,000
3	30-Jun-21	$3,000
4	15-Dec-22	$4,000
5	01-Jan-24	$5,800
6	01-Jan-25	$6,900
7	01-Jan-26	$8,200
8	01-Jun-28	$9,500
9		
10	IRR	5.24%

business's actual work. The manager's tasks include finding deals, executing them, making money, and getting out. The **Limited Partnership Agreement (LPA)** lays out the terms and conditions (rights and obligations of the partners, investment policy and restrictions, duration of the partnership, fees, and profit allocation, etc.).

The following are features of a limited partnership:

- **Fund life:** Limited partnerships have a finite life, usually ten years plus extensions (resulting in a typical duration of 12–14 years).

- **Tax transparency:** Limited partnerships are tax-transparent, i.e., their profits are not taxed but flow through the partners who pay taxes depending on their jurisdiction and tax status.

- **Investment period:** New investments can usually be only made during the first 4–6 years of a partnership's life. GPs are usually given the option to extend the investment period by 1 or 2 years.

- **Cash flows:** While investments in mutual funds or listed investment vehicles are usually paid-in in full, the sub-scribed investment amount in a limited partnership is merely an obligation, and funds are called and returned by the General Partner at its sole discretion.

- **Lock-up:** Partners cannot exit the partnership or return their partnership interests during the life of the partner-ship. As partnership interests are not listed, investors are thus locked into an illiquid investment.

- **Capital at work:** While the investment amount in a mutual fund or listed vehicle is fully invested throughout the holding period, the capital contributions to a limited partnership are stacked over time (as are the distributions). The average capital invested in a fund is usually less than 50%, with a peak funding rate rarely exceeding 75% subscribed capital.

Performance Measurement

To assess the performance of a limited partnership, the cash flow pattern needs to be considered, which requires a time- and money-weighted performance measure.

In a discounted cash flow analysis, IRR is a discount rate that makes the net present value (NPV) of all cash flows equal to zero. This internal rate of return (IRR) is different from the ROI used to calculate the performance of liquid investments, which is time-weighted only.

The IRR formula solves the discount rate that sets all the cash flows (positive = distribution and final period NAV, negative = capital calls) to zero. It measures the performance while money is invested in the private equity partnership. But the opportunity cost of holding the money until it is called is ignored.

The example illustrates the impact of comparing a limited partnership's cash flow to a mutual fund's ROI. Both investments result in the same absolute gain ($30). Still, the cash flow pattern of the PE partnership "worked harder" to achieve that gain as the time the monies were invested was shorter than the five-year investment horizon of the mutual fund investment.

Thus, the IRR number is significantly higher than the ROI number. Mixing the two numbers can lead to incorrect conclusions when comparing asset class returns. As soon as you invest in a mutual fund, the value of your money can rise or fall immediately.

(continued)

The performance of a limited partnership is usually negative for some time. First, the partnership pays fees and expenses. Investments are held at cost until value-creation increases valuations and real gains when an asset is sold. As value creation takes time, partnership NAVs show the value of investments after fees and expenses, which means a negative IRR until value gains happen. The resulting performance pattern is called the "j-curve."

Box 4.2   Limited Partnerships: Cash Flows and IRR

Private market investments don't help investors' overall performance during the startup phase of a program as the IRR is usually negative until a mix of valuation gains and exits moves performance into positive territory (Figures 4.12–4.13).

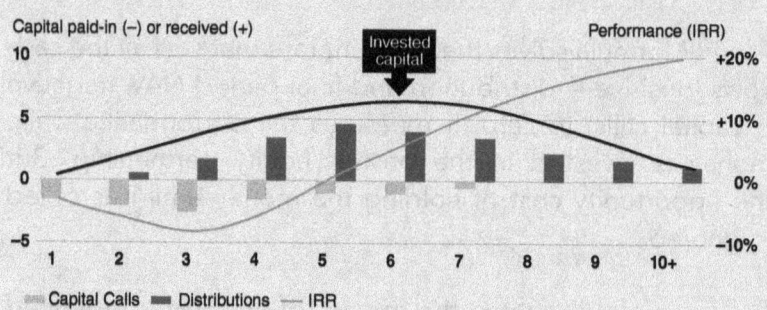

Figure 4.12   Cash flow profile of a limited partnership over time—cash flow during holding periods are material.

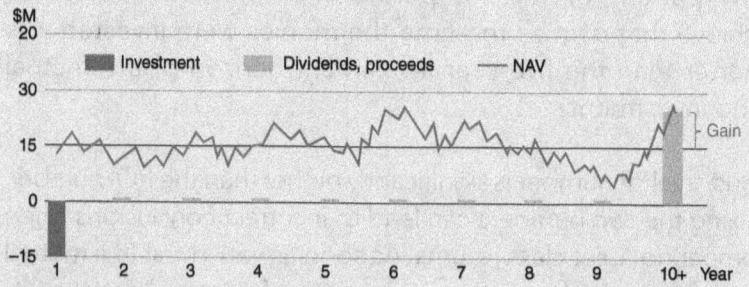

Figure 4.13   Cash flow profile of a mutual fund investment—cash flows during holding period are not material.

Box 4.3   Limited Partnerships: Fee Structure and Waterfall

Figure 4.14 portrays the waterfall structure of the fees in a limited partnership.

Key features of fee and incentive structures are:

- **Management fee:** Private market funds typically charge an annual management fee of 1–2% of the subscription amount during the investment period and on the net asset value after that.

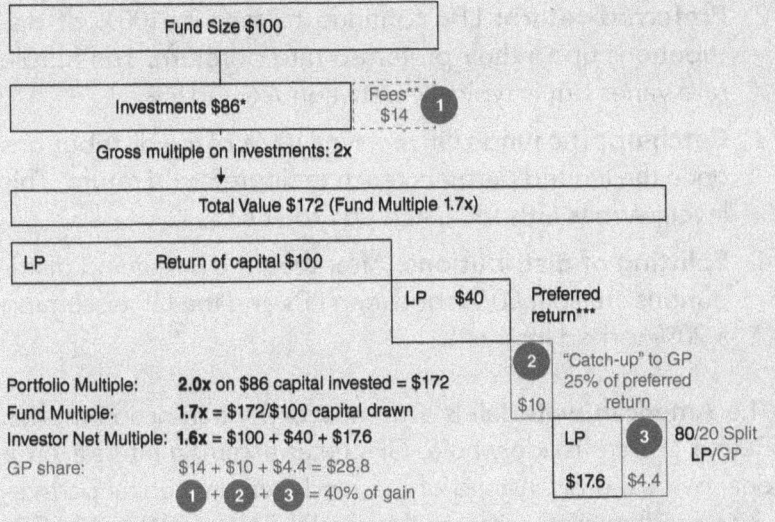

Notes: *The effective investment amount is assumed to match the fund size post fees and expenses.

** The fund has a 12-year lifespan, inclusive of extensions. The management fee is computed based on committed capital for the first 5 years and on NAV for the subsequent 7 years. The NAV is estimated to average 50% of the fund after year 5. Additionally, there's a one-time fund establishment cost of 0.4% of the fund size. The calculation follows the formula: ((1.6% * 5 + 1.6% * 0.5 * 7) + 0.4%).

*** The preferred return is 8% per annum (not compounded for simplicity), with an assumed average portfolio investment holding period of 5 years, equating to 40% of paid-in capital, which equals the fund size.

Figure 4.14   Illustrative allocation of private market funds' distributions.

(continued)

- **Carried interest:** This is a performance fee for GPs. The GPs typically receive 20% of the total profits, although lower rates may apply.
- **Waterfall:** This describes the hierarchy of distributions received by LPs and GPs. In a **European private equity waterfall**, GPs do not receive carried interest until all limited partners' capital contributions, including unrealized investments, have been recovered and their preferred rate of return has been attained (see example in Figure 4.14).

Most equity waterfalls have four distinct tiers:

1. **Return of paid-in capital:** LPs receive 100% of distributions until their initial investment is repaid.
2. **Preferred return:** LPs continue to receive 100% of distributions up to their preferred rate of return. The hurdle rate varies but is typically between 7% and 9%.
3. **Catch-up:** The fund's GP receives 100% of the distributions once the limited partners reach their preferred return. This level permits GPs to "catch up" to LPs.
4. **Splitting of distributions:** After that, the remaining distributions are split 80/20 between LPs and the GP (assuming a 20% carried interest).

The **American waterfall** is a transaction-by-transaction model. Before LPs are made whole, GPs receive carried interest on a deal-by-deal basis instead of the fund. Venture capital partnerships predominantly employ this model. This model favors GPs because they typically receive much faster carried interest from the fund. In addition, LPs are exposed to a greater degree of risk, as they may not reach their hurdle rate before sponsors receive carried interest. Many US venture capital partnerships typically have no hurdle.[76]

---

[76] The description of European and American waterfalls is based on Kastelberg (2019).

Carried interest is typically based on realized returns, which means that the GPs receive a percentage of the profits generated from the sale of the portfolio companies in which they have invested. The use of carried interest is intrinsically linked to the use of limited partnerships as an investment vehicle. Limited partnerships have a limited life, which means that they have a set time frame for making investments and a requirement to exit those investments and return capital to the LPs. By tying the GPs' compensation to realized returns, the LPs can be confident that the GPs are motivated to generate strong returns and to exit investments in a timely manner.

Permanent capital vehicles, on the other hand, do not have a limited life and do not have the same obligation to exit investments and return capital to investors. This creates a different set of incentives for the GPs, and as such, the use of carried interest based on realized returns may not be appropriate. Instead, carried interest in these vehicles may need to be based on some form of net asset value (NAV) development or on a deal-by-deal basis where the carry is applied only to those assets that have been sold.

In summary, carried interest is a compensation structure that is closely linked to the use of limited partnerships as an investment vehicle with a limited life and an obligation to exit investments and return capital. While carried interest may not be appropriate for permanent capital vehicles with unlimited life, alternative compensation structures can be used to incentivize GPs to generate strong returns and manage investments effectively.

PART II

Booms and Busts

Chapter 5

Private Equity During the 1980s

5.1 VENTURE CAPITAL

Fundraising

Venture capital (VC) assets under management (AuM) increased from $2.5 billion managed in 1977 to $31 billion in 1989. At the end of the decade, there were 392 active VC firms compared to about 92 at the start of the decade.[1] But the venture capital industry was just part of the financial ecosystem of startup financing, and private wealth still played a significant role in it. Paul Gompers uses estimates from Wetzel,[2] which suggests that 250,000 wealthy individuals were active in the informal risk capital market and invested between $20–30 billion annually during the 1980s.

---

[1] Metrick and Yasuda (2010). Estimates of the number of venture firms active during the 1980s vary considerably with Gompers (1994) putting them at 225 in 1979 to 674 in 1989.
[2] Wetzel (1987).

Given the repeated waves of disruptive innovations that created new industries, venture capital would have a tremendous impact in enabling high-tech in California despite having "missed" the initial formation of the Silicon Valley cluster. By 1992, West Coast venture capital had become one of the nation's centers for entrepreneurial activity and received 48% of all venture capital financing.[3]

VC firms had evolved, becoming more specialized and professional entities. They embraced staged investments, where capital was injected into startups in multiple rounds, contingent on achieving specific milestones. VC firms fostered collaboration by involving each other in more promising deals during later investment rounds. This strategy not only supported the growth and success of startups but also reduced risk for investors. Another significant aspect of VC financing that had become a standard was the concept of temporary ownership. Venture capitalists aim to nurture startups, aid in their growth, and eventually exit their investments, often through initial public offerings (IPOs) or acquisitions.

New venture capital firms formed in the USA during the 1970s and 1980s include Menlo Ventures (1976), New Enterprise Associates (1977), Matrix Partners (founded as Hellman Ferri Investment Associates in 1977), Sevin Rosen Funds (1981), Accel Partners (1983), Battery Ventures (1983), Draper Fisher Jurvetson (1985), and OrbiMed Advisors (1989).[4] Investors' willingness to support a growing number of venture capital firms and their funds was fueled by several high-profile initial public offerings (IPOs). The relaxation of ERISA rules increased investments by pension funds. Tech IPOs peaked at 173 in 1983, a level they would not reach again for 12 years.[5] The market for initial public offerings was choppy during the 1980s, and banner years were followed by years with few IPOs, particularly after the 1987 stock market crash.[6] Initial public offerings (IPOs) during that decade included Apple (1980), followed by Amgen, Biogen, LSI, Compaq, and Lotus Development (all 1983), as well as Microsoft, Oracle, Sun,

---

[3] Gompers (1994).
[4] Piscione (2013). OrbiMed is one of the few VCs solely focused on biotech and healthcare and New Enterprise Associates, founded by Dick Gramlich who started his venture career in 1969 as a General Partner with Arthur Rock and Co. , was one of the first firms targeting later funding rounds.
[5] Neuman (2015).
[6] Pollack (1989).

and Adobe (all 1986). Those examples show that as far as venture capital financing is concerned, there is a significant time lag between the early round financing and the headline-grabbing IPO.

Deal-Making

Investment amounts were about $3 billion p.a. from 1983 onwards. Despite this level of activity, venture capital lacked direction and conviction about what the next big theme would be. The hardware boom had quietly ended, and large software investment opportunities for the emerging personal computer sector were mainly an opportunity during the 1970s. Overall, software and services, communications, and biotech investments increased while investment in hardware, and semiconductors fell during the 1980s.

The chase for a winning business model occasionally led to overinvestment and mini boom-and-bust cycles caused by what P. Gompers of Harvard University described as "herding." He cites disk drive investments. VCs liked the disk drive industry because it was innovative and open to change. By 1983, more than 70 disk drive startups had received venture capital, up from 12 in 1981. Competition lowered prices and profits, while fixed R&D spending remained the same, affecting these companies' valuations (Table 5.1). P. Gompers identified a distinction between established and freshly started enterprises that he termed "grandstanding," which he defined as a bias to realize profits earlier to show

Table 5.1 VC/PE investment by type of financing

	Seed & start-up	Expansion & later stage	LBO
1980	25%	75%	0%
1981	23%	77%	0%
1982	20%	68%	12%
1983	17%	71%	12%
1984	21%	67%	12%
1985	15%	69%	16%
1986	19%	58%	23%
1987	13%	69%	18%
1988	13%	68%	20%

Source: Gompers (1994).

investors realized gains and, as a result, give up some upside on their successful deals.[7]

The heightened investment activity, growing fund sizes, and a larger number of venture capital firms were all indicative of a decade that ended with venture capital moving past adolescence. Regarding returns, based on somewhat incomplete data, it appears that venture capital returns during the 1980s were below those achieved during the 1970s. Better data covering the vintage years from 1984 onwards, examined by Steven Kaplan et al., suggest that median internal rates of return (IRRs) were around 6.6% in 1984 and increased steadily to 14% in 1989.[8] Vintage year returns during the 1980s thus appear relatively moderate.

The vertically integrated computer industry was replaced by a horizontal, layered, and distributed industry. Its first iteration was a client-server architecture with Windows clients interacting with Unix-based relational database servers. Commercial electronic design automation (EDA) systems began appearing in various industries. Companies like LSI Logitech were pioneers in EDA. A mere decade or two earlier, EDA software was a proprietary tool for heavy industries.[9]

The move toward desktop PCs increased the need for networks, as connecting PCs made them more valuable. Companies such as 3Com (Ethernet), Oracle (relational database software), and Sun Microsystems (Unix operating systems and the Network File System) enabled the connectivity of distributed computing as well as auxiliary functionalities such as data backup and storage. LSI Logitech was Cisco's debut product, originating from technology developed on Stanford University's campus.[10]

Accel Partners used a sector approach that proved critical in choosing investments, such as UUNet. They focused on early-stage technology startups, particularly in software and hardware, looking for disruptive tech and visionary founders. In 1993, Accel invested in UUNet, a then-unknown startup in the emerging ISP field, attracted by its faster, more reliable internet technology

---

[7] Gompers (1994).
[8] Harris, Jenkinson, and Kaplan (2015).
[9] Janeway (2018).
[10] Mallaby (2022).

LSI LOGIC, MILPITAS, CA (1981)
Founders: W. Corrigan, M. Bohn, J. Koford,
B. O'Meara, R. Walker (all from Fairchild).
Funding from Sequoia Capital and Menlo
Ventures.

SUN MICROSYSTEMS, SANTA CLARA, CA
(1982) Founders: V. Pratt, S. McNealy,
A. Bechtolsheim, V. Khosla (all from
Stanford), B. Joy. No early venture
rounds recorded.

CISCO SYSTEMS, STANFORD, CA (1984)
Founders: L. Bosack, S. Lerner (both from
Stanford). Funding from Sequoia Capital.

DELL, ROUND ROCK, TX (1984)
Founded by Michael Dell. No early
venture rounds recorded.

UUNET, ASHBOURNE, VI (1987)
Founder: R. Adams. Funding from M. Kapor
(founder of Lotus), Accel, Menlo, NEA

AOL, NEW YORK, NY (1985)
Founders: S. Case, J. Kimsey, et al.. Funding
from Kleiner Perkins

Figure 5.1 Some prominent startups of the 1980s.
Source: Lsi Logic Corporation; CISCO SYSTEMS, INC.; Uunet; Sun Microsystems;
Dell; America Online Inc.

and visionary founder, Rick Adams. UUNet's global operations in Europe, Asia, and the USA aligned with Accel's global focus. Accel would go on to invest in several startups related to data communication, such as AOL, during the 1990s (Figure 5.1).[11]

The VC sector's growth attracted financial institutions and corporations to establish in-house VC teams. Banks sought to capitalize on investment opportunities using their balance sheets or earn fees by offering venture capital investment services. Corporate VCs aimed to invest strategically, gain a competitive edge, access new markets, or form partnerships. However, competition, regulatory changes, and economic challenges made fundraising and deal-making tougher. Paine Weber and General Electric divested or closed their in-house VC operations, influenced by these factors. Other institutions like Chemical Bank and Continental Illinois National Bank focused on established enterprises. Specialist firms,

---

[11] Accel Partners was established in 1983 and guided by its founders A. Patterson and J. Schwartz, whose vision of the "prepared mind" emphasized sector specialization and industry research intending to be able to anticipate trends. Initially, that meant focusing on telecoms and communications, for which they raised a dedicated fund in 1985 (Mallaby, 2022).

not generalist asset managers or corporate investors, continued to dominate the private market industry. The increased money inflow also split VC companies, with some raising lesser amounts and focusing on early rounds. Other firms focused on later investment rounds and increasing fund sizes. Early-stage funding fell from 25% of overall venture capital investments at the start of the decade to 12.5% at the end.[12] Pioneers in VC investing like J. H. Whitney & Company, Warburg Pincus, Patricof & Co. (since 1972 Apax), Welsh, Carson, Anderson & Stowe, Merrill, Bain Capital, and TA Associates began to adopt a "generalist" investment style.[13]

5.2   THE LBO BOOM DURING THE 1980S

The US Economy During the 1980s

In 1979, Paul Volcker became chairman of the Federal Reserve Board. When he took office in August, year-over-year inflation was running above 11%, and it was generally accepted that reducing inflation required drastic increases in interest rates.[14] The Volker monetary tightening and the high interest rate that resulted caused a short recession in 1980, and again from July 1981–November 1982 in what was termed a double-dip recession (Figure 5.2).[15]

But the recession of 1982—combined with falling oil prices—had one crucial benefit: it curbed runaway inflation. In addition, Ronald Reagan introduced the Economic Recovery Tax Act of 1981 (ERTA), providing significant tax cuts to encourage economic growth.[16] Conditions started improving in late 1983; by early 1984, the economy had rebounded, and the United States entered one of the most extended periods of sustained economic growth since World War II. Consumer spending increased in response to the federal tax

---

[12] Gompers (1994).

[13] A generalist strategy may include late-stage financing, growth capital, and LBOs (Neuman, 2015).

[14] In early 2022, it sounds eerily familiar as US inflation for 02/22 has reached 7.9% and West Texas Intermediate is around $110.

[15] Csiszar (2019).

[16] Some provisions of the 1981 Act were reversed by the Tax Equity and Fiscal Responsibility Act of September 1982, which was passed after the economy went into recession again and amidst a mounting government deficit. Reagan agreed to a rollback of corporate tax cuts and a smaller rollback of individual income tax cuts. The 1982 tax increase undid a third of the initial tax cut.

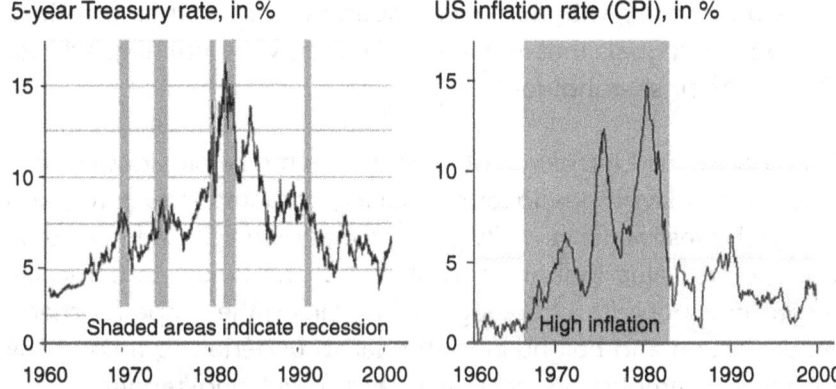

5-year Treasury rate, in %   US inflation rate (CPI), in %

Figure 5.2   Inflation and 5-year treasury bond rates skyrocketed during the 1970s and 1980s.

Source: Bureau of Labor Statistics via FRED. Graph created by Sam Marshall, Federal Reserve Bank of Richmond.

Note: In October 1973 and January 1974, the nominal price of oil doubled. April 1979 marks the beginning of the 1979 oil price surge; in February 1981, the price of imported crude oil peaks.

Table 5.2   Economic and stock market indicators for 1970–1990 (%)

Time	S&P 500/w div. reinvested, nom. return	S&P 55/w div. reinvested, real return	CPI inflation avg. p.a.	GDP growth (real), avg. p.a.	10y Treasury bond yields (end of period)
1971–1980	8.4	0.3	8.1	3.2	12.4
1981–1990	13.9	9.0	4.9	3.3	8.1

Source: Inflationdata.com; S&P calculator (dqydj.com).

cut. Over five years following the start of the recovery, GDP grew at an annual rate of 4.2%.[17]

The annual inflation rate remained between 3–5% from 1983 to 1987. The momentum would last until the "Black Monday" sell-off of October 19, 1987. Even considering the stock market crash of 1987, annual stock market returns during the 1990s were 13.9% (S&P 500/w dividends reinvested) (Table 5.2).

Corporate Raiders: From Managerial Capitalism to Shareholder Value

In 1982, investors looked back at a decade of barely positive real stock market returns. Many large companies were regarded as

---

[17] Ellis (2008).

underperformers, with management entrenched in their positions and pursuing goals that in the eyes of many were not aligned with those of their shareholders.

In his book, *The Outsiders*, author W. N. Thorndike provides colorful examples of lavish headquarters, stifling corporate structures, and wasteful investments in vanity projects that made CEOs focused on shareholder value look unconventional at the time.[18] In particular, larger firms benefited from legislation limiting the scope for share-holder action and heightening the bar to undertaking a company takeover. Examples are securities laws (regulating tender offers), ERISA (the Employee Retirement Income Security Act, preventing pension funds from holding more than 5% of a company), and mutual fund tax laws (putting higher taxes on concentrated holdings).[19]

The term "managerial capitalism" was introduced in 1984 by Alfred D. Chandler Jr. to describe this form of capitalism, where a managerial elite controls corporations without having a significant stake in them.[20] The agency problem that arises from the separation of ownership and management was recognized.[21]

But a new breed of investors emerged that saw an opportunity to unlock value in some of those firms and to overcome the barriers to change. It seemed to be worth a try. Those investors became known

---

[18] Thorndike Jr. (2012).

[19] Reference is made to the Williams Act of 1968, the Employee Retirement Income Security Act of 1974 (ERISA), the Investment Company Act of 1940, which, while promoting disclosure and diversification, also had the potential effect of reducing the likelihood of shareholder activism and, together with the Celler-Kefauver Act of 1950, resulted in increased protection of management against being replaced by shareholders or as a result of a takeover of their company.

[20] Chandler (1984).

[21] E. Englander and A. Kaufman analyze the agency problem arising from the separation of management and ownership of a company and provide a good overview of research on the topic as well as covering the political discussion of anti-takeover legislation (Kaufman and Englander, 1993). They also cite research by Eugene Fama and Michael Jensen who conclude that the costs of the managerially run firm were far greater than others had calculated (Fama and Jensen, 1983). Jensen is cited with the observation that managers cannot readily diversify their risks outside the firm (like stock owners), so they seek to reduce a firm's market risks by retaining earnings rather than paying out excess corporate cash (Jensen and Meckling, 1976). The latter point is also made by LBO firms who would highlight the cash flow discipline imposed by leverage.

as corporate raiders.[22] The term goes back to Louis E. Wolfson, an American financier credited with creating the modern hostile tender offer.[23] In a 1956 TIME magazine article, he was described as a corporate raider, probably the first time this label was used and it stuck.[24] The fact that Wolfson later became a convicted felon after being prosecuted for securities law violations did not help to establish that veneer of respectability for financiers engaged in (hostile) takeovers. In common language the term "raider" is associated with theft or piracy, which is very unhelpful to understand the activity.[25]

Those corporate raiders focused on undervalued companies with stable and predictable earnings, readily identifiable business units that caused underperformance, and the use of high leverage to finance their acquisitions. After the conglomerate boom of the 1960s, many companies could be considered a target. While corporate raiders are often portrayed as an investor category, there were considerable differences in their objectives and approach. As investors, they operated in an M&A market dominated by traditional corporate actors that used similar tactics and would not refrain from submitting competing bids or proposing unsolicited bids.[26]

---

[22] Later referred to as "activist investors," which sounds more friendly. Likewise, the language reflects a bias when it comes to takeover bids. Coming from a corporate buyer, a bid would be called unsolicited rather than "hostile" if it had no support from management.

[23] The main consequence of a bid being considered hostile is practical rather than legal. If the board of the target cooperates, the bidder can conduct extensive due diligence into the affairs of the target company, providing the bidder with a comprehensive analysis of the target company's finances. In contrast, a hostile bidder will only have more limited, publicly available information about the target company available.

[24] TIME magazine, June 25, 1956.

[25] The *Cambridge English Dictionary* defines the term as "someone who enters a place illegally and usually violently and steals from it" (2022).

[26] In 1983, KKR was outbid by Esmark whose chairman was Donald Kelly in the acquisition of Norton Simon where both KKR's and Kelly's bids were triggered by an initial proposal of the chairman of Norton Simon to take the company private. Kelly's winning bid was considered friendly as the board recommended it. In 1984, Kelly and KKR proposed a buyout of Esmark but were outbid by Beatrice Foods, a company that was later acquired by KKR and Kelly (who became CEO) in 1986 (Baker, 1992; Potts, 1983).

Corporate raiders would buy shares to gain voting rights and influence company leadership and management. Sometimes management would respond by finding a friendly investor (a "white knight") willing to buy out the raider at a premium (a practice known as "greenmailing"). This would allow the raider to sell out the shares and pocket a quick trading profit.

Saul Steinberg's agreement with Walt Disney Productions, concluded in 1984, was perhaps the best-publicized negotiated repurchase of shares from an "unfriendly" shareholder.[27] Sometimes the investor would aim for acquisition by making a tender offer and, after taking the company private, proceed with the selling of the assets, realizing a profit from the sum of the parts being larger than the valuation of the company. Carl Icahn,[28] for example, used this "asset-stripping" after his TWA acquisition. Victor Posner employed the same strategy and used an operating company he owned with solid cash flows to acquire stakes in unrelated businesses not unlike a traditional conglomerate.[29] Nelson Peltz[30] acquired Triangle Industries Inc. in 1983 with the idea of using it to execute a roll-up strategy in the packaging sector that he aimed to build into a Fortune 100 industrial company. Raiders used solicited and unsolicited bids, but their strategy neither involved a break-up nor a quick flip of the companies acquired. Although ultimately unsuccessful and ending in bankruptcy, the Campeau Corporation,

---

[27] Macey and McChesney (1985).

[28] Carl Icahn developed a reputation as a "corporate raider" after his hostile takeover of TWA in 1985. The result of that takeover was Icahn selling TWA's assets to repay the debt he used to purchase the company, which was described as asset stripping (Grant, 2005).

[29] Victor Posner usually placed himself as chairman of the board and president of each company that his holding companies controlled and sat on pension boards that he directed to invest in Posner-owned properties, which led to SEC action against him (*The Economist*, 2002a).

[30] Nelson Peltz remains a successful activist investor to this day: in May 2022, he joined the board of Unilever (the share price rose 7% on the announcement) after serving on the board of Procter & Gamble from 2017–2021 after an acrimonious proxy fight. The share price increased 67% during his tenure (Deveau, 2021).

[31] Robert Campeau, a Canadian developer and entrepreneur purchased two of the most prominent American department store holding companies, Allied Stores and Federated Department Stores, in 1987 and 1988. The combined entity ran over a thousand stores and employed nearly 200,000 people (Raff, 1991) When the company declared bankruptcy in 1991, it was the largest Chapter 11 filing in US retailing history, owing to Campeau's inability to repay $8 billion in debt, which roiled the high-yield bond market.

founded by real estate entrepreneur Robert Campeau,[31] pursued the acquisition of department store holdings, betting on an ongoing consolidation trend in the industry.

While his name does not usually appear along with corporate raiders due to his focus on friendly acquisitions, Warren Buffett used Berkshire Hathaway in a similar fashion. To create a diversified holding company in the late 1960s, he used the cash flows of the core business to pay for the leverage needed to make acquisitions. Buffett built a conglomerate instead of breaking one up and preferred negotiated deals (both majority and minority investments) to hostile takeovers as he did not want to get dragged into auctions. He also used more moderate leverage than what was increasingly usual at the time.

As the takeover boom gained momentum, those corporate raiders were joined by investment banks that built equity positions in target companies and arranged debt financing during the second half of the 1980s. At the height of the boom, arbitrageurs—like Ivan Boesky—would try to benefit from the premium paid for takeover bids, and, in his case, this led to insider trading charges and a felony conviction.[32]

Tax Overhaul and Deregulation as Catalysts for the 1980s M&A Boom

The 1980s marked a pivotal era of transformation in the corporate finance landscape, driven by a convergence of legal, tax, and financial changes that catalyzed the rise of leveraged buyouts (LBOs). The Economic Recovery Tax Act (ERTA) of 1981 played a significant role by incentivizing asset sales to reset depreciable asset basis and adopt a more accelerated depreciation schedule known as the accelerated cost recovery system (ACRS).

Further bolstering this trend was the Installment Sales Revision Act of 1980, which strategically promoted asset sales through installment sales, reducing the tax burden for sellers. This approach was

---

[32] Ivan Boesky, a former American stock trader, became infamous for his prominent role in an insider trading scandal that occurred in the United States, where he speculated on potential takeover targets based on inside information from Drexel Burnham Lambert and other financial intermediaries. He was sentenced to three years in prison, and that scandal reinforced the perception that the takeover business and the fortunes made by many people must be somehow illegal.

exemplified by the sale of a corporation's depreciable asset acquired for $50 million, where accumulated depreciation of $15 million led to a tax basis of $35 million. Upon selling the asset at its market value of $75 million, a $40 million gain was realized, with $15 million recaptured as ordinary income and the remaining $25 million as capital gain.

In addition, 1982 witnessed the issuance of new antitrust guidelines by the Reagan administration, which took a more lenient stance on mergers.[33] In 1978, the US Department of Labor also relaxed certain of the ERISA restrictions, under the "prudent man rule," thus allowing corporate pension funds to invest in private equity, resulting in a major source of capital available to invest in venture capital and other private equity.[34] Additionally, many of these same corporate pension investors would become active buyers of the high yield bonds (or junk bonds) that became increasingly important in leveraged buyout transactions after 1985. While ERISA regulates private sector employee retirement benefit plans, its impact on public plan governance and investments was nevertheless substantial and resulted in the adoption of investment guidelines and policies that provided the basis for an increased participation of public pension funds in private equity.[35]

Myron S. Scholes and Mark A. Wolfson (1990) examined the impact of tax reform and observe that ERTA and the Sales Revision Act fostered a resurgence in M&A activity, prompting the average annual dollar value of mergers and acquisitions between 1981 and 1987 to reach a staggering $118.4 billion. This was more than 4x the value observed in the six years preceding the 1981 Act. The M&A resurgence was especially pronounced in going-private transactions, which experienced a remarkable 14-fold increase in average annual dollar volume during 1981–1986 compared to the six years prior to the passing of ERTA. The peak of this boom occurred in 1986 when the M&A boom culminated in a bonfire 1986 when the Tax Reform Act (TRA) was passed that reduced tax benefits for corporate sellers across the board. Deal-making surged before the new rules became effective on January 1987, ushering in a record-breaking period of mergers and acquisitions, with a remarkable $64.65 billion recorded in the fourth quarter.[36]

---

[33] Ellis (2008).
[34] Taylor (1981).
[35] Mitchell and Hustead (2021).
[36] Scholes and Wolfson (1990).

However, the TRA of 1986 presented a unique twist, favoring foreign acquisitions of US businesses. This preference was rooted in the Act's heightened shareholder-level tax on capital gains. Investors from countries with integrated tax systems or favorable treatment of capital gains found the US market increasingly attractive, as their foreign tax base allowed them to avoid the capital gains tax. While offsetting a decrease in domestic demand, this foreign demand also characterized the growing globalization of capital markets, which was one aspect of this transformative era in corporate finance.[37]

The 1980s served as a case study showcasing how tax and regulatory changes influenced the buyout industry's growth opportunities. Over five years, favorable tax regulations benefited domestic buyers and insiders (management), capitalizing on information advantages about asset value. This environment facilitated transactions that aimed to unlock value through asset sales and subsidiary divestitures, exploiting the concept of the parts being more valuable than the whole. Post-1987, the tax regime was again adjusted, and some critical benefits decreased. US assets grew appealing to foreign buyers while domestic acquisitions waned. This rapid shift highlights the fluidity of value creation strategies, target sellers, and buyers. Success in private markets stems from investors' skill in recognizing and adapting to these evolving conditions.

Leveraged Buyouts

Many acquisitions were not hostile as investors negotiated with management or the board the takeover of a company—which became known as leveraged buyout (LBO), and would then be recommended to shareholders. Sometimes the existing management wanted to submit a bid and look for a partner to finance the deal. This was referred to as a management buyout (MBO), and the two terms MBO and LBO are often used interchangeably.

The purchase of Gibson Greetings in January 1982 by former US Treasury Secretary William E. Simon and a group of investors along with management is an early example. The company was acquired for $80 million, of which only $1 million was rumored to have been contributed by the investors. By mid-1983, just 16 months after the

---

[37] Ibid.

original deal, Gibson completed a $290 million IPO, and Simon made approximately $66 million. The Gibson Greetings investment's success attracted the broader media's attention to the nascent boom in leveraged buyouts.[38]

The Emergence of the High-Yield Bond Market

Leading Wall Street firms involved in mergers and acquisitions avoided arranging takeover bids involving their clients because it would compromise their relationships. Chemical Bank, which didn't issue corporate bonds, became a leading provider of leveraged loans. Investors proposing a takeover could also raise subordinated debt from insurance companies, but they required strict covenants, limiting their appeal.[39]

In the 1970s, Drexel Burnham Lambert was a second-tier investment bank; at its peak, it was the fifth-largest investment bank in the United States. The creation of the high-yield or junk bond market contributed to its prominence. Drexel Burnham Lambert, led by Michael Milken (see Box 5.1), began financing (hostile) M&As in the early 1980s.

Box 5.1   High-Yield Bonds and Takeovers

Before Drexel Burnham Lambert's pioneering use of junk bonds in corporate takeovers, high-yield corporate bonds were mostly a result of so-called fallen-angel businesses. These firms had previously issued investment-grade debt before suffering a decline in their credit profile, resulting in a downgrade to a rating below BBB-, the lowest rating available for investment-grade debt. High-yield bonds were also used by smaller firms that could not obtain an investment-grade rating.

Michael Milken (Figure 5.3) was appointed head of Drexel Burnham Lambert's bond trading department in 1971.

---

[38] Crittenden (1983).
[39] *American Banker* (1993).

Figure 5.3   Michael Milken at the New York offices of Drexel Burnham Lambert in 1978.
Source: Neal Boenzi/*The New York Times.* ReduxPictures lincense #0023804.

That rise to prominence resulted from its creation of the high yield or junk bond market. He recognized a tremendous opportunity in the underserved market for "junk bonds."

While junk bonds earned significantly higher rates of return than investment-grade bonds, investors also viewed them as more likely to default. Milken's research established that junk bonds offered an acceptable default rate in exchange for higher yields. He began to convince an increasing number of institutional investors—savings and loan organizations, pension funds, insurance companies, and mutual funds—to purchase them. In addition, hedge funds became an emerging new group of investors and they also invested heavily in high-yield bonds. For example, Steinhardt Partners was estimated to have over $5 billion in assets under management at its peak, while Soros's Quantum Fund was estimated to have over $10 billion in assets during the 1980s. These hedge funds played a significant role in the growth of the junk bond

(continued)

market and helped finance many of the leveraged buyouts and hostile takeovers of the time.

Drexel Burnham Lambert's junk bond sales was fueling the 1980s takeover boom. More than $30 billion in junk bonds were issued in 1986, up from $15 billion in 1985. The junk bond market grew from $10 billion in 1979 to $189 billion in 1989. Milken's businesses accounted for at least half of the firm's income, and he made $550 million in 1987. At the time it was the highest annual compensation ever.[40]

Then came the downfall. Ivan Boesky was convicted of insider trading in 1986 and implicated Milken and Drexel Burnham Lambert. 1988 saw securities fraud charges against Milken and Drexel Burnham Lambert. Milken left Drexel Burnham Lambert in 1989 after it declared bankruptcy.

It was the first Wall Street bankruptcy since the Great Depression. Milken pleaded guilty to six securities fraud charges in the same year. On February 18, 2020, President Trump pardoned him. Increased default rates and Drexel Burnham Lambert's demise shut down the market for almost a year. The market recovered in 1990 and reached $567 billion in 1999.[41]

Drexel Burnham Lambert raised a $100 million for Nelson Peltz in 1984 to provide credibility for his takeover attempts, the first major blind pool raised for this purpose.[42] That same year another raider, T. Boone Pickens (Figure 5.4) used his small Mesa Oil Company to acquire Pioneer Petroleum. His hostile bid for much larger Gulf Oil, financed in part by $2 billion in Drexel Burnham Lambert junk bonds in 1984, sent a signal that even very big companies could now become the target of a takeover bid.[43] Milken also helped finance Nelson Peltz's takeover of Triangle Industries.

---

[40] *Los Angeles Times*, September 11, 1989.
[41] Stone (1990), Steward (1992).
[42] Kelley (1990).

Figure 5.4   T. Boone Pickens. TIME magazine cover, March 4, 1985.
Source: © TIME. https://content.time.com/time/magazine/archive/covers/
1985/1101850304_400.jpg

These transactions marked the beginning of a trend, where raid-ers used high-yield bonds to finance takeovers of companies. Wall Street firms like Bear Stearns and Salomon Brothers also played a significant role in financing leveraged buyouts and takeovers using junk bonds. One of the transactions that Salomon Brothers helped finance was the leveraged buyout of the Beatrice Companies.

Kohlberg Kravis Roberts & Co. (KKR)

Unlike the corporate raiders that often used holding companies to make acquisitions, KKR established institutional funds (limited partnerships) that provided the equity capital and built a franchise

---

[43] Despite being unsuccessful, this bid made Pickens several hundred million dol-lars when Gulf Oil sold out to Chevron Oil for $13.2 billion, as the company's white knight (TIME, 1985). His various transactions are chronicled in (Pickens, 1987). As a corporate raider, Pickens became a leader of the budding "shareholders' rights" movement (Steinberg, 2019).

with institutional investors. As was the case in venture capital, limited partnerships were well suited for tax-exempt institutional investors as they were tax transparent and not subject to corporate taxation. In addition, the leverage applied would reduce the taxable earnings of portfolio companies during the holding period. The reduction of taxable profits and the focus on equity value creation through subsequent de-leveraging conveyed another tax benefit. Early investors included public pension funds such as Oregon PERS, Washington State Investment Board, and the Michigan State Employees Retirement System. As the assets of those public pensions grew rapidly, it was a franchise that would prove crucial for the increasing fund sizes that KKR raised. Over time the buyout model of KKR would prove superior to the holding company model employed by corporate raiders as it was more scalable. A crucial aspect of KKR's success was a keen understanding of the shifting institutional landscape. KKR's rise to prominence was not solely a result of their financial acumen but also their accurate assessment of the growing influence of pension funds. Specifically, KKR recognized large public pension plans' pivotal role in this investor category. By nurturing solid relationships with these influential entities, KKR gained a pivotal funding advantage that propelled them to the forefront of the private equity landscape. Fast forward three decades, the landscape of the private markets industry experienced another seismic shift, this time propelled by the ascent of sovereign wealth funds (SWFs).

By 1984, KKR had put together four investment funds, which grew from $32 million in 1978 to $1 billion in 1984. As their funds grew, KKR became increasingly aware of the opportunities in arranging leveraged buyouts of large publicly held companies. Their funds could be leveraged by a factor of ten, making large firms a target for a KKR takeover.

The fact that KKR used limited partnerships to raise capital also ensured that portfolio companies would be held temporarily. KKR was not to replace an existing conglomerate by creating a new one. Their typical target holding period would be in the range of four to six years. Limited partnerships also provided an alignment of interest between investors and their managers as KKR would invest alongside its limited partners and receive a performance fee only once a portfolio company was successfully sold. The same applied to officers and directors of the acquired companies. There was no cross-financing of deals within or in between partnerships, as can be the case in a holding company structure. Value creation strategies focused on undervalued companies that could be broken up or undergo a restructuring that might involve cost cutting, improvement in efficiencies, asset disposals, and new acquisitions to those portfolio companies.

Buyouts Are Getting Larger: Beatrice Foods

KKR took control of Beatrice Foods[44] in April 1986 in a $6.2 billion leveraged buyout—the largest buyout ever at the time.[45] The management of Beatrice Foods initially resisted the takeover attempt, but eventually, due to mounting pressure from shareholders and the increasing price of Beatrice Foods' stock, they agreed to sell the company to KKR. The price represented a 53% premium over the stock price of the company pre-announcement. Shareholders gained $1 billion. It was funded with $3.3 billion in bank debt, $2.5 billion of junk bonds arranged by Drexel Burnham Lambert, and existing debt of $1.05 billion assumed. Common stock held by KKR was $400 million, and management stock and warrants accounted for another $17 million. By 1987, initial disposals allowed Beatrice to pay down virtually all of the bank debt. After various rounds of spin-outs and disposals, Beatrice Company was sold by KKR in June 1990 for $1.34 billion plus $1.8 billion in debt. It resulted in an annual rate of return for KKR and its investors of 78% with a realized value of $1.8 billion (4.5x).[46]

In addition, KKR received management fees from its fund, merchant banking fees, board remuneration, and other fees. In 1986, KKR's reported fees were $45 million. These figures were seductive; investment bankers, including the "bulge bracket" Wall Street firms, put their concerns of offending their corporate clients aside and rushed into the LBO arena. Merchant banking activity surged from 1986 to 1988, with investment banks leveraging their capital for equity

---

[44] Beatrice Foods was a major US food processing company that became the owner of brands such as Avis Car Rental, Playtex, Shedd's, Tropicana, John Sexton & Co, Good & Plenty, and many more.
[45] Cole (1985).
[46] All numbers are quoted from (Baker, 1992).

positions in LBOs. In 1986, equity financings accounted for just 13% of M&A value. However, within two years, that figure had risen to 25%.[47]

In bidding for Beatrice Foods, KKR showed its readiness to mount contested bids where it saw an opportunity and the ability of buyout firms to target larger companies. One of KKR's founders, Jerome Kohlberg, opposed entering a highly leveraged bid for Beatrice. Unable to convince his partners (and with many other differences over how the firm should do its business), Kohlberg decided to leave KKR in 1987, and he went on to found his own private equity firm called Kohlberg & Company, which followed a more conservative investment strategy aligned with his own preferences and like KKR is still successful today.[48]

Following the Beatrice Foods deal, KKR raised $5.6 billion for its 1987 investment fund, 53% of which came from 11 public pension funds, including an $800 million commitment from the Oregon Public Retirement System.[49] Under the leadership of Henry Kravis and George R. Roberts, KKR aggressively pursued larger deals.

"The Winner's Curse": RJR Nabisco

In 1988, KKR bought the snack and tobacco producer RJR Nabisco for $25.1 billion. Despite being labeled a hostile takeover, the company's board of directors supported the final bid. This record-setting LBO captured widespread media attention, making headlines and appearing on prime-time TV. It is often considered a symbol of the takeover frenzy that characterized the 1990s. As one of the last major buyouts of the 1980s, it marked a significant milestone while also signaling the beginning of the end for the takeover boom that had commenced nearly a decade earlier.

The event was chronicled in the book (and later the movie), *Barbarians at the Gate: The Fall of RJR Nabisco*.[50] Shearson

---

[47] Kaufman and Englander (1993).
[48] J. Kohlberg founded Kohlberg & Company in 1987 as a mid-market buyout firm.
[49] PEI (2008).
[50] Burrough (1989). *Barbarians at the Gate: The Fall of RJR Nabisco* is a 1989 book about the leveraged buyout (LBO) of RJR Nabisco, written by investigative journalists, Bryan Burrough and John Helyar. The book is based upon a series of articles written by the authors for *The Wall Street Journal*. The book was made into a 1993 made-for-TV movie by HBO, also called *Barbarians at the Gate*.

Lehman Hutton and Ross Johnson, the CEO of RJR Nabisco, had announced that they would take RJR Nabisco private at $75 per share. The KKR counteroffer at $90 was at the upper end of analysts' valuations and thus could be considered fair compared to management's offer ($75), derided as an attempted steal.[51] RJR's management team, working with Shearson Lehman and Salomon Brothers, submitted a bid of $112, a figure they felt would enable them to outflank any response by Kravis's team. KKR's final bid of $109, while a lower dollar figure, was ultimately accepted by the board of directors of RJR Nabisco (Figure 5.5).[52] At $31.4 billion of transaction value, RJR Nabisco was the largest leveraged buyout in history until the 2007 buyout of TXU Energy by KKR and Texas Pacific Group.

RJR Nabisco possessed a range of consumer brands like Oreo cookies, Ritz crackers, and Del Monte fruits and vegetables, as well as a tobacco business featuring the Camel and Winston brands. Before the acquisition announcement, its stock was priced at $56 per share, considered undervalued. This low valuation stemmed from its tobacco business, which traded at a reduced multiple

Figure 5.5 Henry Kravis (left) and George Roberts (center front) with their advisors preparing the final bid for RJR Nabisco, November 29, 1988.
Source: Bloomberg Quicktake.

---

[51] Bolt (1988).
[52] Burrough (1989).

despite its strong cash generation capabilities.[53] But the final price paid was almost double the share price pre-acquisition and is thus an example of a "winner's curse." KKR's offer stood out for its size and the epic bidding war with management. They recognized that there was little margin for error and immediately started to dispose of assets to repay debt.[54] To dispose of RJR Nabisco's assets was a long process and the deal was showing signs of strain.[55] While it was reported that KKR's investors had lost $730 million on RJR Nabisco, KKR did not lose money on the acquisition, but the investment did not meet the initial high expectations and generated lower-than-anticipated returns. It took 15 years for KKR to exit the deal entirely.[56] As of 2008, KKR's 1987 fund had a portfolio IRR of 12%. Without the RJR Nabisco deal, the portfolio IRR would have been 25%. The deal is also reported to have generated $22 billion in returns to banks, junk bond investors, and preferred shareholders.[57]

Between 1980 and 1989, there were 2,385 leveraged buyouts valued at around $245 billion. During this time, KKR completed only 28 LBOs, but remarkably, four of those ranked among the top 10 buyout transactions of the 1980s.[58] At its peak, KKR-owned companies, including RJR Nabisco, Safeway, Owens-Illinois, and Duracell had annual sales greater than those of Chrysler, Texaco, or AT&T and employed nearly 400,000 people.

---

[53] The threat of giving the FDA more power to regulate big tobacco was affecting the valuation of tobacco stocks after the Comprehensive Smokeless Tobacco Health Education Act of 1986 was passed.

[54] Greenhouse (1989).

[55] Within a year of the buyout, the junk bond market, which KKR had relied on to refinance its debt, began to dry up. Moody's downgraded RJR's debt in 1989, which raised borrowing costs, and KKR was compelled to make a $1.7 billion equity infusion. In 1993, Philip Morris reduced the prices of its Marlboro cigarettes and started a price war. From 1994, the threat of tobacco-related class action lawsuits became bigger and prevented KKR from selling the tobacco business. They swapped the stake in RJR with consumer goods conglomerate Borden and engineered a turnaround. In 2004, KKR sold its remaining assets to Apollo Management (PEI, 2008).

[56] Norris (2004).

[57] KKR's 1982 fund was their best performing fund as of 2008 with a portfolio IRR of 48% according to investor presentations (PEI, 2008).

[58] This section draws on an excellent description by Allen Kaufmann and Erni Englander of the takeover boom and the early days of KKR (Kaufman and Englander, 1993).

5.3   TAKEOVERS: DID THEY WORK OUT?

Because of the high leverage of many 1980s transactions, deal failures in the 1980s received so much public attention that it is instructive to examine performance data from that era. Figure 5.6 shows that buyout performance during the 1980s was very good and IRRs from the mid-1980s to the mid-1990s surpassed those of the decade that followed.[59]

Figure 5.6 shows that the capital-weighted average of the funds' performance shown is much better than the median during the early vintage years. Larger funds—those involved in large take-over transactions—outperformed. Steven Kaplan et al. also found that during the 1980s, buyouts outperformed stock market investments.[60] In hindsight, those early investments in the buyout industry turned out well for investors. An earlier research report authored by Steven Kaplan and Jeremy Stein looked at 124 acquisitions and found that companies' cash flows generally increased

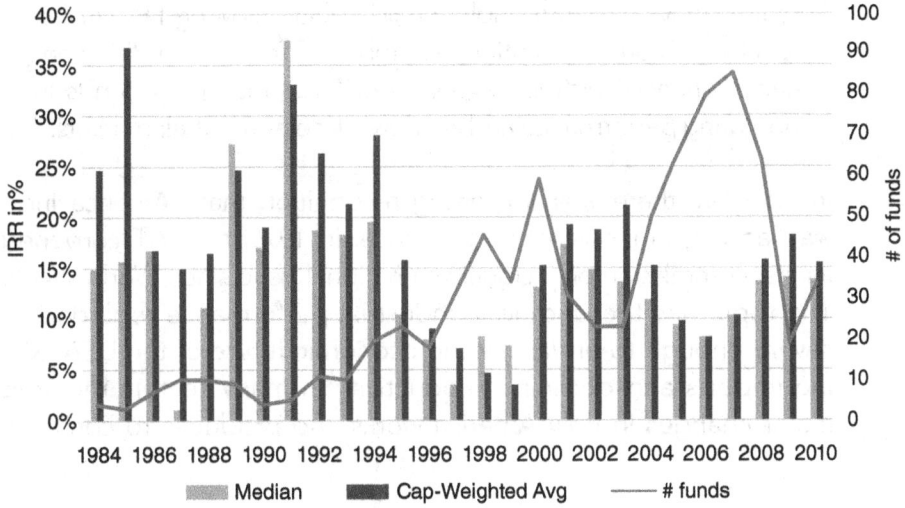

Figure 5.6   Internal rate of return and # of US buyout funds raised by vintage year.
Source: Harris, Jenkinson, and Kaplan (2015); data: Burgiss Group.

---

[59] The 1980–1983 vintages are not covered in the data but appear to have generated good returns based on anecdotal evidence.
[60] Harris, Jenkinson, and Kaplan (2015).

after the takeover, suggesting that after the LBO, cost savings and efficiency gains did materialize. They caution that later deals were more aggressively priced and more susceptible to financial distress.[61] Figure 5.6 also shows that the number of funds raised (fundraising cycle) is lagging the performance cycle, i.e., after good vintage years the fundraising increases.[62]

The United States Federal Reserve Board of Governors also produced evidence that leveraged transactions performed far better than many believe. In 1993, J. Helwege from the Board of Governors of the FED and T. Opler from the Southern Methodist University published a study that examined the performance of 47 large LBOs completed between 1987 and 1990. They showed that the 1990–1991 recession did not derail these LBOs and that banks did not suffer large losses due to the leverage provided for those transactions. The authors continue:

> In fact, cash flow increased by 9.8% after adjustment for industry trends in the average LBO in our sample. While 28% of firms examined in this study experienced financial distress, the majority of firms have reissued publicly-held equity, allowing LBO investors to cash out. In addition, a number of firms which did experience financial distress, experienced subsequent rebounds in operating performance and are now successful in their markets.[63]

In addition, there was a growing recognition that "America Inc." was lagging in industrial performance. In 1996, the MIT convened its first commission on a significant national issue since World War II. The topic was the decline in industrial performance regarded as severe enough to endanger the economic future of the USA. Rising imports and declining productivity in many sectors required major changes in how America works and produces to compete

---

[61] Kaplan and Stein (1993).
[62] The number of funds in the Burgiss database covers between 30–45% of funds raised in the USA during that vintage year. If more funds mean larger overall commitments the relationship between fundraising and performance indicates that new commitments follow the performance trend.
[63] Quoted from Helwege and Opler (1993).

internationally. There was thus a sense that those takeovers were part of the shock that the US economy needed.[64]

Establishment of Important Buyout Firms

As a result of its pivotal role in large transactions, including some record-setting LBOs, KKR became the most prominent LBO firm in those days. It established a brand recognized by the public in the USA and overseas. But KKR was not alone. It faced competition from existing and increasingly from new competitors established during that decade. The heightened leveraged buyout activity and increasing investor interest led to a significant increase in the number of private equity firms. According to some estimates, there were 24 active LBO firms in the USA in 1980. At the end of the decade that number had increased ten-fold to more than 240.[65] Many buyout firm founders had backgrounds in investment banking and had worked on financing and executing leveraged buyouts and hostile takeovers. The newly founded firms included the likes of Blackstone and Carlyle Group that would become direct challengers to KKR's dominance in size and prominence (Figure 5.7). In Europe, the leveraged buyout (LBO) and private equity industry developed more rapidly in the United Kingdom than in Continental Europe in the 1980s. This was due to a well-established financial and legal infrastructure, including a deep pool of investment banks and law firms that could support LBOs and private equity deals and the fact that the UK capital markets were more developed than those of Continental Europe. Continental Europe also had a more restrictive legal and regulatory environment and cultural resistance to LBOs and private equity. The United Kingdom also had a sizable pension fund market in relation to its economy. Still, in 2001, the total assets held by pension funds in the UK exceeded those in the United States when measured as a percentage of GDP, with figures of 73% compared to 62%.

---

[64] The findings of the Commission on Industrial Productivity assembled by MIT were published in the book *Made in America*, which became a bestseller (Dertouzos, Lester, and Solow, 1989). Another book that discusses in detail the impacts of the manufacturing decline on trade, technology, and economic transition that had a strong impact in the 1980s was *Manufacturing Matters* (Cohen, 1988).
[65] *The Economist* (2016).

Figure 5.7 **(a) David M. Rubenstein, co-founder and co-chairman of the Carlyle Group, speaking at an event of SCM Strategic Capital Management in the late 1990s. (b) Stephen A. Schwarzman, co-founder, and CEO of Blackstone at a conference in Zurich in 2009.**
Source: Courtesy of Hepp (author).

This ready access to domestic institutional capital clearly bestowed a fundraising advantage upon UK firms.[66] Over time, however, the private equity industry would develop in Continental Europe and private equity firms would become active across the region.

Among the major firms founded in this period were:

- CVC, a European buyout firm, 1981
- Bain Capital, 1984
- Advent International, 1984
- Hellman & Friedman, 1984
- Hicks & Haas, later Hicks Muse Tate & Furst, and today HM Capital (and its European spinoff Lion Capital), 1984
- First Reserve Corporation, the first private equity firm focused on the energy sector, 1984

---

[66] OECD (2005).

- Blackstone, 1985
- Permira, a European buyout firm, 1985
- Doughty Hanson, a European buyout firm, 1985
- GS Capital Partners, 1986
- H&Q Asia Pacific, an Asian buyout and private equity firm, 1986
- BC Partners, a European focused firm, 1986
- The Carlyle Group, 1987.

At the End, a New Beginning

The world had changed by the end of the 1980s. A nearly decade-long stock market boom had pushed up valuations, making it more difficult to find undervalued targets. Many new competitors were formed in the buyout industry, and investment banks now provided acquisition debt and equity financing.

But corporations had strengthened their anti-takeover defenses and taken steps to make their companies less appealing to hostile bidders. Some states introduced "poison pills,"[67] debt covenants, supermajority voting requirements, and other measures to discourage hostile takeover bids. In addition, several US states introduced various forms of new anti-takeover laws that made it more difficult to launch a hostile takeover bid.[68]

The takeover boom also changed the way corporations were managed. Traditional actuarial valuation methods were replaced by a cash flow–based approach to evaluate business units. Management used business units' cash flows and the corporation's cost of capital as the discount rate to value those businesses and to assess whether their excess returns met targets. Units that failed to pass this test were sold.[69]

---

[67] Poison pills allow the board of directors to issue additional shares that existing shareholders could buy at a discount. This increases the number of shares the acquirer would have to buy (Kaufman and Englander, 1993). Alternatively, a company might issue cheap preferred stock that is convertible to common stock if the company is acquired. However, some research suggests that those safeguards were much less effective than thought when tested in court, and that they may actually increase the likelihood of a successful takeover, which would be another example of unanticipated consequences of regulation (Cain, McKeon, and Solomon, 2014).
[68] Fortier (1989).
[69] *The Economist* (1991).

Corporations also paid out more cash and increased their leverage. But Figure 5.8 shows that leverage increased less during the 1980s compared to the 1960s and early 1970s before the takeover boom. After the 1990s, the trend reversed, and leverage declined again. The takeover boom did, therefore, not mark the beginning of a secular trend toward ever-increasing leverage, as some critics feared.

At the end of the 1980s, investors became wary of investing in takeover schemes through equity or high-yield bonds, and their withdrawal occurred dramatically in 1989 when the junk bond market crashed. The collapse of the Savings & Loan industry, which was a significant junk bond investor, and the scandals involving Michael Milken and Drexel Burnham Lambert were factors leading to the demise of the junk bond market.[70] In addition,

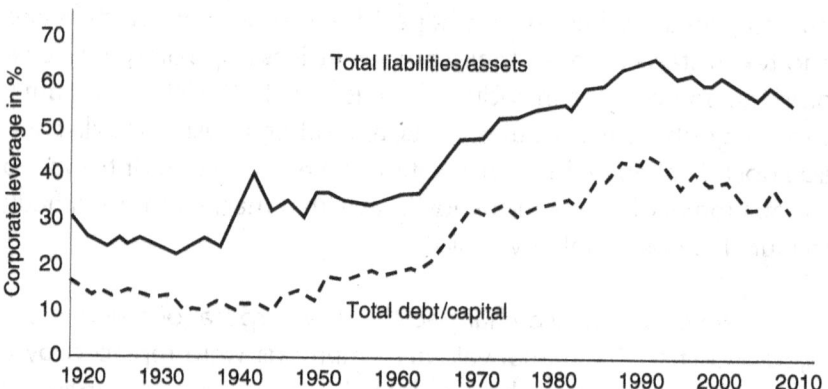

Figure 5.8   Development of US corporate leverage and total liabilities/assets.
Source: Graham, Leary, and Roberts (2014); data: Compustat and Moody's *Industrial Manuals.*

---

[70] The Savings and Loan Crisis of the 1980s and 1990s caused the failure of 1,043 of the 3,234 savings and loan associations (S&Ls) in the United States from 1986 to 1995. This contributed to the woes of the high-yield bond markets as many savings and loan associations were heavily invested in them. When interest rates rose, the savings and loans found that their lending income was below their borrowing cost and they tried to close the gap by investing in junk bonds. While this was not the only factor that triggered the crisis, it contributed to it and, from the perspective of the high-yield market, resulted in a drop in demand and pressure on prices as the positions of the savings and loan associations were liquidated.

the number of defaults increased, and new offerings deteriorated in quality.[71]

Trading volumes and liquidity also declined, with Drexel Burnham Lambert filing for bankruptcy in February 1990.[72] After rising from less than $1 billion in 1980 to more than $60 billion in 1988, the buyout transaction volume declined to less than $4 billion in 1990.[73]

From now on, the buyout firms needed to adapt to an environment where leverage might play a lesser role and come with higher costs and stricter covenants. Competition was more intense, and undervalued assets were harder to find. KKR made it a point to raise larger funds—always the largest fund—in quick succession. Apart from commercial considerations and prestige, there was a logic to that. By outclassing competitors with the size of their funds, KKR could target companies too big for others to acquire. In a world where undervalued public companies came in all sizes, this was a way to outrun the competition. But even then, this logic had its limits. KKR's 1987 investment fund accounted, by some estimates, for one out of every four dollars of the estimated $20 billion in equity dedicated for leveraged buyouts. Still, they faced formidable rivals in any contest, and RJR Nabisco had shown that it only takes one determined opponent to start a bidding war.

The Critics Were Not Convinced

During the 1980s, the media ascribed the "corporate raid" label to many private equity investments, particularly those that featured a hostile takeover of the company, perceived asset stripping, major layoffs, or other significant corporate-restructuring activities.[74]

---

[71] *Los Angeles Times*, September 11, 1989. The liquidity crisis of the Campeau Corporation, a holding company that included Bloomingdale's, Abraham & Straus, and Jordan Marsh, sent junk bond markets into a tailspin as investors feared rising default rates (Richter, 1989). It happened just a month after Michael Milken, who was indicted on racketeering and securities fraud charges, got fired, and Drexel Burnham Lambert settled record civil fraud charges and was effectively put under SEC administration (Vise and Coll, 1989).
[72] Eichenwald (1990).
[73] Kaplan and Stein (1993).
[74] Thackray (1986).

A widespread fear at the time was that some companies had taken on so much debt they would not be able to pay the interest on it if a recession occurred. Congress questioned whether the rising corporate debt-to-equity ratios, incited by the LBOs, imprudently mortgaged America's manufacturing base.[75] As a result, jobs would be lost, and long-standing firms would disappear. The value-add of buyouts and takeovers was questioned and the public equated it with asset-stripping or greenmailing. In this view, takeovers only enriched some investors while distracting management from implementing sound strategies and improving productivity. As early as 1984, LBOs were a target of strong criticism by Paul Volcker, then chairman of the Federal Reserve, and John S.R. Shad, chairman of the US Securities and Exchange Commission. The concern of policymakers and regulators did not abate. In 1989, the SEC Chairman D. Ruder said that the root cause of LBOs was the growth of the junk bond market. Restrictions on the deductibility of interest from corporate earnings and other measures were discussed, but there were few changes in legislation.[76] Lack of action probably stems from the realization that there are two sides to the issue: on the one hand, the conflict of interest between management and shareholders and the agency cost that result, and, on the other, the risk that businesses will increase their leverage, cut back on R&D, and make other cuts to generate cash, which could erode their long-term competitiveness and resilience.[77]

The 1980s ended with the buyout industry under intense scrutiny from institutional investors, public officials, labor, and the general public. As time went by, much research was conducted that looked at highly leveraged deals and their outcomes for stakeholders. A consensus emerged that the de-conglomeration during the late 1970s and 1980s made the US economy more competitive. However, higher debt levels, like those observed in the late 1980s, might reduce companies' resilience during a recession.[78] But these risks did not create a systemic danger for the US economy. They

[75] Kaufman and Englander (1993).
[76] Hinden (1989), Rosenblatt (1989).
[77] Fortier (1989).
[78] Frequently cited studies are Fortier (1989), Shleifer and Vishny (1990), Kaplan and Stein (1993).

needed to be seen in the context of the value created for existing shareholders and LBO investors (including public pension funds).

While buyouts suffered from the image of asset strippers and buccaneers, the major firms gained name recognition, and this new style of investment undertaken by LBO firms gained support from institutional investors. The negative perception of LBOs lingered much longer overseas, where nothing comparable to the US takeover boom had occurred.

LBOs in Europe

The European private equity industry started gaining momentum in the early 1980s, with the UK regional trade association (the BVCA) and its European equivalent (the EVCA) founded in 1983. The industry's rapid emergence then began in earnest, with regional venture capital associations following in France and Germany over the decade.

A feature of European private equity that sets it apart from the USA is that many firms started as in-house teams of banks such as Schroders, Phillips & Drew, or Barclays Bank. Initially, the focus was on venture capital which is also the case for early independent firms like Apax Partners. It was not until the 1990s that buyouts became the main activity of those firms.

Deals during the 1980s were primarily done in the UK. In 1988, the combined value of UK buyouts approached £4 billion (approximately $6.25 billion), up from £270 million in 1984 and the UK accounted for almost 80% of the European buyout volume.

In an article in the *Harvard Business Review*, John Kitching used interviews and data filings to explore some aspects of the European LBO landscape during the 1990s. The study found differences between LBOs in the UK and the USA. US buyouts make more aggressive use of high-yield debt. On average, junk bonds account for 37% of the total LBO purchase price in the US compared to 7% in Great Britain. Meanwhile, loans and notes from vendors, a trivial source of financing for US buyouts, account for 8% of the purchase price in UK buyouts.[79]

Regarding the performance of European buyout funds, there is no robust data to make meaningful comparisons. Still, as the US buyout performance during the decade showed a good performance for most vintage years and relative outperformance versus public markets,[80] one might assume this holds for UK buyouts as well.

5.4   PRIVATE REAL ESTATE

Real estate investing was another area that benefited from the Economic Recovery Tax Act of 1981 (ERTA), the Tax Reform Act of 1986, and the economic boom. Aside from lower tax rates, an Accelerated Cost Recovery System (ACRS) was implemented, which allowed commercial property investors to depreciate a building over 15 years—a period significantly shorter than its economic life. Previously, the standard tax period was 40 years.[81]

Before ERISA, US pension funds allocated to real estate were very limited. This contrasts with other countries where pension funds' real estate investments accounted for more than 20% in Japan and Switzerland and around 15% in the UK. The oil supply shocks and the inflation of the 1970s changed that mindset and caused plan sponsors to consider alternative asset classes that might supply some insurance against broad economic shocks.

Real estate was just such an asset class, as its performance indicated inflation protection and attractive returns over the long run. The Prudential Insurance Company led the way in developing vehicles that facilitated investment in real estate. The company had its own portfolio of real estate holdings. It took its better-located, newer, higher-quality office, retail, and apartment properties (later labeled as core assets). It placed them into what was then referred to as an open-end commingled real estate fund. Prudential would manage the fund—called the Prudential Property Investment Separate Account, or PRISA—as the general partner (GP) that earned fees as a percentage of assets under management, with

---

[79] Kitching (1998).
[80] Harris, Jenkinson, and Kaplan (2015).
[81] Garner (2008).

plan sponsors investing as limited partners (LPs). Other strategies involved the repositioning (renovation) of real estate or outright new development. Those strategies are referred to as value-add or opportunistic funds. US pension funds started investing right at the beginning of the biggest real estate development boom of the twentieth century. Office construction, for example, increased by 221% between 1977 and 1984.[82]

Developers like Fisher Brothers, Tishman Speyer, Bruce Eichner, and Larry Silverstein (Figure 5.9) constructed numerous midtown office towers in New York, following trends elsewhere. In 1983, Tishman Speyer completed $300 million worth of construction, ranking it among the top 10 commercial developers in the country. That year, the 58-story skyscraper Trump Tower in Midtown Manhattan was completed. During the 1980s, Hines expanded its thriving Houston operation into additional American cities. Like buyout firms, real estate developers relied on the robust debt market to finance their undertakings rather than establishing funds that raised equity capital from institutional investors. Many developers used limited partnerships to raise development capital. But this capital was usually provided by private or corporate investors, and pension funds played a limited role in funding value-add or opportunistic partnerships.

This building boom ended when the Savings & Loan (S&L) crisis unfolded from 1986 to 1995. The S&L crisis crippled the construction and real estate (CRE) sector's traditional debt and equity capital suppliers. With traditional capital sources sidelined or gone forever, the entire commercial real estate sector was severely financially distressed in the early 1990s.[83]

Sam Zell (Figure 5.9) established the first of four Zell-Merrill real estate funds using a private equity structure. The fund closed at $400 million in 1988. It was followed by Boston-headquartered AEW Partners—founded in 1981—which raised its first opportunistic fund ($875 million). The Zell-Merrill funds were some of the first opportunistic real estate partnerships with mainly institutional

---

[82] Riddiough (2021).
[83] Carlo, Eichholtz and Kok (2021).

Figure 5.9 Two iconic real estate entrepreneurs: Sam Zell (left) was the forefather of the modern REITs in 1968 and created the largest office space portfolio in the US. He sold Equity Office to Blackstone in 2007. Larry Silverstein acquired key Manhattan office buildings in the late '70s and '80s, as well as the original World Trade Center complex in 2001, which he re-developed after 9/11.

Source: https://www.youtube.com/watch?v=nsViaAOvlC l (not attributed).

investors providing equity capital. These funds benefited from the real estate market downturn at the end of the 1980s and focused on real estate debt and distressed property sales.[84] Other opportunity and distress funds were established in the early 1990s in response to the S&L crisis.[85] Over time, opportunistic real estate investing, as it came to be called, achieved significant success when strategically focusing on undervalued asset plays or distressed opportunities.

---

[84] Corfmann (2015).
[85] Riddiough (2021).

Chapter 6

The 1990s: Dotcom Boom and Bust

The longest recorded economic expansion in the USA was sandwiched between the brief recession in the early 1990s and the dot.com bubble crash between 2000–2002. The fall of the Berlin Wall in 1989 signaled the end of the Cold War. In commerce, the momentum of change was bolstered further with the establishment of the World Trade Organization (WTO) in 1994 and subsequent trade liberalization treaties, which made markets more accessible and opened up entirely new markets to international competition. The stock market had one of its strongest decades in post-war history. The annual return of the S&P 500 averaged 17.5% in nominal and 14.5% in real terms from 1991–2000.

6.1 INTERMEDIARIES IN PRIVATE MARKETS

From the early 1980s onwards, pension plans began shifting large portions of their portfolios away from fixed-income securities and toward equities. The change in allocation occurred slowly at first but picked up speed through the 1990s.[1]

For the growing interest of institutional investors in the asset class to translate into investments, a few barriers needed to be overcome. The idiosyncratic aspects that set private markets apart from traditional public market investments challenged many prospective investors. Access to private markets is difficult due to a lack of publicly available information. While there are thousands of managers and hundreds of funds raised each year, knowing which funds are in the market, evaluating and comparing track records, and gaining access to sought-after funds is not straightforward. As the industry matured, a network of intermediaries, consultants, and service providers emerged to help investors to bridge the information gap and to provide access to investment opportunities. Intermediation has been a critical driver of growing institutional investment in the asset class.

The increase of the investor base was facilitated by a growing network of intermediaries. Additionally, investors began to collaborate to share best practices for investing in the new asset class (Figure 6.1). In the early 1990s, the Institutional Limited Partner Association (ILPA) began as an informal networking association for investors in private equity funds. Over time the organization would grow into an important private markets investor advocacy group.[2]

Investors new to the asset class often sought out an advisory firm's assistance to help them create an investment case. Over time advisors developed toolsets to budget commitments and integrate private equity investments in multi-asset frameworks. They also became increasingly involved in manager selection.

Advisors became known as "gatekeepers"[2] due to their role in the selection of fund offerings on behalf of their clients. Investors often regarded them as an extension of their portfolio management team. While the investor often maintained the final decision, i.e., discretion over manager and allocation decisions, many other

---

[1] Pew Trust (2014).
[2] As of 2021, ILPA had 575+ member organizations representing more than $2 trillion in private equity AuM.

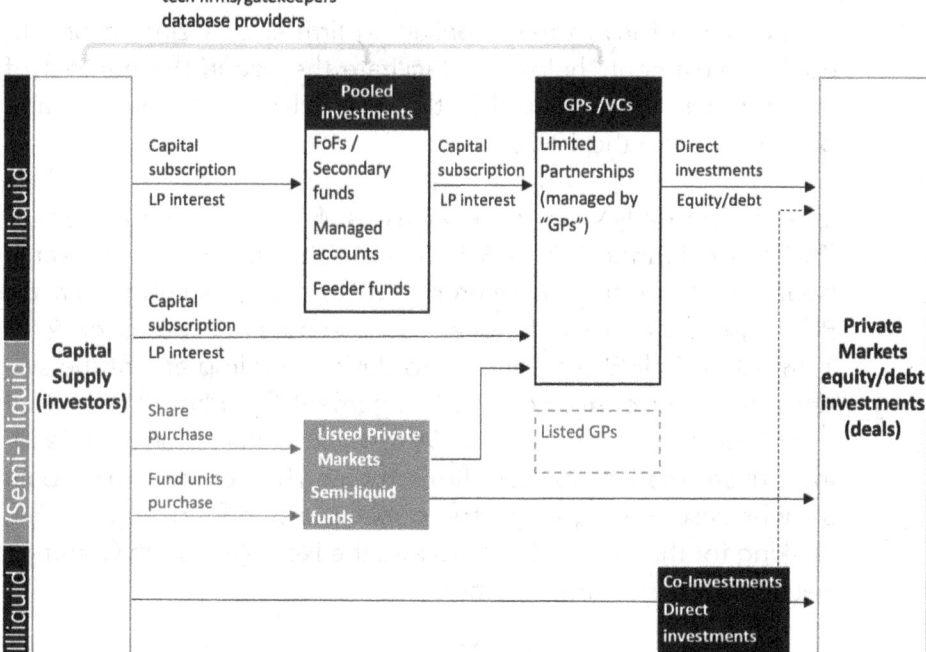

Figure 6.1   The private market ecosystem.

Note: The chart shows the sources of capital for the private markets industry and the different access routes available to investors to gain exposure to portfolio investments. The most common access route is a subscription to a limited partnership that may either act as a FoFs (investing in other partnerships) or directly invest in portfolio companies. Business services and service firms include providers of research, portfolio accounting and management systems, benchmarks and data services, fundraising support (placements agents), or due diligence information.

aspects of the investment process were managed through investment advisors.

Investors use advisors to help them to understand the asset class and its risk and return characteristics. Once they allocate capital to private markets investors also have to decide whether to hire internal staff or external service providers to handle the frontoffice, middle-office, and back-office tasks involved in the investment process. Public pension funds, in particular, often find it challenging to build and maintain an in-house team capable of managing private market investments, were required to obtain independent second opinions and thus became frequent users of consultants and other service providers. The representation of multiple clients gave GPs bargaining to negotiate terms of conditions with GPs.

A Growing Role for Advisors

A new type of investment consulting firm specializing in private equity investments helped to facilitate the rise in the number of investors who participated in the asset class (both venture and buyouts) during the 1990s.

One of the early full-service advisors, Pacific Corporate Group (PCG), was founded in 1979 by Christopher Bower as a research boutique. Over time it offered investment consulting services. PCG's public pension fund advisory experience dates back to 1989, when CalPERS retained it to design and implement the system's Alternative Investment Management Program.[3] Leslie Brun established Hamilton Lane in 1991, which is still among the leading private market advisory firms today. The company also built a client base among very large public pension funds in the USA, working for the likes of CalPERS and the New York State Common Retirement Fund, among others.

European advisors who helped institutional investors in the region launch their private equity programs included SCM Strategic Capital Management in Switzerland (est. 1996, since 2015, Mercer Private Markets), Feri Trust in Germany (est. 1987), Albourne (est. 1994), and Altius Associates (est. 1987, since 2018, Mercer Private Markets) both in the UK.

Stepstone Advisors (est. 2006) was the first of those gatekeepers to develop a strong brand among institutional investors in Asia. In 2010, Monte Brem, the company's founder, moved to Beijing. Subsequently, Andy Tsai, the former head of alternative investment at Cathay Life Insurance Company in Taiwan, joined their Hong Kong office in 2012. By offering segregated accounts or FoFs, gatekeepers transitioned into asset management. In the case of SCM/Mercer Private Markets, the share of assets under management (AuM) in total assets advised was more than 90%, and in the case of Hamilton Lane, discretionary AuM reached $106.4 billion in 2021. Table 6.1 lists some prominent gatekeepers, as of 2021. The list serves as an illustration and is not complete. It should not be viewed as an industry ranking.

---

[3] Information provided on PCG's corporate webpage.

Table 6.1   Some prominent gatekeepers, data as of December 2021

Gatekeeper	Founded	Assets monitored/advised in $B	Headquarters
Cambridge Associates	1973*	270**	Boston, MA
NEPC	1986	1'500	Boston, MA
Hamilton Lane	1991	900	Philadelphia, PA
Callan	1986	<30	San Francisco, CA
Wilshire Private Markets	1989	>100	Santa Monica, CA
Albourne	1994	n.a.	London, UK
Portfolio Advisors***	1994	15	Darien, CT
Stepstone	2006	570	La Jolla, CA
SCM Strategic Capital Management/ Mercer Private Markets	1996	>20	Zurich, Switzerland
Pacific Corporate Group	1979	n.a.	La Jolla, CA

Source: Crunchbase, corporate webpages.
Notes: The list serves as an illustration and is not complete. It should not be viewed as an industry ranking. Assets may be advised on a discretionary or non-discretionary basis.
*Year of incorporation as a multi-asset investment consultant, the start date of private market advisory services is not disclosed,
**Commitments advised since 1980,
***(Portfolio Advisors, 2007).

Generalist investment consultants like Cambridge Associates or Wilshire have also built significant private markets businesses, serving endowments and foundations.

Other Service Providers

Even institutions that don't use consultants may use alternative service providers, such as accounting software or software as a service (SaaS) for portfolio management and benchmarking. Investran (est. 1985),[4] Burgiss (est. 1986),[5] and eFront (est. 1999),[6] are among the most widely used firms in that area. Those firms are not only providing software or SaaS but also analytics based on the fund data

[4] Since 2004, part of SunGard.
[5] Since 2020, part of MSCI.
[6] Since 2019, part of BlackRock.

maintained by their investing clients. Database providers such as Thomson Reuters, VentureExpert/Thomson Reuters (since the late 1960s), VentureSource (est. 1994),[7] and research boutiques, such as Preqin (est. 2003), PitchBook (est. 2006),[8] and Crunchbase (est. 2007) offer access to market intelligence and performance data. It should be noted, however, that none of those databases provide a full overview of the market as even the largest databases cover only about 40% of funds raised in any given vintage year. Databases may differ in sample size, strategy representation, or geographical coverage and thus performance metrics and other analytics do vary.

Assisting managers with fundraising was a service provided by placement agents. Several banks established private placement groups to maintain a network with investors, gauge their interest in different private market strategies, advise GPs on presenting themselves (pitch books and data rooms for due diligence), and organize roadshows. But there are also independent organizations that were established for this purpose. In the USA, Eaton Partners, founded in 1983 by Charles Eaton, ranks among the oldest firms in the private placement business. In Europe, Helix Associates (since 2005, part of Jefferies International Ltd.), founded in 1993 by Lord Charles Cecil and Campbell Lutyens, founded in 1988 by John Campbell and Richard Lutyens, were among the early independent firms active in that space.

Tables 6.2 and 6.3 list placement agents and service providers. The lists only show some prominent examples and should not be viewed as an industry ranking. Furthermore, omissions of firms are not intentional.

During the 1970s and 1980s, US pension funds and endowments primarily adhered to a conservative investment model, with a notable focus on domestic equities and fixed income. To become substantial contributors to private markets, they needed to depart from the traditional "60/40" model. This transition was significantly guided by advisors, gatekeepers, and various service providers, as investing in less liquid assets like private equity presented notable challenges.

---

[7] Since 2020, part of CB Insights.
[8] Since 2016, part of Morningstar.

Table 6.2   Law firms and placement agents used by LPs and GPs, data as of December 2021

Law firms	# of private capital fund formation assignments*	Placement agents	# of private market funds serviced*
Kirkland & Ellis	>800	Credit Suisse Private Fund Group	>350
King & Wood Mallesons	>500	PJT Park Hill	>200
Goodwin	>400	Mercury Capital Advisors	200
Simpson Thacher & Bartlett	>400	UBS Investment Bank Private Funds Group	200
Clifford Chance	400	MVision Private Equity Advisers	200
Debevoise & Plimpton	>300	Lazard Private Capital Advisory	>150
Cooley LLP	>300	Eaton Partners	150
Burness Paull	>300	Evercore Private Funds Group	130
Proskauer	>300	Atlantic-Pacific Capital	>120
Ropes & Gray	>250	Campbell Lutyens	>100

Source: Preqin Service Providers Alternative Asset 2021, data: estimates of Preqin.
Notes: The table only shows some prominent examples, and serves as an illustration, and should not be viewed as an industry ranking. Law firms also serve LP clients but those numbers are not included.
*Several funds serviced or formation assignments may be linked to the same manager.

Table 6.3   Fund administrators and software and service providers, data as of December 2021

Fund administrators	# of private market funds serviced*	Portfolio mangement software & software as service	# of clients**
SS&C GlobeOp	>700	Burgiss Group (MSCI)	1000+
Alter Domus	>600	eFront (BlackRock)	800+
Standish Management	500	iLevel (S&P)	700+
State Street	>300	Investran (SunGuard)	500+
IQ-EQ	300	Allvue	400+
Gen II Fund Services	300	Quva	n.a.
Citco Fund Services	>250	CEPRES	n.a.

Source: Preqin Service Providers Alternative Asset 2021, data: estimates of Preqin.
Notes: The table only shows some prominent examples, and serves as an illustration, and should not be viewed as an industry ranking. Omissions of firms are not intentional.
*Fund administrators also serve LP clients but those numbers are not included.
**Data based on information of the corporate webpages as of 2022.

However, for gatekeepers and consultants to advance their business, a shift in the prevailing investment paradigm was necessary. This transformation was facilitated by the increasing acceptance of non-traditional assets, a trend that gained momentum as some peers and industry leaders achieved success through investments in private equity. The success of Yale's endowment and its role in promoting the adoption of alternative investments in institutional portfolios is often cited as an exemplar (see Box 6.1).

Box 6.1   The Yale Investment Model

The Yale endowment was worth $1 billion in 1985 when David Swensen (Figure 6.2) started managing it; by 2021, its value had increased to $42.3 billion.

The increasing interest by endowments and foundations in private equity and other forms of private market investments was a result of the growing popularity of the "Yale Model" of investing developed by David Swensen after he joined the endowment in 1985. He stressed that "liquidity is a bad thing to be avoided rather than a good thing to be sought out, since it comes at a heavy price in the shape of lower returns."[9]

Figure 6.2   David Swensen.
Source: investments.yale.edu.

[9] Swensen (2000).

Compared to more traditional portfolios, the Yale model is characterized by a high exposure to illiquid asset classes such as private equity. The performance of the Yale endowment's portfolio was widely recognized and became a reference for an asset allocation that includes private equity and other illiquid assets. The Yale model became so popular that it is sometimes referred to as the "Endowment Model" as well.

The division of a portfolio into five or six roughly equal buckets, each of which is invested in a different asset class, is a key component of his strategy. The Yale Model is characterized by its extensive manager diversification and emphasis on equities, avoiding asset classes with low expected returns such as fixed income and money market investments. His insight that pursuing liquidity is undesirable for institutions with long investment horizons and should be avoided was novel at the time.[10]

As a result, the Yale Model has a very high exposure to asset classes like private equity, compared to more conventional portfolios. The Yale Model is also distinguished by a heavy reliance on outside investment managers, and the investment team focuses on asset allocation and manager selection. Yale is also idiosyncratic in its thinking about market niches and strategies to explore. That often (at least initially) created the problem of finding managers to put those portfolio views into practice.[11] Yale thus had to be prepared to back management teams early on, and Swensen was once described as becoming a "venture capitalist of venture capitalists." However, his readiness to support new teams was not limited to venture capital. Different types of private markets investments played a big role in Yale's investment portfolio.[12]

(continued)

---

[10] Ellis (2020).
[11] Yale Investment Office (2022).
[12] Wigglesworth and Kasumov (2021).

Yale uses modern portfolio theory to determine the desired portfolio weights. Still, they argue that one should use discretion and consider qualitative factors to account for the limitations of mean-variance analysis, particularly the low predictive value of parameter estimates derived from historical data and the volatility and volatilities' instability. He also recommends that the model has some constraints imposed (but not too many). Any change in portfolio composition from a quantitative analysis should be implemented gradually over time. Instead of providing point estimates for the weighting of various asset classes, quantitative modeling of alternative investments is thus seen as a tool to draw investors' attention to potentially profitable asset allocation changes.[13]

Control of Risk

Risk management includes using simulations to confirm the resilience of an asset allocation under various scenarios (Figure 6.3) and regular portfolio rebalancing (to the extent that the weighting of liquid investments permits it). However, Yale also emphasizes qualitative aspects, such as the involvement of trustees with relevant experience in the investment process (which takes time).[14]

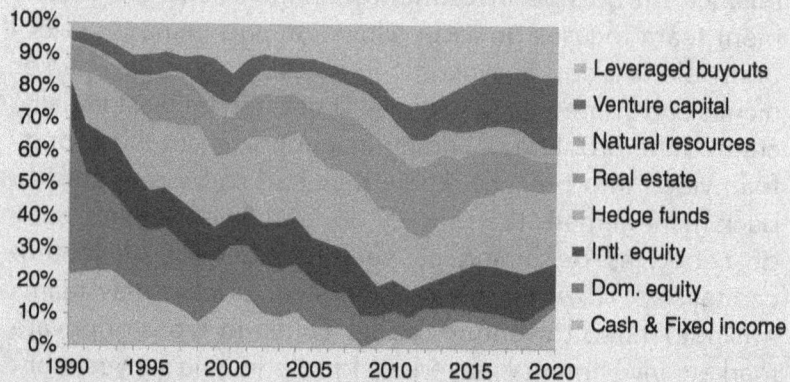

Figure 6.3   Yale asset allocation, 1990–2020.
Source: Yale Investments Office (www.investments.yale.edu).

---

[13] Lerner (2015).
[14] Orr (2019).

Yale built long-term relationships with managers. Unlike typical institutional manager relationships, which last about three years, Yale's management relationships frequently last eight years or longer. Swensen disagreed with evaluating manager relationships based on short-term performance indicators because strong managers can have bad years while underperforming managers can have good years ahead of them.[15]

Many investment professionals recognize the Yale Model's three-decade success. However, putting the strategy into practice requires skill sets from the trustees and investment team that many other institutions might not have. According to a 2023 Forbes analysis, the average endowment size in the USA is $1.2 billion, significantly surpassing the median of approximately $203.4 million.[16] This distribution of assets suggests that the vast majority of endowments—due to their rather small AuM—contend with varying challenges regarding internal management resources, constraints on manager access, and limitations in raising capital for liquidity demands. Consequently, the applicability of the Yale Model is diminished, particularly in light of Yale's asset under management (AuM), which is 40x greater than the average, with most endowments not even close to that size. Yale demonstrated tenacity when the liquidity crisis during the GFC hit. The institution issued (tax-exempt) bonds rather than selling assets to meet some of its liquidity needs. This is something that pension funds or insurance companies may be unable to do for regulatory reasons. Therefore, David Swensen's success cannot be replicated by everyone, and numerous attempts to do so have failed.[17]

(continued)

---

[15] Heaton (2021).
[16] Nietzel (2023).
[17] Wigglesworth and Kasumov (2021).

While the Yale Model may not be an approach to be followed by all institutions, its vital characteristic—a very significant weighting of illiquid private market investments—did trigger a debate in the financial industry and among institutional investors. This debate focused on whether the traditional emphasis on liquid investments is still a good paradigm. This debate would intensify during the next two decades when the low-interest rate environment would render the conventional public bond/public equity asset allocation unsustainable for many institutions.[18]

6.2 FUNDS OF FUNDS (FoFs)

Rather than investing directly in the limited partnerships raised by buyout, venture capital, and other private market managers, a funds of funds (FoFs) holds a portfolio of limited partnership interests. This form of investment can thus be described as a multi-manager investment approach. The original business model of private equity FoFs was to raise capital for a limited partnership that would participate in several newly formed limited partnerships of private equity managers ("primary commitments") and then to manage the fund of funds until the liquidation of the underlying partnership interests.

In a market where minimum limited partnership subscriptions start at $5–10 million and sometimes reach tens of millions, even mid-sized institutions may struggle to build a diversified portfolio of direct partnership investments. FoFs allow smaller investors to gain exposure to more funds and achieve a broader manager diversification than their budget would allow them to do if they opted for direct investments. FoFs thus "scale up" their portfolio. In addition, there are issues of know-how and resources, deal-flow, and access. FoFs as a solution may thus be viewed as an alternative to

---

[18] First published in 2000, David Swensen's book, *Pioneering Portfolio Management*, became a bestseller and helped to establish private markets as an asset class, which institutions should consider.

working with a gatekeeper. Dependent on the governance of an institution, the delegation of investment decisions may sometimes be more appropriate than working with a gatekeeper.

But even large investors with sizable in-house teams managing large pools of capital have been investing in FoFs. Doing so allows them to "scale down" their portfolio, investing in smaller funds or niche sectors their in-house team would not consider due to capacity constraints. Given these characteristics, it's not surprising that the FoFs industry is nearly as old as the private markets industry and has been an important intermediary since its inception. Table 6.4 gives an overview of FoFs managers.

Adams Street Partners' history goes back to 1972 when First Chicago Investment invested in startups alongside many of the earliest venture capital firms. Since the arrival of T. Bondurant

Table 6.4   Overview of FoFs managers, data as of December 2021

FoFs managers	Private markets AuM, in $B		Headquarters
	2006	2021	
Stepstone	n.a.	$134	La Jolla, CA
Ardian (formerly AXA Private Equity)*	$35*	$130	Paris, France
Hamilton Lane	n.a.	$106	Philadelphia, PA
Pathway Capital Management	$21	$90	Irvine, CA
LGT Capital Partners	$23	$89	Pfaeffikon, Switzerland
HarbourVest Partners	$18	$75	Boston, MA
AlpInvest Partners	$42**	$55	Amsterdam, Netherlands
Portfolio Advisors	n.a.	$38	Darien, CT
Pantheon Ventures	$23	$55	London, UK
Adams Street Partners	$24	$50	Chicago, IL
Goldman Sachs Capital Partners	$24	$40	New York, NY
Horsely Bridge	n.a.	$29	San Francisco, CA

Notes: The table serves as an illustration and is not complete. It should not be viewed as an industry ranking. Omissions of large FoFs managers are not intentional. It does not include managers that started as secondary specialists but includes gatekeepers that disclose a substantial FoFs/managed account business. Data from corporate webpages.
*Captive with substantial funds from Axa insurance;
**Captive held by two Dutch pension funds that contributed the majority of AuM;
***(Horsley Bridge, 2021 accessed).

French in 1980, the firm focused on FoFs, which makes it the industry's oldest FoFs provider and Chicago the birthplace of the private equity funds-of-funds industry.[19]

HarbourVest Partners, Boston, and Horsley Bridge, San Francisco, followed in 1982 and 1983. Horsley Bridge was the first firm to focus on venture capital, while HarbourVest was co-founded by Brooks Zug and is a pioneer of international FoFs investing (Figure 6.4). HarbourVest made the first European partnership investment in 1984, and its first specialized international FoFs was formed in 1990, the same year the firm opened its London.

These firms not only showcased to US investors opportunities abroad but also promoted the asset class to overseas investors and supplied capital for local GPs.

Before co-founding HarbourVest Partners (previously known as Hancock Venture Partners) in 1982, Brooks Zug and Ed Kane were investing capital on behalf of John Hancock Mutual Life Insurance Company and built a portfolio of ten venture capital funds from 1978 to 1981. The track record they established during those four years was brief but very strong, primarily due to the significant ascent of technology stocks, which transitioned from lows in the mid-to-late

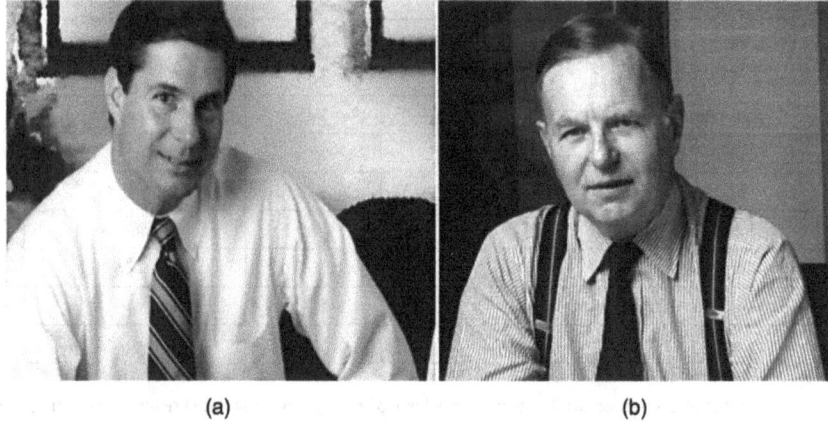

(a)   (b)

Figure 6.4   The Boston connection—two pioneers of international investing.
(a): Brooks Zug, co-founder of HarbourVest, ca. 1994. (b): Peter Brooke, co-founder of TA Associates and founder of Advent International.
Source: HarbourVest, Advent International.

[19] Adams Street Partners (2022).

1970s to peak values in the early 1980s. In an anecdote that illustrates how the spirit of cooperation among General Partners (GPs) extends beyond Silicon Valley, Brooks Zug recalls a pivotal moment in 1982. He invited Peter Brooke, who co-founded TA Associates and later Advent International (see following) to join him in a crucial meeting with the IBM pension plan, aiming to highlight the quality of individuals in whom HarbourVest would invest in their inaugural fund. Following that meeting, when IBM committed $50 million, Peter consistently reminded him of the significant role he had played in the successful launch of the new firm and the fundraising for its first fund.

Advent International was founded by Peter Brooke, who spun Advent out of TA in 1984. His intention was to create an international investment platform through a network of foreign venture capital firms where it held a stake in the GP and sometimes even helped to establish those firms. Unlike HarbourVest Partners, which invested in other GPs' funds, Advent International co-invested directly in deals with those foreign venture partners. But the vision was similar: to provide diversified access to foreign opportunities for (initially) US investors. The HarbourVest/Adams Street FoFs model prevailed, while Advent International changed its model to invest globally directly, and pivoted from venture capital to mid-sized buyouts as a GP through its own offices and investment teams. The first overseas office was Advent International Ltd. In London in 1989, it gave it the first presence in Europe among US GPs.[20] The author has had several occasions to engage in discussions with the founders of Advent International and HarbourVest. Their commitment to spotlighting investment prospects and fund managers operating beyond US borders has played a pivotal role in globalizing private markets investing. These individuals are distinguished for their enthusiasm for this asset class and contributions to the industry's growth.

Pantheon Ventures (1982, UK) is one of the early European FoFs providers. Over time, FoFs not only participated in newly founded funds but also did secondary investments and co-investments in Europe. As in the USA, European managers expanded their geographical focus. Pantheon Venture made its first investment in an Asian private equity fund in 1983 and established a Hong Kong office in 1992.

---

[20] Advent International was also a pioneer in establishing some co-investment programs where LPs of FoFs managers such as SCM Strategic Capital Management would directly invest in deals alongside Advent International across several funds.

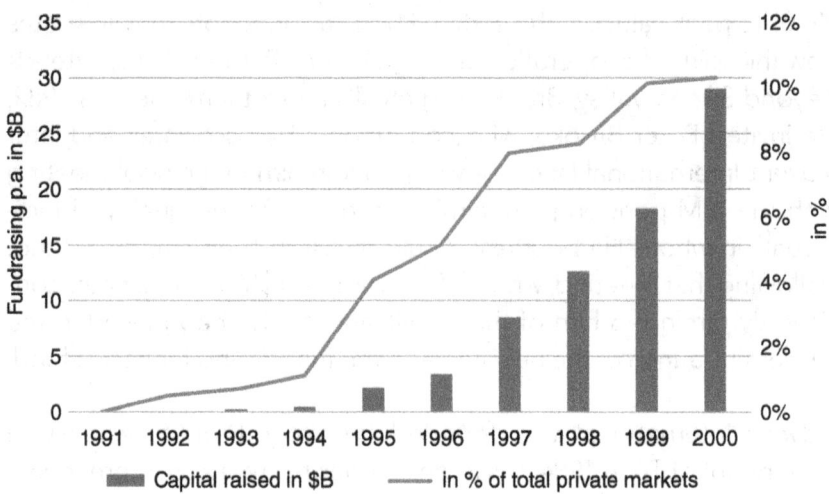

Figure 6.5   FoFs capital raised in $B and in % of total private markets, 2001–2007 p.a.
Source: Adapted from 1991–2000 (Del Ponte, 2005).

During the 1990s, the local FoFs industry in Europe expanded as many institutions did not want to build in-house capabilities or found it difficult to recruit experienced managers to invest in private equity (Figure 6.5).

With its asset management expertise and a large number of domestic pension funds, Switzerland became a European hub for managers that provided institutional investors with private market investment options.

LGT Capital (1994), Partners Group (1996), SCM Strategic Capital Management (1996),[21] Adveq (1997),[22] Unigestion (1997), and Capital Dynamics (1998) acted as catalysts for the growth in number and capital allocations of European investors to private markets. They were joined by peers from other European countries such as French Axa Private Equity (1996)[23] or Dutch AlpInvest 1993).[24]

The rise of FoFs closely tracked the rise of institutional investment in the asset class and its growing adoption outside the USA. Preqin

---

[21] Since 2015, part of Mercer Private Markets.
[22] In 2017, acquired by Schroders.
[23] Today trading as Ardian since a management buyout in 2013.
[24] Reference is made to AlpInvest Holding N.V. that was merged with NIB, a private market manager established by two Dutch pension funds. In 2011, AlpInvest was acquired by the Carlyle Group.

data shows that the share of FoFs in overall private market fundraising increased to about 10% of total capital raised in 2000 (Figure 6.5).[25]

6.3   SECONDARIES FoFs

As the private equity market developed, new niches within the private equity industry began to emerge. In 1982, the Venture Capital Fund of America was the first private equity firm to acquire secondary market interests in existing private equity funds.

Secondaries FoFs mainly acquire partnership interest from investors in existing funds. Secondaries FoFs managers' value proposition sets them apart from traditional FoFs, which place emphasis on their manager selection skills and invest in funds during their establishment phase. In contrast, for secondaries FoFs, the primary driver of performance lies in their ability to identify and evaluate interests in existing limited partnerships and acquire them at a discount to Net Asset Value (NAV) from limited partners looking to exit their investments. Transactions that may involve numerous partnership interests in one portfolio transaction. This segment is thus commonly regarded as separate from the traditional FoFs' business, and fundraising, deal, and exit volumes are reported separately.

Sellers of private-equity investments sell the investments in the fund and their remaining unfunded commitments. By its nature, the private-equity asset class is illiquid. It is intended to be a long-term investment for buy-and-hold investors, and exit from such an investment can only be found through a privately negotiated transaction. Early pioneers offering Secondaries FoFs include: Coller Capital, UK (1990), Arcis, France (1993), Landmark Partners (1989),[26] Partners Group (1996) and Lexington Partners (1994),[27] both US.[28]

The specialist secondary market players did not have a market to themselves for long. Traditional FoFs managers, who had previously focused on primary fund commitments, would soon add secondaries FoFs to their offering or incorporate the strategy into their main funds. Due to their larger fund sizes, it only took a partial allocation to secondaries for FoFs to become significant competitors. An allocation to secondary transactions became a standard part of the FoFs offering.

---

[25] Preqin (2021a).
[26] Since 2021, part of Ares Capital Management Group.
[27] Since 2021, part of Franklin Templeton.
[28] *Private Equity News* (2019), Kreuzer (2003).

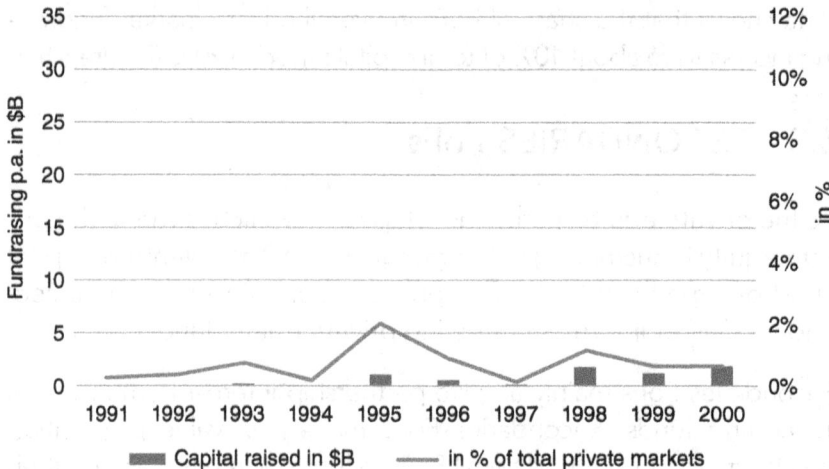

Figure 6.6   Secondaries FoFs: annual capital raised in $B and in percentage of total private markets, 1991–2000.
Source: Black (2018); Capital Dynamics (2016); Jefferies (2021).

The fundraising numbers (Figure 6.6) show that the secondaries FoFs started in the mid-1990s but raised much smaller amounts of capital than traditional FoFs. As many investors were new to the asset class, the priority was to build investment programs through commitments to new partnership offerings rather than through transactions in the secondary market. One reason was that trans-action volumes were initially low, and investors wondered whether secondaries FoFs would allow them to build diversified portfolios. In addition, the 1990s were boom years for private equity and few investors saw a need to sell their fund interests as most of them were in the early stage of building up a portfolio.

6.4   LISTED PRIVATE EQUITY (LPE)

Since initial attempts to use listed investment companies failed to establish themselves as access routes to private equity invest-ments in the USA during the 1950s and 1960s (ARD and SBICs), investments in private equity are mainly accessed through unlisted limited partnerships.

But committing to a partnership was not for everybody. Some insti-tutions had no policy provision for this type of investment, oth-ers struggled with high minimum commitments, and there were also retail investors seeking exposure to the asset class. Com-pared to investments in limited partnerships that require minimum subscriptions of $5 million upwards, investments in shares do not require large sums of money. Unlike partnerships that can usually only be offered to qualified investors, shares can be bought by the general public, including retail investors. Buying and selling them is much more straightforward than subscribing to a limited partnership or selling limited partnership interests in the secondary market. When private equity investment gained traction in Europe, attempts were made again to use listed investment companies to attract capital for the asset class. There are three types of private equity firms that are part of the LPE universe:

1. **Investment companies:** An investment provides mainly access to fund participations, with the investment company typically acting as an LP in limited partnerships. This is the listed equivalent to traditional FoFs.

2. **Investment companies that provide access mainly to individual deals:** Those companies are usually established by a GP rather than a FoFs manager and are the listed equivalent to a private market partnership.

3. **Management companies:** An investment allows shareholders to participate in revenue significantly generated by management fees and carried interest. (IPOs of management companies will be discussed in more detail in Chapter 7.)

Some of the LPE firms would combine some or all of the attributes in this list.

Examples of the first category of FoFs-type listed companies are Pantheon International Plc. (est. 1987) in the UK or Princess Holding (est. 1999) managed by Partners Group AG.

The second category of listed investment companies that invest directly in deals include 3i Group Plc following the successor of the Industrial and Commercial Finance Corporation (founded in 1945).[29]

[29] 3i went public on the London Stock Exchange (LSE) in 1994 and was included in the FTSE-100 index for a time. In 1999, the firm began aggressively to move into early-stage investments, which after initially being successful, led to heavy losses once the dotcom boom turned into a bust. It took the firm almost a decade to unwind its venture portfolio. During the dotcom boom, some US firms such as Internet Capital Group or GMGI raised capital from the public to invest in startups. CHMI invested in AltaVista, Engage, Lycos, and GeoCities and became a NASDAQ 100 company. It is still trading today as Steel Connect (STCN) (Ivashina and Lerner, 2019; Klein, 2023).

This makes it the oldest listed private equity company doing both direct and fund investments and like ARD it had mixed objectives, i.e., generating attractive return and supporting private enterprise during the reconstruction after the war. 3i Plc is still an active multinational private equity and venture capital company based in London. Another example in the UK is Schroder Ventures International Investments Trust (est. 1996).

In other countries, similar companies were listed on local stock exchanges, such as Private Equity Holding AG (established as Vontobel Private Equity Holding 1997, PEHN.SW), which is a hybrid of category one and category two above, as it invests in direct investments and in partnerships.

Partners Group AG not only manages listed private equity companies but also became the first major private equity manager to do an IPO in 2006. It falls into category three as it is a management company. IPOs of management companies gained momentum after the Global Financial Crisis (GFC) and are thus discussed in more detail in Chapter 7.

Generally, this segment of listed investment companies is more important in Europe than in the USA. In 1993, the global market capitalization of one of the oldest indices—the LPX Composite index—was EUR 8.9 billion (Figure 6.7).[30] The capitalization of the LPX Composite was approximately 10% of total private markets AuM at that time. At the end of the 1990s, driven by the demand of retail investors, there was a significant increase in new listings of private equity investment companies, which caused the sharp increase in LPX market capitalization until 1999 to EUR 68.58 billion or roughly 20% of total private market AuM.[31] When using indices such as the LPX for benchmarking traditional private market funds (limited partnerships), it is necessary to ensure that the listed private market benchmark only includes listed fund vehicles and not listed managers to provide a "like-for-like" comparison.

---

[30] The LPX (Listed Private Equity Index) series were launched in 2004 on the basis of exchange-traded private equity companies. The indices track the performance of listed private market companies and the index capitalization is provided by LPX AG.

[31] Bilo, Christophers, Degosciu, and Zimmermann (2005), Tegtmeier (2021).

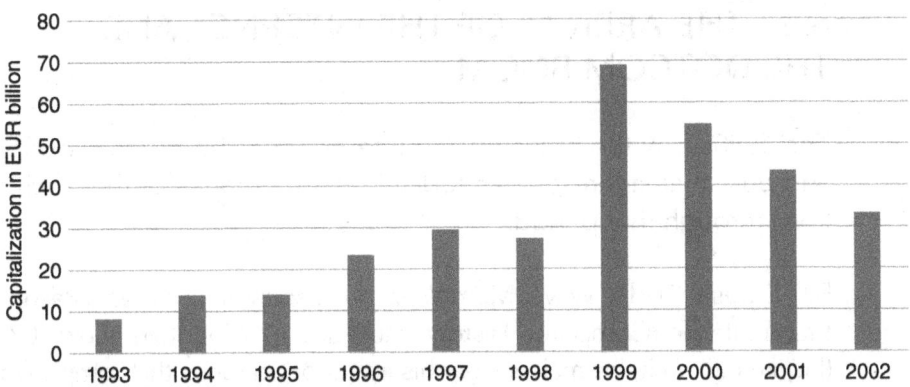

Figure 6.7   Market capitalization of the global LPX Composite index 1993–2002 in billion EUR.
Source: Adapted from LPX Group, LPX Composite Private Equity Index.
Note: The LPX listed private equity companies are those with a certain level of market capitalization and liquidity.

Despite having a sizable market capitalization, the listed private equity sector or structured products have not significantly impacted the landscape of private equity investment. Doriot's American Research & Development Corporation (ARD) provided lessons on the drawbacks of listed private equity, limiting its appeal to institutional investors. The experience in Europe a few decades later was no different. The listed investment companies are often thinly traded and valued at a significant discount to NAV. This increases price volatility while the share price performance does not fully reflect the underlying investments' performance. In addition, corporate taxes apply, which make listed private equity unattractive for tax-exempt investors, such as pension funds.

Over the years, there have also been attempts to broaden the investor base by offering other innovative formats to access private equity investments and, by doing so, to address the requirements of regulated pools of capital. For example, Partners Group used convertible bond structures for its Princess and Pearl Holdings with a guaranteed rate of return and downside protection through an insurance arrangement with Swiss Re that resulted in an AA rating by Standard & Poor's. Those features made those convertible bonds eligible for the investment of cover stock reserves of German insurance companies, which allowed Partners Group to tap a new source of capital.[32]

---

[32] Partners Group (2007, 2014).

6.5   THE ARRIVAL OF THE INTERNET AND THE DOTCOM BOOM

The 1990s saw the arrival of the internet and the dotcom boom and bust that still resonates today in the memories of those who lived through that period.

Bill Gates's "Tidal Wave Memo" is on display in a video presentation at the Computer History Museum in Mountain View, CA (Figure 6.8). In it, he makes clear his intention to focus the company's efforts online with immediate effect and "assign the Internet the highest level of importance," going on to call it "the most important development to come along since the IBM PC was introduced in 1981."

The 1993 release of Mosaic and subsequent web browsers during the following years gave computer users access to the World Wide Web, popularizing the use of the internet.[33] Between 1990 and 1997, the percentage of households in the United States owning computers increased from 15% to 35% as computer ownership progressed from a luxury to a necessity and the growing computer literacy benefited internet usage.[34] This marked the shift to the Information Age, an economy based on information technology. Internet companies that would provide access, search engines, and social and e-commerce services started to emerge in the mid-1990s.

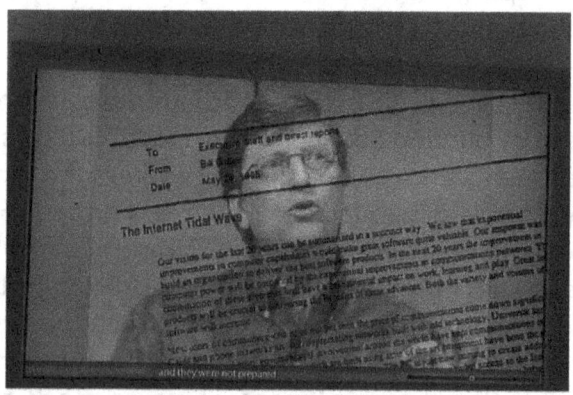

Figure 6.8   Bill Gates's "Tidal Wave Memo."
Source: CHM / Mountainview / CA.

---

[33] Kline (2003).
[34] US Department of Labor (1999).

AOL was one of the early pioneers of the internet in the mid-1990s. It originally provided a dial-up service to millions of Americans. By 1995, AOL had about three million active users.

Founded in 1994, Yahoo! represented the internet as far as many early users were concerned—a webpage that offered (free) email, information and news, search, and messenger. A one-stop destination for many internet users.[35] Even Microsoft used Yahoo! search until 2006.[36]

Netscape was founded in 1994 and developed one of the first commercial web browsers that made it easy for people to access the World Wide Web. After only 16 months and still unprofitable, it went public in 1995. Netscape made an incredibly successful IPO (closed 250% above the IPO price on the first day of trading) which symbolizes the point in time when the internet transitioned from being primarily a tool for academia and tech enthusiasts to becoming a mainstream platform for information, commerce, and communication. The Netscape IPO is called "the Netscape Moment" as it marked the beginning of the dotcom boom and a remarkable surge in public excitement and enthusiasm surrounding internet-related companies and technology during the late 1990s (see Figure 6.9).[37] A combination of rapidly increasing stock prices and confidence that the companies would turn future profits created an environment in which many investors were willing to overlook traditional metrics, such as the price-earnings ratio, and base their confidence on technological advances, leading to a stock market bubble.

Investors were eager to invest, increasingly at any valuation, in any dotcom company. The IPO boom reached its peak in 1999. Examples of dotcom companies are:

- **TheGlobe** was a social networking site founded in 1994 and went public on November 13, 1999, with shares closing up more than 600% from their offering price.[38]

---

[35] Yahoo!'s latest chapter is still unfolding. In May 2021. it was sold (together with AOL) by Verizon to private equity firm Apollo for $5 billion.
[36] Lump (2015).
[37] *The Economist* (2010).
[38] Kawamoto (2002).

Figure 6.9 Marc Andreessen on the cover of *Time magazine*, February 19, 1996, vol. 147, no. 8. The Silicon Valley entrepreneur in sweater and jeans became the symbol of the 1990s.
Source: TIME/Marc Jones. https://content.time.com/time/covers/0,16641,19960219,00.html

- **Priceline**, which offered unsold airline seats to online customers, went public in March 1999 at $16 per share. It reached $88 on its first day of trading before closing at $69. The closing price implied a market capitalization of $9.8 billion, making it the largest first-day valuation of an internet company at that time.

- **Qualcomm** developed the industry standard for mobile communication and thus the basis for 3G and 4G networks. Its shares increased in value by 45% on the first day of trading when it went public in 1991. In October 1999, its share price reached an intra-day high of $92, a 172x increase over its IPO price.[39]

The boom was not confined to the USA. Investors got excited about dotcom IPOs all over the world. The Neuer Markt in Frankfurt, the

---

[39] After the dotcom boom turned to bust, its share price dropped by 85% and would only reach the previous high again in April 2020.

Nouveau Marché in Paris, and Euronext in Amsterdam came into existence as pendants to NASDAQ while cities competed to be the Silicon Dublin, Berlin, Paris, Tallinn, etc. of Europe.

An example that was even made into a movie,[40] Biodata (founded by Tan Siekmann)—a company that developed network security components—went public on the German Neuer Markt in 2000. The shares issued at EUR 45 were initially listed at EUR 240 and posted the highest subscription profit ever achieved on the Neuer Markt. On the first day of trading, the price continued to rise to EUR 302; the peak price of EUR 439 a short time later gave the company that claimed sales of around EUR 23.5 million a market capitalization of over EUR 2 billion.[41] After a consolidated loss of EUR 70 million in the first nine months of 2001, Biodata filed for insolvency in November 2001.[42]

A Gold Rush

In 1999, 12 internet companies that went public increased in value by more than 1,000%. From 1990 to 1999, there were 5,724 IPOs (not all of them internet-related), which exceeded the IPO count for the next two decades—combined—by 1,455 offerings, or 34%.[43] Between 1995 and 2000, the NASDAQ Composite stock market index rose 400%. It reached a price-earnings ratio of 200, dwarfing the peak price-earnings ratio of 80 for the Japanese Nikkei 225 during the Japanese asset price bubble of 1991.[44] Even though the NASDAQ Composite rose 85.6% and the S&P 500 increased 19.5% in 1999, more stocks lost value than gained value as investors switched to internet stocks (Figure 6.10).[45]

An unprecedented amount of retail investing occurred during the boom, and stories of people quitting their jobs to trade on the financial market were common. The news media took note of

---

[40] *Weltmarktführer—Die Geschichte des Tan Siekmann*, a film by Klaus Stern, produced for the German public television (ZDF), was released in 2004 and is also available on Netflix.
[41] ChannelPartner (1999).
[42] Kuri (2001).
[43] Brewer (2020).
[44] Teeter (2017).
[45] Norris (2000).

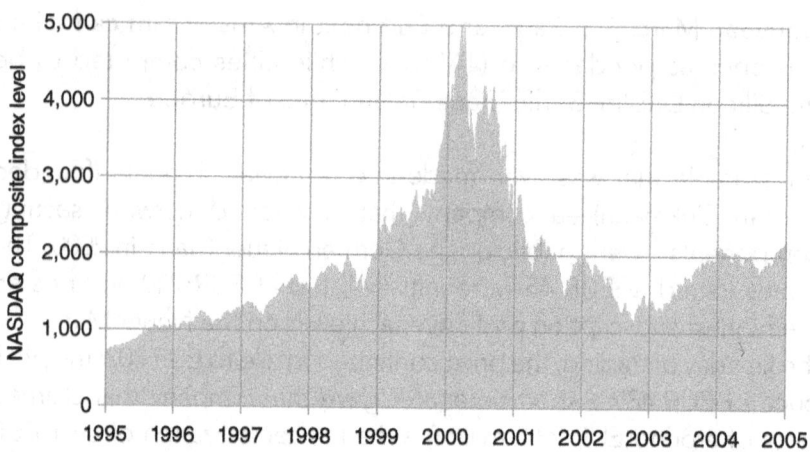

Figure 6.10 The NASDAQ Composite Index 1995–2005.
Source: Adapted from NASDAQ.

Note: The NASDAQ Composite index spiked in the late 1990s and then fell sharply as a result of the dotcom bubble burst. Founded in 1971, "Nasdaq" was originally derived from the abbreviation for the National Association of Securities Dealers Automated Quotations. Initially, it functioned as a mere "quotation system," but in 1998, it made history as the first stock market in the United States to conduct online trading and is particularly known for listing technology-based companies.

the public's desire to invest in the stock market; an article in *The Wall Street Journal* suggested that investors should "rethink" the "quaint idea" of profits, while CNBC reported on the stock market with the same level of suspense as many networks provided to the broadcasting of sports events.[46]

Blitzscaling, 1990s-Style

The arrival of the internet also came with a change of the investment paradigm. Clayton Christensen's theory of disruptive innovation and the "scale fast, get big or get lost" investment paradigm of the dotcom era represent two very different approaches to business growth and innovation.

Disruptive innovation, as described by Clayton Christensen, is a process by which new technologies or business models emerge and ultimately displace established players in an industry. This

---

[46] Wysocki (1999).

often happens in a bottom-up manner, as smaller or newer companies are able to identify and serve previously overlooked customer needs or segments, while larger incumbents are often constrained by their existing business models and processes. Christensen emphasizes startup growth, but he stresses that startups should prioritize growth only if it helps them become profitable and competitive.

In contrast, the startups of the dotcom era aimed to rapidly scale their user bases and achieve massive valuations through aggressive investment and marketing strategies. This approach was often characterized by a focus on user acquisition over profitability. Most dotcom companies incurred net operating losses as they followed the example of Yahoo! and AOL, which spent heavily on advertising and promotions to build market share or "clicks" and "user traffic" as fast as possible. Internet startups used mottos like "get big fast" and "get large or get lost" to reach ubiquity.[47] These companies had a business plan that promised to "change the world"; they offered their services or products often for free or at a loss to gain that market share with the expectation that they could build enough brand awareness to charge reasonable rates for their services in the future.[48]

Behind the "growth over profits" mentality and the aura of "new economy" invincibility was a belief that in network industries, the "winner takes all" logic forces startups to race for scale before competitors achieve it. The investment thesis behind it was Metcalfe's law. Coined by Robert Metcalfe, the inventor of Ethernet, Metcalfe's law states that the value of a communications network is proportional to the square of the number of connected users of the system, i.e., a single phone is useless, but the value of the system increases with every phone connected. Only later, with the globalization of the internet, was this law taken to apply to users. The mental shortcut taken by some was that if the value of the network follows a power law, so must the value of the companies that have a presence on the web as the number of their users increases. This argument was used across the board regardless of whether the

---

[47] Berlin (2008a).
[48] McCullough (2018a).

company would provide network access, an online wine store, or a social network. To dash for growth, VCs would induce founders to accept large amounts of capital—often more than they asked for.

The First "Super-Round"

SoftBank participated in a Series B round with $5 million in late 1995. Four months later, SoftBank President and CEO Masayoshi Son made a move never seen before by offering another $100 million for an additional 30% of the company. Within four months, the valuation of Yahoo! had increased from $40 million to $300 million. The founders said they did not need the money but were told that if they did not accept the investment, Son would invest in their competitors, Lycos and Excite. With this convention-breaking move, M. Son took the logic of "winner takes all" to the consequence: who has the most money wins. But it also taught early-stage investors (in this case, Sequoia) the lessons that they might consider raising larger funds to be able to match such bids and avoid the dilution, which they would otherwise face. Branded internet companies faced an imperative to grow, creating an opportunity for investors to provide growth capital.[49] This was an extreme example of a trend of pouring increasing amounts of money into startups—frequently more money than founders were prepared to handle. This led some companies to spend lavishly on elaborate business facilities and luxury vacations for employees. Upon the launch of a new product or website, companies would organize "dotcom parties" (Figure 6.11).[50]

In October 1999, 199 internet stocks that were tracked by Morgan Stanley's analyst M. Meeker had a combined valuation of $450 billion. But the total annual sales of these companies came to only about $21 billion and the collective losses totaled $6.2 billion.[51]

---

[49] Masayoshi Son went on to bet on at least 250 internet startups between 1999 and 2000 and placed large bets in later rounds of Geo-Cities, Webvan, and E*Trade (though in a post-IPO round as E*Trade had already gone public). Several of the transactions were hugely profitable; for example, Son is reported to have more than doubled his money when Yahoo! went public less than a month after his investment. SoftBank and Yahoo!'s story is quoted from S. Mallaby's book, *The Power Law* (Mallaby, 2022).

[50] Cave (2000).

[51] Quoted from McCullough (2018a).

Figure 6.11   (a) Razorfish founders Craig Kanarick and Jeff Dachis threw a party at which—allegedly—drag queens served 4,000 White Castle burgers to guests. (b) Have times changed? WeWork has been known for its extravagant Halloween parties (scene from WeWork's 2015 party).
Source: Vimeo / Insider Inc.

At the height of the boom, it was feasible for a promising dotcom firm to go public via an initial public offering (IPO) and receive a significant amount of money even if the company had never earned a profit—or, sometimes, no revenue. Employee stock option holders became instant paper millionaires when their firms went public.[52]

As the bubble grew bigger, rising VC activity in Europe and receptive IPO markets prompted US VC companies to invest abroad. Several prominent US GPs, including Benchmark, Sequoia, Accel, and others, opened European offices in 1999–2000.

6.6   THE TELECOM BOOM

But the stock market boom was not confined to internet companies, which, in terms of total investment amounts, attracted less capital than cable and telecom companies. Home internet mainly was dial-up (VPN) in the 1990s. Even that was unavailable to most US households. Cable and mobile infrastructure development was hampered by a decade-old underestimation of its commercial potential (see Box 6.2). While the telecom boom is

---

[52]Smith (2012).

often compared to the nineteenth-century railway mania, there was a significant difference: the railway mania led to new legislation to regulate the construction and operation of railways. In contrast, the telecom boom was enabled by deregulation of the industry. The US Telecommunications Act of 1996 deregulated the communications sector and allowed any company to compete. Many firms seized the opportunity and built networks. Government went beyond deregulation and promoted the expansion of networks. The Telecommunications Act also provided funding for high-speed internet and rural and low-income telecommunication infrastructure expansion. Likewise, through the TEN-Telecom program, the EU provided incentives to modernize telecom infrastructure in Europe to create a single market for telecommunications services and support the development of advanced technologies like high-speed internet and mobile communications. For investors, it seemed like a safe bet and many investors were drawn to the telecom sector due to the rapid growth and supposed high profitability of the industry. Compared with dotcoms, telecom companies seemed to be developing tangible assets that had to be valuable in the Information Age:

- fiber-optic networks
- routers and other telecom equipment
- satellites
- wireless systems
- upgraded telephone and cable TV networks capable of providing high-speed internet connections.

New and existing telecom firms expanded due to capital inflows. Digital infrastructure received $1.6 trillion in equity and $600 billion in bonds. Equipment makers invested $500 billion. However, investor "herding" caused overinvestment and overcapacity, duplication, and price competition comparable to the nineteenth-century railway mania.

Investors loved telecom and cable companies. Deutsche Telekom's IPO in November 1996 was a highlight (Figure 6.13). The going-public of Deutsche Telekom had unprecedented publicity and

Box 6.2 How to Get the Future Wrong

In the mid-1980s, when AT&T was still a monopoly, it asked McKinsey & Company about the number of cell phone users by 2000. McKinsey wrote a study that concluded that the number of cell phone users would not exceed **900,000** by 2000. Based on that report, AT&T decided it was a niche business and left it to the regional Bells to invest in signal towers for cell phones. McKinsey underestimated the market as the number of users in 2000 would turn out to be **109 million**.[53]

Had AT&T obtained different intelligence and taken the lead to build up a national cell phone network, the infrastructure would have been in place to benefit from mobile connectivity and data transmission that came when 3G and 4G licenses became available. But AT&T decided there was not much future to it.[54]

The reason AT&T did not pursue the mobile network opportunity is an example of underestimation of the potential of new technology, including the desktop PC, laptops, cellular phones, and the spread of the home internet. The addressable market assessment was based on current features and capabilities. What was overlooked was the rate of technological progress (which is frequently exponential) and its implications for product features, design, and capabilities that would become available only a few years later. When McKinsey & Company published its report, the Motorola 8000X was introduced. Christened "the Brick" by its users, it weighed 2 pounds and had 30 minutes of talk time and 3 hours of standby time.[55] Six years later in 1991, a pocket-sized Motorola MicroTAC Lite model had a talk time of up to 45 minutes or 24 hours of standby time and 2½ hours talk time with an extended-life battery.

---

[53] *The Economist* (1999a), Sorkin (2013).
[54] Lozano (2019).
[55] Ray (2015).

Figure 6.12   Underestimated technology: mobile phones and PCs.
Source: Motorola; laptops: https://en.wikipedia.org/wiki/History_of_laptops.
Pictures: commons.wikimedia CC.04.

Contemporary observers frequently underestimated the potential of new technology, whether it was the cell phone that was deemed a product only for high-powered executives or traveling sales people[56] or the laptop that the *New York Times* regarded as a niche product[57] (Figure 6.12).

Figure 6.13   German Finance Minister Theo Waigel (left), German Minister of Post and Telecommunications Wolfgang Bötsch (center), and Deutsche Telekom CEO Ron Sommer (right) celebrate the successful IPO on November 18, 1996.
Source: Frankfurter Allgemeine Zeitung GmbH. Copyright Owner: *Frankfurter Allgemeine Zeitung*, Ullstein Bild #00018169, Licence nr. 053559.

---

[56] Rajiv (2017), *The Economist* (1999a).
[57] Sandberg (1985).

marketing for a German IPO.[58] A-List television personalities and government officials promoted the "Volksaktie"—the people's share. Of the more than 2.5 million subscribers, over 650,000 were first-time stock investors in a country traditionally wary of equity investments. Only 25% of households owned stocks in 2021, compared to 50% of US homes. Everything started well. Deutsche Telekom rose 700%.[59] When governments in various countries started to hold auctions to allocate radio frequencies for third-generation (3G) mobile telecommunications services between the late 1990s and the early 2000s, the competition to secure those licenses to extend mobile phone offerings from voice to text and data was intense among telecom companies. Spectrum auctions for 3G in the United Kingdom in April 2000 raised £22.5 billion. In Germany, in August 2000, the auctions raised EUR 50 billion.[60] Equity analysts of major investment banks issued seemingly unbiased research reports that supported dotcom and telecom revenue growth projections. Many analysts distorted the facts to help their firms with investment banking. WorldCom had Goldman Sachs's highest equity rating in May 2001, two months before bankruptcy.[61]

6.7 VENTURE CAPITAL

The boom in internet companies and buoyant IPO markets led to a massive increase in VC activity and propelled the growth of the VC industry.

The IPO boom for internet companies had several effects:

1. **Deal-making and fundraising:** The capital invested by venture capital firms was almost a mirror image of the NASDAQ performance. Startups received $3.6 billion in 1994 and that number would rise to a peak of $108 billion in 2000.[62] Fundraising for venture capital funds showed the same trajectory: from around $6 billion at the beginning of the decade, it increased to $106.6 billion in 2000—a record that would stand for 20 years

---

[58] WDR (2021).
[59] *The Economist* (1999a).
[60] *The Economist* (2002b).
[61] Ellis (2008).
[62] Metrick and Yasuda (2021).

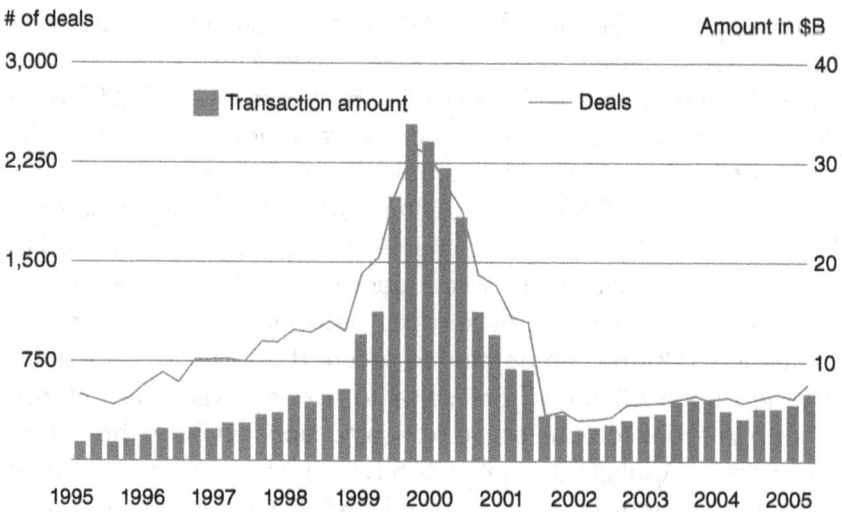

Figure 6.14 Quarterly US venture capital investments, 1995–2005.
Source: Adapted from www.pwc.com/us/en/technology/moneytree.

(Figure 6.14). Both trends are linked as an increase in fundraising was the basis for the increase in startup funding.

2. **Fundraising follows performance:** The performance of venture funds increased from the 1990s until 1997 to new levels. Figure 6.15 shows Burgiss data used in the study by Steven Kaplan et al., and the number of funds in the database shows a pattern that is representative of the overall market.[63] What is clear is the shift of the curve displaying the number of funds for each vintage year. New commitments increased after the vintage years that showed outstanding performance, and new commitments are concentrated in vintage years that posted inferior returns. The best performing vintage years were funds launched during 1993–1996, before the dotcom boom really got momentum.[64]

3. **Time from startup to IPO only declined late during the boom:** Contrary to a widely held belief that Netscape was typical in going public less than two years after it was founded, venture-backed IPOs had a median age of eight to ten years, which was in line with the previous decade. The median age of IPOs was more

---

[63] Harris, Jenkinson, and Kaplan (2015). The Burgiss database covers about 30–40% of funds closed in each year, which represents probably 70–80% capital raised due to the concentration of fundraising and the likelihood that larger funds are captured in the database.
[64] Harris, Jenkinson, and Kaplan (2015).

than six years during 1990–1998. This changed when the boom got going. During 1999–2000, firms that did an IPO got younger. The median age of an IPO firm dropped below five years.[65]

4. **The number of active venture capital firms more than doubled:** The number of active venture capital firms in the USA increased from 400 in 1990 to almost 900 in 1999. Collectively those firms managed $261 billion compared to $30 billion in 1980.[66] (NVCA, 2004). The barrier to entry, i.e., to become a venture capitalist, is relatively low, as one does not need a large fund to invest in early rounds. Indeed, many venture capital firms got established toward the end of the boom when fundraising exploded in 1998–2000.

5. **The performance of venture capital funds was very good.** Steven Kaplan et al. demonstrated that the vintage years 1989–1997 showed average multiples (TVPIs) of 2.5x or more, with a peak of 5.9x average multiple in 1996. Only the last three vintage years, 1998 and 2000, failed to return capital with multiples below 1x.[67] Venture capital funds outperformed public benchmarks in seven out of nine years during the stock market boom (Figure 6.15).

6. **Larger funds performed better than smaller funds:** Another interesting fact that is illustrated in Figure 6.15 is the difference between cap-weighted and median VC returns. If a fund size factor is positively influencing returns, it suggests that established firms (longer track record, more experience) did better as they are the ones that raised larger funds.[68]

7. **Venture performance was driven by IPOs:** In 1999–2000, venture-backed IPOs made up 60% or more of all IPOs, up from 30% in the 1980s and 1990s. Venture capital firms were able to fund and quickly exit many firms because stock investors were willing to subscribe to IPOs of companies without "proof of concept" that their business model would generate revenue and profits. This transferred the risk of a business model failing to public market investors.

---

[65] Gompers and Lerner (2001).
[66] NVCA (2004).
[67] Harris, Jenkinson, and Kaplan (2015).
[68] The observation that better performing managers have larger funds is also found in Robinson et al. (2011).

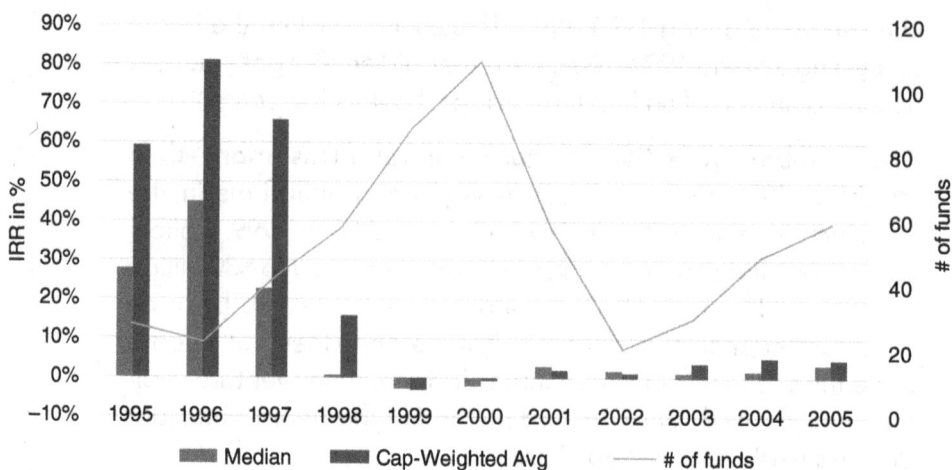

Figure 6.15   Internal rate of return and # of funds raised: US venture capital funds by vintage year, IRR p.a.

Source: Adapted from Harris, Jenkinson, & Kaplan (2015); data: Burgiss Group.

Figure 6.15 shows an increase in fundraising after years of good performance. Despite concerns that the influx of new commitments may have lowered vintage years' performance, the dotcom bust following the 9/11 stock market slump would have happened regardless. In the past, fundraising booms led to overinvestment and herding, which resulted in funding and high valuations for businesses with no viable business model. Although the performance trend remained the same, the excessive capital deployed during those poor vintage years worsened the damage to investors due to their lack of time diversification.[69]

But not all venture capitalists are equal. While the study mentioned earlier does not disclose the names of the venture firms in the sample, one might assume that more established managers raise larger funds. This assumption appears fair, given investors are drawn to managers with a track record of outperformance. Highly regarded venture capitalists are expected to attract more and better deal flow as a result of their increased visibility. Because they have more expertise, they are expected to be able to provide direction and support for their portfolio firms, such as coaching and financial aid, and so increase the likelihood of the venture's

---

[69] See Harris, Jenkinson, and Kaplan (2015). This pattern has also been demonstrated by Eric Sirri and Peter Tuffano in their study of mutual fund flows and they demonstrated investors' reaction to prior performance information. They showed that investors react asymmetrically, investing disproportionately more in funds when performance was very good during the prior period (Sirri and Tuffano, 2002).

success. Academic research confirms the importance of reputation and experience in achieving superior returns.[70,71]

This conclusion is supported by benchmark data from Cambridge Associates, which captures the performance of 459 funds for vintage years 1996–2000 and finds that funds smaller than $150 million performed badly compared to the pooled average of all funds, and funds smaller than $50 million performed the worst, while funds larger than $150 million significantly outperformed the pooled average of the sample.[72] One had to invest in established firms, that continued to have restricted access, and hold commitment budgets steady with the aim of achieving time-diversification of capital deployment rather than following the fundraising boom to catch what was a very successful decade for venture capital.

Investors ignored both rules as many first-time limited partners joined first-time funds. Results plummeted after the dotcom bubble burst.

European Venture Capital

The heightened VC activity was not confined to the USA. Unlike the takeover boom of the 1980s, which was mainly a US phenomenon, the dotcom boom and the surge in venture capital activity also happened in Europe.

Results in Europe were very good, too, during the boom years of the 1990s. The pooled IRR of 48% for the 1996 vintage year suggests that the performance pattern in Europe was similar to the USA. However, the downturn in 2001 seemed to have been more severe as the pooled IRR for 2001 was recorded as –30%.[73] The European performance was also relevant for US investors as they provided about 30% of the capital for European private equity funds (including venture capital).

---

[70] Krishnan (2011), MacMillan (1989), Haagen (2008), Tykvová (2018).
[71] This ties in with more recent research that shows persistence in venture capital return, i.e., firms with previous funds in the top quartile are more likely to achieve future performance in the top quartile of performance, see Kaplan, Harris, Jenkinson, and Stucke (2013).
[72] CA (2017).
[73] Bottazzi, Da Rin, van Ours, and Berglöf (2002) use pooled IRRs (aggregation of all cash flows) and not the median or capitalization weighted IRR displayed in Figure 6.15 showing US VC returns. The numbers are therefore not directly comparable and using them can only give an indication of performance trends in Europe compared to the USA.

In the early 1990s, the annual number of European venture capital funds that closed ranged from 10 to 30. However, by the year 2000, this number had skyrocketed to 228, reflecting the fundraising boom and growth in the number of active venture firms in the United States (Figure 6.16 and Figure 6.17). The expansion of the venture capital industry in Europe was a sign of increased investor interest and a growing recognition of the potential of venture capital to generate significant returns.

Differences Between European and US VC Landscapes

European venture capital investing during the 1990s was distinct in several ways:

- **Size:** The European VC sector was much smaller. During the height of the boom in 1997–2000, European venture capital investment amounted to about $43 billion compared to $199 billion in the USA during the same period.[74]

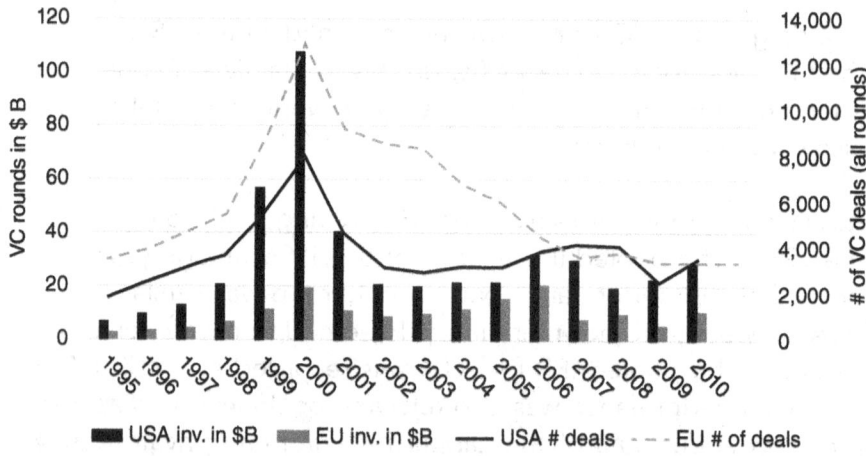

Figure 6.16   Number and volume of VC deals, 1995–2010 in the USA and Europe.
Sources: NVCA data (Bottazzi et al., 2002; Wilson, 2015). European data after 2006: Invest Europe/EVCA (Invest Europe, 2022).
Note: European VC activity data was inconsistent between sources. Deal counts vary greatly. Thus, it is uncertain whether Europe has more venture deals (rounds) than the USA, but its number of deals is higher relative to AuM.

---

[74] It is difficult to state the actual fundraising number for European VCs during the 1990s as many larger firms pursued "generalist" strategies that included venture, growth, and buyout financing. EVCA puts the funds raised in 1999 at about €25 billion. Raade and Machado (2008) and the EIB estimate that total fundraising during 1990–1999 amounted to €100 billion (Christofidis and Debande, 2001).

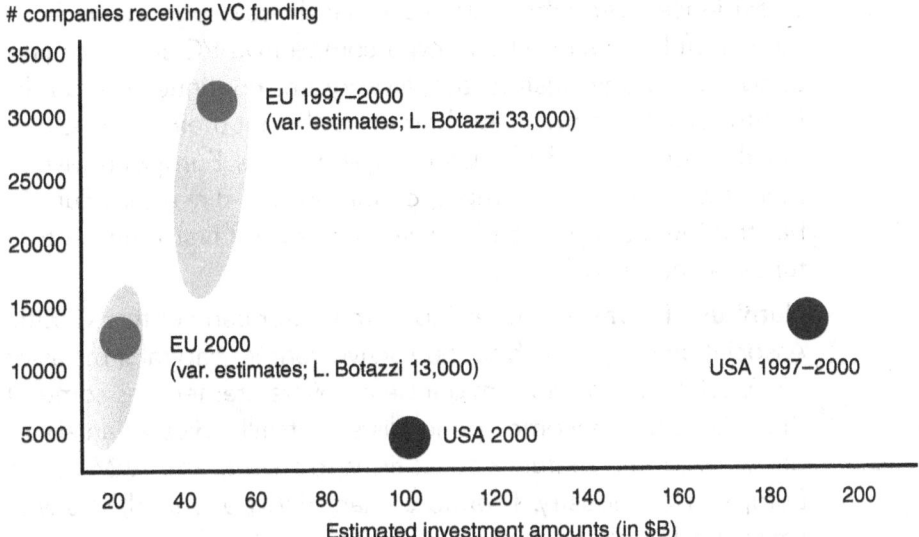

Figure 6.17 VC funding (all stages) and investment amount in $B in the USA and EU.
Sources: Bottazzi et al. (2002), Preqin, Unquote, Crunchbase, and various others have been used by the author to get a range of estimates. Dubocage and Rivaud-Danset (2010) put the number of EU funding rounds in 2000 at 18,000. Note the number of companies might include double-counting if several rounds took place. Counting investment rounds based on GP data may result in multiple counts if more than one GP participates.

- **Role of captives:** Captive and public funds play an outsized role. Venture capital firms dominated VC investment in the USA, while in Europe, captive funds of banks and other corporations accounted for roughly 50% of activity.[75]

- **Government support:** For first-time funds, government incentives (at the country and European level) targeted VC funds. The belief was that more venture capital means more innovation. As a result, many funds were raised that received "special LP commitments" from public sources, enabling funds to launch with limited backing from financial investors.[76] Despite the lack

---

[75] Including captive funds, venture capital investment in Europe was $91 billion during 1997–2000.
[76] Data from Bottazzi, Da Rin, van Ours, and Berglöf (2002), who have published an in-depth study on the subject. Data estimates vary. For example, the size of government sponsorship of venture capital funds ranges from 5% of total commitments to 25% (Bottazzi, Da Rin, van Ours, and Berglöf, 2002; EIB, 2016). Examples of public sources of capital are the European Investment Bank or the special LP commitments conducted by state-owned German Kreditanstalt für Wiederaufbau (KfW) through their "INVEST" and mezzanine funding facilities. This has continued into the 2020s (Lang, 2010; Metzger, 2016; EIB, 2016).

of evidence over almost 30 years that those programs had any meaningful impact on building a competitive VC sector or creating technology clusters, those programs continue. The public institutions that administer them proudly tout their role in building the venture and startup ecosystem. The European Investment Bank (EIB), for example, continues to believe that Europe has too few VC firms and taxpayer support for first-time venture funds is necessary.[77]

- **Number of firms:** Membership of the European Venture Capital Association suggests about 500 active venture capital firms as of 1990. While this number might be an overstatement, as some of those firms had become "generalists,"[78] it still indicates an abundance of (small) venture capital firms relative to the AuM of the European VC industry. Therefore, many (inexperienced) VCs with small checkbooks were likely running around doing small deals.

- **Number of deals:** Various sources suggest that the number of venture capital deals in Europe was greater than in the USA during 1997–2000.[79] While this is unlikely and may include companies that received government startup aid and other mezzanine-type funding from banks, the number of venture deals was certainly very high relative to the size of the VC industry.

- **Focus:** The fact that early round investing accounted for as much as 40% also suggests that rather too many companies are funded relative to the industry's size.

- **Cooperation:** There were fewer syndicated deals. Many European VC-backed firms had only funding from one venture firm, indicating a lack of peer validation of investments between venture capital firms.[80]

---

[77] The European Investment Fund of the European Union stated in a report that government intervention that addresses the shortage of venture capitalists is necessary and highlights their support of first-time funds (EIB, 2016).

[78] Reference is made to firms like Apax or Cinven that historically focused on venture capital but changed their strategy to become a generalist that substantially pivoted toward growth and buyouts.

[79] The number of companies may include double counting as the same company may have received funding in different years. The EIB estimates about 18,500 companies that received venture capital during 1997–1999 (Christofidis and Debande, 2001). While numbers are all over the place, the key fact remains that relative to the size of the European VC industry, there were many more startups funded.

[80] In the USA, venture capitalists participate in each other's deals in second and further rounds to get external validation, to diversify, and to have better visibility where the winners might be (Gompers and Lerner, 2001).

- **Geographic fragmentation:** Mostly venture capital firms, and the startups they funded were domiciled in the same country. The European venture capital scene at the time was best described as a fragmented collection of country markets rather than a continental market. Partly this is due to the risk of double-taxation for funds investing cross-border.[81]

The Dotcom and Telecoms Bust: What Went Wrong?

In January 2000, AOL announced a $180 billion merger with Time Warner. The idea was to combine Time Warner's remarkable book, magazine, television, and movie production capabilities with AOL's 30 million internet subscribers (Figure 6.18). With telecom and cable companies expanding access to the internet, the future potential of content and distribution looked almost unlimited.

NASDAQ peaked on March 10, 2000, at 5,048.62, a level it would not reach again until March 2015.[82] But in January, investors who applauded the AOL Time Warner merger did not see that coming.

Figure 6.18   AOL chairman and chief executive, Steve Case (left), and Time Warner's chairman and chief executive, Gerald Levin, announce the merger of the two companies, in New York.
Source: AP images.

---

[81] EIB (2016).
[82] IB (2021).

There were also warning signs in the telecom sector after a 3G spectrum auction in the United States in 1999 had to be re-run when the winners defaulted on their bids of $4 billion. The re-auction netted 10% of the original sales prices. The telecom companies' assessment of the value of the networks they were building was based on high expectations for user numbers, internet commerce, and the arrival of new economy business models. This, in turn, reinforced investors' excitement for internet companies for whom the sky seemed to be the limit as far as their business models were concerned.

But, in 2000, investors turned bearish on the prospects of the new economy due to several factors, including high valuations, lack of profitability, accounting scandals, increased competition, an economic downturn, and the dotcom bubble burst, which led to the failure of many technology companies. Reasons for the failure are:

- **Overestimation of revenue growth:** The content and connectivity theory, or old and new economy, was based on the expanding number of households with high-speed internet connections (Figure 6.19) and how quickly online enterprises might gain revenue and take market share from established companies. Both bank analysts and firms overestimated customer and revenue growth, which led to inflated valuations. The internet boom and telecoms bust share this feature.[83]

- **The internet was painfully slow:** European and Asian users learned to connect to the internet before the USA got up because it slowed to a crawl. One could download a movie if the VPN connection held for three hours. Internet commerce was increasing slowly because consumers found it disappointing. E-commerce adoption expanded slower than internet

[83] Goldman Sachs and other firms were subsequently found guilty in federal court of breaking the industry's accepted rules of conduct and securities laws in the notorious "analysts case." The case centered on the issuance of bullish research reports that promoted dotcom IPOs despite internal misgivings about those firms' business models and revenue prospects. Goldman Sachs was the most successful underwriter of dotcom firms during 1999–1H 2000 with 65 IPOs. Some 40% of those offerings fell quickly below their offering price, a much higher ratio compared to the IPOs underwritten by other investment banks at the time. Goldman Sachs was fined $110 million, while Morgan Stanley paid $125 million, and the two firms, together with eight other defendants, were required to separate research and investment banking into different organizational units. Quoted from Ellis (2008).

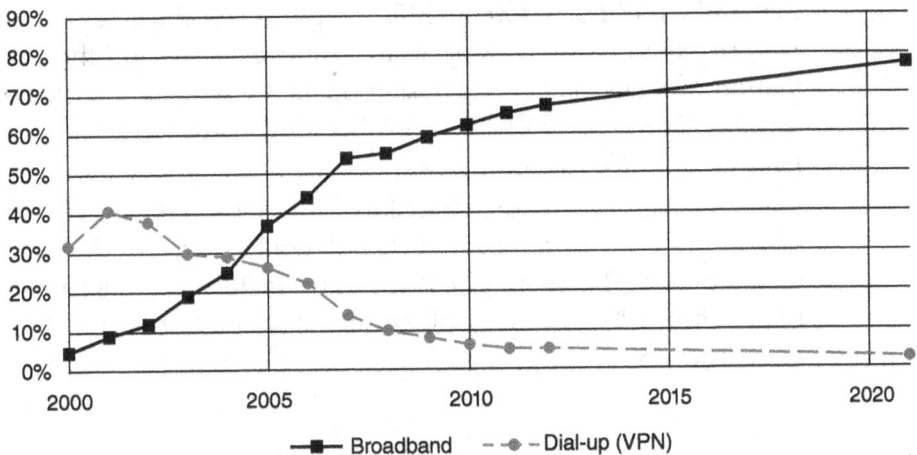

Figure 6.19   Trends in home internet access: the percentage of adults who have broadband vs. dialup, 2000–2012.

Source: Adapted from Pew Internet, American Life Project Surveys, (McNally, 2017).

Note: The chart shows that only from 2005 onwards did broadband access reach dial-up access and only at the end of the first millennium did the coverage include the majority of the population.

users during the decade. In the 1990s, e-commerce also faced a lack of trust in online transactions, insufficient infrastructure for online payments, and a restricted range of products and services.

- **Overinvestment in digital infrastructure:** By 2000, internet connection providers were engaging in price wars as they realized there wasn't enough business, which is a pattern seen before in the history of telecommunications, including telegraph and landline phone networks. This also mirrored developments during the nineteenth-century railway boom and busts.[84] The ultimate cause of the telecom bust was that too many competitors decided to build large and expensive networks for which there was little demand.[85]

- **Overinvestment in internet startups:** Too many internet startups were funded, making it difficult for them to grow profitably due to intense price competition and a fragmented market. The IPO boom created a demand for dotcom companies that neither had to be profitable nor show a compelling business model. The venture capital industry delivered by funding businesses

---

[84] Starr (2002).
[85] *The Economist* (2002b).

that fit the mold of a dotcom IPO company. The chase for a winning business model led again to overinvestment and the formation of many similar business models, for example in online retailing (see Box 6.3 Online Wine Retailer: Wine.com).

- **Leverage in the telecom sector:** When financing became hard to find as the bubble burst, the high debt ratios of these companies led to bankruptcy. Even if default could be averted, investors suffered. The share price of Deutsche Telekom fell to less than half its IPO price. It took about ten years to reach its IPO price again.[86]

Box 6.3   Online Wine Retailer: Wine.com

One area that received attention from the beginning of the commercial use of the internet was the online retailing of wine, which emerged early on as an example of innovative, internet-only business models. Several years later, however, expectations still were not met, with online sales making up only a tiny fraction of overall sales. In 2000, online wine retailing accounted for $100 million, or approximately 0.5% of the total US retail sales, only half of the 1% average share of online commerce). Early estimates of growing the share of online retailers to 5–10% (or $1.4 billion to $2.9.billion) in 2005 proved to be wildly optimistic.[87,88]

Wine.com, formerly known as Virtual Vineyards, exemplifies the consolidation following the dotcom boom (Figure 6.20). Founded in 1994, Virtual Vineyards sold its first bottle of wine online in 1995. Investor David Harmon acquired the company in 1999 and rebranded it as Wine.com. Financial difficulties led to its sale to eVineyard, which eventually reverted to the Wine.com name. In 2004, private equity firm Baker Capital acquired a majority stake for $20 million. Despite financial challenges, the company managed to raise capital and experienced a failed sale at a $75 million

---

[86] *The Economist* (2022a).
[87] Gebauer and Ginsburg (2003).
[88] Swartzberg, Solomon, and Berkman (2000).

Figure 6.20   Wine.com.

valuation. In 2018, it secured $32.5 million in financing from Goldman Sachs.[89] Over time, the company became the largest online wine retailer in the USA, albeit falling short of anticipated valuation levels.[90,91]

An Epic Correction Exacerbated by Fraud

The dimensions of the collapse in the telecommunications industry during 3/2000–3/2002 are staggering. The Dow Jones communication technology index dropped 86%; 23 telecom companies went bankrupt.

Stock markets would take a second hit after the terrorist attack on September 11, 2001, followed by a sharp plunge in the stock market, causing a $1.4 trillion loss in market value.[92]

Then came the Enron scandal. In October 2001, the company declared bankruptcy. The Enron Corporation was an American

---

[89] Baker Capital (2004), Cision PR Newswire (2018).
[90] Information provided on the corporate history of Wine.com is based on Hapgood (1996), Farr (2013), and Peters, (2022).
[91] Tan and Deveau (2020). During the pandemic its revenue got a boost and tried to raise additional funds in 2021 at a reported valuation close to $1 billion but no closing has been reported.
[92] Johnson (2000).

energy company that became the largest seller of natural gas in North America by 1992. Enron pursued a diversification strategy to grow further, expanding into broadband services. The company owned and operated a variety of assets, including gas pipelines, electricity plants, paper plants, water plants, and broadband services across the globe. The company was hiding debt in special purpose vehicles and overstated its revenue from its broadband assets. Those inflated revenue numbers may have also lent credence to the boom in internet companies and their soaring valuations. The discovery that those revenue numbers were fake further undermined trust in the viability of many internet startups and their business model. Its accounting firm, Arthur Andersen, was effectively dissolved. Enron was cited as the most extensive bankruptcy reorganization and biggest audit failure in US history.[93]

In the summer of 2002, the even bigger bankruptcy of WorldCom roiled the markets.[94] Again, accounting irregularities and inflated earnings related to their cable business played a role and resulted in criminal investigations and, ultimately, prison sentences for senior executives. In July 2002, WorldCom, America's second-biggest long-distance phone company and the largest mover of internet traffic, went bankrupt following a massive accounting fraud. It was the biggest corporate bankruptcy in US history.

By the end of the stock market downturn of 2002, stocks had lost $5 trillion in market capitalization since the peak. At its trough on October 9, 2002, the NASDAQ-100 had fallen 78% from its peak. It would take 15 years for the NASDAQ to surpass its previous height, which it did on April 24, 2015.[95]

Over the next year and a half, the number of internet companies that saw the value of their stock drop by 80% or more was in the hundreds. Many of those companies went bankrupt, delisted, or were acquired for token amounts compared to their peak valuations. The same happened to internet companies that were still private, and many of them were held in the portfolios of venture capital funds. It is estimated that at least half of those companies

---

[93] Bondarenko (2022).
[94] Beltran (2002).
[95] Glassman (2005).

were sold or had gone under. By some estimates, Silicon Valley alone lost 200,000 jobs during the following years.[96] Fundraising for US venture capital averaged about $20 billion p.a. during 2001–2005, less than 20% of the funds raised in 2000.[97] As a result many VCs failed to raise successor funds and thus could no longer provide additional funding rounds. While it is difficult to provide a reason why the markets turned when they did, it is relatively straightforward to identify why the lofty valuations in the telecom and internet sector were unsustainable.

Meet the Survivors

The industry faced challenges such as declining revenues and increased competition, leading to mergers and acquisitions among major players. This resulted in fewer, larger companies dominating the market. Additionally, advances in technology, such as the widespread adoption of smartphones and the growth of internet services, also reshaped the industry. Major consolidators included AT&T, Verizon Communications, and Deutsche Telekom. These companies acquired smaller competitors and expanded their market presence through mergers and acquisitions. These consolidations allowed them to increase their market share, improve their competitiveness, and diversify their services offerings.

Deutsche Telekom, which had the biggest IPO in 1996 and also saw its share price plummet after the dotcom bust, is still Europe's largest mobile and internet operator. Deutsche Telekom benefited from post-2000 sector consolidation and acquisitions. T-Mobile USA held 24% of the US wireless market in 2022.[98] Despite its resilience, investors' patience was tested as Deutsche Telekom's shares were trading barely at their IPO price by the year's end of 2021, which was still around 80% below their March 2000 peak. Deutsche Telekom then had a 12x P/E, down from 35x in 1999.[99]

---

[96] McCullough (2018a).
[97] NVCA (2022).
[98] CSI Markets (2022).
[99] GuruFocus (2022).

Verizon Communications, which traces its origin to a joint venture established in 1999 between Bell Atlantic and Vodafone Airtouch PLC, also saw its share price collapse by more than 60% in 2002. Thereafter, Verizon acquired several wireless phone companies and assets across the USA, and the company is today the largest wireless company in the United States.[100] Despite the strong growth of its business, it took 12 years for its share price to reach its peak of 1999 again. But its stock kept rising and exceeded its dotcom peak by 2.5x in 2021.

During the dotcom boom, while many internet companies went out of business, there was consolidation among tech companies across various sectors. In the e-commerce sector, consolidation was driven by the need to achieve economies of scale, increase market share, and offer a wider range of products and services to customers. Amazon, Walmart, and eBay emerged as dominant players. In the search and online advertising sector, consolidation was driven by the need to acquire technology and expertise to improve search algorithms and better target advertising, with Google reaching pole position. The consolidation in the social media sector was driven by the need to acquire user data and increase network effects, with Facebook thriving through acquisitions and organic growth. Some of the survivors and key players that emerged from the consolidation include:

- Amazon
- Google (now Alphabet)
- Apple
- Facebook (now Meta)
- Microsoft.

These companies have since become dominant in their respective industries and have continued to grow and expand their reach. They have also acquired smaller companies to increase their market share and enhance their product offerings. Some of those companies are among the most valuable companies in the world today (Figure 6.21).

---

[100] Reuters (2013b).

NVIDIA, SANTA CLARA, CA (1993)
Founders: Jen-Hsun Huang (AMD, LSI Logic), Chris
Malachowsky (HP, Sun), Curtis Priem (Sun). Seed-
round provided by Sequoia.

YAHOO!, STANFORD, CA (1995)
Founders: David Filo (Stanford), Jerry Yang
(Stanford)
Funding from Sequoia.

JUNIPER NETWORKS, MOUNTAIN VIEW, CA (1996)
Founders: P. Sindhu, B. Liencres (Sun
Microsystems), Funding from Kleiner Perkins.

TENCENT, SHENZHEN, China (1998)
FoundersCharles Chen, Chenve Xu, Jason Zena, Pony
Ma, Zhidong Zhang. Initial funding by IDG Technology
Ventures and PCCW a division of a South African media
company.

AMAZON, BELLEVUE, WA (1994)
Founders: J. Bezos
Funding: 20 individuals, Kleiner Perkins.

EBAY, SAN JOSE, CA (1995)
Founder Pierre Omidyar (Claris/Apple, Ink
Development). Funding of $6.7 million for
series A provided by Benchmark.

Google, MELO PARK, CA (1998)
Founders: L. Page, S. Brin
Funding: A. Bechtolsheim (Sun Microsystems),
Kleiner Perkins, Sequoia.

PAYPAL, PALO ALTO, CA (1998)
Founders: P. Thiel, Y. Pan, K. Howery, L.
Nosek, M. Levchin. Funded by Nokkia
Ventures, Idealab Ventures, DB, GS

ALIBABA, HANGZOU, CHINA (1999) Founders: Jack
Ma, Joseph C. Tsai, Zhang Ying, Trudy Dai et al.
$5 million seed financing and led by Goldman Sachs,
Eight Roads Ventures, and a further $20 million
investment by Softbank that same year.

Figure 6.21   Startups with more robust business models, such as eBay, Google, and Yahoo!, survived in the USA, and Tencent or Alibaba survived in China.
Source: Nivida; Yahoo; Juniper; Tencent; Alibaba Group; Amazon; eBay; Google Inc.; PayPal.

They were joined by a group of Chinese startups that were founded in the late 1990s.[101] In the USA, companies like Google, PayPal, and Amazon were able to survive the dotcom boom due to their strong

---

[101] China did not experience a dotcom boom in the 1990s as the Chinese economy was still in the early stages of its transition to a market-based system, and the country's telecommunications infrastructure was not yet fully developed. In the late 1990s and early 2000s, China began to develop its internet infrastructure and liberalize its telecommunications market. This paved the way for the growth of the internet and e-commerce industries in China. Many Chinese internet companies emerged in the early 2000s, such as Baidu, Alibaba, and Tencent, and they started to gain traction in the market.

cash positions, a focus on their core areas rather than trying to be all-encompassing platforms, and the introduction of revenue-generating services. In Google's case, AdWords, introduced in October 2000, marked the beginning of Google's revenue generation from advertising. Confinity launched a money-transfer service in March 2000 (when it was renamed PayPal), which started to generate revenue from transaction fees for online payments. These factors allowed them to maintain investor confidence, weather the storm, and emerge as successful and enduring companies.

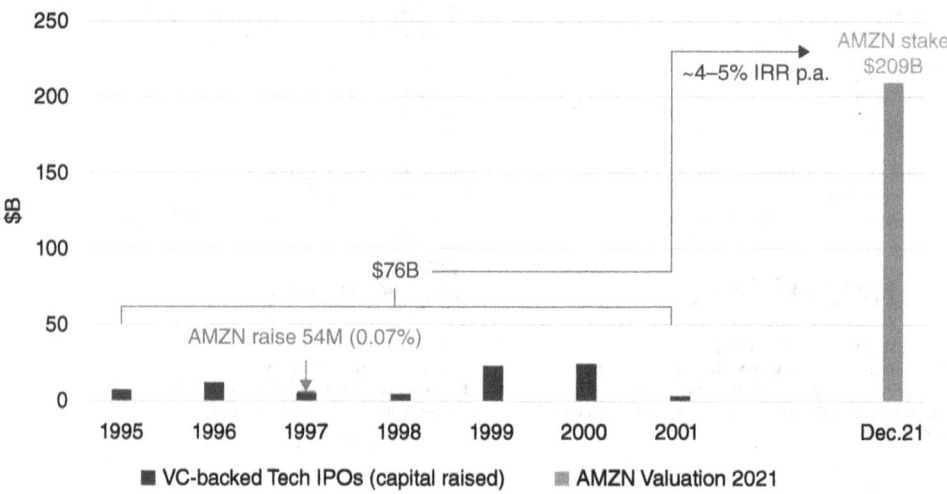

Figure 6.22 VC-backed IPOs during 1995–2000 (new capital raised on IPO) until 2021—Amazon alone would have turned a profit.

Source: NVCA (2011), Kawamoto (1997); display and calculations by the author.

The success of some companies that went public during the dotcom boom, such as Amazon, also challenges the conventional belief that the boom was a losing game for investors. Amazon's initial public offering in 1997 raised $54 million and gave the company a market value of $438 million, demonstrating that the dotcom boom was not necessarily a losing proposition for all investors.[102] Between 1995 and 2000, venture-backed IPOs raised about $76 billion in new capital.[103] If one had bought all the shares at the

---

[102] Kawamoto (1997).

[103] NVCA (2011). It is difficult to provide an exact figure for how much new capital was raised by all venture-backed IPOs during the dotcom boom as it depends on how the data is defined, but it is estimated that around $70–80 billion was raised from the public through venture-backed IPOs during the dotcom boom. This number excludes shares offered by insiders that increased the offering to the public.

IPO and held them indefinitely, assuming all companies except Amazon were losses, one would still own Amazon shares, which were offered at $54 million (total capital raised at IPO) and reached a market value of $209 billion in 2021, when Amazon was worth $1.69 trillion. Overall, investments in dotcom IPOs over a 12.7-year cap-weighted holding period yielded an 4–5% annual return and at least a 2.75x multiple on investment. This thought experiment, which ignores any gains from other IPOs of the dotcom era shows that a bubble may not be irrational (see Figure 6.22).

European VCs: Overheating and Then Running Out of Steam

European venture capital emerged in the 1990s. Many venture funds were receiving capital for the first time from first-time investors. Banks and corporates as investors played a stronger role, compared to the USA. This resulted in structural differences between the US and European venture capital markets that had dramatic consequences. There were too many venture firms with too little capital, and that development partly reflects the presence of public actors that pursued a mission to "get venture capital going" by acting as LPs in funds. As a result, too many deals were usually done in-country with a lack of focus—probably also due to lack of resources—to identify "best-in-class" opportunities Europe-wide. Captive funds played an outsized role, and as those funds would mostly shut down after the dotcom bust, this aggravated the decline in deal-making after the dotcom bust.

Because European VCs spread their investments across a larger number of firms, they struggled to provide later-round financing. The challenge in Europe, according to one observer, "is not finding your $1 million or $10 million startup money; rather, it's securing a $50 million or $100 million funding round. This is where it gets difficult."[104] The unicorn boom in the second decade of the millennium would serve as proof of this claim, as US venture capital firms accounted for a sizable portion of the late-round funding that created European unicorns.

The prospects of European startups receiving additional funding rounds to help them reach a critical size were thus much worse

---

[104] Source prefers to remain anonymous.

than for US startups. Investors faced more write-offs as companies were running out of money. Posting heavy losses GPs would find it difficult to raise successor funds, which aggravated the lack of capital that the European industry faced after the bursting of the dotcom bubble.

In hindsight, few European VCs were established during the 1990s that made it to the top ranks of venture capital firms. One example is Index Ventures, which originated in a Swiss bond-trading firm called Index Securities. Index Ventures was officially founded in 1996 by Neil Rimer, David Rimer, and Giuseppe Zocco, when they raised a pilot fund of $17 million. A $180 million fund followed in 1999. In 2005, Index Venture's third fund raised Euros 300 million; just two years later, it raised a further EUR 350 million for its fourth fund. This is the continuity in fundraising that established US firms showed after the dotcom bust, but very few European firms were able to do.[105]

Performance is clearly one of the reasons for this discrepancy. As reported by Harris et al.,[106] European venture capital underperformed US venture capital by a very wide margin for the vintage years 1994–1999, and that underperformance continued for the vintage years 2000–2010, although the gap narrowed somewhat.

From 1994–2010, European venture capital barely exceeded a public equity return, regardless of the benchmark (S&P 500 in $ or MSCI Europe in EUR). Unsurprisingly, US investors focused on US funds, while many European investors did the same or abandoned the asset class altogether.

Even more than 20 years later, the share of European venture capital investments in later rounds is substantially smaller than in the USA. An analysis of British venture capital in 2021 gave the UK venture capital industry a 14% share in global financing rounds up

---

[105] Powell (2001), Butcher (2011). Today Index Ventures is still one of Europe's most recognized venture capital firms with headquarters in London and San Francisco. In 2021, it was among the top 20 venture firms globally with about $4 billion AuM. Past investments include Dropbox, Facebook, Etsy, and Skype.
[106] Harris, Jenkinson, and Kaplan (2015).

to $1 million but only a 6% share in financing rounds between $1 million to $100 million. Nothing has changed since the 1990s.[107]

What Was Left Behind?

The corporate bankruptcies and the failure of numerous telecom firms around the world not only caused investors losses that were 10x bigger than the dotcom bust but also raised systemic fears due to the loan exposure of the banking system. In 2000, A. Greenspan advocated reducing interest rates after the dotcom bubble burst. He did so again in 2001 after 9/11, the World Trade Center attack (see Chapter 7 for details), continuing a trend of declining interest rates that had started in the 1990s. Fueled by excessive debt, the telecom crash proved to have greater significance by contributing to the subsequent economic recession. In contrast, the losses resulting from the dotcom crash were of lesser magnitude and had a milder impact on the overall economy. When seeking historical parallels, the dotcom boom shared similarities with the English Patent Boom, while the debt-fueled telecom boom bears a greater resemblance to the South Sea and Mississippi bubbles.

Further consequences of the dotcom crash were the passing of the Sarbanes-Oxley Act on July 30, 2002, and NASDAQ raising the bar for a listing.[108] The new listing requirements and the increased reporting and disclosure requirements combined increased the cost of being a public company and lengthened the time it took to become IPO-ready. VCs had to brace for longer holding periods before IPOs, with fewer IPOs, and consequently lower IRRs going forward.

VCs had to rethink their funding plans as there was no hope for an exit of many of those companies, and it would take much longer and require more funding to see those firms through. Faced with heavy losses, venture capital firms struggled to raise new funds, and fundraising in the United States fell by more than 90% until 2002. It took until 2021 for US VC funds to break the previous record of $106 billion raised in 2000, when they raised $121 billion.[109]

---

[107] *The Economist* (2022b).
[108] Among the provisions were a minimum capitalization of $160 million, a three-year earnings record and outside board representation (Marquit, 2021; NASDAQ, 2022a).
[109] Metrick and Yasuda (2021).

The collapse in deal volumes after 2000 meant that much of the uninvested capital—the dry powder—could not be invested during the investment periods of the funds. LPs not only experienced poor performance on their invested capital but also paid fees for money that, in many cases, ultimately was not called to be invested.

Some of the best and worst vintage year performances in recorded history can be found during the ten years from 1992 to 2002. Many investors, especially those who had invested in venture capital for the first time and were drawn in by the high returns of prior funds, soon realized that the funds they committed to would not only fall short of those spectacular returns but frequently failed to show any return at all. The industry declined as many investors excluded venture capital from their asset allocation.

In the 1990s, internet companies offered various services and pioneered many business strategies that would later prove successful. A closer look at online wine retailers shows how slow revenue growth and a lack of follow-on funding have affected many dotcom companies. Many ran out of money and went bankrupt or were acquired cheaply. Even when more capital was raised, earlier investors were squeezed. Holding periods became very long with an IPO or acquisition at an attractive valuation a distant prospect. The investment splurge also showed the perils of overfunding, which undermines the likelihood of success of the collective investments made in a certain sector or sub-sector as the market becomes too fragmented (see Box 6.3 Online Wine Retailer: Wine.com).

After the dotcom boom of the late 1990s, many startup founders learned that the interests of venture capital firms and startup founders can be misaligned. The dotcom boom was characterized by a frenzy of investment in internet-based companies, with many venture capital firms pouring money into startups with little regard for their long-term viability. Founders may have been told by VCs who still had a substantial war chest they were no longer funded because their model was considered to not work anymore. Some VC funds closed and others shifted their focus. A fund's overall prospects may have cost startups funding and attention. As venture capital firms reset their investment strategies, startups suffered.[110] Funding

---

[110] Zider (1998).

companies or business models in anticipation of an IPO before any-one discovers their lack of viability might have contributed to such an outcome. It also highlights a timeless reality: VCs (along with their startups) are essentially merchants of hope. The Amazon example serves as a reminder that the journey to profitability can be pro-longed, even for companies that ultimately succeed. Considering the time constraints imposed by limited partnerships, the ability to go public before a definitive path to profitability is established becomes a prerequisite for generating attractive returns.

Impact on Venture Capital Terms and Conditions

Carried interest is a form of compensation paid to investment executives like private equity and venture capital managers. The managers receive a share of the fund's profits—typically 20% of the total. The experience of the dotcom boom and bust did raise some questions about the legal terms of the partnership agree-ments. In particular, provisions that define the rules for distribu-tions and the calculation of carried interest. A distribution in-kind describes a private market fund distribution that comes in the form of shares rather than cash.

Previously, non-domestic investors and smaller LPs frequently pushed for provisions prohibiting in-kind distributions. They found it costly and time-consuming to sell small share allocations, espe-cially when they were listed on an exchange that was not in the investor's domicile country.

During the dotcom boom, investors and fund managers increas-ingly preferred in-kind distributions, when a portfolio company completed an IPO as share prices often started trading signifi-cantly above their IPO price. GPs were increasingly granted the flexibility to distribute securities to their limited partners rather than sell them. This also can be tax-advantageous, depending on the limited or general partners' tax status.

After the markets turned, that mechanism reversed: when inves-tors received distributed shares, they could be worth a fraction of their "distributed value." Venture capitalists compute car-ried interest using distributions. How is that value determined? IPO? Distribution date share price? Several days before the distribution? Does it matter if the stock is restricted or not? The answers to these questions affect the size of the carry or even whether there is one.

GPs valued the flexibility to do in-kind distributions since it allowed them to avoid selling (occasionally) sparsely traded securities without altering the market price. Both a block sale by the fund and the notification of distribution to investors could hurt the price.[111] After the dotcom bust, investors insisted on the European model for calculating carried interest, i.e., performance incentives based on the entire portfolio and not on the US VC model—a deal-by-deal basis.[112]

6.8   BUYOUTS: AN INDUSTRY LEARNING NEW SKILLS

Beginning roughly in 1992, three years after the RJR Nabisco buyout, and continuing through the end of the decade, the fundraising for buyout funds grew steadily during the 1990s as more institutions began allocating capital to private equity and the emerging FoFs industry recruited additional investors. In 1991, new commitments were estimated at $18 billion, while in 1999, that number increased to about $50 billion.[113] The year 2000 was a bumper year for fundraising with $61 billion in new commitments.[114] Funds also got larger. In 1997, Blackstone completed fundraising for its third private equity fund, with approximately $4 billion of investor commitments.[115] In 1996, KKR completed the fundraising for what was then a record $6 billion private equity fund, the KKR 1996 fund.[116]

---

[111] P. Gompers and J. Lerner (1998) constructed a set of over 700 transactions by 135 funds over a decade-long period, based on the records of four institutional investors. They found significant increases in stock prices prior to distribution and abnormal negative returns immediately after the distribution, pointing to conflicts of interests and governance issues that should be of concern to investors.
[112] The "European Model" is also used by US buyout firms and thus the model using deal-by-deal carry is really a US venture capital model. Top-tier US venture firms did, however mostly maintain the deal-by-deal carried interest model.
[113] Del Ponte (2005).
[114] *Mergers & Acquisitions* (2001).
[115] *New York Times*, October 10, 1997.
[116] Zippia (2022c).

This reflected the growing role of private equity in institutional portfolios, with LPs increasing by number and also by type as pension funds and wealthy private investors were joined by more endowments and foundations as well as insurance companies and banks.

But buyout firms had to consent to the changes to the terms and the conditions those investors demanded in order to continue to raise money. In many limited partnership agreements in the past, there were no restrictions on diversification or single investments. Since then, maximum single investment limits of 15% and other diversification guidelines have become the norm. Provisions that required at least a partial "fee-offset" were prompted by rather high merchant banking and other fees assessed to portfolio companies on top of the management fees paid by investors. Finally, the terms and conditions demanded by investors made it clear that hostile takeovers were no longer permitted.

This all meant that deals would get smaller and more numerous. In addition, both providers of debt and investors that committed the equity in buyout funds eschewed very high leverage, which raised the question of what the comparative advantage of buyout firms would be in such an environment. Financial engineering alone was no guarantee of future performance as the past had seen many instances in which selling shareholders could get a large share of any undervaluation through competitive bidding. In addition, corporations had learned to adopt some of the strategies used by leveraged buyout (LBO) firms, which reduced the number of targets available for the public in private transactions.

This required a new business model, and LBO firms started to brand themselves as buyout firms. How transactions were done and what opportunities were targeted changed. Buyout firms would acquire companies in bankruptcy, co-invest with existing owners, and address complex ownership issues. With leverage reduced, sectors with strong earnings growth potential but higher revenue volatility became more attractive. As the focus shifted from revenue stability to revenue growth, operational plans that took a granular look at the potential for operational improvement became more common. This required differentiated skills in addition to the financial engineering and M&A skills that had been honed during the previous decade's takeover boom. It also led to more staffing that posed a management challenge in its own right.

KKR, the pre-eminent buyout firm of the mega-takeover period, had still only seven partners and a total of 20 investment professionals in 1990.[117] Even during the second decade of the millennium, having only a handful of deal-makers for each billion dollars under management was still not atypical. But they also had a sizable portfolio to manage as it took longer to exit those deals. In combination with smaller deal sizes and more complex and varied value-creation plans, organizations had to grow.

To recruit the talent and to scale up the buyout activities from close-knit firms with a few partners in a conference room to a complex investment organization spanning multiple locations and time zones was a challenge. Any buyout firm would have to manage this transition if it were to continue successfully.

Indeed, questions about how many board seats each partner held, the ratio of investment professionals to the proposed number of deals, the presence of portfolio management and operational support groups, and the plausibility of the proposed fund size would become common items on LPs' due diligence questionnaires. Then there was the question of allocation of carried interest within firms: Would it be pooled or deal-related? Would the deal-team "own" the deal? Should responsibility be transferred to a portfolio management team, responsible for managing and improving the performance of portfolio companies post-investment, or was a hybrid structure appropriate? As the funds grew in number and size, managing those funds through deliberate use of capital recycling,[118] bridge financing to delay capital calls, and other means that

---

[117] Kaufman and Englander (1993).
[118] Proceeds from investments realized early during the investment period can be used to finance new investments and thus allow capital to be used twice, instead of reducing the amount of unfunded capital by returning the proceeds to investors and issuing a new capital call.

enhance IRRs became increasingly common. The growth in central services such as HR, legal and compliance, or IT that came with larger firm size and (often) an expanding office network created additional challenges for incentives and sharing of carried interest and its vesting within those firms. The growth of those organizations also created a widening gap between the ownership of the management company that was typically tightly held by a group of founders and the more widespread allocation of carried interest. Some buyout firms met these challenges and moved ahead while others failed to adapt and (over time) would lose ground.

But the changing deal-making also allowed new firms to rise to prominence. The Thomas H. Lee Partners acquisition of Snapple Beverages, in December 1992, is often described as the deal that marked the resurrection of buyouts.[119] To broaden its geographic reach, Snapple needed more money. The business had been looking for a corporate partner for a while, but its three founding partners were adamant about maintaining control. Finally, Thomas H. Lee reached an agreement with Snapple to purchase 70% of the founders' shares. The sellers were given guarantees that they would keep running the business. While it was a control deal, it shared many characteristics with growth equity including the lack of additional leverage being put on the balance sheet.

This arrangement gave Snapple Beverages the money to pay for the nationwide distribution of its products. Snapple's market share increased, and it started a push to sell its products in foreign markets in 1992, despite the threat of competition from Coke and Nestea, which Nestlé released in February 1992. Through an initial public offering (IPO) in December 1992, 17% of Snapple's stock was made available for $20. As a result of the high demand, the company's stock price rose to $33 on the first day of trading.[120] In 1994, Thomas H. Lee made 32x its equity investment when it sold its stake in Snapple.[121]

---

[119] *New York Times*, April 3, 1992.
[120] *Baltimore Sun*, December 16, 1992.
[121] *Forbes*, July 9, 2022.

David Bonderman[122] and James Coulter completed a buyout of Continental Airlines in 1993 through their nascent Texas Pacific Group (today, TPG Capital). Coulter and Bonderman raised $66 million to acquire a controlling interest in Continental in April 1993. Bonderman brought the airliner out of bankruptcy through a $9 billion reorganization and reversed the company's fortunes considerably. Continental's operating income surged to $716 million in 1997 from a loss of $108 million during the year preceding the buyout. More important for the future capital-raising efforts of TPG, Bonderman was hailed as Continental's savior. By 1998, TPG had generated an annual internal rate of return of 55% on its investment.[123]

TPG also invested in high-tech companies, which other buyout firms rarely considered. They saw that the sector was growing and that IT businesses were expanding while cash flows and sales remained volatile. TPG was among the first buyout firms to broaden their focus on deal opportunities to include technology buyouts. Lucent Technologies (an AT&T subsidiary) announced the sale of its Paradyne business in 1996. TPG bought Paradyne with $52 million in equity and $123 million in debt, installed new management, and split the company into two separate businesses. Paradyne Networks and GlobeSpan went public in 1999, netting TPG and its investors $1 billion in profits (with some equity retained).[124]

The emphasis on distinguishing between financial engineering and operational value creation in buyout deal-making is often overstated. In reality, the significant leverage in such deals compels managers to pay close attention to improving net cash flows and implementing operational enhancements. However, the landscape of buyout deal-making underwent substantial changes after the turn of the millennium. This evolution encompassed various

---

[122] David Bonderman, previously worked for Robert Bass, targeting investments in financially troubled companies, those with labyrinthine financial structures, and companies facing an uncertain regulatory future. These investments had very different characteristics from the undervalued but stable cash flow producing companies that LBO firms focused on during the takeover boom.
[123] Fundinguniverse (2022), Jones (2000).
[124] Jones (2000).

company situations, including minority stakes, expansion financing, buy-and-build, and turnaround efforts. It extended into previously unexplored sectors such as technology and companies that did not have the stable cash flow characteristics preferred by LBOs during the 1990s.

6.9   UK LBOS BECOME PAN-EUROPEAN

Historically, the UK was the dominant European market, with a share in total European transaction volume of over 60%. This reflected the importance of the City of London as a financial centre after the Big Bang deregulation launched by the Thatcher government in 1986 and the UK stock market as the largest in Europe and included a broad segment of midcap stocks. In 1992, the Maastricht Treaty took effect and, with it, the prospect of a European currency and better integration of European financial markets. As the processes of economic activity became more intertwined in the European Union, it became easier to execute cross-border acquisitions and to obtain debt financing for those deals, activity in other European markets increased.

As other European markets became more active, the UK share in buyout transaction volumes would decline to about 50% by the end of the millennium. European investors were initially slow to commit capital to private equity. Still, several banks established in-house private equity teams that provided equity and debt financing for buyouts and sometimes the lead transactions. In 1991, Phillips & Drew and Barings Brothers established such teams, followed by Swiss Bank Corporation (today UBS) with SBC Private Equity and NatWest Private Equity in 1995.

Over time, UK firms such as Candover, Bridgepoint (a spin-out from NatWest), Doughty Hanson, Permira, Apax, Cinven, CVC, and BC Partners as well as some firms that had been established outside the UK, such as Nordic Capital and EQT, became pan-European firms and competed for deals with country-focused managers (at the smaller end of the deal size spectrum).

Those firms were able to build a track record that was on a par with US firms (Figure 6.23), and the experience helped to build an LP

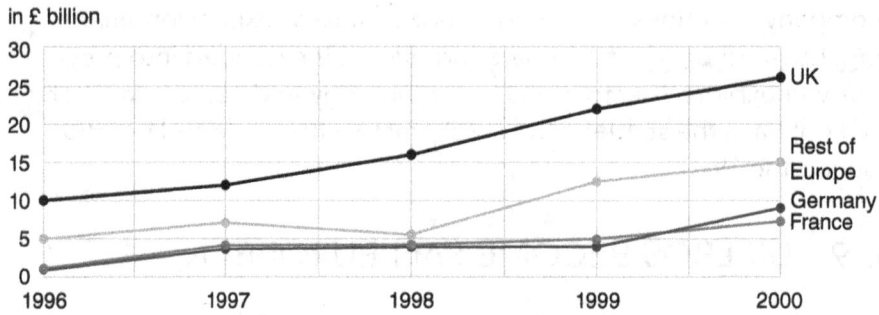

Figure 6.23   European private equity investment by deal value.
Source: Unquote 2005.

base and grow the industry over time. During the 1990s, European buyouts outperformed US buyouts; during the first decade of the millennium, their performance was about equal.[125]

The European firms were joined by US buyout firms opening offices in London.

Toward the end of the 1990s, US buyout firms establishing a European presence included Warburg Pincus (1997), Clayton, Dubilier & Rice (1998), KKR (1998), and Blackstone (2001). Some invested from their global funds, while others established regional funds. Regarding their local presence, some firms operated only from London while others opened offices in various locations in Continental Europe as well.

Performance of Buyouts

Buyout funds had a strong decade, beating the stock market in each vintage year during 1990–2000. The strongest year as far as relative performance goes is the vintage year 2000. In terms of performance, a number of academic studies have looked at the returns generated by private equity funds during the 1990s. For example, a 2002 study by Kaplan and Schoar found that private equity funds raised during the 1990s outperformed public equity markets by a significant margin. Specifically, the study found that

---

[125] Harris, Jenkinson, and Kaplan (2015).

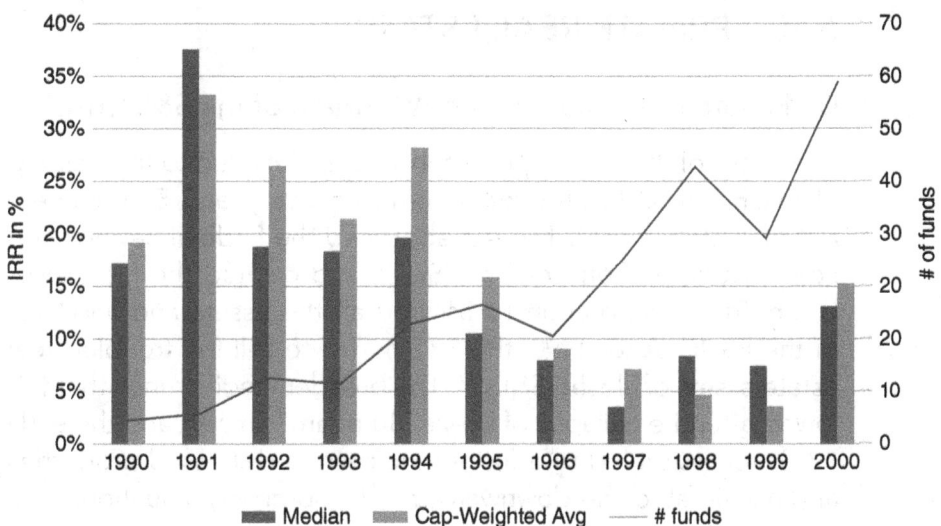

Figure 6.24   IRR and number of funds raised: US buyout funds by vintage year, IRR p.a.
Source: Harris, Jenkinson, & Kaplan (2015); data: Burgiss Group.

private equity funds raised during the 1990s had a median net internal rate of return (IRR) of 16.6%, compared to 9.9% for the S&P 500 over the same period.[126]

The private equity industry saw strong absolute performance until 1995, which declined afterward. Despite this, institutional investors investing directly or through FoFs kept increasing their private equity allocations, as seen by the steady growth of funds raised. Preqin data shows that capital raised globally by private equity funds grew from $13.3 billion in 1990 to $70.2 billion in 1999, reflecting a 20.2% compound annual growth rate (Figure 6.24).[127]

After the dotcom meltdown, investors became even more focused on buyouts as their main private equity strategy. This shift in focus benefited buyouts and the industry entered the new millennium poised for growth. The combination of changing investor attitudes, increased regulatory scrutiny, and the availability of cheap debt financing created a favorable environment for buyouts and helped to spur its growth.

---

[126] Kaplan and Schoar (2005).
[127] Preqin (2020).

6.10   PRIVATE REAL ESTATE

US Private Real Estate in the Aftermath of the S&L Crisis

The onset of the savings and loan crisis in 1986 led to the passing of the Financial Institutions Reform, Recovery, and Enforcement Act of 1989 (FIRREA). The Act abolished the Federal Savings and Loan Insurance Corporation (FSLIC), and created the FRT Resolution Trust Corporation to assume all the assets and liabilities of the FSLIC. After 1990, the FRT began to sell the troubled real estate assets of closed S&Ls.[128] The broader credit crunch that followed after the collapse of Drexel Burnham Lambert and the early 1990s recession led to a further increase in distressed properties and accelerated the downward trend of property valuations (see Chapter 5).

In the late 1980s, Sam Zell and a few others raised institutional capital for limited partnerships to acquire distressed properties. However, subsequent funds were created specifically to acquire property at distressed valuations, frequently by participating in Resolution Trust Corporation–organized block sales of troubled assets. Again, the limited partnership was used, complete with terms and conditions, in particular, fee structures, waterfalls and carried interest that were often identical to private equity limited partnerships.

In the early 1990s, Starwood Capital raised $52 million and acquired 7,000 multifamily units through the purchase of equity and distressed debt from the Resolution Trust Corporation within 18 months. Other private real estate managers such as Goldman Sachs Whitehall Funds, Colony Capital Fund, and Morgan Stanley's MSREF also raised funds, often attracting capital from other financial institutions such as Lehman Brothers and Bankers Trust, who initially invested their own capital in opportunistic funds and only raised funds from third-party investors later.[129] In 1991, with housing at a historic low,

---

[128] Wikipedia (2022c).
[129] All fund information in this paragraph quoted from Douvas (2012).

Blackstone bought several residential properties with the help of a RTC consultant, Joe Robert. Soon after, Henry Silverman, who would later become the founder of private equity firm 54 Madison Partners, teamed up with Blackstone to acquire a number of hotel businesses.[130] These deals were the beginning of Blackstone's real estate business.[131] Blackstone's first European deal—the acquisition of the Savoy Group in the UK—was also partly real estate-related.[132]

After the initial success of the early funds, additional opportunistic funds were raised:

- Apollo Real Estate Partners I ($500 million in 1993).
- Blackstone Real Estate Partners I ($335 million in 1994).
- Westbrook Fund I (a spin-out from MSREF) ($684 million in March 1995).
- Lone Star Opportunity Fund[133] ($247 million in March 1995).

The Resolution Trust Corporation wound down by December 1995. The real estate opportunity in the United States consisted of acquiring and managing hard assets—renovation/rehabilitation and lease-up—while utilizing significant leverage. Capital was returning to the market, and institutional owners started to adjust their portfolios by selling assets. Real estate investment trusts (REITs) were forming to recapitalize troubled developers and re-lever with public debt as market liquidity returned. The real estate market had recovered, rental growth had resumed, and investment activity turned to value-add strategies, making investments in capital-starved assets that needed enhancement. Blackstone's purchase of the Watergate complex in August 1998 for $39 million, which included three luxury apartment buildings with more than

---

[130] Zippia (2022c).
[131] Schwarzman (2019).
[132] Goldsmith (1998).
[133] Lone Star was founded by John Grayken in 1995 and its origins trace back to a joint venture between an investment group and the Federal Deposit Insurance Corporation in 1993, called Brazos Partners, L.P., which was later renamed Lone Star Opportunities Fund.

600 apartments, penthouses, and townhouses, as well as two office buildings, is an example of such an opportunistic investment.[134]

Europe Was Next

In 1996, Western Europe recovered from an economic downturn, leading Lehman Brothers, Cargill, and LaSalle to form a joint venture to acquire a distressed debt portfolio in France from Barclays Bank. As the European economy recovered, demand for commercial real estate grew, leading to opportunities for developing and upgrading existing properties. This led to the establishment of several pan-European or international funds, including Doughty Hanson, Orion, Europa Capital, Soros Real Estate Investors, and Blackstone International. Apollo International and Patron Capital followed.[135]

Opportunities in Japan and Other Parts of Asia

In 1998, non-performing loans in Japan came into focus as the country's economy entered a period of recovery similar to that of Europe five years earlier. Since 1990, Japan had endured the most severe and protracted economic crisis in modern history. The Japanese Financial Services Agency (SFA) increasingly compelled lenders to be strict with weak borrowers, thereby forcing many businesses to restructure or face insolvency. Lone Star, MSREF, Grove International, Starwood, Westbrook, and Whitehall were among the global funds that entered the Japanese market early on. DaVinci Realty ($434 million in November 2002), Aetos ($840 million in December 2002), and Secured Capital Japan ($118.6 million in 2004) raised dedicated funds for Japan. These funds acquired non-performing loans and physical property from corporate restructurings in Japan and expanded to include other Asian countries later. By 2003, non-performing loans in Japan totaled $1.2 trillion, in China, $500 billion, in South Korea, $300 billion, and in Taiwan, $40 billion.[136]

---

[134] *The Journal Record* (1998).
[135] All fund information in this paragraph quoted from Douvas (2012).
[136] Ibid.

Unlike buyouts or venture capital, opportunistic real estate funds mainly relied on financial institutions, family offices, and some endowments for capital. Between 1995 and 2000, each year, between 10 and 60 opportunistic real estate funds were raised and fundraising did not exceed a maximum of $10 billion per year.[137] In the 1990s, pension funds avoided investing in real estate partnerships due to past losses. In addition, pension funds hold real estate investments mainly to receive long-term income and the development of the REITs market provided a chance to invest in core property and participate in the market recovery from 1995 onwards. The rapid shift in geographical focus among opportunistic real estate investors underscores the cyclical nature of deal flow suitable for applying buyout-type transaction models in real estate investing. This cycle is closely tied to forced sellers, often driven by debt market disruptions or regulatory changes. However, the spectrum of available value-creation strategies in this context is comparatively narrower when contrasted with corporate buyouts. While GPs face the challenge of deploying capital when market conditions require this type of replacement capital, LPs need to ask whether a steady allocation to opportunistic real estate is warranted, given the cyclical nature of the opportunity set.

---

[137] Sahling (1991).

Chapter 7

A Private Markets Boom Between Two Crises

The new millennium started with a severe stock market correction after the bursting of the dotcom and telecom bubbles that led to a recession. In response, the Federal Open Market Committee (FOMC) began to lower interest rates from 6.5% in late 2000 to 1% in June 2003–2004. In addition, the FOMC changed its preferred measure of inflation twice in the early 2000s, effectively loosening monetary policy considerably.

The FED's move to support the financial markets became known as the "Greenspan Put."[1] The actions of the FED were also referred to as "back-stopping the market."

---

[1] Miller (2002).

Figure 7.1   Alan Greenspan, Chairman of the Federal Reserve Board, in 2005.
Source: Financial Services Committee / Wikimedia Commans / Public domain.

Low interest rates and abundant liquidity provided by the FED resulted in booming debt markets. Thus began the "free money" era of central banking, coupled with a belief of investors that the FED would support markets.

At last, the economy started to grow again, and Alan Greenspan (Figure 7.1) began to raise the federal funds rate in mid-2004, eventually by more than four percentage points. The period until 2007 mainly saw positive economic growth fueled partly by an unfolding housing boom and supported by low inflation rates that helped the expectation of continued low interest rates. This happened not only in the USA but in most major western economies. The stock market entered five years of positive return that averaged 11% p.a., which is about equal to the long-term rate of return p.a. since 1945.[2] Despite rising interest rates, long-term bond yields continued their decline. The 10-year treasury bond yield stood

---

[2] The stock market performance during that decade reflects the two major corrections after the burst of the dotcom bubble and later in that decade during the Global Financial Crisis (GFC).

at 6.8% at the beginning of 2000 and declined to 2.2% in 2008. As bond yields reached historic lows, investors were looking for alternative sources of income. Insurance companies and pension funds used actuarial rate of return assumptions that were not available in the bond markets anymore. Investors with liabilities to fund faced the most vital impetus to "search for yield." Asset owners, particularly large pension funds, would increasingly look at alternative assets to close the income gap resulting from low bond yields. Of those institutions, the ones that already had invested in private markets started to increase their allocations, while others became new investors in the asset class.

A study by the Pew Charitable Trust that looked at asset allocation trends of 70 US public pension funds showed that between 2006 and 2011, alternative investments had increased from 11% to 23% of plan portfolios. The majority of this growth came from more significant investments in private equity. The study found that the Oregon Public Employees Retirement System and the Washington Public Employees' Retirement System had the highest reported private equity allocation. Both reported more than 20% of their assets in private equity.[3]

Another group of investors that became increasingly significant was sovereign wealth funds (SWFs). In 2012, the Sovereign Wealth Fund Institute estimated that the total assets of these funds increased from $500 million in 1990 to more than $5 trillion in 2012. This asset growth was not just the result of existing funds getting bigger but also their growing number. Some of the largest SWFs established during 2000–2010 include Mubadala Development Company (2002), Qatar Investment Authority (2005), Korea Investment Corporation (2005), Australian Future Fund (2006), Investment Corporation of Dubai (2006), and China Investment Corporation (2007).[4] While not all SWFs are the same, as a group, they became significant private markets investors. In 2012, SWFs invested 9% of their assets under management (AUM) in private markets such as real estate, infrastructure, or private equity funds—representing

---

[3] Pew Trust (2014).
[4] Bernstein, Lerner, and Schoar (2013).

about 10% of the total assets committed to private markets. At the end of 2017, this figure had risen to 30%.[5]

European institutions were slower in adopting private market investments. UK pension funds, for example, accounted for only 5% of funds raised by UK private equity firms in 2005. In contrast, overseas pension funds accounted for 26% during that year. UK pension funds that were allocated to private equity had average allocation of about 3% in 2007—about half the allocation of US pension funds that had a private equity program. Only after 2010 would private equity allocations of UK pension funds reach 6%.[6] Pension funds in other European countries showed similar trends. In Continental Europe, 37% of pension funds had a private equity allocation as part of their investment strategy or were planning to introduce it in 2005, compared to only 13% in 2001.[7]

In Europe, the increase in private market fundraising and deal-making was thus mainly driven by capital from outside Europe. At the same time, domestic institutions provided the bulk of the capital in the USA. In Asia and other parts of the world, significant pension funds and SWFs participated in the asset class. However, much of their capital was invested outside their home countries or regions.

But overall institutional participation in private markets increased steeply from 2004 onwards. It seemed that a switch was flipped, and the Yale Model of investing became a mainstream concept for institutional asset allocation. Whether an institution decided to participate in the asset class or not—it became an asset class you could not ignore.

Occasionally the rise in global interest in the asset class would even surprise the GPs themselves. The head of investor relations of a major European buyout fund recalled receiving a call from NPS—the national pension fund of Korea—expressing a desire to invest in the latest fund offering. That GP did not even have Korea on their list when they did a roadshow to raise funds. But on they

[5] Hannah and Sy (2016).
[6] Pensions Investment Research Consultants (2007).
[7] Avery (2002).

went, and while in Seoul, they also visited KIC—the Korean Investment Corporation. Both institutions became limited partners in the fund but only after they accepted a cut-back of their desired investment amount, which was unavailable due to the fund's maximum size limit (the "hard-cap"). Thus, momentum was building that would change the industry from a cottage industry to a major force in the capital markets during the decade ahead.

7.1 FUNDS OF FUNDS (FoFs) TAKE OFF

The influx of new investors was facilitated by a growing FoFs industry that offered a diversified gateway to the asset class, which was convenient for new investors that lacked a network of GP relations and had no experience in selecting private market managers. Fundraising between 2004–2007 boomed and FoFs became the second largest source of capital after pension funds and ahead of SWFs.

The growing prominence of FoFs that accounted for more than 25% of total capital raised for private equity in 2004 gave a boost to many smaller private equity firms (Figure 7.2). The focus of FoFs to diversify and to demonstrate their network compelled them to invest in country funds and to look at private equity globally. They acted as catalysts for the globalization of private equity investing.

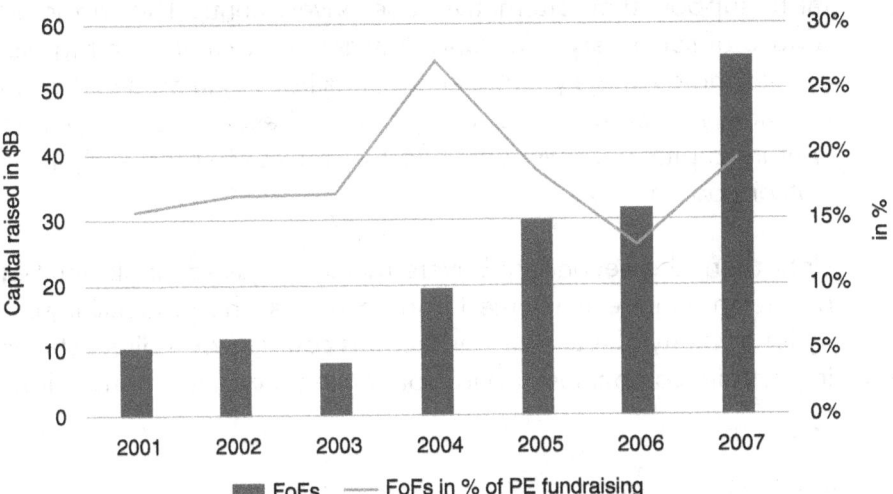

Figure 7.2 FoFs capital raised and share in private equity fundraising, in $B and in %.
Source: Adapted from Preqin.

Investors in those funds achieved internal rates of return (IRRs) that were on average around 10% for vintage years 2001–2003 and then declined to around 6% for vintage years 2004–2007, according to a study by Steven Kaplan et al. that uses both Burgiss and Preqin data.[8] Those performance numbers were below what is commonly expected from private equity (PE) investments, but one must note that the distribution of outcomes around the average was relatively broad. FoFs first commit to partnerships, which then make investments. This implies that capital deployment is slower than a direct partnership, and a lot of capital would be invested during 2007 and 2008, just before the onset of the Global Financial Crisis (GFC).

7.2 SECONDARIES FoFs

The stock market crash at the beginning of the millennium and losses on bonds impacted many financial institutions' balance sheets. Some cash-strapped investors turned into forced sellers of their private equity holdings to generate liquidity. The pressure to sell such holdings also came from regulators. In the late 1990s, regulators in the USA (followed by European regulators later) changed the capital requirements for commercial banks and insurance companies, forcing these institutions to set aside more capital to support their alternative asset investments. This triggered a wave of secondary sales, and that deal flow came with big discounts and gave the young Secondaries FoFs industry a boost.[9] In addition, numerous corporations that had established corporate venture capital units were looking for an exit after the end of the dotcom boom.

Until then, the secondary buyers mainly acquired single limited partnership interests sourced from investors who required liquidity for a variety of reasons. Transactions could involve direct stakes in portfolio companies or participation in funds. Now transactions

---

[8] Kaplan, Jenkinson, Harris, and Stucke (2017).
[9] Probitas Partners (2004).

came in the form of entire portfolios, often representing transaction amounts of several hundred million dollars.[10]

Figure 7.3 shows that fundraising for Secondaries FoFs was much less than for traditional FoFs (see Figure 7.2). Fundraising accelerated after 2000. It peaked during 2003–2004, followed by a relative decline that was much more pronounced than the relative decline in traditional FoFs' fundraising. This points to the more opportunistic nature of secondaries and suggests that investors switch from primary to secondary investments during times of upset as they anticipate more opportunities in the secondary markets.

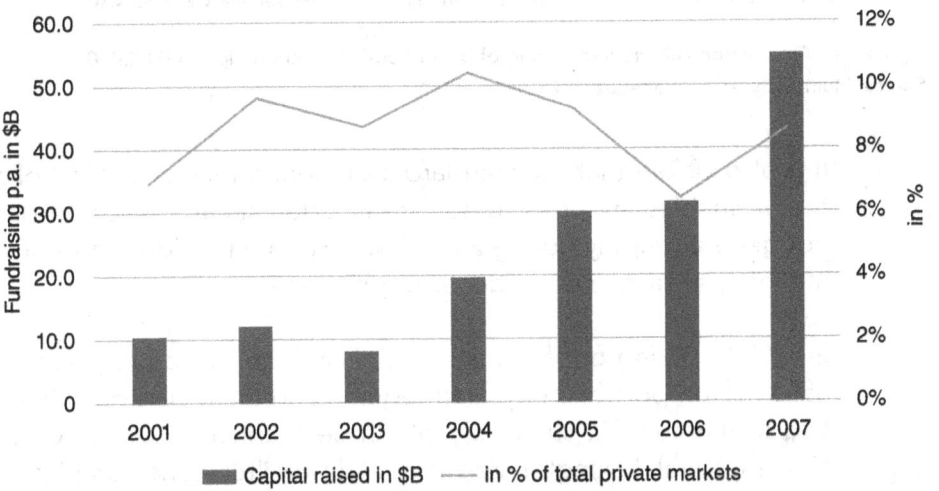

Figure 7.3 Secondaries FoFs capital raised and share in PE fundraising, in $B and %.
Source: Capital Dynamics (2016); Black (2018); Jefferies (2021).

Figure 7.4 illustrates the increases in discounts during 2008–2009 and the surge in transaction volumes during that time. To do those transactions, secondaries FoFs needed more capital. The annual fundraising, about $5 billion from 2001–2003, increased to an annual average of $12 billion from 2006–2008, and individual funds became bigger too (see Figure 7.3).[11]

---

[10] In one of the earliest portfolio transactions, the Crossroads Group acquired a $340 million portfolio of direct investments in large- and mid-cap companies from Electronic Data Systems in 1999 (Cawley, 1999).

[11] For example, Coller Capital raised a record-setting $4.5 billion fund in 2007—twice the size of its predecessor fund. By 2008, secondary deal volume had almost doubled from 2004 levels, to $16.4 billion (Verdun and Chang, 2018).

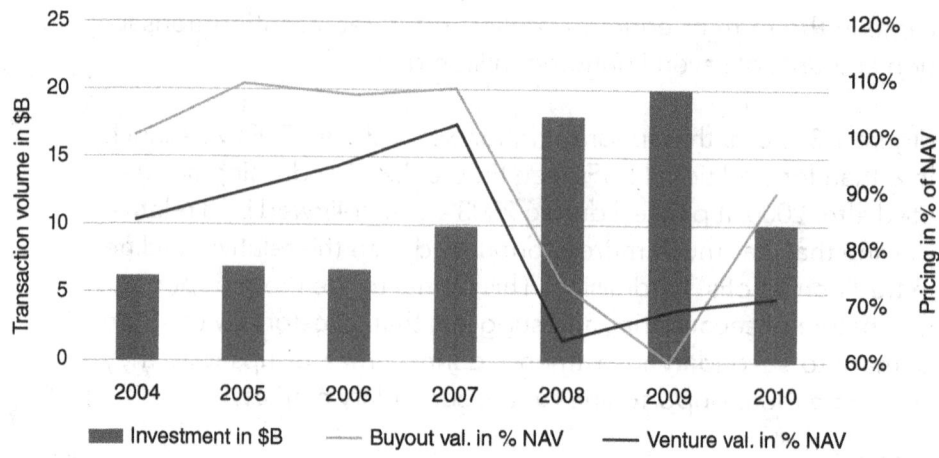

Figure 7.4   Transaction volume and pricing of buyout and VC secondaries, 2004–2010.
Source: Multiplicity (2018); Jefferies (2021).

It is also visible that the standard argument for secondaries FoFs that it enables investors to acquire LP interests at a discount did not generally apply during 2004–2007. Boom times do not generate many attractive secondaries opportunities.

In 2000, Lexington Partners and Hamilton Lane acquired a $500 million portfolio of private equity fund interests from Chase Capital Partners (a subsidiary of Chase Manhattan Bank), while Coller Capital, Lexington Partners, and Hamilton Lane completed a purchase of over 250 direct equity investments valued at nearly $1 billion from former NatWest Equity Partners.[12]

Those transactions are examples of typical portfolio transactions made during that time and the sellers involved. Many large financial institutions (e.g., Deutsche Bank, Abbey National, UBS AG) sold portfolios of direct investments and "pay-to-play" participation in various partnerships established to gain merger and acquisitions (M&A) assignments. Technology companies (but not only those)[13] had established in-house venture teams during the 1990s to get a foothold in promising acquisition targets and identify breakthrough technologies. They, too, wanted to shut down those private market units and sell the investments held on their books.

---

[12] The Royal Bank of Scotland (2000).
[13] Even the oil company Shell and some utilities had in-house venture teams.

If the holdings were venture capital fund interests or direct investments in startups, a management buyout (MBO) was unlikely for the management team as the portfolio often had no hope of achieving a performance that could be used as a track record. In that case, a special purpose vehicle (SPV) was created to manage the liquidation of the portfolio. The team would be taken over and work for the secondary fund that purchased the investments. For example, in 2007, Royal Dutch Shell and Coller Capital announced the sale of 45% of a newly created Shell Technology Ventures Fund 1 BV. The new fund took over Shell's existing portfolio of 34 technology investments and the investment team from Shell that would continue to manage the investments.[14]

If the team was buyout-focused, it would often seek to do an MBO and start a business with a contract to manage the legacy portfolio. At the same time, a large secondary fund would acquire the portfolio and thus become its limited partner. For example, Bridgepoint, a UK-based mid-market buyout firm, was founded as NatWest Private Equity Partners as part of NatWest Group. The firm was renamed Bridgepoint Capital in May 2000, following a management buyout.

After the initial surge driven by forced sellers, the secondary market landscape began to change in the mid-2000s. Public pension plans began to sell assets from their private equity portfolios. In 2004, the State of Connecticut pension plan became one of the first pension funds to sell in the secondary marketplace.[15] In 2005, the California Public Employees Retirement System (CalPERS) decided to create a "legacy portfolio" of non-core assets and manager relationships. When it sold the portfolio in 2007, the NAV was $2.1 billion. The Ohio Bureau of Workers Compensation followed with a sale of $400 million in PE-interests and Harvard sold a portfolio with an estimated value of $1.5 billion in 2009.[16]

The increase in fundraising was a reflection of performance. Capital was deployed when discounts were high (pricing < 100% NAV), and the evidence points to significantly better IRR performance of secondaries FoFs compared to FoFs that focus mainly on primary funds. The time to payback of capital was

---

[14] Shell Technology Ventures (2007).
[15] Verdun and Chang (2018).
[16] Anson (2009).

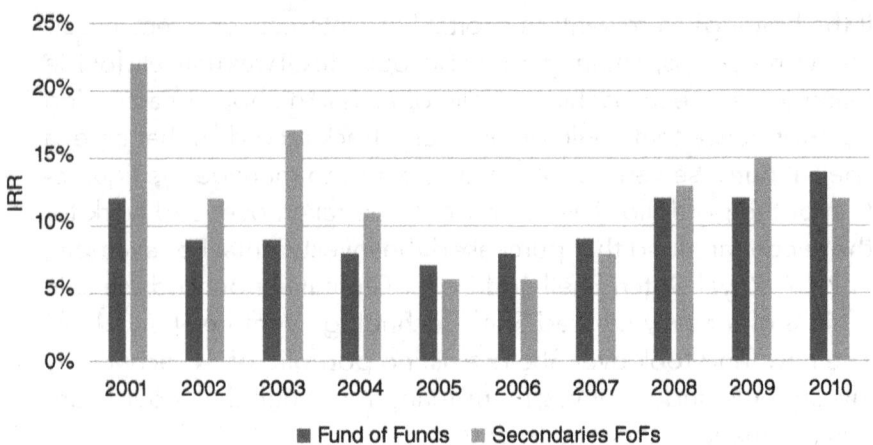

Figure 7.5 Median IRRs by vintage years for FoFs and secondaries FoFs.

Source: Burgiss, cited from Kaplan, Jenkinson, Harris, and Stucke (2017), Auerbach and Shivanada (2017).

Note: The data used comes from different sources and samples are restricted and may not be representative. It should also be noted that the dispersion of returns is wider for primary FoFs than secondaries FoFs.

substantially shorter for secondaries FoFs, reportedly achieving the return of paid-in capital (total value to paid-in (TVPI) = 1) in less than seven years compared to 11 years for traditional FoFs for vintages 2002–2010, which explains the outperformance (Figure 7.5). But this observation also serves as a point of caution. The data presented in Figure 7.5 shows IRRs for vintage years 2001–2010 as of year-end 2016. Due to the slower pace of building a portfolio even a FoF of vintage year 2009 or 2010 is considered quite young as some of the underlying funds may still be in their investment period. Traditional FoFs may thus have been "too early to tell" due to their longer time to return capital, while secondaries FoFs already had substantial realized returns. This leaves open the possibility that the performance gap would narrow over time.

Characteristics of Secondary Transactions

Traditionally a secondary buyer would look for funds:

1. That are significantly invested, as this means that the NAV is relatively high, which makes any discount more meaningful.

2. That have assessable portfolios (no black box).

3. Where the payback time may be short.

Such purchases of middle-aged funds preserve the upside while saving a significant amount of fees (management and set-up fees that do not go into the NAV) on top of any discount to NAV. A discount applied also results in an immediate performance (IRR) uplift for the buyer as the transaction is booked at NAV. Secondaries thus help investors to flatten their "j-curve," i.e., the initial period of negative performance of a PE investment resulting from fees and expenses not being compensated by valuation gains.

The last point is also something to keep in mind when analyzing the performance track records of FoFs. Marketing material often shows the percentage of selected funds that are "top quartile" against a vintage year peer group (which shows primary fund returns). Due to the discount and shorter holding periods, secondary purchases may move fund investments into the top quartile bucket, due to the performance boost the discount provides. The same fund held as a primary investment might not make the grade. While the numbers may be correct, they are not proof of manager selection skills.

The earlier a fund interest is purchased, the smaller those benefits are as the transaction moves closer to a primary fund commitment (this may still be attractive, particularly when investors get access to restricted funds). Buying already mature funds reduces these benefits too (apart from the fee savings) and increases the likelihood that some break-out deals are already realized.

The potential benefits of a secondary purchase are shown in Figure 7.6. Curve A shows the cash flow development of the primary investor. Curve B illustrates a secondary transaction that occurs 5 years into the fund's life at a 10% discount. In this scenario, the secondary buyer attains a higher Total Value to Paid-In (TVPI) ratio due to the discount on Net Asset Value (NAV) and the saved fees payable before the acquisition date. Additionally, the transaction leads to a significantly higher Internal Rate of Return (IRR) compared to primary investors achieve, mainly because of the shorter time to pay back.

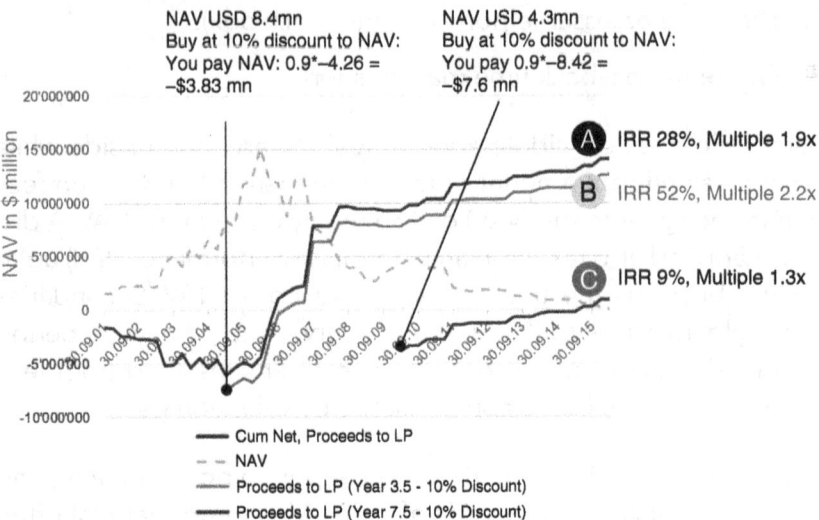

NAV USD 8.4mn
Buy at 10% discount to NAV:
You pay NAV: 0.9*–4.26 =
–$3.83 mn

NAV USD 4.3mn
Buy at 10% discount to NAV:
You pay 0.9*–8.42 =
–$7.6 mn

Ⓐ IRR 28%, Multiple 1.9x

Ⓑ IRR 52%, Multiple 2.2x

Ⓒ IRR 9%, Multiple 1.3x

—— Cum Net, Proceeds to LP
-- - NAV
——— Proceeds to LP (Year 3.5 - 10% Discount)
—— Proceeds to LP (Year 7.5 - 10% Discount)

Figure 7.6 **(A) Cumulative cash flow of a PE fund (28% IRR) compared to the same fund bought after 5 years (B) or 9 years (C) at a 10% discount. While both second-ary buyers make money the late buyer (C) gets a lower IRR as substantial gains were distributed prior to the acquisition date.**
Source: Data based on a $15 million commitment to a buyout fund.

In contrast, Curve C represents a secondary transaction taking place later, specifically 9 years into the fund's life. While the dis-count percentage is the same, in dollar terms, the price reduction is smaller due to the lower NAV. This lower NAV results from some highly profitable exits before the transaction date. Consequently, the secondary buyer misses out on those lucrative investments and achieves a relatively low multiple and IRR compared to the primary investors who participated in these profitable deals. Curve C illustrates that secondary transactions don't always guarantee superior performance; they can vary in outcomes.

To understand the timing issues and risks, one needs to understand the performance characteristics of the underlying portfolio invest-ments. Unfortunately, the data required to do such research has not been readily available in the past. Still, new insights could be gained with the more recent availability of good-quality deal-level data.[17]

---

[17] Kaplan et al. (2020) have used data provided by Burgiss, a global provider of data and analytics to investors in PE funds (limited partner investors or LPs), which are gathered from the financial reports of general partners (GPs) to LPs who are Burgiss clients.

Steven Kaplan et al. looked at over 45,000 portfolio companies of private equity funds. In the following quote, some interesting findings are given:

> Focusing on realized buyout deals, mean (median) multiple is 2.28 (2.07) but that a fifth of multiples are essentially zero and a few holdings are exceptionally profitable. Such highly dispersed outcomes mean that overall performance in private equity is dependent on the success of a relatively limited number of investments, especially in VC funds but also in buyouts. Large investments appear to have lower performance for buyouts but not for venture capital. Average performance appears to drop off for exits past 4 years for buyouts, but not for VC. Perhaps surprisingly, the average duration (from investment to realization) of exited investments is essentially the same in buyout and venture. However, the duration of investments is highly variable, more so in VC. While the median duration is five years in both venture and buyout funds, there is a long "tail" of investments that take much longer to exit than the typical ten-year assumed life of a PE fund implies, with a small percent stretching to 15 years or more.
>
> (Kaplan, Brown, Harris, et al., 2020)

These results confirm similar observations from other scholars and practitioners. While most investors know that venture capital returns are highly skewed (Pareto distributions), it is sometimes ignored that this is also true (albeit to a lesser extent) for buyout and growth investments. Diversification in the public markets is primarily understood to be a risk management concept in which an investor mitigates performance risk by not putting all of one's eggs in one basket. The distribution of deal-level returns suggests that it is also an opportunity to harness the return in private markets. Gaining exposure to many investments increases the likelihood of not missing those "break-out" deals that drive returns. This suggests that the number of funds held in a portfolio should be large, as this increases the likelihood of benefiting from break-out deals.

Steven Kaplan et al. also find that winners come early, and investing in a fund where those early exits have already occurred reduces the expected return. Once the remaining portfolio has a holding time of more than four years, it greatly reduces the chance that the residual portfolio will match the initial performance of a fund. Setting a low discount or even a premium to a fund that has shown excellent performance by the time the acquisition is made might result in overpaying for past performance that is not indicative of the future.

VC funds show somewhat different dynamics. Write-offs come early and thus buying a stake in a VC fund is *a priori* attractive as a more mature portfolio is somewhat de-risked. This, however, is not the case during a boom when the NAV might reflect valuation gains of later rounds. Buying elevated valuations at a discount may still leave secondary buyers looking at losses while primary investors just face reduced gains.

Uncertainty surrounding the remaining holding period and the potential of tail-end positions—"left overs"—generates an incentive for limited partners to sell their fund holdings. At the same time, purchasers need to apply a discount to take on that risk and meet their return target when acquiring a residual portfolio that may be devoid of break-out deals but includes challenged investments.

But not only LPs but GPs too should be looking to sell tail-end holdings and close a fund (mainly if IRR and TVPI are already at or above expectations) rather than waiting it out.

For the primary fund, the IRR is the same but the TVPI would decline (not displayed) from 1.94 to 1.81 due to the discount. However, this is compensated by the shorter holding period, i.e., that money is received earlier. For the secondary fund the transaction would result in an IRR of 26% and a TVPI of 1.58. While the TVPI is somewhat low, the gain resulted in a holding period of just four years.

Both investors, as well as the GPs, increasingly used the secondary market. By 2006, active portfolio management had become far more common, and an increasing number of investors had begun to use the secondary market to rebalance their private equity portfolios.

Traditional secondaries typically have a lower TVPI, faster payback, and higher IRR. Primary fund investors contemplating a sale must consider whether the earlier return of capital is worth the discounts. This depends on the investment opportunities available to investors. Investors buying a secondary stake must decide whether to prioritize IRR or TVPI, particularly when some successful deals have already been realized. Secondary investors are motivated by j-curve mitigation, faster capital deployment, and payback but often have lower absolute gains (TVPI) and thus face an IRR vs. TVPI trade-off.

7.3 LISTED PRIVATE EQUITY: MANAGERS' IPOs

The new millennium saw an increase in private markets management companies that sought additional capital from third-party investors and went public. The IPOs of private markets firms changed the universe of listed private markets significantly, as those management companies would eventually dominate the listed private markets universe.

In the early days of private equity investing, management firms were small organizations with a limited number of employees, usually operating out of one or two offices. They raised funds in sequence, and while management fees were paid to the management company, the carried interest would be distributed and vested to partners and other investment team members, based on a revised schedule for each new fund raised. Fees were supposed to cover the cost of the operations, but with management fees as high as 2% of the funds raised, these fees became arguably a source of profits and provided an incentive to grow AuM. This changed as funds became very large, and management fees and transaction fees far outstripped the cost of operations and overhead. The value of the management company was not in focus as it was traditionally regarded as a pass-through vessel and the partners' stake in the economics of the business was determined by their share in the carried interest.

Ownership of the management company was usually more concentrated than the participation in carried interest. To illustrate the point, Apax Partners & Co Ventures Holdings Ltd was more than 90% owned by ten shareholders in early 2001. At that time, the firm had 32 partners in five offices that would receive carried interest.[18] In 2007, the firm had 50 partners in eight offices.[19] Apax's AuM increased from $3 billion in 2001 to $20 billion in 2007.[20] Due to the surge in AuM, management companies became increasingly valuable and, on top of the NPV of the cash flows they received from the active partnerships, management companies would acquire brand value and a franchise that boosted their valuations.

It became increasingly implausible that junior partners could buy out departing partners at anything approaching "fair value" and the owners of management companies faced the questions of (1) how to create liquidity for themselves, and (2) how to widen the participation of key employees in the value created of the franchise in addition to the carried interest they received from the funds they invested?

Multi-strategy Firms Require Different Incentives

Management tasks relating to the management company were typically assigned to a senior partner who acted as *primus inter pares*. Important decisions would be taken by consensus in a partners meeting. This started to change as the private market business became increasingly global and some firms became multi-strategy firms, i.e., they raised funds in different private market asset classes and offered different product types such as traditional partnerships, FoFs, or even listed investment companies. These developments raised profound management issues that firms needed to resolve to stay successful. As firms got bigger, they increased their staffing size. Apart from the geographical expansion of large private equity firms, there was a product dimension as well. As firms leveraged their brand recognition and financial resources to develop strong

---

[18] Information based on archive material of the author. In addition to partners, other team members, directors, and entities would receive carried interest as well.
[19] Davies and Wilkes (2013).
[20] Apax (2022).

fundraising capabilities, they also expanded into new investment sectors such as infrastructure, private real estate, and later private debt, and occasionally even hedge funds and FoFs (more on the rise of mega-firms, see Section 7.5). KKR grew from 20 employees in 1990 to about 700 employees in 2010 and its peers showed a similar trend. The Carlyle Group employed 500 investment professionals in 14 countries in 2005.[21] This was already a large number but in 2013 the Carlyle Group employed more than 1,450 people in 34 offices across six continents.[22]

Scale prevents the continuation of the partnership governance at some point in time. It is beyond the scope of this book to explore the solutions that different organizations found to adapt their governance and organizational design to the needs of a rapidly growing and diverse business. But it is worthwhile highlighting some of those issues as they go some way to explaining the trend toward seeking outside investors that started during the first decade of the new millennium and accelerated after 2010.

Challenges of growing general partner organizations:

1. **Governance:** Delegation of decisions to management and involvement of equity owners of the management company and deal partners.

2. **Incentives for partners in managerial roles that are removed from deal-making:** Management renders a service to the organization at large and not to individual funds as deal partners do.

3. **Capital allocation across multiple jurisdictions and incentives for deal partners:** In the past, carried interest was only partially allocated at the outset of a new fund. However, partners (and non-partners) would receive additional carried interest in a fund once a deal was approved. Given that deal opportunities

---

[21] Messer Industry GmbH (2005).
[22] Carlyle Group (2022).

are cyclical, particularly in smaller markets, how is the objective of retaining your deal-makers in those markets balanced with an incentive structure that rewards deal-making?

4. **Resource allocation across product lines:** How do you reallocate resources within the organization if you are active in multiple product lines? For example, if you want to transfer deal partners from your buyout fund to a newly formed special situations fund in the middle of the former's investment period. Does the deal partner receive carried interest in both funds, or do they have to give up some carry in the buyout fund? To illustrate the challenge: the Carlyle Group's 1,450 employees have $185 billion of assets under management across 122 funds and 81 fund of funds vehicles as of September 30, 2013.[23]

5. **Growth of balance sheets:** Organizations may have to grow their balance sheets and retain earnings to fund their expansion, which increasingly includes making acquisitions and providing GP commitments to their funds.

As a result, the validity of a partnership as the ownership model for a private equity firm had to be re-assessed by those large multi-strategy firms as they were considering appropriate incentives and compensation schemes for their organizations.

To address those issues, private equity started to consider opening the partnership to external investors (selling a "GP stake") or becoming a listed partnership or corporation (IPO). GPs pursued both routes from 2007 onwards, and the trend accelerated after 2010.

Selling GP Stakes

While not listed as private equity, the sale of GP stakes was driven by some of the same dynamics that led to the IPOs of management companies and, in several cases, a precursor to going public. An early example of selling a GP stake was the acquisition of a

---

[23] Ibid.

20% stake in Blackstone by Japanese bank Nikko Securities for a $100 million investment in 1988 (valuing the firm at $500 million).[24] But such a sale of a GP stake remained rare and only gained momentum after, in September 2007, the Carlyle Group sold a 7.5% interest in its management company to Mubadala Development Company, which is owned by the Abu Dhabi Investment Authority (ADIA) for $1.35 billion. The transaction valued Carlyle Group at approximately $20 billion.[25] Next followed an announcement in January 2008 that Silver Lake Partners had sold a 9.9% stake in its management company to the California Public Employees' Retirement System (CalPERS) for $275 million.[26]

This trend gained further momentum when funds that specialized in acquiring GP stakes, "funds of firms," were established. Funds like Dyal Capital Partners, which started as a division of Neuberger Berman in 2011, or Blackstone's Strategic Capital Holdings in 2013 are two initiatives that created additional sources of capital for GPs seeking outside investors. These and other firms raised billions of dollars in capital for vehicles that are dedicated to buying GP minority stakes.[27]

A GP stake sale creates liquidity for partners, aligns key investors as strategic partners, and establishes a valuation for future fundraises or IPO. It also allows GPs to raise funds for expansion. Traditionally, carried interest was vested with individual team members and partners, but assigning it to the management company increases the revenue stream and valuation while reducing the share of carried interest for the investment team.

If purchased before an IPO, GP positions permitted limited partners to partake in fee and (perhaps) carried interest revenue streams and any valuation gain. Buying a GP investment by another private equity firm is often a precursor to an acquisition.

---

[24] Qint (1988).
[25] Sorkin (2007).
[26] Sorkin (2008).
[27] Bain & Company (2020). Dyal Capital is reported to have made investments of more than $10 billion during the decade after its foundation (Vandevelde, 2021).

Selling a GP stake became an option available to both smaller GPs and large firms. According to Preqin data, more than 300 GP stakes were sold during 1988–2020—most of them since 2005. The majority of GP stakes have been sold by buyout firms, followed by FoFs, and prominent buyers were "funds of firms," which accounted for 50% of all deals, followed by sovereign wealth funds and private equity firms.[28]

IPOs of Private Market Firms

Although some publicly traded private equity entities existed before, 2006–2007 saw the beginning of a trend of large private market firms seeking a listing. One key impediment stopping private market firms becoming corporations was the resulting taxation of corporate profits compared to a limited partnership in the USA and other jurisdictions. In Switzerland, however, tax-efficient holding structures are available while carried interest is taxed as income. Swiss resident managers can generally only benefit to a certain extent from a tax-exempt capital gain or privileged dividend income, which reduces the incentives to use a partnership structure for management companies. This explains why Partners Group (Figure 7.7) already was incorporated as a company and did the first IPO of a major private markets manager.

On March 24, 2006, Partners Group Holding AG went public on the SIX Swiss Exchange, with founders and management retaining substantial ownership. Partners Group historically provided FoFs (primary and secondary) and other structured investment solutions before it pivoted toward direct investing—one of the only large firms to have made this pivot successfully. Since 2007, the firm also added private real estate development with the purchase of Pension Consulting Alliance's discretionary real estate asset management business.[29]

Its evolution is thus similar to other large private market firms. Its history and strategy illustrate the playbook for mega-firms that went public. However, there were two differences: unlike the US

---

[28] Fogelström and Gustafsson (2021).
[29] Partners Group (2007; 2008).

Figure 7.7   The founders of Partners Group. From left to right: M. Erni, U. Wietlisbach, and Alfred Gantner.
Source: Schweizer Illustrierte.

firms that did their IPOs as listed partnerships (see as follows), Partners Group was listed as a joint stock company. This had the advantage that the general public could buy its stock. Also, its revenue mix was tilted toward stable management fees rather than volatile performance fees due to its heritage as a FoFs manager. Both factors, i.e., a broader investor base and less volatile earnings, explain to some extent the outperformance of its stock compared to other GPs that went public.[30]

Fortress Investment Group went public in February 2007. While not a pure-bred private equity firm, its IPO set a value bar for firms that invest heavily in private markets.[31]

On June 21, 2007, Blackstone went public as a listed limited partnership[32] (Figure 7.8), selling a 12.3% stake in the company for $4.13 billion, in the largest US IPO since 2002.[33] But the

[30] Lietz and Andrade (2016).
[31] Seymor (2007).
[32] In 2019, when the corporate tax rate was reduced from 35% to 2%, Blackstone changed from a publicly listed partnership to a C-type corporation, becoming a taxable entity (Rubinstein, 2021).
[33] Anderson (2007).

Figure 7.8 Blackstone co-founders Stephen A. Schwarzman and Peter G. Petersen.
Source: Blackstone.

performance of its shares was initially disappointing. A year after the IPO, S. Schwarzman complained that the market had undervalued Blackstone.[34] Performance fees often account for over 50% of Blackstone's reported earnings in the past, and as they are more variable, investors seemed unwilling to value them highly. In addition, Blackstone (like most US PE firms that went public) chose a listing as a publicly listed partnership. This made it difficult for many investors to own the stock given (potentially) complex tax considerations.

Less than two weeks after the Blackstone IPO, rival firm KKR filed with the SEC in July 2007 to raise $1.25 billion by selling an ownership interest in its management company.[35] KKR had previously listed its KKR Private Equity Investors (KPE) private equity fund vehicle in 2006. The onset of the credit crunch and the resulting shutdown of the IPO market would dampen the prospects of obtaining a valuation that would be attractive to KKR, and the flotation was postponed. In 2010, KKR finally went public. Apollo Global Management and Carlyle Group followed in 2011 and 2012.

---

[34] Kandell (2021).
[35] Anderson and Michael (2007).

For buyout firms that extolled the virtues of private ownership, seeking a public listing is counter-intuitive. Why would private market firms submit to the scrutiny, disclosure, and reporting requirements of an IPO? First, the mega-firms' growth in the first decade of the millennium made it unrealistic for founding partners to pass on their stakes at a stock market valuation to the next generation of partners. IPOs were attractive for maximizing founders' wealth. When selling a GP stake, there are limitations to opening a partnership to external investors. One might invite one or two LPs to buy a GP stake, but it becomes unwieldy if too many external investors are invited into a private partnership.

An IPO is also good for brand building. It was the author's experience that Partners Group could surge ahead in the Swiss market after their IPO as many of their (happy) institutional shareholders also would give "their manager" preference for allocations to their investment funds. Also, an IPO allows for raising additional equity for acquisitions or longer-term investments. The permanent capital argument.[36] Finally, private markets firms, as public companies, can introduce stock-based incentive schemes to align senior employees with the organization. Multi-product mega-firms can shift human resources between product areas. This favors share-based incentives' flexibility.

Private market firms are not immune to the pressures of being a public company. As they became public companies, their outlook changed, and their alignment with their limited partners weakened because they had to serve an additional master—the public shareholder. Stable management fees are valued higher than the more volatile performance fees, resulting in disappointing post-IPO stock performance. Management fee generation drove shareholder value. Blackstone's fee-related earnings, for example, went up from one-third in 2017 to about two-thirds in 2021. One of the obvious moral hazards of becoming a public company is

---

[36] Blackstone's history provides two examples of opportunities that require a larger balance sheet. In 1988, Blackstone was invested in the roll-up of Larry Fink's Blackrock Group but sold its stake in 1994. With sufficient permanent capital Blackstone might have held on to it, and its 40% stake would be worth about $16 billion in mid-2022 (Banerjee, 2013). Schwarzman offered to buy a stake in Bloomberg back in 1988, but was ultimately thwarted by Mike Bloomberg's stipulation that he should never sell the stake and stay a partner for life (Oguh, 2020).

to turn into an "asset gatherer" that prioritizes growing fee revenue over maximizing the value of the investments.[37] Investors are watching the trend of their private market managers to become public companies with some unease and realize that this has implications for the relationship between GPs and LPs that will only become apparent over time.[38]

7.4   VENTURE CAPITAL IN THE POST-DOTCOM ERA

Following the dotcom bust in 2002, venture capital (VC) firms became more cautious in their investments, shifting their attention to later-stage startups with proven revenue streams. They also began to focus more on criteria such as customer acquisition cost and lifetime value rather than just valuing companies based on future market size. Furthermore, as fewer funds were raised, the quantity of money invested by VC firms declined. As a result, fewer companies were funded, and those that were, received less money. The industry also became more specialized, with some firms concentrating on specific industries, such as biotech or enterprise software.

In the USA, venture capital investment activity remained subdued for many years after the dotcom bust and the NASDAQ crash that started in 2000. NASDAQ remained well below its peak of 1999 throughout the first decade of the millennium, and the few IPOs of venture-backed firms happening hardly created headlines. In a report on the best venture capital investments of all time, only Google's and Genentech's IPOs fall within the post-dotcom period until 2010, and nothing pointed to the social media and technology boom of the second decade of the millennium. Facebook had only 12 million users in 2006 when it was still concentrated on the college market, and there was a danger it would fizzle out when introduced to the general public.[39]

---

[37] This agency problem has been highlighted by various scholars (Kaplan and Schoar, 2005; Phalippou, Gottschalg, and de Silanes, 2009).
[38] See, for a discussion Fogelström and Gustafsson (2021), Mustafina and Nacksten (2020).
[39] CB Insights (2019).

The number of funds and amounts raised were only a fraction of the late 1990s. Many venture firms stopped raising new funds and became "zombies," living off the management fee of previous funds but otherwise not engaging in new investments. By some estimates, the number of active venture capital firms in the USA declined from more than 900 in 1999 to less than 750 in 2010.[40] While this does not look like a big drop in active firms, it hides the fact that a considerable number of those firms did not raise a new fund and were living off the management fee of their previous funds. Fundraising during 2001–2005 declined by about 50% compared to 1996–2000 and the number of new funds raised showed a similar pattern.[41]

A report published in 2009 by the Kauffman Foundation concluded that the venture capital model was broken, due to low performance, failure to beat public markets, and misalignment of interest due to high management fees. The opinion that venture capital had lost its relevance was widely shared at the time.[42]

In Europe, numerous venture firms also failed to raise new funds, captive funds stopped investing, and captive teams were often disbanded. Between 1995 and 2010, European venture capital investment was, on average, approximately one-quarter of the size of investment in the USA. As European VCs continued to disperse funds more broadly through smaller deals compared to their US peers, they found it challenging to provide the required later-stage financing. A report from the European Venture Capital Association acknowledges the problem. Looking at its data, it appears that during 2003–2009 less than 20% of investments made by European VCs went to follow-on rounds, while in the USA, that proportion was more than 40%.[43] As a consequence, there was less deal sharing among European VCs and less concentration of investments in companies that had reached certain milestones and thus had better odds of success, which would have boosted success rates and thus performance.

The continuation of deal activity in Europe was partly driven by investments by US venture firms which became significant players in later stage financing rounds.

---

[40] The NVCA reports 800 active venture capital firms for 2010 (NVCA, 2022).
[41] Metrick and Yasuda (2021).
[42] Wilhelm (2012), Kedrosky (2009).
[43] EIB (2016).

Table 7.1 Kleiner Perkins Caufield & Byers funds closed during 2000–2010

Fund	Fund size in $M	Year
Kleiner Perkins Caufield & Byers XIV	650	2010
Kleiner Perkins Caufield & Byers XI.A	150	2009
Kleiner Perkins Caufield & Byers XIII	700	2008
Kleiner Perkins Caufield & Byers XII	625	2006
Kleiner Perkins Caufield & Byers XI	400	2004
Kleiner Perkins Caufield & Byers X	625	2000

Source: palico.com/funds/kleiner-perkins-caufield-byers.

If you worked in one of the old venture firms located on Sand Hill Road during those years, you might not have noticed the decline in the industry or even regarded it as a positive. As one general partner of a storied venture capital firm put it, "the tourists had left." Established VCs, however, continued to raise capital and invested. Kleiner Perkins's fundraising is shown in Table 7.1.[44]

The Sarbanes-Oxley Act (SOX) of 2002 was passed in response to the corporate accounting scandals of the early 2000s, and imposed new or expanded requirements for all US public companies and accounting firms. The SOX compliance costs and increased liabilities for firms going public made it less attractive for venture-backed firms to pursue an IPO. NASDAQ made several changes to its rules listing requirements in order to improve the quality of companies listed on the exchange and to increase transparency for investors. These changes to NASDAQ's listing requirements had the effect of making it more difficult for companies to list on the exchange, particularly for those that were not yet profitable or had lower market valuations.

The fact that firms have to wait until they are more mature when they go public has also meant that they do so at substantially higher valuations. Firms needed more private capital as they went along the path to profitability and the need for such late-stage equity infusions tilted the balance from VCs toward growth

---

[44] Woodmann (2022).

financing (see next section). Investors that traditionally focused solely on the public markets also saw that they were missing out on the capital gains that companies such as Facebook, LinkedIn, and Salesforce garnered while still private and started to provide the capital needed to extend the runway needed by startups to become viable IPO candidates.

The extended holding periods and the lack of exits, as well as the fact that many late-rounds were done at lower valuations ("down-rounds"), impacted VC performance, which was significantly below buyout returns and generally considered unsatisfactory by investors. In 2013, Reuters posted the headline "Venture capital kingpin Kleiner Perkins acknowledges weak results" and went on to report that "the 41-year-old firm built a reputation by backing technology titans such as Amazon.com Inc., Netscape and Sun Microsystems, but recent investments in Zynga Inc., Groupon Inc. and other companies have worked out less well."[45] The biggest wins for Kleiner Perkins (and Greylock) during those years was the Google IPO (2004) and Genentech (2009).

But there were new opportunities on the horizon. One opportunity set was geographic—venture capital and growth financing in China. New Enterprise Associates first invested in China in 2003 and opened an office in 2005. Sequoia Capital China and India were founded in 2005. Sequoia Capital closed its first China-focused fund at $250 million in 2005 and followed with Sequoia Capital China II ($250 million) and Sequoia China Growth I ($500 million), both launched in May 2007. In 2007, Kleiner Perkins raised a $360 million fund focused on China and announced the opening of offices in Shanghai and Beijing.[46]

The technology sector, particularly software and internet-related businesses, saw substantial investments. By the mid- to late 2000s, software as a service (SaaS) had established itself as a mainstream delivery model for enterprise software, and it continued to gain popularity and momentum in the following years. Furthermore, the early 2000s saw a wave of SaaS companies such as Salesforce,

---

[45] Quoted from (Reuters, 2013a).
[46] Auchard (2007).

founded in 1999, and had its initial public offering in 2004. Other companies like Workday, ServiceNow, and Zendesk also went public around that time.[47]

Developing the technology for startups became cheaper. The open-source movement made outsourcing R&D and technology development cheaper. Free software tools and rentable computer resources decreased the upfront cost of producing enterprise software, while cloud-hosted commercial software allows for the frictionless deployment of updates and incremental functionality. However, scaling up takes more time and money. The market fragmented as centralized IT departments lost control and budget and business divisions took over purchase decisions. This makes it more complex and more expensive to develop channels for these dispersed clients and offer solutions instead of technology, as those business unit customers lack the technical skills to deploy and maintain complicated code.[48]

Another opportunity set came in the form of the mobile internet. Handheld mobile computing, pioneered by the Newton (1993), Palm Pilot (1997), and Blackberry (1999), found limited appeal until they could be interconnected via wireless and mobile operating systems. They would soon be eclipsed by the widespread success of the Apple iPhone (2007) and App Store and Google Android-based products (2008). Looking back, it seems relatively easy to spot the trend behind the momentum toward mobile, with three strong drivers: a dramatic fall in both communication and electronic storage costs and a significant increase in computing power. There was also a clear focus on consumer tastes and preferences over enterprise solutions. These factors transformed what were once common cell phones into handheld computers, with the ability to run large applications and do things better than most computers just a few years earlier.[49]

The telecom boom created the infrastructure needed for internet maturity. After the telecom bust, internet bandwidth oversupply

---

[47] Fryer (2023).
[48] Janeway (2018).
[49] O'Gorman (2015).

allowed new companies to offer sophisticated services at low prices. Despite internet usage doubling every few years, bandwidth costs dropped 90% by 2004. Up to 85% of US broadband capacity remained unused in 2005, allowing for the widespread distribution of new internet-based services and e-commerce through inexpensive capacity.[50]

But to use this connectivity one needs a computer. It is often overlooked that personal computers only became a common household item in the 2000s, as revealed by data from the US Census Bureau. Specifically, in the year 2000, more than 50% of American households reported owning a computer for the first time, compared to just 8.2% in 1984. By 2015, the number had risen to 78.0%.[51] Despite the excitement of the dotcom era, with hindsight, it took about two decades for consumers to fully grasp the benefits of owning a computer at home. The adoption of personal computers mirrors the adoption of electricity that also saw a significant gap between early adopters and its ubiquity. It took several decades for electricity to become a common household item, as many people were initially skeptical about its benefits and saw it as an unnecessary luxury. In comparison, the dotcom and telecom boom both accelerated the roll-out of networks (even if capacity was not used) and accelerated the us of PCs at home. It did have a positive effect on people's ability to use the internet and complete tasks online, with the number of websites growing from 17 million in 2000 to roughly 200 million in 2010.[52] And there was more to come: by 2009, the number of unique users of mobile phones had reached half the planet. The ITU reported 3.8 billion activated mobile phones in use and 3.4 billion unique users of mobile devices in 2010. Mobile internet data connections were following the growth of mobile phone connections, albeit at a lower rate. In 2009, Yankee Group reported that 29% of all mobile phone users globally were accessing browser-based internet content on their phones.[53]

Many Europeans and Americans were already using fixed internet when they tried mobile. India's first internet use was on a

[50] McCullough (2018b).
[51] U.S. Census Bureau (2017).
[52] Data on broadband usage and price trends cited from McCullough (2018b).
[53] Yankee Group report cited in Hamblen (2010).

mobile phone. In regions where the PC wasn't the first internet device, growth was fastest. This was due to mobile phone adoption. For example, a Morgan Stanley report stated that Pakistan and India had the highest mobile phone adoption growth in 2006.[54] And then there was China, which had come out of nowhere to 155 million mobile internet users as of June 2009.[55]

These dynamics heralded globalization of the addressable market for internet-related services, which could be developed quickly because the digital economy faced much lower entry barriers than traditional goods and services. New venture capital opportunities arose when social media became popular. Despite being low-key during those years, the venture capital backed some future industry giants. Opportunities arose where the people were, which meant Asia. Social media, mobile internet, and e-commerce in China attracted foreign investors.[56]

Rise of Angel Investing and "Founder-Friendly" Terms

In the aftermath of the dotcom boom venture capital had something of a reputation problem with investors and entrepreneurs alike. A study by Bob Zider found that venture capitalists (VCs) primarily focused on "middle" portfolio companies, rather than on their best or worst performers. He also noted that the financial incentive for VC partners is to manage as much money as possible, leading to less time for nurturing and advising entrepreneurs.[57] Paul Graham, co-founder of Y Combinator, criticized the venture capital industry for its short-term focus and lack of support for early-stage startups. He also argued that venture capitalists were becoming increasingly risk-averse, avoiding investments in early-stage startups with high potential but also high-risk.

In his book, *Zero to One*, Peter Thiel, co-founder of Founders Fund (Figure 7.9), claims that most venture capitalists are not interested

---

[54] Morgan Stanley Research (2009).
[55] *China News* (2017).
[56] EIOPA (2022), EIB (2016).
[57] Zider (1998).

Figure 7.9 Peter Thiel, the German-born entrepreneur, venture capitalist, and hedge fund manager was a co-founder of PayPal, Palantir Technologies, and was an early investor in Facebook.
Source: Gage Skidmore, CC BY-SA 3.0, https://commons.wikimedia.org.

in funding truly innovative companies, but rather in investing in companies that are copying existing business models. He says the industry is not interested in funding new technologies or new ways of doing things, but rather in companies that are simply riding existing trends. Thiel also suggested that venture capitalists do not add much value to startups beyond the capital they provide, and that they should stop mentoring founders. In his view, VCs are too diversified and by spending most of their time on middling companies, they miss really outstanding opportunities.[58] These criticisms had a real-world impact since they frequently came from previous entrepreneurs who were now prepared to finance businesses and offer a different relationship with founders than traditional venture capital. While it is difficult to determine the total amount invested by angel investors in US startups during the 2000s with precision because data on angel investments is not consistently reported or tracked, some estimates suggest that the total amount of angel investments in the USA increased significantly between 2005–2008, with annual

---

[58] Thiel and Masters (2014).

investment amounts ranging from $20 billion to $50 billion. Among prominent angel investors of that time were:[59]

- Ron Conway, an investor in firms such as Google, PayPal, and Ask Jeeves.
- Dave McClure, whose investments include Dropbox and Twilio.
- Chris Sacca, a seed investor in Twitter, Instagram, and Uber.
- Keith Rabois, who backed Square and PayPal.

And, of course, Peter Thiel, who participated in Facebook's Seed round and went on to make other angel investments.

Startups had additional options for raising capital and could delay a Series A funding round with VCs. During the 2000s, the equity stake for angel or seed-round investors in a company varied considerably, although it was typically in the 10–30% range. As angel investors signed more extensive checks, founders' bargaining power strengthened, and VC share allocations in Series A fundraising rounds fell to at most 25%—sometimes as low as 10%.[60]

Angel investors were distinct from traditional venture capitalists in that they provided "founder-friendly" startup finance. Angel investors imposed fewer restrictions and did not require board seats. Instead of limiting founders' voting rights, angel investors agreed to super-voting rights for founders that allowed them to maintain control after many investment rounds, sometimes even after an IPO. Angel investors also ceded their voting rights to founders, which increased their control even more.[61] Thus, VCs' and founders' bargaining power had reversed from previous decades. Not only did angel investors become more numerous and were writing larger checks but some angels even began to raise funds to finance startups at earlier stages than was typical

---

[59] RSCM (2010).
[60] Ortmans (2016).
[61] Examples of super-voting shares are Mark Zuckerberg, the founder of Facebook, who holds Class B shares in the company that gives him 10 votes per share; Evan Williams, the founder of Twitter, who held super-voting shares in the company that gave him 10 votes per share; and Larry Page and Sergey Brin, the co-founders of Google, who held Class B shares in the company that gave them 10 votes per share. Elon Musk, the founder of Tesla, holds super-voting shares in the company that gives him 20 votes per share. Jack Dorsey, the founder of Twitter, held super-voting shares in the company that gave him 20 votes per share.

for institutional venture capital investors. As an example, Y Combinator (YC) was founded in 2005 as a startup accelerator that provides seed funding, mentorship, and resources to early-stage startups. The organization runs two three-month accelerator programs per year, during which startups receive an investment of around $150,000 in exchange for 7% equity. During this time, startups receive mentorship and resources from a network of successful entrepreneurs and investors, and participate in weekly dinners with guest speakers and networking events.[62] Peter Thiel's Founders Fund, also known as FF, invests in early-stage companies across a wide range of industries. It invested in a variety of technology companies during the 2000s, including companies such as Airbnb, Lyft, Palantir Technologies, and Stripe. Both FF and Y Combinator are known for their founder-friendly terms and their willingness to make investments without board representation.

Traditional venture capitalists were confronted with this new reality and also had to accept lower equity stakes at higher valuation as round A financing shifted due to the abundance of seed financing. Typical Series A equity stakes were less than 25% thus continuing a declining trend that could be observed over several decades in line with the growth and maturation of the VC industry.

But some experts argue that this increased involvement of angel investors has led to a decline in governance in venture capital-backed companies due to "founder-friendly" terms that are often included in funding agreements.[63] This can lead to a lack of alignment between the interests of the company's founders and its investors, as the founders may prioritize their own interests over those of the investors. Furthermore, boards that are dominated by the company's founder can lead to a lack of oversight and accountability. This can negatively impact the company's performance.

So, at the end of the first decade of the new millennium, the power had shifted: the VC model established in the late 1960s and early 1970s relied on a degree of control that was outsized relative to its capital contribution. VCs could force exits, engineer mergers, replace founders as CEOs and monitor spending trends closely. Angel investors broke that hold on governance not by replacing it

---

[62] Janeway (2018).
[63] Fan (2022).

but by diluting it and giving founders much more control over their companies. VCs continued to hold a valuable role as coaches and mentors to startups, and their capital and involvement remained highly sought after. The investment of a top VC was seen as a strong endorsement, increasing the odds of a startup's success. However, their impact was often more subtle, as VCs exercised influence from the backseat rather than asserting control rights that put them in the driver's seat.

Growth Financing and Non-traditional Investors

During the 2000s, the startup ecosystem underwent a significant transformation that was marked by a shift in the way startups were funded. Prior to the 2000s, venture capital (VC) had been the dominant funding source for startups, with early-stage investments being the focus of most VC funds. However, with the dotcom bust in the early 2000s, the IPO market for startups dried up, leaving many VC-backed companies without a clear path to exit.

As a result, investors began to turn their attention to later-stage growth financing as an alternative to IPOs. Growth equity, which involves investing in mature companies that are experiencing growth but are not yet ready for an IPO or acquisition, began to play a larger role in the startup ecosystem (Figure 7.10). This type of financing provided capital to startups that had already proven their business models, but still needed additional funding to scale and reach profitability. The importance of growth financing was

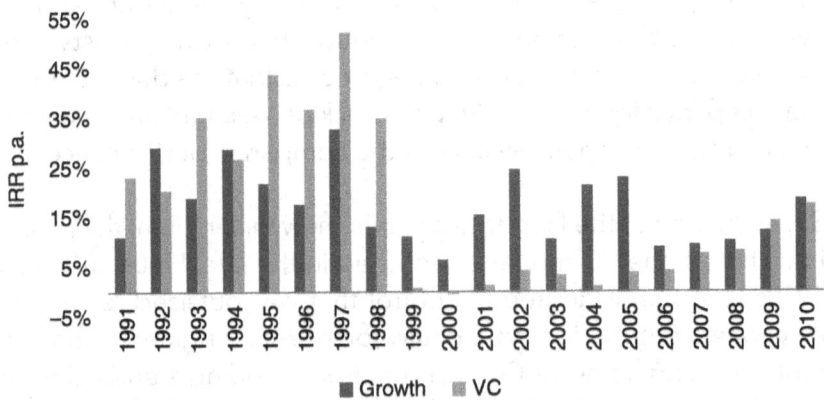

Figure 7.10   Pooled IRRs of growth financing and VC funds, 1991–2010.
Source: Burgiss data, as of December 2022, the performance data has a later cut-off date, which has led to discrepancies in VC performance data compared to other sections of the book. This is because the data reflects the pressure on valuations that occurred after 2021.

further highlighted by the fundraising crunch that many VCs faced during this time. With limited capital available for new investments, VCs needed to keep their existing portfolio companies private for longer, which meant that growth financing became even more crucial for startups seeking to scale.

In the startup ecosystem, non-traditional investors such as private equity firms and strategic investors were increasingly drawn to growth equity investments, primarily because of the potential for high returns in later-stage startups. SoftBank, a prominent player in the industry, had already been investing in late-stage deals since the 1990s and continued to do so in the 2000s (Figure 7.11).

LINKEDIN, SAN JOSE, CA (2003)
Founders: R. Hoffman, K.Guericke, J. Vaillant, A. Blue, E. Ly (all from PayPal). With seed funding from colleagues at PayPal followed by Sequoia.

BEIDU, BEIJING (2000)
Founders: R. Li, E. Xu. Funding of $1.2 million series A through Peninsula Capital and Integrity Partners. Google joined in Series C.

SKYPETALLINN 2003
Founders;N. Zennström,J. Friis. Funding from Index Ventures.

SPACEX, HAWTHORNE, CA (2002)
Founder: E.Musk.
Funding: from Paypal co-founder L. Nosek, Future Ventures Fund, Valor Equity Partners.

FACEBOOK, CAMBRIDGE, MA (2004)
Founders: C. Hughes, A. McCollum,D. Moskovitz, E. Saverin, M. Zuckerberg. Funding: Peter Thiel (PayPal), Accel Partners, Index Ventures.

TESLA MOTORS, SAN CARLOS, CA (2003)
Founders: E. Musk (PayPal),M.Eberhard, M. Tarpenning et al.. Funding: Threshold, Valor Equity, Technology Venture Partners et al.

YOUTUBE, SANMATEO, CA (2005)
Founders: J. Karim, C. Hurley, S. Chen (all from PayPal).
Funding from Sequoia Capital.

AIRBNB, SANFRANCISCO, CA (2008)
Founders: B. Chesky, N. Blecharczyk, J. Gebbia. Funded by Y Combinator, Greylock and Andreessen Horowitz.

TWITTER, SANFRANCISCO, CA (2009)
Founders: J. Dorsey, E. Williams, N. Glass, B. Stone.Funding from Union Square Ventures, Spark Capital, Benchmark.

WHATSAPP, SAN JOSE, CA (2009)
Founders: B. Acton, J. Koum (both from Yahoo!).
Funding from Sequoia Capital.

Figure 7.11   Some of today's most successful startups were launched during the 2000s.
Source: LinkedIn.

The shift toward growth financing in the 2000s was significant for the startup ecosystem, providing an alternative source of funding for startups that were struggling to secure an IPO. It also paved the way for new financing models that would emerge in the following decade. Growth equity investments proved to be a fruitful and viable option for later-stage startups and attracted a diverse range of investors. The success of growth financing ultimately contributed to the emergence of new financing models and cemented its role as a prominent part of the startup funding ecosystem.

7.5   THE BUYOUT BOOM

In 2003, the US private equity sector had spent the previous two and a half years reeling from crises and was severely limited by a lack of credit supply.

In Europe, the deal-making environment was a little better as financing was easier. This allowed the closing of some significant acquisitions. Yellow Pages was sold to Apax and Hick Muse for $3.5 billion in June 2003, followed by a £1.75 billion acquisition of road assistance and car insurance provider AA by CVC and Permira in 2004—the first large buyouts since the onset of the crisis.

But in the USA, some developments would also help buyouts regain their momentum. The Sarbanes-Oxley Act of 2002 established a new set of rules and regulations for publicly traded companies that reduced the attractiveness of being a public company—at least in the eyes of their CEOs and board members.

As one submission to the SEC put it in 2005: "it has significantly raised the cost of doing business [. . . and] it has also changed management and director priorities, reducing overall productivity. It has also increased the perceived risk of being a company director. . . ." (SEC, 2005). Many big firms considered private equity ownership as potentially more appealing than remaining public for the first time.

In addition, the bond markets reopened due to lower interest rates and the liquidity provided by the Federal Reserve, resulting in reduced borrowing costs and a resumption of lending that improved the ability of private equity firms to finance larger acquisitions.

Mega-Buyouts During the Boom Years of 2003–2007

Fundraising had been slow during 2000–2003 as investors recovered from the losses during the stock market crash. Given the difficult economic and financial market environment, nothing pointed to the first decade of the millennium being a bumper period for buyouts. But then things changed from 2005 onwards, and fundraising accelerated. Average annual capital raised for buyout funds increased enormously from $55 billion in 2001–2003 to about $240 billion yearly for 2006–2008. As venture capital fundraising stagnated at a low level—barely exceeding $50 billion in its peak year in 2008—asset flows drove that growth to the buyout industry.

Buyouts began a resurgence that saw some of the largest leveraged buyout transactions in history, and in some ways, it was a return to its past (Table 7.2). The surge in deal volumes in 2006–2007 resulted in record deal values that were driven by a credit bubble inflated by low interest rates.

The "golden age" of private equity was fueled by a global liquidity surge from return-hungry investors. The market for leveraged loans reached new heights as a result of investor demand for structured finance instruments such as collateralized loan obligations (CLOs). The financing of multibillion-dollar buyouts was made possible by favorable debt market and fundraising conditions. The public-to-private deal had a comeback, and the investment playbook often resembled the takeover boom of the 1980s. Among the largest buyouts of this period are hospital group HCA (2007), property REITs Equity Office Properties (2007), and electricity provider TXU (2007), which in 2022 still held the record as the largest leveraged buyout ever.

Deals would involve companies that had fallen out of favor in the public markets and were undervalued, growing businesses that needed capital to expand, subsidiaries of multinationals that came up for sale, and also included infrastructure and real estate assets.

Burger King—though not among the largest transactions but one of the largest deals at the beginning of the decade—is an example of a repeat take-private transaction that could be observed for several deals.

Table 7.2   Most of the largest buyouts were done 2005–2007

Portfolio Company	Investors	Year	Public-to-private	Asset class	Location	Deal size $ billion
TXU	TPG. KKR, GS	2007	Yes	PE	US	45
Equity Office Properties	Blackstone	2007	Yes	RE	US	40
Medline	Blackstone, H&F, Carlyle, Abu Dhabi, GIC	2021	No	PE	US	34
HCA	incl. KKR, Bain Capital	2007	Yes	PE	US	33
Clear Channel	Bain Capital, TH Lee	2007	No	PE	US	26,7
Hilton Intl.	Blackstone	2006	Yes	IS	US	26,3
First Data	KKR	2007	Yes	PE	US	25,7
Altel	Atlantis Hldgs.	2007	Yes	PE	US	25,1
RJR Nabisco	KKR	1989	Yes	PE	US	25
Kinder Morgan	incl. Carlyle, AIG	2006	Yes	PE	US	21,6
Freescale	incl. Carlyle, Permira, TPG	2006	Yes	PE	US	17,6
Harrah's Ent.	TPG, Apollo	2006	Yes	PE	US	17,1
TDC	incl. Apax, Providence	2006	Yes	PE	EU	15,8
Thames Water	Macquarie	2006	No	IS	UK	15,2
Hertz	incl. CD&R, Carlyle	2005	Yes	PE	US	15
BAA	incl. Ferrovial, CDP	2006	Yes	PE	UK	13,9
Univision	incl. Providence, TPG	2006	Yes	PE	US	13,6
Proofpoint	Thoma Bravo	2021	Yes	PE	US	12,3
SunGard	incl. KKR, Silverlake	2005	Yes	PE	US	11,3
...						
Burger King	3G Capital	2002	Yes	PE	US	2,2
Burger King	TPG, KKR, GS	2010	Yes	PE	US	3,3

Legend: PE = Buyouts; IS = Infrastructure
Source: Partners Group Annual Report 2006, Sender and Crooks (2014), James (2010); chart modified and updated to include post-2007 buyouts by the author.

To do large deals, private equity firms needed to raise ever larger pools of capital. Blackstone raised the largest private equity fund of that period, with a final closing size of $21.7 billion announced in August 2007. The fact that the largest deal was a natural resource play and the second largest deal a real estate investment—both done by traditional buyout firms—shows that the distinction between these sub-asset classes had become somewhat blurred.

Club Deals and Secondary Buyout Transactions

One development that concerned investors and regulators alike were syndicates formed by buyout firms to submit "Club deals" for large transactions. These triggered fears of collusion and led to a debate about whether there was a decrease in competition. Many studies found no evidence for a price effect due to club deals and also touched on the fact that those deals are usually contested by other firms or rival syndicates and strategic buyers.[64,65,66]

Another phenomenon that continued to be discussed in the press and among investors was the increase in transactions where (different) buyout firms acted as both buyers and sellers ("sale to GP"). While limited partners of the selling fund are agnostic to who the buyer is, they may (and did) worry whether the acquired company had enough upside, given that value creation had already taken place. The share of such "secondary buyouts" was always higher in Europe. Up to 40% of all transactions fell into that category, while the share of secondary buyouts in the USA was usually well below 30%. In many conversations the author had with GPs, they pointed out that they were willing to pay a slight premium for a company that was previously private equity owned. They reasoned that PE-owned companies often have better financial management systems in place and the risk of bad surprises—those "skeletons in the closet"—was lower in their experience.[67]

---

[64] One study using a sample of completed LBOs of US publicly traded companies (mostly before 2006), found that target shareholders receive approximately 10% less of pre-bid firm equity value, or roughly 40% lower premiums, in club deals compared to sole-sponsored LBOs. This result is, however, based on a sample that mostly includes firms with low institutional ownership (Officer, Oguzhan, and Sensoy, 2010).

[65] Buyout syndicates are also just one participant in the M&A market and the market share of buyout firms in the M&A market was between 9% and 17% with a peak of 21% in 2006.

[66] Barrachi (2008).

[67] SCM Strategic Capital Management AG has analyzed client portfolios to address concerns that secondary buyouts were underperforming and found no evidence for that. This view was also shared by many GPs asked about the issue.

But the high share of secondary buyouts indicates a persistent issue—the conflict between value creation dynamics and the fixed fund life of limited partnerships. While there is no evidence that secondary buyouts are performing worse than buyouts acquired from strategic sellers, there are studies that suggest that value is lost if a fund becomes a forced seller at the end of the fund life.[68] Efforts to solve that problem would continue.

Mega-Firms Invest Across the Private Markets Spectrum

The increase in deal size and transaction volume was enabled by a boom in fundraising and by increasing fund sizes. A small group of (buyout) firms decoupled from the broader market and managed to grow AuM at a breakneck pace. In July 2006, Blackstone announced the closing of Blackstone Capital Partners V (BCP V), with total commitments of $15.6 billion, creating the world's largest private equity fund at that time, a record it broke when it announced an additional closing that brought total capital committed to $21.7 billion in August 2007.[69] In June 2006, Blackstone announced the closing of Blackstone Real Estate Partners V (BREP V) with capital commitments totaling $5.25 billion, creating the largest real estate opportunity fund ever raised. This was followed by Blackstone Real Estate Partners Europe III, which closed at EUR 3.1 billion.[70] Carlyle raised its first infrastructure fund at $1.15 billion in 2007. In addition, the Carlyle Group raised funds focused on Asia, Japan, mezzanine funds, and financial services funds. When Lou Gerstner, former chairman, and CEO, replaced Frank Carlucci as chairman of the Carlyle Group in January 2003, the firm, which had been founded 15 years earlier, had accumulated $13.9 billion of AuM.[71] In 2010, this amount increased by $106.7 billion in 84 funds.[72] A few other firms showed the same pattern. The size of their flagship funds in the "core" strategy increased dramatically while those firms also expanded by raising billions of dollars for "secondary" strategies. Large private market firms like Blackstone, Carlyle, KKR, and Apollo had become one-stop shops for alternative investing.

---

[68] Sousa (2010), Degeorge, Martin, and Phalippou (2013).
[69] Blackstone (2007).
[70] Blackstone (2006).
[71] Zippia (2022a).
[72] Carlyle Group (2011).

Not all those new business areas turned out to be profitable for investors. A study by Bain & Company looked at 105 private equity firms that added additional investment areas to their activities before the 2007–2008 financial crisis. Only 30 of those firms continued to raise funds in all the areas they were active before the crisis, while the rest abandoned at least some activities (one might assume because they did not deliver the returns expected).[73] While so far there is no "size effect," i.e., a robust negative relationship between increased fund size and returns, Harris et al. provide evidence that the "core" fund styles of GPs perform better than "secondary" style funds that are launched later.[74]

Differences in AuM growth among private market firms can be attributed to varying success in establishing track records for newly added strategies. Investors should avoid relying solely on brand names even when investing in a firm's flagship fund and be even more critical when considering recently introduced strategies outside a firm's core area of expertise.

Globalization of Buyouts

The new millennium also saw more activity in Continental Europe, including Eastern Europe. During the 1990s, private market investing was concentrated in the USA, followed by the UK, which was home to about 60% of buyout transaction volumes. But at the end of the decade, the UK share in total European transactions declined to about 40% as other Continental European markets showed more activity. But this evolution was slow in coming. In Germany, the total annual buyout transaction volume barely reached EUR 500 million in 1999, while in France, a buyout transaction volume of EUR 600 million was recorded in 1997.[75] But similar to the USA, the search for alternative sources of return driven by low-interest rates compelled more European institutions to look at private equity. The disappointing experience with venture capital in the late 1990s shifted institutional demand to buyouts. The growing interest of local investors allowed home-grown teams to

---

[73] Bain & Company (2020).
[74] Harris, Jenkinson, Kaplan, and Stucke (2020).
[75] Data on German and French buyout cited in Söffge (2016) and Le Nadant and Perdreau (2006) respectively.

raise increasing amounts of capital and poised the industry for growth in the new millennium.

The emergence of more flexible funding structures and the ability of the market to repackage, trade, and sell down credit risk, which has enabled debt providers to spread risk more widely, facilitated deal-making for buyout firms. Buyouts also gained more accept-ance in markets where financial buyers were traditionally viewed with skepticism. Besides the pan-European funds that were mostly headquartered in the UK, country funds played an increasing role in the mid-market. Managers like CapVis (focused on Switzerland and Germany), Orlando (Germany), Gilde (The Netherlands), Mercapital (Spain), PAI Partners, LBO France, Euromezzanine (all France), IK Investment Partners (Scandinavia) were able to signifi-cantly grow their asset bases and attract international LPs.[76]

Additional momentum came from EU-enlargement that created opportunities in Central and Eastern Europe where the private sector was expected to show "catch-up growth" and transforma-tion as a result of the integration of those economies into the European market. The same investment thesis drove interest in Russia. While those markets did not have a significant local investor base, firms like Innova Capital (Poland), Genesis Capi-tal (Czech Republic), Euroventures (Hungary), MCI, Mid Europe Partners (Central and Eastern Europe) or Baring Vostok (Russia) are some of the prominent names that were supported by non-domestic investors, which included European institutions as well as US investors.[77]

Another frontier opening for private equity was Asia. The first lev-eraged buyouts were recorded in South Korea and Japan in the late 1990s, and from 2003 these markets comprised over 90% of leveraged buyout transactions recorded in the region.

In 1997, Advantage Partners raised its maiden fund from a group of Japanese institutional investors. Despite being formed in 1992,

[76] Invest Europe (2020).
[77] Barings Bank was a UK-based merchant banking firm that failed after a trader (Nick Leeson) engaged in a series of unauthorized and risky trades that went sour in 1995. Its private equity business was spun out of bankruptcy and resulted in Baring Vostok and Baring Asia being formed through MBOs.

it took Advantage five years to raise a fund. Only a regulatory change in 1996 allowed a holding structure to acquire majority stakes in a Japanese company.[78] Unison Capital followed in 1998. Foreign LPs gained familiarity with Japanese private equity as several high-profile banking deals were done from 1998 onwards by foreign GPs.

Following the Asian Financial Crisis of 1997, a number of distressed opportunities occurred in the financial sector. As an example, the Long-Term Credit Bank of Japan was nationalized in 1998 and sold in 2000 to a group led by US-based Ripplewood Holdings and the bank was renamed Shinsei Bank. When the deal was exited in 2005, it reportedly achieved a 12x return.[79] Opportunities to acquire distressed banks also became available in Korea. Lone Star, for example, acquired Korea Exchange Bank in 2003 and sold it to HSBC and Hana Financial Group, a deal that led to a tax dispute between Lone Star and the Korean government. Domestic GPs, however, were only established following the 2004 Law on Private Equity Capital Gains Tax and Fund Formation that clarified fiscal and structural parameters for private equity firms.

In India, ChrysCapital launched the first domestic growth capital fund with a closing size of $64 million in 1999 and focused initially on smaller deals due to its fund size. A first opportunity which was seized by foreign GPs to do larger transactions emerged in the Indian mobile telecom sector in the early 2000s when foreign GPs closed some $1 billion deals, including Bharti Infratel by Goldman Sachs, Temasek, and Macquarie, and Idea Cellular by TA Associates, Citigroup, GLG Partners, and Sequoia. Warburg Pincus reportedly made almost $1.1 billion on its 18% stake from a $300 million investment carried out between 1999 and 2001 into Bharti Televentures, renamed Bharti Airtel. But opportunities remained limited due to lending restrictions on control deals.[80]

In Australia, Quadrant raised its first fund in 1996, followed by Archer Capital Pacific Equity Partners in 1998. Other markets followed: Seeing the opportunity to set up the first fund in Vietnam to focus uniquely on investing in private companies, Mekong Capital

---

[78] Blind and von Mandach (2021).
[79] Sharma (2020).
[80] Ibid.

launched Mekong Enterprise Fund (MEF) in 2002. Smaller Asian markets were also targeted by regional funds such as Baring Asia[81] (est. 1997, HK), Navis Capital (est. 1998, Kuala Lumpur/HK) and Affinity Equity Partners (est. 2002, Seoul/HK).

In Asia, private equity firms faced unique challenges such as legal and cultural barriers to takeovers and a focus on growth capital rather than buyouts. Additionally, Asian private equity funds were initially funded by foreign capital due to limited participation from local investors. Despite this, fundraising increased significantly from $4 billion to $45 billion from 2001 to 2010, with most capital coming from outside the region. Local funding came initially from large pension funds and sovereign wealth funds such as Singapore's GIC or Korea's NPS.

Then there was China. In 1995, China's State Council approved the Administrative Measures on the Establishment of Chinese Industrial Investment Funds Abroad, encouraging on-shore financial and non-financial companies to set up funds off-shore and invest in China. The early years of the new millennium saw the establishment of several prominent Chinese private equity firms and the start of investment activity by some older HK-based firms, including H&Q Asia (1985, HK), Walden International (est., HK), CDH (est. 2002, Beijing), Hony Capital (est. 2003, Beijing), Qiming (est. 2005, Shanghai), and Fountainvest Partners (est. 2007, HK). In addition, Asia Alternatives, one of the first local FoFs focused on Asian private equity funds, was founded in 2005 in Hong Kong. For the large US buyout firms, having established offices in Europe from the late 1990s onwards, it was now Asia that turned into focus as well. In 2005, KKR opened offices in Hong Kong and Tokyo, and Carlyle opened three offices in Beijing, Mumbai, and Sydney in 2005 alone. Other large buyout firms both from the USA and Europe would join them.

Funds focused on the rest of the globe (mostly on South America and MENA) raised $3.5 billion in 2001 and $24.5 billion in 2008.[82]

---

[81] EQT announced that it intends to acquire Baring Asia in 2022.
[82] Preqin (2021a).

In South America, Brazil became the most active market and some of the most important regional PE firms have their headquarters in São Paulo. Leader of the pack is Advent International (the São Paulo office was opened in 1997 by Patrice Etlin) that invested in the region not only $8 billion in dedicated LATAM funds raised until 2021 but also from Advent International's global funds. Other prominent firms in Brazil are GP Investimentos (est. 1993) and Patria Investimentos (est. 1988).

Investors' decreasing home bias in the private equity industry mirrored the trend in bonds and stocks since the 1980s. The lack of private equity transaction activity and domestic funds in their home markets further encouraged non-US limited partners to invest in US funds. Local SWFs, including the Kuwait Investment Authority, the Abu Dhabi Investment Authority, SAMA Foreign Holdings, Public Investment Fund, the Qatar Investment Authority, the Dubai Investment Corporation, and Mubadala, both based in Dubai, soon rose to prominence as LPs from the MENA region. However, it took some time for a local GP base to grow, and local deal activity was minimal. Super-return conferences developed into major industry events (Figure 7.12).

The burgeoning growth of the private equity industry became evident through transforming annual events like the SuperReturn conferences into major gatherings. These conferences attracted thousands of delegates who joined to network and listen to panel discussions and presentations led by experts and industry leaders (Figure 7.12).

Figure 7.12 Super-return conferences developed into major industry events.
Source: LinkedIn, KNect365 Finance/Flickr.

Trends in Partnership Terms and Conditions

- **Investment periods:** As funds got bigger, the investment period became longer too. Managers were able to propose longer investment periods to assuage the fears of their investors that the capital might not be invested. Investors seemingly preferred this to a smaller fund size, which would have resulted in cutbacks on their commitments. For the managers, this was also a way to compensate for reduced headline fees— typically below 1.5% rather than the buyout industry average fees closer to 1.8%, as longer investment periods delay the time, after which the calculation basis switches from committed capital to NAV.

- **Longer fund life:** The very large funds (> $12 billion) typically have a 5–6-year investment period and not the fixed 4-year period that used to be. Add to that 1- or 2-year extension rights, and the expected fund life is probably 15 years rather than the 10-year fixed life advertised. Investors already had the experience of having funds longer on their books than 10 years and might expect that holding periods would get even longer.

- **Key man provisions:** As GPs sold stakes to third parties, investors needed to address the commitment of their founders as well as the impact on incentive structures and perspectives of more junior (but often important) team members. The multi-strategy firms often abolished key man provisions. It became progressively impossible to link investment outcomes to individuals. As a result, investors' due diligence standards and objectives started diverging, depending on the size of the manager. For large managers the link between deal-makers and performance weakened due to the size of their teams.[83]

- **Management fee offsets:** The extent to which monitoring, transaction, and other portfolio company-related expenses, paid to the GP are offset against management fees. These clauses have become more common as transactions got bigger and investors started to scrutinize the additional income that managers derived from their portfolio companies.

- **Catch-up clause:** This clause is meant to make the manager whole so that their incentive fee is a function of the total return

---

[83] As of 2022, Blackstone listed more than 40 MDs/Senior MDs for its private equity business alone on its webpage.

and not solely on the return in excess of the preferred return. For example, if the preferred return were 8% and the manager had a 20% performance fee subject to a catch-up, the distributions would flow as follows: the investor would receive an annualized 8% preferred return and their capital back. The manager would then receive 100% of distributions until they receive 20% of all annualized profits. The catch-up percentage has often been negotiated to a number below 100% and sometimes eliminated completely.

7.6   PRIVATE REAL ESTATE

After the Greenspan rate cuts, the economy grew, and demand for commercial property increased, leading to higher valuations. Lower interest rates also prompted a shift in capital flows toward real estate. As fixed-income investments, such as bonds, offered lower yields, real estate with its potential for income generation and capital appreciation, became an appealing option for institutional investors (Figure 7.13).

Figure 7.13   The real estate boom.
Source: lzf / Shutterstock.

While the real estate boom unfolded globally, the housing boom in the United States during the 2000s had some distinct character- istics that set it apart from housing booms in other countries as it was driven by subprime mortgages, which expanded the pool of eligible buyers and caused an unprecedented increase in house prices. Fannie Mae and Freddie Mac's practices, and despite warnings about them, led to a huge increase in subprime mort- gage volume.[84]

Several factors contributed to the growth in mortgage lending:

1. Expansion of subprime loan purchases by Fannie Mae and Freddie Mac and Securitization (mortgage-backed securities).[85]

2. Rise of off-balance-sheet entities for banks to grow leverage.[86]

3. Growing demand for collateralized loan obligations (CLOs) using risky mortgages as collateral to construct investment- grade tranches (Figure 7.14).

4. Global savings glut flowed toward US safe assets, including mortgage-backed securities, driven by the search for yield.

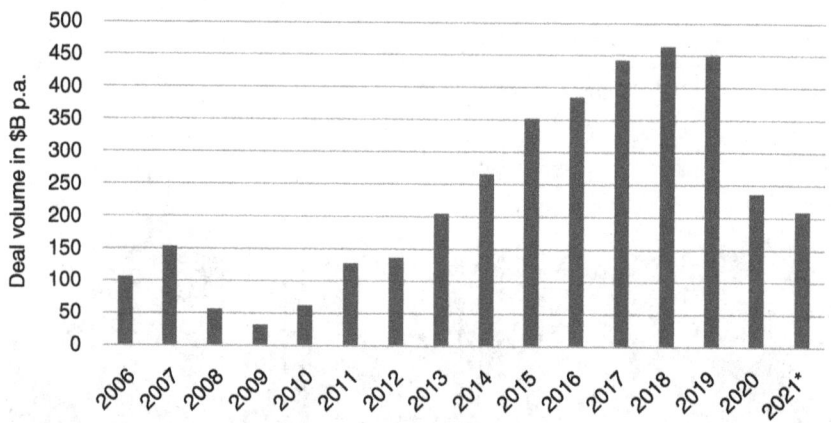

Figure 7.14 Commercial mortgage-backed security (CMBS) issuance, 1996–2010. More than $450 billion CMBS were issued in 2006–2007.
Source: Adapted from NAREIT.

---

[84] The FBI warned as early as 2006 that increasing mortgage fraud accompanies the growth of subprime mortgages (FBI, 2007).
[85] Loutskina and Strahan (2009).
[86] Acharya and Richardson (2021).

A building boom resulted from the expansion of development activity to deliver the required inventory, leading to an increase in real estate partnership fundraising and investment activities.[87] Real estate partnerships often employed leverage of 50–80% and teamed up with local developers/landowners in joint ventures with double-promotes.[88]

Fundraising

The combination of increased institutional demand and improved liquidity resulting from the rate cuts had an upward effect on property valuations. As institutional investors sought real estate assets, the demand-supply dynamics shifted, leading to increased competition and bidding for properties. This heightened demand, coupled with favorable financing conditions, boosted the capital gains that could be achieved through development strategies and created a favorable fundraising environment for private real estate funds. North American annual fundraising for private real estate funds grew from $9 billion in 2002 to almost $70 billion in 2008. The Institutional Real Estate 2007 Plan Sponsor Survey, conducted by Kingsley Associates, showed that more than 68% was targeted for value-added and opportunistic investments, which illustrates the shift toward higher-risk strategies late in the cycle.[89] Large mega-firms were able to raise multibillion-dollar funds, which allowed them to target large portfolio transactions and set the stage for a return of public-to-private deals on a scale not seen since the 1980s.

In Europe, annual fundraising also increased from $4 billion in 2002 to a peak of $30 billion in 2007. Real estate markets were already sinking when fundraising peaked (Figure 7.15).

The Real Estate Buyout: Public-to-Private Transactions

The real estate boom increased investors' risk appetite and resulted in a significant increase of opportunistic private real estate funds

---

[87] Bernanke et al. (2011).
[88] A double-promote is a two-tier performance (and management fee) system. The joint venture would provide a profit share to the local partner prior to any gains being transferred to the real estate manager's limited partnership, which would then be eligible to carry interest.
[89] Jacobius (2007).

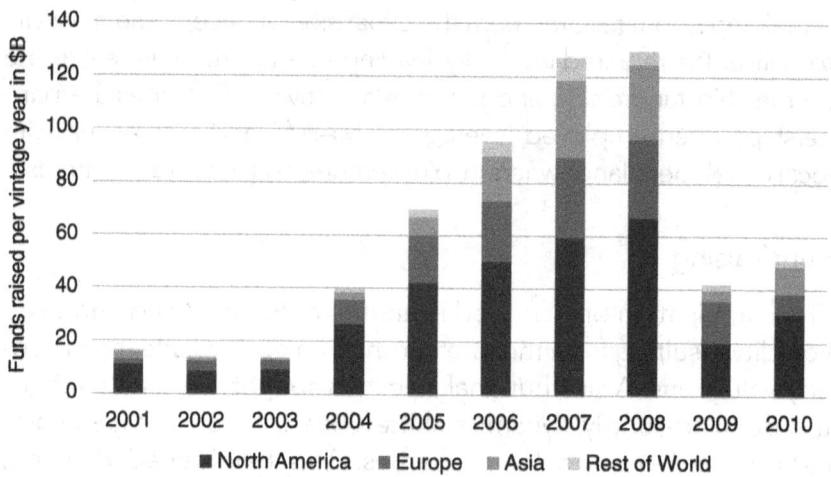

Figure 7.15   Annual capital raised by private real estate funds by geography, 2001–2010, $B.

Source: Adapted from Preqin Pro.

Note: Real estate debt, secondaries and FoFs are excluded.

raised. An opportunistic real estate fund is an investment vehicle that focuses on taking advantage of unique and time-sensitive opportunities in the real estate market. The real estate boom during the 2000s provided an environment of rising valuations that could lead to potentially high returns. Opportunistic real estate funds typically have a higher risk profile than other real estate investments, such as core or value-add funds, as they may involve higher leverage greater uncertainty and often require active and hands-on management to maximize returns. This can involve property repositioning, redevelopment, or other value-add strategies.

Private equity (buyout) firms found an edge in opportunistic real estate compared to traditional developers due to their financial expertise, access to capital, and exit strategy knowledge. Joint ventures allowed buyout firms to leverage their financial and operational expertise, and developers contributed their deep knowledge of the (local) real estate industry. The large (buyout) mega-firms entered the market through their real estate platforms. They targeted large portfolio transactions—sometimes public-to-private acquisitions of listed developers or real estate investment trusts (REITs)—to capitalize on undervalued assets or to unlock value by repositioning the properties and increasing rental income. The opportunity for some became buying core-like assets with high leverage and holding them just long enough to make improvements, then selling at a much lower cap rate.[90]

Numerous public-to-private transactions began to occur in 2004 as a result of arbitrage opportunities created by price disparities between the public and private markets involving real estate companies, both large and small, throughout the 2000s. These deals could involve REITs, property development firms, or other entities operating in the real estate sector. In these transactions, value is unlocked by minimizing overhead expenses and maximizing leverage for a scalable platform. The private owner can utilize greater leverage than the public company and convert expensive corporate unsecured property debt into securitized CMBS financing. Additionally, the conversion of public C-corporations to REITs or LLCs can eliminate double taxation. In public real estate companies, the combination of operating and property businesses muddled the values of each portion. By separating the business into an operating company and a property company (an "Op-Co" and a "Prop-Co"), the property company was assigned a higher multiple, making the property company's parts initially more valuable than the business as a whole.[91]

Moreover, the actual value of land and other non-income-generating assets is frequently understated in public valuations. Eliminating public company costs, consolidating operations, and outsourcing are ways to reduce overhead expenses. Improved operating margins, cost reductions, revenue maximization, and space re-measurement are examples of operational enhancements. As assets that are not central to the longer-term strategy are liquidated, this strategy can result in a rapid return of capital.

Public-to-private transactions differ from opportunistic real estate investment strategies that emerged after the savings and loans (S&L) crisis. Instead of acquiring undervalued assets during market disruptions and holding onto them for recovery, public-to-private transactions focus on acquiring companies whose stock prices don't reflect the actual market value of their assets (Figure 7.16). The strategy involves unlocking value by selling individual assets. This approach capitalized on the availability of low-cost debt, unlike the tighter lending conditions following the S&L crisis, and

---

[90] Lienemann Associates LLC (2004).
[91] Douvas (2012).

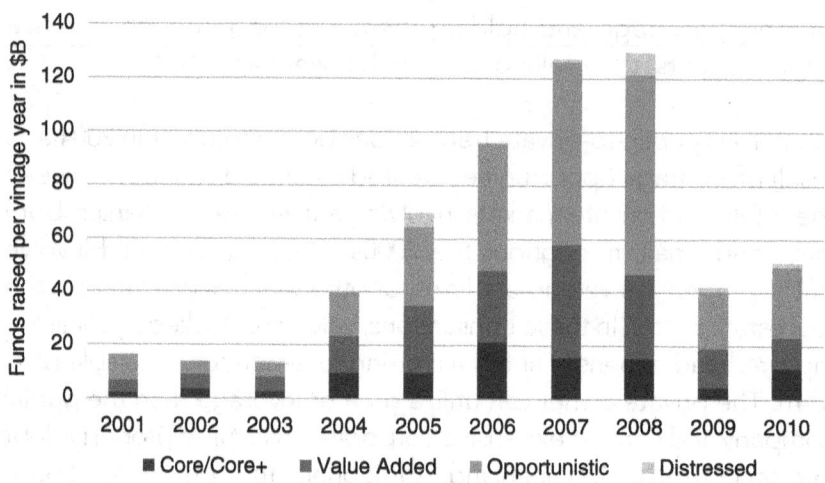

Figure 7.16 Annual capital raised by private real estate funds by strategy, 2001–2010, $B.
Source: Preqin Pro.

relied on the ability to quickly liquidate portfolios. For those who sold prior to the onset of the September 2008 global financial crisis, returns were often spectacular.

With its large funds, Blackstone was well positioned to capitalize on this opportunity. Capitalizing on its prior experience with hotel assets, Blackstone acquired Extended Stay America, Prime Hospitality, Boca Resorts, and Wyndham Hotels between 2004 and 2005. Blackstone's acquisition of Equity Office Property Holdings (EOP), led by Jonathan Gray, at the time the largest leveraged buyout ever, was the privatization that signified the market peak. Blackstone closed on this $38.7 billion acquisition in February 2007, using the remaining BREP V capital, necessitating an immediate $11 billion BREP VI raise to fund the remaining 43% of the equity (see Box 7.1).

The transaction was a standard public-to-private transaction, and the value creation strategy was predicated on dividing the portfolio into more valuable pieces than the sum of the parts. This was a rerun of the highly levered deals of the 1980s and the ability to sell assets quickly and reduce leverage was the key to success.[92]

---

[92] In October 2007, the Blackstone Group acquired Hilton Hotels Corporation through its Blackstone Real Estate Partners (BREP) V fund. The acquisition was made in partnership with other Blackstone funds, including Blackstone Capital Partners V. The $26 billion acquisition of Hilton marked one of the largest leveraged buyouts in history.

Private real estate investing during the 2000s was characterized by strong performance and growth, driven by several factors. One of the primary drivers was the low interest rate environment that prevailed during the early and mid-2000s, which made borrowing cheaper and more accessible. This allowed real estate investors to leverage their capital and take advantage of attractive investment opportunities.

When the credit markets froze with the onset of the GFC, private real estate faced particularly severe challenges. One notable example was Apollo Global Management's acquisition of Realogy (Anywhere Real Estate Inc., NYSE: HOUS), a real estate franchising and brokerage company, in 2007 for $9 billion. The acquisition was financed primarily with debt, and as the financial crisis hit, Realogy's business suffered due to the collapse of the housing market and declining home sales. In 2009, Realogy was forced to restructure its debt, with Apollo and other lenders agreeing to exchange their debt for equity in the company. Apollo ultimately retained a significant ownership stake in Realogy, which has since rebounded and become one of the largest real estate companies in the world. The example demonstrates that real estate deals involving acquiring existing businesses faced similar challenges and presented a risk profile typical of traditional buyouts. However, several public-to-private transactions relied on valuation arbitrage, with the primary strategy being the quick disposal of assets to unlock their value.[93]

Those who were not able to sell fast suffered from the combined effects of leverage and severe value declines. Another approach to creating value, which had been employed earlier in the German public housing privatizations (see next section), involves acquiring substantial residential property portfolios to narrow the disparity between existing rents and market rates. Nevertheless, the experience gained from privatizing German public housing tells us that this process unfolds at a considerably slower pace than the divestment of undervalued assets. In one scenario, you are selling buildings, while in the other, you are negotiating rent adjustments for apartments. The differences between these two strategies are

---

[93] *Wall Street Journal*, December 18, 2006, Hayes (2009), Massoudi (2012).

illustrated by two (famous) real estate transactions that took place near the end of the real estate boom. The transactions were the acquisition of Equity Office Properties (EOP) by The Blackstone Group (see Box 7.1) and the acquisition of Stuyvesant Town by Tishman Speyer and BlackRock (see Box 7.2). The EOP transaction relied on the swift sale of multiple sub-portfolios, while the Stuyvesant transaction attempted large-scale rent conversion. The results of these transactions showed that peak-of-cycle transactions made at high valuations can have very different outcomes depending on the speed at which value-creation strategies can be implemented for de-leveraging.[94]

Box 7.1   Equity Office Properties

During the early 2000s, EOP's stock traded at a discount to its net assets, around 25% The reason for its lagging stock price could have been the diverse range of its holdings, from NYC office buildings worth billions to industrial properties in California, which carried varying values based on their net operating income. An EOP acquisition would require streamlining its portfolio by selling assets and exiting the remaining grade-A properties at full value.

Blackstone, in a deal led by Jonathan Gray (Figure 7.17), purchased Sam Zell's Equity Office Properties Trust (EOP) in February 2007 (including debt). Blackstone upped their original offer of $47.50 to $55.50 per share for a total amount of $38.7 billion. Blackstone had leveraged its buyout with $32 billion of debt plus $3.5 million in equity bridge financing, leaving $3.2 billion of equity.

Equity Office Properties, with over 500 properties and 100 million square feet across the USA, held the top spot for office building management in the country at the time. Blackstone reached an agreement on the final price, which included the ability to reach out to potential buyers during negotiations. This move helped Blackstone arrange sales and minimize

[94] All fund information in this paragraph quoted from (Douvas, 2012).

Figure 7.17 Jonathan Gray started as an investment analyst at Blackstone, fresh out of college in 1992 and later rose to head the firm's real estate group before he became President and COO of Blackstone in 2018.
Source: Blackstone.

transaction risk. Based on pre-arranged sales some assets did not even become part of the EOP portfolio; seven Class A Manhattan office buildings sold concurrently with the completion of the EOP transaction (Figure 7.18). By doing so, it improved the geographical footprint of the portfolio, showing that the decision of what you keep is as important as what you sell. It's worth noting that the debt structure of the Equity Office Properties acquisition allowed for pre-payment with minimal penalties. This feature enabled Blackstone to sell off many of the properties in the months following the acquisition without incurring significant costs. This flexibility in the debt structure played a crucial role in reducing risk and optimizing the portfolio. The acquisition of EOP is widely regarded as one of the most significant and successful real estate private equity transactions.[95] It was reported that the sale yielded a $7 billion profit from the EOP buildings.[96]

(continued)

[95] Yeh (2018).
[96] Kandell (2021).

Figure 7.18   Three of the seven Class A Manhattan office buildings that New York property developer Harry Macklowe bought from EOP for $7 billion in the Blackstone acquisition.

Sources (left to right): 1301 Avenue of the Americas, Americasroof, wikimedia.org CC BY-SA 3.0; One Worldwide Plaza, Jim Henderson, wipikedis.org - public domain; 527 Madison Avenue, wikimapia.org - open source.

Box 7.2   Stuyvesant Town

Stuyvesant Town and Peter Cooper Village's 11,200 units are home to a 25,000-strong middle-income population, making it Manhattan's largest apartment complex by far (Figure 7.19). Assumptions about gains through efficient management, combined with the belief that the complex has latent gentrification potential, led Tishman Speyer and BlackRock to pay $5.4 billion.

The deal was 80% debt-financed, but the property's income supported only a fraction of the interest expense. The impact of the 2008–2009 recession and what might have been a miscalculation of repositioning potential led to only a small increase of market-rate units.[97] When a judge ruled that certain tax subsidies prohibited an owner from converting any rent-regulated units to market rates, Tishman turned over control of Stuyvesant Town to lenders in early 2010.[98]

---

[97] Staley (2010).
[98] Eide (2013).

Figure 7.19   Peter Cooper Village and Stuyvesant Town apartment complex.
Source: AP images.

Among investors, Singapore's GIC, the Church of England, and CalPERS all lost significant amounts of money.[99]

In October 2016, Blackstone Property Partners LP and Ivanhoé Cambridge, a subsidiary of the Caisse de dépôt et placement du Québec, invested $5.3 billion in Stuyvesant Town and Peter Cooper Village.[100] The purchase was funded by $2.7 billion in low-interest debt from Fannie Mae and $144 million from the Public Housing Development Corp. The new owners pledged to maintain 5,000 moderate-income units for 20 years and limit rental increases for 1,400 flats to 5% per year for five years after 2020. In 2022, a tenants' group won a lawsuit granting rent-regulated status to those 1,400 flats. It's unclear if the owners will appeal in early 2023.[101] Stuyvesant Town serves as a prime example, highlighting the challenges that investors face when seeking to bolster the financial returns of large residential portfolios, specifically when dealing with rent control or other tenant protection mechanisms. This is a time consuming where it takes years to grow revenue.

---

[99] *New York Times* reporter Charles V. Bagli's book, *Other People's Money* (Bagli, 2013).
[100] NYC (2015).
[101] Gonella (2023).

The German Property Acquisition Spree

The trend of acquiring large real estate portfolios was not confined to the USA. In 2004–2005, Germany was facing increasing budget deficits, high unemployment, and low economic growth following years of economic stagnation. The opportunity was to buy German housing companies and portfolios from corporations and the state, which needed to generate cash. The investment rationale for these acquisitions was based on the opportunity to obtain a "bulk discount" by acquiring assets at valuations that were considered undervalued. Furthermore, there was potential to increase rental income and sell the portfolio in parts to prominent listed core real estate companies, which were experiencing growing investor demand in the low-interest-rate environment.

The German government and industry owned an estimated three million residential units (14% of the residential market). In 2004 alone, more than 220,000 residential units were sold in four major transactions, the largest of which was Fortress's acquisition of the German housing company GAGFAH, from the German social security and pension agency. Others were the GSW purchase by Cerberus/Whitehall, and ThyssenKrupp Immobilien by MSREF/Corpus, Blackstone buying WCS—each for more than €1 billion (Figure 7.20). From 2002 to 2004, the number of residential units acquired increased from 20,000 to more than 260,000.[102] In 2007, German property investment transaction volume hit a record $116 billion, with half of the buyers being funds from the UK and the USA.[103]

The German Federal Government published a study in 2007 that looked at the role of foreign funds buying large property portfolios in Germany and lists some US firms among the most significant buyers.[104]

According to some market analysts, residential real estate in Europe, particularly Germany, was undervalued compared to the United States. Public housing companies and public housing have been rapidly declining due to the state's and local governments' ongoing budgetary issues in Germany. Additionally,

---

[102] All fund information in this paragraph quoted from Douvas (2012).
[103] CNBC (2008).
[104] Lorenz-Hennig and Zander (2007).

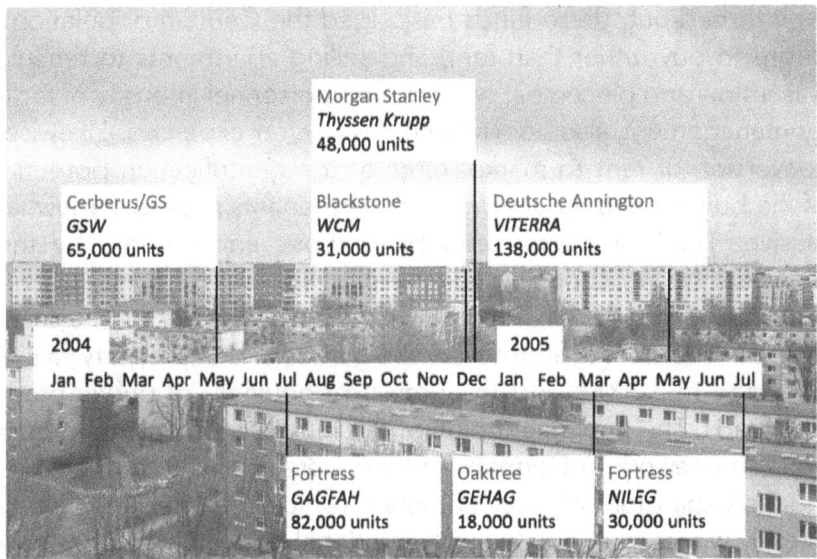

Figure 7.20 Major German residential property portfolio acquisitions by foreign funds, 2004–2005.

Legend: buyer (gray), SELLER (black, italics): GAFA was a listed real estate company, GSW, GAGFA and GEHAG were public non-profit housing companies, WCM, Thyssen Krupp and Viterra are corporate sellers, and NILEG was bank-owned real estate holding. There have been other large portfolio transactions not displayed here.

Source: Deutsche Bank quoted in Kofner (2006). Credit/Copyright background picture: Housing blocs and buildings around Alexander Platz in Berlin, Germany. Shutterstock Stock Photo ID: 2325065879, license no. 166969566.

many industrial companies were eager to sell their real estate holdings, viewed as non-core assets, because they no longer saw a need to provide company housing. As Germany had the lowest home-ownership rate in Western Europe, there seemed to be the potential to convert rent-controlled apartments to condominiums, and in addition, the ability to acquire properties.[105]

The biggest potential was seen in (former) social dwellings that offered publicly subsidized social housing and the highest potential for rent increases to market levels. This was, however, restricted by "social charters."[106]

---

[105] Kofner (2006).

[106] These charters were part of some deals and included protection clauses providing dismissal protection, rent controls, protection against luxury upgrading, and rebates for tenants willing to buy their apartments. Subsequently, there were some legal disputes as buyers were accused of reneging on those commitments. One example was the dispute between GAGFAH, owned by Fortress Group and the city of Dresden, in which it charged GAGFAH had violated tenant protection agreements. The lawsuit led to a $52 million settlement in 2012 (Reuters, 2012).

As it turned out, these funds misjudged the German population's desire to buy rather than rent, and selling apartments to tenants was a slow and piecemeal process. The personnel intensity of facility management also constrained savings on expenses. Likewise, conversion of rent to market rates or the gentrification potential of the buildings to attract more affluent tenants proved somewhat elusive. Thus, problems resembling those encountered by the Stuyvesant transaction limited operational value creation. If operational value creation did occur, it had a slow start and had a small impact. What drove returns were the general rise in property values since the mid-2000s and the growing popularity of public property funds. The implementation of the real estate investment trust (REIT) framework in Germany in 2007 was a catalyst, further driving the expansion of listed real estate vehicles. These vehicles had already witnessed heightened institutional demand amid the low-interest rate environment. The private real estate funds could either acquire additional properties to improve diversification before an IPO or sell their housing portfolio to public real estate funds that expanded beyond traditional commercial real estate sectors, such as office and retail, into residential property. Beyond Germany, the emerging European REITs market provided an exit channel once the scale and geographical diversification were achieved.[107]

The key drivers of return were:

1. Rising property valuations (until 2007).

2. The ability to acquire undervalued properties at a discount through a bulk transaction.

3. Financial engineering.

4. Improving the geographical diversification through add-on acquisitions, which was a condition of successful public market exit (REITs).

For many investors, the ultimate exit would be delayed by the GFC. Cerberus and Goldman Sachs, for example, only started exiting their 2004 investment in GSW through an IPO in 2011. During 2011–2012 they sold their stakes in GFC at a total valuation of approximately EUR

---

[107] In 2003, France was among the first to introduce a REIT regime among the European countries, followed by the UK, Germany, and Luxembourg in 2007 (Jerndal and Varga, 2018).

8.7 billion, compared to their acquisition price of EUR 1.8 billion.[108] Fortress floated GAGFAH on the German stock exchange in 2006 and raised $1.1 billion, but it took the firm until 2014 to fully liquidate its holding. It was estimated that Fortress funds garnered proceeds of $3.8 billion on a total equity investment of around $2.9 billion or a 1.8x multiple over a ten-year holding period.[109]

A second opportunity was non-performing loans that presented an opportunity similar to Japan's in the late 1990s. In 2004, German banks sold off bad loans with an estimated face value of $13 billion to $16 billion, with Lone Star purchasing up to two-thirds of the total. The prominent US players had the market almost to themselves as they had gained the experience to acquire and manage sizable non-performing loan portfolios in the USA during the aftermath of the S&L crisis. In one of the most significant transactions of its kind, Hypo Real Estate Group, a spin-off of HVB Group sold troubled loans with a face value of $4.8 billion to Lone Star in a single transaction.[110]

Emerging Markets

When investors started to worry about high valuations in developed market assets in 2006, attention shifted to emerging markets. Brazil, Russia, India, and China (BRIC) economies, jobs, and real wages grew quickly, and several demand drivers provided opportunities for new development. Increasing urbanization demanded new office, industrial, residential, retail, and hotel properties. Business travel and tourists increase demand for new hotels, especially those catering to domestic clients. The IT boom and Western and multinational companies' offshoring fueled India's economic growth, while solid commodity exports fueled Russia's and Brazil's economic growth. China transitioned from foreign investments and exports to private consumption. In 2007, Tishman Speyer became the first US manager to launch a China-focused fund, which closed on $884 million.[111] It was the first foreign group to close an RMB-denominated fund for domestic investors five years later. Gaw Capital (the Gateway Capital funds) and Winnington Capital followed by raising China-focused funds. But those managers faced

---

[108] PE Online (2012).
[109] Zacks Equity Research (2014b).
[110] Douvas (2012).
[111] Campbell (2021).

fierce competition from well-connected local developers that often had access to cheap debt financing. As a result, capital deployment was initially slower than expected.[112]

In 2006 and 2007, FIRE Capital, IREO, JPMorgan, Kotak, Red Fort, SUN Apollo, Tishman Speyer, and Xander raised capital for funds focused on India.

Jensen, Marbleton (sponsored by Alfa Capital and JER), and Rutley Capital raised funds in Russia. Brazilian Capital, GTIS, Hines, Paladin, Patria, Prosperitas, Tishman Speyer, and Vision Brazil raised funds in Brazil. While these markets were all affected to some degree by the global financial crisis, most of these funds could withstand the downturn better than funds in mature markets due to more robust market fundamentals and lower leverage.[113] But investors in markets like India and Brazil had to cope with foreign exchange losses on their investments once their currencies weakened against the dollar after 2009.

The Tide Turned

The tide turned when the real estate market corrected in 2006–2007. Several cities and areas that had seen the most rapid expansion between 2000 and 2005 began to see significant foreclosure rates.[114] Economists argued that the housing industry's downturn and the loss of consumption might result in a recession, but as of mid-2007, that had not yet happened.[115] In a paper he presented to a Federal Reserve Board economic symposium in August 2007, Yale University economist Robert Shiller warned, "The examples we have of past cycles indicate that major declines in real home prices—even 50% declines in some places—are entirely possible going forward from today or from the not-too-distant future."[116] When that finally happened, banks had to write off their loan portfolios and stopped providing new construction loans or rolling over old ones. This caused developers to fail and investors lost big on real estate equity and debt.

---

[112] Zeng (2018).
[113] Douvas (2012).
[114] Christie (2007).
[115] Bureau of Economic Analysis (2007).
[116] Quoted in Shiller (2021).

To avert equity and debt losses, banks and servicers extended numerous real estate loans between 2009 and 2011. This tactic was made viable by regulatory changes, such as a provision that restricted write-offs of the portion of loans that was greater than the value of the property as long as interest payments were made. The 2008 financial collapse punished the most heavily leveraged funds. Due to underwhelming results and Dodd-Frank restrictions, most investment banks that had real estate private equity platforms shut them down. This allowed for the entry of new actors with the expertise to purchase loans and loan portfolios, execute loan workouts, and manage real estate assets.[117]

Have Private Real Estate Funds Pulled Their Weight?

The performance of private real estate investments has displayed notable cycles, with historically, the most favorable results being realized during market corrections, when property owners found themselves compelled to sell due to financial distress. Funds that started investing after the onset of the S&L crisis throughout the 1990s and during the early years of the new millennium and from the cap rate compression that occurred did very well (see Figure 7.21).[118] But for investors that started investing during the property boom, returns were not satisfactory. Professor J. Pagliari Jr. from the University of Chicago looked at fund performance during 1996–2012 and argues that, overall, highly leveraged opportunistic funds only narrowly outperformed comparable low-risk funds.[119]

To evaluate the performance of private real estate investing, it is beneficial to examine the playbook of a developer. The initial equity investment occurs when acquiring land or an existing building. Equity is necessary to finance the acquisition, cover interest expenses, and fund building permit-related costs, in addition to any portion not covered by property loans. The second funding event takes place when construction begins, typically years later depending on jurisdiction and project size. Construction loans

---

[117] Levitin and Wachter (2017).

[118] The Partners Group data seems consistent with data from Burgiss Group for value-add and opportunistic real estate partnerships of vintage years 2007–2011, which includes both US and non-US funds. It shows a pooled IRR of 5% as of year-end 2020. Data quoted in Mercer (2021).

[119] Pagliari (2013).

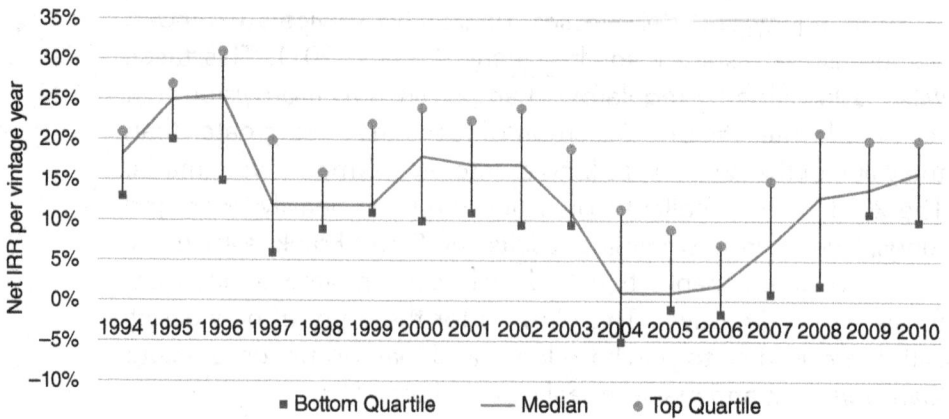

Figure 7.21 **Private real estate performance (IRR) by quartile, vintage years 1994–2010.**

Source: Adapted from Monfared, Persistency in Alternative Asset Strategies.

Note: The earlier vintage years until 2003 have few observations, and the quartile boundaries may thus be not meaningful. However, the performance pattern and median net IRR appear consistent with the Partners Group Thomson Reuters Private Real Estate Index data as of December 31, 2011. They should therefore provide a good feel for the performance pattern of private real estate.

partially finance the construction phase, with loan terms dependent on transaction risk mitigated by leasing agreements or off-plan sales. Since land often does not generate significant capital gains during the project duration, development value creation primarily arises from the difference between construction value and the on-sale value of the property. However, this margin is unlikely to yield the 2x capital gains typically targeted by opportunistic funds. While multiples may be lower than in buyouts, the equity investment duration tends to be shorter due to sequential investments land acquisition, planning, permitting, and construction. Real estate development may thus generate high internal rates of return (IRR) rather than high multiples. While investors may find a deal-level multiple of 1.3–1.5x appealing—witnessed by the many private and institutional direct investors that have achieved good results over long periods—it becomes insufficient when delivered through a private equity-type fund with fee and carried interest structures similar to buyouts. During booms, developers often rely on land price increases for additional upside and off-plan sales or leasing agreements ahead of construction to minimize the equity requirement.

Investors should carefully consider whether the use of leverage by opportunistic real estate funds aligns with the investment strategy or if it is primarily driven by the aim to achieve private equity like returns to justify the fee structure. High leverage may be justified during distressed periods when assets can be acquired below replacement value and downside risk is limited. However, the same approach is unsuitable for pure development, which plays a more prevalent role during economic booms. In the latter scenario, developers risk having insufficient equity once the valuation cycle turns, and the debt burden may become unsustainable until a recovery phase ensues. Those boom-and-bust cycles keep repeating, which led to the term "opportunistic real estate." Historically, investing during difficult times has produced superior vintage-year returns. Although this was not the case during the 2000s real estate boom, the next big window of opportunity for distressed real estate investing was right around the corner.

7.7 INFRASTRUCTURE

Equities and bonds issued by infrastructure businesses have long been included in institutional portfolios. Investors commonly access infrastructure assets in two ways: either by investing in securities listed on global exchanges or by investing directly in the assets themselves and/or through pooled investment vehicles. Similar assets can be accessed via listed or unlisted markets.

For example, Melbourne Airport is owned by unlisted investors, while Sydney Airport (SYD:ASX) or Frankfurt Airport (Fraport AG (FRA.DE) are owned and operated by public companies. Several Spanish motorways are owned by publicly traded Abertis Infraestructuras, S.A. (ABE.MC). In contrast, the Indiana Toll Road and Chicago Skyway are owned by institutional investors and were previously held by private infrastructure partnerships (see Box 7.3). The same applies to water utilities: Thames Water is owned by unlisted investors, while American Water Works (NYSE: AWK) is publicly listed. To reflect the listed infrastructure universe, several new infrastructure indices (capturing only publicly listed infrastructure securities) have emerged since the mid-2000s. In December 2021, the Dow Jones Brookfield Infrastructure Index consisted of 101 companies with a market capitalization of around $2.2 trillion. The sector breakdown shows that utilities, energy generation, and communication are the main sectors of

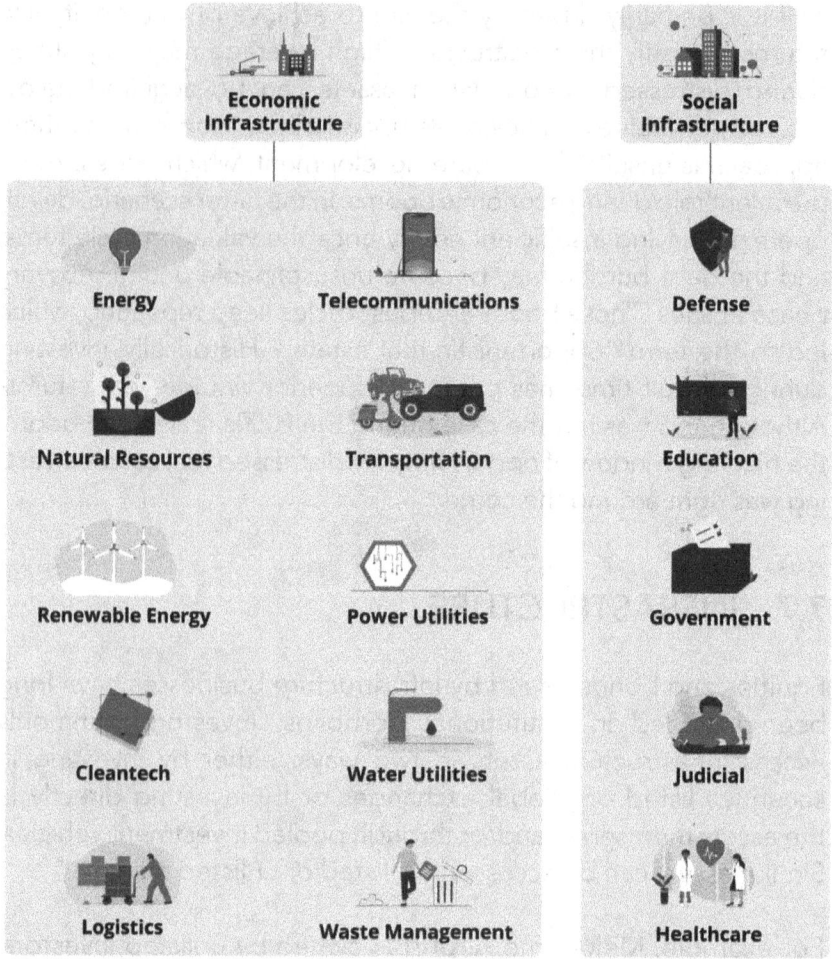

Figure 7.22   Infrastructure sectors.
Source: Adapted from Preqin, 2022a.

listed infrastructure.[120] Listed infrastructure is therefore a significant sector of the public markets.

Infrastructure comprises public and private physical structures such as roads, railways, bridges, tunnels, water supply, sewers, electrical

---

[120] About 60% of investors use listed IS indices as benchmarks for their private market infrastructure portfolios (Amec et al., 2019). Among the most widely used indices are the UBS Global Infrastructure & Utilities Index, the S&P Global Infrastructure Index, the Dow Jones Brookfield Global Infrastructure Index and the FTSE Global Infrastructure Index. For a description, see Maple-Brown (2015), Wang et al. (2023).

grids, and telecommunications (including internet connectivity and broadband access). Infrastructure may be owned and managed by governments or by private companies. Generally, most roads, major airports and other ports, water distribution systems, and sewage networks are publicly owned, whereas most energy and telecommunications networks are privately owned. Investments by private capital investors were concentrated in economic infrastructure, i.e., transportation, energy, and telecommunications. Other sectors, such as renewable energy, cleantech, logistics, waste management, and social infrastructure, only gained significance after 2010.

Dedicated infrastructure funds were first set up in the mid-1990s in Australia, following the One Nation program of infrastructure development introduced by the government and carried out from 1991 to 1996 in the aftermath of the early 1990s recession (Figure 7.23). It involved the privatization of assets in Australia, including electricity and airports.[121] Landmark transactions included electricity assets in the State of Victoria and airport privatizations by the federal government. Australia was also an early adopter of the PPP model; many such partnerships involved large transport projects, particularly urban toll roads and tunnels. Infrastructure investing in

Figure 7.23   Australian port owned by IFM investors.
Source: cefc.com.au.

---

[121] Infrastructure Partnerships Australia (2017).

Australia was traditionally outsourced to external fund managers. Australian banks were pioneers in packaging privatized and other infrastructure assets into mainly listed fund vehicles.[122]

Therefore, the privatization of Australian assets stood at the beginning of a new, specialized infrastructure asset class, which quickly extended to Canada. Some Canadian pension plans, notably the Ontario Teachers' Pension Plan (OTPP) and the Ontario Municipal Employees Retirement System (OMERS), were early investors in infrastructure in the late 1990s and early 2000s, second only to Australian superannuation funds. Other funds followed, and the average allocation of Canadian pension plans was 5% of total assets in 2012. As in Australia, there is usually a "size effect", i.e., large pension plans made substantial investments in infrastructure, while small and medium-sized pension funds had little or no private infrastructure allocation.[123] The Canadian funds also showed a preference for direct investments. According to Preqin (2011), 51% of institutional Canadian infrastructure investors make direct investments, the highest figure in the world. Direct investments come with lower fees compared to investments through funds. Dyck and Virani report a mean figure of 0.44%, while the Canada Pension Plan Annual Report notes a mean of 0.39% on their infrastructure NAVs. This is considerably lower than the 1.5% on committed/invested capital that infrastructure partnerships charge according to a Preqin report.[124]

The "Canadian Model," in which large pension funds make direct infrastructure investments and indirect investments through specialized funds, started private investing in the asset class, i.e., not using listed closed-end vehicles common in Australia. Typically lacking the size of the large Canadian pension plans the Australian model of indirect investing also became a template for investors in Europe and the United States in the early 2000s. Investments were accessed through limited partnerships that used terms and conditions that were copy-pasted from buyouts and other private market investments. Little thought

---

[122] Inderst (2009).
[123] Inderst (2014).
[124] Preqin (2011, 2015c); Dyck and Virani (2012).

was given to whether this form of ownership was suitable for assets that come with the promise of stable long-term cash flows.

Infrastructure funds witnessed significant growth in the number of funds closed and capital raised during the 2000s. At the end of the decade, AuM for private infrastructure funds totaled $167 billion, or around 6.8% of the total private market AuM (Figure 7.24).

Investments in infrastructure have characteristics that appealed to yield-starved investors seeking additional diversification and alternative sources of income in their portfolios and rising institutional demand fueled fundraising but finding investable assets posed a challenge. In infrastructure investing, a distinction is made between "greenfield infrastructure" (developing a new asset) and "brownfield infrastructure" (acquiring an existing asset that may require additional investment for capacity enhancement, upgrading, etc.). Greenfield investment is riskier as it involves development (obtaining building permits, dealing with objections by stakeholders or construction delays, and cost overruns). Greenfield investment also comes with a delay until the stable cash flows that investors are looking for can be delivered, as the asset needs to be operational before it can generate cash flows. As many deals involved greenfield projects, there was the issue whether investments in infrastructure funds would provide the attributes cited below.

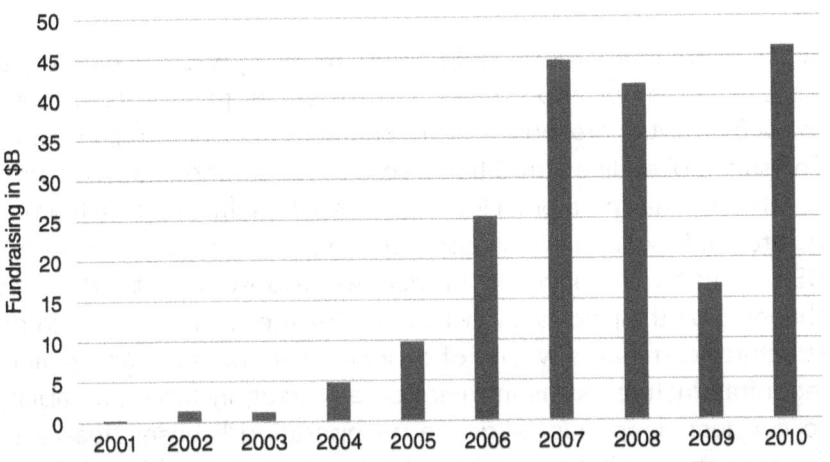

Figure 7.24   Unlisted IS fundraising, 2000–2010, in $B.
Source: Adapted from Preqin.

Key characteristics that investors frequently cite as reasons that attract them to the asset class are:

1. The long duration of many concessions of many infrastructure investments made them an attractive asset class for investors that needed to fund long-term liabilities.

2. Strong free cash flow, since operational assets usually have low operating and maintenance expenses as a percentage of revenue received.

3. Consistency of cash flow due to infrastructure assets' durability, which generally exceeds two decades, and the predictable and consistent long-term income flows well-suited to fund long-term liabilities.

4. Barriers to entry result in stable demand. Because infrastructure assets provide essential services, demand for them is often steady over time. There is also a barrier to entry due to the high cost and complexity of developing infrastructure assets.

5. Inflation protection due to provisions to adjust fees in line with consumer price inflation (CPI) or another measure of inflation.

When infrastructure investing started to gain traction in Europe and the USA in the mid-2000s, investments were offered through limited partnerships. Some Australian managers, such as Macquarie, became significant players due to their home market experience (see as follows).

In 2007, Britain's largest cable company, NTL, was to sell its network of communication masts and towers as part of its strategy to focus on its core business of electricity and gas transmission. The sale looked like a traditional spin-off, and various buyout firms considered making a bid. However, when the infrastructure team at Australia's Macquarie Bank approached the advisors of one of the US buyout firms looking at the deal to propose a joint bid, it was shunned by their advisors at Lehman Brothers. Macquarie's infrastructure team had a wealth of experience in investing and financing infrastructure assets in their home market, including an ability to conduct deep due diligence on operating licenses, leases or concessions, capital expenditure budgets, creditworthiness of customers, and scrutiny as well as the re-negotiation of service-level agreements that underpin the responsibility and liability for operating the asset.[125] Two years before, NTL sold the Australian part of its broadcast business to Macquarie Communications Group (MCG) and Macquarie was on the lookout for similar opportunities in Europe.[126]

Macquarie sought stable, long-term businesses that paid steady dividends, using high leverage and long-term debt with credit insurance to reduce risk. They, convinced investors that infrastructure lending was safer than buyout loans and they accepted lower yields, longer maturities, and higher loan-to-value (LTV) ratios than traditional LBO financing would deliver.

Not being able to partner with one of the buyout firms looking at the deal Macquarie decided to bid on its own. As Macquarie entered the bidding process, it approached it with the mindset of long-term project financing that combined high leverage with asset-based loans that had lower yields compared to LBO financing. It was thus able to offer a higher price, which resulted in its acquisition of NTL's UK wireless business. Macquarie then took full ownership of the company in 2007 and renamed it Arqiva, which became one of the UK's leading communications infrastructure and media services providers.[127] The US buyout firms were somewhat shocked to lose the deal to a player relatively unknown outside Australia.

The deal was one of the largest infrastructure transactions at the time, demonstrating the potential for private investment in essential infrastructure assets. In 2007, Macquarie's $4.9 billion acquisition of National Grid Wireless was another significant milestone for the firm.

However, large transactions involving mature traditional infrastructure were comparatively rare. When fundraising increased strongly during 2006–2008, managers' primary difficulty was locating assets and deploying funds.

---

[125] The anecdotal evidence as well as a description of the skills that allowed Macquarie to be successful in the bid for National Grid Wireless are discussed in Khajuria (2022). But long-dated loans with high leverage can also put infrastructure investments in peril (see Box 7.3 on the Chicago Skyway).
[126] Wright (2004).
[127] Kavanagh (2018), Harrison (2004).

Few privatizations of operational assets meant greenfield investments were common. However, such investments require substantial development before cash flow, which is contrary to the goal of committing to the asset class for long-term cash flow stability. The incentive structure of limited-life funds and private equity-type carried interest motivates GPs to sell assets upon completion rather than holding them for cash flow.[128]

There is a perception that brownfield infrastructure is less risky than greenfield infrastructure, with terms like "core," "value-add," or "opportunistic" being used to describe investment strategies. However, applying these real estate terms to brownfield or greenfield projects can be misleading. Similar investments, such as toll roads in different countries, can have significantly different risk profiles (see Box 7.3).

Box 7.3   Toll Road Privatizations: A Tale of Two Outcomes

Toll roads are a classic example of stabilized, long-term brownfield assets with recurring and inflation-protected revenues. In 2004–2006, toll road concessions were auctioned in both the USA and France. In a study undertaken by Harvard University and the University of Barcelona, Germa Bell and John Foote analyzed the reasons for the different valuations obtained by the Chicago Skyway and Indiana Toll Road concessions in the USA and the French motorways.[129] Both countries enjoy high country ratings, and the transactions were comparable in size and complexity. In many respects, the roads and the auction

---

[128] Some infrastructure partnerships have been established with a fund life of 15 years plus extensions but that does not fully resolve the issue of fund life limitations and creates a strong moral hazard that managers of underperforming funds sit on the assets to maximize fee income.

[129] Bell and Foote (2007). The authors analyzed this paper analyzes the main features of the Chicago Skyway and Indiana Toll Road concessions in the US and the Autoroutes du Sud de la France (ASF), Autoroutes Paris-Rhin-Rhône (APRR) and Société des Autoroutes du Nord et de l'Est de la France (Sanef) concessions in France.

(a)   (b)

Figure 7.25 **(a) Autoroute Paris-Rhine-Rhône. (b) Chicago Skyway**
Sources: (a) Autoroute Paris-Rhine-Rhône / wikimedia commons / Public Domain / CC-BY 3.0; (b) Josh Evnin / Flickr/ CC BY 3.0.

Country	Country rating S&P	Type	Terms of the auction				
			Seller's objective	Duration	Toll increases*	Leverage restrictions	Maintenance requirements
USA	AA+	Privatization	Price	99 years	Greater of CPI or GDP	No	General maintenance standards
France	AA+	Privatization	Price + consumer welfare	23 years	capped at 70% of CPI	Yes, max. 40% of transaction value	Specific maintenance budget (verified)

Figure 7.26 **Comparison of US and French auction terms.**
Note: *Both concessions had a schedule of fixed toll increases for some years.

processes were similar. There were two key differences, however: Compared to the terms of the French auction, the two US concessions had a much longer duration and came with no leverage restrictions. In addition, toll increases (indexing) and maintenance requirements (minimum criteria versus specific investment budgets) were different (Figure 7.26). The terms of the auction (Figure 7.26) and the buyers' assumptions and winning bid (Figure 7.27) reflect the bid for Chicago Skyway and the bid for the Autoroute Paris-Rhine-Rhône (APRR). In 2005, the Skyway concession was purchased by Cintra Infraestructuras of Spain and Macquarie Group of Australia. Their bid of $1.83 billion was nearly $1 billion higher than the second-highest bid. The winning bid for APRR was also won by consortium led by Macquarie (Figure 7.27).

(continued)

Asset	Buyers' growth assumptions			Winning Bid			
	Toll increases (in %)	Traffic growth (in %)	Operating expenses (in %)	Leverage / EBITDA multiple	Price/ EBITDA multiple	Buyer	Transaction date
Chicago Skyway	4.0	1.2	2.2	35x	60x	Cintra, Macquarie	2004
Autoroutes Paris-Rhine-Rhône (APRR)	1.2	0.2	3.5	6.9x	12x	Effiage, Macquarie	2005

Figure 7.27   Buyers' assumptions and winning bids for the US and French toll roads.

There are disparities in the assumptions for traffic growth and operating expense growth between the Chicago Skyway and the APRR toll roads. These differences, despite the long duration of the Chicago Skyway concession, did not account for the varying valuations proposed by the same bidders for the US and French toll roads, as noted by Bell and Foote in 2007. The bidders' revenue growth assumptions could be too optimistic, and this would have a more pronounced impact on the Skyway concession due to the less aggressive traffic growth assumptions for French toll roads. However, it's worth noting that the winning bidders' traffic growth projections for the Chicago Skyway proved accurate.

The authors argue that the key factor contributing to the divergence in valuations is the substantially greater leverage employed in the US transaction (Figure 7.27). They assert that if a leverage cap, akin to that of the French toll roads, had been implemented, it would have raised the weighted cost of capital from 9.4% to 11.7%. This change in the cost of capital would have had a significant effect on valuations, particularly considering the long duration of the US concessions.

The outcome of the privatizations could not have been more different. Investors paid 12x EBITDA for APRR and 60x EBITDA for the Chicago Skyway. Several bidders were involved in both the French and the US privatizations. The fact that Macquarie won concessions in France and the USA rules out the greater fool explanation for the difference in prices paid.

By 2015, the owners of Chicago Skyway had run into cash flow problems and struggled to service its debt. Despite those challenges, the owners were able to sell it at the end of the year to the Canada Pension Plan Investment Board (CPPIB), Ontario Municipal Employees Retirement System, and Ontario Teachers' Pension Plan. They each bought a one-third stake for a total of $2.8 billion, resulting in a one-billion-dollar profit on exit. The investors were thus rescued from possible insolvency by the yield compression and its effect on the NAV of their long duration concessions that facilitated a profitable exit to a consortium of several Canadian pension plans in 2016. The original syndicate that won the auction is still managing the French concession as of 2022 but Macquarie had sold down its stake to other shareholders and exited its remaining holding in APRR in early 2020.[130]

When governments balance privatization sales proceeds with consumer welfare by imposing price increase caps or requiring specific maintenance budgets, higher valuations put more financial pressure on the concessionaire. Toll roads represent a typical case of long-term infrastructure assets whose value is assessed through discounted cash flow analysis. They serve as a demonstration of how auction terms can affect valuations and the risk characteristics of otherwise similar transactions (see Box 7.3).

As noted by Kempler, S. (2020), private infrastructure transactions can command substantial premiums compared to the valuation multiples seen in publicly listed infrastructure. The example of toll roads serves as a reminder that it is essential to acknowledge the vast differences in risk profiles among investments in the same asset type, with one of the primary drivers of these disparities being the capital structure.

---

[130] Sociétés de Vinci Autoroutes (2022).

For instance, owners of the Chicago Skyway encountered difficulties in meeting their debt obligations, and some other toll road operators even faced insolvency. This experience highlighted that assets promising stable, inflation-protected cash flows have their own set of risks. To determine the value of an asset, one must make revenue projections over several decades, as even slight deviations from these forecasts can significantly impact free cash flows. Even without price competition and amidst a period of decreasing interest rates that boosted asset values, investments in infrastructure carried the potential risk of insolvency.

Indeed, assets often commanded higher valuations upon exit or emerging from bankruptcy than the initial purchase prices paid by investors. This phenomenon can be attributed to the extended duration of these assets, which resulted in significant valuation uplifts as a consequence of the secular decline in interest rates and yield compression.

In the words of Maple-Brown (2023), who analyzed numerous private infrastructure deals, "Unlisted infrastructure managers have historically been willing to employ higher levels of leverage to enhance equity returns. The combined factors of increased leverage, rising asset prices, and a widening valuation gap between assets in the publicly listed and private markets have significantly contributed to overall performance."

But the terms of concessions and other quasi-monopolistic assets are just one aspect of investment risk. Many infrastructure assets, such as airports, ports, and waste management companies, are businesses that face competition, swings in demand of the business cycle as well as high operating costs. Their risk profile is thus very different from assets that require mainly a sunk-cost investment up front with limited overhead and maintenance expenses. Cyclical businesses in the infrastructure space are no different from other companies that buyout firms target. Unsurprisingly, there has been a considerable overlap with buyout and infrastructure firms investing in airports, power transmission companies, or waste management companies, to name but a few. Real estate funds would invest in warehouses, logistics, or student housing as did infrastructure funds. Natural resource funds invest mid-stream, i.e., in pipeline and storage facilities, which are also a target for infrastructure funds.[131] Investors in private markets found themselves exposed to infrastructure deals without intentionally including the asset class in their portfolios. This raised doubts about the necessity of an additional allocation to infrastructure. Some deals labeled as "infrastructure" were essentially regular buyouts.

What is clear is that during the first decade of the millennium, many deals done by private infrastructure funds did not involve the acquisition of stabilized cash flow generating assets (brownfield) but rather investments in projects that required development or assets that had cyclical revenue and operated in competitive markets (Figure 7.28).

Investor surveys of that time indicate that investors were unhappy with the partnership format as it often forced the managers to sell assets once they generated recurring cash flows due to their fund life constraints.[132] Fee structures and terms in infrastructure funds were criticized for incentivizing managers to use excessive

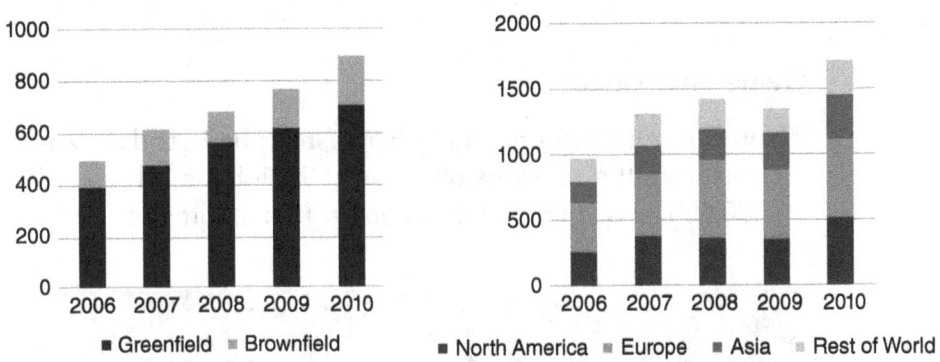

Figure 7.28 **2006–2010 infrastructure deals by stage and geography, # of deals.**
Source: Adapted from Preqin.

---

[131] Bridgepoint, a European mid-market private equity firm, bought Leeds-Bradford airport in 2007, while Global Infrastructure Partners bought London City Airport in 2006.
[132] Preqin (2011).

leverage, which reduced investment resilience during economic or credit market downturns. Consequently, major institutional investors preferred making direct investments and often acquired assets from infrastructure funds, as seen in the case of London City Airport (Box 7.4). While limited partnerships may be suitable for greenfield projects that may have a capital gain objective, they were not suitable to hold assets for stable long-term cash flows. To address this, managers needed to develop investment solutions that align with long-term objectives, as discussed in Chapter 8.

Box 7.4   London City Airport: When the Sky Has Its Limits

Airports are a classic example of a traditional infrastructure project. Until the pandemic, their revenue from passenger handling (take-off and landing rights, luggage handling, etc.) was considered a steady and expanding source of income due to increased air traffic. London City Airport (LCY), which opened in 1988, illustrates such an investment (Figure 7.29).

Ownership History

When Dermot Desmond, an Irish investor, purchased the airport from the previous owner in 1995, it handled around 500,000 passengers per year. It had a limited route

(a)   (b)

Figure 7.29   (a) London LCY in the 1990s and (b) LCY Airport Expansion Project.
Source: British Midland Airways and Bechtel.

network due to the airport's short runway. The airport's expansion increased the range of planes flying to LCY, there was growing business with private jets, and the connection to Docklands Light Railways made the airport more accessible. When Desmond sold his interest in LCY in 2006, 2.5 million passengers traveled through LCY annually.

In 2006, AIG Financial Products and GIP paid £750 million for London City Airport—32x more than Desmond had spent 11 years earlier. The new owners created a three-phase plan to increase passenger capacity to 8 million between 2015 and 2030.

The plan's first phase, submitted in 2007, was much delayed due to several protests and lawsuits. After eight years, Boris Johnson (then Mayor of London) intervened, and the final permission was issued in 2016. Even so, LCY was sold in 2016 to a Canadian consortium that included Alberta Investment Management Corporation (AIMCo), OMERS, the Ontario Teachers' Pension Plan, and other investors for £2 billion, or 2.7x AIG's and GIP's initial investment.[133]

A Challenged Business Model

London City is one of England's priciest airports, with an unusually high dependence on passenger and landing fees, which amount to 80% of revenue compared to 60% at Heathrow. Given the average flight length at each airport, LCY's high aeronautical income per passenger makes it initially unattractive to airlines (Figure 7.30).

Generally, airports serving more long-haul destinations will charge more than those offering more short-haul flights. The growth of passenger volumes was driven by business travel

(continued)

---

[133] Hepp (2021).

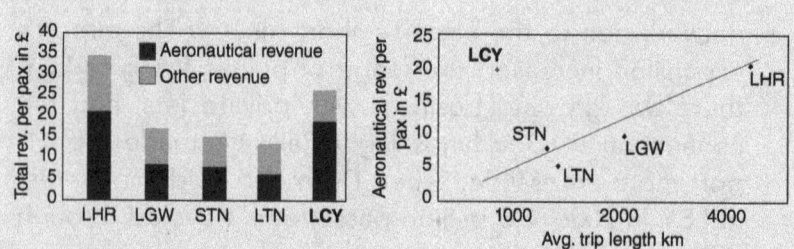

Figure 7.30   (a) Revenue per passenger (GBP) for London's Heathrow (LHR), Gatwick (LGW), Stansted (STN), Luton (LTN), and City (LCY) airports in 2013. (b) Revenue per passenger per average trip length, 2013*.
Source: Data: (CAPA, 2014).
Note: *Nearest to financial year 2013.

and passengers' willingness to buy premium tickets to reduce their commute to the financial hubs of the City of London and Canary Wharf. This is an illustration that even pure play infrastructure investments carry commercial and business cycle risks that limit the predictability of returns.

Long-haul jets require more expensive infrastructure, such as longer runways, more extensive stands and gates, and larger luggage handling equipment. Aeronautical fees tend to be higher at airports that serve many long-distance routes. The ability of airlines to recuperate costs via fares is also higher for longer trips as those tickets cost more to begin with. LCY has the shortest average trip time of all London airports, which makes its aeronautical fees uncompetitive for discount carriers.

BA offered the only long-haul service to New York JFK through Shannon. But in 2016, BA announced that it would terminate one of its two daily long-haul flights to New York City due to cost concerns, which was dashing hopes that LCY might attract more long-distance flights.

To alleviate the reliance on aviation fees, the new owners suggested expanding the terminal by 400%, increasing revenue from retail, catering, and lounges. These plans, however, were thwarted by the COVID-19 epidemic, and construction work was halted indefinitely in August 2020. The speed and extent of business travel recovery following the pandemic are challenging to forecast, with Brexit adding to the uncertainty.

The postponement of terminal construction will also prevent a diversification of income streams for the foreseeable future, putting the airport in danger of having too few aircraft connections if business travel does not rebound and airlines terminate services.[134]

The example shows that airports are exposed to demand swings, and their revenue mix makes them more or less attractive to specific aviation industry segments. LCY, for instance, is not viable for discount carriers. Its traffic growth was driven by full-fare business traffic to London and the willingness of passengers to pay a premium to reach an airport close to the Canary Wharf and the City of London. While the airport had been a good investment for several infrastructure investors, it has recently run into trouble due to the changes brought by the COVID-19 pandemic and, possibly, Brexit. The example also shows that very large institutional investors are an important exit channel for an asset held by infrastructure funds. Airport investments were made by buyout funds and infrastructure funds, and this is not evidence of a lack of asset class integrity but reflects the fact that even undisputed infrastructure investments can have characteristics that are closer to traditional buyouts than the stable and predictable long-term return that is commonly associated with the asset class.[135]

7.8 NATURAL RESOURCES

Natural resources refer to a hybrid asset class that includes venture capital (exploration), private equity (trading, production, and service businesses), and infrastructure investment risk profiles (transport, storage, renewable energy) (Figure 7.31). It is, therefore, no surprise that private natural-resource investment began as a sub-category of private equity and infrastructure, eventually growing into its own category. Despite the increase in fundraising and investment activity since the mid-2000s, natural resources remained a niche segment (see Figure 7.32).

---

[134] Ibid., CAPA (2014).
[135] Reportedly, as of early 2023, OMERS had written down its stake in London City Airport to zero.

Figure 7.31   Natural resources.
Source: Preqin.

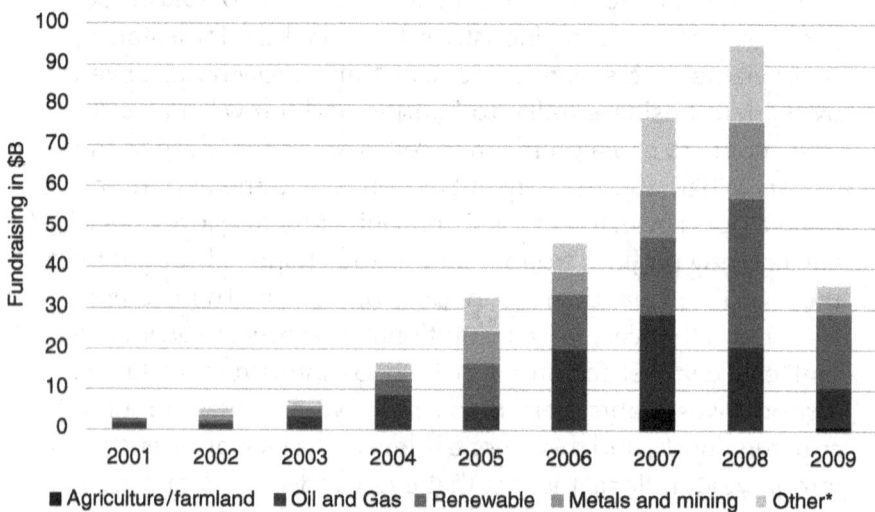

Figure 7.32   Natural resources capital raised, vintage years 2001–2009, $B.
Source: Preqin.
Note: *Other includes water and diversified funds.

Energy (both traditional and renewable) is the biggest sector within natural resources, with agriculture, timber, mining, and water playing very minor roles (Figure 7.32). Within traditional energy, shale gas extraction and storage, pipelines, processing, and distribution provided opportunities for both natural resources and infrastructure funds in recent years. These investments have very different risk profiles. Midstream activities such as petroleum product storage, processing, and transportation (operating tanker ships, pipelines, or storage facilities) are more cyclical and sometimes negatively correlated with energy prices.[136] In contrast, pipeline operators, for example, may charge a volume fee, resulting in economics somewhat unrelated to oil or gas prices. Refining, distributing, and retailing are examples of downstream investments in petroleum products. Funds

[136] Exploration (upstream) is typically the riskiest part of the business due to its high exposure to oil and gas prices and high project risk.

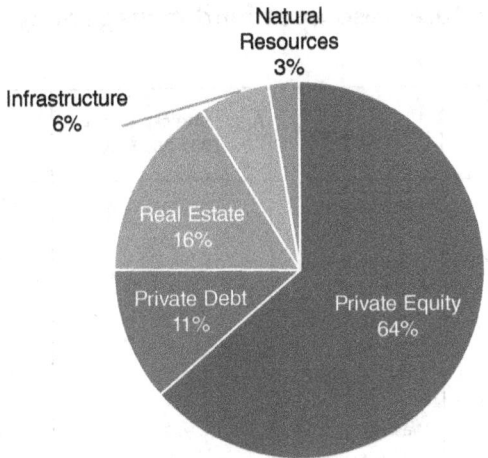

Figure 7.33   AuM of private market asset classes as of year-end 2010 (total $1.7T).
Source: Adapted from Preqin.

investing in traditional energy raised about $116 billion during 2001–2009 and those funds were mainly focused on North America. Funds targeting renewable energy raised a total of $130 billion, of which two-thirds were targeting opportunities in Europe.

Private equity investments in renewable energy are more common in Europe than in the USA (Table 7.3). There the sector benefited from EU and national government initiatives that provided subsidies, guaranteed feed-in tariffs, and tax benefits for renewable energy.[137] However, despite the buzz, there is little in the way of performance data that would allow us to assess the performance of private equity investments in renewable energy during the first decade of the millennium. But anecdotal evidence points to a mixed picture as policy reversals, changes in subsidy regimes, and other factors caused investor losses.[138] The USA also has a long history with solar energy (as one might expect, given the climate in many states). Solar One was built in 1981 as the world's first pilot solar power tower. However, due to the cheap cost of conventional energy and the relative lack of incentives, solar energy and other renewable energy installations have been slower to acquire traction in the US energy market than in Europe.

---

[137] Germany, for example, had the world's greatest installed photovoltaic capacity until 2014. Additionally, it ranks third in the world in terms of installed wind capacity, with 59 GW in 2018, and second in terms of offshore wind capacity, with over 4 GW.
[138] In 2011, Spain slashed its subsidies to solar and wind industries, creating huge losses for investors (Webb, 2011).

Table 7.3 Top 12 natural resources fund managers by capital raised in 2007–2017

Firm	Headquarters	Aggregate capital raised 2007-2017, $B	Other activities
EnCap Investments	Houston, USA	28	Infrastructure, Growth Capital
Global Infrastructure Partners (GIP)	New York, USA	26	Infrastructure
Brookfield Asset Management	New York, USA	25	Real Estate, Infrastructure
Riverstone Holdings	Tornoto, CAN	28	Specialist
EIG Global Energy Partners	Washington, USA	13	Infrastructure
NGP Energy Capital Management	Irving, USA	13	Infrastructure
First Reserve	Greenwhich, USA	13	Infrastructure
ArcLight Capital Partners	Boston, USA	11	Infrastructure
Energy & Minerals Group	Dallas, USA	11	Specialist
Energy Capital partners	Short Hills, USA	10	Infrastructure
Carlyle	Washington, USA	10	Multi-strategy
Macquarie Group	Sydney, AUS	8	Infrastructure

Source: Preqin (2017a), data as of 12/2017.

The first oil- and gas-specific PE firms in the United States were established in the late 1980s in Texas. Houston-based EnCap, Enervest, and Dallas-headquartered Natural Gas Partners were the pioneers of this genre of private equity investments in natural resources in the USA. Other forms of finance tend to target "proven" operations in the oil and gas industry by focusing on established businesses with producing, rather than potential, hydrocarbon reserves. The shale gas boom provided momentum for natural resources funds that would invest in emergent producers that needed capital to develop their oil and gas properties. This would be done by providing mezzanine or growth capital and thus provided investors to invest through private equity or private debt vehicles. In 2000, shale gas provided only 1% of US natural gas production; by 2010, it was over 20% (Box 7.5).[139]

---

[139] Field (2021).

Box 7.5 The Shale Gas Boom

Increased access to new and enormous natural gas reserves through fracking has substantially increased US shale gas output since 2007. In 1997, Nick Steinsberger, an engineer of Mitchell Energy, applied the slick water fracturing technique, using more water and higher pump pressure than previous fracturing techniques.[140] This new completion technique made gas extraction widely economical in the Barnett Shale and was later applied to other shales and started the "shale gas boom" in the USA (Figure 7.34). Technological breakthroughs have led to a sharp increase in shale gas production in the United States from 11 billion cubic meters in 2000 to 137.9 billion cubic meters in 2010, accounting for 23% of natural gas production.[141] In 2009, the United States surpassed Russia to become the world's largest producer and resource country of natural gas. By 2010, shale gas accounted for 23% of US gas output.[142]

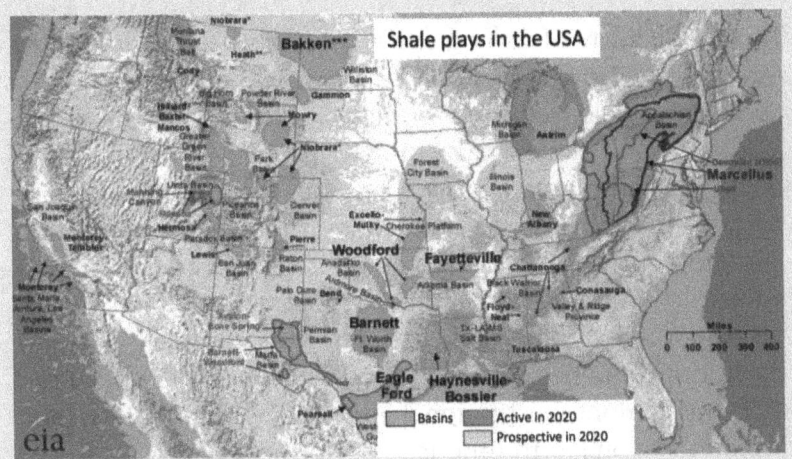

Figure 7.34 EIA map of shale gas fields in the USA.
Source: US Energy Information Administration / Wikimedia Commons / Public Domain.

(continued)

---

[140] Russell (2014).
[141] DePamphilis (2014).
[142] US Energy Information Administration (2010).

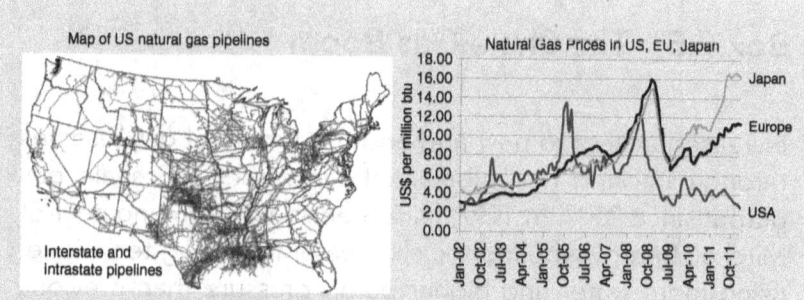

Figure 7.35   Map of US gas pipelines and gas price chart, 2002–2011.
Source: US Energy Information Administration / Public Domain.

Oil and gas prices experienced an upward trend during the 2000s, with surging oil and gas prices in 2005 and 2008 (Figure 7.35). The primary cause for the rise in oil prices in the 2000s was growing Chinese demand. Besides the high and growing demand, additional variables affecting supply and pricing were at play. These included, most notably, the sharp depreciation of the US dollar between 2000 and 2008, which had a pro-cyclical effect since oil is traded in this currency.[143]

The productivity of drilling shale gas wells has grown due to advances in moving drilling rigs between neighboring areas and using single well pads for many wells.[144]

Shale gas production growth has been supported by significant investments in additional pipelines, liquefaction and storage facilities as well as terminal and transportation infrastructure to facilitate the product's distribution. Natural resource funds and infrastructure funds equally pursued these opportunities. While shale gas development occurred in other nations, institutional investors concentrated their investments on North American opportunities.

---

[143] Cardillo (2012).

[144] One of the consequences of shale gas exploration was the development of "tight oil" or shale oil production in deep underground shale beds (Fetzer, 2014). During the oil and gas price boom it became commercially viable to expand shale gas exploration and production, which were accompanied by significant improvements of technology that helped to bring the price of production down (Energy Information Administration, 2011).

For natural resources funding, the acquisition of oil and gas assets in the US basins as well as midstream infrastructure required to condition and deliver product from the wellhead to market offered many attractive investment opportunities. Investments are often minority stakes, i.e., growth capital to fund further acquisitions or expansions. Exit routes are IPOs or a sale to corporate buyers, such as an oil major. But the sector is also the focus of infrastructure and buyout funds, which are quick to move in when the opportunity is there. In August 2006, for example, Carlyle Group and its Riverstone Holdings affiliate partnered with Goldman Sachs Capital Partners in the $27.5 billion acquisition of Kinder Morgan, one of the largest pipeline operators in the US (Mouawad, 2006).

It is noticeable that the list of the largest natural resource fund managers includes prominent infrastructure managers such as Global Infrastructure Partners and Brookfield and multi-product firms such as Carlyle.

The performance of natural resource funds launched during the millennium's first decade was very volatile, with median returns in the low single digits and numerous funds losing money. This was often caused by the large oil and gas price swings that hurt many investments in the traditional energy sector. In renewables (both solar and wind), backtracking of governments regarding feed-in tariff guarantees invalidated many business plans and caused significant losses too (Global Subsidies Initiative, 2010).

7.9 SOME LESSONS LEARNED FROM 30 YEARS OF PRIVATE MARKET DATA

During the 2000s, the private markets industry experienced growth, innovation, and heightened investor interest. Buyouts were particularly prominent during this time, with firms raising substantial amounts but other private market sectors, such as opportunistic real estate or infrastructure, gained in significance. At the eve of the onset of the Global Financial Crisis, private markets had emerged as an "industry," with many participants maturing from small partnerships into institutions expected to outlast their founders. This achievement was underpinned by a track record of consistently outperforming public markets over long periods. Much of the academic research and investor experience in this asset class reflects private equity, particularly within the USA. This is because newer segments of private markets and private equity outside the USA often lack the length and depth of historical data required to form robust conclusions. Data quality, or the lack of it, had a critical impact on the findings of earlier research papers on outperformance, as R. Stucke described in his paper "Updating History."[145]

In October 2014, Steven Kaplan published "Private Equity Performance: What Do We Know?" in the *Journal of Finance*. The authors found that buyout funds showed on average, a 3–4% annual outperformance. Venture capital had shown strong results during most of the 1980s and 1990s but after the late 1990s, venture capital funds underperformed public markets.

Investors have come to understand that private market returns follow cycles, with strong years often succeeded by weaker ones. Certain strategies, like venture capital, might face extended periods of underperformance, whereas others, such as opportunistic real estate or secondaries, flourish due to distressed asset opportunities and limited liquidity. This makes their performance especially responsive to market conditions and asset availability. In contrast, buyouts are influenced by market trends too but primarily driven by the success and growth prospects of individual companies. Yet, investors also grasped the benefits of diversification over time. During bullish market phases, surging AuM suggest increased capital commitments to private markets to maintain desired portfolio allocations Bull markets coincide with robust M&A activity, leading to heightened deal-making and realization of portfolio assets which can turn a private markets program cash flow positive, thereby reducing the NAV of existing fund commitments and compounding

---

[145] Phalippou and Gotschalk (2006) found that when correcting for high valuations of unrealized portfolio, companies private equity returns showed an underperformance compared to public equity results. Higson and Stucke (2012) discovered severe anomalies in the underlying data. Funds continued to be part of the database with their last available valuation carried forward unchanged after updates from GPs stopped or were not available anymore from public sources. Those funds were still used to make performance comparisons.

the under-allocation issue. To mitigate this effect investors often commit more capital, i.e., their commitment pacing is pro-cyclical. Practitioners' experiences and academic research discourage, however, commitment strategies that mimic the fundraising cycle.

AlpInvest/Carlyle's Peter Cornelius puts it bluntly: "A market-neutral strategy aiming at maintaining a constant market share in the fundraising market leads to the worst outcome."[146] The negative relationship between the fundraising cycle and performance has also been documented in several other studies.[147]

Harris, Jenkinson and Kaplan report: "cyclicality in private equity performance that associates high levels of fundraising with lower subsequent fund performance."[148]

But commitment pacing, i.e., the budgeting of annual commitments is just one challenge. How many funds to add to the portfolio, should investments be concentrated with a few managers or widely spread is another important decision investors face. Diversification in the public markets is primarily understood to be a risk management concept in which an investor mitigates performance risk by not putting all of one's eggs in one basket. Many investors base their view on the diversification of systematic stock risk that underpins the CAPM. The literature suggests that 30–50 different stocks essentially eliminate unsystematic (diversifiable) risk.[149] Even today, many GPs make that point.

A study by Adams Street Partners examined 26,322 portfolio companies from 964 partnerships. It shows a Pareto distribution, i.e., few events dominate the outcome (Figure 7.36). VC returns are driven by positive outliers ("break-out deals"). Somewhat more surprising, this holds for buyouts as well. A little more than 20% of buyout deals account for 100% of the gains. The

---

[146] Quoted from Brown et al. (2020).

[147] See, for example, Robinson and Sensoy (2016).

[148] Quoted from Harris, Jenkinson, and Kaplan (2014). Phalippou, Gottschalg and de Silanes (2009) found that deal-making is a significant driver of returns: investments held at times of a high number of simultaneous investments underperform substantially.

[149] For example, Evans and Archer (1968) suggest that additional diversification gains rapidly declines after holding more than 10 stocks. Statman (1987) suggests that diversification benefits (after transaction cost) persist for holdings of 30–40 stocks.

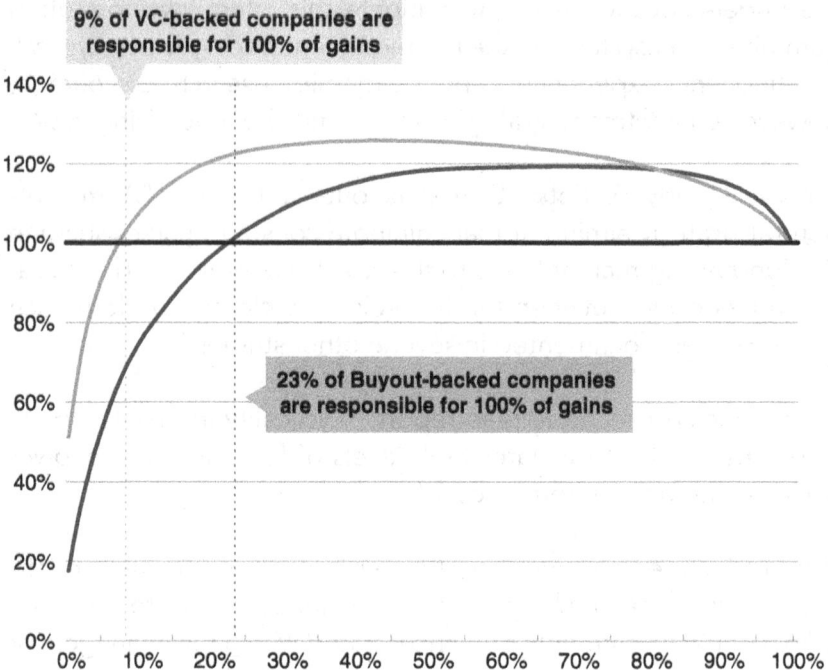

Figure 7.36   Company contribution to total gain, cumulative in %.
Source: Adams Street Partners.

Note: Based on the underlying data set of companies in which Adams Street has invested on a primary basis, as of 3/31/2021. The data set consists of 26,322 portfolio companies from 964 partnership funds from Adams Street.

rest is mostly returning money (while in VC write-offs are a high percentage).

Their result is consistent with VC FoFs manager Horsley Bridge Partners, who looked at 7,000 startups financings of vintage years 1985–2014 in their database and found that 5% of the deals generated 60%t of their total gains.[150]

Research by A. Buchner et al. found highly skewed deal-level outcomes that deviated substantially from a normal distribution to measure total fund risk.[151]

---

[150] Mallaby (2022).

[151] Buchner, Mohamed, and Schwienbacher (2016) looked into deal-level and fund-level cash flow data based on 18,256 unique investments in portfolio companies done by 769 VC and buyout funds during the 1980–2009 period from the Center for Private Equity Research (CPERES) database.

WHAT DOES THIS MEAN FOR INVESTORS?

The fact that breakout deals drive buyouts and venture capital fund performance has implications for diversification. So, a fund with 20–40 investments should not lose money (in buyouts). However, beyond risk mitigation, power law distributions—the most commonly known being the 80/20 law of the Pareto distributions, have essential implications for diversification. In a power law distribution, a small number of investments or assets have a disproportionately large impact on the overall performance of a portfolio. A few highly successful investments can significantly contribute to portfolio returns, while most investments may have little impact. Getting exposure to a sufficient number of deals is therefore essential. Figure 7.37 uses Swiss statistics on male height and wealth declared in tax returns and illustrates that normally distributed outcomes such as the height of the average person require a relatively small sample to estimate the average for a much larger population. If one is looking at average wealth one notices that by missing even a tiny number of very wealthy individuals the estimate for the national average wealth is underestimated. In order to have a high probability of actually achieving median or average

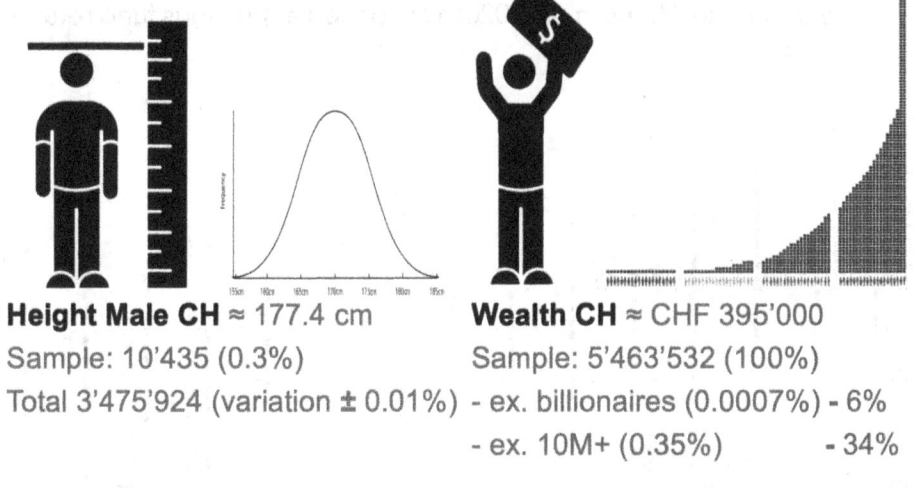

Height Male CH ≈ 177.4 cm
Sample: 10'435 (0.3%)
Total 3'475'924 (variation ± 0.01%)

Wealth CH ≈ CHF 395'000
Sample: 5'463'532 (100%)
- ex. billionaires (0.0007%) - 6%
- ex. 10M+ (0.35%)   - 34%

Figure 7.37 What do power laws mean? Estimating height and wealth.
Source: Bundesamt für Statistik (30.10.2020). Die Schweizerische Gesundheitsbefragung 2017 in Kürze—Konzept, Methode, Durchführung and Bundesamt für Statistik Vermögen natürlicher Personen 2019.

returns in private markets, one needs to aim for exposure to hundreds of deals in buyouts and thousand or more deals in venture capital, which is vital to return capture as it increases the likelihood of not missing those "break-out" deals that drive returns. This also suggests that the number of funds held in a portfolio should be large. Furthermore, suppose investors that use FoFs or separately managed accounts allow a manager to add some venture to a predominantly buyout-focused strategy. Adding a few VC funds will, however, not give exposure to the (large) number of deals required to have a high probability of achieving median VC industry returns. A better course of action would be to use a part of the commitment and invest in venture-focused FoFs that have a higher likelihood of giving exposure to a critical number of deals.

There is also little scope for GPs to concentrate investment in companies that exceed expectations in buyouts. The bet is made up-front. Relying on a limited number of deals to generate a fund's returns leads to a broader range of performance outcomes compared to public market funds. This emphasizes the significance and inherent risk of manager selection (Figure 7.38).

Recent research papers find that buyout fund performance is only modestly persistent and more robust pre-2001 than thereafter while VC funds tend to have a somewhat higher and more stable persistence. Harris et al. (2020) also looked at previous fund returns

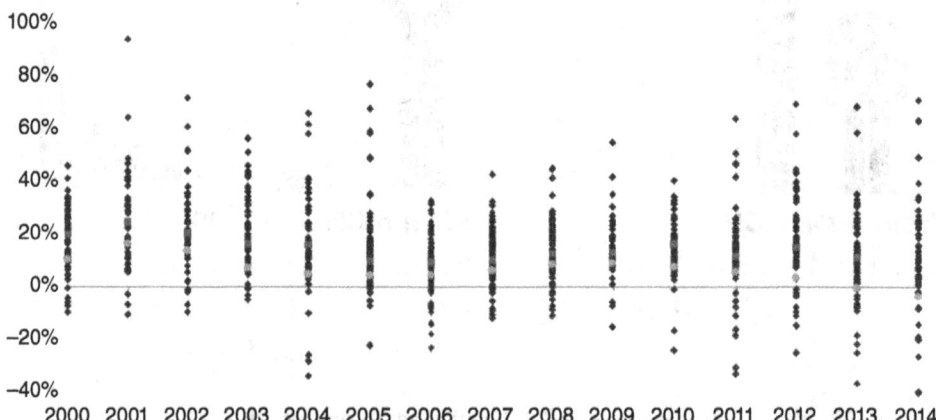

Figure 7.38   Net IRR of buyout funds globally by vintage year.
Source: Preqin (buyout funds data as of most up-to-date figures, the chart does not show funds with a net IRR >100% and <–40%), Mercer analysis as of December 2016.

reported when a successor fund was launched. The authors find that those interim results—both absolute, and relative versus a public benchmark or a peer group—have very little predictive value with regard to final outcomes. Using fund returns at that stage shows no persistence for buyouts and significantly smaller persistence for VC funds. It may seem logical to consider the performance of the most recent fund when making decisions about a commitment or re-up to a new fund offering from a manager because it is the most up-to-date information available. The assumption is that the performance of the manager's previous fund is indicative of their capabilities and track record. However, this logic overlooks the fact that the interim results of a predecessor fund have very little predictive value.[152] VC is somewhat of an exemption as there are a number of firms that have shown an ability to serially achieve top-quartile performance with their funds (Table 7.4). But access restrictions prevent most investors from investing with those managers.

Table 7.4 Examples of consistent top-performing venture capital fund managers

Firm	Headquarters	# of funds in database	# of funds in top quartile
Battery Ventures	US	11	8
Summit Partners	US	11	6
OrbiMed Advisors	US	5	5
Co-Win Ventures	China	7	4
Matrix Partners	US	6	4
The Column Group	US	4	4
Sequoia Capital	US	4	4
Benchmark Capital	US	3	3
CyanhillCapital	China	4	3
Kleiner Perkins	US	6	3
AJU IB Investment	South Korea	3	2
Index Ventures	UK	3	2

Source: Preqin 2019 global private equity and venture capital league tables, data as of December 2019.
Note: Given that many high-performing VCs are access-restricted, one must assume that they are underrepresented in databases, and the data shown in the table is thus incomplete.

---

[152] There are a few buyout or growth equity managers who have shown persistence that is comparable to top venture firms: TA Associates, Vista Equity Partners, Thomas Bravo, Bain Capital and Hellmann and Friedman are such examples.

Investors face the challenge of building portfolios that give them exposure to a large number of deals—possibly in the thousands and to spread their investments across a large number of funds. A few insights stand out after decades of investing:

- **Implementation takes time:** Investors must have a patient, long-term perspective as it takes time to fill an allocation and even more time to see results.

- **Manager selection is crucial but manager (and fund) diversification is even more important:** Choosing the right private equity manager is a critical factor in achieving favorable returns and there is no magic formula. Historical performance is at best a weak indicator of future results, making it important to assess a manager's strategy, team, and track record comprehensively. But due diligence is better in identifying weak or improbable performers rather than finding the next top-quartile fund.

- **Diversification drives returns:** Investments across different funds, vintage years, industries, and geographies can help mitigate risk and is crucial to capture performance that follows a power-law distribution. Power-law distributions require large samples, which means lots of deals in a private markets portfolio.

- **Resources:** Private markets investing requires resources and, given minimum subscription amounts are typically in the $5–10 million range, this requires commitment budgets that only very large investor can muster.

- **Pooling investments:** FoF-type solutions should not be avoided because of their additional fee layers if the alternative is a more concentrated portfolio with exposure to fewer deals as this reduces the probability of achieving or exceeding market returns.

- **Alignment of interests:** Ensuring alignment between investors and fund managers is crucial.

Investors learned that a steady build-out of their private market programs and a focus on consistent capital deployment with the aim of gaining access to many deals are crucial for success. In the decade to come, that quest to cast the net wider, find cost-effective solutions to do so, and find new ways of cooperating among investors and between LPs and GPs would shape the role of intermediaries and the private markets industry.

PART III

Becoming Indispensable

Chapter 8

The GFC and the Surge of Private Markets

In Spring 2007, the UK bank Northern Rock announced at its AGM that it was the best capitalized bank in the UK, and would be returning "surplus" capital to shareholders. And according to internationally agreed risk calculations, it was indeed the best-capitalized bank in Britain. The risks weights mandated by regulators assumed that mortgages were among the safest assets one could invest in; however, if you stripped out the risk weighting, the liabilities of Northern Rock were eighty times its equity capital.

—John Kay and Mervin King (2020)

Figure 8.1 People queuing outside a branch of Northern Rock to withdraw their savings due to fallout from the subprime crisis. After the first run on a British bank in 150 years, Northern Rock was nationalized in February 2008.
Source: AP images.

8.1   THE GREAT FINANCIAL CRISIS AND ITS IMPACT

The financial crisis of 2007–2008, known as the Global Financial Crisis (GFC), was the worst economic downturn since the Great Depression of 1929, according to the International Monetary Fund (IMF).[1] This "perfect storm" included expansive lending to low-income homebuyers, excessive risk-taking by global financial institutions, and the implosion of the US housing bubble. The value of mortgage-backed securities (MBS) related to American real estate and a complex network of derivatives linked to those MBS plummeted. The mortgage crisis severely harmed financial institutions all across the world.[2]

---

[1] Gopinath (2020).
[2] Wharton (2008), Williams (2010).

Then came September 2008. Fearing a meltdown in the US housing market, the US government took direct control of Fannie Mae and Freddie Mac—the two government-sponsored enterprises at the epicenter of the mortgage crisis. This was done by putting them into conservatorship on September 6, 2008. The US government would ultimately provide $191.5 billion in government funds to avert a collapse.[3]

On September 15, 2008, Lehman Brothers filed for bankruptcy. A day later, insurance giant AIG received a government bailout—the first of several—of $85 billion (see Box 8.1).[4] On September 26, 2008, Washington Mutual was put into liquidation—then the largest banking failure in US history. An international banking crisis unfolded across all major economies. Hank Paulson, US Treasury Secretary at that time, wrote "Tuesday, September 16, 2008 . . . Peer Steinbrück, the German finance minister, called to say that it was unthinkable AIG could go down. Christine Lagarde, the French finance minister, echoed his view: everyone was exposed to AIG, and its failure would be catastrophic."[5] From December 2007 to June 2009, the US economy lost over 8.7 million jobs. In the months after the recession began, the unemployment rate peaked at 10%, and American households lost over $16 trillion in net worth.[6] To keep the global financial system from collapsing, governments engaged in massive bailouts of financial institutions and adopted other market-supporting monetary and fiscal measures.[7]

---

[3] From 2012, the two companies have given the Treasury all their profits and as of the first quarter of 2019, have paid the government $297 billion—well above the $191.5 billion in government funds they received (Schroeder, 2019). As of 2022, the two firms were still government-owned.

[4] Banking failures are described in Stackhouse (2017). The total size of the bailout grew to $182 billion. As was the case with Fannie Mae and Freddie Mac, the government would ultimately make a profit on its investment.

[5] Paulson (2010), p. 233. his view: everyone was exposed to AIG, and its failure would be catastrophic."

[6] Data job losses and household financial losses cited in CBPP (2018) and Vo (2013).

[7] Sakelaris (2014).

Box 8.1   AIG: Too Big to Fail

Even before the GFC, AIG's relationship with its regulators and supervisors was rocky. In 2005, AIG was the subject of several fraud investigations by the Securities and Exchange Commission (SEC), the US Justice Department, and the New York State Attorney General's Office. Chairman and CEO "Hank" Greenberg was dismissed in February 2005 because of an accounting scandal.[8] The New York Attorney General's investigation culminated in a $1.6 billion fine against AIG and the filing of criminal charges against some of its executives.[9]

But AIG (Figure 8.2) continued to expand through acquisitions, international expansion, and a new product line—credit-derivatives default insurance. AIG insured tens of billions of dollars' worth of derivatives against default but did not attempt to minimize the risk through reinsurance. It then used the deposit collateral for the derivatives insurance it

Figure 8.2   AIG headquarters on 175 Water Street, New York City.
Source: American International Group / Wikimedia commons / Public Domain.

---

[8] *Insurance Journal*, November 24, 2004.
[9] Talton (2018).

received from clients to secure loans used to buy mortgage-backed securities.

When the mortgage market collapsed in 2007–2008, AIG was forced to pay insurance claims while compensating for losses in its collateral accounts. Following the announcement of heavy financial losses and a drop in the stock price, CEO Sullivan resigned on June 15, 2008. On September 17, 2008, the US government installed a new chairman of the board to oversee the restructuring. CNN Money reported on September 17, 2008, that the situation was so dire that an AIG bankruptcy was possible. AIG was far larger and more complex than Lehman Brothers, and releasing all of its assets simultaneously would have caused a meltdown of the financial system. Experts also raised doubts about the existence of sufficient qualified investors that could acquire the firm and its subsidiaries.[10]

The bailout: on September 16, 2008, the Federal Reserve Board provided AIG an $85 billion two-year loan to prevent its bankruptcy and further stress on the global economy. On November 10, 2008, the FED restructured its aid package and provided additional funds to the Treasury. After those changes, the total bailout was $180 billion.[11] AIG's size was decreased by the sale or spin-off of a number of assets.

By 2012, AIG had returned the US government $205 billion. The Financial Stability Oversight Council ruled in September 2017 that AIG was no longer a systemically important financial institution (SIFI) as a nonbank financial firm.[12]

Some developing economies, including China, Brazil, India, and Indonesia, grew significantly during the GFC. Europe faced a banking and sovereign debt crisis. The latter's impact was longer-lasting than the housing bubble's implosion and financial system spillover.

---

[10] Paulson (2010), who also references the CNN Money reporting.
[11] Agelides (2011).
[12] Amadeo (2020).

The European sovereign debt crisis was another element in this drama. It began in late 2009 when the Greek government revealed that its budget deficits were far more significant than previously estimated—again, fake accounting was the root cause of the crisis. Still, this time it was sovereign accounting rather than the corporate variety.[13] Greece requested external assistance in early 2010 and was granted a bailout package by the European Union (EU) and the IMF in May 2010. European nations launched a variety of financial support measures both in early 2010 and late 2010, including the European Financial Stability Facility (EFSF) and the European Stability Mechanism (ESM).[14] The European Central Bank (ECB) also aided in the resolution of the crisis by cutting interest rates and offering low-interest loans totaling more than one trillion Euros to keep money flowing between European banks. On September 6, 2012, the ECB reassured financial markets by offering limitless free support for all Eurozone nations participating in an EFSF/ESM sovereign state bailout/precautionary program, via yield-lowering Outright Monetary Transactions (OMT).[15]

Fear and Panic

Writing about these events in hindsight, one must not forget to mention the fear and panic that prevailed in those years (Figure 8.3). Savers staged bank runs in various countries and withdrew deposits. In Switzerland, some pension funds bought physical gold or withdrew cash balances from UBS—the country's largest bank—to make deposits with (public) cantonal banks as they feared the country's largest bank would go under. This was not just paranoia. In Iceland, all three of the country's major privately owned commercial banks defaulted in late 2008 with assets equal to more than 11x the national GDP.[16] The unthinkable became the norm. People were afraid to lose their savings, their pensions, and even their life insurance contracts as that sector was wobbling too.

---

[13] *The Economist* (2008).
[14] Robinson (2010).
[15] ECB (2012).
[16] *The Economist* (2008).

Figure 8.3 **The floor of the New York Stock Exchange on Sept. 29, 2008, when the Dow Jones industrial average and the S&P 500 each recorded its worst decline as measured in points.**
Source: Associated Press / Alamy Stock Photo.

There were doubts whether the Euro or even the European Union would survive another year.

As panic spread, general partners (GPs) received calls from limited partners (LPs) imploring them not to dare to send a capital call. Stocks or loans were stuck as banks negotiated bail-out programs. Trust in counterparties evaporated as nothing appeared certain anymore. For most people who experienced the GFC, it was the most brutal and scary episode (economically speaking) in their life.

Regulatory Response(s)

In 2010, the Dodd-Frank Wall Street Reform and Consumer Protection Act was enacted in the USA as a response to the crisis to "promote the financial stability of the United States." It set financial industry rules in place and also initiatives to prevent mortgage businesses and lenders from taking advantage of customers. Dodd-Frank gave new tools to the toolkit of the US government for regulating and enforcing laws against banks and financial intermediaries (Figure 8.4).

Figure 8.4   Screenshot showing the opening of Panel 4 hearing on April 20, 2010, of the US House Financial Services Committee to investigate the Lehman Brothers Banking failure.

Source: National Cable Satellite Corporation/ C-Span.org; https://www.c-span.org/video/?293077-4/2008-lehman-brothers-failure-panel-4 / last accessed July 14, 2023.

The Basel III capital and liquidity standards were also adopted by countries worldwide. A successor to Basel II became effective in 2004 as a response to the dotcom and telecom busts. One of the key elements of Basel III was strengthening capital requirements intended to make the banking system more resilient. While Basel II also imposed a minimum total capital ratio of 8% on banks, Basel III increased the portion of that capital that must be in the form of Tier 1 and Tier 2 assets from 8% to 10.5%. Basel III also eliminated an even riskier tier of capital, Tier 3, from the calculation.[17]

The GFC showed how interconnected the financial system had become. Banks had to be rescued, and insurance companies—once

---

[17] Tier 1 capital includes equity and retained earnings. Tier 2 capital comprises revaluation reserves, hybrid capital instruments, subordinated term debt, and loan-loss reserves. Basel III also required banks to maintain a countercyclical capital buffer or rainy-day fund of 0% to 2.5% of their risk-weighted assets. So they'll have more capital during a recession when they face greater potential losses (BIS, 2019, 2020; Moody's Analytics, 2011).

a byword for prudence and solidity—were in distress too. Apart from the $180 billion bailout of AIG, about 63 failures and near misses of European insurance companies prompted regulators in all major markets to act.[18]

Solvency II was the new European set of rules implemented in the following years. The new rules strengthened the Solvency Capital requirement, which is the sum of funds insurance and reinsurance companies must hold to have a 99.5% confidence they could survive the most extreme expected losses for a year. Capital required needs to be calculated on a market-based approach, meaning that assets and liabilities would be valued at the amount they can be exchanged for, transferred, or settled in the market.[19]

A divergence between regulatory perspectives and investor sentiments became apparent, as investors would subsequently proceed to augment their allocations to private markets wherever feasible, despite the regulators' stance on heightened capital requirements discouraging such allocations. This contrast in views is particularly noteworthy, given the private markets' demonstrated resilience during the GFC and their ability to curtail portfolio volatility, as discussed in the next section. Additionally, no retrospective evidence indicates that escalated leverage resulted in an upsurge of default rates, despite high-profile cases that implied the contrary.

Impact on the Financial Sector

At its core, the GFC was a crisis in the financial sector, in particular, the banking and insurance sectors. As the economic crisis progressed and rescue packages were agreed upon, banks faced massive write-downs on their loan books (up to $3.5 trillion, according to some estimates).[20] This adjustment occurred more quickly in the United States than in Europe, where banks took years to repair their balance sheets and raise extra equity to comply with stricter capital requirements. As a result, new loan activity declined, and

---

[18] EIOPA (2018).
[19] EIOPA (2022).
[20] BIS (2010).

banks mainly abandoned the financing of mid-market leveraged acquisitions during the next decade, particularly in Europe.

Banks also sold stakes in private equity partnerships, which they had joined to develop ties with GPs to support their leveraged lending operations. As was the case ten years ago with in-house venture capital teams, the in-house private equity teams would be spun off or liquidated, with the private equity fund portfolio put up for sale. This was a repeat of forced selling observed after the dot-com bust. The only difference this time was that insurance companies joined banks as forced sellers.

Insurance firms faced capital requirements for private market investments twice as high as those for listed shares, effectively shutting them out of the market. In 2013, Axa Insurance spun off its private equity business as Ardian.[21] Allianz and other larger insurers also reduced the scale and ambition of their private market units as well, focusing them more on third-party business and away from on-balance sheet investments.

Impact on Private Markets Valuations

The Preqin private market performance index, which is based on reported net asset values (NAVs), fell to a low of 72% in March 2009 (December 2007 = 100), with vintage years 2006–2008 being most impacted (Figure 8.5). Buyouts and private real estate saw the greatest correction while infrastructure initially continued rising and barely dipped below an index value of 100 once it started correcting in 2009. Once the public markets recovered, private market performance edged upwards. The exemption was private real estate, which continued its downward trend well into 2010 (Figure 8.6).

---

[21] *Financial Times*, September 29, 2013.

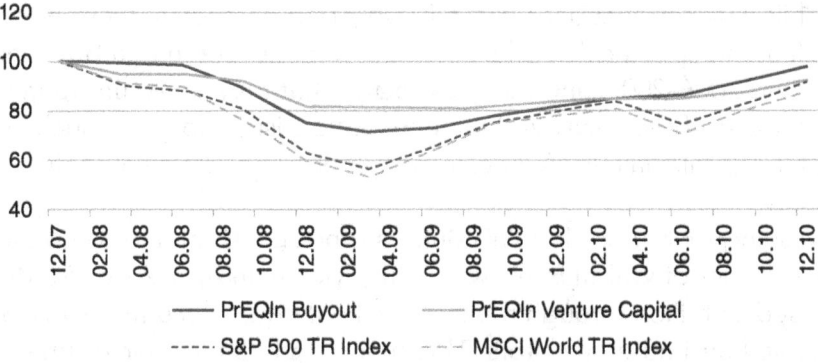

Figure 8.5   Private equity strategies vs. public market performance during the GFC.
Source: Adapted from Preqin, data as of 2022, indices rebased to December 27, 2007 = 100.

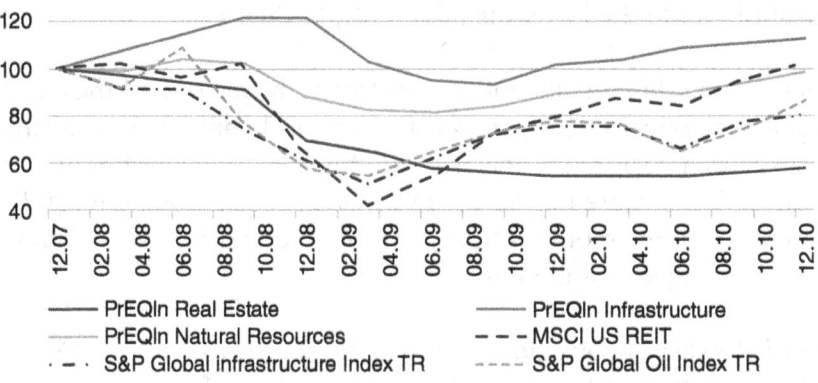

Figure 8.6   Other private market strategies vs. public market performance during the GFC.
Source: Adapted from Preqin.

As long as investors were not compelled to sell in the secondary market where discounts to NAVs often exceeded 30%, the decrease in valuations of private market investments was significantly less severe than the correction of the public markets. This was partly due to the accounting valuation methods used to calculate the net asset values (NAVs) of non-traded assets. For many investors, this relative stability during valuations during the GFC and the fact that any downward revision would only be recognized with a three- to six-month delay when those quarterly reports were issued was welcome. The experience that private market investments can contribute to the portfolio's stability would influence future portfolio decisions.

While NAV corrections were relatively benign overall, there were still some spectacular failures. There were several mega-buyouts during 2006–2007, and many expected that they were sure to fail. But most of them survived the economic crisis, and a few, such as the hospital chain HCA, have even generated substantial profits.

Washington Mutual, Inc. (WaMu), a savings bank holding company and owner of WaMu Bank, was a GFC victim. In April 2008, WaMu raised $7 billion through the direct sale of equity securities to TPG Capital and other investors. TPG made a $1.35 billion investment in WaMu. In mid-September 2008, the Office of Thrift Supervision seized WaMu Bank and placed it into the receivership of the Federal Deposit Insurance Corporation (FDIC). The FDIC then sold most of WaMu Bank's assets to JPMorgan Chase.

As a result, TPG lost its entire investment. It was one of the most significant private equity write-offs ever and certainly one of the fastest, as it happened only five months after the investment was made.[22] There were no more deals of similar size done until 2021. Lenders became more cautious, and regulators discouraged banks from funding leveraged transactions.[23]

The $45 billion acquisition of the Texas energy behemoth TXU in 2007—the largest leveraged buyout in history—had also been a costly investment for its private equity owners and debt holders alike. Energy Future Holdings was the largest of the so-called mega-buyouts between 2005 and 2007. The $8.3 billion equity invested in the deal had been wiped out. KKR was holding its Energy Future Holdings investment at 10 cents on the dollar, according to a securities filing in 2012 (see Box 8.2).

---

[22] Washington Mutual (2008), Davis (2008), Lattman (2008, 2012).
[23] ECB (2017), Tan (2015).

Box 8.2   Not Too Big to Fail: Energy Future Holdings (TXU)

Energy Future Holdings Corporation was a publicly traded electric utility corporation based in Dallas, Texas (Figure 8.7). The corporation generated most of its electricity through coal and nuclear power facilities.

From 1998 until 2007, the corporation was known as TXU Corporation until it was acquired by KKR, TPG Capital, and Goldman Sachs Capital Partners in a $45 billion leveraged buyout (including assumed debt). When it became a private firm in the largest buyout in history, it was renamed Energy Futures Holdings (EFH).[24] At the time of the purchase, the buyout firms invested a combined $8.3 billion in equity (implying an 80% leverage including assumed debt) but likely syndicated part of that to other investors, financial documents indicated.

Due to prior divestitures of natural gas assets, the EFH takeover, which left TXU with a debt load of more than $40 billion, was a bet that natural gas prices would climb, providing a

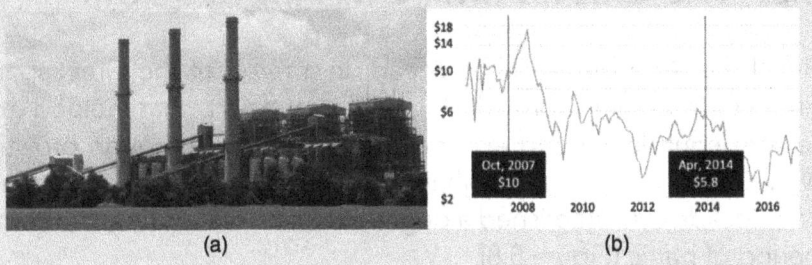

(a)   (b)

Figure 8.7   (a) Martin Lake Power Plant, Tatum, Texas. (b) Henry Hub natural gas spot price, 2008–2016.
Source: (a) www.commons.wikipedia.org, L.D. Moore. CC BY-SA 4.0; (b) www.macrotrends.net.

(*continued*)

---

[24] Snowberg and Henderson (2019).

competitive edge for its coal-fired power plants. Rather than that happening, natural gas prices decreased precipitously.[25] In addition, the Sierra Club and its supporters started the "Beyond TXU" campaign to persuade retail power consumers to move away from TXU toward alternative retail electricity suppliers that produce "greener" energy.[26]

The impending maturity of a substantial amount of debt, considerable financial losses, and credit rating downgrades, forced the company to file for bankruptcy on April 29, 2014.[27]

The EFH bankruptcy was the largest for a private equity-backed corporation since the Chrysler Group's demise in 2009. However, some asset revaluations during the following years increased the potential of a significant, if not complete, recovery for debt holders.[28] Private equity firms invested in EFH had to write down their investments and reportedly lost over $7 billion during the bankruptcy proceedings. However, the restructuring process allowed them to recover some value, although not all.

8.2   THE GREAT PRIVATE MARKETS BOOM

But there were better times ahead. In a rerun of the Greenspan Put, central banks provided liquidity support that helped to restore confidence and economic momentum. Although growth would turn out to be somewhat weaker compared to the previous two decades, it established a degree of investors' optimism after a period of panic (Figure 8.8).

The primary effect of the monetary stabilization efforts was a turbocharged repetition of the liquidity injection administered after the dotcom bubble burst. After the GFC, the continuous slow

---

[25] Chediak (2013).
[26] Garland (2013).
[27] Schnurman (2013).
[28] Sender and Crooks (2014).

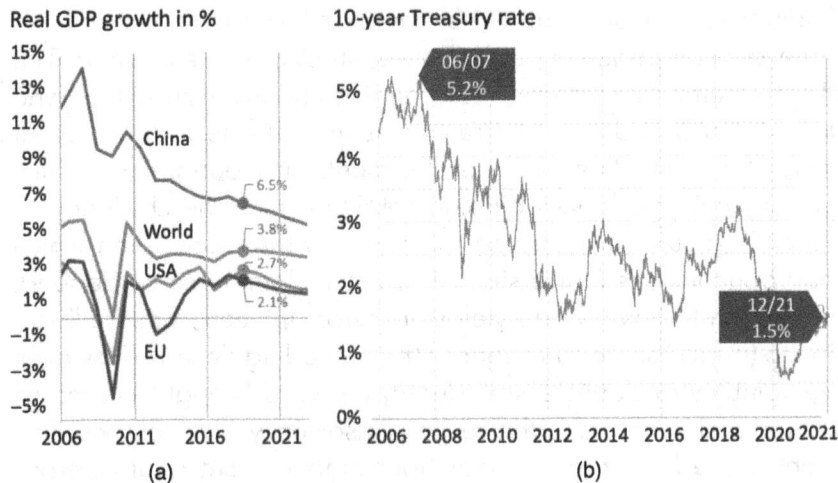

Figure 8.8 Economic growth and interest rates 2006–2021. (a) Real GDP growth (%). (b) 10-year Treasury rate.

Source: Adapted from Euromonitor International, Macrotrends.

growth and low inflation environment compelled central banks to combat deflation with loose monetary policies, which in Europe also relieved several deeply indebted Euro member states. The COVID-19 outbreak and the monetary and fiscal response it necessitated thwarted efforts to tighten monetary policy. It had a lasting impact on interest rates, with short-term rates in major economies approaching zero and long-term bond rates falling dramatically—some reaching negative territory, as was the case in Switzerland and later Germany. Even a few years before, the notion that you must pay governments or investment-grade issuers to take your money would have seemed ludicrous to seasoned market observers, yet it happened.

As a result, institutions worldwide, particularly pension funds and insurance companies that needed to fund contractual liabilities, had to re-evaluate the role of bonds in their portfolios. They faced the challenge of ensuring sufficient cash flow and adequate returns in the new environment of low or negative interest rates. There was even a question of fiduciary duty and liability: Are you exposed to litigation as a trustee or board member of a pension fund or insurance company if you approve investments that would result in a guaranteed loss due to negative interest rates? The search for yield turned into a scramble in the second decade of the twenty-first century.

Traditionally, most institutional investors' portfolios comprised three key components: public bonds, stocks, and real estate. The effect of ultra-low interest rates on liability-driven investors who use market-based discount rates was an increase in the present value of their liabilities. Even endowments and foundations, which typically have no legally binding liabilities, face the challenge of generating sufficient cash to maintain contributions upon which their beneficiaries (universities, hospitals, charities, etc.) depend. In reaction to lower bond yields, investors increased their allocation to (public) shares throughout the preceding decade. However, the volatility of public assets during the GFC brought numerous institutional investors to the verge of insolvency. This "black swan" event caused a surge in correlations among asset returns, eroding the anticipated advantages of diversification, underscoring the complexity of risk that extends beyond the scope of merely one or two standard deviations from historical performance.[29]

When investors experienced near-zero or even negative bond yields in many advanced economies, they had essentially four options:

1. **Do nothing and maintain the current situation:** This would result in maintaining a bond allocation that delivers no return or even losses (at zero or negative rates). The consequences, however, made that approach unworkable since maintaining the status quo would have required pension funds, for instance, to reduce their expected returns to a point where the required increases in contributions or reductions in benefits would have been unacceptable to their plan members.

2. **Increase your cash reserves and wait for bond yields to recover to their long-term averages:** This "wait and see" stance required a belief that central banks would be able to reverse the monetary stimulus in the near future. However, the relatively sluggish recovery of economic growth and low inflation did not support the notion that interest rates would rise rapidly.

3. **Invest in traditional asset classes, such as real estate and public equity that benefit from low interest rates:** But in the early years following the GFC, real estate was viewed with

---

[29] The concept of black swan events was popularized by the writer Nassim N. Taleb in his book, *The Black Swan: The Impact of the Highly Improbable* (Taleb, 2007).

skepticism, as this asset class was at the center of the mortgage crisis that precipitated the GFC and the volatility of public equities cautioned investors.

4. **Identify and add new ("non-traditional") asset classes** with attractive risk-return profiles to diversify and maintain expected returns without exceeding risk restrictions.

Harvesting the Illiquidity Premium

Academic researchers and major pension fund consultants[30] were advocating exploiting the illiquidity premium.[31] The argument goes that many institutions are long-term investors, and by focusing excessively on liquidity (which they do not need), they forgo the additional profits that come with embracing illiquidity and growing the proportion of illiquid assets in their portfolio. Increasing portfolio share of illiquid investments was an application of the Yale Model of investing to large pools of capital, i.e., pension funds and insurance companies.

As previously shown, private market investments also had more minor valuation corrections than public markets during the GFC due to the actuarial valuation methods used. While it is debatable whether those valuations represent fair market value, i.e., a price at which investors could sell those investments—it turned out that many investors liked the degree of stability that private market investments brought to their balance sheets.

Private market investments thus combined the attractive features of promising additional return without excessively elevating balance sheet volatility. For investors that concluded that their portfolio was more heavily weighted toward liquid investments than their circumstances required, increasing the proportion of illiquid assets became an attractive portfolio choice.

Consequently, the repositioning of investment portfolios favored private market assets the most. Since the end of the GFC, the number of institutional investors in this sector has expanded

---

[30] Mercer (2015).
[31] For example, some studies (Ang, Papanikolaou, and Westerfield, 2013; Schwartz and Tebaldi, 2006; Tirole, 2011) did look into the return premium that can be realized through illiquid investments.

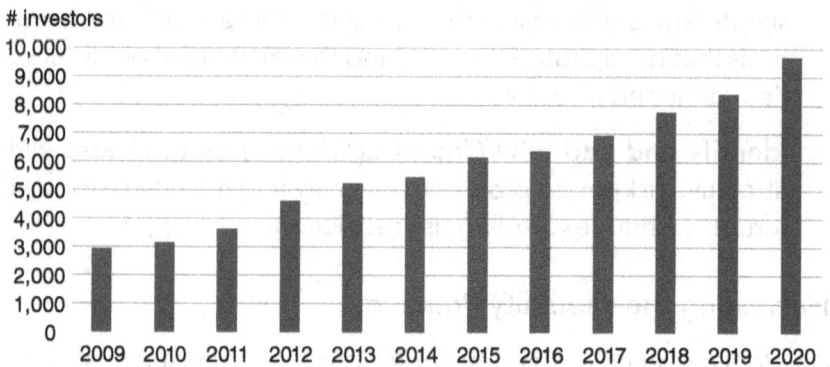

Figure 8.9 **Number of active private equity investors, 2009–2020.**
Source: Preqin.

significantly and SWFs gained in prominence (Figure 8.9). New investor categories, such as high-net-worth individuals and, most recently, retail investors, have joined their ranks.

Previously, investors faced a cash flow crunch when the Global Financial Crisis led to a backlog of portfolio companies that couldn't be exited. However, when markets stabilized, there was an increase in exit volumes that exceeded the volume of new capital calls, resulting in the NAVs of existing investment programs shrinking during 2010–2014. The issue became how to maintain allocations. Additionally, the S&P 500 experienced one of the longest bull runs since WWII from 2010 to 2021, which increased AuM and thus required higher private market allocations due to the denominator effect. The combined effect of rising AuM and declining private market NAVs due to a surge in distributions fueled demand for new fund offerings even further, forcing investors to increase their commitment budgets to maintain their allocation (Figure 8.10). This demand persisted throughout the decade, with many types of investors still being significantly under-allocated relative to their target allocations as of 2021.

Over time, market fluctuations of total assets under management (AuM) may cause deviations from the target allocation for individual asset classes ("denominator effect"), and illiquid investments' portfolio weight may run counter to the overall trend due to their lagged and somewhat muted valuation adjustments. The magnitude of the shift in portfolio weights can be exacerbated through

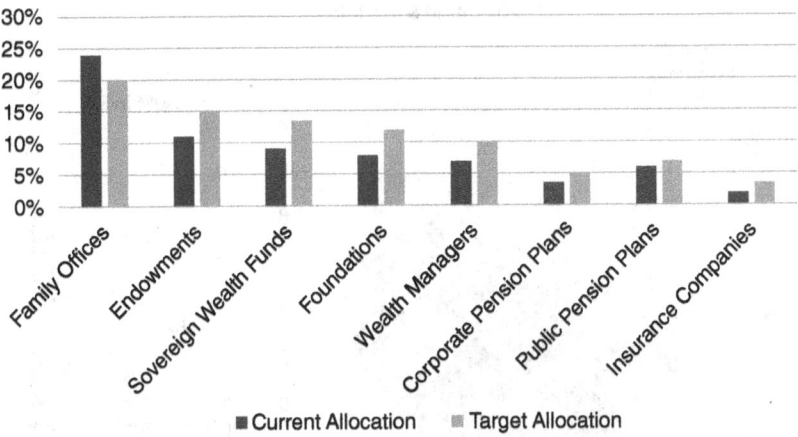

Figure 8.10   Actual and target allocations to private equity in 2021.
Source: McKinsey (2022); data: Preqin.

the exclusion of illiquid assets in a portfolio rebalancing. As the decline in asset values is usually not of the same magnitude across asset classes, a portfolio rebalancing is required to restore the target allocation. Additionally, private market investments tend to adjust their valuations slower, which means that the portfolio allocation of private market investments tends to increase during a market downturn while it falls behind target during an upturn. Balancing the benefits of harvesting the illiquidity premium, which involves seeking higher returns from less liquid assets, with the potential drawbacks of reduced liquidity is a strategy that requires careful analysis of an investor's investment objectives, risk tolerance, and liquidity needs.

8.3   A $10 TRILLION ASSET CLASS

The pursuit of higher yields and the strategic shift of institutional portfolios away from conventional bond investments led to a rapid increase in fundraising activity from 2017 to 2021. During 2000–2021, AuM increased by approximately 12% per year, and during 2016–2021, this growth accelerated to around 18% per year. The AuM of the private markets industry increased from $2.7 trillion in 2010 to about $10 trillion, representing approximately 16% of the MSCI World Index's capitalization in 2021 (Figure 8.11).

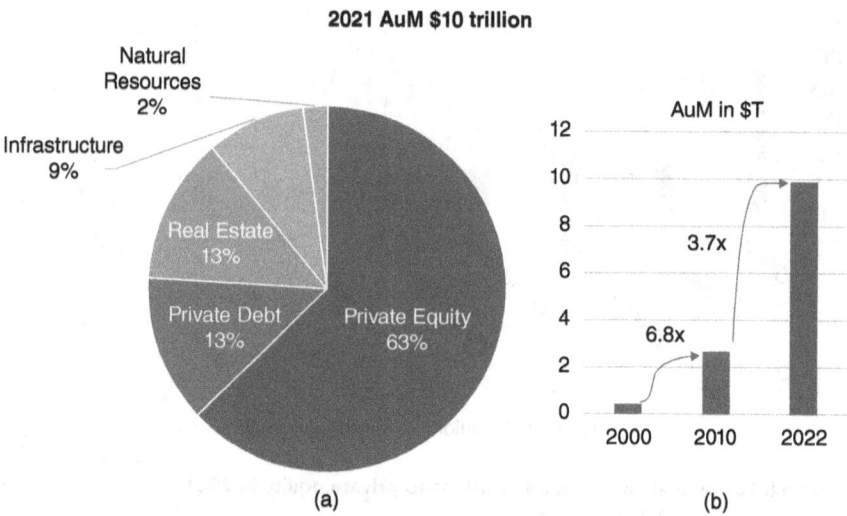

Figure 8.11 **(a) Global private market AuM by strategy (%). (b) AuM in $T. Data as of year-end 2021.**
Source: Adapted from Preqin, PitchBook.

Compared to 2009, the annual fundraising volume of 2021 was 4x higher.

The fundraising boom benefited buyout funds and other asset types in the private market. Infrastructure raised its percentage of total AuM from 6% in 2010 to 9% by 2021. This was mirrored by a comparable decrease in private real estate, which is not surprising, given that this asset class was the most hit by the GFC. The share of private debt in total private markets' AuM increased by 2%, but the important shift was the increase in senior loans and direct lending at the expense of distressed and mezzanine strategies, which both have equity-like risk profiles. Investors had previously regarded private debt investment as an optional add-on to their private equity allocation. Following the GFC, private debt filled the gap in senior loan financing for mid-market transactions caused by the banks' withdrawal from that space. Private debt became a separate allocation with a focus on yield in the ultra-low interest rate environment. Private equity's share in total private markets AuM remained stable, but there, too, were substantial changes within the asset class with venture capital/growth financing regaining favor following a decade of low fundraising numbers. Geographically, North America (USA) continues to dominate most private market

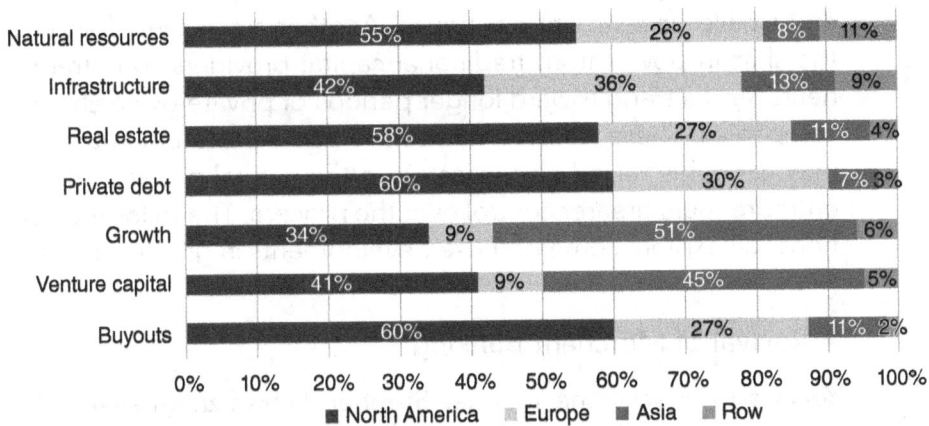

Figure 8.12 Private market AuM by region, 2021 (%).

Source: Adapted from Preqin.

Note: Natural resources based on fundraising 2010–2021; for growth capital and venture capital other sources indicate that North America has replaced Asia as the largest region due to strong fundraising in 2018–2021.

investing areas. Europe comes in second place behind the USA in all private market strategies except venture capital/growth financing, where Asia (China) matched or even exceeded activity in the USA and put Europe in third place (Figure 8.12).

Private markets have matured into a diverse asset class, embodying a broad spectrum of investment strategies across the risk spectrum. This success has transformed the traditional cottage industry into a landscape increasingly dominated by large asset managers. Likewise, the growing prominence of very large institutional investors had an impact on the LP-GP relationship. As a result, novel forms of implementation and intermediation emerged that, sometimes, depart from the conventional LP-GP model. These include funds of firms, co-investment, continuation funds, and platforms that allow private investors to access alternative assets. Direct investment has become more popular, empowering investors with greater control over their investment decisions and reducing the role of intermediaries. Furthermore, the line between traditional private market investment managers and other types of investors has become increasingly blurred, and permanent capital and ownership extension have gained importance. The private markets industry has also become more institutionalized, resulting in a widening gap between large, publicly traded multi-strategy managers and smaller investment boutiques. Another significant change is the shift in power from traditional capital providers to entrepreneurs, and a trend toward longer periods of private ownership for companies. These developments have had a profound impact on how capital is raised and invested in the capital markets, giving entrepreneurs greater control over the process. The following sections will explore some of these developments in greater detail.

A Revival of Merchant Banking

Years ago, Blackstone founder Stephen Schwarzman shared his perspective on Blackstone's identity with the author, emphasizing that he did not view it solely as a buyout firm. At a later point, when questioned about the envisioned valuation of his newly public company, he responded that it would exceed that of Goldman Sachs. Connecting these two statements took the author quite some time. While it may not initially seem remarkable for a former investment banker to gauge his firm's stock performance against a major investment bank, comparing the current mega-firms in the private markets arena and traditional investment banks offers intriguing insights and hints at the direction the industry may be taking.

Investment banking is known for specializing in capital markets and facilitating a wide array of financial transactions across diverse products and services, serving a broad clientele. Much like private market firms, investment banks had humble beginnings as partnerships.

During the late nineteenth and early twentieth centuries, those firms got increasingly involved in raising equity for their clients, and moved on to engineer the formation of large industrial conglomerates, often structured as trusts or holding companies, to gain control and monopolize various sectors. As previously discussed, figures like J. P. Morgan and his firm, J. P. Morgan & Co., played pivotal roles in establishing these trusts. They helped consolidate and restructure major industries such as railroads and steel. They wielded significant influence within these trusts through board seats and substantial equity ownership acquired via "founder's shares" or outright purchases.

Investing in equity and securing a substantial portion of the trust's upside resembles the private equity model, where investment managers as general partners and gain additional upside through carried interest. In both scenarios, the fund manager exerts significant control over the acquired companies, shaping these entities' strategic direction and decisions. This parallel underscores how historical developments in investment banking share similarities with contemporary private equity practices.

However, a critical distinction between those trusts and modern partnerships lies in their fundamental nature and objectives. The trusts of the past were characterized by their indefinite lifespan, designed for long-term ownership of acquired companies within a specific industry. Value creation was achieved through mergers that generated synergies and ended price wars. These trusts aimed for enduring control and consolidation.

In contrast, contemporary private equity funds pursue temporary ownership and maintain a diversified portfolio across industries. Portfolio companies remain distinct entities, and the aim is often to enhance their performance and value before divestment.

The era of old-world investment banking, often called merchant banking, saw banks holding significant equity stakes in firms they advised and the funds and trusts they established. While shareholdings were treated as separate investments, a portfolio-oriented approach became evident when banks began to encourage the companies they were involved with to engage in various forms of cooperation, which may have included acting as suppliers for infrastructure investments financed by the same banks or adopting new technologies that these financial institutions were endorsing. This approach shares similarities with the modern-day practice of private equity firms providing portfolio companies with support and centralized services, holding "CEO days," and is illustrated by the regular dinners hosted by Masayoshi Son with the CEOs of his portfolio companies to encourage them to do business with each other. This era ended with the passage of the Glass-Steagall Act in 1933. This legislation separated commercial banking from investment banking activities and imposed restrictions on merchant banks. In contrast, investment banks were generally prohibited from holding substantial ownership interests in companies they advised on mergers, acquisitions, or other financial transactions, as well as those they managed as trustees. This separation aimed to eliminate potential conflicts of interest and maintain the integrity of financial advisory services by preventing banks from having financial interests that could influence their advice to clients.

Consequently, modern investment banking underwent a significant transformation, shifting its core focus toward trading and market-making activities. The deregulation of capital markets, exemplified by the British "Big Bang" of October 27, 1986, marked a pivotal moment. It unleashed international competition, decreased trading costs through electronic trading and the abolition of fixed commissions, fueled a surge in trading volumes, and introduced a new dimension to securities trading with the growing importance of derivatives.

This evolution heightened the significance of market-making and proprietary trading in the business models of investment banks. Many investment banks decided to go public to accommodate the expanding balance sheets and compete effectively. Going public allowed them to raise the equity capital required to thrive in this evolving environment. However, expanding balance sheets, increasing leverage, and pivoting toward market-making and proprietary trading also made their business riskier.

The changing business model of investment banks created an opportunity for firms specializing in advising companies and holding equity stakes in them, with the capability to acquire these companies through external funds established for that purpose. Leveraging the limited partnership structure as an investment vehicle enabled these firms to capture upside potential while allowing them to maintain streamlined balance sheets and operate with minimal equity.

This model can encompass other asset classes, including infrastructure, real estate, and private debt. The historical practices of the old merchant banks, which engaged in a diverse range of asset plays, serve as a clear precedent for such diversification in the modern financial landscape.

The opportunity did not go unnoticed by traditional financial intermediaries. During the first decade of the twenty-first century, there was a notable trend where banks and insurance companies positioned themselves as competitors in private markets. The Gramm-Leach-- Bliley Act of 1999 repealed key provisions of the Glass-Steagall Act, which had previously enforced the separation of commercial banking, investment banking, and insurance activities. Banks, including investment banks, began showing heightened interest in the private equity sector. However, this trajectory was abruptly disrupted by the Global Financial Crisis (GFC), which exposed vulnerabilities in the banking system that led to a reconsideration of the risks associated with financial activities.

The Volcker Rule, a pivotal provision of the Dodd-Frank Wall Street Reform and Consumer Protection Act, enacted in 2010, significantly reshaped the industry. It restricted proprietary trading by banks and their affiliates, including investment banks, and imposed limitations on their investments in and sponsorship of hedge funds and private equity funds. This rule indirectly impacted the equity investments of investment banks by placing constraints on their trading and investment practices.

The more restrictive regulatory environment also resulted in increased capital requirements and intensified regulatory oversight. These factors collectively enhanced the competitive advantage of private market firms, which were not subject to the same level of regulatory constraints as banks and could operate more flexibly.

However, seizing opportunities in the private markets still necessitated larger balance sheets than the pass-through profit model typically employed by traditional private market firms organized as limited partnerships could provide. As a result, an increasing number of private market firms opted to go public through initial public offerings (IPOs) after 2010. This move allowed them to access public capital markets and strengthen their balance sheets to pursue opportunities in the evolving financial landscape.

During the second decade of the millennium, the largest of those firms increasingly resembled the merchant banks of old days, and those mega-firms dominated the private market industry and increasingly disintermediated traditional investment banking not only in the higher risk-return space of private equity-type investments but increasingly also in lower-risk strategies, such as senior lending or core property and infrastructure investing through evergreen or long-dated fund structures. In addition, the acquisition of insurance businesses provided a new funding source—at least in the US. The industry model of relying on committed capital through limited partnerships has proven a powerful way to raise temporary capital, which was instrumental in control transactions, enabling private market firms to wield managerial influence and capture a substantial share of the potential upside with minimal equity investments. As the industry shifted towards a multi-strategy framework, the need for larger balance sheets became evident, as GP investments increased with large funds and M&A become more frequent, often targeting specialized fund managers or asset gatherers, including insurance companies.

8.4   MEGA-FIRMS DOMINATE THE INDUSTRY

In Section 7.5, we discussed the emergence of mega-firms after 2005 and their significant impact on the private markets industry. These firms managed over $100 billion in assets under management (AuM) by the end of the first decade of the new millennium, and their transaction, management, and performance fee income far surpassed that of comparable mutual fund revenues. Though large in the private markets context, these firms were mid-sized in the broader asset management world. The 2008–2009 financial crisis slowed AuM growth but helped these firms gain fundraising market share.

In the years following the resumption of fundraising, the industry witnessed larger funds and consolidation. From 2015–2021, the top 20 fundraisers accounted for a considerable percentage of venture capital, private equity and real estate, private debt, and infrastructure commitments. Furthermore, multi-strategy firms often topped the list of fundraisers in multiple areas, leading to a concentration of fundraising and assets under management.

Many of the large private market firms went public during the 2020s, following the path set by Partners Group, Fortress Management, and Blackstone in the previous decade. This transition to going public has provided private equity managers with access to permanent capital that can be used to invest and grow their businesses.

Although private markets are still a cottage industry, with over 1,000 active firms globally in buyouts alone, the industry has become dominated by a few mega-firms such as Blackstone or Carlyle, who have assembled a portfolio of businesses that represent all facets of private markets. Specialist firms have given way to diversified firms that generate substantial revenue. Blackstone's $22.5 billion revenue in 2021, surpassing that of BlackRock's $19.4 billion, highlights this shift.[32] In the private markets industry, a handful of firms have emerged as giants over the past two decades. For instance, Blackstone, the largest private markets firm, reported AuM of $880 billion at the end of 2021, a staggering figure that includes $279.5 billion in real estate, $261.5 billion in private equity, $258.6 billion in credit and insurance, and $81.3 billion in hedge funds. This underscores the significant growth in size and scope of the multi-strategy firms that have transformed into mega-firms. In March 2021, Blackstone surpassed the market capitalization of Goldman Sachs, a testament to the increased significance of private markets firms in the financial world.[33]

Big private market brands benefited from the GFC in three ways:

1. In the face of heightened uncertainty, investors prioritized renewing their investments with the funds managed by large and well-established mega-firms at the expense of allocating resources to funds operated by smaller organizations or backing first-time funds.

2. Their varied product offerings and swift product expansion enabled them to benefit from the rising demand for inventive investment strategies, such as private debt, growth financing, and ESG-themed investments.

3. Lenders scaled back their activities and deliberately supported larger deals, favoring mega-firms and their substantial funds. This decision benefitted the mega-firms and further bolstered the prominence of their large funds.

Top private market managers went public and established permanent capital structures for stable funding and diversification with low-risk, income-focused strategies. Blackstone, for example, introduced new products (real estate investment trusts (REITs) and collateralized loan obligations (CLOs) to boost assets and attract

---

[32] Figures obtained from corporate announcements for 2021.
[33] Gara (2020).

Table 8.1   Large private markets managers in 2021

Name	Founded	Country	AuM in $ billion, as of 2021
Buyouts/Real Assets			
Blackstone	1985	USA	881
Brookfield Asset Management	1997	Canada	698
KKR	1976	USA	459
Apollo	1990	USA	455
Ares Management Corp.	1997	USA	306
The Carlyle Group Inc.	1987	USA	301
Partners Group	1996	Switzerland	127
CVC Capital Partners	1981	UK	122
Macquarie Asset Management	1985	Australia/UK	117*
TPG Capital	1992	USA	109
EQT	1994	Sweden	73
VC/Growth			
Tiger Global Management	2001	USA	125
Sequoia	1972	USA	85*
Andreessen Horowitz	2009	USA	35*
New Enterprise Associates	1977	USA	25*

Source: Company reports, as of December 2021.
Note: *AuM as of 2022. AuM figures may include other alternative investments and liquid asset strategies.

investments. This trend demands incentive adjustments, such as NAV-based or deal-by-deal carried interest. An increased focus on asset gathering can also be seen in venture capital, where firms like Sequoia have expanded from early-stage financing to later-stage and growth financing and added specialized funds in industries like healthcare, financial technology, and clean energy. With $85 billion in assets under management, Sequoia is a prime example of the changes happening in the venture capital industry (Table 8.1).

8.5   THE RISE OF PERMANENT CAPITAL

Your LP Becomes Your Competitor

It was only possible to raise huge amounts of capital with the continuing support of large institutional investors. However, some of these institutions started to build sizable internal investment teams, sometimes larger than the managers that sought their commitments.

Since the 1990s, Ontario Teachers has been at the forefront of what is known as the "Canadian Model." Back then, it brought more of its investments in-house.[34] Other large funds quickly followed suit, establishing teams to handle transactions independently. Ontario initially utilized this strategy for infrastructure investments, but it has since been extended to all private market asset classes. On more significant transactions, the funds frequently participate as "co-sponsors" with private market firms. This allows them to control their investments more, save on costs, and accelerate capital deployment. The Canadian Model also became a blueprint for many sovereign wealth funds around the world. The critical elements of the Canadian Models are:

1. Investments in internal resources and management teams with competitive salaries and incentive structures.

2. Preference for direct deals and willingness to provide capital when long holding periods are required.

3. A flexible asset allocation that often uses factor risk models to manage overall investment risk and not sticky asset allocation limits for individual asset classes. This approach also allows them to add new investment strategies quickly to their portfolio.

To understand the implications of this shift and its effect on the private markets sector, a closer examination of sovereign wealth funds (SWFs) is crucial. By 2022, there were 98 active SWFs, with 38 formed after 2010. Combined, they managed $10.38 trillion in assets.[35] While this is less than the $60 trillion AuM of pension funds, a look at the largest 300 institutional investors illustrates their significance: As of 2021, the 300 largest institutional investors included 123 public pension funds ($9.5 trillion of assets) and 25 SWFs ($7 trillion in assets) with another 152 corporate pension plans and collective pension

---

[34] For the past 25 years, a number of public pension funds in Canada have followed what is globally referred to as the "Canadian model." Quoted from (Clarke, 2019) who also discusses some challenges. The Canadian Model is associated with a focus on independent and professional governance, investing in private assets, active management of public equities, and internalization of investment activities to avoid high external management fees. See World Bank (2017) and *The Economist* (2012) for descriptions.

[35] Aguliar (2023).

schemes representing $7.2 trillion. Evidently the growing prominence of SWFs has significantly increased the number of ultra large capital pools active in the asset class.[36] Notably, GIC and Temasek (in Singapore) and Abu Dhabi Investment Authority (in the UAE) ranked among the top 10 private equity investors, collectively contributing $202 billion.[37] SWFs and public pension funds expanded their investments in private markets from 10% in 2008 to 22% in 2020 with SWFs displaying higher allocations. Traditionally, SWFs, like other institutional investors, began by allocating capital to externally managed limited partnerships. Despite public pension funds representing larger overall commitments, SWFs displayed the highest median commitment ($50 million vs. $22 million) and together with very large public pensions favored larger funds, contributing to the consolidation of fundraising and enabling mega-firms to amass significant assets. The bias toward large GPs and their funds was driven by a need to deploy significant amounts of capital and access platforms that could provide ample co-investment deal flow.[38]

In doing so, SWFs followed the example of Temasek, where co-investments with GPs already comprised 25% of its pre-crisis portfolio and grew to 40% by 2015. Co-investment capital surged 11-fold by 2018.[39] Leveraging their influence, SWFs negotiated better terms and control, and opted for SMAs instead of making direct capital commitments to funds, with an estimated 40% of sovereign wealth funds' investments being directed into SMAs rather than the primary partnerships of general partners.[40]

Despite their strong internal management capabilities, large institutional investors continue to invest through external managers to utilize their strategic relationships for co-investments and further penetrate overseas markets (Table 8.2). To continue receiving their commitments, managers were required to grant extensive co-investment rights and collaborate with these investors as deal-consortium partners.

---

[36] Thinking Ahead Institute (2022).
[37] Megginson et al. (2023).
[38] Ibid.
[39] Bortolotti and Scortecci (2019).
[40] Preqin (2018).

Table 8.2   Some of the largest institutional investors in private equity

Name	Country	Investor type	Private equity assets $ billion, as of 2020
Ontario Teachers	Canada	Pension fund	$42
CPPIB	Canada	Pension fund	$94
CalPERS	USA	Pension fund	$30
WSIB	USA	Pension fund	$25
Texas TRS	USA	Pension fund	$23
CalsSTRS	USA	Pension fund	$23
NYSCRF	USA	Pension fund	$22
OPERF	USA	Pension fund	$19
SBA Florida	USA	Pension fund	$15
OMERS	Canada	Pension fund	$14
CIC	China	Sovereign wealth fund	$160
ICD	UAE - Dubai	Sovereign wealth fund	$158
Mubadala	UAE - Abu Dhabi	Sovereign wealth fund	$100
HKMA	China - HK	Sovereign wealth fund	$93
Softbank VF I	Japan	Investment Company	$87
PIF	Saudi Arabia	Sovereign wealth fund	$66
KIA	Kuwait	Sovereign wealth fund	$50
QIA	Qatar	Sovereign wealth fund	$45
Temasek	Singapore	Sovereign wealth fund	$39
GIC	Singapore	Sovereign wealth fund	$39

Source: Izelis (2020), annual reports.
Note: Softbank VF I is predominantly investing captial from SWFs.

Co-investment rights were also not new. GPs offered them to LPs in the past to close transactions that exceeded their fund's single investment limits. For very large LPs, however, co-investment rights became a prerequisite for fund subscriptions. As allocations grew, co-investments and direct investments gained importance as a means of implementing private market programs for SWFs and large pension funds alike. The $478 billion California Public Employees' Retirement System (CalPERS) reported in 2022 that it had earmarked over half of its $12.3 billion private-equity commitments for co-investing and SMAs.[41]

---

[41] Preeti (2022).

The journey of SWFs and very large pension funds in private markets involves robust LP-GP relationships, with co-investments as both an intermediary step to direct equity investments and as the core pillar of building diversified portfolios.[42] The role of SWFs and large pension funds as limited partners and their contribution to industry funds as LPs might not sustain the previous growth, given their pivot toward direct investing, but they will continue to grow their presence in the private markets' ecosystem as potent deal-making competitors or collaborators. For large private market firms, to have strategic relationships with SWFs has become a major enabling factor to sustain their large fundraises.

Institutional direct investors differ from traditional private market managers who establish limited partnerships to raise capital. Unlike limited partnerships, these investors are not constrained by finite fund life restrictions and the ensuing transient ownership, allowing them to hold investments for much longer than the customary four to seven years. This lack of a finite investment horizon provides a competitive advantage in situations where more permanent capital is needed, but it can also create conflicts of interest. For instance, when the general partner wants to sell due to the end of a fund's life, the co-investor may prefer to hold onto the investments for their unrealized potential.

Continuation Funds

Previously, investors expected managers to exit portfolio holdings fast, but as it grew more difficult to deploy capital, longer holding periods became acceptable. Occasionally GPs would ask their LPs to transfer an investment to a successor fund but that would result in carried interest being paid on the transaction value—essentially the valuation the GP put on the deal, and result in lengthy investor advisory board meetings, if not an LP vote in both funds to approve the transaction, and was thus rarely done. After 2010, private equity investors became more receptive to the idea of extended ownership and wanted to hold onto their investments for longer. They supported continuation funds because an environment of rising valuations allows them to generate additional returns and increase the value of their assets. The fact that limited partners found it difficult to reach their allocation target motivated

---

[42] Bortolotti and Scortecci (2019).

them to "keep what you have."[43] Continuation funds offer private equity investors a way to achieve long-term investment goals while also reducing costs associated with frequent buying and selling of assets and eliminating the transfer pricing problem, at least for those LPs that participate in the continuation fund. They provide a predictable source of capital for follow-on investments, which adds stability and predictability to the private equity business.

GPs can transfer deals to a continuation fund, allowing investors to continue owning the investment and participating in its upside. Secondaries funds offer replacement capital for investors who want to exit and, by doing so, validate the transfer price. This type of transaction has expanded significantly since 2018, and by 2021, it comprised most secondary sales. Many private market firms, including VC firms, have established continuation funds. For instance, Audax announced the Audax Private Equity Continuation Fund in January 2021, which comprises $1.7 billion in capital commitments and funded the purchase of four portfolio companies from Audax Private Equity Fund IV, a 2012 vintage fund with $1.25 billion in capital commitments.[44] Other firms that have established continuation funds include Ares, Apax Partners, Carlyle, General Atlantic, Warburg Pincus, TPG, and KKR, to name but a few. Overall, Private Equity International reported that more than a third of the biggest private equity (PE) firms have used continuation funds to extend the ownership of assets held in their funds.[45]

The initiative for such GP-led transactions as the name suggests usually comes from the GP. The motivations for these transactions vary, but in general, continuation funds allow the manager and investors a combination of liquidity, i.e., returning cash to current LPs that opt out and the ability to prolong the holding period. Rather than focusing on "problem" investments, assets transferred to continuation funds are likely to be the best performers of the main fund and can therefore be considered a growth or momentum play. GPs are able to retain exposure and/or management of what is typically a

---

[43] Given that many LPs faced cutbacks on their desired allocations in new funds and were below target allocation, it was counterintuitive to sell private assets already held. The influence of investment budgets on institutional investment behavior is often underestimated.

[44] The transaction was led by secondaries managers AlpInvest and Lexington Partner as well as Hamilton Lane (Carlyle Group, 2021).

[45] Baruch (2021).

high-quality asset or share of assets to provide additional capital for their portfolio companies over an extended period.

This allows for continued valuation growth and investment in asset classes such as infrastructure or real estate with a longer-term outlook.[46] As infrastructure and real estate investments are sought-after assets for investors seeking stable yield and inflation protection, a continuation fund provides a means for investors to benefit from those characteristics once the asset is de-risked. It is only a small step that separates an asset specific continuation fund from a permanent investment vehicle that might own a portfolio of such assets. Funds that invest in stabilized assets might attract capital from incomeoriented investors that see this as a way to gain exposure to the long-term revenue generated by these assets.

The trend of establishing continuation funds is expected to increase and has already spread beyond buyouts to infrastructure. In 2021, the transaction volume of GP-led secondaries, i.e., capital raised for LPs that do not want to participate in a continuation fund, was estimated at \$62 billion, after \$26 billion in 2019 and 2020.[47] As some GPs raise replacement capital from existing LPs who mainly do not opt out, one might conclude that the AuM of continuation funds exceeded \$200 billion at year-end 2021.

GPs that establish a continuation vehicle for single or multiple assets often request that "rolling" investors provide additional cash commitments to the continuation fund at the outset (for fees and expenses, follow-on investments, etc.) as well as permission for some reinvestment of proceeds. Terms can differ significantly (Figure 8.13).

Tiered carried interest starts at 10–15% for lesser returns and rises to 15–20% for greater yields after internal rate of return (IRR) or total value to paid-in (TVPI) requirements are met. Lower percentage fees than primary funds or budget-based management fees are normal. Private equity/special situations fund last 5–7 years, while primary funds last 12–15 years. Regarding the GP investment, the GP invests the carried interest and management incentives in the continuation vehicle.[48]

---

[46] Forestner and Young (2021).
[47] Capital Dynamics (2022).
[48] Clifford Chance (2020).

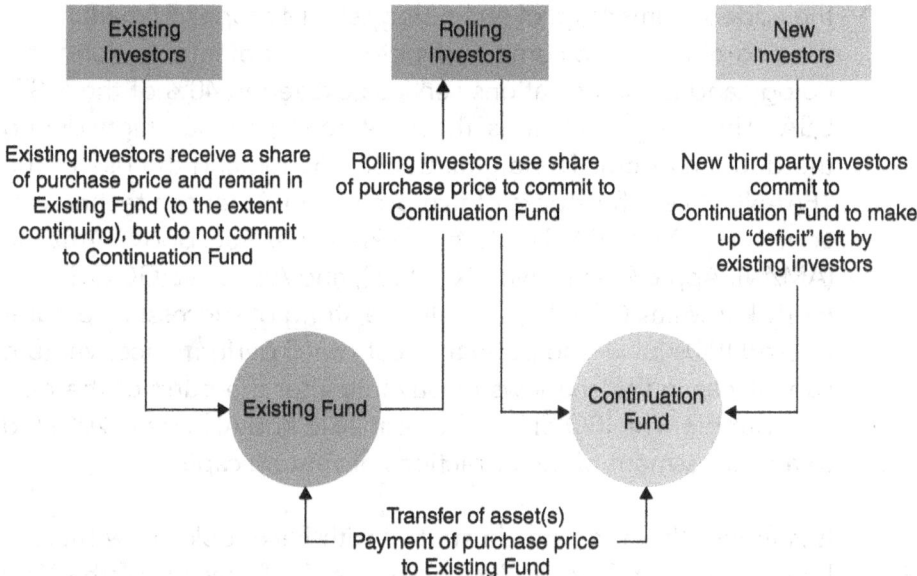

Figure 8.13   Structure of a continuation fund.
Source: Adapted from Clifford Chance, 2020.

Terms depend on fund assets, target holding periods, investor base, investor bargaining power, and sponsor economics. When continuation funds have a long duration, investors must consider liquidity options, tax considerations, and sometimes the shift from capital gain to income as a significant part of total return. Governance, conflict of interest, and sponsor (GP) management duties must also be addressed.

Outside investors, such as secondaries FoFs that weren't LPs in the fund, provide independent valuation validation and liquidity for investors who don't want to participate in the continuation fund. Continuation vehicles increase the importance of fee income versus carried interest for GPs. This is a development worth watching.

8.6   THE TECHNOLOGY BOOM AND THE RISE OF THE ENTREPRENEUR

If you were born into the millennial and Gen Z generations, you came of age as investors during a period of extremely muted inflation and the longest bull market in history. While low interest rates and low inflation led to increases in asset prices across the board, the added momentum of technology stocks propelled markets. At the end of 2021, the combined index weight of information technology and communications services exceeded 40% of the MSCI USA. This weight exceeds those sectors' previous high during the dotcom boom. The digital transformation and the rise of the "FAANG," i.e., the stocks of five prominent American technology companies: Meta (META) (formerly known as Facebook), Amazon (AMZN), Apple (AAPL), Netflix (NFLX), and Alphabet (GOOG) (formerly known as Google), as well as a string of successful venture-backed IPOs have also been a boost to VC performance. Venture capital was in the shadows of buyouts after the burst of the dotcom bubble. The IPO of Facebook in 2012 and Alibaba in 2014 led to a reassessment of the attractions of venture capital.

It is fitting, that the decade started with Facebook—now Meta—founder and CEO Mark Zuckerberg as TIME Person of the Year and eleven years later that accolade went to Elon Musk, who co-founded PayPal and went on become the founder, CEO, and chief engineer of SpaceX, angel investor, CEO and product architect of Tesla, Inc., owner and CEO of Twitter, Inc. (now known as X), founder of The Boring Company, co-founder of Neuralink and OpenAI. Over the course of the decade Musk became not only the world's richest man but in the words of TIME editor-in-chief E. Felsenthal, "a person with extraordinary influence on life on Earth, and potentially life off earth too" (Figure 8.14).[49]

It may sound hyperbolic, but it reflects their impact, which has been global and rapidly scalable due to the reach of technology and their rise is an economic and cultural phenomenon. While the tech entrepreneurs during the dotcom boom made headlines due to their fast success—from college to multi-millionaire—the new crop of tech magnates caught the public imagination through their impact on society and focus on radical and ambitious goals such as colonizing Mars or connecting the world through the internet. Musk and Zuckerberg also stand out in their approach to leadership and public persona. They are known for their unconventional and sometimes controversial statements and actions, which have helped shape their personal brands and contributed to their influence. In this, they are as much a product of the technological revolution that they personify as its trailblazers.

---

[49] Romo (2021).

Figure 8.14   TIME covers: (a) Mark Zuckerberg, founder and CEO of Meta, on the cover of *TIME Magazine*, December 27, 2010. (b) Elon Musk, founder and CEO of Tesla, Space X, and owner and CEO of Twitter (X), on the cover of TIME magazine, December 27, 2021.
Sources: (a) Martin Schoeller for TIME. https://content.time.com/time/covers/ 0,16641,20101227,00.html. (b) Mark Mahaney for *TIME*. https://time.com/person-of-the-year-2021-elon-musk-choice/.

Their desire to shape the world in significant ways translates into bold vision and ambitious goals. They inspire people to think beyond current limitations and thus their impact on innovation and entrepreneurship has been far-reaching and transformative, inspiring new thinking and shaping the future. Working for a startup has become fashionable as a career launch pad, while funding or working for a private markets firm has become the preferred career path for MBA graduates from top-ranked business schools.[50] Arguably one has to go back to the early twentieth century, the railway barons, steel, oil, and car magnates for the last time when entrepreneurs enjoyed a vaguely similar high profile. They have also faced a stream of criticisms, which highlight the challenges and responsibilities faced by tech entrepreneurs and the impact they have on society.

This reflects the ambiguity of the unfolding digital revolution, which has profoundly changed how we live and work and created

---

[50] In 2022, 12–26% of MBAs graduating from HBS, Wharton, Booth, or Stanford took jobs in private equity or venture capital (Ingram, 2023).

trillion-dollar companies. But excitement about seemingly limit-less opportunities is mixed with concerns about privacy, security, and the impact on jobs and employment.

Zuckerberg and Musk are also examples of the media's winner adulation, which is amplified by social media. This reflects the asymmetric nature of gains and losses involved in launching new businesses: the failure of a promising startup is not significant enough to warrant media coverage. The consequent focus on the more exciting and memorable success stories distorts the realities of launching a new venture, leading to an overestimation of the likelihood of great success.

Facebook, Inc., held its first public offering on Friday, May 18, 2012. The IPO made it the first company in US history to top $100 billion. On September 19, 2014, Alibaba's initial public offering (IPO) on the New York Stock Exchange raised $25 billion, giving the company a market value of $231 billion.

In retrospect, when describing a significant trend (or calamity), one always looks for a "moment" that started it. Usually, things are not that simple, but the 1990s had its "Netscape Moment," so let us call this the "Facebook Moment." Looking back, it marked the beginning of the great technology boom during the second decade of the new millennium until the end of 2021. The Facebook IPO did not immediately start a bonanza. There was lots of initial skepticism from market commentators and analysts. The Verge concluded that its valuation "looks way out of whack. The company earned around $1 billion last year, which means its price-to-earnings ratio, a common method for evaluating stocks, is roughly 100 to 1."[51]

Analysts judged Facebook as not profitable enough, growth aside. At the time, it was thought to be reasonable not only to demand that tech companies are profitable at IPO but they were benchmarked to far more mature public companies in terms of profit metrics.[52] Initially, the skeptics must have felt validated as Facebook's shares primarily traded below their initial public offering (IPO) price for over a year, which explains why it did not spark a tech company IPO boom, similar to what occurred after the Netscape IPO. But its IPO demonstrated the valuation that a digital platform business could achieve.

---

[51] Quoted in Popper (2012).
[52] Wilhelm (2017).

The Stock Market Recovery and the FAANG Boom

While the stock market recovery following 2008 was first driven by the resumption of economic growth, low interest rates, and low inflation, the technology sector turned into the main driver of stock market returns from 2015 onwards. By that time Google and Facebook showed strong profits, i.e., Google reported a net income of $16.4 billion, and Facebook reported a net income of $3.7 billion. Both companies experienced significant growth in their respective advertising businesses, which was a major driver of their strong financial performance in 2015.[53] These results changed investor sentiment and led to high demand for technology stocks. Jim Cramer, the host of CNBC's *Mad Money*, coined the phrase "FAANG" in 2012.[54] It became a catchphrase for a group of technological companies that included Meta (META) (formerly known as Facebook), Amazon (AMZN), Apple (AAPL), Netflix (NFLX); and Alphabet (GOOG) (formerly known as Google).

Over the decade until 2021, the S&P 500 saw significant growth with an annual 15% total return (dividends reinvested). The NASDAQ, which had not come close to its dotcom high during the millennium's first decade, began quickly to recover from its decline during the GFC in early 2011. In 2014, it reached a new high at year-end and continued its strong performance throughout the decade (see Table 8.3).

What started as a recovery from the decline during the GFC became one of the biggest bull runs in history. Both NASDAQ and the S&P 500 became increasingly dominated by a few constituents.

That dominance increased over time. In 2020 and 2021, the broad market performance was driven by few stocks: 31% of the S&P 500 performance in 2021 and 63% of its performance in 2020 were due to the top five stocks by market capitalization. This contribution reflects the weight of those companies and the fact that some have achieved a trillion-dollar market cap in a relatively short period (Figure 8.15).[55]

---

[53] In 2015, Facebook's (now renamed Meta) revenue in 2015 was 360% its revenue in 2012, while Amazon's revenue was up 75% over the same time. Data source: Statista.
[54] Groww (2023).
[55] Firestone (2022).

Table 8.3 S&P 500, NASDAQ and their tech sub-indices, performance, and capitalization in $ trillion

	2010	2021	1H 2022
S&P 500 Index (INDEXSP:.INX)	1258	4766	3776
S&P 500 Tech Index (INDEXSP-45)	365	3091	2248
S&P 500 Index change in % p.a.	2010–2021: 10.8%		-21%
S&P 500 Tech Index change in % p.a.	2010–2021: 20.1%		-27%
S&P 500 Capitalization in $T	$11	$40	$32
S&P 500 Tech capitalization in $T	$2	$12	$9
S&P 500 Tech in %	19%	29%	28%
NASDAQ Total (INDEXNADAQ:.IXIC)	2269	15645	10998
NASDAQ Tech (INDEXNASDAQ: NDXT)	1105	9575	6358
NASDAQ Total change in % p.a.	2010–2021: 17.5%		-30%
NASDAQ Tech change in % p.a.	2010–2021: 20.3%		-34%

Source: spg.global.com, nasdaq.com, bloomberg.com.
Note: performance numbers are based on price indices and not total returns, i.e., no dividends included or reinvested. The 1H 2022 column show the index level as well as the 1H 2022 performance.

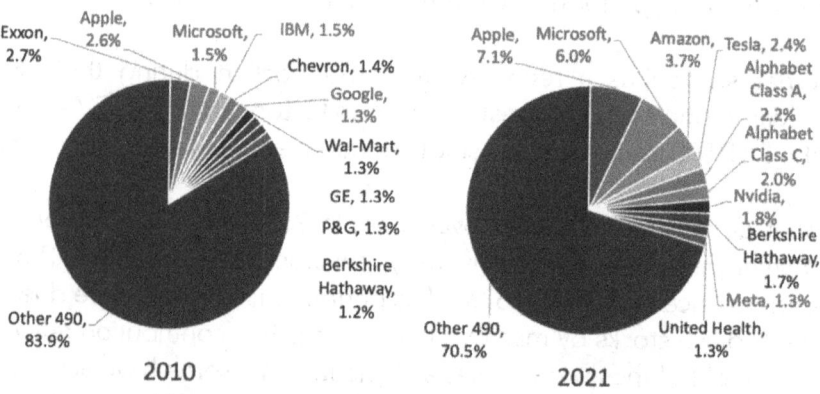

Figure 8.15 Composition of the S&P 500 in 2010 and 2021 (cap-weighted).
Source: Statista.com as of 02/2022, chicaelmoh (2020).

The FAANG stocks (Facebook, Apple, Amazon, Netflix, and Google) have seen a surge in valuations due to their increasing profitability. Despite being commonly referred to as technology stocks, these companies are not exclusively in the technology sector, and many rely on commoditized technological resources that are not unique to the industry. For example, Walmart's e-commerce revenue is estimated to be $75 billion for 2021, but it is not considered a technology company.[56] Likewise, Amazon and Netflix are not included in the S&P 500 information technology index. But if you Google it, you will find Amazon and Netflix in many listings of technology stocks. For investors to draw valid conclusions from the tech boom, it is thus important to understand why the FAANG stocks created so much excitement and high valuations while Walmart did not. Equally important is the question why the surge in valuations did not happen during the previous decade as the FAANG stocks mainly include companies that went public much earlier, such as Apple (1980), Google (2004), Amazon (1997), and Netflix (2002), with Facebook (2012) being the exception.

It started with hardware. In 2012, Apple saw a substantial increase in revenue driven by the popularity of the iPhone and other product lines. By 2015, their total revenue reached $233.72 billion. The widespread adoption of smartphones and high-speed mobile internet expanded market opportunities for companies like Facebook, Google, and Amazon, whose user/advertiser business models thrived.

Moreover, companies like Apple and Amazon generated revenue from various sources, including subscription services, paid apps, e-commerce, and transaction fees. In 2015, significant advances in cloud computing, mobile devices, and data analytics reached a crucial stage, leading to accelerated profitability and high investor expectations for ongoing innovation and expansion.

With the rise of profits of customer data-driven business models, the value of customer data as a driver of revenue growth has become increasingly recognized by investors. Companies possessing extensive and high-quality customer data started receiving higher valuations. The combination of accelerated profitability and the valuation of customer data-rich companies contributed to the technology share boom. Targeting users based on their profiles

---

[56] Junglescout (2022).

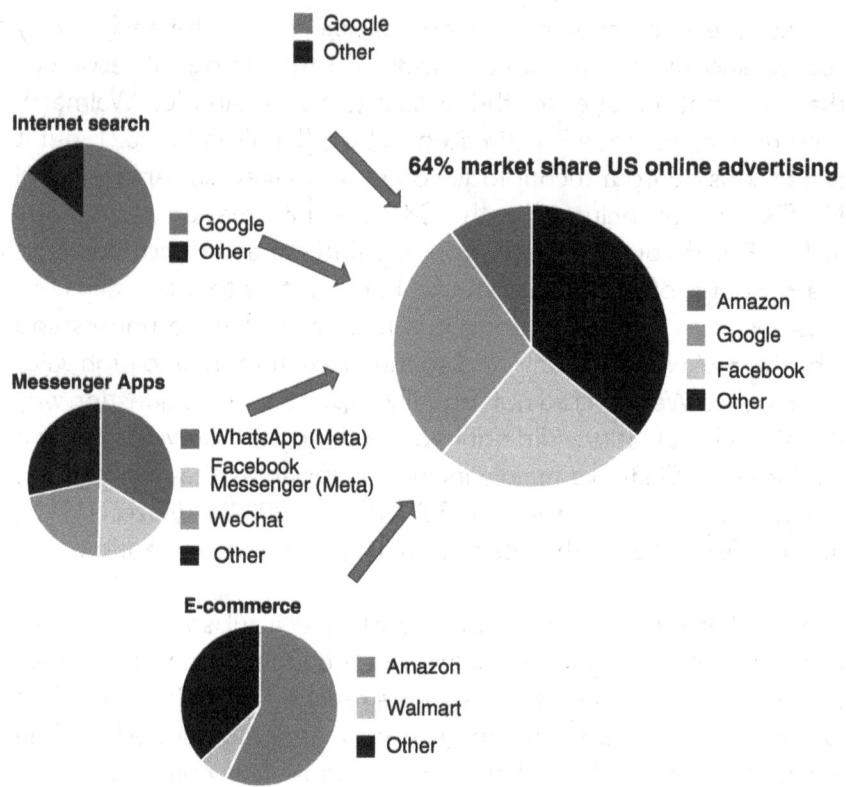

Figure 8.16 Follow the money: leading competitors for online advertising.
Source: Messenger apps: (Similarweb, 2022), online advertising: (Mordor, 2022), web browsers: (Statcounter, 2022), e-commerce: (Statista, 2022), internet search: (Statcounter, 2022).

became central to business models, where collecting and analyzing user data was the core activity. Any services or products offered are auxiliary—and often free.[57] This phenomenon underscored that, in digital platforms, the primary customer was not the end user but rather, to a considerable extent, the advertising industry. The sector's expansion was fueled by a transition of advertising expenditure from traditional media to digital platforms, where a small group of dominant companies held sway (Figure 8.16).

However, the robust performance of FAANG stocks in the stock market did not trigger a boom of initial public offerings (IPOs) for venture-backed startups until late in the cycle. The requirements

---

[57] Colin (2015).

imposed by both listing regulations and investor sentiment necessitated companies to exhibit a clear and achievable path to profitability to ensure a successful IPO. The listed tech companies
did, however, become more acquisitive as they sought to defend
and expand their market positions and to keep users active on
their platforms. As a result, merger and acquisition (M&A) activity increased, which raised the valuations of private companies
and offered high-return exit opportunities for venture capitalists
(Figure 8.16). Thus the initial effect of the technology boom was
not an IPO boom for venture-backed startups but an M&A boom
that lifted valuations and increased exits—both leading to higher
IRRs for long-suffering venture capital funds and their investors.
A second effect was that VCs started to back companies that
sought to emulate the success of the FAANGs.

A (Not So) New Investment Paradigm

The theory went that to be considered the dominant actor in the
digital economy, all that is required is faster development and the
ability to overwhelm competitors.[58] A key presumption underlying this investment approach is that investors are able to identify
promising startups that focus on large addressable markets and
support them by a rather aggressive strategy to gain market share.
This resembles the 1990s, when internet startups used the motto
"get big fast" and "get large or get lost."[59]

Both in the past and the present, the primary emphasis has been
on expanding the customer base rather than solely focusing on
revenue or profits. This approach stems from the unique characteristics of business models and markets in the digital space:

- **"Winner takes all" dynamics:** In some markets, dominant players can achieve significant revenue and profit growth due to
"quasi-monopoly" rents.
- **Economies of scale:** Profitability increases rapidly after a certain
amount of turnover, thanks to high incremental margins.

---

[58] LeBlanc (2016).
[59] Cited from Berlin (2008).

- **Double-sided network effects:** Platforms benefit from attracting more participants, as the value of the service grows with the number of users.
- **Data as a valuable asset:** Collecting more data enables firms to improve their offering, react faster to market trends, and better target customers. Machine learning algorithms also improve with more data.
- **Virality:** Users can help acquire new customers, reducing the cost of customer acquisition over time (Figure 8.17).

Amazon achieved the validity of its business after a somewhat accidental entry into the cloud business through its cloud services platform AWS, driving its profitability and contributing 76% of its total profits in 2021.[60] Despite these idiosyncratic elements of its success, Amazon's massive post-IPO valuation increase made it a

Figure 8.17   Reid Hoffman was an early investor in Facebook, helped to found PayPal, and launched LinkedIn in 2002. In his book, Blitzscaling: The Lightning-Fast Path to Building Massively Valuable Companies (Hoffman and Yeh, 2018), he describes the strategy of rapidly building out a company to serve a large and usually global market, to become the first mover at scale.
Source: Kelly Sullivan / Stringer.

---

[60] Aran (2022).

textbook example of the new investment paradigm for tech companies. This created a "too big to miss" mentality among investors who wanted to repeat the success of the "Big Five" in winner-take-all markets.

Author Al Ramadan called such firms "category kings" as they seek to define, develop, and dominate new markets.[61] To set this flywheel in motion, firms must grow rapidly, strive for market dominance, and acquire incumbents and other new entrants.[62] This observation is confirmed by Hammer (2017), who found that inorganic growth strategies are planned components of the investment case rather than the result of opportunistic behavior during the holding period.[63] Kaplan and Strömberg also identified that the ability to accelerate growth through acquisitions is a crucial component of a VC's investment thesis.[64]

So here is where the tech boom differs from the dotcom boom. Previously, established public technology corporations would purchase startups to expand their technology and service offerings. Acquisitions have always been a vital exit strategy for VCs. Large tech firms have been serial acquirers of large and small startups. Microsoft, for example, had acquired 210 companies, including 45 during the preceding five years until mid-2022, according to Mergr, a platform that tracks those acquisitions. A total of 13 acquisitions came from private equity firms.[65] But mergers and acquisitions among startups occurred mainly after venture capitalists declined to sponsor destructive price wars or after a boom had turned to bust by acquiring companies at bargain prices to bolster the survivor's position.[66] VCs had learned to use M&A after the dotcom boom ended and when consolidation provided a way to create stronger businesses out of the carnage. The difference was that those acquisitions often required minimal capital as many of the acquisition targets were not viable on their own.

---

[61] Ramadan (2014).
[62] The importance of outgrowing competitors and the role of acquisitions therein is discussed in Kenney (2019) and Solomon (2015).
[63] Hammer (2017).
[64] Kaplan and Strömberg (2000).
[65] Mergr (2022).
[66] A more recent example reported in Mallaby (2022, p. 364) was DiDi's acquisition of UBER China in 2016, which was engineered by TPG and Benchmark after UBER lost $2 billion in China.

During the tech boom, "buy and build" or "inorganic growth" methods were essential to many startups' business models.[67] The fact that startups would be serial acquirers before they went public was a new trend that differed from the 1990s. In 2021, there were 527 transactions where venture-backed startups acquired other venture-backed startups or did a merger, up 90% and 50% over 2020 and 2019, respectively, according to a Crunchbase data query.[68] This time, acquisitions did not come cheap and were often done at peak valuations.

The Rise of the Non-traditional Investor

While late-round and pre-IPO investments by institutional investors became increasingly frequent from 2000 onwards, the developments that took place since 2017 are on a different scale and can have wide-ranging implications for the venture capital industry and capital markets going forward. During the dotcom boom, companies were rushing to do an IPO to get the capital needed to fund their quest for market share and brand building. After the Facebook IPO in 2012, the tech startup IPO market did not immediately open because the stock price of Facebook dropped significantly after its IPO, which made many investors wary of investing in other tech IPOs. In addition, the SEC introduced new rules and regulations in response to the JOBS Act (Jumpstart Our Business Startups Act) in 2012. While the intention of the JOBS Act was to make it easier for small businesses to go public by loosening certain SEC regulations and disclosure requirements, some of the rules have had the opposite effect. Several additions to the Act made in 2016 have made it easier for private companies to stay private, for example, by increasing the shareholder number threshold for registration and reporting.

This reinforced a preference for founders who wanted to maintain control over their firms without the regulatory burden and the restrictions that come with a public company. Startups were thus compelled to stay private longer and to seek the necessary funding through private investor rounds. But the traditional venture rounds were too small to implement the scale of expansion and acquisitions that some startups envisioned. So, investors with deep pockets were required.

---

[67] For a discussion of buy-and-build as a PE value creation strategy, see Hammer (2017) and for the role of acquisitions in the creation of unicorns, see Kenney (2019).
[68] Crunchbase News (2022).

Then came the establishment of the SoftBank Vision Fund in 2017 (today in its second edition).[69] SoftBank contributed $28 billion to the Vision Fund, which raised $100 billion—more than 30x larger than the biggest venture fund at that time. In a testament of the growing prominence of SWFs in venture and growth financing the Vision Fund's funding originated mainly from Saudi Arabia's Public Investment Fund (PIF) with $45 billion, and UAE's Mubadala with $15 billion. This event signaled a profound shift in the allocation strategy of SWFs' capital. Gradually and consistently, SWFs increased their investments in startups, particularly directing capital toward technology companies. They fully embraced disruptive innovation as a key investment theme. Previously a minor component of SWFs' portfolios in 2020, venture capital surged to encompass 40% of SWFs' total private equity deals in 2019 and has continued to expand since then.[70]

In conjunction with other non-traditional institutional venture capital investors, SWFs contributed significantly to the record-breaking investment levels observed in the VC industry in 2020 and 2021. Their escalating participation provides insight into why startups choose to remain privately held for extended periods. Softbank astutely recognized this emerging dynamic and understood the transformative role that SWFs would assume within the venture ecosystem.

Even during the dotcom boom Masayoshi Son had been prepared to write large checks to build up companies to global market leaders and by doing so put down a challenge to the more incremental venture capital model (Figure 8.18). But now with the resources of SoftBank and the Vision Fund, he could push the concept of "funding whatever it takes" to new heights.

The investment pattern that followed was characterized by rapid deal-making in many companies and, over time, large capital infusions that may exceed $1 billion—larger than most funds of venture capital firms. SoftBank invested around $84 billion in startups

---

[69] Masayoshi Son launched SoftBank in 1981 as a software distributor. He made a string of large bets on internet companies such as Yahoo! E-Trade, Excite, GeoCities or Webvan. After initial successes the end of the dotcom boom resulted in estimated losses of $70 billion during the dotcom bust of the early 2000s. After the dotcom bubble burst, SoftBank sold several of its non-core assets, such as its Japanese telecom business, to raise cash and reduce debt. Additionally, SoftBank made strategic investments in companies, such as Alibaba and Yahoo! Japan, which helped the company recover and grow.
[70] Bortolotti and Scortecci (2019).

Figure 8.18   Softbank Group Corp. CEO Masayoshi Son announces the group's earnings at a news conference.
Source: Tomohiro Ohsumi, Getty Images #1205730885, license nr. 2092940244.

between 2017 and 2021. It was already the world's largest tech investor before raising a $30 billion sibling to the $98.6 billion Vision Fund in May 2021. Its more than 300 technology investments span from early-stage businesses to established behemoths like Byte Dance, OneWeb, and Grab.[71]

Several other investors copied its concept, most notably hedge funds like Tiger Global Management and Coatue Management, which are "crossover funds" that invest in both public and private markets.[72, 73] They brought a new "spray can" approach to venture

---

[71] The SoftBank Vision Fund, a venture capital fund founded in 2017 that is part of the SoftBank Group, held more than 300 portfolio investments in 2021.

[72] Tiger Global started in 2002 by investing in Chinese web portals that went public just before the dotcom bubble burst and were no longer covered by Wall Street analysts. After that Tiger Global established a partnership vehicle to expand its investment in (illiquid) private companies. But their model evolved compared to the early China investments as they changed from value-driven to a momentum investor (Mallaby, 2022). Tiger Global Management holds more than 1,000 portfolio companies across 10 funds at year-end 2021. This is like trying to win the lottery by buying all the tickets.

[73] Coatue Management LLC is a technology-focused investment manager led by founder and portfolio manager Philippe Laffont, who was previously with Tiger Global Management. Coatue invests in public and private markets with a focus on technology, media, telecommunications, consumer, and healthcare sectors.

capital (the managers would dispute that characterization), which is worlds apart from the nurturing and partnering with startups that traditional venture capital firms advertise.[74] Apart from doing many deals and investing in early rounds, they were also providing massive amounts of late-round financing. The abundance of capital that was a result of the new entrants in the startup financing space has led to heightened expectations of founders regarding funding amounts, raised concerns about overinvestment or funding too many startups with the same business model ("overfunding"), and weakening governance, as too much money came with too few strings attached.

From customary players, such as Temasek, GIC, and SoftBank's Vision Fund to emerging key contributors like Mubadala, the Australian Future Fund, and Qatar Investment Authority (QIA), SWFs engage in co-investments alongside prominent venture capital firms. These include traditional VCs, such as Sequoia Capital and New Enterprise Associates, hedge funds, like Tiger Global Management, asset managers, and investment firms, such as Fidelity and Goldman Sachs, which are expanding the VC landscape to potential new partners. Consequently, the venture capital industry has broadened its horizons to encompass later and more substantial funding rounds, fostering greater confidence among ultra-large institutional investors.

Sequoia Capital, for instance, has co-invested in 87 deals with at least nine distinct SWFs, showing a preference for transactions involving the Vision Fund, Temasek, and GIC. Tiger Global Management has partnered with six different SWFs, while New Enterprise Associates has participated in co-investments across 43 deals with eight distinct SWFs.[75]

The convergence between specialized venture capital funds and institutional direct investors, asset managers, or hedge funds was gaining momentum due to the rise of mid-to-late-stage investment

---

[74] In 2021, Tiger Global led a funding round on average every four working days out of five in 2021. Insight Partners—another crossover fund—was not far behind, its three-person team has been involved in roughly 200 deals in three years—around 65 deals a year—leading a round every three working days per week. SoftBank led more than two investments every week on average, according to Crunchbase (2022).

[75] Aguliar (2023).

rounds. This trend is two-fold: specialized VC funds are amassing larger funds or raise dedicated growth financing vehicles to support successful startups in subsequent stages, and sizable institutional investors aim to tap into earlier rounds to secure access to late-stage super rounds, venturing into areas they had not explored before.

This new type of investors was termed by VCs "non-traditional investors," a group that included private equity firms and growth financing funds, hedge funds and the Vision Funds, which previously had limited venture involvement. Together those non-traditional investors went from investing $144 billion in 2020 to $260 billion in 2021, and the increased involvement of non-traditional investors is estimated to have reached 44% of global venture activity in 2021, up from 20% in 2002.[76] As a result of numerous late-stage funding rounds, the number of unicorns has increased, and many of those unicorns are ten years old or even older. For a startup, staying private has become a viable option.[77] Unicorns not only boosted the exit environment for early-round investors, but they also acquired other companies to establish dominance, which created an exit channel for startups held in other VC funds. Non-traditional investors led some VC firms to engage in growth financing, resulting in larger late-stage financing rounds. Sequoia Capital launched its first growth financing fund in 2006, and Andreessen Horowitz (a16z), Peter Thiel (Founders Fund), and Battery Ventures followed suit, making seed investments and large bets in unicorn companies. These firms gained a reputation for offering founder-friendly term sheets.[78] The multi-stage investment approach requires large pools of capital: Andreessen Horowitz was managing $54.6 billion as of Q1 2022 and Sequoia Capital was reported to manage $85.5 billion.[79]

SoftBank Group's Vision Fund played a key role in transforming these mega-deals into the "new normal" for ambitious companies. This led to the unicorn phenomenon, i.e., more than 1,100 startups valued at $1 billion or more at the end of 2021. As funding

---

[76] Huff-Eckert (2022), *The Economist* (2021f).
[77] *The Economist* (2019).
[78] Metrick and Yasuda (2021).
[79] Loizos (2022).

rounds became more numerous and were done at steeply increasing valuations, investors that participated in earlier rounds saw a quick increase in the valuations of their investments.

Large private funding rounds not only eliminated the need for fast-growing companies to go public but also offered other advantages. Founders and early-stage investors could get full value for their shares compared to IPOs that were usually priced at a discount. Late-round investors were also founder-friendly, allowing founders to maintain or strengthen control over their company through super-voting shares and additional board seats. Additionally, late-round investors could provide liquidity to early-stage investors or employees by buying out their stock options or VC stakes.[80]

But often, VCs did not want to sell and were happy that the company received private funding, and they would continue to participate in further value increases and not have to distribute or sell shares, as would have been the case in an IPO. Yahoo! provided a template both by doing the first $100 million round (with SoftBank) and, second, by creating massive gains for Sequoia and its investors because it did not liquidate its shares soon after the IPO but slowly over time. As Michael Moritz put it, the secret was "just learning to be a little patient."[81] But investors in his fund can also buy shares in the public market and by doing so participate in the continued growth of valuations without paying carried interest. The question here is whether Moritz had a mandate to be "a little patient."

Institutional investors struggled with new digital economy companies staying private longer and having high valuations, causing concerns about missed value creation. While this trend was enabled by large pension funds and sovereign wealth funds it has

---

[80] Private exchanges, such as SharesPost or NASDAQ Private Market, have evolved to accommodate those who wish to buy or sell their interests. This has also created opportunities for institutions seeking direct investments or secondaries funds that acquire those stakes (Black, 2018).

[81] Mallaby (2022) reports that M. Moritz stretched share distribution from their investment in Yahoo! Until November 1999—more than three years after the IPO—by which time its stock traded 14x more than the price of its floatation. M. Moritz is quoted there (p. 161).

a ripple-through effect as more institutions established in-house programs for technology growth financing. For many institutional investors, the opportunity to invest large sums of money in the venture capital space was too tempting to ignore.

One result of the growing influence of investors who could invest directly from their balance sheets, unencumbered by fund term restrictions, was that the idea of temporary ownership was starting to lose significance.[82] Temasek in Singapore, for example, invested across financing stages and was reported to have invested $4 billion in VC rounds in 2021. It also established an incubator to provide financing for seed and startup rounds.[83] Thus, the arrival of non-traditional investors put the spotlight on permanent capital.

If this observation needs confirmation, it comes from one of the most prestigious venture capital firms in Silicon Valley. Sequoia Capital (Figure 8.19) announced in 2022 that it will revamp its fund structure by establishing a singular, permanent structure called The Sequoia Fund. The fund will invest in public equity and allocate

Figure 8.19   Sequoia headquarters on Sand Hill Road in Menlo Park California.
Source: Gado Images / Alamy Stock Photo.

---

[82] It needs to be said, however, that not all the late-stage financing came from permanent capital sources. The Vision Fund is a limited partnership with a 12-year fund life, and Tiger Global Management, as well as other growth equity investors in the technology space, do invest in capital pools that have a limited life.
[83] SWF (2021).

capital to closed-end sub-funds. In decline are the 10-year return cycles that pushed GPs to liquidate holdings based on set timelines rather than the timing of the GP.[84] Softbank illustrates both the potential and the risks that come with building massive exposure in the technology space. Its portfolio was valued at a staggering $1.1 trillion in mid-2021, according to PitchBook.[85] As of 2021, the portfolio's performance has been remarkable and the Vision Fund had distributed $38.7 billion to LPs within five years of the fund's launch.[86] But when investors started questioning whether many of the once high-flyers of the tech boom had a clear path to profitability, SoftBank itself posted a $13 billion annual net loss and reported a record $26.2 billion loss at its Vision Fund in 2022.[87] As these privately-funded companies grow into multi-billion-dollar entities, their valuations limit potential M&A options, leaving an IPO as the only means of liquidity. However, the cyclical nature of the IPO market can extend holding periods if market sentiment changes. Non-traditional investors with longer investment horizons may be better placed to wait for the next IPO window than VCs with their fund life constraints. These challenges may not be significant in a thriving market but become more pressing during downturns.

8.7   THE UNICORN BOOM

The emergence of unicorns, i.e., startups with valuations of a billion dollars or more, reflects the new investment paradigm that believes smaller financing rounds followed by acquisitions or IPOs are not the most effective way to achieve success. Late-stage venture rounds became more frequent, larger, and often exceeded $1 billion, which resulted in the creation of billion-dollar startups. As of 2015, there were around 140 unicorns and that number had increased to around 340 unicorns in 2018 before it exploded to more than 1,100 in 2021, according to Crunchbase data (see Box 8.3). This pattern illustrates that the unicorn phenomenon turned into a frenzy in 2021. According to Crunchbase, there were 168 unicorns that raised funding rounds of $1 billion or more between 2019 and the first half of 2021. This includes both primary and secondary funding rounds.

[84] Matney (2021).
[85] *The Economist* (2021b).
[86] SoftBank (2022).
[87] Nussey (2022).

Box 8.3   Unicorns

The Crunchbase Unicorn Board counted over 1,100 active unicorn firms worldwide. Yahoo!'s $1 billion investment in Alibaba in 2005 was the first unicorn round recorded, and Facebook is still the most valuable company that achieved unicorn status before going public.[88]

Throughout their existence, these unicorn enterprises have raised more than $700 billion in financing, and, in 2021, they set a new record by exceeding $4 trillion in valuation for the first time. That is more than twice the value of the world's unicorns by the end of 2020, so the formation of unicorns was not linear but exponential at the end of the valuation cycle in 2021 (Figure 8.20). The average valuation of the unicorns was $3.6 billion while the median valuation was $2.5 billion, which suggests that the valuation of unicorns as a group follows a power law too.[89]

The unicorn club also includes 59 "decacorns" valued at $10 billion or more. Three of these decacorns are the world's most valuable private companies, with valuations above $100 billion: ByteDance ($180 billion), Ant Group ($150 billion), and SpaceX ($100 billion).

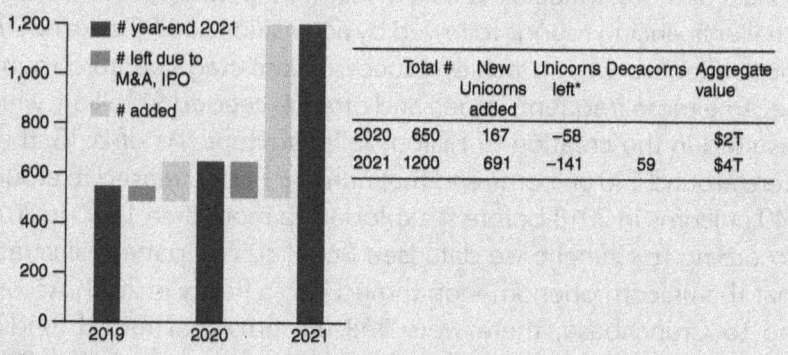

	Total #	New Unicorns added	Unicorns left*	Decacorns	Aggregate value
2020	650	167	−58		$2T
2021	1200	691	−141	59	$4T

Figure 8.20   Value ($B) and growth (#) of unicorns.
Source: CB Unicorn Board, as of January 2022.

[88] Teare (2022b).
[89] *The Economist* (2021d).

Unicorns provided an exit channel for VCs to sell to late-stage investors and extend the period a company could stay private. Approximately 60% of 2021 unicorns were based in North America. China has roughly 16% of all unicorns, followed by India with 6%, and Germany with 2.5%.

In Europe, there were nearly 150 unicorns in 2021, quadrupling the previous year's total. The developing markets have also seen many startups experience rapid valuation growth and enter the unicorn club, although at much smaller numbers.[90]

Investments in unicorns were dominated by traditional VCs in the early rounds but non-traditional investors in later "super-rounds."

Even though VCs often used later rounds to exit their investments, at least in part, many funds still carry significant positions in those highly valued firms. While they may be diversified in terms of capital invested, their final fund outcomes will—at least in some cases—heavily depend on the realization of those highly valued portfolio companies.

Investors were willing to participate in late rounds at high valuations as the IPO market seemed to offer substantial upside over pre-IPO valuations. Correa et al. analyzed 44 unicorns that went public on NASDAQ (21) and NYSE (23) between 2013 and 2017, looking at the valuation increase of a unicorn IPO compared to its pre-IPO valuation. The average pre-IPO valuation of a unicorn was $2.9 billion, and the average IPO valuation was $4 billion, a 35.7% increase. At the end of the first trading day, their average valuation was $4.5 billion, which declined to $4.2 billion after 120 trading days.[91] Reminiscent of past booms, participating in late-stage rounds and subscribing to IPOs of unicorns was a profitable strategy—as long as the boom lasts. Participating in the unicorn trend is seen by institutional investors as a desirable way

---

[90] Bryan (2022).
[91] Correia, Vidigal, and Dionisio (2021). The average age of those companies was 9.5 years at IPO.

to invest in the digital transformation of the economy, as venture capital funds face oversubscription and restricted access. Companies with an IPO valuation of over $1 billion raised 10x the money of private rounds from 2017 to 2021. As of late 2021, the 1,100 unicorns had raised a total of $700 million with a final valuation of $4 trillion.[92] It is unlikely that all of these private unicorns will achieve a 10x multiple over money raised—it implies an aggregate IPO value of $400 trillion or more than 3x the capitalization of the NYSE in 2021. But many investors at the time stood to gain in the event of an IPO due to the expected valuation gain. As investors engage in various rounds at differing valuations, many might even experience gains if the IPO valuation ends up being lower than the previous round before the IPO.[93]

SoftBank's Vision Fund made one of its largest bets in the We Company (formerly WeWork), based on the belief that flexible office space would disrupt traditional real estate. WeWork attracted heavy investment as the potential leader in this space, with funding rounds reaching record sizes, including a round of over $4 billion, including debt financing (see Figure 8.21). The private market's optimism doesn't always carry over to the public market, as evidenced by WeWork's unsuccessful $60 billion IPO in 2019. The public market had concerns about the sustainability of WeWork's unprofitable business model, which led to the IPO's failure. In 2020, WeWork merged with a SPAC at a much lower valuation of $9 billion. Despite the low public market valuation, WeWork continued to receive funding from private investors, causing significant losses for those who invested at a higher valuation.[94] In total, the We Company had received more than $26 billion in debt and equity funding as of mid-2022.

---

[92] Teare (2022d).

[93] Ibid.

[94] The We Company scrapped plans for an IPO in 2019 after investors raised concerns over its business model and corporate governance and its founder and then-CEO Adam Neumann. SoftBank, one of its key backers, put a $49 billion valuation on the company at the time of the planned IPO. In 2021 The We Company went public through a de-SPAC merger that put its valuation at $9 billion. The shares closed 13% higher after the merger (Subin, 2021). Thereafter it share price declined as investors questioned the firms ability to turn around and The We Company filed for bankruptcy in November 2023. After the IPO was canceled in 2019, Adam Neumann, the firm's founder, was replaced as CEO and subsequently left the board of the We Company. Neumann founded Flow in 2022, with financial backing from Andreessen Horowitz, a prominent Silicon Valley venture capital firm, to focus on the residential real estate market.

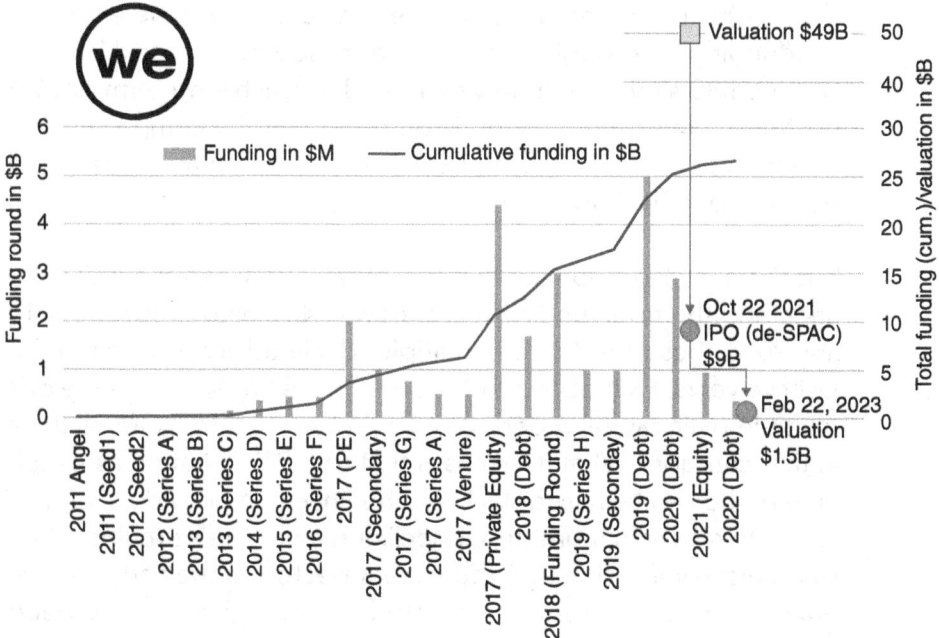

Figure 8.21   The We Company: an example of the perils of overfunding.
Source: Adopted from Crunchbase data as of June 2022.

But the unicorn boom also generated a string of success stories. As of 2021 the most valuable private companies globally included ByteDance ($140 billion), SpaceX ($127 billion), Shein ($100 billion), Stripe ($95 billion), and Canva/Checkout.com (tied for fifth place at $40 billion). Fintech is the most commonly represented industry among unicorns, followed by internet software and services, e-commerce and direct-to-consumer, and health.

Are Unicorns a Successful Model for Investors?

A series of successful IPOs have shown that unicorns can go public at valuations higher than the amount raised, as well as significantly higher than their post-money valuations from the last private funding round. However, the abundance of unicorns raises doubts about whether this trend can be sustained for the many that are still private. One concern is the issue of "overfunding," where entrepreneurs receive excessive funding without sufficient accountability measures. This not only raises governance concerns for investors, but also the belief that overfunding undermines the cost and spending discipline.

CB Insights published a research report to examine the effects of overfunding.[95] To begin, startups that raised more than $100 million pre-IPO almost uniformly struggled to reach long-term growth post-IPO and were consistently outperformed by companies that raised less capital. This is an issue for post-IPO shareholders and post-merger SPAC investors.

But there is also evidence that the spread between the IPO valuation and the total funding received was declining. Between 2013 and 2018, those exit-to-raise multiples declined across all ranges in just five years. Exits above $1 billion took the hardest hit as the exit multiple over capital raised went down from 16x to 7x for all IPOs in that category. What it means is that the IPO valuation as a multiple of the capital raised declined. But investors provide capital at very different valuations and a declining exit-to-raise multiple can still achieve very attractive returns for investors in the early rounds. But late-stage investors that invested at very high valuations need to ask themselves whether the upside in the event of a successful IPO will be enough to compensate for the downside.

As the *CB Insights* report points out:

> News outlets often only report sky-high valuations as they are more prominent eye-catchers than in-depth data. But even high-profile exits such as Uber IPO at $82bn valuation represents just a 3.3x multiple on its massive $24.7bn raise over 22 funding rounds. That is less than half the typical capital efficiency for a company of that size, let alone Uber's clear struggle in achieving a profitable model and sustainable growth as a public company (CB Insights, 2019).

Traditionally venture capital is an investment strategy that benefits from a few outsized successes to compensate for the majority of investments that generate no or only modest returns. Sequential funding rounds aimed to limit losses and concentrate capital in more promising ventures as the odds of success become more visible over time. There is a reason why "fail often, fail fast" is a creed

---

[95] *CB Insights* looked at over 500 VC-backed US tech companies that have exited for more than $100 million between 2013–2018 (*CB Insights*, 2019).

of traditional venture financing. In recent years startups expanded their funding fast and achieved soaring valuations that made many of them unicorns. But their business models are unproven, and they're still burning cash.

These high-valuation super-rounds may not indicate increased odds of success. Late-round funding lacks results visibility. Flying blind is a bad idea, and given how much has been invested in unicorns, late-round investors may struggle to make a return. Longer timelines allow companies to delay the need to achieve profitability to validate their business model while investors may feel pressured to participate due to fear of missing out on potential value creation.

Unicorns: How Will a Bubble Affect Venture Capital?

The creation of unicorns was driven by a fear of missing the next Meta or Amazon. Its targets have been companies that address large numbers of users and provide digitally enabled services previously impossible to construct or deliver—ventures like Uber, Airbnb, or DoorDash. Informed investors think unicorns are overvalued—regardless of whether they are invested in them, used later rounds as an exit mechanism, or otherwise benefit from the relentless increase in valuations that this stampede of money has caused. Kaplan et al. published survey results from nearly 900 venture capital professionals, revealing that 91% of their respondents believe unicorns are overvalued—slightly or significantly. This was back in 2016 before the momentum toward unicorns gathered speed. The core contradiction of the unicorn phenomenon is the willingness of investors to pay premium prices for illiquid investments that resemble the IPO valuations seen during the dotcom boom. The difference is that the late-stage investors still need an IPO to realize a profit.

Historically, IPOs have been valued at discounts of 15–25% to their first trading day closing prices[96]—during the dotcom boom, even much higher, and IPO subscribers could reasonably hope to sell their share allocations at a profit for as long as the boom lasted. In the past, private placements as an alternative to late-round

---

[96] Lehmann-Hasemeyer and Streb (2016).

financing were often priced at 40% discounts compared to public companies. However, current "super-rounds" have not shown any valuation discount. By staying private, the funding avoids public equity market regulations and provides certainty in receiving peak valuation, making it an attractive option for founders and early-round investors. This eliminates the valuation risk inherent in an IPO offering price.[97]

Only a small percentage of unicorns are profitable, and their loss-making business models have been called into question by many observers. There is also evidence that being a "tech company" was a categorization exploited to justify investments and valuations where those concepts do not apply.

There is a group of enterprises dubbed "fake tech." These include capital-intensive companies like The We Company, which is primarily a landlord for freelancers and companies. The word "technology" appears 110 times in the S-1 filing for their (aborted) IPO.[98]

The Economist reports on another example, Casper, which sells mattresses. As reported, its co-founder, Neil Parikh, declared in 2016, "We consider ourselves a tech company first." Stock market investors valued it as a mattress retailer. In February 2021, it was listed at $575 million, less than half its $1.1 billion private valuation.[99]

But unlike the funding squeeze that followed the dotcom crash, the VC industry is well-funded this time. According to PitchBook data, the industry's cumulative, or undeployed cash, was around $222 billion at the end of 2021, a record high. Tech startups also raised a lot of money, according to Preqin, $476 billion and *CB Insights* $612 billion, in 2021 alone. *The Economist* reckons that the 70 largest unicorns can cover their burn rates until 2025. This ties in with the fact that secondary pricing for unicorns declined less than the broader stock market.[100] With a shift in investor focus

---

[97] Janeway (2018).
[98] Lopato (2019)
[99] *The Economist* (2020a), Preqin and *CB Insights* quoted therein.
[100] *The Economist* (2022f).

on lower valuations and profitability, there was already a slowdown in startups joining the unicorn club in 2022 compared to the previous years as 308 private startups crossed the threshold in 2022 through November, compared to 596 overall in 2021, according to PitchBook data.[101]

One can expect an increase in acquisitions as startups backed by investors seek consolidation. The reluctance of investors to provide more funding at high valuations will impact unicorns, leading to significant down rounds or failure. Once backers face substantial losses on their portfolios and redemption requests from their investors (in fund vehicles that provide a degree of liquidity), they will become more selective in their investments. This will be especially true for non-traditional investors, and many entrepreneurs may discover that funding can be easily gained and lost.

But this process will take time and will only start to gain momentum in a few years. In the meantime, one might experience a lull as acquisitions are put on hold with the expectation that targets will get cheaper. It depends on how investor attitudes, the stock market, and the economy develop—time will tell. As of 2023, the lack of large exits, combined with falling tech valuations and slower startup investment, has made the case for funding a Series D round or later much harder. These factors have contributed to pushing US investment at this stage to its lowest point in years and in the first quarter of 2023, total Series D investment was down 92% from the peak. According to data from Crunchbase, prominent investors, known for their active participation in large, later-stage funding rounds, have ceased leading Series D rounds.

Notable examples include Tiger Global Management and Soft-Bank Vision Fund. Based on Crunchbase data, these two firms served as lead investors in Series D rounds a total of 43x in 2021 and 2022. However, as of mid-2023, neither firm had led a single round at this stage.[102] This trend indicates that non-traditional investors, who have experienced significant valuation losses in their portfolios, may no longer play the substantial role they once

[101] Rubio (2022).
[102] Glasner (2023b).

did as providers of capital. A reduced involvement of these investors could impact the availability of capital for unicorns, making it challenging for them to secure the necessary funds to continue their growth and operations. Similar observations apply to sovereign wealth funds (SWFs). Whether their commitment to allocating substantial capital to startups will persist remains to be seen, considering that the SWFs' rapid shift from real estate to late-stage startup financing after 2015 was quite abrupt, there is a possibility of history repeating itself.

In the pursuit of achieving unicorn status and driven by intense competition, startups increasingly granted liquidity preferences to secure large funding rounds, which give investors in that round a choice between a pro-rata share in exit proceeds or a preferential repayment of their invested capital.[103] As a result, when unicorns face a cash crunch or consolidation, certain stakeholders may bear the consequences. Earlier-round investors, lacking the protective measures to oppose such concessions, often went along to ensure their portfolio company's viability in a competitive market. If subsequent funding rounds do not materialize or the company fails to achieve a favorable exit, late-round investors may receive substantial payouts while earlier investors may lose part or all of their investment.

Contrary to conventional wisdom, VC investors may thus not be protected by their lower entry valuations and may bear the brunt of the losses in the event of an exit that falls below the peak valuation. On the other hand, investors who have a liquidation preference may have a better chance of recouping their initial investment—despite having paid peak valuations. This dynamic challenges the notion that lower entry valuations provide a substantial cushion for early-round VC investors. While a unicorn bubble burst may not pose systemic risk, it could lead to significant write-offs and prompt institutional investors to re-evaluate their private market

---

[103] A liquidation preference determines the order and the amount VCs get paid in the event of an exit or liquidation. A 1x liquidity preference for investors in a particular series gives them the right to receive their invested capital before any other investor or founders get paid according to their ownership stake.

strategies, in particular their allocations to VCs. Relying on a few investments for outsized returns over a long-term horizon may not be viable if many holdings are lost. It is uncertain if current stakeholders in unicorns can hold their surviving positions for decades if a significant number of their investments fail.

8.8 SPACs

A special purpose acquisition company (SPAC) is a blank-check company formed for the purpose of merging with a private company to make it a public entity.

Compared to an IPO, the SPAC is much less risky for the target company. In a SPAC acquisition, the target company only needs to sign a deal with the SPAC for a fixed amount of money at a negotiated price. Whereas if the company decides to go down the IPO route, the target company is uncertain about the size, price, or even potential demand.

The SPAC boom in 2020–2021 appeared to come out of nowhere. While SPACs were utilized in the previous decade, their impact was limited, and they faded into oblivion after 2007, most likely due to their poor performance.[104] But memories are short and SPAC IPOs did not entirely vanish and saw a steady increase in numbers from 2017 and then in 2020–2021 surge (Figure 8.22), which led to NASDAQ hitting a record of 1,000 IPOs, with over 60% of new listings in 2021 being SPAC IPOs.[105] Total capital raised jumped from nowhere to $80 billion in 2020 and $162 billion in 2021.

One of the main appeals of SPACs was their ability to allow companies that were not yet profitable to go public. After the dot-com era, stock exchanges implemented new listing requirements that demanded a history of operations and a minimum level of

---

[104] Looking at 127 SPACs that completed a merger since 2003, Tykvova and Kolb (2016) find that SPAC firms are associated with severe underperformance in comparison to the market, the industry, and (comparable) IPO firms.
[105] Bazerman and Patel (2021).

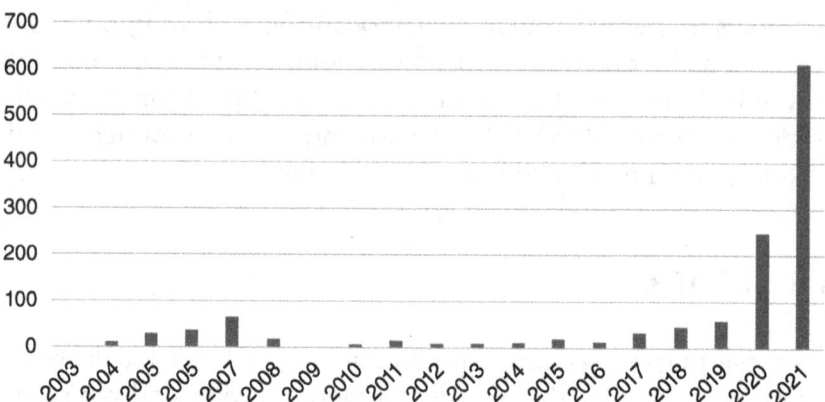

Figure 8.22   Number of special purpose acquisition companies (SPACs) IPOs in the United States from 2003 to 2021.
Source: Adopted from Statista.

capitalization.[106] Both NASDAQ and later the NYSE introduced "tailored listing standards" that accommodated blank check companies with no operating history. SPAC IPOs and their capitalization had lower equity and capitalization requirements compared to a traditional IPO, which broadens the universe of IPO candidates to smaller VC-backed companies.[107]

SPACs also seem to provide their targets with higher valuations, quicker access to funds, lower fees, and fewer regulatory

---

[106] For example, NASDAQ states as a requirement for an IPO, "The company must have aggregate pre-tax earnings in the prior three years of at least $11 million, in the previous two years at least $2.2 million, and no single year in the prior three years can have a net loss" (NASDAQ, January 2022). If a business doesn't meet cash flow or revenue requirements, it can still meet listing requirements for NASDAQ if it has assets and equity. The market capitalization requirement is $160 million—as long as total stockholder equity is $55 million and company assets total at least $80 million. This is a much smaller size threshold than one would find for traditional IPOs. As subsequent mergers do not fall under rule 5305 or 5405 in the case of NASDAQ, startups that would not meet the standards for a traditional IPO, i.e., a revenue and profit track record, could obtain a listing.
[107] In a memorandum issued by the SEC's Office of the Investor Advocate to NASDAQ, it was pointed out "[that] in 2005, the American Stock Exchange (now NYSE American) began listing SPACs pursuant to generic listing standards that did not require operating histories, and then in 2008, NYSE and NASDAQ obtained Commission approval to list and trade SPACs pursuant to more tailored listing standards" (SEC, 2022).

obligations.[108] This development was very relevant for the venture capital industry as it provides an alternative exit route for startups to become public companies. SPACs are often created by private equity funds, well-known tech investors, or executives from major public companies, who act as sponsors. The sponsors' reputation is crucial as it signals their ability to source, vet, and assess the potential of a high-performing (tech) company and its leadership. For example, according to SEC filings, Khosla Ventures formed four blank-check companies, and other venture capital firms followed. In that context, SPACs can also be used to continue ownership of a portfolio company like the continuation vehicles that became increasingly popular among private market firms.[109] The amounts shown as SPAC IPOs do overstate their war chest for acquisitions as investors in the SPAC IPO have the right to redeem their shares. There is little risk of losing the original investment because cash is put into a trust that invests in US treasuries and shareholders can ask for their money back by redeeming their shares at any point. It is estimated that more than 50% or more of investors redeemed their SPAC shares in 2019–2020.[110]

De-SPAC mergers became a significant exit route for VC-backed companies in 2020 and exit values overtook IPOs of venture-backed companies (money raised) in 2021. While VC-backed IPOs are a significant part of IPO activity, in particular, when compared to tech and biotech IPOs a category into which most VC-backed IPOs fall, the larger role of de-SPAC mergers during 2020–2021 is eye-catching (Figure 8.23).

The key comparison is between the volume of de-SPAC mergers and IPOs, as both result in venture-backed company exits while a SPAC IPO just creates a cash box that is available but yet unused

---

[108] Unlike a company undergoing a traditional IPO, SPACs do not provide services or sell products and therefore have no business operations data to provide to initial investors. When the SPAC identifies a prospective target company to merge with, it sends out a proxy statement to its shareholders, which often includes "forward-looking statements" regarding anticipated performance or financial projections of the post-merger company. This suits private companies with no clear path to profitability, that can use projections relating to their business in their filings that would be much more restricted in a traditional IPO (Barton and Ward, 2021).
[109] Khosla Ventures filed for a number of SPAC mergers: (Khosla Ventures, 2021a, 2021b, 2021c).
[110] Gompers and Kaplan (2022).

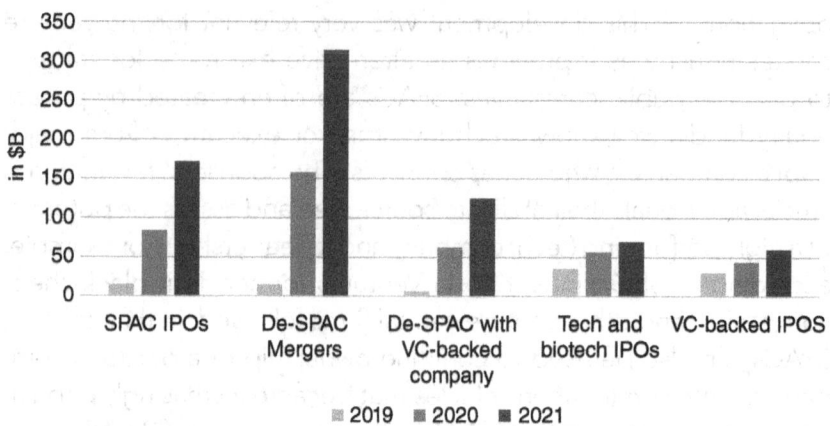

Figure 8.23 Venture-backed public market exits: IPOs and de-SPAC merger volumes, 2019–2021.

Source: VC-backed public exits National Venture Capital Association (NVCA) and PwC MoneyTree, SPAC-IPO and de-SPAC volumes (White & Case, 2023) and SPAC Insider.

for such an outcome (Figure 8.23). However, De-SPAC mergers represent a full exit as the entire company is bought, while IPOs are only partial exits as they only concern shares made available to the public and don't account for the company's total valuation. As VCs can sell or distribute additional shares after the IPO, the magnitude of the liquidity event is understated by looking just at the IPO offering. The numbers highlight the increasing significance of public exits for VC-backed firms toward the end of the decade and the prominent role of de-SPAC mergers in 2021 when 107 VC-backed companies merged with SPACs (after the IPO) in deals worth more than $100 billion.[111]

How SPACs Work

A special purpose acquisition company (SPAC) is a company that has no commercial operations and is formed strictly to raise capital through an initial public offering (IPO) for the purpose of acquiring or merging with an existing company. In an IPO, a company hires bankers to sell shares to primarily institutional investors at a predetermined price. SPACs reverse this. Investors fund a shell company. It then seeks out an unlisted target company to merge with and will raise the second round of investor funding to complete the deal. There are two distinctive events after the formation

---

[111] For an analysis of market trends in 2019–2021, see Kunthara (2021b); Hu, Parry, and Rubinstein (2022); Macintosh (2022).

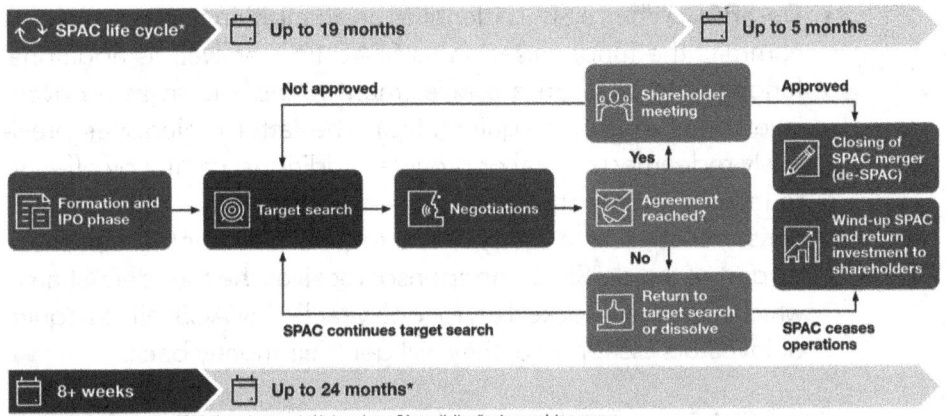

Figure 8.24 SPAC lifecycle.
Source: Adapted from White and Case, 2023.

of a SPAC: (1) the SPAC IPO, and (2) the de-SPAC, when a business is acquired (Figure 8.24).

- **Formation/sponsor:** Generally, a SPAC is formed by an experienced management team. SPAC shares are usually 20% founder(s) shares and 80% IPO public shares.
- **SPAC IPO:** IPO investors receive redeemable shares and warrants as a sweetener. Those warrants detach from the shares and can be kept or traded in the secondary market, even when a shareholder redeems. Typically shares are usually issued at $10 with warrants that have a conversion price of $11.5. There is one warrant for ten shares. In 2021, warrants traded in a range of $0.50–1 for SPACs whose shares price did not differ significantly from their IPO price.[112] SPACs have a two-year time frame to close a merger as otherwise the SPAC is dissolved and the money returned to investors.

  Although SPACs are perceived as a means of providing access to high-performing tech companies to the general public, the reality is that more than 70% of SPAC IPO funding comes from a limited group of hedge funds.[113] Hedge funds would participate in the IPO and redeem their shares afterwards but keep warrants.[114]

---

[112] However, shares can trade up significantly based on the announcement or an expectation of a specific merger (Lipschultz, 2022).
[113] Gompers and Kaplan (2022).
[114] Gahng, Ritter, and Zhang (2021). The authors calculate that for redeeming shareholders, this represents a mean annualized return of 11.6%.

- **De-SPAC:** When a SPAC identifies an acquisition target, it typically commits the funds raised in its SPAC IPO, as well as additional funds raised by a private investment round known as a private investment in public equity (PIPE). The latter replenishes previously redeemed capital or provides additional capital by offering to invest in newly created shares—sometimes at a discount. The consummation of a merger also requires shareholder approval. As part of the de-SPAC the sponsor receives the founders' shares, which are usually locked up for one year.[115] If SPACS fail to acquire or investors disapprove, they will get their money back.

When SPACs merge, they treat their shares as being worth $10 each, and in their proxy statements, they describe those shares directly or indirectly as being worth $10.[116] But the net cash underlying SPAC shares—and hence, the cash that will be invested in a target—tends to be substantially less than the $10 that those investors originally contributed and can be as low as $6, i.e., the target company has almost to double for investors to start making a return.

It has been argued that in a de-SPAC merger, those who maintain their stake in the merged company or come in before the merger, which often includes retail investors, are taking on both the risks of a potentially poor deal and substantial dilution from the founders' shares and free warrants that have been handed out to early backers.[117] Gahng et al. point out that the warrants that were issued to the initial subscribers of the IPO plus the high award of founders' shares for the sponsor act as a drag on performance even when the merged company is successful.[118]

A study by Klausner, Ohlrogge et al. (2022) found that SPACs lost 12% value in 6 months and 35% in a year from January 2019 to June 2020 while NASDAQ rose 30%. They conclude that the odds work against SPAC investors, in particular, pre-merger investors due to dilution.[119] The free shares handed to the sponsors are viewed by some as incentivizing them to pursue a merger even if the target firm is less than

---

[115] Deloitte (2023).
[116] Lipschultz (2022).
[117] Alija and Kruppa (2021).
[118] Gahng, Ritter, and Zhang (2021).
[119] Klausner, Ohlrogge, and Ruan (2022).
[120] Goldstein (2022).

promising, because sponsors stand to benefit even if the share price falls. Some SPACs addressed this problem by issuing fewer warrants to make them more attractive to post-merger shareholders.[120] These issues have caused a backlash from the SEC that has issued rules that aim to prevent the circumvention of minimum capitalizations or issuance rules by making shares redeemable as well as requirements to improve disclosure and comply with filing rules that govern IPOs.[121, 122]

Target corporations must comply with SEC rules that require a documented review of projections, independent validation, cautionary language, and disclaimers to avoid potential liability.[123] The fact that the SEC has deemed the underwriters of a blank-check offering to also be underwriters of the SPAC's subsequent purchase of a target firm has raised liability concerns and heightened the prospect of lawsuits being filed against those underwriters by investors.[124] Goldman Sachs stopped dealing with most SPACs in May 2022 due to increased regulatory scrutiny, causing doubt on the fate of funds raised for blank-check vehicles.[125] The league table (Table 8.4) shows the ranking difference when comparing the entire period 2019–2021 to 2021 in isolation. In 2021, the major investment banks had already largely retreated from underwriting SPAC IPOs.

To track the performance of these stocks, PitchBook has created an index that follows the public performance of de-SPAC stocks. This de-SPAC index only considers the price of companies after the reverse merger has been completed and the ticker has been changed, excluding any price movement that may occur during the blank-check vehicle's journey from issuance to announcement to transaction completion (Figure 8.25).

---

[121] In October 2021, the SEC instructed auditors to account more strictly for public shares in SPACs and classify redeemable shares as temporary equity, causing SPACs to fall below the minimum equity requirement of NASDAQ's Capital Market tier, resulting in them being moved to the Global Market tier with no equity requirement (Sen, Prentice, and Hu, 2021).
[122] The SEC adopted new rules in March 2022 requiring SPACs to give more disclosures and register as investment companies, in some cases, subjecting them to tougher regulations, providing investors with comparable levels of protection (Kaufman and Kavanaugh, 2021).
[123] Weiner and Hunter-Reay (2021).
[124] Natarajan (2022), Barton and Ward (2021).
[125] Hu, Parry, and Rubinstein (2022), Natarajan (2022).

Table 8.4 Top 10 league table of underwriters of US tech-focused SPACs, 2019–2021

2019-2021			2021		
Underwriter	Volume ($M)	% Share	Underwriter	Volume ($M)	% Share
Cantor Fitzgerald	1,003.2	11.9%	Cowen	5.3	15.2%
BofA Securities	820.8	9.8%	Barclays	287.5	8.2%
Credit Suisse	797.8	9.5%	BTIG	253	7.2%
BTIG	633.1	7.5%	Chardan	229.8	6.6%
Cowen	614.6	7.3%	Needham	180.4	5.2%
Deutsche Bank	493.8	5.9%	Oppenheimer	179.4	5.1%
Goldman Sachs	438	5.2%	Nomura	179.4	5.1%
Morgan Stanley	417.1	5.0%	EF Hutton	173.1	5.0%
Stifel Nicolaus	364.2	4.3%	JP Morgan	172.5	4.9%
Jefferies	299	3.6%	BofA Securities	172.5	4.9%

Source: SPAC Research (2022).

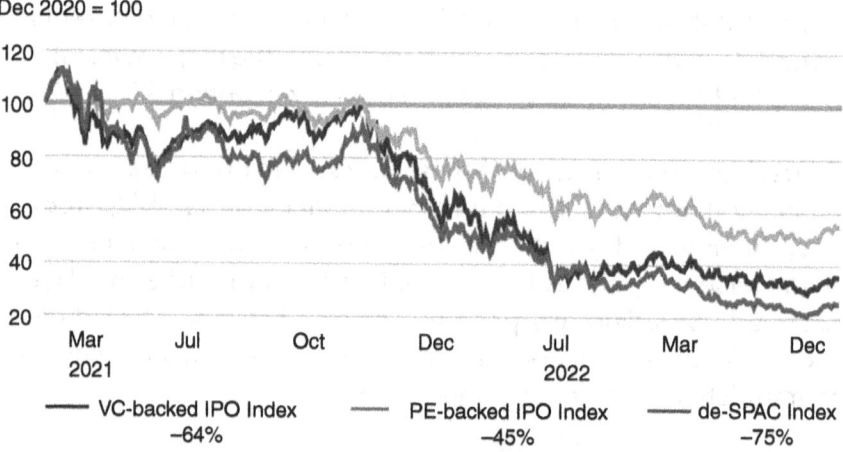

Dec 2020 = 100

VC-backed IPO Index −64%   PE-backed IPO Index −45%   de-SPAC Index −75%

Figure 8.25 Relative performance of the de-SPAC index compared to VC- and PE-backed IPOs December 2020 (= 100) to January 2022.
Source: Adapted from PitchBook, 2023.

With hindsight, venture-backed IPOs and de-SPACed companies had a powerful rally from April 2020 until mid-February 2021. Then a massive correction took place, despite the still positive performance of the overall market (S&P 500 and NASDAQ indexes). It is evident from Figure 8.25 that de-SPACed companies have underperformed venture-backed or private equity-backed IPOs. Many de-SPAC mergers were priced in the valuation climate of 2020 and 2021, which included some of the highest multiples in history. Their underperformance is putting pressure on SPACs to deliver on their promises. The ability to include future projections in prospectus documentation was promoted as a feature to entice companies to contemplate a reverse merger with a SPAC; nevertheless, altering public market attitude may have caused this tactic to backfire on many de-SPACed companies. While macroeconomic developments did not help, it is mainly the re-assessment of the plausibility of many of those companies' growth prospects and their ability to become profitable at all that drives their valuations downwards. The dynamics are thus not different from the bust of the dotcom boom, and the outcome may be similar too.

8.9   THE INVESTMENT LANDSCAPE HAS CHANGED

The period leading up to 2021 has not only set new records in fundraising, deal volumes, and exits but has also witnessed a rapid trend toward the emergence of mega-firms and the participation of non-traditional investors. These two trends are interrelated. While statistics indicate an expansion in the number of LPs, resulting in a broader investor base, the sources of capital have paradoxically become more concentrated due to the increasing prominence of SWFs and higher allocations from large public pension funds (PPFs).

The rise of these ultra-large investors has played a dual role. First, it has facilitated mega-firms' ascent, amplifying their share in global fundraising and overall AuM. Second, these influential players are also part of a new breed of non-traditional investors, which through their direct investment activity or by providing significant capital to entities outside the conventional GP sphere, reshaped the system of entrepreneurial finance.

Another defining aspect of these non-traditional investors and their backers is their extended investment horizon, leading them to favor avoiding the limitations imposed by traditional limited partnerships' conventional fund life constraints. Prominent private market managers increasingly taking the form of listed corporations have also made that shift, as their valuations benefit from the

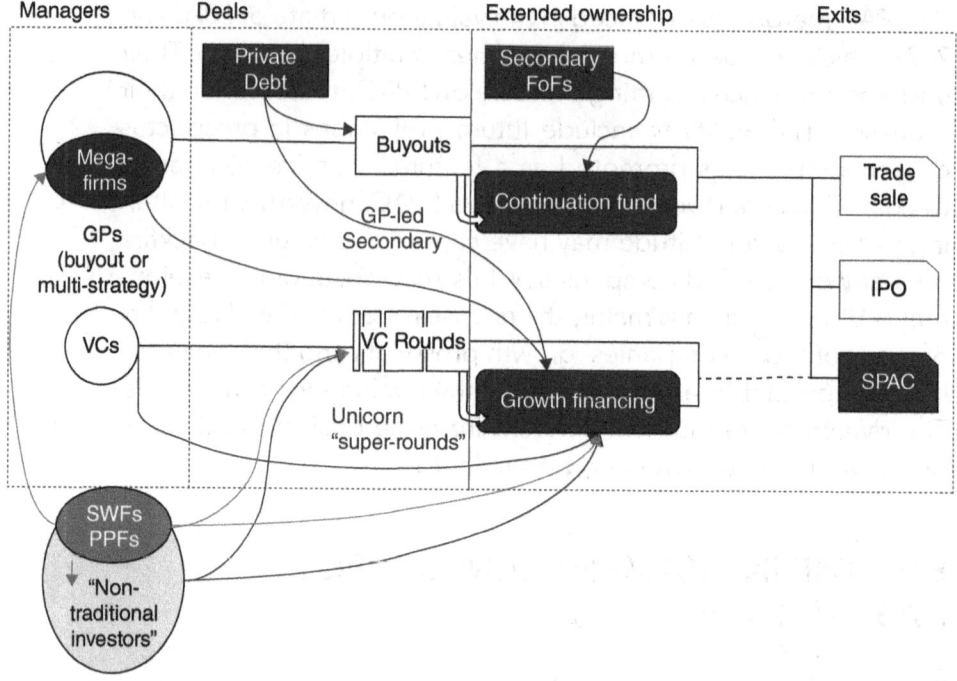

Figure 8.26 The changing landscape of private markets investing.
Source: Adapted from Preqin.

extension of holding periods and a gradual shift toward permanent capital and the predictable fee income that goes with it.

Figure 8.26 highlights the elements that are a departure from how private markets worked until the GFC. The emergence of private debt as a significant source of leverage, mega-firms due to consolidation, and the use of "super-rounds" in VC financing drove growth financing in the USA. It enabled the increase in GP-led secondaries that establish continuation funds. Continuation funds have been widely used to extend ownership of promising assets. Investors struggling to reach their private market allocation were happy to hold on to what they have and for those that wanted liquidity secondaries FoFs provided replacement capital. Growth capital played a similar role in startup financing that enabled firms to stay private longer, raise huge amounts of capital in super late-stage rounds, which led to unicorns and decacorns. Lastly, SPAC IPOs and de-SPAC mergers provided GPs with an additional exit route for their funds' investments and access investors that were (again) ready to back public listings of still unprofitable companies. These shifts, gaining traction since 2017, mirror the increasing influence of SWFs and large public pension funds (PPFs) as capital sources and direct players in private markets.

Private market firms have broadened their sources of capital and some have become global institutions with extensive scope, allowing them to be leaders in different segments of the private markets. The venture capital industry experienced a split, with some firms continuing to focus on specific financing stages, while others are developing capabilities across the spectrum of deal sizes and have significantly increased their AuM.

Private market strategies expand into lower risk profiles. The largest private market firms established evergreen funds that deploy capital in strategies that are more income-oriented or require longer holding periods.

The move toward permanent capital is just one aspect of a departure from traditional LP-GP model, entrenched across diverse private market strategies and rooted in the fee/carried interest framework originating from private equity. Investors aiming for steady, inflation-protected returns in the infrastructure sphere contemplate the transient ownership and capital gains focus inherent in partnership-based investments, raising concerns about alignment with their goals. The growing popularity of platforms providing access to stable assets, often through evergreen or extended-maturity vehicles with liquidity options, reflects the ongoing pursuit of investment solutions better attuned to investors' objectives. Notably, such platforms often emerge from collaborations of like-minded investors, such as IFM Investors (Australia) or AIP (Denmark), both pension fund-owned or Caisse de dépôt et placement du Québec (Canada), which extends its in-house capabilities through third-party mandates.

In private debt, the use of significant in-fund leverage has risen as the focus shifted from riskier mezzanine and distressed debt to senior lending. This leverage trend at the fund level might be driven by general partners aiming to achieve private equity-like returns to rationalize the private equity fee structure. Unsurprisingly, large investors prefer SMAs, allowing them to negotiate fee arrangements that reflect a more conservative risk-return profile due to lower leverage. As the industry evolves, the challenge of offering solutions that differ from the traditional LP-GP model to reflect the unique aspects of various private market strategies will get bigger due to the growing demand for income-oriented strategies. One consequence of this trend is the continued quest for lower fees as investors seek implementation options outside the traditional GP-LP model.

These developments are market-driven, i.e., it is ultimately the investor that shapes those trends. Whether it is the rising interest in co-investments or the investment of resources to do direct deals, there has been a noticeable desire by investors to get closer to the action and to accelerate capital deployment by doing deal-level investments.

The growing trend of major LPs investing directly reflects the high fees and performance incentives commanded by GPs. Alongside the rise of co-investments and SMAs, SWFs are also showing a growing interest in collaborative investing by joining or establishing investment platforms, like QIA's Global Infrastructure Investment Platform, ADIA's Real Estate Investment Platform or Alaska Permanent Fund's Capital Constellation (venture capital), while also increasing direct investments. If these platforms gain traction with other institutions as a more affordable option, pressure on fees for traditional private market funds could increase and accelerate the consolidation of an industry that is still populated by thousands of small GPs.[126]

The trend toward permanent capital has not prevented evolving strategies within private markets to improve speed and access to public markets. SPACs provide private equity firms with a new way to take a portfolio company public through an IPO. The surge in SPAC IPOs and the subsequent growth of de-SPAC mergers highlight how investors are still eager to support companies even before establishing a track record of profitability. This showcases the adaptability of capital markets in finding new solutions. However, it raises the question of whether the regulations and stricter

---

[126] IFSWF (2022).

listing requirements introduced after the dotcom bubble might have unintentionally led to an alternative approach, where the odds might be stacked against public investors in ways that don't quite compare to regular IPOs. Their sustainability must be questioned unless changes are made to their economic model.

8.10   THE NEW FRONTIER: ACCESSING PRIVATE WEALTH THROUGH (SEMI-) LIQUID FUNDS

Private wealth, with over $50 trillion in capital, is a new frontier for private markets, which has relied on institutional finance. Private markets are being added to the services of banks and asset managers for high-net-worth individuals (HNI) and, in some cases, retail investors through acquisitions, joint ventures, or investments in their in-house teams. Due to large minimum commitments that create barriers for smaller investors, market penetration remains limited, but amended legislation, novel products, and GP distribution capabilities are changing this. According to a recent survey, more than 30% of private market managers intend to have a retail-oriented vehicle within the next five years In 2020, just 9% had a dedicated retail or HNI offering and estimates for the AuM of those vehicles range from $60–100 billion as a number of the large private markets asset managers that previously catered only to an institutional client base are developing more accessible products.[127]

In the past, private markets investments assets have been accessible only to large institutional investors due to the complexities of investing in the asset class and high minimum commitment amounts for limited partnerships. Past attempts to overcome that barrier focused on listed private markets investment companies but "semi-liquid" private-market investment vehicles, popularly known as evergreen vehicles, have developed into a rapidly growing sector. Partners Group brought the first product to market in 2001, and since then other managers such as Blackstone, Starwood, Apollo, Carlyle, KKR, Ares, EQT, Partners Group, and Stepstone followed in recent years.

---

[127] Preqin (2020).

Investing in (semi-)liquid fund structures that focus on private equity or private debt can offer potential advantages but also introduce distinct considerations and risks. Here are the key factors to ponder when choosing between traditional limited partnerships and permanent investment vehicles that typically offer a degree of liquidity.

Fund Structure

Investors need to gain a comprehensive understanding of the specific fund structure under consideration. Some funds provide partial liquidity options, allowing investors to redeem a portion of their investments periodically. Conversely, others impose lock-up periods, prohibiting redemptions until a predetermined maturity date.

Capital Deployment

In the case of permanent vehicles, although they grant exposure to an existing portfolio, they may face challenges when returning capital from underlying investments is not immediately reinvested. This can result in the accumulation of cash balances, which may affect overall fund performance.

Leverage

Many permanent vehicles use lines of credit to bridge investments until capital is returned from the existing portfolio. While this enhances the efficiency of capital deployment, it incurs costs and, during periods of declining net asset values (NAVs) and reduced distributions, may increase the risk of fund "gating," wherein redemptions are suspended.

Entry and Exit Rules

Liquid funds may have queuing systems and transaction fees for entry or exit. They may need to hold cash or sell assets to meet redemptions, and the latter can result in discounts during market downturns. In contrast to limited partnerships, permanent funds must decide how to distribute losses from these discounts when selling within the fund. This can create concerns about a mass exodus if departing investors can redeem at NAV while the remaining investors bear secondary market losses.

Fee Structures

As permanent vehicles do not return capital to investors unless they redeem them, it is essential to scrutinize how performance fees are calculated. The traditional carried interest on realized returns may not be an appropriate formula. Also, management fees may be assessed based on NAVs, including leverage, potentially making them higher than headline numbers suggest.

Easier Distribution to Private Investors

Regulation has eased to broaden the scope for distribution of (semi-)liquid funds to private investors. Examples of new regulation in Europe include the European Long-Term Investment Fund (ELTIF) and in the UK the planned Long-Term Asset Fund (LTAF). Both structures provide a regulated means for sophisticated retail investors to access private asset investments. In the USA, the Department of Labor has ruled that 401K plans could invest in private equity, further clarified in January 2022 to be subject to plan suitability.

Legal and Regulatory Matters

Structures used for evergreen private markets closed-end funds include Delaware Statutory Trusts in the USA and in Luxembourg an open-ended investment company with variable capital (Société d'investissement à capital variable; SICAV) or fixed capital (SICAF) in Europe. In both the USA and Europe, limited liability companies (LLCs) are also a popular choice for evergreen or semi-liquid funds. Some jurisdictions also allow limited liability partnerships (LLPs) with no fixed end date, allowing for an evergreen structure. If a corporate legal structure is used, it often comes with different share classes and investors need to understand the rights and obligations assigned to each share class and their implications for the overall fund structures. For distribution to private investors, additional registration and passporting requirements apply. Regulatory provisions can significantly influence fund operations, reporting obligations, and investor safeguards.

Tax Implications

Tax consequences of investing in private market funds may not only diverge from those of publicly traded assets but also may differ between fund structures, due to the elections for tax treatment those vehicles have made.

Summary

The future will reveal if these patterns will persist throughout a downturn and consequently have a long-term impact on the private markets industry. Some of the developments detailed in the preceding sections are not new but have occurred in earlier cycles. Other patterns are new, although they may be influenced by the exuberance around technology investments and the sector's valuation. Chapters 9 and 10 will delve deeper into the trends and evolution of the sub-asset categories that constitute private markets during the ten years preceding 2021. Moreover, they will present a perspective on potential future developments.

Chapter 9

Responding to Shifting Dynamics: Intermediaries, VC, and Growth Financing

In the decade until 2021, private market investment has surged due to low-interest rates, private markets' resilience during the Global Financial Crisis (GFC), liquidity abundance, and increased investor participation. Approximately 70% of endowments, foundations, and pension funds have embraced private market investments, with penetration likely peaking in 2021. Traditional capital sources may not outgrow their assets under management (AuM) trend, prompting general partners (GPs) to explore alternative pools such as insurance and retail.

Sovereign wealth funds (SWFs) play a key role, driving trends toward co-investments and direct investments, resulting in a concentrated investor base dominated by ultra-large participants. This shift aims to reduce fees and extend asset retention beyond the conventional LP-GP model. This chapter examines how intermediaries have responded to these changes and analyzes private market managers' transition to public entities, introducing shareholders as a new stakeholder group and impacting operational frameworks.

The profound effects of the technology boom on venture capital and growth financing are also discussed in this chapter.

9.1   FoFs: THE CHANGING LANDSCAPE OF INTERMEDIARIES

The market share of funds of funds (FoFs), which numerous institutions used to access the asset class, declined as investors sought direct ties with GPs. To some extent, this is an expected evolution in a maturing asset class. Investors become more experienced and comfortable, leading to higher allocation and a growing emphasis on in-house resources. The latter is often a condition for the former as investors require more influence in the investment decision and portfolio-building process when allocations are increasing, and an asset class moves from a "side-show" to a significant part of the overall portfolio. The changing appeal of FoFs was also somewhat the consequence of a reevaluation of the cost-benefits of FoFs (see Box 9.1). This reflected a broader trend among investors after the GFC to save management fees. While large investors shifted from partnership commitments to direct investments, many smaller and mid-sized investors shifted from FoFs to direct partnership investments and (pooled) co-investments.

To remain competitive, FoFs providers have resorted to offering larger investors separate managed accounts (SMAs) with much lower fees instead of slashing headline management fees. There has also been an increase in tiered fees, the use of secondaries, and co-investments that mitigate the "j-curve" and earn higher margins.

As selecting primary fund commitments became commoditized, larger players moved into higher margin strategies like secondaries or co-investments and expanded the coverage of other private markets asset classes (private debt, real assets). The upward

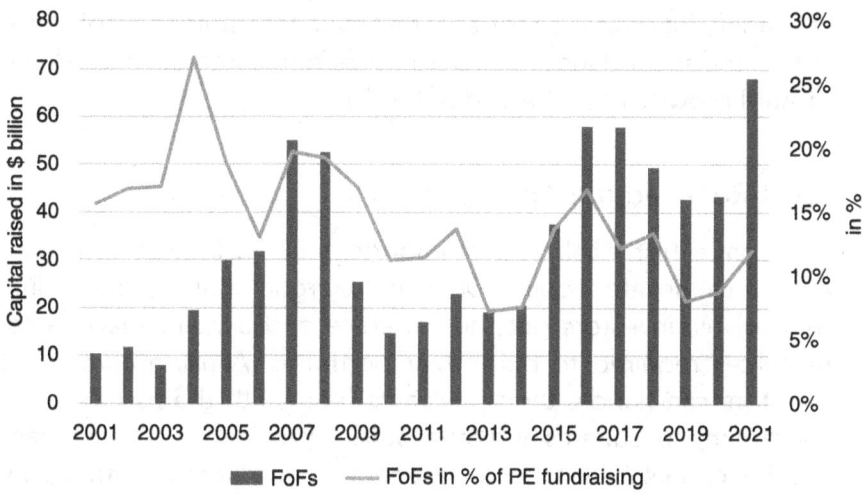

Figure 9.1   FoFs capital raised per vintage year and share in private equity fundraising, in $B and in %.
Source: Adapted from Preqin.

trajectory toward higher-margin businesses was accompanied by heightened M&A activity.

By the end of 2021, the private markets FoFs industry had over $800 billion in AuM, with more than $600 billion held in private equity FoFs. Fundraising was about $450 billion during 2010–2021.

However, the growth of fundraising masks the relative decline of FoFs as their share in total fundraising fell to low single digits after the GFC (see Figure 9.1).[1] In the previous decade, FoFs accounted for 15% or more of private equity fundraising, a market share they did not recover despite the growth in the number of investors.

For example, HarbourVest, one of the leading global private markets FoFs managers, closed its US-focused flagship HarbourVest XI fund in 2022 at $2.6 billion—a result that was not much different from HarbourVest VII, a 2002 vintage year fund that closed at $2 billion. In contrast, their secondaries FoFs, Dover Street X, closed at $6 billion in 2020.[2] The different outcome for primary and

[1] Data: Preqin (2021a; 2022a).
[2] Data: Crunchbase.

secondary fundraising illustrates that even for traditional FoFs providers, the secondaries FoFs business had become the main driver of AuM growth since the end of the GFC.

What Reduced the Appeal of FoFs?

FoFs have historically been important in facilitating investors' access to private equity. One could argue that as the industry evolves, investors get the expertise and acquire the internal resources required to build their portfolios. A rising number of investors can handle their programs often with the assistance of investment consultants and other service providers. Separate managed accounts (SMAs), co-investments, and direct private equity programs are all being used by investors in addition to the traditional FoFs investment model.

Unlike venture capital–focused FoFs, buyout-focused and growth capital-focused FoFs have not generally promoted their access to restricted funds as a key selling point in the past and highlighted their manager selection skills. The evidence of that past performance is no indicator for future results (weak persistence) in most private market strategies—apart from venture capital—undermined the selling point that in-depth track record analysis translates into better fund selection.[3] Still, access and network might become more relevant as even big buyout funds became increasingly access-restricted during the fundraising boom.

In-house expertise and technology can be more easily justified with higher private-market allocations, as the double fee layer of funds of funds favors in-house solutions as investment amounts increase.

Historically, management fees for funds of funds were typically in the range of 0.8–1% of committed capital/net asset value (NAV), and carried interest was charged between 5–10%. However, since 2010, there has been a trend of declining management fees, with 0.5–0.8% being more typical, although some funds-of-funds managers have maintained higher fees. Carried interest on primary

---

[3] The evidence for the persistence of returns, i.e., how strong past performance is as an indicator for future success will be discussed in more detail in Section 9.4.

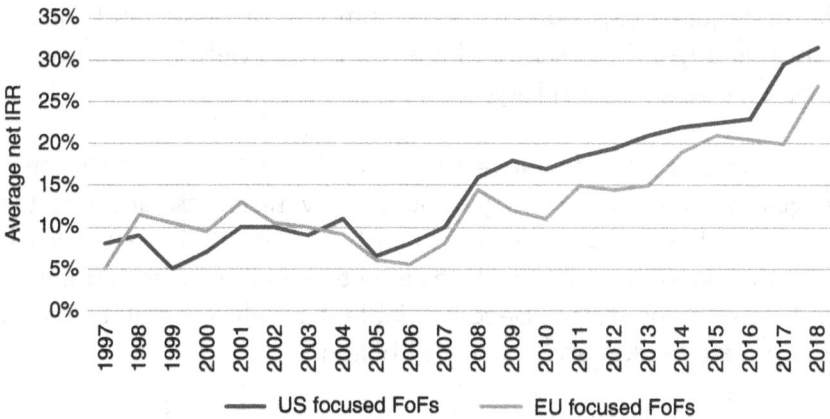

Figure 9.2 Europe-focused and US-focused PE FoFs: average net IRRs as of September 2022.

Source: Adapted from Monfared (2022d); data: Preqin as of September 2022.

Note: IRRs per vintage year since inception as of Q3 2022. Small sample size is low until 2003 and thereafter mostly exceeds 10 funds for Europe-focused funds and 30 funds for the US-focused fund in each vintage year. Performance differences may reflect differences in strategy exposure.

commitments has largely disappeared, but it still remains in the range of 5–10% for secondaries and co-investments. Tiered fee structures, which offer fee cuts for investors committing larger amounts, have also become more prevalent. Overall, these trends suggest that margins have decreased significantly over the past decade (Figure 9.2).

FoFs posted rather low returns during the first decade of the millennium but performance increased substantially post-GFC.

Despite investors' decreasing appetite for funds of funds, these funds continue to provide a valuable service. They offer a diversified portfolio to smaller investors who may not be able to manage an extensive private equity program independently and provide manager access. This is particularly relevant for investors who are new to the asset class and may not have a manager network. Such investors also receive a significant backoffice benefit, funds of funds generate far fewer capital calls and distributions than their underlying portfolio of participations in limited partnerships. In addition, investors face a trade-off between cost savings and increasing their probability to capture successful deals that drive performance. The latter requires exposure to large numbers of deals (and funds), which is beyond the scope of many investors without resorting to pooled investment vehicles.

The growing role of co-investments and direct investments often requires establishing special purpose vehicles to address tax issues and other concerns, which further raises the bar after which in-house management becomes effective. In the author's opinion, in-house teams start to become viable if a multi-year allocation to the private market approaches $1 billion.

Box 9.1   Are FoFs Value for Money?

In 2017, Steven Kaplan et al.[4] published a study on FoFs' value-add and compared the performance of 294 funds of funds to both public equity markets and direct fund investing techniques (Figure 9.3). Their key findings are summarized as follows:

- Buyout and generalist FoFs do not beat direct fund invest-ment strategies and didn't earn their fees, compared to direct fund investments. But FoFs still beat public markets.

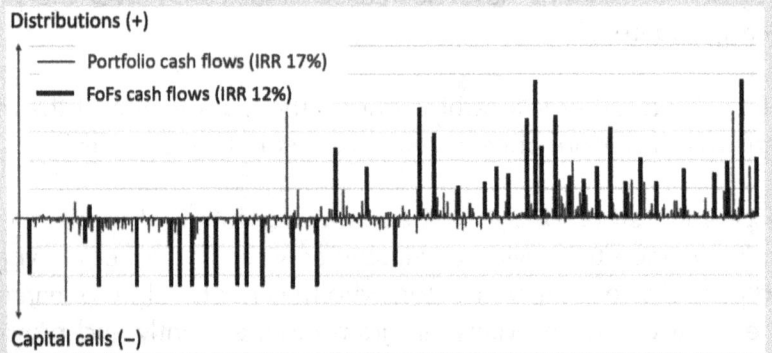

Figure 9.3   **Comparison of FoFs and portfolio cash flows over a fund's life.**
Source: Adapted from SCM Strategic Capital Management AG.

---

[4] Kaplan, Jenkinson, Harris, and Stucke (2017). The sample included 135 buyout, 87 generalist, and 72 venture capital FoFs cash flows, and 1,828 direct funds (net of all management and performance fees). Their study used verified cash flow data from Burgiss on both FoFs and direct funding.

- Performance of FoFs in VC ≈ direct VC investing.[5]
- Funds of funds hold an average of 26 funds and make commitments mostly in years 2 and 3, implying limited time diversification.
- Buyouts FoFs hold fewer funds than generalist or venture capital FoFs, which the authors attribute to venture capital funds' greater performance dispersion.
- The fee concern is somewhat mitigated by lower fees, and carried interest on primary commitments is rarely charged nowadays.[6] The difference in multiples is much smaller than the gap between the portfolio and the IRR net to investors.

A private equity fund generates 3.5 cash flow events per year (capital calls, repayment of capital and capital gains). Assuming 26 funds, investors would face 91 capital calls/distributions a year versus 4–5 for FoFs, limiting cash flow events, which benefits investor back offices.

Cash balances reduce performance. Up to half of the performance difference to direct fund investments seems to result from cash balances. FoFs managers now use lines of credit to minimize cash drag, which was often limited or excluded in fund agreements in the past.

The New World of Intermediaries

Faced with declining margins, FoFs managers had essentially three strategic options:

1. **Scale-up:** Acquire competitors or get acquired to gain scale and build assets.

2. **Introduce higher margin products:** Adjust your product offering to include higher margin/higher growth sectors such as secondaries or direct investors. Getting there may also involve merger and acquisition (M&A) activity to bring in additional expertise in products, markets, and regions.

---

[5] This is also confirmed in (McElhaney, 2017).
[6] Preqin (2017c).

3. **Gain access to new distribution channels:** Get acquired by a more extensive platform or enter joint ventures that provide access to new investors by geography or segment

Examples of M&A transactions illustrate each of these options:

- In 2005, Capital Dynamics acquired MAN Group's private equity business to broaden its asset base and increase its footprint in the UK.[7]

- In 2007, Partners Group acquired US real estate advisor Pension Consulting Alliance, a private markets real estate advisor, to strengthen its offering in the real estate space. Partners Group also acquired the team of German mid-market buyout firm German Capital to expand Partners Group's direct investment activities in Europe and to expand its Munich (Germany) office.[8] Many observers felt that for a FoFs manager to move into direct investments would cause a conflict of interests and potentially—by becoming a competitor—access issues to the funds of other GPs. But the strategic pivot toward direct investments, capitalizing on the information advantage it had from years of primary and secondary investing, proved successful, and Partners Group increased its AuM from about $28 billion in 2010 to $127 billion in 2021.

- In 2017, Hamilton Lane acquired Real Asset Portfolio Management; a company focused on real estate, natural resources, and infrastructure. In 2021, they announced the acquisition of 361 Capital to expand its presence and capabilities in the US private wealth channel.[9]

- In 2023, FS Investments (formerly Franklin Square), an FoFs provider targeting individuals and financial advisors as well as smaller institutions, merged with Portfolio Advisors and institutional FoFs managers to create a $73 billion platform in what can be described as an expansion of asset class expertise for FS Investments and access to a distribution channel into wealth management clients for Portfolio Advisors.[10]

---

[7] PEI (2005).
[8] Fruchbom (2007), PEI (2010).
[9] Hamilton Lane (2017; 2021).
[10] CISION PR Newswire (2023).

The traditional FoFs model was and still is attractive to new entrants such as investment consulting firms or traditional asset managers. Compared to fees earned in managing traditional assets, the revenue generated with a private market FoFs business—even at today's reduced fees—is very attractive. Those new entrants were buying private market investment platforms and FoFs businesses and working with established providers to leverage their distribution networks.

After the financial crisis of 2007–2008, traditional pension fund advisors (Mercer, Watson Wyatt), strategy consultants like Bain & Company, McKinsey & Company, or Oliver Wyman, joined investment consultants and specialist gatekeepers to provide private markets advisory and sometimes even asset management services. According to a Preqin study from 2010, there were over 300 advisors worldwide, with about 20 probably accounting for most of the non-discretionary AuM advised. The proportion of institutional investors that use an external consultant to assist with their investments was about 60% during the new millennium's first decade, with more than 80% of public pension funds using consultants.[11]

Marsh & McLennan Companies, Inc.'s subsidiary Mercer announced completing the acquisitions of SCM Strategic Capital Management in 2014, and in 2018, Pavilion Financial Corporation in 2018.[12] These acquisitions were part of a strategy to diversify into asset management, notably higher margin private market FoFs services. With their 2022 fund of fund offering closing at $4.8 billion, these acquisitions were successful in enabling Mercer's entry into the private markets FoFs business.

And then there were the large buyout firms adding FoFs offerings to their portfolio of products. In the past, such acquisitions would probably have met internal resistance among general partners fearing a dilution of their margins. But in the new world of listed

---

[11] Preqin (2010a).
[12] The SCM acquisition is discussed in Zacks Equity Research (2014a); Pavilion Capital Corporation is a full-service investment consulting firm that had previously acquired Altius Associates, a UK-based private equity advisor and LP Advisors, a US-based private markets service provider (NASDAQ, 2018). Mercer's FoFs business in reported in Private Equity Wire (2022).

private market firms with the higher multiples assigned to stable revenue, such considerations changed:

In 2011, AlpInvest, the Dutch FoFs and secondaries specialist, was sold to Carlyle Group. Blackstone followed in 2013 with the acquisition of CS Strategic Partners, the FoFs business of Credit Suisse.[13]

Larger asset management groups have particularly shown an interest in the private equity FoFs businesses in recent years. These firms recognize that despite the challenges faced by the industry, diversifying into private equity products alongside their other offerings can offer benefits. Private markets were the busiest area of deal-making for big mutual fund firms in 2021. That year saw a number of acquisitions by large generalist asset managers, such as Franklin Templeton's purchase of Lexington Partners for $1.8 billion in late 2021 and T. Rowe Price's $4.2 billion acquisition of Oak Hill Advisors. There was also Fidelity's purchase of a minority stake in Moonfare, which is a web-based platform that distributes individual fund offerings to registered HNI users and allows minimum subscriptions of $100,000.[14,15] Previously Vanguard entered into a partnership with HarbourVest Partners in 2020.[16] These are examples of the entry of mainstream and often retail-oriented asset managers into the private markets business.

BlackRock, the world's largest asset manager, has been quietly building an alternatives business. It has grown AuM to $320 billion, more than all but the three largest alternative managers. Half its business is private credit, much of the rest in property and infrastructure. The firm also has a growth-equity partnership with Temasek, a Singaporean sovereign wealth fund. Previously in 2019, BlackRock bought eFront, a portfolio management software platform for private market investments, and prior to that, Swiss Re

---

[13] PEI (2011), Carlyle Group (2011), Private Banker International (2013).
[14] Ricketts (2021).
[15] Moonfare (est. in 2016) is a German fintech platform which allows private individuals to invest into private equity funds. As of mid-2022, it claimed that 2,800 investors have used their platform to subscribe to $1.8 billion with individual commitments starting from $50,000 in more than 50 fund offerings.
[16] *The Economist* (2022d).

Private Equity Partners, the FoFs business of the Swiss reinsurance group, in 2012.[17,18]

Banks and other wealth managers also acquired FoFs managers. For example, Schroders, the UK's biggest listed fund manager, bought Swiss manager Adveq in 2017.[19] Swiss secondary manager Montana Capital Partners was sold to PGIM, the global investment management business of Prudential Financial, in 2021.[20]

When one considers the additional investments made by banks and traditional asset managers in in-house resources to provide product offerings for wealth management clients, it is clear that a variety of new players, most notably large traditional asset managers and banks, are moving into the private markets FoFs space.

Making Fund Distribution to Private Investors Work

Historically, a $10 million minimum LP commitment has been fairly standard for limited partners (LPs) investing in private equity or venture capital funds (with some managers requiring an even higher amount). Each investor causes onboarding and servicing costs for the life of a fund, beginning with lawyers reviewing subscription agreements, Know Your Client (KYC), tax, and other documentation, and continuing with ongoing work related to facilitating capital calls, redemptions, dispositions, custom LP financial reporting, and so on.

Managers provide individual investors with access through traditional 401Ks (in the USA) to feeder funds, which are also used as a solution in wealth management and private banking to provide access to funds for investors, ranging from $50,000 to $1 million. Banks and other financial intermediaries have established feeder funds that pool those commitments and aim for an overall size that not only meets the funds' minimum subscription requirements but also allows the operation of those feeder funds as a profitable business (Figure 9.4). Many asset managers and fund administrators are heavily investing in new technology that automates

[17] eFront (2019).
[18] Lenz and Staehelin (2012).
[19] Copley (2017).
[20] PGIM (2021).

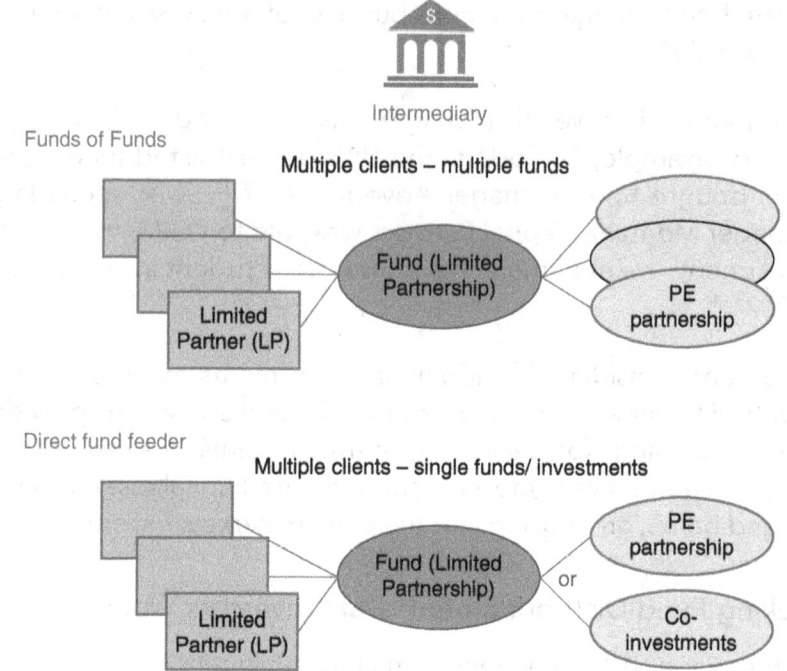

Figure 9.4   Feeder funds and their purpose as used by banks and wealth managers.

investor onboarding and fund lifecycle operations, lowering the cost of investor servicing.[21]

To begin with, unfunded capital must be tracked and blocked in some form to ensure that a client is not in default, as this might put the entire feeder in default (unless there is some cross-default protection).[22] Banks and asset managers can only share KYC and tax information with the GP to the extent of local rules and regulations

---

[21] CAIA (2022).

[22] A cross-default provision essentially stipulates that if some participants in a pool are in default, the default penalties of the partnership where the pool is invested only apply to the capital share of defaulting investors. As the feeder acts as a single LP in an underlying fund, failure to have those provisions in place could result in an outcome where the default of a single participant affects the entire feeder and all its investors as default penalties would kick in. The non-defaulting participants in the pool would surely hold the sponsor of such a feeder fund liable for damage that would occur.

permitting, which sometimes requires not only authorization by the client but also approval by the regulator.

Reporting and entry of NAV into general portfolio accounting systems must be possible, and the sponsor must be able to track and verify the accounting done by outside administrators. The fund administration business has not always kept up with the requirements of private market funds. A lack of digitalization and reliance on spreadsheets to support manual processes strain those providers as their business grows. In many cases, sponsors found that even though the administration for feeder funds is outsourced, sponsors still needed a reconciliation process to identify and fix errors and omissions which are more frequent than one would like.

A further cost factor is related to substance requirements that are increasingly demanded to domicile a FoFs or feeder structures in a jurisdiction. As distribution becomes increasingly regulated or passported, traditional lower-cost solutions such as the Channel Islands, the Cayman Islands, or the Virgin Islands are increasingly out when distributing such products to non-US investors. Fund structures for US investors are still predominantly domiciled in Delaware. Regulated jurisdictions such as Luxembourg gain market share but require local presence, meaning that local staff needs to perform at least some risk management, monitoring, or investment functions and it is no longer possible to fully delegate all those activities to another jurisdiction. For larger firms, that is not a problem, but smaller sponsors may face the need to open an office and hire local staff, which increases the revenue threshold for a FoFs or feeder funds business to become profitable.

In Table 9.1, initial and ongoing expenses for feeder funds are shown, excluding management fees, with fees often based on the net asset value (NAV) and subject to minimum amounts that increase the fee burden (Figure 9.5). Larger fundraising for a feeder fund may result in a decline of NAV in later years, leading to a higher fee burden.

Table 9.1   Overview of feeder fund cost items (estimates) and the impact of NAV on the fee load in percentages, without management fees

Luxembourg (AIFMD compliant)				Operational cost in % of NAV p.a.
Cost item	Amount p.a.	Type/frequency	Minimum p.a.	
Legal including Filing	150,000	set up		
Administration	19,250	set up		
Fund administration	0.07%	quarterly NAV	30,800	
Custody	0.04%	quarterly NAV	27,500	
Legal costs	5000			
Audit fees	27,500	annually fixed		
Domicilation fee	22,000	annually fixed		
Director's fees	10,000	annually fixed		
Tax fees				
Other costs	20,000	annually		

Source: Estimates of the author based on quotes from service providers.
Note: Terms can vary over time and the display should be used as an illustration. The table does not include costs related to a local office and staff to meet substance requirements as those costs are spread over various funds. Management and incentive fees are not shown as those are revenue from a sponsor's perspective.

9.2   CO-INVESTMENTS AND DIRECT INVESTMENTS

LPs became increasingly eager to co-invest with GPs to accelerate capital deployment. In the past, LPs were offered larger deals, as smaller deals have less room for "sharing" from a GP's standpoint. During 2015–2021, between 5% and 10% of buyout deal volume was co-sponsored by limited partners.[23] Co-investment provisions inside letters are typically negotiated between limited partners (LPs) and general partners (GPs) in private equity funds. LPs are investors who contribute capital to the fund, while GPs are the managers who invest the fund's capital in portfolio companies.

---

[23] Troutman Pepper (2022). Other sources put it even higher when other private market asset classes are considered.

Co-investment provisions allow LPs to invest alongside the fund in specific portfolio companies, providing them with the opportunity to potentially generate additional returns and also reduce the fees paid to the fund. These provisions are often negotiated in side letters, which are agreements between LPs and GPs that are separate from the funds main legal documents, such as the limited partnership agreement (LPA).

Many large institutional investors, including the Canada Pension Plan Investment Board, the Abu Dhabi Investment Authority, the New York State Common Retirement Fund, the Teacher Retirement System of Texas, and the Washington State Investment Board, have dedicated co-investment programs that allow them to invest alongside private equity funds in various deals. These models help investors gain additional investment opportunities and potentially reduce fees paid to private equity funds.

Co-investments are typically structured as separate entities (SPVs) from the main private equity fund and offer investors the opportunity to invest directly in individual private equity deals. This can provide several advantages to investors, such as lower fees, greater control over the investment, faster capital deployment, and the ability to customize exposure to specific deals or sectors. The disadvantage of co-investments is that they are frequently not available to smaller investors and that there may be a lack of diversification. There was also concern about possible overrepresentation of deals at the end of a valuation cycle (when activity is very high) and a bias toward more risky or larger deals. Academic research has shown, however, that there is no evidence for adverse selection (see Box 9.2). According to several investor polls conducted by Preqin, most LPs believe, however, that the performance of their co-investments exceeds their fund portfolios (Figure 9.5 and Figure 9.6).[24]

---

[24] This has been confirmed by various surveys and sources: (Preqin, 2015a, 2017b), (Duksin, Van Hock, Schuster, and Jordan, 2021).

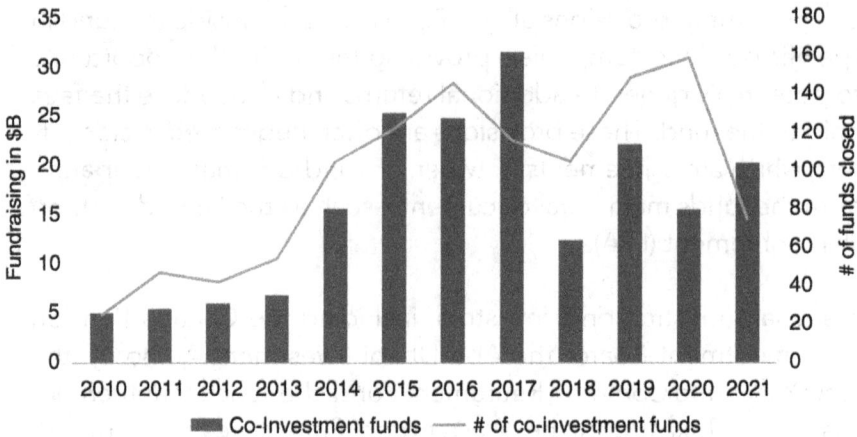

Figure 9.5   Co-investment funds raised, 2010–2021, in $B and number.
Source: Troutman Pepper (2022); data: Preqin.

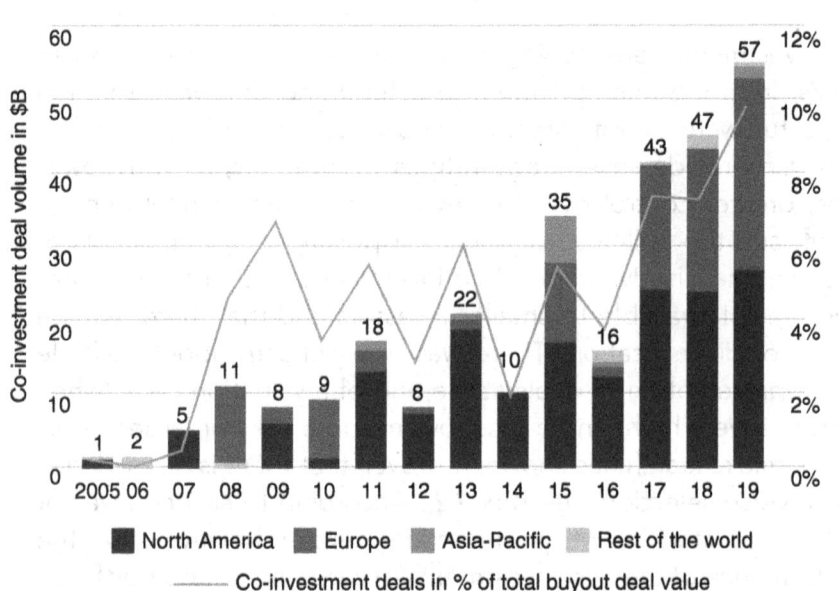

Figure 9.6   Global buyout co-investment volume, in % of total transaction volume.
Source: McKinsey (2022).

Notes: Includes add-ons, excludes loan-to-own transaction and acquisition of bankrupt assets based on announcement date; includes announced deals that are completed or pending with data subject to change; based on number of deals from 2015 to 2019.

Geography based on target's location; excludes real estate and infrastructure. Deal volume number may vary from other parts of the book due to different data sources.

Box 9.2   Co-investments: Adverse Selection?

Braun et al. use a sample of 1,016 co-investments made by 458 investors (buyout and VC). They used data from Burgiss and deal-level cash flow data from three funds of funds managers over the period 1981–2010. In 320 deals, more than one LP participated as a co-investor. The co-investment deals were associated with 464 different funds, which, in total, made 13,430 investments. Therefore, 7.6% of deals in the sample of funds were co-investments.[25]

Main Findings

Co-investments outperform fund investments significantly for buyout and venture capital and the authors' findings correct earlier research that co-investments underperformed.[26] The authors use a participatory monitoring and evaluation (PME) ratio to measure relative performance. PME > 1 indicates outperformance, and a ratio of 1.1 indicates that the total gain was 10% more than the benchmark. The average buyout co-investment outperforms fund deals by 0.10–0.29 (net) PME. The PME is a ratio that measures total outperformance versus a benchmark. In VC, co-investments outperform other fund investments by 0.19–0.39. But fund investment also shows a PME > 1 for both buyout and venture capital funds, which indicates outperformance of the funds in their sample. Figure 9.7 is the author's illustration of their findings.

Fee Savings Drive the Result

As long as fees are only paid during the holding period of an agreement, outperformance persists. Due to fees charged on committed capital, most co-investment funds will not produce the returns investors expect.

(continued)

---

[25] Braun et al. (2017).
[26] Reference is made to Fang, Ivashina, and Lerner (2015).

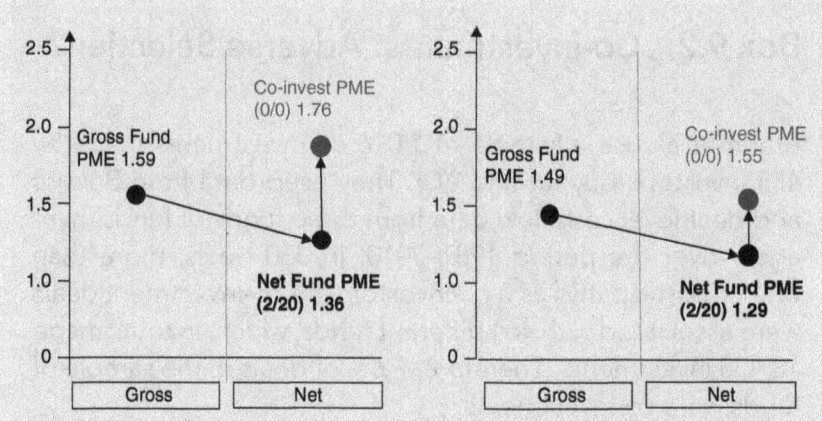

Figure 9.7   Relative performance of buyout and VC co-investments.
Source: Braun et al. (2017).

Other Observations

Deal size drives co-investment offerings: large deals are significantly more likely to be offered for co-investment. One needs to use cap-weighted PMEs to capture this effect (Figure 9.7). There is no evidence of adverse selection or return differences between existing LPs and non-LPs participating in a co-investment.

It is important to note that co-investments carry the same risks as other private equity investments and may require a significant commitment of time and resources to manage effectively. As such, they may be more suitable for experienced private equity investors and institutional investors who have the resources and expertise to manage these investments.

As co-investments tend to be allocated to bigger investors, there has been an increased demand for co-investment fund vehicles as smaller LPs aspired to follow the example set by those ultra-large LPs. Both traditional FoFs providers and advisors have seized the opportunity to use their "buying power" to gain access to co-investments and make them available to their clients through fund offerings. During 2017–2021, more than $100 billion was raised for such "funds of deals," which somewhat contradicts the fee-saving goal. Examples are Hamilton Lane, a gatekeeper that offers co-investment solutions as part of its product suite, or HarbourVest, an FoFs manager that has a dedicated co-investment program.

Direct non-sponsored investments by LPs in private equity refers to investments made by LPs in private equity deals without the involvement of the private equity firm that is managing their main investment fund. This allows LPs to invest directly in specific deals and bypass the traditional fund structure. Investors doing direct deals or co-investing with GPs, needs to consider that the returns generated in private equity are characterized by a Pareto distribution, where a few successful deals drive the overall returns. As a result, investors must build a portfolio of a fairly large number of investments to capture the outsized returns generated by a few of these deals. Research has shown that to maximize the potential benefit of co-investments, an average investor should aim to diversify and build a portfolio of at least 20 but ideally many more deals (see Box 9.2).

9.3 SECONDARY MARKETS

With the GFC unfolding, the secondary market began a new phase. As the supply of LP interests for sale began to outpace demand and the outlook for a leveraged buyout and other private-equity investments deteriorated, the secondary market's pricing level plummeted significantly. Discounts to net asset value widened to 30% and briefly approached 60% (see Figure 9.8).[27]

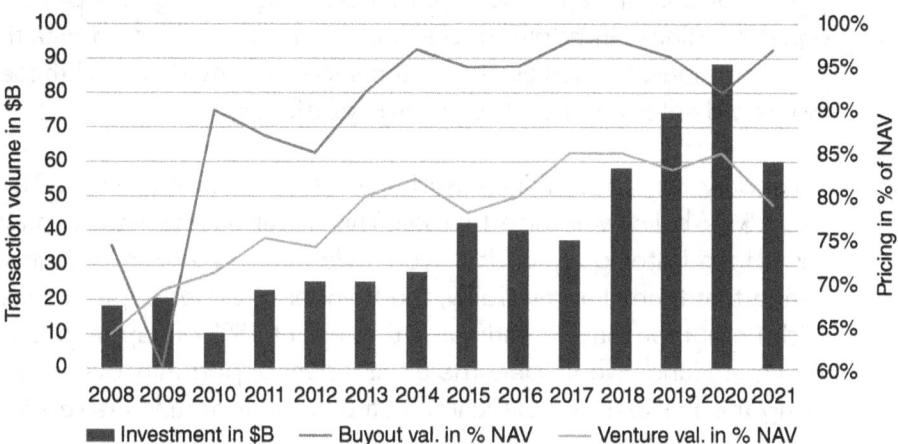

Figure 9.8   Secondary transaction volume p.a. in $B and discounts to NAV for buyouts and venture funds.
Source: Hege and Nuti (2011; Jefferies (2021); Greenhill (2022).

[27] Hege and Nuti (2011).

Many sellers had huge overcommitments to existing private equity programs and significant unfunded commitments that were causing liquidity issues in certain situations.[28] Financial institutions such as Citigroup and ABN AMRO, as well as AIG and Macquarie affiliates, were among the top sellers.[29] They were joined by some of the large endowments. Harvard Management Company was reported to be looking to unload roughly $1.5 billion in private equity stakes in the secondary market, but with discounts as high as 40% it is unclear how much was ultimately sold.

But even secondary buyers did not want to catch a falling knife. When buyout discounts became huge in 2009, several large secondary players halted their acquisitions. Buyers who had committed to secondary purchases began to utilize material-adverse-change (MAC) clauses in their contracts to back out of deals they had signed merely weeks earlier.[30] In 2010, the discounts to NAV started to stabilize but with the onset of the European sovereign debt crisis discounts became larger again and the transaction volumes remained low. After that, volumes recovered, with the average annual transaction volume at $25 billion between 2012–2014. While initially, sellers' motivation was driven by a mixture of a cash crunch and overexposure, a new driver gained importance: regulatory pressure. Banks and insurance companies faced higher capital charges from Basel III and Solvency II standards, so they started liquidating their private equity holdings. In addition, pension funds and sovereign wealth funds continued to sell assets on the secondary market, and those sellers did enter the market with large portfolios.[31]

Secondary fundraising increased considerably. From 2009–2015, about $136 billion was raised in total. This was about 8% of the capital raised for private equity funds (buyouts, venture and growth financing) during that time. Jeremy Coller, the founder of Coller Capital, once told the author that he estimates that about 15% of capital raised in primary funds would become a secondary opportunity over time. Using this number as a benchmark, the amount of funds raised for

---

[28] Marshall (2008).

[29] Hege and Nuti (2011).

[30] PE Online (2008). The proposed secondary sale was first reported in *The Harvard Crimson* (2009).

[31] PE Online (2012), Bloomberg (2012).

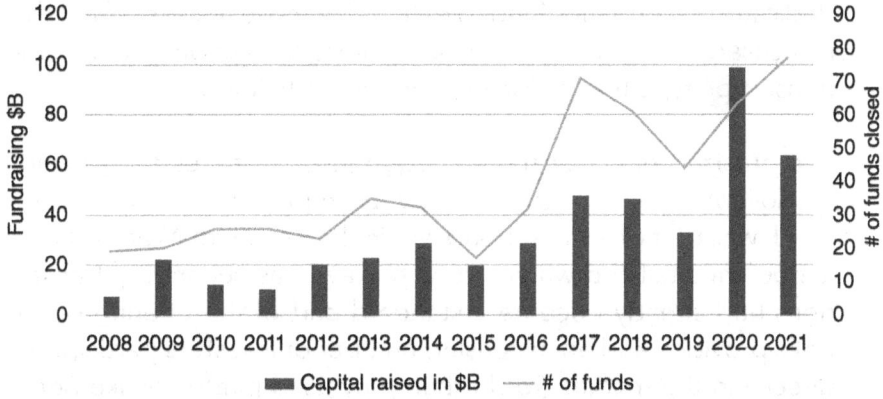

Figure 9.9 **Private equity secondary fundraising, 2008–2021, in $B and # of funds.**
Source: Capital Dynamics (2016); Jefferies (2021); Secondary Investor (James, R.) (2022).

secondary funds looked reasonable. The trend toward larger funds was also in line with the rising number of larger portfolio transactions, including dozens and sometimes more than one hundred partnership interests that became available as large institutions started to unwind their positions. But then, from 2017 onwards, fundraising increased. During 2017–2021 more than $300 billion was raised and 2020 saw a record with $99 billion raised. Secondaries FoFs' total new commitments were about 10% of total private market fundraising, slightly above the average of 8% for the last 20 years.

The spike in fundraising in 2020 was, however, remarkable as it was driven by five mega funds that collectively raised $61 billion—more than the total secondaries fundraising in any other year (Figure 9.9). One of those funds was Coller Capital XIII with just over $9 billion, plus a credit secondaries fund that closed at $1.4 billion. That year also saw AlpInvest Partners complete fundraising for its seventh secondaries program, reaching a hard cap of $9 billion and Ardian closed its flagship secondaries FoFs ASF VIII at $19 billion—then the largest secondaries FoFs ever raised.[32] The pattern persisted. Blackstone announced the final closing of its latest global secondaries strategy, Strategic Partners IX (SP X), and its maiden GP-led continuation fund strategy, Strategic Partners GP Solutions, in January 2023 (SP GPS). SP IX has $22.2 billion in total obligations, whereas SP GPS has $2.7 billion in total commitments. SP IX is the world's largest

---

[32] Crunchbase (2022).

dedicated secondaries fund to date.[33] The move to raise a fund that is focused on GP-led secondaries reflects the growing role of this transaction type that is discussed further as follows.

The outsized effect of those mega funds illustrates the growing consolidation of the FoFs industry (both primary and secondary), which was part of a wider trend within the private markets industry. It does not tell the whole story, however, as secondary transactions had already become a standard part of the offering of any FoFs provider, and an increasing number of investors participated directly in the market. To do that, they used platforms like Setter that post limited partnership interests for sale.[34]

Investors can often exercise a "preemption right" to submit a matching bid in funds where the investor is already a limited partner. Preemption rights are nowadays a standard provision in many limited partnership agreements.

So, there was more competition for deals. Deal volume in 2015–2017 did increase somewhat, but not on a scale that would justify the substantial increase in fundraising. Discounts were also small, as one would expect, given the bullish market environment and investors' demand for the asset class. The environment was generally benign, with funds showing good performance. But secondary funds have also become a way to get diversified access to the asset class and, given that returns have been attractive, they have become a staple in many investors' allocations and benefit when commitment volumes increase. But that capital had to find new opportunities as the traditional opportunity set of buying partnership interests at a discount was limited and, given the small discounts, may not even have been that attractive compared to the past.

Sales to GPs, GP-Led Secondaries, and Continuation Vehicles

Transactions involving GPs on both sides of the deal were always regarded with some suspicion by their investors. Given that the

---

[33] Blackstone (2023).
[34] Institutions can register on the Setter platform and obtain due diligence information that allow them to evaluate and submit a bid.

company has supposedly been put in shape and is run very well, all the low-hanging fruits must have been exploited by the previous owners' private equity, and thus, the upside for the new owners must be limited. While there is no evidence that companies bought from a PE vendor underperformed compared to those acquired from other seller types, the suspicion lingered that a purchase from a GP is a second-best exit.[35]

But if this is not the case, why is the GP not holding on to the portfolio company, harvesting the additional upside that the new owner must expect? The answer is that limited partnerships have a maximum lifespan that restricts the managers' holding period of portfolio investments. In a relatively illiquid closed-end investment vehicle, investors wanted to be sure to get their money back—the earlier, the better (Figure 9.10).

Historically, such GP-led secondaries were a means of doing just that: moving unrealized portfolio investments out of a fund that

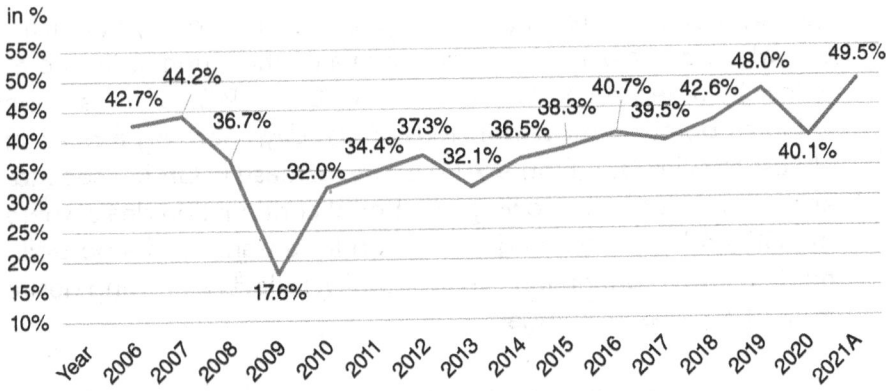

Figure 9.10   Sales to GPs in % of total number of exits.
Source: Adapted from Preqin.

---

[35] Responding to client requests, SCM Strategic Capital Management analyzed the performance of deals acquired from a GP and compared them with deals obtained from other seller types several times during the 1990s and 2010s. There was no evidence that such deals showed a worse performance and private equity managers often pointed out that they like to buy companies from other PE firms as they usually come with no bad surprises. Management teams already understand private equity ownership and have often established better financial controls and reporting than those found with companies that were acquired from other vendors.

was approaching the end of its lifespan. Sometimes it implied that the remaining assets were performing below expectations or even in distress, struggling to make exits, and GPs were thus unable to close the fund within its (extended) lifespan. In recent years, there has been a significant shift in the use of secondary markets. Instead of using them as a liquidity option, GPs are now using them to extend their ownership over portfolio investments. This approach involves migrating portfolio assets into continuation funds, allowing GPs to extract additional value from their best-performing assets.

A New Role for Secondary Funds

Secondary funds play a role in such GP-led secondaries, which are different from the sale to GP discussed before. GP-led secondaries describe the sale of one or several portfolio holdings to a secondary buyer at a discount—typically at the end of a fund's life to close the fund or to roll over assets in a continuation vehicle to extend the ownership period, which involves secondaries FoFs as they frequently supply the replacement capital required to buy out investors who do not want to participate in a continuation fund (see as follows). GP-led secondaries were at or below 20% of transaction volumes before 2016 and increased steadily, reaching a peak of almost 50% in 2021 (Figure 9.11).[36] The increase in GP-led secondaries was driven by a growing number of continuation deals where the GP (and some existing LPs) opted for a transfer of a portfolio holding into a continuation vehicle, which reflects a growing desire to hold on to assets longer.

The large proportion of secondary transactions suggests that FoFs are investing more assets in individual transactions instead of a diversified portfolio. This leads to less diversification, reduced discounts, and fee savings, and a closer resemblance to a co-investment or direct investment strategy. Investors should be aware of this shift when considering the role of secondaries in their private market portfolios.

---

[36] Shi (2022).

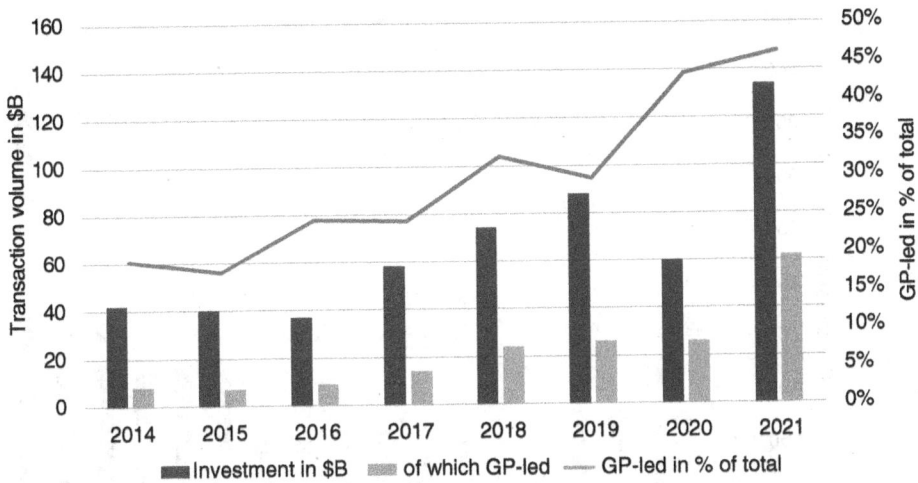

Figure 9.11   GP-led secondary transactions drove transaction volumes toward the end of the decade.
Source: Adapted from Capital Dynamics, 2022.

9.4   LISTED PRIVATE EQUITY (LPE)

After the global financial crisis (GFC), private equity markets rebounded strongly. Listed private markets consist of closed-end private market investment businesses that invest directly in deals or engage in limited partnerships (listed FoFs) and public management companies (GPs). Morningstar, PitchBook, LPX, and S&P track this sector. The S&P listed private equity index had 78 constituents because of fee float, liquidity, and capitalization filters. At the end of 2021, the LPX global composite index had 120 constituents. Management companies dominate private market capitalization (GPs), and listed FoFs are mainly buyout-focused.[37]

During the GFC, the capitalization of the LPX global composite index fell from its previous peak of EUR 83 billion in 2006 to about EUR 23 billion at the end of 2008. It took until 2013 before the LPX reached a new high. At the end of 2021, the index had a capitalization of EUR 396 billion after an enormous rally during that year (Figure 9.12). This capitalization, however, is still smaller than the listed infrastructure or real estate sectors.

---

[37] Data LPX and S&P.

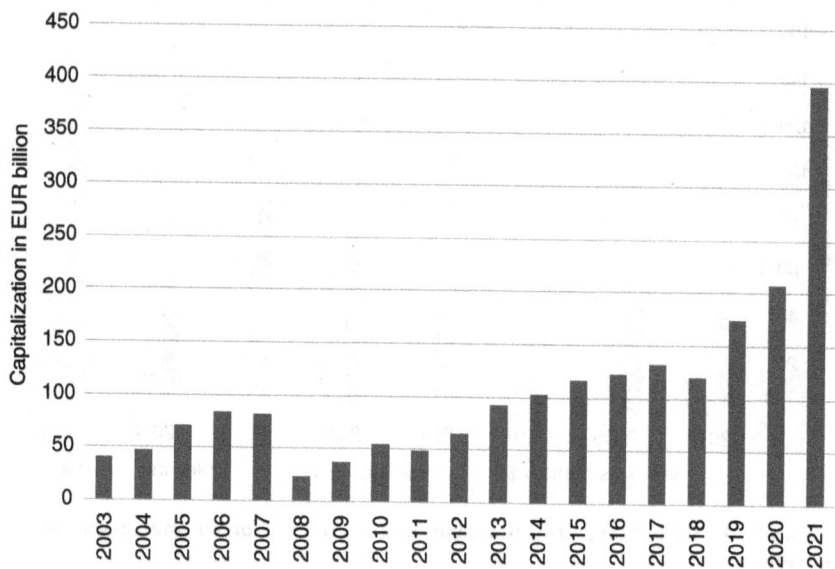

Figure 9.12   Market capitalization for global LPE, 2003–2021, in EUR billion.
Source: Adapted from CAIA, 2022; data: LPX Group, LPX Composite Listed Private Equity Index, updated April 2022.

The performance of their investments was not the driver of the growth of listed private equity as a sector. The most heavily capitalized companies in the index are management firms, such as Partners Group Holding, Blackstone, and other large private markets managers. IPOs of other large GPs contributed to the increase in capitalization as 10 of the 17 largest cap stocks have gone public since 2010. The segment of listed management companies drove the jump in market capitalization in 2021.

Ares became a publicly traded partnership in May 2014, and EQT broke a half-decade lull in such listings in 2019. Bridgepoint (UK), Blue Owl (USA), and Antin Infrastructure Partners (France) were all listed in 2021.[38]

In January 2022, TPG had its IPO on NASDAQ at a $10 billion valuation. The companies on the following list account for more than 50% of the total capitalization of the two benchmarks mainly used to track listed private markets companies, i.e., the LPX Composite

---

[38] Wiggins (2022).

and the S&P Listed PE index. Table 9.2 lists the prominent market firms that have gone public and the date of the IPO.

High valuations are a recent occurrence, though. Until 2017, after ten years as a public firm, Blackstone's share price had lingered mostly below its IPO price. Stephen Schwarzman of Blackstone. could not hide his frustration with public markets when he addressed Blackstone stockholders, "As most of you know, I have been racking my brain to make sense of this disconnect." Blackstone was not alone, however. KKR & Co. Inc., Carlyle Group Inc., Apollo Global Management Inc., and Ares Management Corp. had a lackluster early performance of their stocks too.[39]

One of the key factors that subdued the valuation of listed private market managers is the low multiple assigned to performance fees that are regarded as volatile and unpredictable.

Table 9.2 List of prominent private market firms that have gone public

Name	IPO date	Ticker
Pantheon International	1987	LON:PIN
3i Group Plc	1994	LSI:III
Intermediate Capital Group	1994	LON:ICP
Brookfield Asset Management	1997	NYSE:BAM
Partners Group Holding AG	2006	SWX:PGHN
Blackstone	2007	NYSE:BX
KKR	2010	NYSE:KKR
Apollo Global Management Inc.	2011	NYSE:APO
Carlyle Group	2012	NASDAQ:CG
Oaktree	2012	NYSE:OAK
Ares Capital Corp.	2014	NASDAQ:ARCC
Hamilton Lane Inc.	2017	NASDAQ:HLNE
EQT	2019	STO:EQT
Owl Capital Inc.	2021	NYSE:Owl
Antin Infrastructure Partners	2021	ANTIN:EN Paris
Bridgepoint Group Plc	2021	LON:BPT
TPG	2022	NASDAQ:TPG

Source: Bloomberg.

---

[39] Wiggins and Gara (2022).

Historically, Blackstone's income was more related to performance fees than Partners Group's, whose earnings came mostly in management fees, and its share underperformed until 2015. But the difference in the revenue mix decreased as Partners Group pivoted toward direct investing, and the share price performance of Blackstone caught up. For 2021, Partners Group had reported a share of performance fees of 46% in revenue compared to Blackstone's 33% share of performance fees for 2021 (Table 9.3). So, both companies have become more similar in that they are generally tradable by the investing public and display a similar dependency on performance fees.[40] The share prices of other listed private markets managers such as Carlyle Group or KKR have shown similar trajectories.

A second factor may have also driven this share price catch-up: broadening the investor base. In 2018, after the US corporate tax rate was lowered to 21% from 35% in 2018, several US private market firms converted from publicly traded partnerships into a C-corporation, including Carlyle Group, KKR & Co. Inc., Ares Management Corporation, and Apollo Global Management. Under the so-called C-corp structure, those firms pay corporate taxes on revenue to enable investors such as mutual funds and index trackers to buy the stock. The broadening of the potential investor universe coincided with the public's growing interest in the asset class.[41]

Table 9.3   Share price development of Partners Group and Blackstone since 2007 (%)

	Partners Group Holding AG (PGHN:SW)	Blackstone Inc. (BX)	S&P Listed PE Index
12/31/07–12/31/15	14.9%	10.6%	-2.5%
01/04/16–06/30/22	18.9%	25.9%	11.4%
01/03/22–06/30/22	-42.6%	-28.0%	-30.0%

Source: Bloomberg.

---

[40] Revenue numbers were obtained from the presentations to shareholders that both companies published for the full year 2021.
[41] Roumeliotis (2019).

Listed private equity can thus be a way to gain exposure to a GP (like buying a GP stake). The share price of listed management firms is driven by AuM growth and the resulting management fees, which are very stable due to the closed-end nature of their funds and performance fees that tend to come in lumps and are hard to predict. While their founders may complain about the stock market not understanding performance fees, their share price performance overall has been solid and reflected the enormous growth of the industry and their businesses over the last 20 years. It is the performance of those management companies that also drives the overall performance of the listed private market indices.

An example helps to understand the dominance of management companies in listed private market indices: the iShares Listed Private Equity UCITS ETF reflects the return of the S&P Listed Private Equity Index. With 78 holdings as of mid-2022, it is well diversified (Figure 9.13). But management companies dominate the index's capitalization.[42]

Rather than an alternative to traditional partnership investing, these indices primarily reflect management firms' valuation trends. Those shares are also the most liquid. A closer look at two exchange-traded

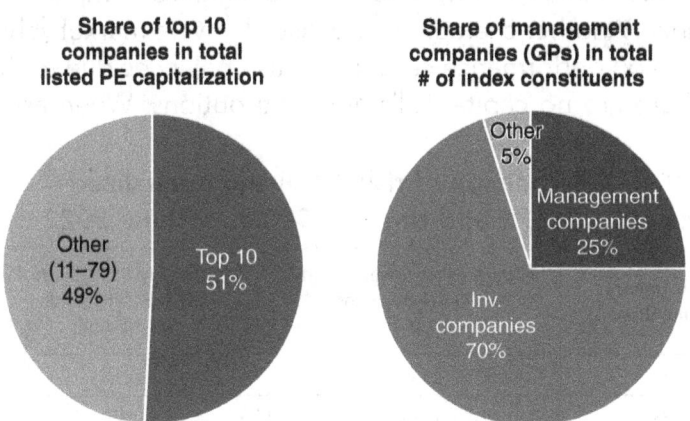

Figure 9.13   Concentration of the S&P listed private equity index
Source: Adapted from S&P.

---

[42] Khajuria (2022).

funds (ETFs) that track the S&P 500 and the S&P listed private equity sector clearly shows a weak performance of listed private vehicles designed to provide access to the asset class for the general investing public. The performance over shorter and longer horizons fails to beat the S&P 500 and comes with substantially higher volatility (see Table 9.4). In addition, listed investment companies pay corporate earnings tax—a disadvantage compared to tax-transparent limited partnerships. Tax-exempt investors, such as pension funds cannot recoup the corporate earnings tax.

To understand the lackluster performance of listed PE investment companies, one must primarily look at their share price relative to their NAV performance. Table 9.5 illustrates that discounts to NAV are persistent. Discounts on listed private equity companies are unrelated to capitalization, manager brand, NAV performance, tax rates, or the exchange. It's puzzling why these firms aren't taken private to sell underlying holdings in the secondary market. Listed PE benchmarks are inadequate to reflect performance and unsuitable as a benchmark for traditional private markets.

Since the days of the American Research and Development Corporation it has been apparent that listed investment companies are not a suitable investment vehicle for private market programs due to discounts to NAV, which have a significant impact on performance. Another characteristic of listed private market vehicles is the drag on performance caused by cash balances due to the fact that there are no capital calls and distributions. When assessing

Table 9.4   Comparison of risk (STD) and annualized returns of Listed PE and the S&P 500 as of June 2022

Performance annualized	iShares Listed Private Equity UCITS ETF (dividends distributed)	iShares Core S&P 500 UCITS ETF USD (dividends distributed)
1Y	-19.4%	-10.9%
3Y	6.4%	10.3%
5Y	7.1%	11.0%
10Y	10.7%	12.4%
STD	28.4%	18.6%

Source: BlackRock (July 23, 2022), performance data as of June 30, 2022.

Table 9.5   Share price and NAV performance of two listed PE investment companies

	Private Equity Holding (PEHN.SW)		HarbourVest Global PE (HVPE.L)	
	Share price performance in % p.a.	NAV performance in % p.a.	Share price performance in % p.a.	NAV performance in % p.a.
12/31/07–12/31/15	0.7%	10.4%	n.a.	n.a.
01/01/16–06/30/22	3.2%	9.0%	10.5%	17.3%
01/03/22–06/30/22	-20%	31%	-19%	13%
Disc. to NAV 06/30/22	-49%		-43%	
Market Cap	$0.2B		$ 2.1B	

Source: Bloomberg.

the share price performance of publicly traded private equity investment companies in comparison to limited partnerships, it is important to recognize that any perceived underperformance may be overstated. This is because the Internal Rate of Return (IRR) tends to be higher than the period Return on Investment (ROI) due to variations in calculation methods. The figures in Tables 9.4 and 9.5 are ROIs, not IRRs.

9.5   VC DURING THE TECHNOLOGY BOOM

After regaining some momentum since 2005, the GFC caused another setback for the VC industry as new deals declined from their small comeback at the end of the previous decade. Investors were anxious, and the performance figures did not look promising. Nothing foreshadowed the massive shifts that were about to take place, transforming the venture capital business beyond recognition. If anything, it appeared that the best opportunities might be found outside of the United States, specifically in China.

Then the tide turned for venture capital. While the Facebook IPO created a headline exit for angel investors like Peter Thiel and firms like Greylock Partners and Accel Partners, its lackluster share price performance failed to ignite an IPO boom. Neither did VCs get an immediate boost. Still in 2013, the *Harvard Business Review* published an article that questioned VC's ability to create value.[43] Facebook's 2012 IPO, the largest US IPO of a venture-backed company at the time, helped validate the tech startup model. Its high valuation led to more investment in the tech industry and continued funding growth for startups. The growth of Facebook and other FAANG companies' earnings and valuations also increased M&A activity, boosting startup valuations (Figure 9.14). Facebook's purchase of WhatsApp showed that VCs found a profitable exit path again.

Facebook Buys WhatsApp

With its shares' high valuation and substantial cash resulting from the IPO, Facebook had the means to make large acquisitions. In July 2012, Facebook acquired Instagram for $1 billion and started a conversation with WhatsApp founder Jan Kou, which, in February 2014, led to the acquisition of WhatsApp. The initial bid was $16 billion, of which $12 billion would come in the form of Facebook shares. The final bid was increased to $19.6 billion—adding $3.6 billion to the original price and Facebook share prices rose 14% when the deal closed in October 2014. The acquisition

Figure 9.14   The spectacular valuations of some tech IPOs added momentum to the technology boom: traders work during the IPO for Chinese ride-hailing company Didi Global Inc on the NYSE floor in New York City, U.S., June 30, 2021; UBER results; Facebook IPO.

Sources: Associated Press Alibaba IPO # 592783983279; Reuters, Alamy # 2G5XGCT; # 19150715087121; Shannon Stapleton, Reuters, Alamy # 2CM914W.

---

[43] Mulcany (2013).

surpassed Google's $3.2 billion purchase of Nest Labs and Apple's $3 billion Beats Electronics takeover and gave Sequoia—an early round investor—a 5,000% return.[44]

It was the largest acquisition of a tech startup ever, and the rationale of the purchase was not driven by a desire to add revenue and profit. In 2013, WhatsApp lost $138 million, of which about $98 million was due to stock compensation and brought in $10.2 million in revenue. In preparation of an IPO, WhatsApp introduced a $1 subscription fee in 2013 as an independent company. Keeping the app ad-free required revenue and for a company to go public, investors need a profit history.[45] Facebook valued the company at about $2.9 billion and declared the remaining $15.3 billion of its original bid to be "goodwill value," i.e., an intangible.[46] WACC and FRCF/FCFE-based valuation models would give an even lower valuation range of $1.8–2 billion.[47] But Facebook was not alone in applying a substantially higher valuation than WhatsApp's operational metrics suggested, as it was fending off a $10 billion bid from Google.

User growth and access to developing markets where internet connectivity was sparse and where WhatsApp was already widely used were the fundamental motivation behind the acquisition.[48] Facebook's acquisition was based on the premise that focusing on user numbers rather than profitability can unlock tremendous value and the subscription fee was abolished.[49] Facebook integrated its

---

[44] Mallaby (2022).
[45] The subscription fee was abolished in early 2016 as it required a credit card which would have limited the growth of users, in particular, in markets and among audiences where credit card penetration was low (Hern, 2016).
[46] Wagner (2014).
[47] Bentes and Costa (2018) use the discounted cash flow method and weighted average cost of capital (WACC) based discounts of the free cash flow to equity (FCFE) and free cash flow to firm (FCFF)), i.e., the cash flows available to, respectively, all of the investors in the company and to common stockholders to determine a valuation range that results from a Monte Carlo analysis of input parameters. The authors arrive at an average valuation of about $1.8–2.0 billion. Leaving the details of the valuation method and the question of alternative approaches aside, it is clear that the price paid by Facebook was way above what any CAPM valuation approach would suggest and the motivation behind the deal must therefore have been driven by factors that had nothing to do with WhatsApp's financial metrics.
[48] Prior to its acquisition by Facebook in 2014, WhatsApp co-founder Brian Acton had publicly stated that the company was planning to go public (Olson, 2018).
[49] Deutsch (2022).

services to take advantage of network effects and access these mobile user bases.

The acquisition of WhatsApp by Facebook in 2014 is widely considered to have created a "herding effect" among venture capital (VC) firms, where investors followed the lead of Facebook in making investments in similar companies and technologies.[50] This phenomenon was driven by a combination of factors, including the perception that Facebook's acquisition validated the value of WhatsApp's technology, the belief that similar companies and technologies would generate similar returns, and a desire to capture a piece of the potential upside in the market. As a result, many VC firms increased their investments in messaging and social media. Although its sector definition is wider, Preqin reports that venture capital investments in the information technology sector jumped from $51 billion in 2014 to $70 billion in 2015.[51]

Two Phases of a Boom

Figure 9.15 shows the increase in exits that reflected the WhatsApp acquisition and some other M&A transactions in 2014.[52] Venture capital had a slow start in returning money to limited partners until 2014. After that, investment activity picked up but payouts

---

[50] It has been shown that heightened acquisition activity in a given industry segment does signal increased valuations and exit potential, which VCs perceive as increased attractiveness of investments in complementary innovation activities, leading to more deals. Prado and Bauer (2022) looked at data about Big Tech startup M&As of VC-backed firms that were consummated between January 1, 2010, and December 31, 2020. Their research suggests that big tech startup acquisitions by companies like Google, Facebook, Amazon, Apple, and Microsoft had a positive impact on venture capital activity. The study found an average increase of 30.7% in the total amount of VC funding toward US-based startups and an increase of 32.1% in VC funding for deals targeting European startups in the quarters following a big tech start-up acquisition.

[51] Preqin (2023b).

[52] Microsoft, for example, had acquired 210 companies, including 45 during the preceding five years until mid-2022, according to Mergr, a platform that tracks those acquisitions. A total of 13 acquisitions came from private equity firms. During 2014, there was a buying spree as both Google and Facebook built out their digital ecosystem and added products and services to their platform. Google acquired Nest Labs, DeepMind, Twitch, and, in 2016, Apigee. Facebook (apart from WhatsApp) acquired Oculus VR and previously bought Instagram in 2012 (Mergr, 2022).

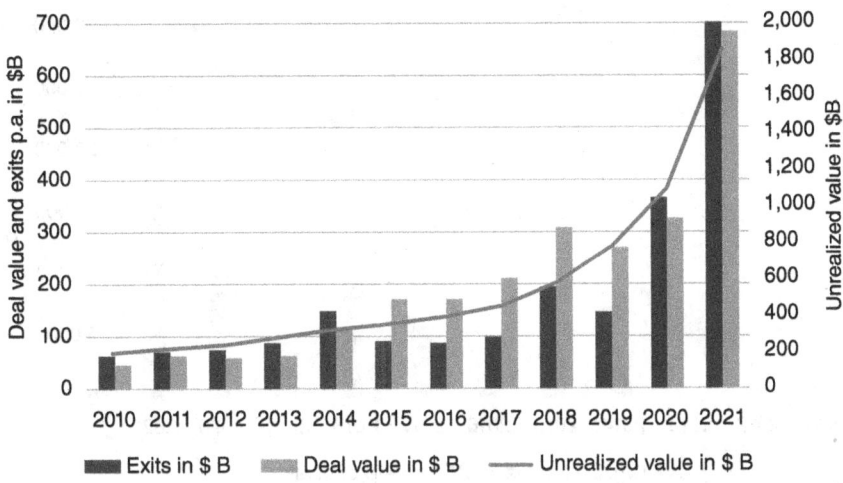

Figure 9.15   US VC exits, deal value, and unrealized value in 2010–2021 (Q3), in $B.
Source: Adapted from Preqin data as of September 2022.

only increased investment amounts again in 2020–2021, when exit volumes reached over $300 billion in 2020, and an all-time high of $700 billion in 2021. The recovery of venture capital thus started with an exit boost in 2014, which was followed by increasing deal activity and valuations before exits surged in 2020–2021.

Average deal volumes increased from an annual average of about $58 billion during 2010–2013 to $166 billion during 2014–2017 and then to almost $400 billion p.a. during 2018–2021 (Figure 9.16). Valuations increased across the board, with seed rounds in 2021 equaling Series A deal sizes from a decade earlier.[53]

As a sign that venture capital had stepped out of the shadows of buyouts where it lingered during the previous decade, the share of venture capital in total private equity deal volume has increased significantly in recent years, altering the overall composition of private equity activity. From 26% in 2006, venture capital's share of total PE deal volume rose to 41% in 2020. The trend is reflected in the record-breaking number of 4,000 startups that raised their first venture round in 2021 in the USA, with the total number of

---

[53] The average seed funding collected by a US startup in 2021 was $3.3 million, more than 5x that in 2010 (Davis, 2021).

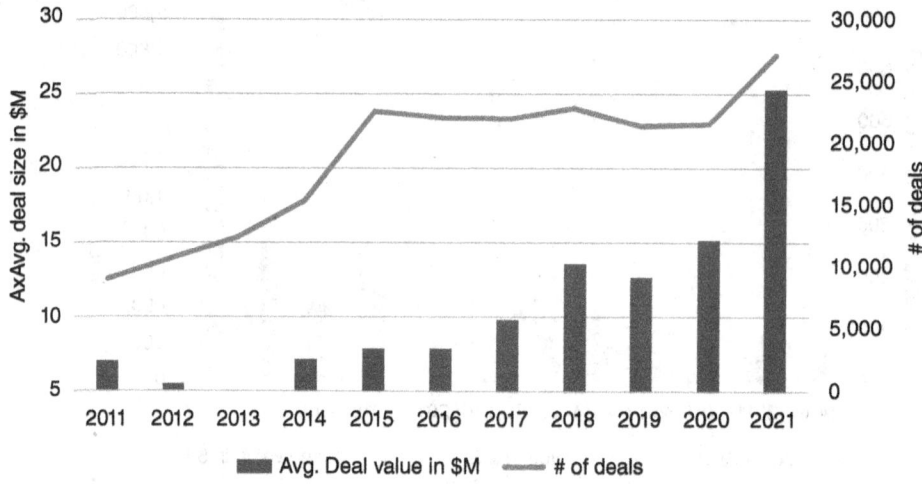

Figure 9.16   US growth in VC deal numbers and deal sizes.
Source: Adapted from Preqin 2023b.

deals reaching an all-time high.[54] Exits and increased deal activity, accompanied by rising valuations, have boosted the realized and unrealized value of VC funds. This, in turn, led to a jump in performance during 2013–2015, as shown in the index of rolling one-year IRRs of US venture capital (Figure 9.17). After many years of poor performance, the VC industry made a comeback.

As in the past, performance did boost fundraising. VC fundraising had been around $40 billion a year between 2010–2014, and after that, it increased rapidly. Between 2018–2021, more than $700 billion had been raised, exceeding the amount raised during the three years before the dotcom bust, culminating in a record of $234 billion in 2021 (Figure 9.18).

With the increase in fundraising also came larger funds and a number of $1 billion+ funds were raised.[55]

The list of the largest funds (Table 9.6) includes managers such as Tiger Global Management, a hedge fund focused on public and private technology companies and, as such, is not strictly a VC fund but might equally classify as a growth fund. In contrast to

---

[54] jdsupra.com (2022).
[55] Data from Preqin and PitchBook.

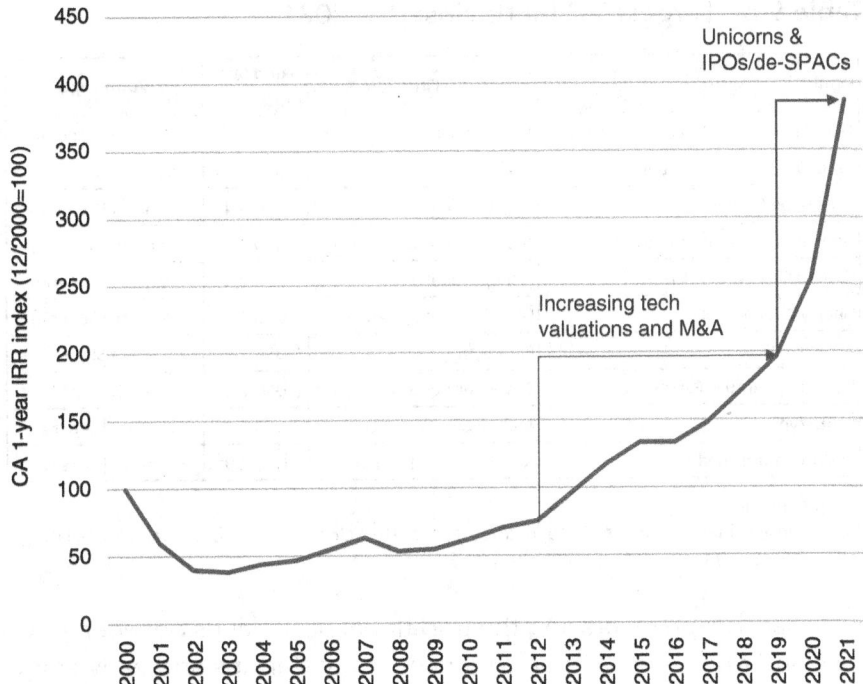

Figure 9.17 US VC one-year rolling IRR (cum. index, 2000 = 1000): a tale of two booms.

Sources: 1999–2017 Cambridge Associates Benchmark Statistics (CA, 2017); 2018–2021 (Preqin, 2023e).

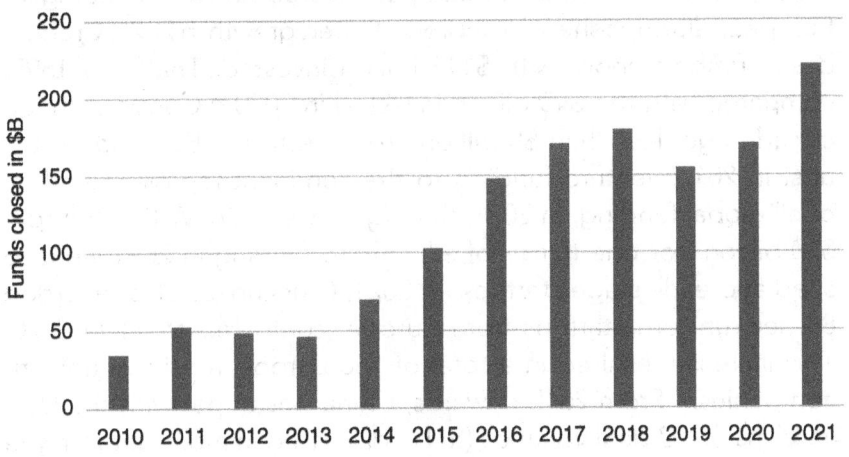

Figure 9.18 VC fundraising globally, 2010–2021.

Source: Preqin data as of September 2022.

buyouts, where certain firms expanded significantly by adopting a multi-strategy approach, the upheaval in venture capital originated externally. Non-traditional investors entered the scene, reshaping

Table 9.6   Largest VC funds closed in 2021

Fund	Firm	Fund Size (bn)	Fund Type
Tiger Private Investment Partners XIV	Tiger Global Management	USD 6.7	Venture (General)
Technology Crossover Ventures XI	TCV	USD 4.0	Expansion / Late Stage
Pioneering Fund VII	Flagship Pioneering	USD 3.4	Venture (General)
Norwest Venture Partners XVI	Norwest Venture Partners	USD 3.0	Venture (General)
ICONIQ Strategic Partners V	Iconiq Capital	USD 2.6	Venture (General)
Liberty 77 Fund	Liberty Strategic Capital	USD 2.5	Venture (General)
Paradigm One	Paradigm	USD 2.5	Early Stage
Bessemer Venture Partners XI	Bessemer Venture Partners	USD 2.5	Early Stage
a16z crypto III	Andreessen Horowitz	USD 2.2	Venture (General)
ARCH Venture Fund XI	ARCH Venture Partners	USD 1.9	Venture (General)

Source: Preqin.
Note: Tiger's final closing was held in 2022, its reported closing size in 2021 was $6.7 billion.

the landscape by erasing the traditional boundaries between public and private investments in technology startups and early-stage and growth financing.

These funding and deal-making trends played out not only in the USA, Europe also saw record fundraising, deal-making, and exit activity, and the venture industry recovered as well. Funding to European startups showed unprecedented growth in 2021, Crunchbase numbers show, with $116 billion invested. That's up 159% compared with the $45 billion invested in 2020.[56] Consider that a decade ago, less than $8 billion was invested in European startups. In 2012, venture funding to the continent represented 13% of all global funding; in 2021, that figure was 18%. Within Europe, $40 billion—or one-third—of all venture funding in 2021 went to seed and early-stage startups. In 2021, Crunchbase also recorded 84 new unicorn startups from Europe, compared to 11 in 2020. This increase resulted in a total of 150 European private unicorn companies.[57] From 2015 onwards, China was at par with the USA in terms of VC deal volumes (to be discussed in more detail in the following section).

---

[56] Crunchbase (2022b).
[57] Teare (2022d).

The Late-Cycle IPO Boom

Amazon had high barriers to entry and low margins and was the only unprofitable FAANG at the time of its IPO, leading to skepticism about its success. It took 14 years to show a cumulative net profit but eventually overtook Apple to become the world's second most valuable company in 2018—making its founder Jeff Bezos the richest man in the world.[58] Amazon set the trend for prioritizing growth over profitability as a new investment paradigm, becoming a poster child for the approach. This led to a tech IPO boom with companies like Zoom, Lyft, Uber, and Pinterest going public with high valuations in 2018 and 2019 as investors backed fast-growing but unprofitable companies. Even excluding the $82 billion valuation of the Uber IPO, the average IPO size was $246 million.[59] VC-backed tech IPOs were more prevalent than during the dot-com boom.[60] Table 9.7 illustrates the heightened activity seen during the decade leading up to the record year 2021.

While the IPO boom did provide significant returns for some venture capital firms, the M&A market remained the dominant

Table 9.7   Median age and fraction of all IPOs and IPOs with VC backing, 1980–2021

Period	# of IPOs	Median age	All VC-backed IPOs #	All VC-backed IPOs %	Tech & Biotech IPOs #	Tech & Biotech IPOs % VC-backed
1980–1989	2047	8	514	25%	595	47%
1990–1998	3614	8	1265	35%	1228	56%
1999–2000	856	5	523	61%	630	68%
2001–2009	919	11	360	39%	311	64%
2010–2021	1650	11	995	60%	534	74%
2021	311	11	175	56%	72	64%

Source: Ritter (2022).
Note on data sources (quoted from Ritter, 2022): The SDC new issues database is updated by reviewing prospectuses on EDGAR and information from Dealogic (post 1991), "Going Public: The IPO Reporter" (1980–1985), and the Howard-Huxster IPO prospectus collection (1975–2006). Tech stocks are defined as internet plus other tech (not including biotech), and data may differ from other sources in the book. As of February 16, 2022.

---

[58] *Financial Times*, March 20, 2018, La Monica (2019).
[59] Potter (2020).
[60] Ritter (2022).

exit route for venture-backed companies. Therefore, in terms of its share in total exit volumes, the IPO boom of 1998–2000 was more relevant to the venture capital industry than the IPO boom of 2020–2021.

There is as yet no agreement whether holding periods of start-ups in the portfolios have decreased as a result of the IPO boom. Kaplan et al. find shorter holding periods, which are similar when comparing buyouts and venture capital. PitchBook and Ritter suggest that the median age of firms that did an IPO has increased significantly since 2000.[61] Janeway argues that by 2017 the average time to IPO of a venture-backed company had exceeded eight years compared to the five to six years typical since 2000 and less than three years during 1995–2000. For M&A transactions the time to acquisition has, however, remained steady at about four years.[62] Some of the IPOs that made the headlines (Figure 9.19) were private for quite a number of years before they went public.

The demand for tech IPOs, increased trade sales, and exit opportunities through SPACs all contributed to the surge in distributions to VC funds and their LPs late in the cycle. This development did not happen gradually. The average exit value in 2006 was $50 million and increased to $119 million in 2019. But, in 2021, the average valuation of VC-backed exits reached $440 million— almost a 9x increase compared to 2006. Exit volumes were not only driven by portfolio companies that went public but also by a parallel development that pointed in the opposite direction: late-stage super-rounds that allowed startups to become multi-billion-dollar companies without going public. As described in Chapter 8, this trend gained momentum after the SoftBank Vision Fund I was established. As a result of numerous late-stage funding rounds, the number of unicorns has increased, which not only drove valuations up across the board but also provided exit opportunities for early-stage investors that sold out to late-round participants. A further exit channel was the sale of a portfolio company to a unicorn.

---

[61] Kaplan et al. (2020), PitchBook analysis from Latta (2017); Ritter (2022). The Pitch-Book analysis only includes data up to 2016, thus missing the impact of the IPO boom on holding periods.
[62] Data based on 2Q PitchBook NCA Venture Monitor quoted in Janeway (2018, p. 91).

FACEBOOK, CAMBRIDGE, MA (2004)
Founders: M. Zuckerberg et al.. Funding:
Peter Thiel, $500'000 seed round. Followed
by investments of Accel Partners, Andreessen
Horowitz, Greylock and Marc Pincus (Zygna)
in Series A. Total funding $16.1 billion.
Facebook had its IPO in 2012 with a valuation
of $104 billion.

PINTEREST, SAN FRANCISCO, CA (2011)
Founders: P. Sciarra, E. Sharp (Facebook),
B. Silbermann (Google)
Series A founding led by Bessemer ventures
in 2011. Total funding $1.5 billion.
Pinterest went public in 2019 at a $10 billion
valuation.

SNAP, STANFORD, CA (2011)
Founders: E. Spiegel, B. Murphy, R. Brown (all
from Stanford University)
Funding: Kleiner Perkins and others. Total
funding $4.9 billion
SNAP went public in 2017 with it share price
up 44% and a valuation of $33 billion.

UBER TECHNOLOGIES, SAN FRANCISCO, CA
(2010) Founders: T. Kalanick, G. Camp Series
A funding round in 2011 was led by
Benchmark. Total funding $25.2 billion.
UBER went public in 2019 at a valuation of $82
billion and made history as the biggest first-
day dollar loss in IPO history in the USA.

Alibaba Group

ALI BABA, HANGZOU, CHINA (1999) Founders:
Jack Ma, Joseph C. Tsai, Zhang Ying, Trudy Daietal.
$5 million seed financing and ledby Goldman Sachs
and Eight roads ventures with a further $20 million
investment by Softbank that same year..
Total funding $8.5 billion.
Alibaba had its IPO in 2014 with a valuation of $231
billion.

zoom

ZOOM, SAN JOSE, CA (2011)
Founder: E. Yuan, (Cisco)
Seed financing and series A led by AME Ventures
and Horizon ventures respectively.
Total funding $276 million.
Zoom had its IPO in 2019 with its share price surging
80% on the first day of trading, resulting in a
valuation of $15.9 billion.

LYFT, SAN FRANCISCO, CA (2012)
Founder: L. Green.
Funding: AF Square, Mayfield Fund, K9
Ventures, Floodgate. Total funding $4.9
billion.
Lyft went public in 2019 with a market
valuation $22.2 billion.

DiDi, BEIJING, CHINA (2012) Founders: Cheng Wei
founded Didi Dache, backed by Tencent. In
February 2015 the company merged with DiDi
Dache, backed by Alibaba to form Didi Kuaidi,
which was later rebranded DiDi.
In 2021 Didi went public on the NYSE, raising
$4.4 billion on a valuation of close to $70 billion
US dollars.

**Figure 9.19 Some of the most successful IPOs of VC-backed startups during
2010–2021.**

Source: Facebook; Pinterest; Snapchat; Uber; Alibaba Group; Zoom; Lyft Inc.; DiDi.

The unicorn phenomenon may thus provide an explanation for
the contradictory findings regarding holding periods of startups in
VC funds. Late-stage super rounds both allow a company to stay
private longer while providing early-round investors with an exit
opportunity. Unlike an IPO or an M&A, which has a measurable exit
date, the later funding rounds allow VCs a partial exit that keeps
the company in the portfolio while most of the money may be off
the table.

Overall, the resulting increase in distributions was not primarily driven by the number of exits but by their higher valuation. But after many years of lackluster returns venture capital was dazzling investors again. Some top-tier venture funds reported spectacular results: Sequoia Capital has been reported to have returned between 8x and 11x invested capital on its three recent funds (Figure 9.20).[63]

With lots of deals still unrealized—at least for the younger vintages—the year-end 2021 pooled IRRs may look optimistic given the downturn that started in late 2021. However, for investors

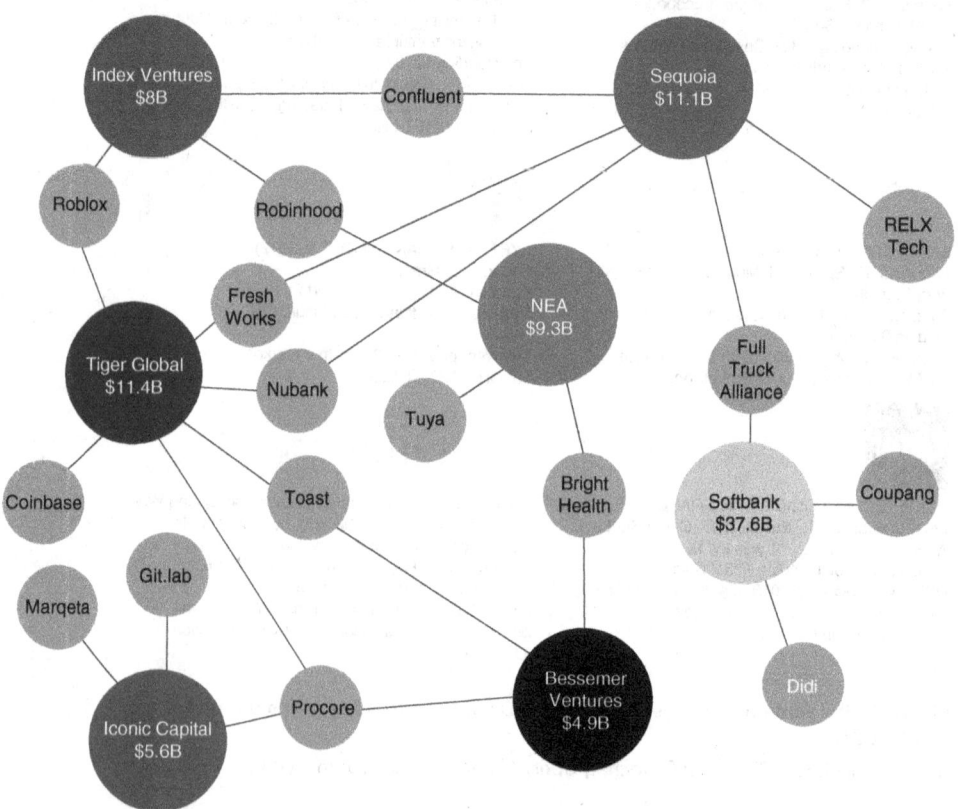

Figure 9.20   Mega IPOs made billions for VC funds (and their LPs): select stakes by GP in the most valuable venture capital-backed IPOs.

Source: Adapted from PitchBook / https://pitchbook.com/news/articles/2021-largest-ipo-vc-investors-performance.

Note: The numbers in the bubbles indicate the aggregate value of the stakes VCs hold in the companies that are connected to them.

---

[63] Russel (2020).

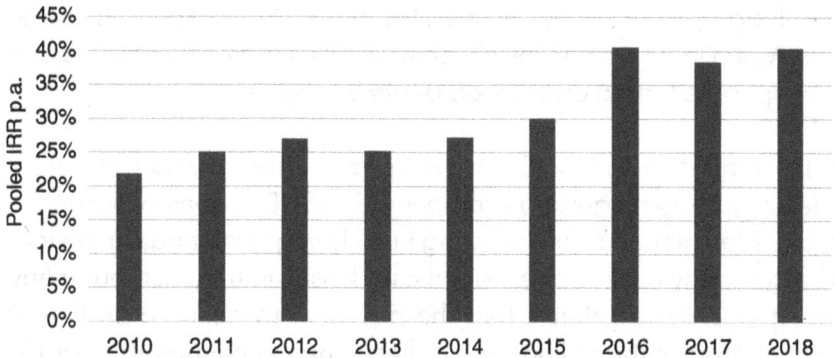

Figure 9.21   Pooled net IRR for VC vintage years 2010–2018 as of December 2021.
Source: Adapted from McKinsey, 2022; data: Burgiss.

that have waited long for good news, the decade delivered them in abundance, and venture capital was the best-performing asset class of private markets in seven out of nine vintage years during 2010–2018 and even the younger vintages showed very strong returns on the back of rising valuations (Figure 9.21).

9.6   LATE-STAGE SUPER-ROUNDS: DOORDASH

Some commentators have dismissed the unicorn phenomenon as a sign of the exuberance of the technology boom. Indeed, it is easy to point out examples where a combination of inflated expectations, weak governance, and "fake tech" claims by startups have caused significant losses for investors. But this is only part of the story as there are also examples of successful outcomes both in terms of valuations as well as the business model that those companies pursue. What cannot be doubted is the changes in the market environment for startup financing that enabled the increase in unicorns. Using DoorDash as an example, a deeper dive into its funding history exemplifies this emerging environment in which both traditional venture capitalists and non-traditional investors are participating. It also helps to focus on the issues investors need to consider when formulating their approach to startup financing going forward.

DoorDash is a technology company that provides an on-demand food delivery platform, connecting customers with local restaurants and food delivery drivers. It operates in the United States, Canada, and Australia. The company has seen significant growth, as more and more people turn to online food delivery services.

In December 2020, DoorDash went public through a merger with a special purpose acquisition company (SPAC). DoorDash was not yet profitable and had been investing heavily in growth and expansion. The company has reported significant losses in the past, but many investors believed that it had the potential to become profitable in the future as the online food delivery market continued to grow.

As of Q3 2022. DoorDash (DASH) reported revenue of about $6 billion, EBITDA of −$600 million and an operating margin of −15%.[64] DoorDash's funding history is a good illustration of the trend that was behind the proliferation of unicorns (Figure 9.22):

- **Many rounds:** 12 funding rounds that raised a total of almost $2.5 billion.
- **Massive valuation increases:** Its post-money valuation after its last round was $16 billion.[65]
- **Many acquisitions:** DoorDash made seven acquisitions. Unicorns often use the capital they raise to grow their business that way.[66] As a result, the market is getting more concentrated. In 2016, the top three food delivery companies held a combined market share of 52% and in 2021 that share increased to 84%.
- **High exit-to-raise multiple:** Its IPO in December 2021 valued the company at $38 billion, which was 2.4x over its pre-IPO valuation and 15x exit-to-raise-multiple.[67]
- **IPO valuation uplift:** DoorDash's stock rose 86% to close the day at $189.51—giving it a $72 billion valuation, which is 4.5x its pre-IPO valuation.[68]

---

[64] Macrotrends (2023).
[65] Crunchbase (2020).
[66] Delivery Hero has acquired 17 companies, including 6 in the five years until 2021 (Traxcn, 2023).
[67] Ponciano (2020).
[68] Griffith (2020), DoorDash stock price at year-end 2022 was below $49.

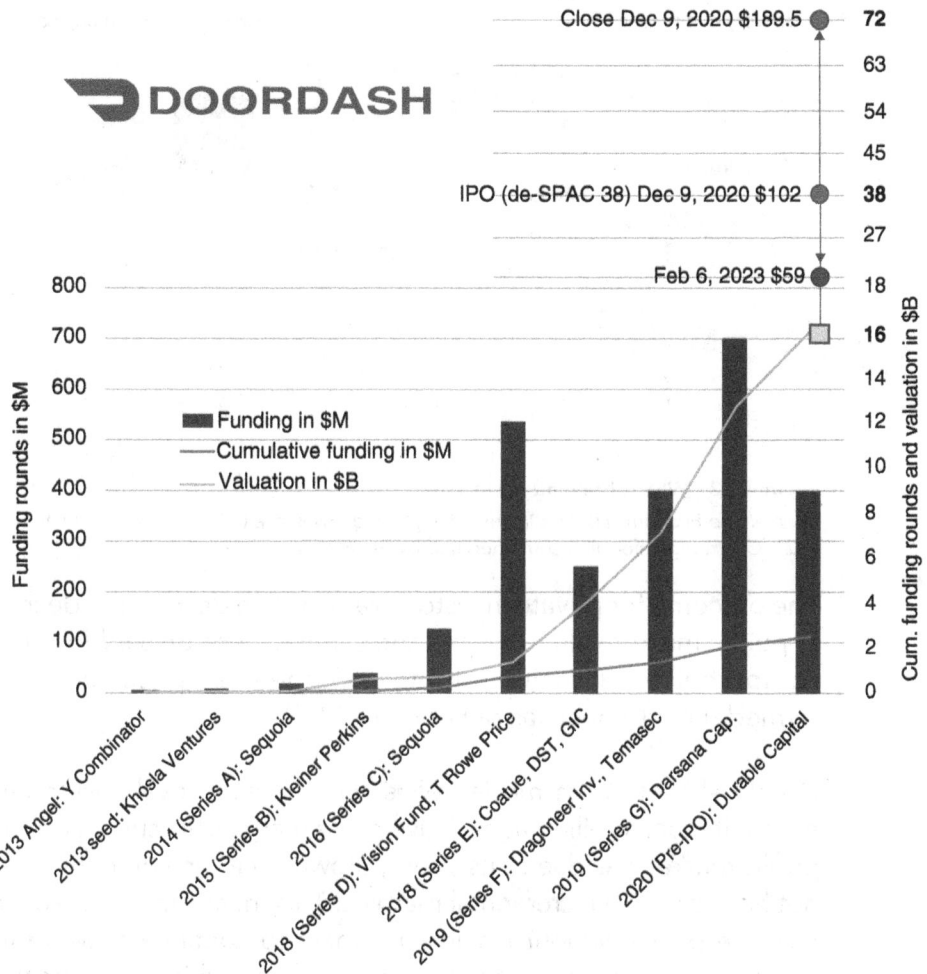

Figure 9.22   DoorDash financing rounds, valuation, and public market capitalization.
Source: Adapted from Crunchbase.

Note: Participants in funding rounds show only lead investors, but there were numerous other investors in the later rounds. Early-round investors are angel investors and traditional venture capital firms while later rounds include SWEFs, hedge funds, and growth financing/crossover funds.

- **A crowded field:** Similar to the dotcom area, this is a very crowded field. There are a large number of competitors and entrants from other domains. DoorDash expanded its market share in the USA to 53% in 2021 but UberEats is a follower with a 26% market share (see Figure 9.23).[69]

---

[69] Macrotrends (2023).

Figure 9.23   Who is bringing my lunch?
Source: The Economist (2021d); Govindarajan and Srivastava (2021). Data as of October 2021. Chart: digitalfoodlab.com, modified by the author.

The outcome for private investors was positive despite the decline in public market valuations but the same cannot be said for public stockholders. Despite a strong start, the share price underperformed the IPO price (as of February 2023).

DoorDash's business model relies on attracting loyal customers, even if it means selling at negative gross margins. Its success in the public market was due to its strong growth, but the company does not have positive incremental margins. This means that it needs to increase prices without losing customers to continue growing its revenue. The verdict on whether DoorDash can achieve this remains open, and it is a relevant issue for many other unicorns that are still privately held. Some investors, like Andy Bechtolsheim, a Silicon Valley entrepreneur and the angel investor who gave Google's founders their first outside investment, are critical: "If you sell a dollar for 80 cents, you can get through it [capital] very quickly," he says. "People tried it in 2000, and it didn't work then either."[70]

Takeaway.com, another prominent delivery company, vividly illustrates the hazards posed by another common trend among unicorns: growth through acquisitions. Initially established as Thuisbezorgd.nl

---

[70] *CB Insights* (2019).

in 2000, the company grew rapidly with positive operating margins from 2003 onwards. It had steady profit growth until 2016, and went public after two venture rounds in 2012/2014. The company acquired competitors as its share price declined due to slower growth compared to other unicorns that expanded rapidly. Nine companies were purchased, including Eat in 2019 (closed in 2020) for $7.8 billion and GrubHub in 2020 for $7.3 billion, resulting in the company being renamed Just Eat Takeway.com and becoming the world's largest food delivery company.[71] Nevertheless, the company's future outlook is still challenging due to a combination of factors, including high leverage, write-downs of its acquisitions, and reduced margins caused by intense price competition. As of February 2023, the company had a market value of around $5 billion after a massive drop in its share price.[72] This illustrates the dangers of overfunding for a venture-backed company as it led it on a buying spree paying what turned out to be peak valuations. But its share price was still above its last round post money valuation and its valuation was a multiple of about 7.5x capital raised in early 2023.

Figure 9.23 points to yet another uncomfortable truth. The operating margin for the sector was about −15% as of October 2020. This is similar to DoorDash's numbers in 2022 and a result of the price war following overinvestment, i.e., the funding of many competitors in the same sector. As these firms are (still) well funded there is no magic bullet that offers a way to quickly squeeze competitors through lower prices. Their cost structures are similar, and there are no significant economies of scale as the delivery business is a physical local business and not a digitally distributed service. Thus, there is only one way to restore profitability and this is to increase rates. The future will tell what this will do to demand but until it happens, we can enjoy our subsidized meals. With the need for consolidation in the sector being evident, there has been increased M&A activity. But without mergers of very large players smaller acquisitions will simply improve the footprint of incumbents without reducing price competition to a point where those companies turn profitable.

---

[71] Wikipedia (2022b).
[72] Ibid., companiesmarketcap.com (2022).

9.7   THE ROLE OF VCs IN THE NEW ENVIRONMENT

The case of DoorDash raises some interesting questions for investors, mainly because it had a good outcome for participants in the private funding rounds. Its funding history and deal terms are not related to the specific sector it operates in but illustrate what has changed in the 40 years since Arthur Rock and others started the venture capital business.

- **Reduced stakes for institutional rounds due to angel investors:** As DoorDash started raising money before non-traditional investors became prominent, it received pre-seed and seed funding from Y Combinator and Khosla Ventures, demonstrating the rising importance of professional angel investors in venture capital that started in the previous decade. The pre-seed and seed round investors' interest in the company was significant compared to investors in the A and B rounds who got about half of the 49% VCs would ask for during the late 1960s and early 1970s.[73]

- **Terms for VCs have become less favorable:** VCs in early and "middle" rounds often were not able to negotiate liquidity preferences or protections against preferential terms given to later round investors.[74]

- **Weaker governance:** VCs are not only getting a lower stake but also losing the power they previously had. Following another trend, DoorDash issued Class B Common Stock with 20 votes per share to founders Tony Xu and Andy Fang.[75] As a result, despite repeated investment rounds, the founders could retain control of the company. This exemplifies the decade-long weakening of governance through founder-friendly terms. In the case of DoorDash, both Kleiner Perkins and Sequoia had representatives on the board, which in this particular case, mitigates the concern about oversight somewhat.

- **Reduced ability to coach founders:** But some doubt whether it matters. Peter Thiel argued for a hands-off approach as truly successful companies have leaders that do not need coaching

---

[73] WURK (2020), Teare (2020).
[74] A liquidation preference determines the order and the amount VCs get paid in the event of an exit or liquidation.
[75] SEC (2020).

by VCs.[76] He advocated a focus on a few bets on outstanding companies and their founders rather than spending time on middling companies. In contrast, Masayoshi Son invested in hundreds of companies held in the Vision Fund, and might claim that he is there when a company takes off and ready to put big money behind it. What they have in common is their hands-off approach. This could not be more different from firms like Benchmark or Greylock who emphasize the support they give to their portfolio companies and their founders. But those firms are also investors in DoorDash, leaving investors to question the practical importance of these differentiating style proclamations.

- **Less attractive risk-reward profile for early-stage investing:** While liquidity preferences were traditionally granted to early-round investors as a safeguard, their usage has increased in late-stage super-rounds. This trend exposes early-stage investors to the risk of loss, even if the exit valuation exceeds their initial investment. Late-stage investors can exercise their right to preferential capital repayment, leading to an imbalanced distribution of exit proceeds. Consequently, this raises concerns about the diminished risk-reward profile associated with early-stage investing in such circumstances.

Questions LPs Must Answer

Does the value-added provided by venture capitalists still justify the fees they charge?

Generally, the combination of a smaller stake with less (or no) control raises questions about the role of traditional VC firms. If they cannot provide guidance and governance, what is their value-add? Are investors paying only for the skill to identify promising startups and gain access to them?

Maintaining an early-stage focus or participating in multi-stage funds?

In response to the challenge presented by non-traditional investors, some VC firms opted to raise substantial funds, enabling them to engage in later rounds or establish separate growth

---

[76] Mallaby (2022), pp. 209–211.

financing funds specifically for that purpose. Conversely, other VC firms chose to maintain their focus on early-stage financing. Investors now face the decision of which approach to support.

Are multibillion-dollar funds able to maintain past performance?

While past studies showed no size effect negatively impacting the performance of VC funds, those related to traditional venture funds were not comparable to the multibillion-dollar funds that some VCs have raised.[77]

How do VCs manage conflicts that might arise from investments across different funding rounds?

Some VCs have decided to move into growth financing by raising dedicated funds while others are increasing the size of their flagship funds. Sequoia was doing the former and came into Series C with a $127 million investment. But that can lead to conflicts of interest as capital pools are at different stages in their fund life and different valuations are participating in the same deal.

Will VCs be able to deal with growing organizational complexity?

As some VCs get bigger and execute different strategies, they face management challenges related to incentives, investment processes, and the growing role of fees and pressure to deploy capital. That is quite a change for an industry that used to cultivate the image of "star investors" and their position on the Midas List.[78]

Are ventures becoming riskier?

VCs previously used a staged investment process and active board roles to mitigate risks in their portfolios. However, the rise of numerous funding rounds with fewer restrictions has shifted control of capital raising and spending to founders instead of VCs. Uber's case serves as an example of the potential dangers that can arise when a company grants excessive power to its founders. The leadership and management approach of Uber's co-founder and former CEO, Travis Kalanick, faced intense

---

[77] Kaplan, Harris, Jenkinson, and Stucke (2013).
[78] Produced by Forbes in partnership with TrueBridge Capital Partners, the Midas List is an annual ranking of the top 100 tech investors.

scrutiny, leading to significant backlash due to allegations of a toxic work culture and questionable business practices. These incidents highlight the importance of robust corporate governance practices to ensure accountability, ethical conduct, and the protection of investors' interests.[79]

Are economic and regulatory frictions reflected in investment cases?

Digital service-based companies have an advantage in scalability and achieving profitability compared to those dealing with physical assets and infrastructure. But economic frictions may still be encountered as existing service providers in different markets have different strengths to resist or well-funded startups can engage in longer price wars. This can lengthen the path to profitability and increase the cost of getting there—both potentially undermining an investment case.[80] Another concern is regulatory frictions that may slow down the expansion of service offerings and increase the cost of compliance. Fintech is another significant sector within the unicorn universe. At year-end 2021, there were about 300 Fintech unicorns worldwide with a combined valuation of $1.8 trillion.[81] Frequently, these companies initiate their operations within a loosely regulated niche. But as they expand their range of services, one should expect greater regulatory scrutiny and increased costs associated with banking regulations and compliance.[82] A further example for regulatory frictions is the increasing focus on data privacy and regulations, which means that non-compliance or data breaches can have significant financial and reputational consequences.[83]

---

[79] Addressing frictions is crucial for business success and requires understanding the political and cultural elements of ecosystems. Uber's scandals led to Benchmark Capital Partners suing founder T. Kalanick. Founders and early investors had super-voting rights, while later-round investors were largely passive, leaving VCs unable to exercise effective oversight or replace the founder as CEO. This highlights the dangers of watering down governance (Mallaby, 2022).

[80] Larson (2016).

[81] Bruene (2022).

[82] Larson (2016).

[83] Companies like Target have used customer data to understand their preferences and needs and C. Duhigg provides an account of Andrew Pole's work at Target in 2002 where he created a pregnancy prediction model, which was so successful that it got Target into trouble. Issues about the limits of data usage and the uneasiness of customers once they realize how much a company knows about them are nothing new either (Duhigg, 2012).

9.8   AI: OPPORTUNITIES AND CHALLENGES BEYOND THE HYPE

During the 2020s, the technology industry experienced a substantial surge fueled by the impressive valuations of major technology companies. These companies' supremacy in their respective sectors, along with their high profitability and margins, became a blueprint for aspiring startups, ushering in the unicorn boom. However, in the early 2020s, a new technology emerged that poses a threat to the profitability of these tech giants and their business models—Generative AI (GenAI). Some experts predict that AI will become the transformative technology of a Fourth Industrial Revolution, bringing about benefits similar to those seen in the internet and mobile revolutions.[84] Sequoia Capital even predicts that "generative AI could change every industry that requires humans to create original work."[85]

Artificial intelligence (AI) has been around for many years, but it experienced a resurgence in the mid-2000s thanks to the growth of big data, cheaper computing power, and deep learning-powered algorithms. Early AI systems were heavily supervised and required a lot of time and effort to train. However, with the growth of big data and the development of more powerful computing, AI has become more capable. With hindsight, the release of OpenAI's language model ChatGPT in November 2022 may turn out to be a pivotal moment. Two months later after being released for free to the public, UBS analysts reported that ChatGPT reached 100 million monthly active users. This milestone was achieved faster than TikTok and Instagram who both took about two years to exceed 100 million active users and demonstrates the rapid adoption and potential impact of AI on a global scale.[86]

In that same month, Microsoft made headlines with their announcement of a $10 billion investment in OpenAI, joining Alphabet, Amazon, Meta, and Apple, among others, in the race to dominate

---

[84] Elliot (2023).
[85] Pennington (2023).
[86] Hu (2023).

GenAI technology.[87] Meanwhile, Alphabet announced layoffs of 12,000 workers and pivoted the company's attention toward GenAI. Google's management even declared a "code red" out of concern that chatbots could replace traditional search engines.[88]

The intense competition among tech giants to introduce AI-related services and capabilities is not limited to the USA, as Chinese tech companies' initiatives such as Baidu's Apollo project and Alibaba's DAMO Academy show that they are also following a similar path.[89] Overall, the investment in GenAI technology and the competition among tech giants signal a growing recognition of the transformative potential of AI, as well as the significant risks for companies that fail to adapt.[90] As such, it is likely that we will continue to see rapid developments and strategic moves in the AI space as companies jockey for position in this increasingly critical arena, which is likely to result in a significant increase in AI-related M&A activity as well.[91]

GenAI requires vast server capacity and computing power—both expensive, which could potentially place pressure on profit margins for tech companies. Additionally, the rise of chatbots and other AI-powered tools could lead to a reduction in the number of ads displayed, thereby impacting a key source of revenue for these companies. As a result, tech giants may face significant challenges in maintaining their profitability in the face of these emerging technologies. In addition, startups may offer cheaper but "good enough" solutions at lower price points. For example, if "ChatGPT writing" is the core, one could offer a stripped-down Word with ChatGPT at a fraction of the cost, and still deliver most

---

[87] Elliot (2023).

[88] *Forbes* (2023b).

[89] Alibaba (2023), Tencent (2023).

[90] Bass (2023).

[91] In 2015, Facebook acquired Wit.ai, a natural language processing platform that allows developers to add voice and text recognition to their apps, while Google acquired the AI research lab DeepMind for a reported $400 million, and Apple followed in 2016 with the acquisition of Turi, a machine learning platform that allows developers to build AI models. The acquisition was reportedly worth around $200 million. More recent acquisitions include SigOpt (Intel), Kustomer (Facebook), Slack (Salesforce), and DeepMind (NVIDIA). Source: corporate announcements/crunchbase.com.

of the value to the consumer.[92] Advances in hardware such as the development of specialized processors designed specifically for AI (AI accelerators) may result in significantly faster and more efficient performance compared to traditional CPUs or GPUs, which will determine in part the margin pressure that the large tech firms may be facing in the future but also determine the pace of adoption of GenAI tools and solutions.[93]

GenAI also shares a characteristic of disruptive innovation observed in the past—the speed of technological change. Due to the rapidly evolving nature of GenAI and its underlying models, techniques, and libraries, what is cutting-edge today may become obsolete within weeks. This reduces the ability of companies to build a sustainable competitive advantage based on their technology while it is also doubtful whether intellectual property can be effectively protected.[94] The rapid pace of creative destruction also hinders differentiation, as competitors can quickly replicate models and work.

The disruptive impact of AI technology extends beyond leading tech companies and also affects AI platforms backed by venture and growth capital, relying on earlier generations of AI technology. A number of these companies already were unicorns in 2021.[95] Despite their success, they face the risk of obsolescence as AI technology continues to evolve rapidly. This highlights the significant technology risk in AI-related investments, where even well-funded startups may struggle to keep pace with the industry's rapid change.[96]

---

[92] This observation is based on a discussion of the subject with Max Rumpf, ETH Zurich & Carnegie Mellon University. That new market entrants offer a product or service that is simpler, more convenient, and more affordable than existing offerings is also a characteristic of disruptive innovation. See Christensen (1997).
[93] Smith (2022).
[94] In 2014, the U.S. Supreme Court looked at the ability to patent software in *Alice Corp. v. CLS Bank International*, 134 S.Ct. 2347 (2014). In its decision, the Court clarified the criteria for the eligibility test for software patents. Ultimately, the Court determined that patents covering certain computer-implemented transactions are abstract ideas and therefore not eligible under patent protections. Quoted from Fisher Phillips (2022).
[95] Examples are UiPath, which automates business processes, SenseTime, a developer of facial recognition, and C3.ai, which offers AI-based solutions for enterprise applications such as fraud detection, each valued at over $3 billion based on their latest funding rounds until year-end 2021.
[96] Temkin (2023).

The expected widespread incorporation of AI across a plethora of applications and the heavy investments of the tech giants in AI have ushered in a reassessment of the prospects of previously funded startups and their business models by VCs. In March 2023, PitchBook released a report indicating that the US VC investments in GenAI alone had increased from $408 million in 2018 to $4.5 billion in 2022.[97] The funding trend in GenAI counters the overall negative trend in VC funding that declined by 36% since Q1 2021 in the USA, according to Crunchbase. The most significant decline was in later rounds and growth financing, which declined by 49% and 73% Q1 2021 to Q1 2023.[98] Valuations of unrealized investments in VC portfolios had already been under pressure since 2021 and the shift of VCs' focus away from traditional models that are now deemed to be less innovative or competitive could accelerate this downward trend. The outcome could be similar to the post-dotcom era, where previously popular business models did not receive funding anymore as VCs shifted their focus toward new, emerging technologies.

The emergence of GenAI has therefore the potential to disrupt the existing market and impact the valuations of large tech companies, make existing VC-funded AI platforms outdated, and leave those unicorn startups struggling to secure funding as investors shift their focus to GenAI-focused startups. As a result, these factors could create significant write-downs on unrealized investments for VC funds and their LPs.

While the emergence of GenAI may increase the valuation risk for existing investments in VC funds, it also presents potential upside opportunities as tech entrepreneurs identify new opportunities and are forming ventures to develop and introduce new AI productivity tools. Examples in the new space are OpenAI, Anthropic ($300 million investment by Google, essentially an OpenAI competitor), CohereAI, or (for images, also started in 2022).[99] Most of them are unicorns already with most funding raised in 2022/2023.[100] Several

---

[97] PitchBook (2023b).
[98] Teare (2022c), Wiggers (2023a).
[99] Victor (2023).
[100] Commentary received from Max Rumpf, ETH Zurich & Carnegie Mellon University as well as a list of companies provided has been used to draft this section and is gratefully acknowledged by the author.

startups in Y Combinator's Winter 2023 batch are developing "ChatGPT for X" AI-powered chatbot.[101] As the technology continues to advance, it may become more accessible to non-experts, much like website and app development has become more accessible with increasingly user-friendly tools and platforms. It is worth noting that all of the companies are focused on providing a conversational, user-friendly experience for their customers, whether that involves automating routine business processes or providing customized support for customer service queries. AI-powered chatbots are designed to be user-friendly and easy to use, often incorporating natural language processing and aiming to make AI more accessible for enterprise use cases.

The surge of funding in GenAI is creating a problem that is all too familiar for VCs: overinvestment due to "herding." This problem is likely to intensify as development budgets become more certain, and the technical skill required to develop AI models declines.

Additionally, the high cost of computing is a significant obstacle to the widespread adoption of AI use cases for businesses. The development and deployment of AI algorithms require significant computing power and storage resources, which can be prohibitively expensive for many companies, especially smaller ones. This may lead to a "5% versus the rest" phenomenon, where only large companies can fully harness the productivity gains through GenAI, similar to the experience of another disruptive technology: electricity.

Another obstacle to widespread adoption is the "black box" problem, where the decision-making process within AI systems

---

[101] "ChatGPT for X" is a phrase that refers to a new generation of startups that are attempting to develop chatbots using advanced AI technology, specifically natural language processing (NLP) models like GPT-3. These chatbots are designed to be highly sophisticated and capable of handling complex tasks, such as customer service or technical support, in a conversational manner. Yuma, for example, is using text-generating AI models to suggest replies to customer service queries that are customized to support agents. Baselit, meanwhile, is using GPT-3 to provide businesses with chatbot-style analytics for their customers, allowing them to perform database queries in plain English. Lasso combines a ChatGPT-like interface with robotic process automation, and a Chrome extension to automate customer service processes (Wigger, 2023b).

is difficult to understand. This highlights the need for transparent AI systems for many business applications that involve processes requiring monitoring by internal audit or compliance. Finally, integrating GenAI solutions with existing systems and processes can be challenging, particularly in industries where legacy systems are prevalent.

Additionally, the path to revenue and profitability for AI investments remains challenging. VC firms support startups developing AI solutions to enhance knowledge management and productivity within organizations. However, these startups face obstacles in training algorithms on client data without compromising company-specific proprietary knowledge. While the AI technology itself may be scalable, the custom solutions developed for one business may not be easily transferable to another, potentially hindering scalability. But companies like GDrive, Dropbox, Sales, and Slack—as well as OpenAI—are working on "enterprise" large language model (LLM) services that help companies to build on top of LLMs.

AI startups have various revenue models at their disposal, including subscription-based, pay-per-use, licensing, commission-based, advertising, and data monetization. Tech giants like Amazon and Microsoft are attracted to the prospect of enhancing their cloud business, while companies like Google or Facebook may invest heavily in AI development and M&A to defend their market share in online advertising. These large players may not necessarily charge users for AI services. Many AI startups are likely to adopt the Software as a Service (SaaS) model, offering AI-powered solutions as a service. They will compete with established tech companies that can spread investments across a wider range of applications, giving them a size advantage. Size may also play a role when it comes to providing customers with affordable computing and server capacity to run these applications. Startups must find a niche with paying customers to succeed. No one knows yet what a sustainable, differentiated business in the AI space looks like, but the disruptive nature (internet-sized transformation) that many VCs and their investors assign to it means that there will be money made if the distribution capability is there to build an audience. For investors, AI presents a bold bet that includes both technology and market risks. AI development costs can be significant. Despite

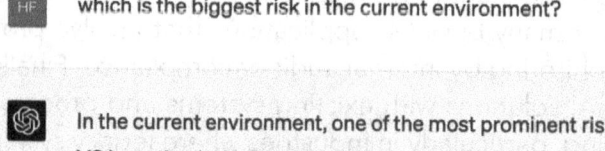

which is the biggest risk in the current environment?

In the current environment, one of the most prominent risks for VC investing in AI startups is the combination of market risk and hype risk. These risks are interconnected, as hype can significantly contribute to market saturation and competition.

Figure 9.24   The biggest risk for VCs investing in AI startups.
Source: ChatGPT / Microsoft Corporation. https://www.openai.com.

the rapid (and often free) adoption of AI models like Chat GPT, the transformative potential of AI may take time to materialize fully. Asked about the biggest risk for VCs investing in AI startups in the current (2023) environment, OpenAI's GPT-4 gave the response shown in (Figure 9.24).

9.9   VENTURE CAPITAL IN CHINA

In 2018, China overtook the USA when it attracted 47% of the world's venture capital investments compared to the 35% share of the USA. China has also surpassed the United States in the generation of unicorn companies, as of 2019. In 2019, Tencent overtook Facebook to become the world's fifth-largest company. It was a watershed moment, a wake-up call for those in the West accustomed to viewing the global tech industry through the prism of Silicon Valley: Facebook, Google, Apple, and Microsoft. From its beginnings in the early 2000s, the country had become the world's second-largest VC market by funds under management.[102] The meteoric rise of Chinese venture capital, which did not exist before the new millennium, mirrored the Chinese economy's transformation.[103]

But how did China VC get there? China did not experience a dotcom boom in the 1990s to the same extent as other countries, such as the United States. Then the Chinese economy was still in

[102] Yang (2018); Lu, Chen, and Fu (2018).
[103] Frederick and Beck, March 18, 2019.

the early transition to a market-based system. The first stock market in China, the Shanghai Stock Exchange, opened for trading in 1990. The Shenzhen Stock Exchange followed in 1991. Before July 1999, the authorities used a quota system for IPOs. The China Securities Regulatory Commission (CSRC) and the State Planning Commission (SPC) determined each year's total IPO volume. The approach favored large state-owned enterprises (SOEs) over small and medium-sized SOEs and private firms, and the quotas were allocated depending on the government's strategic focus. While this system has been modified, IPOs still need approval by the authorities, which favor state-owned enterprises. Y. Qian et al. found that IPOs in China are often underpriced due to the use of fixed-price offerings, resulting in significant first-day trading gains of 172% over the IPO offer price between 1990–2021, compared to only 17.5% in the USA. This practice has contributed to a high incidence of stock flipping in China, which is significantly greater than in other markets. Additionally, the *Harvard Business Review* reported a substantial disparity in IPO valuations between Chinese startups that went public in China versus those that went public in the USA, although this gap has been decreasing over time.[104]

Domestic IPOs have therefore been very expensive for Chinese companies and came with a lack of stability in their investor base. Startups also found it very difficult to obtain credit as the banking system favored SOEs too. Equity was overwhelmingly issued in the form of common stock. Preferred shares with reduced voting rights, stock options, and share-based compensation that are part of the US venture playbook were unknown. ARD and the small business investment companies (SBICs) in the USA reflected a concern that startup financing might get crowded out by the changes in the capital markets and institutional trusteeship of capital. While those concerns were only partly justified in the USA, in China, there was no such question. Startup financing did not exist beyond raising equity from friends and family and an informal network of debt providers that only occasionally included banks.

In the late 1990s and early 2000s, China began to develop its internet infrastructure and liberalize its telecommunications market.

---

[104] Qian, Ritter, and Shao (2022); Zhang, Zheng, and Wang (2019).

It paved the way for the growth of the internet and e-commerce industries. Many Chinese internet companies emerged in the early 2000s, such as Baidu, Alibaba, and Tencent (the "BATs") and started gaining traction in the market. But they had no pathway to obtain the funding necessary to scale up in size to address the vast domestic market or—dependent on their business model—to enter the global stage.

The change came when some international investors noticed that there was an opportunity. China Mobile's IPO on October 22, 1997, on NYSE and the Hong Kong Stock Exchange probably marked the time when international investors noticed the rapid expansion of mobile communications and the internet in China. Regional investment arms of US firms in Asia first realized the resulting investment opportunity in Chinese technology companies.[105]

Lip-Bu Tan was a managing partner at the Walden USA investment fund before founding venture capital firm Walden International in 1987, based in San Francisco and Hong Kong, which invested in Asian startups and started making investments in China during the 1990s.[106] IDG Capital, founded in Boston in 1993, is one of the earliest firms that established a base in China. Quan Zhou, a partner at IDG in Boston, relocated to China once their office was established in 1999 and invested in several successful companies, including Baidu, Xiaomi, and Tencent.[107] The private equity arm of Goldman Sachs, the Principal Investment Area, was investing $200 million in Asian technology companies and—led by Shirley Lin—invested in a range of rising stars in China and, in October 1999, led Alibaba's first round of investments by providing $5 million for a 50% stake, part of which was later syndicated and included SoftBank as an investor.[108] Hans Tung of GGV Capital (2005) was among the first Silicon Valley VCs to move to China full-time, spending eight years investing in companies like Xiaomi and Byte Dance before returning to

---

[105] China Mobile (2023).

[106] *Business Week* (2004).

[107] IDG (2023).

[108] Mallaby (2022). Jack Ma's struggles to find capital had real consequences: when Alibaba had its IPO, he owned 8.8% of the firm—he had to give up a lot of shares to secure financing. In contrast, Jeff Bezos held 16% of Amazon when it went public.

Silicon Valley in 2013. After graduating from the University of Chicago Booth School of Business, JP Gan joined Carlyle in 2000 as a director of its Asian venture fund before joining Qiming Ventures, a Chinese VC founded by Gary Riedel in 2005, where he was a managing partner for 13 years before founding INCE Capital.[109] Those early movers played a role in helping to build the foundations of the Chinese venture capital industry.

Then came the IPO of Tencent, which was listed on the Hong Kong Stock Exchange at a valuation of approximately $10.9 billion on June 16, 2004, followed in 2005 by the listing of Baidu on NASDAQ.[110] China was suddenly hot, and in 2005, Sequoia Capital China, led by Neil Shen, was established, followed by NEA (2005), Draper Fisher Jurvetson (2006), Kleiner Perkins (2007), and Matrix Partners (2008).

To a large extent, China's venture capital ecosystem was forged by American investors bringing their expertise, networks, legal structures and capital to China. Even the Chinese VCs had a US background in their education, professional training, and approach to venture capital.[111] But implementing US private equity culture in China was a complex process due to the lack of developed stock markets for tech startups. But direct foreign investment in Chinese companies was not possible, and the workaround was to incorporate holding companies as well as an operating company that had to be entirely Chinese-owned in the Cayman Islands as conduits for (indirect) investments in domestic Chinese companies. This required side agreements between offshore and domestic companies to create a synthetic equity structure. While this allowed for non-Chinese investment, NASDAQ listing, and stock-based compensation, it was tolerated but never explicitly endorsed by the Chinese authorities, which always made such investments surrounded with an air of uncertainty.[112]

---

[109] *Forbes* (2023a).

[110] Shen (2019).

[111] Mallaby (2022).

[112] In 1995, China's State Council approved the "Administrative Measures on the Establishment of Chinese Industrial Investment Funds Abroad," which in principle endorsed offshore investments, but did not address the acquisition of significant stakes in startups.

The Chinese venture capital industry has always prioritized technology investments even more than its American counterpart. The fact that the market formed after the dotcom boom, when internet access became pervasive and internet-based business models became feasible in the USA, triggered (foreign) investors' interest in funding Chinese startups once the internet really took off. VCs already knew many business models in the USA, which gave them the domain expertise that was missing in China then.[113]

Until 2010, China's private equity market was dominated by overseas (mainly US) VCs, as well as Hong Kong– and Singapore-based firms.

Constraints and impediments have always made investing in China more difficult for international VCs. Capital controls and frequently changing rules could prevent deals from closing or render local LPs unable to meet capital calls. Likewise, the repatriation of profits was sometimes put in doubt or delayed. Despite these obstacles, the opportunities to finance would-be market leaders that could replicate in China what leading tech companies did in the USA seemed too good to miss. A 1997–2018 VC fund study found that Chinese venture capital outperformed its US peers, according to eFront.

Since 2007, renminbi (RMB) funds have been authorized and gained traction among local investors. Since they were authorized in 2014, RMB funds have mostly benefited local GPs such as Hony Capital, CPE, INCE, China Merchants, and Trustbridge, which have acquired market share at the expense of foreign VCs. Often those firms were founded by Chinese partners who worked for foreign GPs either in the USA or in their China offices before they set out on their own.

With the progressive widening of permissions for domestic banks and institutions to engage in domestic private equity (mostly VC and growth finance) after 2011, state-owned banks raised RMB funds in 2012 and competed for deals. As a result, RMB funds

---

[113] Bain & Company (2020).

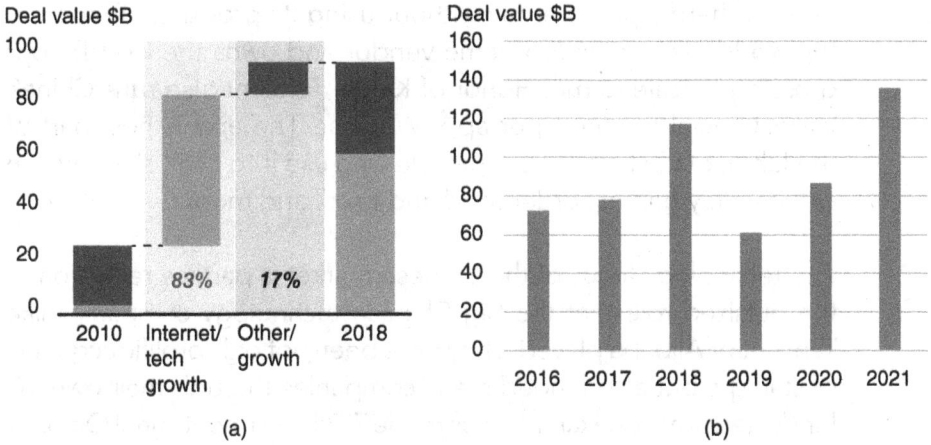

Figure 9.25 (a) Tech sector weight, 2010–2018. (b) Tech sector deal value, 2016–2021, in $B.
Source: Bain & Company, Preqin.

managed by local GPs began to dominate the Chinese VC and PE sector (Figure 9.25 (a)).[114]

Noticeably, while Silicon Valley is naturally focused on the well-known processes of "creative destruction," which include replacing established business models and changing industry structures through technological innovations, China adopts innovative technology to encourage economic catch-up and capitalize on the momentum generated by the country's fast urbanization and economic development.[115]

But the technology focus of the Chinese VC is even greater than in the USA (Figure 9.25). Depending on how the internet/tech growth is defined, one arrives at a share of 40–50% of the 2010–2018 VC deal volume in the USA compared to 80% or more in China.

Founded in 1998 by a group of investors, including Pony Ma, Tencent is arguably the most influential internet firm in China, as

---

[114]Wharton (2009). As described there, in 2011 there were 5,000 group-buying websites in operation, with competitors spending money on ever deeper discounts to attract customers in what was known as the "Groupon War." This was the Chinese equivalent of the overinvestment in disc-drive companies that accompanied the first surge in VC fundraising the US experienced during the late 1970s and early 1980s.
[115]Malkin (2021).

one can hardly go by a day without using its products. Tencent is the world's largest video game vendor and owns the world's top-grossing mobile game, Honor of Kings. Tencent also runs China's largest social media super app, WeChat. The app is now part of the fabric of life for Chinese people who use it to chat, shop, watch videos, play games, order food and taxis, and more.

The technology focus of the Chinese market is partly a reflection of the outsized role that the big Chinese technology companies like Tencent or Alibaba played. They have been not only prolific acquirers of startups but also funded many companies through their own VC funds. Tencent, for example, has made 727 investments until October 2022 and the firm is now one of the largest shareholders in leading tech companies like Meituan, JD.com, DiDi, Snap, and Baidu.

In 2015, Chinese corporate venture investment began to accelerate under a government policy of encouraging entrepreneurship and innovation. During this period, the number of corporate venture capital institutions peaked at 170. In addition, the number of startups and the investment amount also expanded significantly. Since 2016, the total investment of Chinese corporate VCs has been on a par with independent venture capital.[116]

According to Crunchbase, there were about 180 unicorns in China as of March 2022. Considering China's output of unicorns, it appears that China's technology sector generates more spinoffs than its US counterpart. This is reminiscent of the early days of Silicon Valley, which became a cluster due to the numerous spin-offs that Fairchild Semiconductor and other technology firms in the valley generated.[117]

After several years of bumper deal-making, fueled by successful IPOs such as Tencent (2004) and Baidu (2005), followed by Alibaba (2014), and Meituan (2018), the government changed course, and new regulations made it harder for banks and insurers to invest. The rampant deal-making involving financial institutions and SOEs was probably seen to be creating systemic risks. However, the changes extended beyond a mere bubble cooldown. In

---

[116] Zheng and Zhou (2022).
[117] Malkin (2021).

2015, China unveiled Made in China 2025, intending to increase its domestic component share in critical technology sectors. Foreign investment in these sectors has been either discouraged or restricted. In 2021, China implemented a new Five-Year Plan that sets forth guidance and national development goals until 2025. The plan emphasizes adopting civil-military fusion and an all-of-state approach.[118] The catchword is "disorderly expansion of capital," which describes investment activities that are not aligned with the sectors the government prioritizes.[119]

In 2017–2019, the restrictions on RMB fundraising caused a meltdown on a scale comparable to the decline in US venture capital fundraising after the burst of the dotcom bubble (Figure 9.26). Figure 9.26 (a) shows the growing significance of government-guided funds that replaced China VC RMB funds raised from

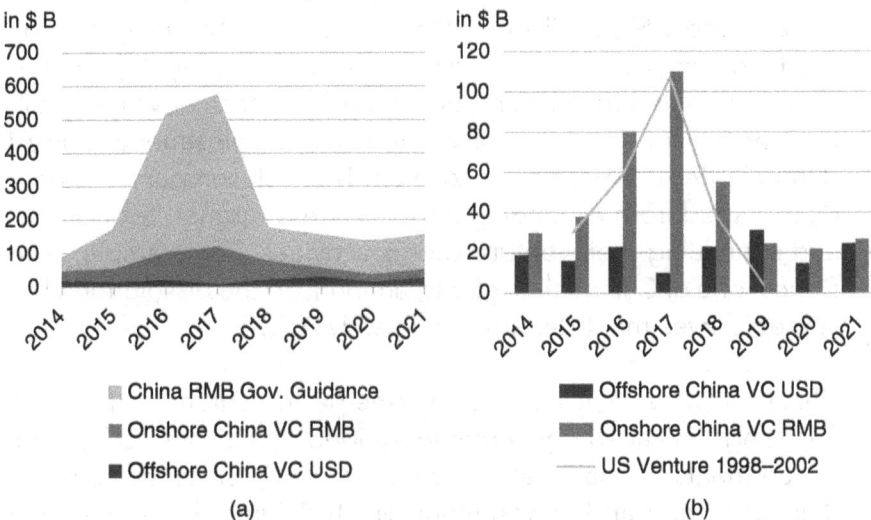

(a)

(b)

Figure 9.26   Offshore and RMB fundraising for venture capital——the onshore RMB boom and bust as on a scale of the dotcom boom and bust in the USA.

Sources: Preqin, zero2IPO Research, (*The Economist* (2022e). 1990s data from NVCA.

Note: The data on RMB funds is patchy at best and cannot be verified. As most RMB funds do not seek foreign investors and regional development funds invest as limited partners with local firms, there are no incentives to report closings or fund sizes to international data providers. The government guidance fund numbers are based on announcements that reflect an intention to commit that capital, which may be subject to change and should therefore not be interpreted as fundraising amounts.

---

[118] Ibid.
[119] *The Economist* (2021e), McBride and Chatzky (2019).

institutional investors. The rise and decline of the domestic RMB funds mirror the fundraising boom and bust of the dotcom era in the USA (Figure 9.26 (b)).

Astonishingly, this was not widely noticed in the international investment community as investment activity resumed, with venture capital investments in China hitting $135 billion in 2021.[120] However, the composition of LPs had changed significantly after 2017. State-guided funds played an increasingly dominant role while the role of SOEs as limited partners and technology companies as venture capitalists declined. The latter due to the clampdown on the large tech companies, including internet conglomerates Tencent, Meituan, Alibaba, and companies in online gaming, private tutoring, and cryptocurrency. This was the first of several high-profile actions against major tech companies. The State Administration for Market Regulation (SAMR) took aggressive steps to combat anti-competitive behavior, levying a record $2.8 billion fine on Alibaba and a $530 million fine on Meituan.[121] The crackdown on the technology sector has impacted Chinese technology enterprises and roiled markets, reducing the firms' market value by billions of dollars. The pace of venture capital investments slowed during 2019–2020 before it recovered. The tech companies appear discouraged from expanding into new areas through acquisitions and continuing their venture capital activities. For example, Byte Dance, one of China's tech giants, announced the dissolution of its strategic investment department in early 2022.[122]

China has also seen new actors emerge in venture and growth financing. So-called "government-guided" funds set up by local governments or national ministries, thrived. Since 2015, more than one thousand government-directed funds have emerged across China. China Venture, a research organization, estimates they amassed around RMB 9.4 trillion (about $1.4 trillion) by the end of 2020. They are replacing conventional domestic LPs such as government-owned enterprises, insurance firms, and banks. The government urged local authorities to form such investment

---

[120] Preqin (2022c).
[121] Liu and Leslie (2022).
[122] Zheng and Zhou (2022).

vehicles to attract entrepreneurs, talent, technology, and ultimately tax income to their areas. Due to a lack of internal investing expertise, most have served as limited partners in private-sector funds. Those government-guided funds have the dual aim to counter the dominance of the large tech firms and to pursue the government's and their regional authorities' development goals.[123]

However, little is known about state-guided funds like the Optics Valley Hi-Tech Venture Capital Guidance Fund ($1.5 billion) or the Enterprise Reform Fund ($11 billion) and the local (Chinese) GPs that may receive an allocation from those capital pools. They do not report their fundraising and deal-making data, and it is not known whether those fundraising numbers are statements of intent by the regional governments that sponsor them or irrevocable capital commitments. But the jump in private companies with state investment has accounted for nearly all of China's increase in newly registered capital. Public investments in private-sector companies surged from $9.4 billion in 2016 to $125 billion in 2020.[124]

Thus, much has changed since 2019, resulting in significant shifts across various sectors. The share of unicorns in e-commerce, fintech, and education technology has declined. In contrast, the number of unicorns in semiconductors, software, enterprise services, health tech, biotech, and AI has seen a substantial increase. These changes highlight that startups operating in government-backed sectors face fewer hurdles as the government's influence has expanded from early-stage financing to IPO.[125]

Given the size of the funds involved, there is a risk that private capital might get squeezed out. There is also a question of whether state funds are as profit-oriented as private funds or accept deal terms that prevent other VCs from participating. Shenzhen's Communist Party Secretary Wang Weizhong reportedly told investors late in 2020 that if they set up a fund in the South China tech hub, the government would bear 40% of their losses.[126]

---

[123] *The Economist* (2020b).
[124] Luong, Zachary and Murphy (2021).
[125] Ibid., *The Economist* (2023a).
[126] *The Economist* (2021a), McBride and Chatzky (2019).

Foreign VCs came under pressure from different sides:

- The Chinese government intensified scrutiny of local companies that receive foreign investment.
- The State Administration of Foreign Exchange (SAFE) passed a series of measures in 2021 that put the repatriation of profits in doubt.
- Many Chinese PE firms have sprung up over the last ten years, gaining know-how and having stronger local networks with the target firms and domestic investors.
- Many companies preferred to work with local PE firms.
- State-backed funds have access and funding advantage without sector restrictions.

Foreign VCs have responded differently to those challenges. Some VCs maintain their presence and continue to receive backing for new funds. In July 2022, Sequoia announced the closing of its latest China fund with $9 billion of committed capital. Accel Partners invests through a joint venture with local partner IDG Capital. NEA invests through its global funds and has backed local funds intending to do co-investments. As reported in the press, Kleiner Perkins has essentially wound down its China operations since 2018.[127]

When Masayoshi Son, SoftBank's founder, decided to invest in Alibaba in 2000, Dick Kramlich convinced his partners at New Enterprise Associates to invest $100 million into Semiconductor Manufacturing International (SMI) in 2003, or Ontario Teachers' Pension Plan Board participated in a $400 million private equity round of JD.com in 2012, the Chinese VC market was a different world from what it is after 2020. Despite the growing challenges for foreign VCs, there is also an opportunity for them to partner with state-guided funds by targeting government-prioritized

---

[127] Fannin (2018). In June 2023, Sequoia planned to split into three independent partnerships, with its businesses in China and India adopting new brands and the firm in the United States and Europe retaining the Sequoia name (Hirsch, 2023a).

sectors. This can help de-risk investments and potentially lead to government procurement and targeted investments for startups, accelerating their path to profitability, particularly for industries and technologies where China aims to strengthen home-grown capabilities.[128]

But new sectors may become off-limits for investors, reducing opportunities and affecting previously made investments. There is also a risk of overfunding and overfinancing in regions competing to become the next hub for industries like AI, novel materials and composites, and high-end robotics. This could potentially lower return prospects even in promising areas. But until 2021, deal-making by foreign and local Chinese venture capital firms suggested that the opportunity still outweighed the risks.[129]

The tensions between the USA and China did, however, decrease the interest of Western investors in Chinese venture capital, despite the fact that in 2021 foreign investors—both traditional VCs and non-traditional investors—were still prominent (Figure 9.27) and continued to invest their existing funds. However, President Joe Biden's executive order in August 2023, which imposes restrictions on new US investments in sensitive

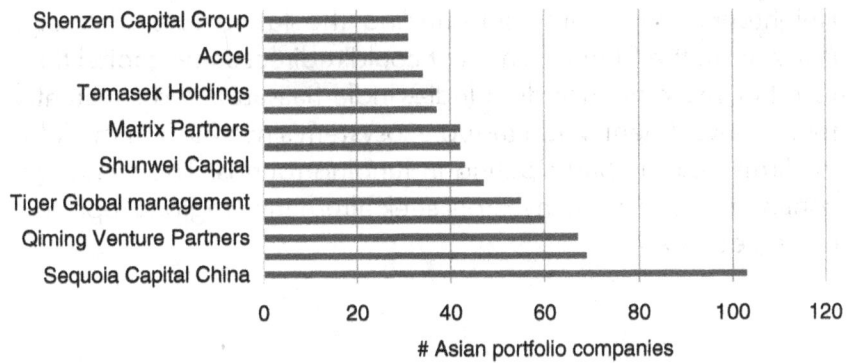

Figure 9.27   Investors' early- and late-stage portfolio counts in 2021 of Asian companies.
Source: Adapted from Metinko, 2022.

---

[128] Reference is made to the 2015 launch of "Made in China 2025" with the goal of increasing the share of domestic components in ten "core" technology sectors (Malkin, 2021).
[129] Bloomberg News (2014), Cheng (2021).

technologies, such as computer chips, and mandates government notification across other tech domains, began the process of US venture investors withdrawing from China. This noticeable trend is highlighted by Crunchbase statistics, which show that predictions for 2023 foresee US startup investors participating in new investments in Chinese startup ventures totaling less than $3 billion—representing a 70% decrease from the levels reported in 2021.[130] Additionally, restrictions on Chinese companies listing in the US could harm the exit environment for Chinese startups. As previously discussed, the Chinese IPO market was much less efficient compared to the US IPO market. Several reforms were implemented to address the Chinese stock market's shortcomings, such as the introduction of specialized stock markets like the STAR Market in 2019 and a transition from an approval-based to a register-based IPO system. The latter has streamlined the IPO approval process, providing startups a faster and more efficient way to access capital. This has led to a sharp increase in new tech IPOs during the 1H 2023. However, despite these efforts to offer more options for companies looking to go public, the Chinese stock markets still lack the depth of the NASDAQ and the Hong Kong Stock Exchange has also not yet emerged as a truly viable alternative.

Heightened uncertainty surrounding the future role of foreign investors in the China VC market could redirect some capital flows to other markets, including India. India has attracted substantial foreign investment in its startup ecosystem since 2015, with global VC firms actively participating in funding rounds. This trend may continue, especially if investors seek alternative regional opportunities (see Box 9.3).

---

[130] Romburgh and Teare (2023).

Box 9.3   India's VC Sector Steps into the Limelight

Figure 9.28   The Stock Exchange (BSE) building at Dalal Street in Mumbai.
Source: BSE India through Wikipedia CC BY-SA 3.0.

As in China, much of the Indian VC industry started taking shape post-1995, backed by foreign capital. The government limited early foreign investments regarding which sectors were open for overseas investment. Over the past two decades, however, the government has slowly relaxed sector limitations, and overseas money has flowed in from investors looking to exploit an underfunded market. From 2006 onwards, prominent US VCs such as Sequoia, Accel Partners, and Matrix Partners started raising dedicated India-focused funds.

VC investments in India started picking up pace in 2005 and accelerated from 2015 onwards, driven by a robust macroeconomic environment. Post-GFC, mobile Internet has been a significant driver of innovation in India. The number of start-ups in India has increased by more than 7x from approximately 7,000 in 2008 to almost 50,000 by the end of 2018.[131] The Bangalore and NCR (Delhi) regions, followed by Mumbai, remain

(continued)

---

[131] KPMG (2019).

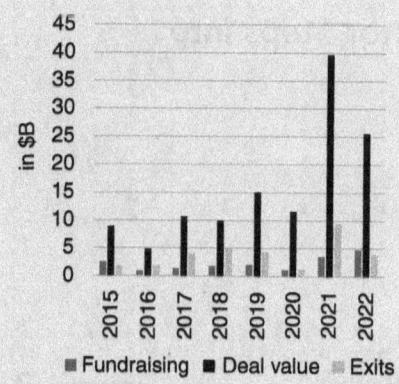

Figure 9.29 Indian VC fundraising, deals, and exits.
Source: Bain & Company, Preqin.

India's hotbeds of venture activity. In fact, Bangalore and Delhi figure among the top 20 global cities for contribution to VC investment growth (Figure 9.29).[132]

With regard to funds that have made India-dedicated investments since 2017, there are about 195 active funds. More than 65% of these funds were launched after 2014.[133] The year 2022 saw record fundraising as multiple investors raised their largest ever India-focused funds: The list includes leading global investors (e.g., Sequoia: $2 billion India-focused fund) and prominent domestic VCs (e.g., Elevation Capital: $670 million; Fireside Ventures: $225 million).[134]

VC deal volume 2015–2022 reached about $127 billion, with the share of Series A investments declining in value terms while Series B and above gained ground. This reflects the fact that the VC ecosystem is maturing, and promising startups are being funded throughout their growth journey. Further, in 2022, India continued to outpace China for the second year in a row in terms of new unicorns created, and reached 100 unicorns in mid-2022.[135]

While historically, most of the venture funds have targeted foreign institutional investors for their fundraising, the domestic LPs base has grown since 2015, with an estimated 30% of capital being raised from about 100 domestic institutional investors/LPs—mainly wealth managers and family offices.[136]

[132] Mamgain (2018).
[133] Mustafa (2019).
[134] Bain & Company (2023).
[135] Ibid.
[136] Preqin (2019).

Furthermore, India also witnessed significant involvement from government agencies and public financial institutions. As the domestic VC ecosystem expands, there has been a decline in the proportion of foreign VC deals. Instead, a notable trend has emerged where co-investment deals are rising. This shift is driven by the sector-specific expertise offered by certain Indian VC funds and the broader origination capabilities of venture capitalists dedicated to India. Foreign venture capitalists can effectively leverage these networks.

Exits from investments in India have posed challenging due to the prolonged time it takes for companies to reach the desired scale and returns. In order to go public through an IPO in India, companies must demonstrate profitability in at least three of the previous five financial years. This requirement prevents the listing of companies that have yet to achieve profitability. Additionally, the Indian IPO market has displayed volatility, with IPOs accounting for approximately 10–40% of total exits since 2015, averaging around 25% of the total exit volume. This volatility has impacted investor confidence and presented difficulties for venture capitalists seeking to exit their investments. As a result, the most commonly utilized exit mechanism by investors has been through mergers and acquisitions (M&A).[137] The lack of high-value IPOs is probably the biggest concern for LPs considering allocations to Indian venture capital.

Performance and returns data availability are challenging as the VC industry is very opaque. Based on available data on 30 funds, Mustafa suggests that the average IRR (in rupee terms) for funds of vintage years 2016–2018 was around 15%. However, one must note that this dataset is relatively small and does not provide a comprehensive basis for comparison.[138] Furthermore, it is possible that IRRs have improved since 2018 due to increasing valuations and exit amounts. Nonetheless,

(continued)

---

[137] Bain & Company (2023).
[138] Mustafa (2019).

the data does suggest that Indian venture capital performance, particularly when expressed in US dollar terms, may be lagging behind that of the United States.

Looking ahead, global investors are expected to continue to hold a favorable view on India due to the positive economic fundamentals, which will create opportunities. According to an investor survey conducted in November 2022, 45% of respondents regarded Indian venture capital as the most appealing opportunity outside of the United States and the European Union. This marks the first time that India has been rated as more attractive than China, with only 19% of respondents considering China the most appealing, a decline from 39% in 2021.[139]

9.10 GROWTH FINANCING

Growth capital, a minority investment strategy for mature companies seeking funds to expand or restructure operations, has been dominant in Asia due to relatively immature capital markets and a high proportion of founder-managed companies. Chinese firms, in particular, struggled to raise enough capital to sustain significant expansions or acquisitions to gain a leadership position in the fast-growing Chinese market. From 2000 to 2021, Asia accounted for 10–15% of global buyout fundraising, while the region's share growth capital fundraising was about 30%. Growth capital is thus the only private market asset class where Asia ranks second after the US in terms of institutional fundraising. The tech sector has fueled growth in capital fundraising and deal activity, with China emerging as a key destination for Asian growth capital (Figure 9.30). The focus on later-stage startup financing in the USA since 2015 could also be observed in Asia and explains the dominance of China as a destination for growth capital in the region.

From an investor's perspective, investing in growth financing was often the second-best proposition. Investors viewed the fact that

---

[139] Preqin (2023b).

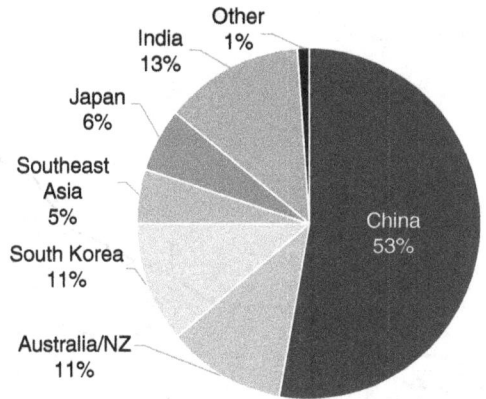

Figure 9.30   Average share of growth financing deal value, 2014–2015, in Asia.
Source: Adapted from Asia Private Equity Review.

growth financing funds often charged similar management and incentive fees as buyout funds as a disadvantage. It was considered a beta strategy as it lacked the potential operational value creation that comes with control ownership and the enhanced returns that come with the use of leverage. Therefore, LPs allocated limited capital to growth financing in regions where no vibrant buyout markets existed. The lack of buyout opportunities in the region drove Asia's traditional focus on growth financing. Accessing the potential of fast-growing Asian economies, especially China, was the motivation for the investments of overseas investors. The line between growth and other PE investment is often blurred, which can obscure fundraising nuances, especially when separating VC from growth financing.

The combination of a growing interest in China and, since 2018, opportunities in technology growth financing in the USA has increased average annual fundraising significantly (Figure 9.31 and Figure 9.32). Despite the increase after the GFC, fundraising still lagged behind other PE strategies: growth equity's annualized growth rate of 9% since 2011 trails the rest of PE's 13%.[140] In China, there was a significant drop in fundraising due to a combination of new guidelines during 2018–2019 that aimed to prevent an over-heating of the market by discouraging domestic institutions to

---

[140] McKinsey (2022), Preqin (2022c).

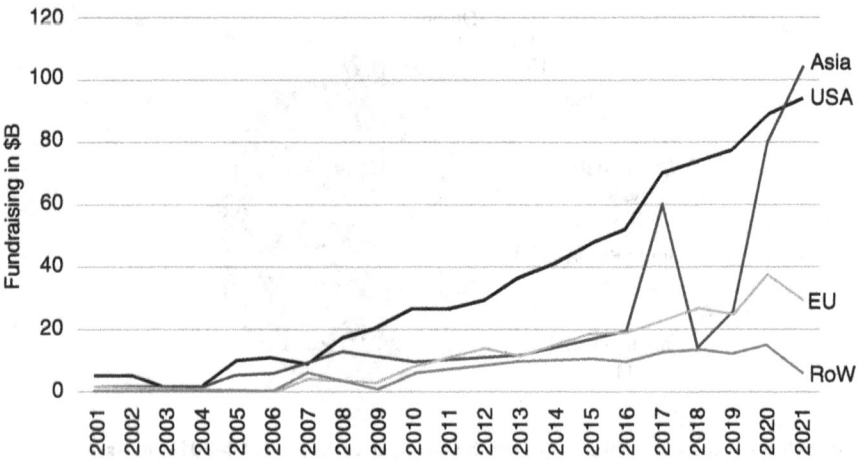

Figure 9.31   Growth equity fundraising by region of focus, $B.
Source: McKinsey & Company; data: Preqin.
Note: The observed decline of growth financing fundraising in Asia Is mainly driven by the drop of fundraising of domestic RMB funds in China that engage in technology growth financing and venture capital.

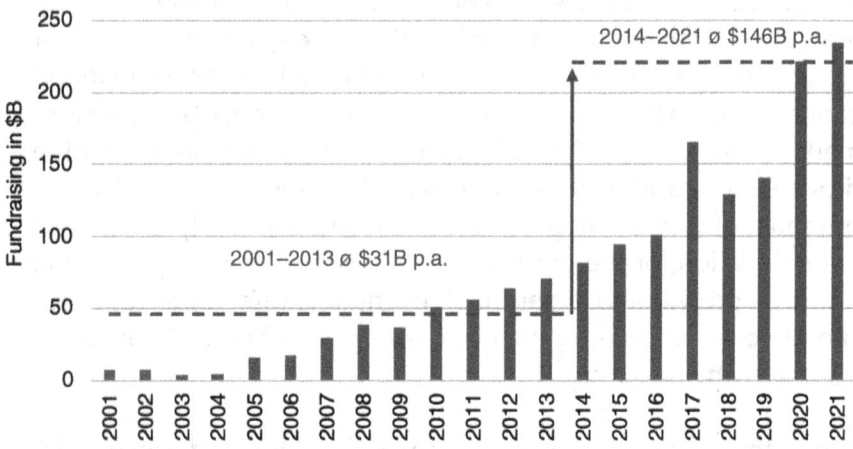

Figure 9.32   Growth equity annual fundraising, in $B.
Source: Preqin (2022c).

maintain their commitment pace to RNB funds and a shift toward state-guided funds that aim to align venture capital and growth financing with state development goals.

Growth Financing and the Technology Boom

Figure 9.33, showing growth financing fundraising trends, suggests a completeness of data that, unfortunately, does not exist.

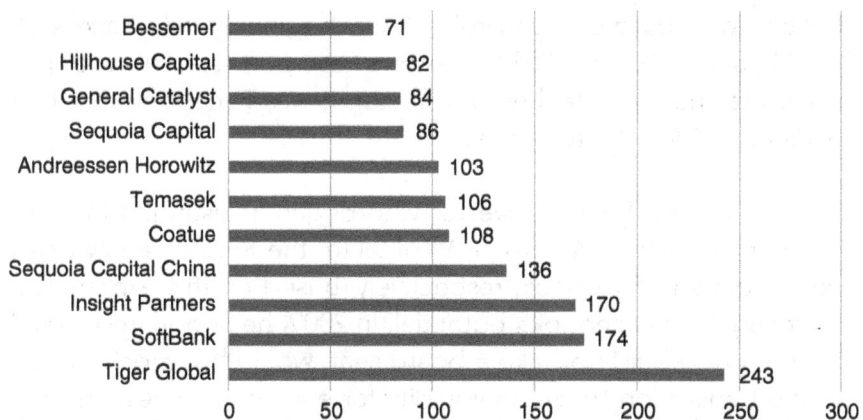

Figure 9.33   Top 15 investors by # of late-stage venture and growth investments, 2021.
Source: Bain & Company (2020); data: PitchBook.

Imagine a seven-year-old company that still likes to be called a startup, which has raised more than $1 billion in more than ten financing rounds. Is their latest round—let's make that a $300 million capital raise—a late-stage venture deal, a venture super-round, or a growth financing deal? Do the fundraising figures encompass hedge funds, state-guided funds, or the investment programs of SWFs? No, they do not. Consequently, private markets fundraising statistics are an imperfect indicator of the capital available for late-stage technology and other forms of (minority) equity investments.

The increase in deal-making and fundraising is directly related to the technology boom. The disruptive power of digital technology and super-financing rounds have pushed growth equity and late-stage venture capital to the forefront in recent years. With it came a muddle of labels that made it difficult to distinguish between growth financing and venture financing capital. In addition, the traditional providers of growth financing have been joined by a range of other investors who battle to control this burgeoning market. Participants include traditional venture capital firms and hedge funds that, as "crossover funds," invest in all stages of startups (Figure 9.33).

How do you classify actors like Tiger Global Management or the Vision Funds of SoftBank?

Following a string of high-profile IPOs, beginning with Facebook in 2012 and Alibaba in 2014, investors have pondered how to gain access to the rising technology sector. It was Facebook that had earlier provided the template.

Yuri Millner is a Russian investor who began investing in internet companies such as Yandex or VKontakte, the Russian equivalents of Google and Facebook, respectively. Based on this experience, he recognized Facebook's potential. In 2009, he negotiated a deal in which he would not take a board seat, would buy stock as part of the transaction to create liquidity for early employees, and the newly issued shares would be issued as preferred stock with a liquidation preference to protect against losses. As Mallaby stated: "In the 1970s, venture capitalists created the concept of building governance around a startup's founder. Now, Millner reversed the model. He was shielding founders from governance."[141]

However, this was only possible because investors in earlier rounds could not negotiate covenants protecting them from the issuance of shares on more favorable terms in later rounds and agreed to "super-voting" founder shares of 10 votes per share, sometimes more, for founders. Investors in further rounds also agreed to assign proxy voting rights that gave Mark Zuckerberg the irrevocable right to vote their shares.[142] Y. Millner, through his investment firm, acquired $200 million worth of company shares for a 1.96% stake, valuing Facebook at $10 billion and secondary employee stock at a lower price. In doing so, he could offer a valuation that made Facebook the most valuable unicorn at that time while paying substantially less than this valuation implies, once the secondary purchase is taken into account. The latter also eased the pressure Mark Zuckerberg might have been under to go public in order to allow key employees to monetize at least part of their stakes. He viewed this investment in a company with the ability to go public as a passive investment.[143] This marked the start of a boom in late-stage growth financing and the arrival of non-

---

[141] Mallaby (2022).

[142] VentureBeat (2023), www.venturebeat.com.

[143] Non-traditional investors charging private equity fees without actively engaging with companies is a concerning trend that could potentially lead to misaligned incentives and suboptimal outcomes for both investors and companies.

traditional investors who would play a significant role in funding private technology companies.[144]

Startups stayed longer private due to an increasing number of financing rounds with previously unheard-of sizes. This provided an opportunity for growth financing to enter the funding of technology startups and participate in those late-stage "super-rounds" that provided investors with an opportunity to increase their exposure to technology companies that were seen as disruptive while simultaneously being able to deploy meaningful amounts of capital. The opportunity for growth capital was to bridge the funding gap between venture capital and the ultimate exit via an IPO or trade sale.

Growth equity has attracted venture capitalists, buyout firms, large institutional investors, and non-traditional crossover funds (Figure 9.34). Limited partners are eager to contribute capital and co-invest in transactions, increasing the amount of capital available for late-stage financing. This trend began following the GFC and gained traction in 2018 when, by some estimates, non-traditional investors provided 30% or more of growth funding. Six of the top 10 buyout managers have formed new growth investment vehicles in the last ten years.

To compete with traditional growth funds and new entrants, venture capital firms also raised increasingly large funds that allowed them to participate in later financing rounds.

The following are some significant players in the tech-focused growth financing area:

1. **The SoftBank Vision Fund:** A venture capital fund founded in 2017 that is part of the SoftBank Group, with over $100 billion in capital. In 2019, SoftBank Vision Fund 2 was founded.

2. **Insight Partners:** The New York–based, global software investment firm closed their twelfth fund at $20 billion in capital commitments and has $80 billion AuM.

---

[144] Mallaby (2022).

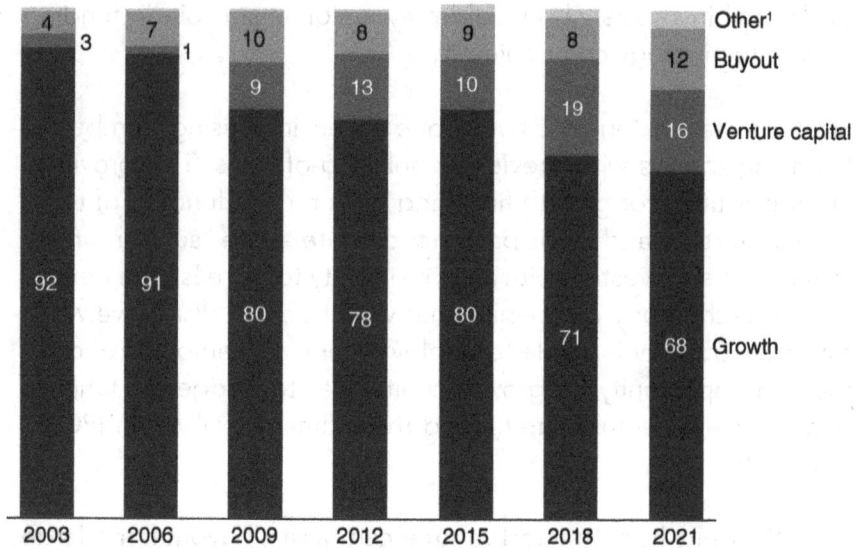

Figure 9.34   Global growth equity fundraising by manager type, 3-year trailing (%).
Source: Adapted from McKinsey, 2022; data: Preqin.
Note: [1]Other includes other PE, real estate, infrastructure, and private debt.

3. **TA Associates:** Founded in 1968, TA Associates is one of the leading global growth private equity firms. Over more than 50 years, TA has raised $47.5 billion.

4. **Summit Partners:** A global alternative investment firm that manages more than $42 billion in capital dedicated to growth equity, fixed-income, and public equity opportunities as of year-end 2021.

5. **Tiger Global Management:** A global tech-focused hedge fund that has raised $12.7 billion for its latest flagship fund (final closing early 2022) to back fast-growing technology companies with investments across all stages.[145]

6. **TPG Growth:** It has a 15-year track record of investing in earlier-stage companies, from traditional minority growth investments to growth buyouts and specialty capital. As of 2021, TPG Growth manages $15.2 billion in assets.

---

[145] Bunker and Cooper (2022).

7. **General Atlantic:** Closed its sixth flagship growth equity fund at $7.8 billion in 2021, bringing total committed capital to $23.8 billion.[146]

8. **Blackstone Growth (BXG):** Blackstone's dedicated growth equity investing platform. In March 2021, the firm announced the final close of Blackstone Growth (BXG), its inaugural growth equity fund. BXG was oversubscribed and closed at its hard cap of $4.5 billion.[147]

But investors have not yet seen results. Growth equity returns have been lower than other PE strategies over the ten years until 2021. The ten-year pooled IRR of vintage 2009–2018 was 13.6% for growth financing, while buyouts achieved a 17.1% IRR. It has to be said that the vintage years 2014–2021, when fundraising surged, may be too early to tell. Still, the performance of technology growth financing in China and the USA will determine whether the strategy can improve returns versus other PE strategies over the long run. Given that valuations have been under pressure since 2022, growth equity stands a larger chance of losing, due to the high valuation points of many investments.

[146] Growth Cap (2022).
[147] Blackstone (2021).

Chapter 10

Buyouts, Private Debt, and Real Assets During the Post-GFC Boom

While buyouts have maintained their role as a staple in institutional private market investment, a standout trend post-GFC (Global Financial Crisis) has been the rising appeal of private debt investments. Investors in private markets thus gained access to income-oriented strategies beyond conventional equity financing. Furthermore, investors increasingly embraced investments that require extended time horizons, such as infrastructure projects, necessitating longer fund lives or evergreen vehicles.

In March 2022, the *Financial Times* revealed that private debt funds held an all-time high dry powder volume, reaching approximately $400 billion.

This chapter examines how buyouts, private debt, and investments in real assets evolved after the GFC. The aim is to look at investment results, trends in deal-making and exits, as shown in the impact of new developments, such as the growing role of sustainable investing.

10.1   BUYOUTS

With the GFC came a lack of debt financing and a disconnect between buyers and sellers regarding valuations. While many potential sellers still had their valuation expectations anchored at 2007 levels, buyers were bracing themselves for further declines from the already low levels in 2008. It was hard to agree on a price and even harder to close a deal or exit a portfolio company. Despite this slowdown, cash-strapped investors still faced more capital calls than distributions—aggravating their liquidity problems.

When the markets recovered after the first quarter of 2009, the backlog of companies that were ready to exit resulted in a surge of distributions that exceeded capital calls (Figure 10.1). The same investors who were previously concerned about funding capital calls were now confronted with the reverse challenge of reaching portfolio allocations, which they would continue to increase while their portfolios shrank due to the heightened exit activity. Increasing commitment budgets and looking for additional channels to put capital to

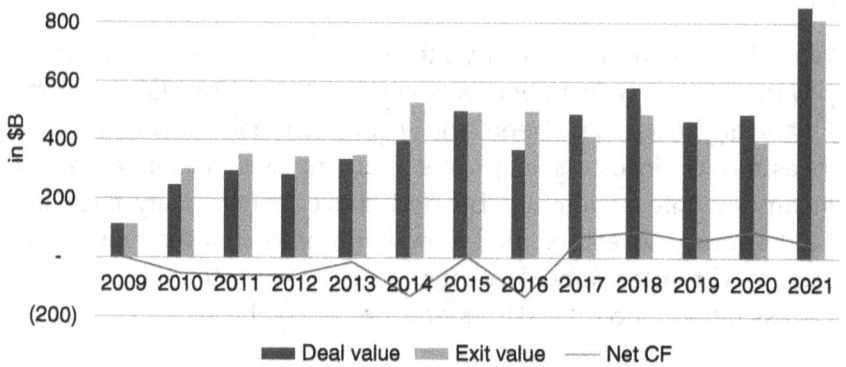

Figure 10.1   PE global deal values, exit values, and net cash flows from 2009– 2021 in $B.

Source: Adapted from Preqin.

Note: Private equity includes growth capital add-on and mergers as well as PIPE deals.

work became a defining feature of the fundraising cycle in private markets during the decade that followed the GFC.

Even in 2021 and despite record deal volumes, many investors were still under-allocated. As limited partners (LPs) continued to fall short of their allocation targets for private market asset classes as the dollar gap between actual and target allocations had widened during the boom due to a combination of increased distributions and strong public market performance.[1] Fundraising increased from $133 billion in 2009 to a peak of almost $390 billion in 2019.

After the markets turned in 2022, the gap between actual and target allocations narrowed due to the denominator effect, i.e., a decline in AuM can increase the relative allocation of illiquid or alternative investments due to their lagged valuation adjustments. But with more than $1 trillion in uninvested capital ("dry powder"), the buyout industry continues to be well positioned to seize any opportunities that a different environment may bring.

The principal beneficiaries of the fundraising boom during the second decade of the millennium have been large buyout firms (Table 10.1). Between 2010 and 2021, the top 20 fundraisers raised approximately half of all new assets (Table 10.2). Although product proliferation is a factor, the 20 firms who have raised the most money in the last decade have done it mostly by raising more and larger flagship funds. The amount of these companies' flagship funds has more than doubled during the five years until 2021, and they have raised money every three years on average.[2]

In 2021, the top 10 funds received almost $150 billion in commitments, setting a record. In both 2020 and 2021, buyout funds dominated the league table. Hellman & Friedman Capital Partners ($24 billion), Clayton, Dubilier & Rice ($16 billion), EQT (€15.5 billion), and KKR Asia ($15 billion) were among the prominent firms that raised substantial private equity funds.[3]

---

[1] McKinsey (2022).
[2] Ibid.
[3] Mendoza (2022).

Table 10.1   Largest fundraisers for private equity, 2010–Q2 2020

Name	Country	Total capital raised $ billion, 2010-2020
Blackstone	USA	143*
Carlyle Group	USA	102.7
SB Investment Advisors	USA	98.7
KKR	USA	87.8
CVC	UK	77.1
Ardian	France	72.1
Thoma Bravo	USA	53.0
SINI-IC Capital	China	52.3
TPG	USA	52.1
Apolo Global Management	USA	50.3

Source: Preqin.
Note: * Blackstone financial data suggests $143 billion instead of $115.9 billion (Preqin).

Table 10.2   Largest buyout/growth funds closed, 2020–2021

Fund	Firm	Country	Strategey	Fund size $ billion
Hellman and Friedman Capital Partners X	Hellmann & Friedman	USA	Buyouts	24.4
CVC Capital Partners Fund VIII	CVC	UK	Buyouts	23.0
EQT X	EQT	Sweden	Buyouts	18.5
Silver Lake Partners VI	Silver Lake	USA	Growth	18.3
Thoma Bravo Fund XIV	Thoma Bravo	USA	Buyouts	17.8
Clayton Dubilier & Rice Fund XI	Clayton, Dubilier & Rice	USA	Buyouts	16.0
KKR Asian Fund V	KKR	USA	Buyouts	15.0
TA XIV	TA Associates	USA	Growth	12.5
Bain Capital Fund XIII	Bain Capital	USA	Buyouts	11.8
Apax X	Apax	UK	Buyouts	11.0
Vintage Fund VII	Goldman Sachs	USA	Buyouts	10.0
Platinum Equity Partners V	Platinum Equity	USA	Buyouts	10.0
Insight Partners XI	Insight Partners	USA	Growth	9.5
Dover Street X	HarbourVest Partners	USA	Secondaries	8.1

Source: Preqin.

Approximately half of the top 20 fundraisers are large multi-asset managers. Consolidation in the buyout industry, which began in the first decade of the new century, intensified and spread to other private markets sectors, such as private lending, infrastructure, and natural resources. In contrast, the barriers to entry for newly formed managers and first-time funds increased. Their share of overall fundraising fell to single digits between 2019 and 2021. Nevertheless, the buyout sector remains tremendously diverse: an average of 260 funds were raised annually from 2019 to 2021, and even allowing for several funds raised by the same organization, it appears that there are more than 1,000 active buyout managers worldwide.

Public-to-Private Transactions

Taking companies private was driving record-breaking transactions. This has been true since the days of RJR Nabisco, and this was especially true in 2006–2007, when those transactions accounted for approximately 45% of overall yearly buyout volumes. Because of the uneven success of those transactions, as well as the substantial exposure of debt holders, investors were hesitant to support such very large acquisitions, and their share of overall buyout transaction volume remained considerably below 20% in most years since 2009. Noticing the paucity of mega-deal activity, Preqin published a research paper in 2014 entitled "Are Public-to-Private Transactions on the Way Out?"[4]

But with valuations rising, deal sizes certainly became bigger. This was felt mostly in the mid-market. In 2021 alone, the number of deals above $1 billion nearly doubled, compared to the previous year. The increase in transaction values was partly a result of the increase in the share of technology acquisitions that come with higher valuations.[5]

2021 also saw the return of the public-to-private deal. Among the 20 largest deals, 10 deals were public-to-private transactions with an aggregate volume of $73 billion, including the more than

[4] Preqin (2014).
[5] Bain & Company (2022).

Table 10.3   Largest buyout deals closed in 2021

Portfolio Company	Investment Type	Investor(s)	Location	Industry	Deal Size $ billion
Medline Industries, Inc.	Buyout	Blackstone, H&F, Carlyle Group, Abu Dhabi, GIC	US	Medical Devices & Equipment	34
Proofpoint, Inc.	Public To Private	Thoma Bravo	US	IT Security/Cybersec.	12.3
Athene Holding Ltd.	Public To Private	Apollo Global Management	US	Insurance	11
PAREXEL International Corporation	Buyout	Goldman Sachs AIMS Group, EQT	US	Biotechnology	8.5
Lumen Technologies' ILEC Business	Buyout	Apollo Global Management	US	Telecoms	7.5

Source: Preqin.

$30 billion acquisition of Medline Industries led by Blackstone, Carlyle, Hellman & Friedman, and GIC (Table 10.3 and Figure 10.2).

The fact that deals have grown larger—even though mega-deals have lost their significance since the GFC—was accompanied by increased leverage ratios, as larger transactions tend to have higher leverage.

Buyout Value Creation and Performance

In 2021, multiples for current deals were at or near record levels, mainly driven by surging asset prices in sectors such as technology. General partners (GPs) who purchased firms at these valuations had to show a strong impact in value creation to fulfill their investors' return expectations. There is, however, some doubt whether the magic is at hand. According to a Bain & Company analysis of hundreds of deals, multiple expansion and revenue growth (rather than margin expansion) are the most critical drivers of PE returns, post-2009. In recent years the revenue growth was driven mainly by acquisitions ("buy-and-build"). Through the strategic acquisition and integration of smaller businesses it was often possible to lower the overall entry valuation as smaller firms tend to trade at lower earnings multiples and to enhance the value of the PE-owned firm

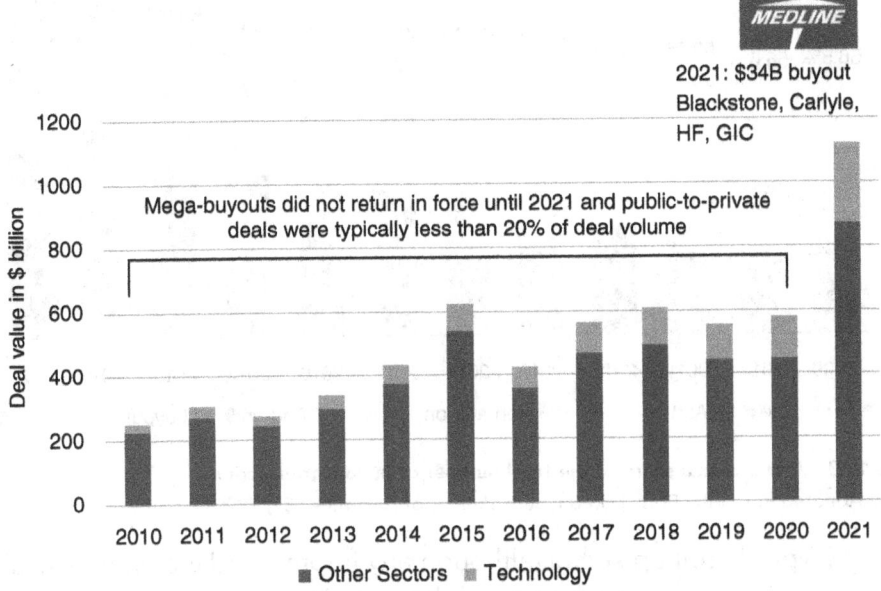

Figure 10.2 **Global buyout deal value, including add-on deals in $ billion.**
Source: Adapted from Preqin Pro; data as of October 2021.

through various means, including cost synergies, and further revenue growth.[6]

Buy-and-Build

Over the last two decades, the value of add-ons as a private equity (PE) strategy has steadily increased. Some 71.7% of US PE deals in 2020 were add-ons (Figure 10.3). Historically, GPs kept add-on platforms for a longer amount of time than other portfolio firms. However, the median exit periods for portfolio businesses with and without add-ons have converged recently. GPs appear to be more adept at adopting buy-and-build strategies and, as a result, shortened holding periods.[7] Roughly one-third of portfolio firms exited in 2020 had completed at least one add-on, and more than 5% had completed more than five acquisitions. An increasing number of these platform companies are serial acquirers, completing dozens or even hundreds of acquisitions with the assistance of a single financial sponsor. The healthcare industry, for instance, is a

[6] Bain & Company (2020).
[7] Bain & Company (2021).

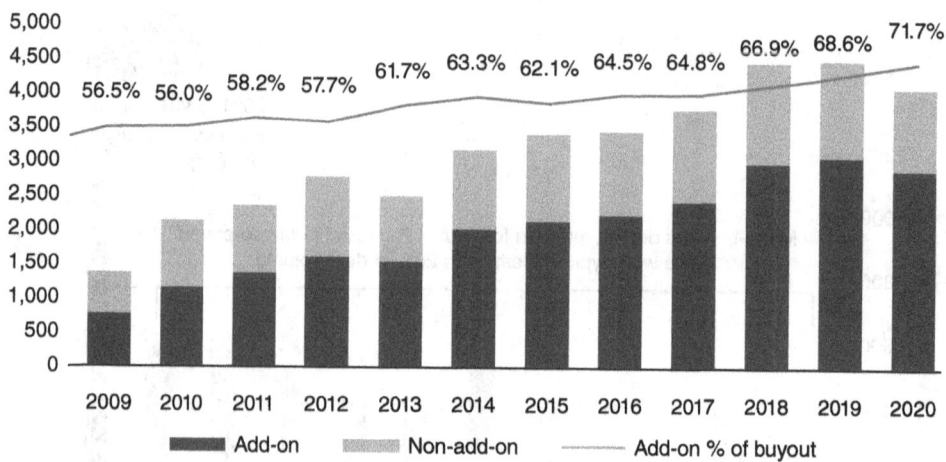

Figure 10.3   Add-ons as a share of the total number of buyout transactions.
Source: Adapted from PitchBook | US Buyouts, data as of December 31, 2020.

"typical" roll-up sector, although any fragmented industry vertical might be a target for a consolidation strategy.[8]

Operational Improvements

In an environment where multiples may stagnate or decline, and leverage become more expensive, financial engineering of value may lose significance. Will portfolio support and operational improvements increase their importance? Long gone are the days when GPs were synonymous with deal-makers and some external operating partners added to the mix. Bain Capital pioneered the systematic use of consulting resources to develop action plans for strategic repositioning or operational improvements. While GPs still retain a (growing) number of operating partners, their internal portfolio support groups have mostly gained significance. For example, Advent International, a global upper mid-market buyout firm, has 37 professionals (vice president and above) listed in this area on their homepage. Bridgepoint, a mid-market buyout firm, provides bulk purchasing, e-auction, and cost management through its subsidiary PEPCO. In 2021, Blackstone had more than 100 professionals supporting portfolio companies in procurement, centralized purchasing of healthcare plans, operations, enterprise technology, or cybersecurity, to name just a few. But these are just

---

[8] Gabbert, Bowden, and Tarhumi (2021).

internal resources that are complemented by operating partners—
often former owners or CEOs of portfolio companies, consultants,
and industry experts—who can be called upon to develop and
help execute action plans relating to a particular acquisition.

Operational support has become a significant part of PE firms'
value proposition. As a result, PE firms are increasingly organized
around industries. Investment experience in particular sectors and
internal and external resources to drive operational improvements
are differentiating factors and constitute "an edge" in deal sourcing and execution that is recognized by GPs and LPs alike. That
expertise is based on past transactions, both those that were consummated as well as those that did not materialize. Each time a
deal is looked at, information on the target company, the sector,
competitors, and clients as well as management teams is collected.
Furthermore, due diligence results in information on operating
and financial metrics, regulatory issues, technology challenges, as
well as yielding an insight into critical negotiating points during
the period between signing and closing a deal.

Value-creation strategies follow trends, such as increased acquisitions in buyouts and venture capital since 2018 or offshoring during the millennium's first decade. The changing elements of such
value creation playbooks also reflect the types of sectors and target companies that GPs focus on, which vary over time.

Operational improvements are rarely the biggest driver of final
value, they are essential when the economic outlook and financial
market conditions deteriorate, and companies need to conserve
cash to meet their debt obligations, as such operational improvements are poised to gain importance in the post-2021 environment.

Governance is also a significant driver of value generation. While
this is more difficult to quantify, it is reasonable to assume that
the alignment of owners, board members, and management can
result in superior performance compared to public companies.
The separation of ownership and control was identified in the economic literature as an important reason for the underperformance
of public versus private companies and studies suggest a significant positive impact of managerial ownership on firm performance

as reported in Ogabo et al.[9] But private companies that are not PE-owned have even less equity ownership of external board members and management than public companies. Schroeder et al. published a survey in the Harvard Law School Forum on Corporate Governance that looked at feedback from 1,100 respondents representing companies in a broad range of industries and revenue sizes on board compensation. Only 26% of private companies offer long-term incentives for directors or management.[10] This picture changes radically when one looks at private-equity owned firms. Paul Gompers and Steven Kaplan estimate that management shareholding increases by a factor of four from going public to private.[11] In a survey published in 2016, Gompers et al. found that PE firms allocate 17% of company equity to management, with the CEO typically getting 8%. Between 1993 and 2007, US-listed company CEOs held, on average, 3.6% of equity.[12]

While concentrated ownership and skin in the game seem to be a significant driver of the value creation that can be observed in PE-owned companies, this has also fueled suspicion that private equity is "hollowing out" companies at the expense of stakeholders, in particular, workers. Unsurprisingly scrutiny of private markets firms has increased with the trend toward the adoption of broader environmental, social, and governance objectives (ESG) by institutional investors.

Performance of Buyouts

Amidst a backdrop of historically low interest rates, buyout funds were well-positioned to secure financing for acquisitions and bolster their returns. Concurrently, rising valuations and active M&A markets presented lucrative exit opportunities. Burgiss data, per year-end 2021, shows that buyout funds from vintage years spanning 2009 to 2018 delivered an average annual internal rate of return (IRR) of 17%, with specific vintage years displaying performance (IRR) within a range of 11% to 28%. Within the private markets landscape, buyouts were the second best performing

[9] Ogabo, Godspower, O., and Tasha (2021).
[10] Schroeder, Masuda, and Schindler (2022).
[11] Gompers and Kaplan (2022).
[12] Gompers, Kaplan, and Muhkarlyanov (2016).

asset class after venture capital. Investors undeniably reaped the rewards of attractive returns coupled with substantial distributions.

ESG and Private Markets Investing

That companies seek long-term value creation by considering the needs of all their stakeholders and society at large is at the heart of the idea of "stakeholder capitalism," a term first used by Klaus Schwab, founder of the World Economic Forum, 50 years ago.[13] The practice of taking environmental, social, and corporate governance issues (ESG) into account when making investment decisions and to encourage companies to act responsibly began in the 1960s as socially responsible investing, with investors excluding stocks or entire industries from their portfolios based on business activities, such as tobacco production or involvement with the South African apartheid regime.

To accommodate this, private equity funds had provided investors with side letters that gave them excuse provisions, i.e., the right not to participate in deals that involved sectors or businesses that were on their exclusion list, and as the investor base grew more global and more diverse, those exclusion rights became more numerous too. But PE firms, in particular, buyout firms, were also in the spotlight as their acquisitions affect many stakeholders.[14] The debate of whether private market investments cause negative externalities and hurt stakeholders started in the 1980s during the takeover boom and lingered. Still in 2005, Franz Müntefering, then chairman of the German Social Democratic Party, accused private equity firms of destroying jobs and compared them to locusts.[15] Even more recently, in 2021, Elizabeth Warren introduced a "Stop

---

[13] Schwab and Kroos (1971).

[14] In Europe, for example, it is estimated that about 23,100 companies are private equity–owned (including venture-backed companies) that employ more than 10 million workers (Invest Europe, 2021).

[15] Müntefering (2005). It has been suggested that Müntefering's remarks referenced the acquisition of family-owned German bathroom fittings manufacturer Grohe through BC Partners in 1999, followed by a sale to TPG and the private equity group of Credit Suisse (Bayaz, 2013). The new owners were reported planning to cut up to 4,000 jobs, which caused outrage. In the end, only 850 jobs were cut and a study commissioned by the German Finance Ministry in 2009 found that PE ownership had benefited the company and created lasting value, as reported in *Die Welt* (2009).

Wall Street Looting Act" and accused the private equity industry of exploiting workers, consumers, and communities.[16]

Buyout firms have encountered headwinds from their limited partners, in particular, public pension funds, where unions have occasionally used their representation on the boards to exert pressure to preserve jobs by passing motions that would have deprived those firms of further investments. In 2010, Permira, a prominent European buyout firm, announced the closure of the Ohio-based plant of its portfolio company, Hugo Boss. It received letters from two large investors, i.e., CalPERS and the Ohio State Pension Fund (OPERS), indicating they would review future investments in Permira funds if the plant closure went ahead.[17] The plant stayed open.[18] Consumer activists and environmental organizations have also targeted private equity firms or PE-owned companies in the past. When TPG, KKR, and Goldman Sachs acquired TXU (which became Energy Future Holdings Corp.), they agreed with the Environmental Defense Fund (ED) and the Natural Resources Defense Council (NRDC) to cancel 8 of its planned 11 new Texas coal-fired power plants as well as several new coal-fired plants in Pennsylvania and Virginia to end a campaign and lawsuits of those NGOs against the company.[19]

---

[16] Warren (2021). Many commentators use the conjecture that private equity–owned companies are ill-equipped to handle an economic downturn because of heavy debt obligations, compared to public companies. While some studies suggest higher bankruptcy rates, for example, McElhaney (2019), the overwhelming evidence finds no compelling proof that job cuts or high debt ratios are the primary drivers of investment return or that leverage applied by PE firms increases the financial distress ending in bankruptcy, compared to non-buyout companies. For example, Strömberg (2008), Ranko (2011), Tykvová and Borell (2012), and Haque (2021).

[17] *Pensions & Investments* (2010).

[18] Meikle (2010). Permira fully exited Hugo Boss in 2015, resulting in a reported gain of $2.7 billion for the firm and its investors—one of their most successful transactions at the time (Bof, 2015).

[19] Global Energy Monitor (2012). The Sierra Club and the Environmental Defense Fund also launched lawsuits in 2007, 2010, and 2011 and Luminant, a subsidiary of Energy Futures Holdings, announced additional coal plant closures in 2011.

LPs and Regulators Increasingly Demand ESG Policies and Disclosure from Private Market Firms

In 2006, the United Nations launched its Principles of Responsible Investing (PRI), which require the incorporation of ESG issues into the investment process. ESG Investing (also known as "socially responsible investing," "impact investing," and "sustainable investing") started from small beginnings. In 2006, 32 asset owners signed PRI, thereafter it has grown significantly, with more than 600 signatories representing more than $120 trillion AuM in 2021.[20] According to a recent survey by ILPA and Bain, more than 50% of LPs have implemented ESG policies for their private market investments.

The narrative changed from the exclusion of some investor-specific sectors to an alignment of the investments with the broader environmental, social, and governance objectives that this group of asset owners has committed to. The PRI signatories committed to incorporating ESG into their investment decision-making process, demanding appropriate disclosure (from companies or investment managers) and promoting the acceptance of ESG objectives within the financial industry.

While ESG considerations are not yet a primary factor in fund screening, they become more important during due diligence and post-commitment monitoring. As a result, private market managers need to provide comprehensive details about how they integrate ESG into their own investment process and the reporting they provide. Enhanced disclosure rules now target institutional investors and their managers. Unlike past regulations that tried to establish rules and regulations concerning particular aspects of corporate activities (labor laws, anti-discrimination statutes, anti-bribery legislation, energy standards), the emphasis is now on nudging the capital providers to adopt ESG standards more broadly. In March 2022, the International Sustainability Standards Board (ISSB), established by the International Accounting Standards Board (IASB), introduced comprehensive global rules for sustainability disclosures for the capital markets. It launched a consultation on its proposed standards. The European Commission announced

---

[20] PRI Association (2022).

in March 2021 a new Sustainable Finance Disclosure Regulation (SFDR).[21] It will come into force by 2023. Following the lead of the Europeans, the SEC published proposals to enhance disclosures by certain investment advisors and investment companies about ESG investment practices in May 2022, "The Enhancement and Standardization of Climate-Related Disclosures for Investors." The scope of the new rules would include many private market managers and their funds.[22]

Some of the newly proposed measures are still being debated, and companies and asset managers have already expressed concerns about regulatory overreach, significant cost increases, and implementation issues. However, the trend is clearly toward more comprehensive and stringent disclosure and reporting requirements.[23] As ESG reporting requirements evolve, investors may increasingly request portfolio-level ESG data to feed into their reporting.

The private (non-profit) Sustainability Accounting Standards Board (SASB) supports the view that ESG integration is still lagging at private market firms. In 2021, SASB reported a survey of 150 private equity firms, of which 88% said they plan to increase their efforts to manage and measure ESG performance among portfolio companies over the next two years. One element slowing down this process is the concern of many GPs (46%) that by using their ESG scoring methodologies, they may be accused of greenwashing.[24] But the SASB finding also signals an intention by the vast majority of firms to move forward.

ESG Adoption Comes with Challenges but May Also Provide Investment and Business Opportunities

Private market firms may find meaningful ESG reporting challenging due to their short target holding period (four to five years), which may not be long enough to achieve measurable effects of ESG initiatives.

---

[21] KPMG (2022b).
[22] SEC (2022a).
[23] Nicodemus (2022).
[24] Cohen (2021).

PE-owned firms are also typically smaller than the average public company. Many PE-backed portfolio companies may lack the resources, expertise, or inclination to prepare sustainability reports. Smaller firms and privately held firms, in general, are also typically not rated. Private market data providers, such as Preqin, who have recently joined the ranks of ESG rating providers, might try to change that. Still, their analysis is only as good as the data they receive from portfolio companies or the funds that own them.

There are also liability aspects that can cause private market firms to proceed cautiously. The lack of external ratings requires GPs to collect and interpret information. Given that there is a general trend toward increased accountability for (financial) projections and forward-looking statements, the risk of being liable for misrepresentation increases once vaguely defined ESG criteria and assessments enter the information provided to investors or buyers of portfolio companies.

But there is a clear trend that private market managers need to provide data on the scope and outcome of their ESG initiatives to meet investor reporting and monitoring requirements as well as to demonstrate ESG adoption in their own organizations. But the trend toward ESG also comes with new possibilities. The large-scale programs recently adopted by the EU and the USA to support the transition to a low-carbon economy will also provide investment opportunities for private market funds and their investors. Private market investors can create value by investing in companies benefiting from increased environmental regulation or a shift in consumer behavior. As in the past, when an undermanaged company became a takeover, an acquisition of a company "to clean up its act" might become a new chapter in the value creation playbook. This has already been done at firms like Carlyle, which has also led an effort to establish a GP-LP initiative to standardize ESG reporting in private markets.[25]

While ESG adoption may be necessary to maintain LP support, launching ESG-themed funds, especially impact funds, can also broaden a GP's product offerings. In 2016, TPG, Bono, and Jeff Skoll

---

[25] Carlyle/CalPERS (2021).

launched the Rise Impact Fund. As of year-end 2021, the Rise Impact Fund and its successor had an AuM of $14 billion.[26] Bain Capital followed suit, launching its own Double Impact Fund at $360 million in 2017, followed by a successor fund of $800 million in 2021. During that year, about $16 billion in impact funds were raised in total, including KKR's $1.3 billion impact fund.[27]

But major private equity firms have also recognized the growing ESG controversy as a potential threat to their fundraising and profitability. The divergent views on ESG increase the risk of negative perceptions by some stakeholders, which could harm the reputation and business of asset managers. This development has important implications for sustainable investing and could impact the bottom line of private equity firms in the years to come.[28] Conflicts, both real and perceived, and disagreements may arise. As ESG becomes increasingly important to investors and new regulations and reporting standards are implemented, the debate around ESG is expected to persist.

10.2   THE GFC AS A CATALYST FOR PRIVATE DEBT

Except for venture capital,[29] the majority of private market investments are executed with a combination of equity and debt. Debt financing—both the structuring of debt and the overall size of the debt package—are crucial determinants of transaction value and, therefore, can be the difference between closing a deal and losing it to a rival buyer. The debt market is cyclical, with periods of abundant low-cost debt followed by periods of expensive, difficult-to-obtain debt. This directly impacts the number and volume of transactions that can be executed. Since the development of the high-yield bond market in the 1980s, private market firms have had a choice between public debt and private loans to finance

---

[26] TPG (2022).

[27] Kreutzer (2020), Businesswire (2020).

[28] Temple-West and Masters (2023), *Wall Street Journal* (2022b).

[29] In recent years private debt rounds have become more numerous in later-stage financing rounds. Nevertheless, Preqin puts the AuM of venture capital private debt at only 1.8% of total private debt AuM (Preqin, 2022e).

acquisitions. The different forms of debt that can be placed with different types of investors increase the availability of capital to execute transactions.

Traditionally, private debt refers to loans that are not listed or traded in public markets. But private debt is also a term used to describe a specific private market investment strategy that raises capital through limited partnerships from LPs to provide debt financing to leveraged buyouts and other private market strategies.

In this section, an overview of the different debt instruments will be provided as well as the factors that influence the capital structure that GPs opt for at the time of investment. Thereafter, the evolution of private debt as an asset class of private markets will be described.

Types of Debt Instruments

Debt is a liability that must be repaid with interest on a predetermined schedule or by a specified maturity date. A holder of corporate debt has no voting rights and does not participate in a company's growth or profits other than receiving principal and interest. However, debt holders are placed above equity investors in the capital structure as their claims have precedence. Claims of debt holders may be secured by property, equipment, or, more generally, the cash flow of the company. A significant benefit for corporate issuers is the tax shield, which refers to the tax deductibility of interest payments. Additionally, the issuance of debt does not dilute shareholders' equity. Restrictive covenants in loan agreements that limit the freedom of a company's owners or management to engage in M&A transactions, sell an asset, or in some cases pay dividends are disadvantages of debt from the issuer's perspective.

Debt instruments traded in public markets are public debt, including commercial paper, medium-term notes, and corporate bonds. The advantage of issuing public debt is the depth of the markets, the liquidity, and the broad investor base. But to issue public debt, companies need a credit rating, must meet disclosure and reporting requirements, and follow regulatory standards that govern the offering of debt to the public. As a result, public debt issuance can be pretty expensive, and public markets cannot be accessed by companies with no credit ratings or those seeking to raise smaller amounts of debt.[30]

The private debt markets refer to loans that are not sold and traded in public markets. The most common forms of private debt are bank loans and other debt instruments distributed through private placements. There are fewer restrictions on private debt compared to public debt, which results in lower issuance costs and allows for flexible structures, limited disclosure, and no rating requirement.

Within private market investing, private debt is most significant for mid-market buyouts. The leverage sought to do such transactions is predominantly raised through private loans (Figure 10.4).

The US leveraged buyout (LBO) market had been very buoyant in the years leading to 2021. The total of outstanding leveraged

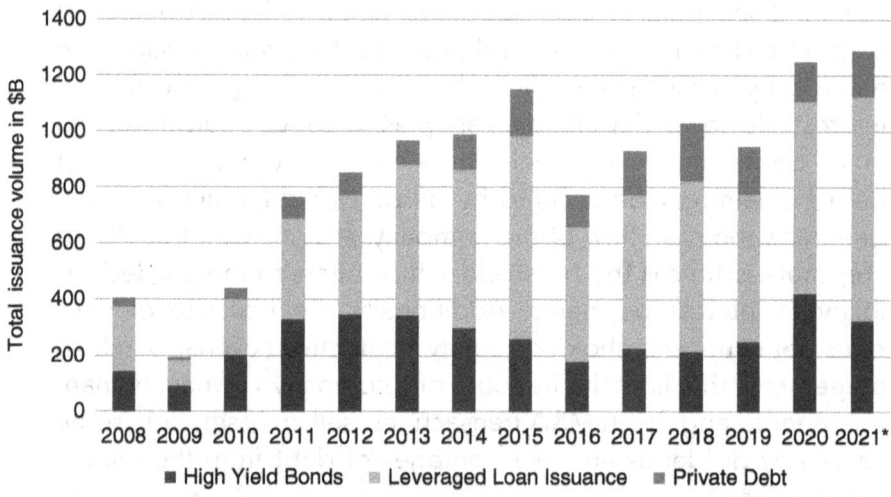

Figure 10.4   US high yield bond, leveraged loan, and private debt issuance, 2008–2021.*
Source: S&P LCD, private debt data Preqin.
Note: * Data as of Q3/2021. *PIK refers to: Payment-in-kind, i.e., a financial instrument that pays interest to investors of bonds or notes with additional securities or equity.

---

[30] Ippolito (2020).

loans is estimated at just under $2 trillion. Of the outstanding loans, $1.3 trillion is held by institutional investors.[31]

The leveraged loan market is the principal source of debt financing for acquisitions. Leveraged loans are arranged by banks that will then syndicate them to investors. A lead bank arranges leveraged loans. Lead banks may act as sole lenders, syndicate the loan by selling parts of the loan to other lenders, or act with other banks in a group of participating lenders. Most leveraged loans are issued as senior loans, which are first in line in the case of default. Senior loans are issued with floating rates at a spread over LIBOR or the Secured Overnight Financing Rate (SOFR), which replaced LIBOR in 2022. Senior loans typically have several covenants that ensure that cash flow is sufficient to cover interest and principal repayments.

Another type of senior loan is an asset-backed loan secured by a specific asset, for example, real estate. Potential losses are tied to the value of collateral asset-backed loans with few covenants, as the focus is on the asset value of the collateral. As leveraged transactions usually involve the assumption of debt already on a target company's balance sheet, asset-backed loans are often part of the overall debt structure. The fact that specific assets may be pledged to specific loans implies a change in the pecking order concerning those assets, even among senior loan holders, which must be reflected in the loan agreement. Likewise, second-lien debt is issued as part of the senior loan tranche but ranks below first-lien senior loans.

Senior loan packages are arranged by banks who act as principal lenders for about 15–25% of the total loan volume. This reflects underwriting restrictions imposed by the FED and later by the European Central Bank of 6x EBITDA. The bank-held tranche includes amortizing term loans and revolving credit facilities. The latter are used to fund working capital requirements. The amortization of term loans and the monitoring of credit lines require systems and infrastructure that other types of investors do not necessarily possess. The remaining 75–85% of a senior loan package are sold

---

[31] *The Economist* (2022d).

as an institutional tranche to insurance companies, hedge funds, and collateralized loan obligation (CLO) or collateralized debt obligation (CDO) managers.[32] The global CLO market reached $1 trillion in size in 2021, split roughly between 80% US and 20% European CLOs.[33] Each CLO is structured as a series of "tranches," or groups of interest-paying bonds, including a significant portion that is rated investment grade—capturing demand from investors that require investment grade loans—along with small pieces of more risky debt and even equity. The term bank loans require amortization while the institutional tranche usually consists of bullet maturities but allows for pre-payment. Leveraged loans can be traded, which is important for banks and CLO or CDO managers who need to be able to adjust their portfolios.

The next layer of the capital structure is subordinated debt, which is typically unsecured. There are different categories of junior debt, and unlike senior debt, which is governed by one credit agreement, junior debt has a separate loan agreement for each issuance. For most large private equity transactions, junior debt takes the form of high-yield bonds, i.e., a public debt instrument (Table 10.4).

Since the days of Michael Milken, high-yield bonds and syndicated leveraged loans have been major forms of acquisition debt. Companies with no (or a very low) credit rating, either because of challenges in their business or because they were highly leveraged, would turn to the high-yield market to issue bonds. As of year-end 2021, the high-yield bond market volume was about $3 trillion—not all related to leveraged buyouts. High-yield bonds are typically used for large multibillion-dollar transactions, and new issuance volume in the USA reached $483 billion in 2021.[34]

---

[32] Data on the relative importance of different types of debt for large LBOs and mid-sized LBOs has been presented in Gompers and Kaplan (2022). A CLO or CDO manager ("collateralized loan obligation" refers specifically to corporate syndicated loans whereas "collateralized debt obligations" can include mortgages or any other type of asset) creates an asset-backed capital structure of tranches with varying risk and return expectations. The CLO manager raises capital from investors to purchase loans, which are then re-packed to represent different credit risks and resold. By doing so, 60% or more are rated as investment grade.

[33] Van Schie (2021).

[34] Columbia Threadneedle (2022).

Table 10.4   Characteristics of private debt, high yield bonds, and leveraged loans

Characteristic	Leveraged Loans			Subordinated Debt	
Instrument	Bank term loan & revolving credit facility	Institutional term loan	Asset-backed loans	Junior debt, Mezzanine	High-yield Bonds (public securities)
Ranking	Senior (first-lien)	Senior (first-lien), sometimes additional second-lien tranche	Senior secured by collateral	Subordinated, unsecured	High-yield debt may be secured by collateral or have other forms of protection
Coupon structure	Floating (Libor/SOFR + x%)			Mainly floating (Libor/SOFR + x%), US mezzanine often fixed rate, cash pay plus PIK*	Fixed rate
Prepayment option	Yes, usually no penalty			3 year non-call rules, thereafter with penalties for the borrower	3-5 year non-call rules, thereafter with penalties for the borrower
Investors	Banks and then syndicated (off-balance sheet)	Institutional investors	Asset-backed lenders, banks	Private debt funds, mezzanine funds, institutional investors	Institutional investors
Liquidity	Low to moderate	Moderate	Low	Low	Moderate
Term	5-7 years (amortizing)	7-8 years (bullet)	5-7 years (bullet)	6-8 years (bullet)	8-10 Years (bullet)
Covenants	Maintenance covenants, both positive and negative		Few covenants, mainly to restrict asset sales	Maintenance covenants, both positive and negative	Few covenants, mainly incurrence
Sources of return	Libor/SOFR +x%, arrangment fee			Libor/SOFR +x%, arrangement fee, warrants	Fixed coupon, market value
Warrants	No			Mezzanine yes	No

Source: Ippolito (2020) with modifications by the author.
Note: *PIK refers to: Payment-in-kind, i.e., a financial instrument that pays interest to investors of bonds or notes with additional securities or equity.

High-yield bonds are significant for US deals while the high-yield bond markets in Europe, and Asia are rather small. Covenants are less effective because companies cannot disclose private information to the dispersed holders of high-yield bonds. Usually, they come only in the form of incurrence covenants that limit specific actions such as a merger or acquisition (M&A) or issuance of new debt. High-yield bonds come with longer maturities—typically eight to ten years—and have no or deferred pre-payment options. Highyield bonds also have a fixed rather than floating rate coupon.[35]

Mezzanine financing also ranks as junior debt and is a hybrid product due to the use of warrants that give investors some upside value of a company. Interest can be paid in cash or as payment-in-kind (PIK), where it is added to the principal value of the loan. Investors could thus hold a non-cash interest-bearing instrument with warrants that make it not only the riskiest debt instrument in the debt portion of the capital structure but also ties their returns significantly to the company's growth in value. Mezzanine, typically unsecured and subordinated, is intended to bridge the gap between senior debt and equity. Mezzanine is a type of patient capital that allows businesses to grow with a lower coupon burden. It is frequently used in LBO deals. Mezzanine is typically longer dated than direct lending and structured to include a fixed-rate coupon (in some cases, floating), payment-in-kind, and warrants. These loans are also commonly not amortized over the life of the debt and thus have a longer duration than senior notes and offer no protection against interest increases. Mezzanine and distressed debt were traditionally a mainstay of private debt investing, and both strategies target downturns in the debt cycle. In 2009, for example, mezzanine accounted for almost 70% of all private debt deals by value. Post-GFC, its share shrank to less than 10% of private debt deal volume during 2019–2021.[36]

Unitranche debt is flexible financing typically used to fund mid-sized buyouts and acquisitions. Unitranche financing uses a hybrid loan structure that combines senior and subordinated debt in one debt instrument. The borrower of this type of loan pays a blended

---

[35]Ippolito (2020).
[36]Preqin (2022b).

interest rate that falls between the rate of the senior debt and sub-ordinated debt. Unitranche loans have only one set of documents between the borrower and the lenders, who enter into an "Agreement Among Lenders" between themselves. They are useful when existing debt packages have to be refinanced and allow the lender to bypass the banking market and lend directly to existing borrowers under a single umbrella facility. If the deal requires a haircut on existing debt, a unitranche offer not only mitigates what might become a costly and protracted recovery but also reduces refinancing and advisory fees, which adds to its appeal.

Factors Driving the Capital Structure of Leveraged Transactions

High leverage is often described as a disciplinary factor that increases pressure on management to improve free cash flow and avoid wasteful spending while simultaneously providing a tax advantage due to the tax shield of interest payments.[37] Those benefits have to be balanced against the heightened risk of default resulting from high leverage if the company faces a decline in earnings. As the market for corporate acquisitions is highly competitive, one can assume that GPs take as much debt as they can get to fund a transaction, which is confirmed in survey results. Gompers and Kaplan (2022) report that more than 65% of GPs stated that they use as much debt as the market might allow. The authors also analyzed LBO data from 2000–2019 and found that in most years equity is about 35% of capital provided.[38] However, it is important to recognize that the amount of leverage employed in private equity deals can vary, based on the sector, the business cycle, and prevailing conditions in the debt market. Understanding that leverage is not a fixed constant in absolute terms or as a multiple of earnings is crucial. Debt can be repaid, restructured, and typically decreases during the holding period of a private equity deal; the level of leverage changes accordingly.

---

[37] For a discussion of research into the effect of higher leverage on corporations, see Kaplan and Gompers (2022).

[38] For a discussion of the trade-off theory that stipulates that industry factors play a primary role in leverage decisions and the market time theory that assumes that overall debt market conditions are the primary driver, see Kaplan and Gompers (2022). Their book also contained information on capital structures for LBOs 2000–2019 that is quoted earlier.

If a transaction is somewhat exclusive, a general partner may tend to be more conservative than the market in using leverage. This is because the GP can offer a lower valuation compared to the outcome of a competitive bidding process. This applies to only a small number of the leveraged transactions closed each year and is more likely to occur for smaller transactions.

The decisions on the capital structure are focused on the overall amount of debt and the composition of the debt package.

The acquisition in 2006 of Hospital Corporation of America, Inc. (HCA) by a consortium of private equity firms led by Bain Capital Partners was the largest LBO of a hospital chain in terms of revenue at the time. The private equity investors put up about $4 billion in equity plus $1 billion in rollover equity, i.e., sales proceeds that were reinvested by HCA's founding Frist family retaining a stake. The remaining 80 percent (approximately $20 billion, including revolving credit facilities) of the purchase price were funded with debt. (Appelbaum and Batt, 2020). Table 10.5 shows the capital structure after the acquisition. The private equity investors considered HCA undervalued because Investors mis-priced HCA for two main reasons: too much focus on quarterly revenue and admissions volatility and the not-yet visible impact of investments in system-wide tools and technology to drive growth and margin improvements (Bain Capital, 2023). The capital structure reflects the ready availability of debt at the time that allowed the buyers to fund the transaction, mostly with longer-dated (and partly low fixed-rate) senior debt with a high leverage ratio. The physical assets (hospitals) were used to obtain asset-backed loans. In 2011, HCA went public again, and the investment was reported to have made a 4x return for the private equity firms (Primack, 2011).

If a buyout's value creation includes significant asset disposals early, a higher level of debt can be justified. Using a revolving credit facility or a short-term financing facility can also play a more prominent role, as de-leveraging is expected to occur rapidly. Value creation strategies that focus on new market entries, new product roll-outs, and other initiatives that take time to implement require a more sustainable debt package. When quick de-leveraging is not viable, there is a risk that debt may have to be carried on the balance sheet for longer than expected. Depending on where the debt

Table 10.5 Example of the capital structure of a large buyout (HCA 2006)

Sources of funds:	$M	Uses of Funds	$M
Senior Secured Credit Facilities		Equity Purchase Price	20214
Asset Based Revolving Credit Facility	1730	Rollover Equity	1065
Revolving Credit Facility	188	Repayment of existing Indebtness	3714
Term Loan A Facility	2750	Retained existing Secured Indebtness	230
Term Loan B Facility	8800	Retained existing Unecured Indebtness	7473
New Notes	1250	Transaction Costs	776
European Term Loan Facility (non-amortizing)	5700		
Retained existing Secured Indebtness	230		
Retained existing Unsecured Indebtness	7473		
Equity	3901		
Rollover Equity	1065		
Dividend	365		
Total Sources of Funds	33452	Total Use of Funds	13258

Source: Warburg Pincus, Ruediger Stucke.

Note: Secured credit facilities describe loans that are asset-backed or otherwise collateralized. Unsecured indebtedness may either be senior or subordinated. Rollover equity describes the reinvestment of some of the sales proceeds into the deal as may be the case for incumbent management who held shares in the company prior to its sale but reinvest in the deal.

cycle is when a transaction closes, this may favor the issuance of high-yield bonds that come with fixed coupons and longer maturities and thus help to defer debt repayment and the impact of rising interest rates on debt serving.

Value creation strategies that focus on serial acquisitions require additional debt at future times. Therefore, part of the debt financing would be in the form of "delayed draw" acquisition financing.

The capital structure of leveraged transactions is also impacted by local rules and regulations. While tax shields are standard in many countries, the rules allowing for loss carry-forwards are very different. The US Tax Cuts and Jobs Act (TCJA), passed in 2018, removed the 2-year carryback provision, extended the 20-year carry-forward provision indefinitely, and limited carry-forwards to 80% of net income in any future year.[39] In France, the 2019 Finance Act limited the deduction of financial expenses to EUR 3 million or a maximum of 30% of the adjusted taxable earnings before

---

[39] Tuovila (2020).

interest and taxes, depreciation and amortization (EBITDA).[40] Limiting tax loss carry-forwards dissuades investors from assuming leverage that causes interest expenses to exceed net earnings as the tax shield is reduced. This can exacerbate reductions in leverage ratios as a reaction to interest rates rises.

Differences in bankruptcy laws, tax regulations, and the regulatory environment of the financial market have led to variations in private market debt financing, depending on the country where the transaction took place and whether a domestic or international buyer invested. Comparing Europe to the United States, one must also take note of the traditional significance of local commercial banks, which results in a more significant role for bank loans in European LBO financing.

Finally, as previously mentioned, the capital structure of leveraged transactions is not static. The capital structure of buyouts and other private market financing evolves, reflecting transaction-specific dynamics during the holding period and the debt market cycle. Financial engineering aims to repay debt during the holding period in order to create equity value. Comparisons of leverage at the time of a transaction with, for example, the average leverage of an S&P 500 company are misleading as they ignore sector-specific aspects as well as variations of the level and structure of LBO debt over time.

In 2009, for example, some transactions were done as "equity-only" as there was no debt available, and those deals were subsequently refinanced when the debt market was receptive again. In contrast, frothy debt markets may require GPs to use large amounts of leverage that compel them to look for transactions that allow for a quick reduction in debt to de-risk the transactions. In 2021, many existing deals were re-leveraged as GPs thought to de-risk by returning equity to their LPs and to lock in low interest rates.[41]

Table 10.5 gives an example of the debt structure of a large buyout at acquisition. Some of the loan facilities may have different

---

[40] PwC (2022b).
[41] Bain & Company (2022).

components with terms targeted at different investors. Part of the financing may be re-invested equity ("rollover equity") from sellers including management. Assembling and structuring these debt packages are a major element of any buyout.

Private Debt as an Asset Class

Before the financial crisis, distressed debt and mezzanine financing dominated private lending. Since the 1980s, such mezzanine or distressed debt funds have existed and were (usually a small) part of the private equity allocation due to their equity-type risk profile. This was private debt as an asset class where GPs raised funds (limited partnerships) from institutional investors. Historically, such private debt partnerships played a marginal role in terms of the overall debt volumes used for private market transactions. Compared to the high-yield bond market and the leveraged loan market, it was a specialized investment strategy that targeted riskier transactions and much smaller issuance volumes. Investors saw the strategy as more of an opportunistic add-on to capture distressed opportunities rather than a staple in their portfolio allocations.

Initially, the GFC provided just such an opportunity. The banking sector saw a massive wave of consolidation with stronger banks acquiring weaker ones. In the USA, the Federal Deposit Insurance Corporation (FDIC) nudged relatively healthy regional banks to clean up their impaired (property) loan balance sheets before making acquisitions. This presented an opportunity for funds to partner with the banks to acquire these portfolios through joint-venture arrangements or to acquire loan portfolios directly.

As in prior cycles, Europe lagged behind the United States—this time by as much as two years. Three and a half years after the crisis began, European banks were still engaged in "extend and pretend" related to the performance of their loans. Although slow in coming, sizable opportunities for funds to acquire non-performing loans from European banks were available for years to come. Many European financial institutions—primarily UK, Irish, German, and Spanish banks—held large portfolios of distressed commercial real estate loans and foreclosed assets on their balance sheets. In total, CB Richard Ellis (CBRE) estimated that some €970 billion in commercial real estate loans were outstanding across Europe, 60% of which are held by UK and German banks. For example, in December 2011, Lone Star Real Estate Fund II acquired a £900 million loan book from UK Lloyds Banking Group. In December 2011, NAMA—a "bad bank" created by the Irish Government to take over property loans from Irish banks—sold a €600 million nominally valued loan portfolio to Orion Capital for €326 million, reflecting a 46% discount.[42]

Beyond the distressed opportunities in the aftermath of the GFC, there were more lasting changes underway that impacted private debt: as banking regulations have become more stringent, there has been a notable shift in corporate lending away from traditional banks. Nonbank intermediaries, such as private debt (PD) funds and collateralized loan obligation funds (CLOs), have emerged as significant players in filling this lending gap. These alternative sources of financing have stepped in to provide corporate loans and bridge the void left by the banking sector's retreat from the small and mid-market lending area following the GFC. Between 2010 and 2020, the share of banks in the lending market for small and mid-sized businesses in the United States decreased from approximately 30% to 20% (Figure 10.5).

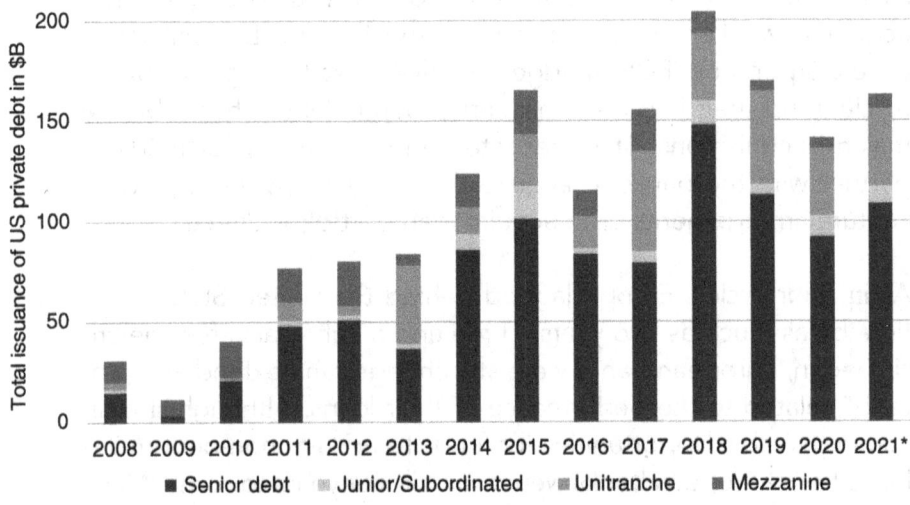

Figure 10.5 Aggregate value of US private debt deals by investment type p.a., 2008–2021.*
Source: Adapted from Preqin Pro data as of June 2021.
Note: * Data for 2021 until Q3 2021.

---

[42] Douvas (2012).

In Europe, a similar trend could be observed. After European banks reduced non-performing real estate loan lending volumes and wrote down such loans due to accounting changes, private debt funds were able to acquire them at discounted valuations. Investors were eager to provide the capital needed to invest in the growing opportunity set for private debt, particularly insurance companies searching for higher yields. Private debt promised similar returns to private equity but with a lower capital charge under Solvency II regulations. Private debt also generated cash flow, which was especially attractive in a low bond yield environment.[43]

Fundraising

Emerging from the GFC, private debt funds—after initially focusing on the distressed and mezzanine opportunities that came with the crisis—found a market meeting the demands of private market firms for senior debt acquisition finance for mid-sized transactions, as banks mainly abandoned this segment. By offering investors a fixed-income alternative that beat public debt yields, private debt repositioned itself from a niche strategy focused on the riskier tranches of the capital stack to a "core" strategy that provided an alternative to bond investments. The low-interest rate environment and the scramble for yield provided the catalyst for a surge in direct lending through private debt funds with an emphasis on lower-risk senior debt.

Fundraising accelerated steadily after the GFC and private debt became one of the fastest-growing private market asset classes. According to Moody's, the global market for private loans more than doubled in size between 2015 and 2021 and is now worth at least $1 trillion—comparable in new loan volume to the US LBO market.[44]

This development happened in the USA and Europe almost simultaneously, but the USA accounts for the majority of deal volume and funds raised (Figure 10.6), and US firms also played

[43] *The Economist* (2022d).
[44] Langton (2022).

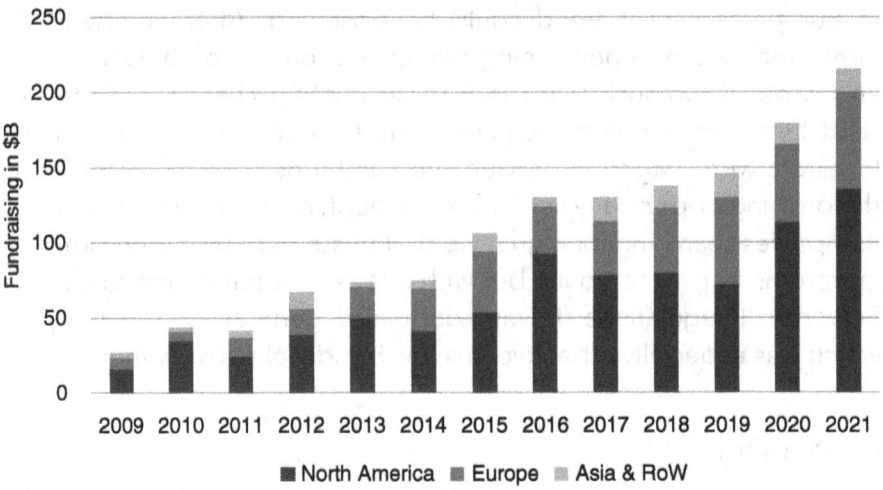

Figure 10.6   Fundraising of private debt funds by geography, 2009–2021.
Source: Adapted from Preqin Pro data as of June 2022.

an important role in the European private debt market.[45] The US share was around 77%, followed by Europe with about 17% of total deal volume.[46] Private debt is funded and held by limited partnerships until maturity. This is different from leveraged loans (LBO loans), which are syndicated. Those loans are also traded in the secondary market, which is usually not the case with other forms of private debt.

Fundraising for private debt funds is highly concentrated. Over the past decade, Ares has led its peers in private debt capital fundraising with $59.9 billion in capital commitments across 25 funds. Goldman Sachs ($47.1 billion) and Blackstone ($44.9 billion) are also among the top managers in the asset class by capital raised (see Table 10.6). The largest 10 funds accounted for 30–40% of total fundraising in most years since 2011 and the top 20 funds sometimes accounted for more than 60% of the total.[47] Overall, US firms dominate the private debt market by the size of their AuM.[48]

---

[45] Ares, for example, established its first European office in London in 2008 and established itself as among the key players in European private debt financing under the leadership of Blair Jacobson.
[46] Ippolito (2020).
[47] Preqin (2023c).
[48] Ibid.

Table 10.6   Largest private debt managers by aggregate capital raised 2011–2021, $B

Firm	Headquarters	Total Capital raised 2011–2021 ($B)
Ares Management	Los Angeles, USA	59.9
Goldman Sachs Asset Management	New York, USA	47.1
Blackstone Group	New York, USA	44.9
HPS Investment Partners	New York, USA	42.8
Oaktree Capital Management	Los Angeles, USA	32.4
ICG	London, UK	29.3
Fortress Investment Group	New York, USA	24.7
Cerberus Capital Management	New York, USA	21.4
Apollo Global Management	New York, USA	21.3
Hayfin Capital Management	London, UK	18.1

Source: (Preqin, 2022e).

The concentration of fundraising reflects investors' objective to deploy larger amounts of capital and a perception that senior lending requires less manager diversification than riskier equity-type strategies. The private debt space is also characterized by the prevalence of SMAs as an alternative to commitments to a partnership, which many larger investors use. SMAs allow large investors not only to negotiate fees but also to have a better control of the risk profile of the underlying investments.

The shift in emphasis that accompanied the fundraising surge between 2010 and 2021 is illustrated by the changing composition of AuM (Figure 10.7), while the growing role of direct (senior) lending is evident from the composition of AuM. The year 2022 may mark a reversal as mezzanine debt hit new highs for fundraising, and exceeded during Q1–Q3 2022 the full-year figures for every year from 2001 to 2021.[49]

---

[49] Ibid.

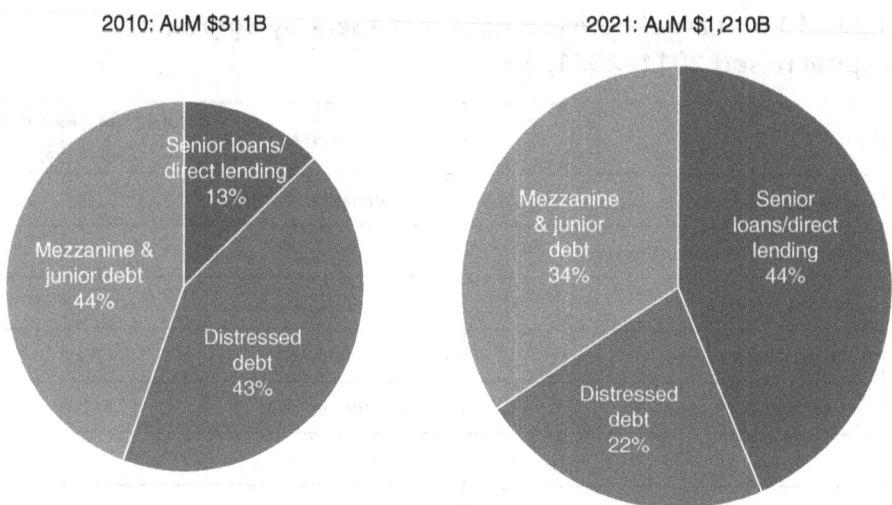

Figure 10.7   Private debt AuM 2010 and 2021 by strategy.
Source: Adapted from Preqin Pro.

An analysis of Cliffwater in 2023 shows that private debt (direct lending) has historically shown a significantly higher yield spread compared to leveraged loans or high yield bonds and less volatility.

The Cliffwater Direct Lending Index (the CDLI) seeks to measure the unlevered, gross of fees performance of US middle market corporate loans. The CDLI is asset-weighted by reported fair value. Current yield equals coupon interest divided by current price, implying that the investor will receive the then current price at maturity and the difference between the then price and stated principal will be lost, presumably because of default. Figure 10.8 also shows the Morningstar LSTA US Leveraged Loan Index, and the Bloomberg High Yield Bond Index from the September 30, 2004, inception of the CDLI through June 30, 2023.[50] Looking at US senior loans, StepStone Group—a global private markets firm—found that loss rate resulted in a 0.17–1% yield reduction during 2010–2019, while in 2005–2009 the maximum yield reduction due to the loss rate was around 2% in 2005 and 2007 for private debt, which makes it a very attractive investment for investors that do not require liquidity

---

[50] Stepstone (2021).

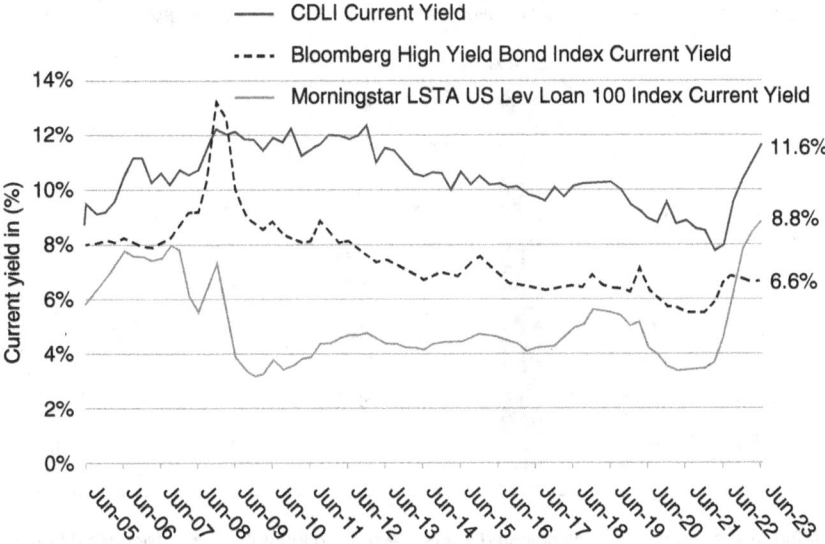

Figure 10.8   CDLI, high yield bond, and leveraged loan current yield comparisons yield (September 2004 to June 2023).
Source: Cliffwater (2023).

for a part of their fixed-income portfolio.[51] Seasoned investors have noted that mid-market loans have a higher recovery rate than high-yield bonds or syndicated loans, resulting in a lower effective loss rate. Allianz Global Investors reported an effective loss rate of less than 1% on their private debt portfolio from 1988 to 2015, compared to roughly 3% for high-yield bonds and somewhere in between for leveraged loans (Figure 10.9).[52] The returns do suggest that mid-market loans generate very attractive returns compared to syndicated leveraged loans or high-yield bonds but the foray into senior loans is relatively new and a prolonged period of higher interest rates and diminished economic growth may provide a stress test with regard to loss rates and recovery rates that is not reflected in past data.

---

[51] Stepstone Global, Internal Database, US First Lien Deals (more than 13,000 transactions and $400bn of invested capital). Loss rates present the annualized vintage loss rates and take into account any principal loss as well as any interest foregone (Audren, April 19, 2023).
[52] Schroff (2021).

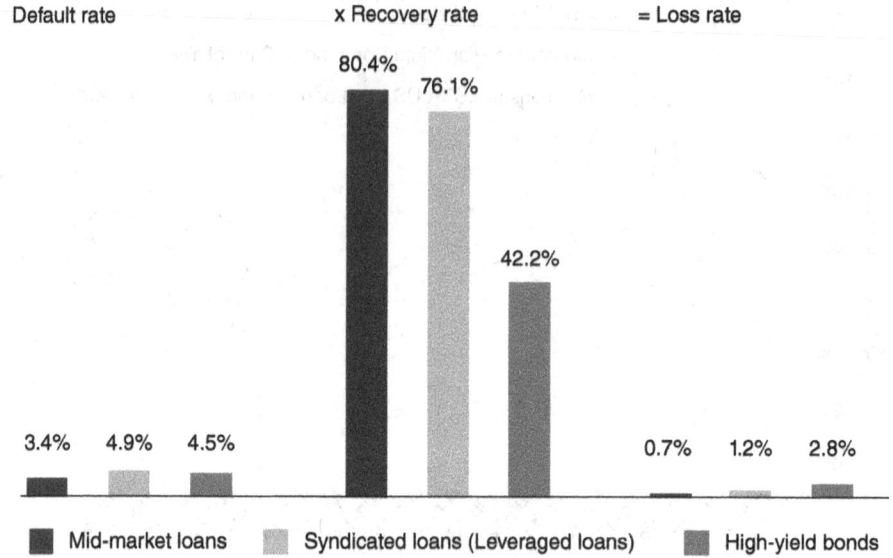

Figure 10.9 Private debt seems to offer attractive loss rates in the longer term (data 1988–2015).

Source: Adapted from Allianz Global Investors; chart based on Dr. Sebastian Schroff, CFA, Global Head of Private Debt, Allianz Investment Management SE, presentation on private debt, CFA Forum, Switzerland, October 25, 2022.

The growing amounts of capital raised by private debt funds have also increased competition, particularly in the US market and as managers were doing larger deals, they left the original sweet spot of the asset class, i.e., lending to mid-market companies that are underserved by banks and the syndicated leveraged loan market, and increasingly compete with large banks by providing an alternative to the syndicated LBO market. The increased availability of private debt financing and the move of private debt funds into large LBO financing are reflected in the gradual decline of yield spreads compared to leveraged loans since 2010 (see Figure 10.8). Those yields are, however, still attractive and institutional demand for (senior) private debt investments continues.

On the supply side, the reversal of the interest rate trend since 2022 increased the cost of debt financing, which made leveraged finance much more expensive for PE sponsors and caused new deal volumes to decline. Some market observers have cautioned that while the cost of loans have increased the large amount of capital raised for private debt funds prevented the industry to adjust spreads sufficiently to reflect a more challenging environment.

Investors therefore need to be aware that in this asset class, as in any other, there can be too much capital and deploying it may be challenging. A mitigating factor is that banks have curtailed their lending books, which may accelerate the trend of private debt to replace traditional bank lending and allow additional capital deployment. (see next section).

What Is the Competitive Edge of Private Debt?

Private debt funds offer more flexible and tailored financing solutions, particularly in mid-market acquisition finance, which banks struggle to match, due to regulatory constraints. The competitiveness of (senior) loans is not immediately obvious as the spreads charged make private debt look expensive versus high-yield bonds and syndicated loans. Indeed, the first foray into direct lending was therefore in small and mid-sized lending where traditional providers of funding retreated. But competitiveness is not just a function of the cost of financing but also determined by the flexibility of debt packages and their covenants, which needs to be understood in order to understand not only the attractiveness of the offering for borrowers but also the effective risks that lenders take when making those loans. The popularity of unitranche investments, which combine senior and junior debt in a single package, has grown due to their flexibility and time-saving benefits. This approach allows issuers to negotiate directly with equity owners or existing debt holders, cutting out multiple counterparties and potentially saving significant fees and recovery costs. Private debt funds possess distinct advantages over traditional leveraged loans arranged by banks, primarily stemming from their efficiency and flexibility in deal-making. Block et al., in 2023, conducted a survey that included 38 US and 153 European private debt managers (GPs) that, based on their AuM, represented at least 35% of the private debt market. The authors found that GPs of private debt funds identified several key advantages that they consider to be the most important factors contributing to private debt:

1. Certainty and speed of execution

2. Higher leverage available

3. Greater flexibility in covenant structures.

4. Sponsor/lender know each other and debt is held to repayment

The rank order of these advantages is consistent between US and European private debt managers. However, the percentage of respondents citing them tends to be higher among US managers than their European counterparts.[53]

This difference may be attributed, in part, to the focus on senior loans, which is more prevalent among US funds compared to European funds. On the other hand, European funds emphasize subordinated debt and loans for expansion. Additionally, US funds primarily focus on buyout loans, while European funds target buyouts, expansion financing, and capital expenditure financing. This highlights a distinct difference in the debt strategies between US and European investors.

US private debt funds commonly incorporate ongoing principal repayments using amortizing loans, while European funds lean toward bullet payments. This distinction implies that US funds directly compete with banks. At the same time, European funds focus on transaction opportunities that fall outside the scope of syndication or are considered too small for banks to pursue. Moreover, the prevalence of amortizing loans and revolving credit facilities in the USA suggests a more competitive overlap with traditional bank offerings (LBOs).

The disparity in fundraising size and loan amounts further illustrates this trend. US private debt managers typically raise larger funds and provide significantly higher loan amounts, with a mean of $226 million while European funds have a mean loan amount of EUR 70 million.[54] This discrepancy indicates that US funds have transitioned from complementing syndicated bank loans to actively disintermediating them, while European funds focus on alternative lending opportunities within their niche.

Debt investors focus on covenants, i.e., contractual clauses that outline specific terms, conditions, and restrictions that borrowers must adhere to during the life of a loan or debt instrument. These clauses are designed to protect the interests of the debt investors and ensure that the borrower maintains a certain level of financial health and stability. Covenant-light loans (or Cov-lite) are financial jargon for loan agreements that do not contain the usual protective covenants

---

[53] Block, Jang, Kaplan, and Schulze (2023).
[54] Ibid.

for the benefit of the lending party (Box 10.1). This has become more common in LBO financing due to competition among lenders, borrower demand for flexibility, and increased investor acceptance. The latter is likely a reflection of the small number of defaults during a favorable economic environment. Covenant-lite leveraged loans made up over 90% of new loans in 2021. While covenants in leveraged loans can be tracked, it is unclear whether private debt has followed this trend, as GPs do not disclose loan terms. According to the survey results of Block et al. (2023), the most significant financial covenants, with a considerable margin of importance, are debt to EBITDA and coverage ratios (including interest coverage, fixed charge coverage, and debt service coverage).

Box 10.1   Mytheresa: The Role of Covenants

Creditors to Neiman Marcus were displeased when its private equity owners transferred Mytheresa—an online fashion retailer—to Neiman's parent company. This potentially puts the assets of Mytheresa out of reach of Neiman's creditors just before the parent company announced it would need to restructure its nearly $5 billion in debt. But the loan agreements gave the owners the right to do such asset transfers. *The Wall Street Journal* reported on July 31, 2020, that Neiman Marcus Group Ltd.'s private-equity backers agreed to relinquish part of Mytheresa, clinching a settlement with creditors and clearing a big hurdle for the bankrupt department-store chain's exit from Chapter 11.[55]

Figure 10.10   Neiman Marcus and Mytheresa.
Source: Neiman Marcus.

(continued)

---

[55] Biswas (2020).

Covenants are often put in place by lenders to protect themselves from borrowers defaulting on their obligations due to financial actions detrimental to themselves or the business. There are two sorts of covenants: maintenance covenants that must be continuously maintained and incurrence covenants, which are tested for specific events (new debt issuance).

Covenants are usually represented as financial ratios that must be maintained, such as a maximum debt-to-asset ratio or other such ratios. Maintenance covenants require that covenants are met at all times. Covenants can cover everything from minimum dividend payments to levels borrowers must maintain in working capital to key employees remaining with the firm. Covenant-lite loans often do not have maintenance covenants, although they typically include incurrence covenants, for example, minimum free cash flow test before a dividend can be paid. Once a covenant is broken, the lender typically has the right to call back the loan from the borrower.[56]

Following is a list of some of the common metrics lenders use as debt covenants:

- Debt / EBITDA
- Debt / (EBITDA—Capital Expenditures)
- Interest Coverage (EBITDA or EBIT / Interest)
- Fixed Charge Coverage (EBITDA / (Total Debt Service + Capital Expenditures + Taxes)
- Debt / Equity
- Debt / Assets
- Dividend Pay-Out Ratio.

During the boom years of 2010–2021, the use of covenants declined, which left debt investors less protected. As the economic environment has been benign, few private markets investments experienced financial distress. It will require a protracted downturn to determine whether private debt investors will suffer due to a lack of protective covenants.

---

[56] CFA (2022).

Private debt investors often have ongoing relationships with borrowers, which can influence the terms of the loan. This could lead to more customized covenant packages that balance flexibility with risk. The sponsors also help with deal quality, with deal sourcing, and in reducing information costs (through repeated interactions). These benefits might allow the private debt lenders to lend more (at higher multiples) and to craft less restrictive covenants, which would give them a competitive advantage versus banks.[57]

While the private debt market may have largely avoided the trend of covenant-lite lending, an uptick in covenant-loose lending during 2020–2021 suggests that funds are seeking to offer more aggressive terms while still meeting investor demands for certain borrower restrictions. This increase is attributed to traditional middle-market players raising large private credit funds of $5–6 billion, forcing managers to finance larger companies and deals and match the banks' aggressive manner in terms and flexibility.[58]

A report by the law firm Proskauer found that for deals arranged in the private debt market, covenant-loose structures jumped to 59% in the first half of 2019, compared to 26% recorded in all of 2018.[59] Acquisitions were often financed with senior loans and no junior or subordinated tranche. This means debt holders may not only lack the cushion that subordinated debt provides, but having multiple funding rounds with senior loans can lead to overlapping claims, diverging investor interests, and a lack of claim hierarchy, which could complicate workouts.[60] In restructuring scenarios, senior loan holders may accept "super-senior" loans that have priority over their existing loans, because they face the prospect of write-downs when little or no subordinated debt is available to provide a cushion. Additionally, the terms and conditions of super-senior loans, such as call and put options or restrictive covenants, can complicate a restructuring process. Investors should examine capital structures carefully and not rely solely on the "senior" classification when examining a GP's track record or portfolio.

---

[57] Ibid.
[58] Brooke (2019).
[59] Montgomery and Iodice (2022).
[60] Biswas (2020).

Leverage and Performance

Both US and European private debt investors target unleveraged gross returns that imply substantial premiums over the comparable risk-free treasuries and investment grade bonds (Figure 10.11).

How do the returns at the deal level translate into net returns for investors in private debt funds? From 2010 to 2021, private debt funds have demonstrated attractive performance, with larger funds generally exhibiting slightly stronger results during most vintage years (Figure 10.12 and Figure 10.13).

Block et al. highlight a notable distinction between US and European private debt funds. It is reported that 95% of US funds utilize

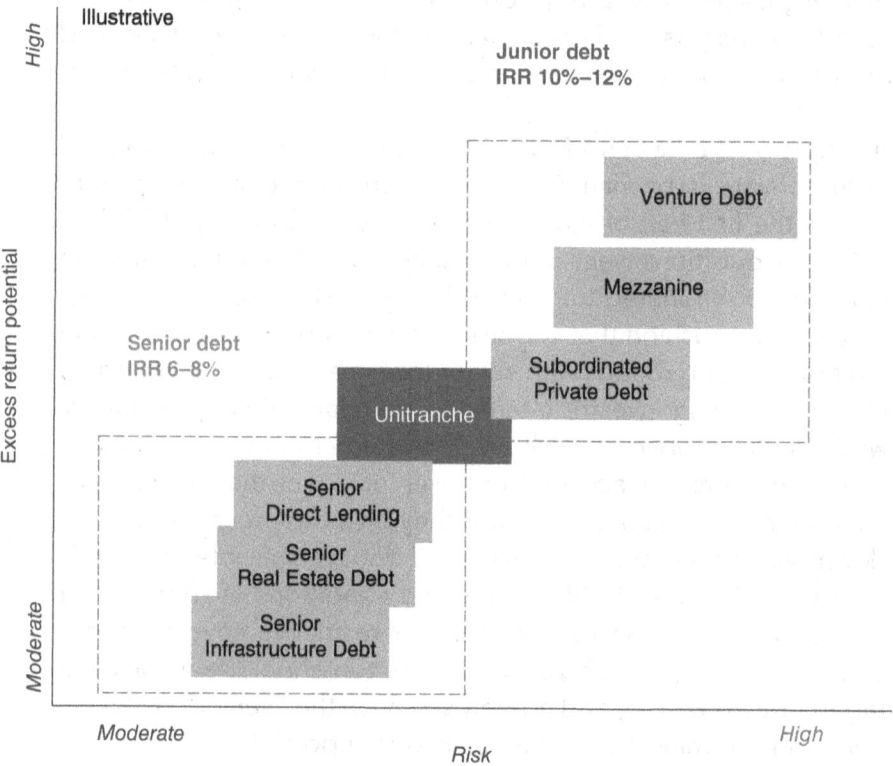

Figure 10.11   Private debt: returns based on indicative pooled net IRRs for vintage years 2008–2018, as of September 2021.

Source: Adapted from Mistry and Ripka, 2017; data: Burgiss Group, Preqin.

Note: IRRs reflect pooled net IRRs of funds raised in 2008–2018, indicating investors' returns from the strategies displayed. These IRRs are not a forecast or indication of return expectations.

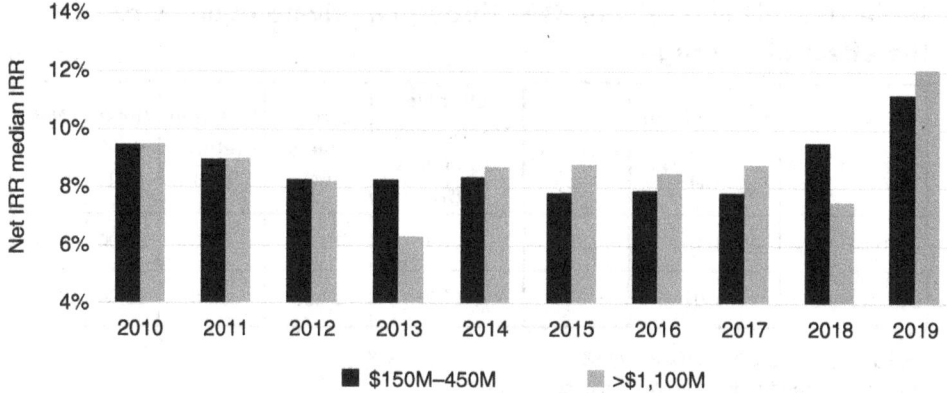

Figure 10.12   Median IRR of small ($150M–1,100M) and large (>$1.1B) Private Debt funds, 2010–2019.

Source: Adapted from Rahnama, 2022c.

Note: Distressed and mezzanine strategies are more represented in the smaller funds. Thus, the performance differential is not a direct size effect but reflects the presence of more risky strategies in the smaller fund bucket, which may be the result of the smaller deal sizes of those strategies.

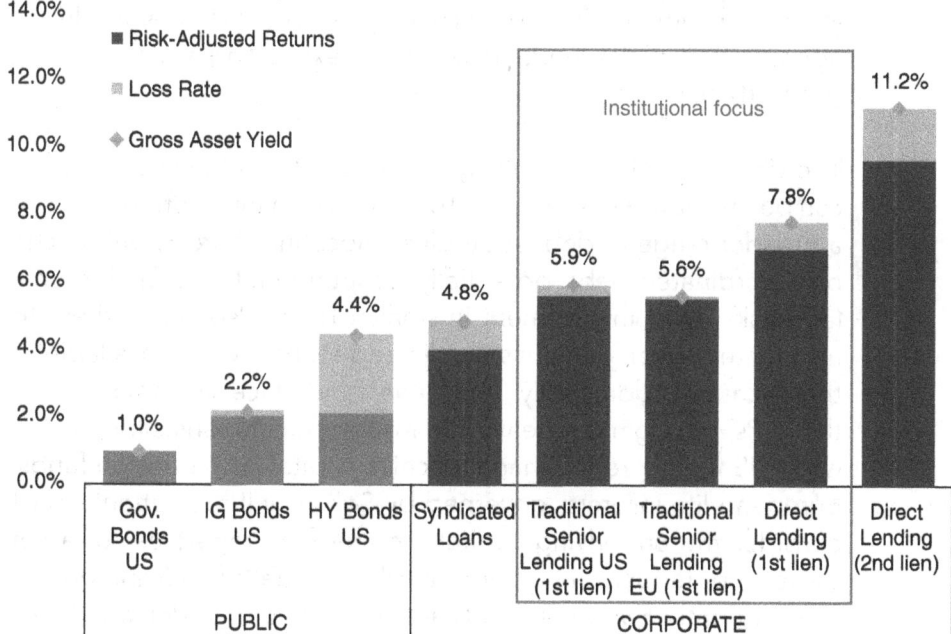

Figure 10.13   Gross asset yields and risk-adjusted returns, January 2010–April 2021, suggest attractive returns compared to the public market.

Sources: Stepstone; "Government Bonds" data based on Barclays US Agg. Treasuries; "Investment Grade Credit" reflects the yield to worst of the Barclays Global Agg. Corporate index; "HY Bonds." data based on CS HY Index; "Syndicated Loans" based on yield (3 years life) on BB rated loans and the Broad index (CS data) minus the historical loss rate since 2010; "Bank Lending" based on Stepstone database. "Direct Lending First Lien" based on average first lien and unitranche loans minus the estimated loss rate for first liens (estimation based on Stepstone internal database), "Direct Lending Second Lien" based on Thomson Reuters, Quarterly MM Private Deal Analysis. Data as of April 2021.

Table 10.7   Doing private debt through a private equity structure: the effect of leverage

	Management fee (%)	Leverage	Effective Management fee on NAV (%)	Carried interest (%)	Preferred return (5%)	Gross yield (%)	Net yield (%)
Average	1.10	1.07x	1.89	13.10	6.10	12.00	8.88
Cap.-weighted	1.07	1.25x*	1.99	12.90	6.30	12.80	9.47

Source: Nesbitt (2022); Cliffwater (2022).
Note: * for large funds leverage can exceed 1.6x.

some level of leverage, with an average of 40% (median of 25%) of total capital, typically, at most 60%. Conversely, European funds tend to employ very little or no leverage, with 67% of funds abstaining from its use.[61] This finding aligns with a study by Cliffwater, which examined 49 direct lending managers collectively managing $541 billion in 2022. The study revealed a 25% average leverage with 90% of the funds surveyed not exceeding a 50% leverage (Table 10.7).[62]

The disparity in leverage usage between US and European funds can be attributed to several factors. European funds often focus on a broader range of debt strategies, allocating more to unitranche or subordinated debt, potentially targeting higher overall returns (and risk). Their involvement in smaller deals also allows them to negotiate higher yields, as syndicated loans are less available in these cases. Additionally, European funds face constraints from their LPs, relying more heavily on insurance companies for capital, while US funds predominantly receive capital from pension funds. European life insurers, governed by Solvency II regulations, must consider the underlying capital requirement, regardless of asset ownership, rendering higher in-fund leverage less advantageous. Consequently, European funds are compelled to underwrite loans with higher target returns to compensate for the limited ability to rely on higher leverage to achieve returns that are attractive to investors once a private equity fee structure (fixed fee and carried interest) is taken into account.

[61] Block, Jang, Kaplan, and Schulze (2023),
[62] Nesbitt (2022).

Investors comparing US-focused funds to their European counterparts must appreciate the different risk profiles risk profiles.
Although the senior loan market yields are attractive, funds need to
generate the returns necessary to warrant the fee and carried interest structure typical in private debt funds. US-focused funds tend
to invest in larger senior loans and employ higher levels of in-fund
leverage than European funds to boost returns. Due to the competitive nature of the syndicated loan market, covenants may be
weak, which also increases the risk for investors. European private
debt managers often focus on smaller deals, which could offer less
competition and potentially better returns and protections. But
European funds' investment strategies also involve placing capital
in the lower end of the capital stack (like second lien and unsecured
exposure). This can boost returns but also comes with higher risk
due to the subordinated position of part of the capital.

In summary, when comparing US-focused funds and European
private debt managers, investors must carefully analyze the differences in investment strategies, deal sizes, leverage levels, and
capital stack positions.

Where Do We Go from Here?

Until 2023, private debt funds delivered returns that resulted in
a substantial spread over traditional forms of leveraged financing as well as investment grade bonds. This is still true despite
higher base rates. Unsurprisingly, private debt is one of the asset
classes where investors still plan to increase their allocations, as
has been shown in various surveys.[63] Private debt funds are set to
disrupt the traditional CLO market by enabling direct participation in loans that meet specific credit requirements without the
involvement of banks and CLO or CDO managers, which has the
potential to transform the lending industry and create momentum
for further growth.

The leading (US) players have been able to raise sizable funds that
compel them to do larger deals, as evidenced in the findings of

---

[63] Preqin (2020; 2023c).

Block et al. that mean loan sizes are higher for the US funds (mean of $226 million) than for the European funds (mean of €70 million).[64] The use of amortizing loans and revolving credit also puts them closer to traditional (syndicated) leveraged loan financing while their equity-based funding model results in a lower risk profile for investors compared to the highly leveraged CMO/CLO structures.

Mega-firms are adapting their approach to deals, evaluating them across various capital pools and trading assets within affiliated funds and may allocate more senior tranches of a deal to funds that target a lower risk/return profile. As a result, private debt is expected to become increasingly important in their overall AuM, as private debt is an ideal investment for semi-liquid, income-oriented funds. The asset class has therefore a lot of potential to gain traction in the insurance and private wealth markets. The preference for PE-sponsored deals, also creates a "win-win" situation for private equity and private debt firms and an opportunity to grow each other's business.[65] The growth of private debt is expected to increase further as banks have stepped back again from underwriting leveraged buyouts as they struggled to sell debt that they committed to before interest rates rose from 2022 onwards.[66] According to estimates by Morgan Stanley analysts, the pullback of regional banks in the United States, particularly in commercial real estate, such as office buildings, may provide another boost to private debt. Property owners in this sector may seek to refinance at least $1.5 trillion in mortgage contracts throughout 2023–2024.[67]

The availability of large pools of capital for private debt may also mitigate the lack of debt financing that has been a typical feature of past downturns. In 2022–2023, leverage levels remained steady despite the rising cost of debt, at just below 7x EBITDA, and debt-to-capitalization ratios and equity-check percentages were roughly in line with the levels observed in 2021, as reported by McKinsey.[68]

---

[64] Block, Jang, Kaplan, and Schulze (2023).
[65] Based on conversations of the author and also discussed in Khajuria (2022); an example is the $5.5B private debt provided by Blackstone and Apollo for Cotiviti (Carlyle) (Platt, March 6, 2023).
[66] Hirsch (2023).
[67] Tan (2023).
[68] FT report: (Fletcher, 2022), (McKinsey (2023).

10.3   REAL ESTATE

Following the GFC, distressed real estate opportunities were slow to emerge in the United States. The initial opportunity was in the distressed real estate debt area as the Federal Deposit Insurance Corporation (FDIC) was initiating the sale of non-performing loans on banks' balance sheets. Since 2008, the FDIC has executed thirty-one structured loan sales, the largest of which was the Corus Bank portfolio sale in October 2009 for $551 million of required equity ($4.4 billion book value) acquired by Starwood.[69] Those debt transactions required the ability to take possession of property and few managers had the necessary platform in place to successfully invest in these often complex asset-disposition transactions. Core property buyers lacked the skill set to engage in complex investments; only a handful had the internal capabilities to perform workouts on large portfolios of very small-balance loans. Further opportunities came from restructurings and recapitalizations.

Opportunistic real estate funds injected fresh capital into the large stock of real estate with capital structures that were "stuck." These structures were burdened by essentially worthless equity, and debt worth far less than face value. In many cases, particularly with loans made by regional and community banks, borrowers provided recourse guarantees, and, for their part, lenders were ill-prepared to take back and operate the respective properties. So, in essence, funds were acquiring assets from distressed sellers, which was in many ways a *déjà vu* of the opportunities that followed the Savings & Loan crisis in the early 1990s. But new banking regulation also meant that financial institutions were shedding their entire real estate investment platforms. In 2010, Blackstone acquired Merrill Lynch's Asian real estate assets and acted as the new general partner for the Merrill Lynch Asian Real Estate Opportunity Fund.[70]

When the economy recovered in 2010, so did the housing market. After falling 33% during the recession triggered by the GFC, housing prices in the USA increased by 51% between 2010 and 2017, with similar recoveries recorded in other countries.[71]

---

[69] Douvas (2012).
[70] Blackstone (2010).
[71] Lerner (2018).

Several factors were driving the recovery of the real estate markets:

- Stabilizing debt markets and the re-emergence of commercial mortgage-backed securities (CMBS) issuance.
- Property demand improvements, as shown in vacancy and absorption trends.
- Favorable commercial property valuations.
- Macroeconomic tailwinds.
- Significant level of capital ready to be deployed for US real estate.

As many of the world's largest investment firms, institutional investors, and pension plans increased allocations to real estate, demand led to a meaningful recovery of property values as yields approached pre-financial crisis levels once more.

Starting in 2009, institutional capital increasingly went into quality and low-risk properties that generate stable and consistent cash flow ("core") in primary US market regions in search of reliable, long-term yield. Public pension plans, such as the California Public Employees' Retirement System (CalPERS), had adjusted their real estate investment strategy to include a greater allocation to core commercial property.[72] This trend was not confined to the USA. In Switzerland, for example, real estate (domestic and international) allocations increased from 9% of total assets in 2009 to 24% in 2021.[73] Increased core allocations did not have much impact on private real estate, which has traditionally targeted real estate market dislocations or development (Figure 10.14). Core strategies play a minor role in private market real estate fundraising as investors opt for more liquid and permanent investment vehicles such as REITs to gain exposure to core real estate.

It is somewhat surprising that core/core+ funds are part of private real estate fundraising at all as there is little scope for earning an illiquidity premium. Being primarily an income-oriented buy-and-hold strategy, one might expect institutions to use open-ended real estate funds or REITs (with large institutions holding real estate directly). LaSalle estimated the size of the market for publicly traded

---

[72] Williams, Brakat, and Braffman (2011).
[73] Swisscanto (2022), Dick (2011).

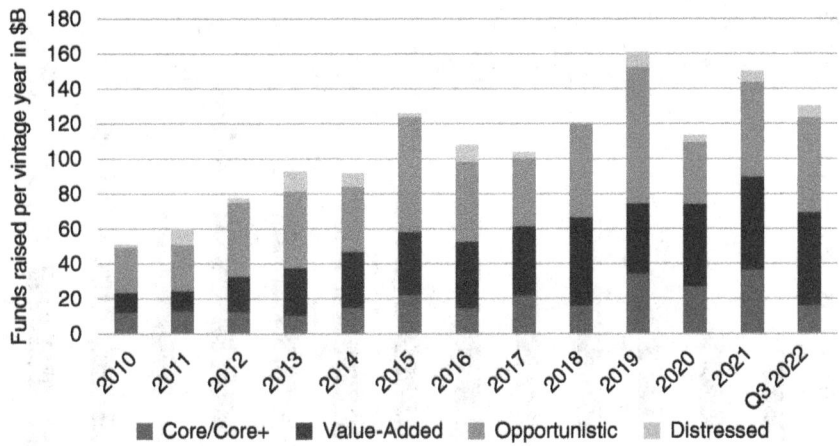

Figure 10.14 Annual capital raised by private real estate funds (opportunistic, value-added, and distressed), 2010–Q3 2022, $B.
Source: Adapted from Preqin.

real estate funds at $4.6 trillion in 2021.[74] This number highlights the difference from other private market asset classes: a deep pool of listed or open-ended fund investment products is available. A limited partnership with its final life is thus not an obvious choice for implementing core/core+ strategies in real estate.

But the strong results of opportunistic funds after the onset of the GFC that were the result of distressed transactions reignited investors' interest in opportunistic funds.

Fundraising surpassed the previous peak of 2008 ($130 billion) in 2019 with $160 billion raised globally. Value-added and opportunistic funds accounted for the largest share of funds raised, with about 75% of total fundraising during 2010–2021.

The fundraising pattern also shows the continued dominance of the US market (Figure 10.15). However, one must notice that US funds often have a global investment focus. Given that the scope for opportunistic real estate strategies is somewhat cyclical, an international investment focus has allowed managers to shift their investment dollars geographically where the opportunities are. Thus, the large share of US fundraising reflects the importance of US mega-firms that tend to raise huge funds but does not necessarily imply that those funds are strictly earmarked for US opportunities.

---

[74] LaSalle (2021).

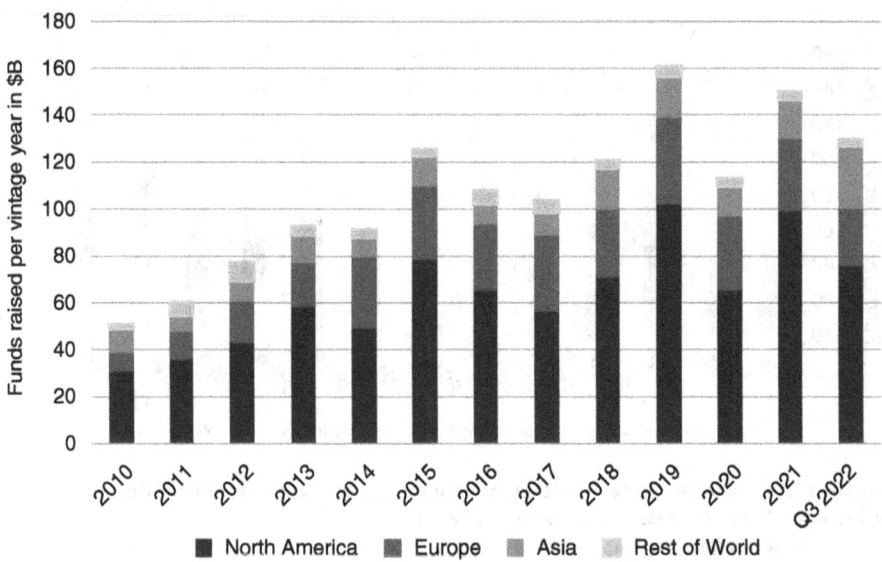

Figure 10.15   Global private real estate fundraising by geography, 2010–Q3 2022, $B.
Source: Adapted from Preqin; data as of January 2022.

Fundraising and the Role of Mega-Firms in Private Real Estate

It turns out that private real estate is not as concentrated as infrastructure or buyouts, but the top 20 fundraisers still raised 41% of total funds on average from 2010–2021. The list of the largest private real estate managers in Table 10.8 shows that several buyout firms are significant players.

Blackstone set a fund-size record in 2019 when it closed Blackstone Real Estate Partners IX at $20.5 billion, followed by Blackstone Real Estate Partners Europe VI ($10.6 billion) and Blackstone Real Estate Debt Strategies IV ($8 billion). Those were the largest private real estate–focused funds raised during 2020.[75]

In 2021, Starwood Distressed Opportunity Fund XII ($10 billion) and Carlyle Realty Partners IX ($8 billion) were the largest funds closed.[76]

---

[75] Oguh (2019).
[76] Preqin (2021c).

Table 10.8 Large private real estate fund managers by fundraising activity over the previous 5 years, as of 2021

Fund manager	Total funds raised $B	Headquarters
Blackstone Group*	198.2	New York, US
Lone Star Funds	60.7	Dallas, US
Brookfield Asset Management	53.9	Toronto, Canada
GLP	32.1	Singapore
CBRE Global Investors	18.5	Los Angeles, US
Starwood Capital Group	28.1	Miami Beach, US
PATRIZIA	16.7	Augsburg, Germany
Carlyle Group	24.3	Washington, US
Angelo, Gordon & Co	15.1	New York, US
Amundi	15.0	Paris, France

Source: (Preqin, 2021c), funds closed in 2021 and 1H 2022 have been added to the total based on Preqin reports.

Note: *The Blackstone number refers to total real estate fundraising 2017–2021 and was provided by the manager.

Deal Activity

Deal volume rose steadily until 2019. The COVID-19 epidemic and uncertainty about interest and inflation lowered deal volume, which thereafter recovered more slowly than other private market asset classes (Figure 10.16).

Office and commercial property (retail and industrial) were dominant in deal activity. Residential property investment increased after 2019 (Figure 10.17).

Traditional Development vs. the "Buyout Playbook"

Compared to buyout-type real estate transactions, capital deployment and the capital structure for real estate development plays are very different. There is a much more significant role for assetbacked loans (mortgage financing), PIK structures to fund development,

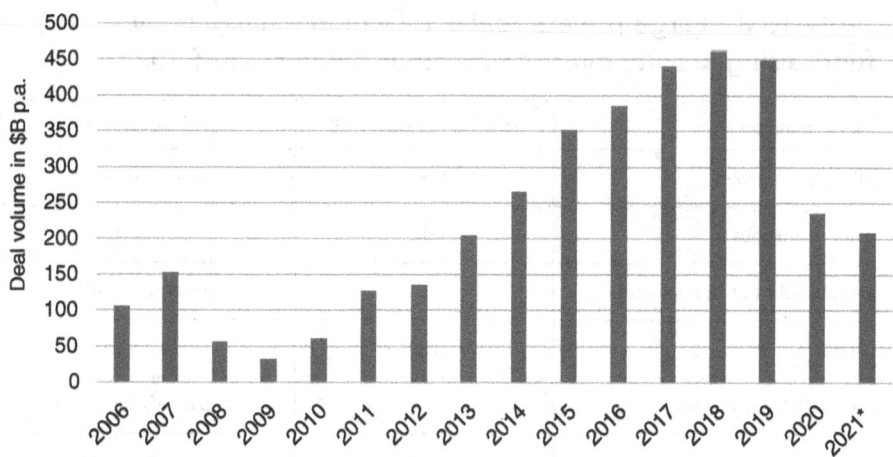

Figure 10.16   Annual deal volume 2006–Q3 2021 in $B.
Source: Adapted from Preqin; data as of January 2022.
Note: *2021 until Q3.

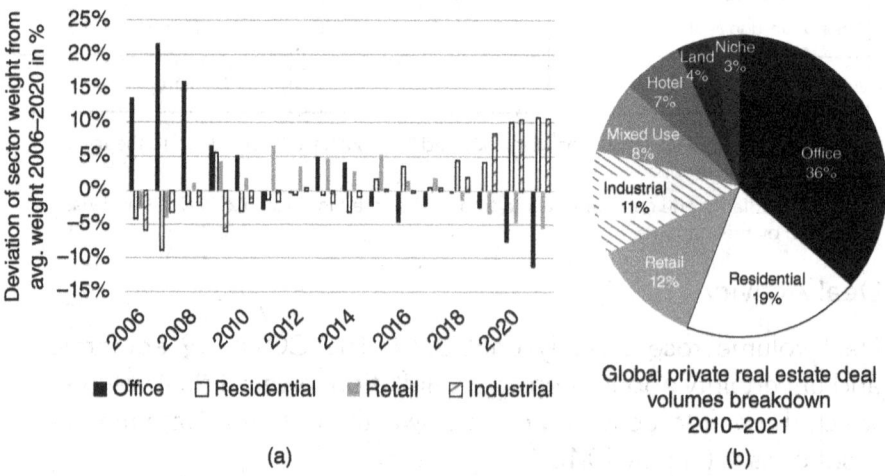

Figure 10.17   (a) Sector over-/under-weight vs. 2006–Q2/2021 average. (b) Global private real estate deal volumes breakdown, 2010–2021.
Source: Adapted from Preqin.

and deferred debt (construction financing). Land purchases are financed through equity and a mortgage, including first and second lien tranches. As the developer receives no cash flow during the planning and permitting stage, intermittent financing through PIK toggle notes[77] or mezzanine financing, is often used to fund

---

[77] A toggle note is a type of payment-in-kind (PIK) loan in which the issuer has the option to defer an interest payment by agreeing to pay an increased coupon in the future. With toggle notes, all deferred payments must be settled by the loan's maturity.

development expenses until the off-plan marketing is underway. Once a good part of the project (typically 50% or more of total square footage) is under contract, the developer receives payments over time (down payments). This allows the developer to replace intermittent financing through a construction loan secured by the down payments from square footage under contract. This often allows a release of equity before the building is completed.

The variable and significantly deferred funding creates a risk that "things will change" between the time of the land purchase and the start of construction or that timelines become much longer than anticipated and debt needs to be refinanced. While average leverage may be lower for development projects over the holding period compared to buyout-type strategies, there are significant refinancing risks, which explains why a surge in failures of developers often accompanies any downturn in the real estate markets.

While generic, Figure 10.18 illustrates a typical development financing and payment schedule for residential development. This timeline becomes significantly longer for larger projects and sometimes exceeds ten years.

Compared to buyouts and distressed real estate, which usually require most of the equity at the acquisition date, the equity requirements for real estate development are staged over time, which boosts IRR even when multiples of total gain are comparatively low. Leverage is typically in the 60–80% range and leverage

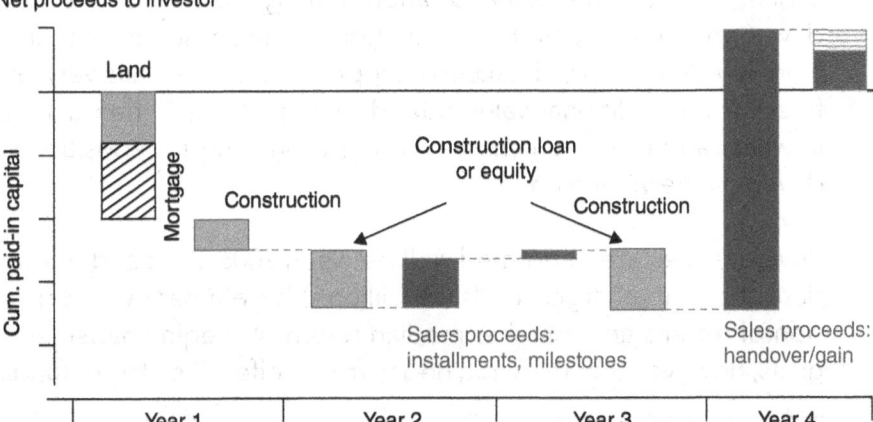

Figure 10.18   Timeline and cash flow pattern of a condominium development project.

tends to be highest during the construction phase; these are peak numbers as construction loans are amortized through sales proceeds. Unlike buyouts or distressed property sales where leverage tends to be highest at the time of acquisition, leverage of development projects is thus more back-ended.

Institutional real estate partnerships are typically not doing the development in-house (although some do) but rather invest in a series of projects, which are joint ventures with developers, and where the fund acts as a sponsor. This results in a double layer of fees as both the developer receives service fees and a performance fee and the GP through the carried interest.

Development, i.e., focusing on building new property, is typically done by smaller and mid-sized GPs while the large mega-firms that have increasingly entered real estate typically use buyout strategies for value creation. Two approaches stand out: roll-ups, i.e., "buy and build" using serial acquisitions, and public-to-private transactions, i.e., buying a portfolio at a discount and selling the real estate assets.

The Blackstone $13 billion acquisition of American Campus Communities, the largest US student housing real estate investment trust, announced in April 2022, epitomizes the type of deal that the largest real estate managers are executing. They are motivated by sector conviction and can impact an entire industry.[78] The transaction is also an example of the growing role of perpetual capital as the transaction was completed by Blackstone Core+ perpetual capital vehicles. The value creation strategy in that deal is new development and possibly acquisitions to increase capacity in a market where demand exceeds supply. Those deals are very different from traditional value-added or opportunistic transactions in which a manager purchases land or a building to reposition or develop a new building.

Private real estate performed well between 2008–2013 and Burgiss data shows that larger funds ($5 billion+) have a narrower dispersion of returns and a higher median return. A Preqin analysis suggests, however, that there is a negative size effect, i.e., larger funds'

---

[78] Benson (2022).

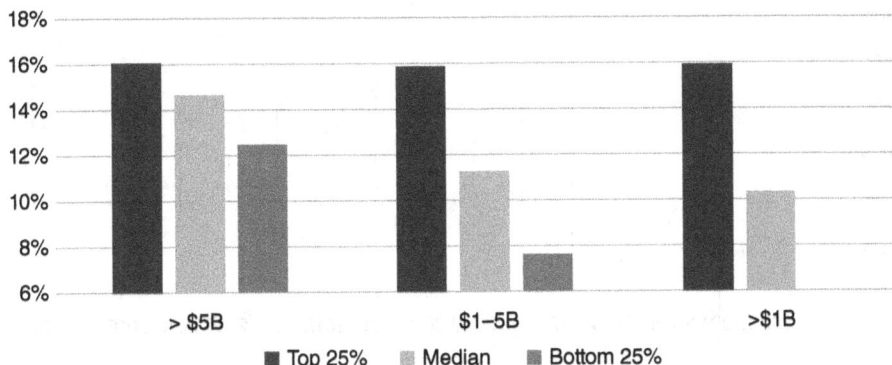

Figure 10.19 Median IRR of real estate funds (average of vintage years 2008–2018).
Source: Adapted from McKinsey & Company; data Burgiss.
Note: Methodology: IRR spreads calculated for funds within vintage years separately and then averaged out. Median IRR was calculated by taking the average of the median IRR for funds within each vintage year.

performance being below those of small funds of $100 million or less.[79] The differing conclusions may reflect sample difference and the different size brackets used as Preqin defines large funds as bigger than $650 million in size. (Figure 10.19).

But over the longer run it is also apparent that private real estate returns have been very cyclical with strong vintage years followed by years with moderate or even negative median returns. Figure 10.20 refers to value-added funds and performance data during the 1990s, based on few observations; the performance pattern is quite volatile.

The value-creation playbook for opportunistic funds that focus on development rests on an ability to identify additional floor space and devise a product that is right for the market and micro-location of the project in the planning stage. It also rests on an ability to go to market quickly, which is contingent on obtaining building permits and managing stakeholders (neighbors, heritage boards, etc.) well to avoid delays and costly additional rounds of approval. After that, it is crucial to secure anchor tenants or off-plan sales to commence a project with the confidence that the take-up of the floor space will be fast. Financing only sometimes provides an edge as the options are relatively straightforward, and asset-backed loans

---

[79] Preqin (2022f).

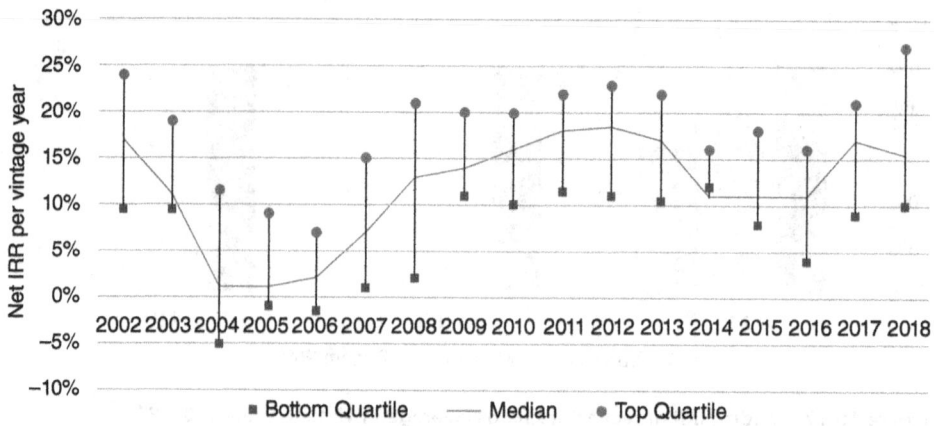

Figure 10.20   Top quartile, median, and bottom quartile net IRR of value-added US private equity real estate funds of vintage years 2002–2018, as of August 2022.

Source: Adapted from Monfared, 2022.

Note: Monfared uses data on US value-added private real estate funds. The earlier vintage years until 2003 have few observations, and the quartile boundaries may thus be not meaningful. However, the performance pattern and median net IRR appear consistent with the Partners Group Thomson Reuters Private Real Estate Index data as of December 31, 2011. The younger vintage years may be too early to tell as they had not had meaningful realizations at the time the performance was measured.

and lending against sales agreement are the most common. This is in contrast to mega-firms that use buyout capital structures and often benefit from lower funding costs than other potential buyers. While development requires intimate local market knowledge as a basis for generating superior returns, portfolio transactions undertaken by the large opportunistic funds are much more driven by financial engineering.

The partial sale of the London Broadgate complex (see Box 10.2) exemplifies a recurring theme that has allowed opportunistic real estate funds to capitalize on opportunities since the early 1990s, when this asset class gained traction among institutional investors: motivated sellers who need to repair their balance sheets but must sell in a market where demand has vanished. To be able to close those deals, you need (patient) equity and debt. The transaction demonstrates how far the industry and its key players have progressed, as the owner of Broadgate was compelled to sell in order to reduce a loan-to-value ratio (LTV) of 47% and the concentration of holdings in the central London office market, while the buyer was able to structure the transaction with nearly 90% leverage.

Box 10.2   Broadgate: British Land Joint Venture with Blackstone

The British Land Company plc is one of the UK's leading property development and investment firms. British Land was heavily invested in the London City office market at the start of the GFC, accounting for 31% of their total portfolio, with Broadgate accounting for 27%. The office complex in London's financial area employs 30,000 people. Broadgate consists of 16 office towers totaling 4 million square feet (Figure 10.21).[80] There was a possibility that UBS, the largest tenant, would refuse to sign a new 700,000-square-foot contract.[81] In addition, and probably most important, British Land's loan-to-value ratio (LTV) had gone up significantly and the firm was under pressure from its banks to de-leverage and had to find a buyer for a part of its portfolio in a market where estimates for 2008–2010 rental decline were in a range of −1 to −20%.[82]

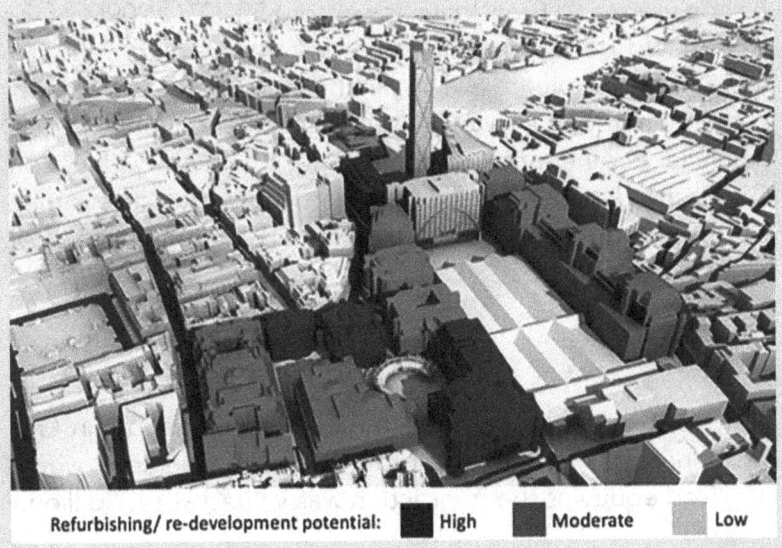

Refurbishing/ re-development potential: ■ High   ■ Moderate   ■ Low

Figure 10.21   Overview of the Broadgate complex.
Source: M3 Consulting, London.

(continued)

---

[80] GLA (2008).
[81] British Land (2009, 2012), Mobelli (2018).
[82] GLA (2008).

A Motivated Seller

British Land wanted to cut its large exposure to the London office market, which became untenable as property values fell during the GFC. After the disposal, British Land's exposure to the City of London declined to 21%, with its share in the Broadgate joint-venture accounting for 16%. Its Group LTV had decreased from 47% in June 2009 to 30% after the transaction closed.[83]

Transaction

Blackstone paid £1.07 billion to buy a 50% stake in Broadgate by forming a joint venture with British Land. That deal was struck with Blackstone putting up £987 million of debt and £77M of equity. Part of the equity and debt was deferred until some buildings under construction/refurbishment were delivered. The leveraged loan package included a five-year £243 million loan at 2.5% over LIBOR secured against 201 Bishopsgate and Broadgate Tower for 55% LTV. £209M of the loan would be drawn only when the construction/refurbishment was completed.[84] This financing package, which was partly inherited, is a case study in value creation through debt (financial engineering) combined with a low entry-valuation. Given the state of the debt market, only the largest players in the opportunistic real estate market are able to close such deals.

Outcome

In 2013, Blackstone sold its stake to the Singaporean GIC, which netted a £600 million profit and a 7.5x multiple over its invested equity as the transaction was valued at £1.7 billion.[85]

---

[83] British Land (2009).
[84] *Financial Times*, September 18, 2008.
[85] *Evening Standard*, August 20, 2013; *Financial Times*, December 23, 2013.

10.4 INFRASTRUCTURE AND NATURAL RESOURCES

The decade to 2021 has seen a surge in the allocation of institutional investor assets to infrastructure investments. Global fundraising for infrastructure (IS) and natural resources (NR) funds rose to an all-time high of $124 billion in 2021, up 23% over the previous year and again surpassed by $139 billion raised during Q1–Q3 2022. Since 2010 until Q3 2022, infrastructure funds raised almost $1.2 trillion in total. Infrastructure (including natural resources) global AUM reached $0.9 trillion in 2021 and was estimated to amount to $1.1 trillion by the end of 2022.[86] This number likely understates the total capital available for funding infrastructure projects, given plentiful "shadow infrastructure" capital targeting infrastructure deals but residing outside infrastructure-mandated funds, including PE funds making infrastructure investments.

Apart from the general scramble for yield, it was the experience during the GFC where infrastructure funds barely dipped below their year- end valuations of 2007 and recovered soon after that, which boosted investors' demand. But there was a supply-side story too. A report published by the IMF in 2020[87] opines that "infrastructure needs far exceed the resources that countries can hope to raise in a fiscally responsible and macroeconomically sustainable way." The growing importance of environment, social, and governance (ESG) investing and opportunities in sectors considered "green" and the general perception of a big infrastructure funding gap that the private sector can profitably address drove the growing interest in the asset class.

In contrast, natural resource funds (NR), whose performance suffered during the financial crisis and subsequently saw the value of many assets drop further as energy prices fell to new lows, went out of favor. After 2015, the forces of performance (low) and

[86] Preqin (2023e).
[87] Schwarz, Fouad, Hansen, and Verdier (2020).

growing ESG investing (putting "dirty fuels" on the defensive). Shareholder pressure on oil majors to reduce their engagement in traditional further eroded the M&A market for E&P.[88] This also worked against managers focused on oil, gas, and mining trying to raise new funds. Those sectors used to dominate NR investing in the USA, followed by other sub-sectors, such as water, farmland, and timber, that are much smaller in terms of capital deployed.

An Asset Class Dominated by Large Players

Institutional investors, such as pension funds, sovereign wealth funds, endowments, and insurance companies, are becoming increasingly crucial alongside governments in providing the capital that finance infrastructure projects. As previously discussed, large investors have increased their share in total private markets fundraising and infrastructure is no exemption. In infrastructure the prominence of large institutions -both as LPs and direct investors- is higher than in any other private markets asset classes. Large public pension funds and SWFs have both high percentage and absolute dollar allocations to infrastructure investing (Table 10.9).

The prominent role of large investors seeking to deploy substantial capital is reflected is mirrored in the concentration of fundraising for the asset class. Between 2010 and 2021, the 10 largest infrastructure funds raised about 30% of total capital each year (Table 10.10), similar to buyouts and real estate.

The top 20 IS managers account for about half of all capital raised during 2010–2021 (Table 10.10). The market also has a significant presence of multi-strategy firms, such as Blackstone, EQT, and Partners Group. Among the top twenty fundraisers from 2006–2021 were eight multi-strategy firms. This reflects a broader trend in private markets that firms with a multi-strategy approach and huge global distribution networks can move quickly to absorb a significant increase in demand in any sub-asset class within private markets.

---

[88] For example, Shell shareholders approved an energy transition strategy in May 2021, and the company continues to be under pressure to accelerate an exit from fossil fuel production and to completely stop new oil and gas exploration (Jolly, 2021; Yergin, 2022).

Table 10.9 IPE top 12 investors in infrastructure, 2020

Institution	Headquarters	Allocation (%)	AuM ($M)	Allocation ($M)	Institution type
CPP Investments	Toronto	9.8	372,978	36,616	Public pension fund
Abu Dhabi Investment Authority	Abu Dhabi	5.0	579,621	28,981	Sovereign wealth fund
Caisse de dépôt et placement du Québec	Quebec City	8.8	286,574	25,219	Public pension fund
Allianz Global Investors	Munich	3.4	711,676	24,197	Insurance company
National Pension Service of Korea	Jeolla-bukdo	3.1	766,041	23,889	Public pension fund
APG	Amsterdam	2.9	695,780	19,862	Public pension fund
Ontario Municipal Employees Retirement	Toronto	2.0	82,326	16,465	Public pension fund
AustralianSuper	Melbourne	1.1	156,548	16,438	Public pension fund
BCI	Victoria	1.0	156,655	15,885	Public pension fund
China Investment Corporation (CIC)	Beijing	1.4	1,045,700	15,000	Sovereign wealth fund
PSP Investments	Ottawa	1.1	133,134	14,378	Public pension fund
Ontario Teachers' Pension Plan	Toronto	8.2	170,847	13,945	Public pension fund

Source: Infrastructure Investor (2021).

Fundraising by Geography

The USA was the most significant destination for IS and NR fundraising followed by Europe in all but one year during 2010–2022 (Figure 10.22). The geographical allocation of fundraising can, however, be misleading as many funds operate globally and thus will allocate capital to the region where opportunities appear most attractive.

Asian private infrastructure funds have made comparatively few investments or raised capital. Due in part to China's Belt and Road Initiative, investors from outside the region have taken a back seat. The program's ambitious goals for record amounts of state- backed development capital may have discouraged private investors from investing in the region out of fear of competition. The Middle East and North Africa (MENA) region also has seen

Table 10.10   Twenty largest IS managers by total capital raised in $B, 2010–2021.

Manager	Country	Capital raised $B
Macquarie Asset Management	UK	75.9
Global Infrastructure Partners	USA	64.8
Brookfield Asset Management	CAN	53
KKR	USA	46.9
EQT	SWE	37.3
Stonepeak Infrastructure Ptnrs.	USA	32
I Squared Capital	USA	22.3
BlackRock	USA	22
IFM Investors	AUS	21.6
AMP Capital	AUS	19.7
Antin Infrastructure Ptnrs.	FRA	18.2
Blackstone	USA	17.5
First Sentier Investors	AUS	16.9
Copenhagen Infrastructure Ptnrs.	DEN	15.4
DigitalBridge Group	USA	14.8
Morgan Stanley Infrastructure Ptnrs.	USA	12.1
Ardian	FRA	12.1
Actis	UK	10.3
Partners Group	CH	8.8
Energy Capital Ptnrs.	USA	8.6

Source: (Infrastructure Investor, 2021).

relatively little fundraising for funds focused on the region and the transaction volume has also been low. Despite being heavily promoted by international organizations such as the World Bank or the OECD, the private market funds have been somewhat tone-deaf to the opportunity.

As Mark Wiseman, former CIO of CPPIB, pointed out:

To really make infrastructure investing attractive in each jurisdiction for us, we need that consistency and predictability of the regulatory framework. When you're investing in quarter centuries, as opposed to the next quarter, that regulatory framework and that consistency must transcend any given government. Because the asset is going to outlive a government . . . By and large, in

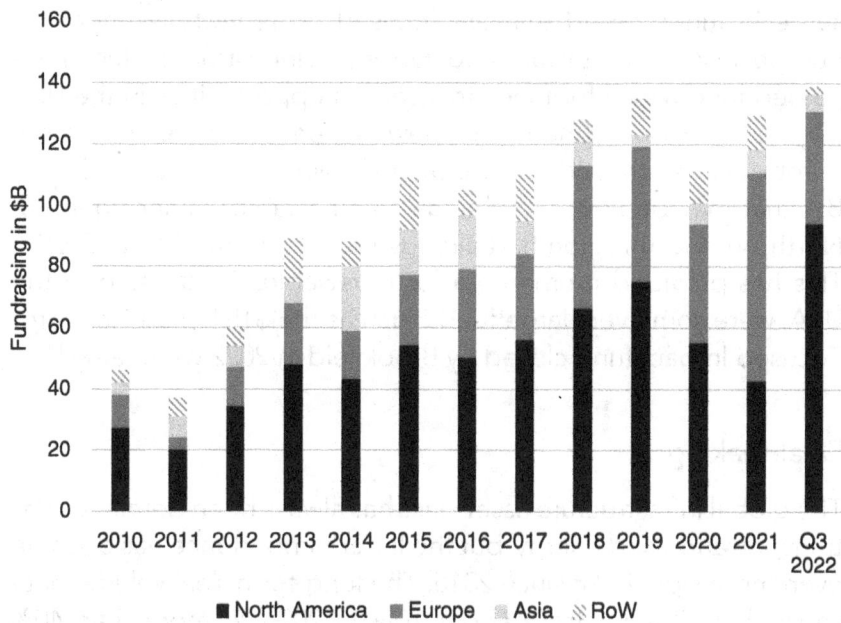

Figure 10.22 Global infrastructure and natural resource fundraising by region, $B. *Source:* (McKinsey, 2022; Preqin, 2023e), data as of December 2022.

emerging markets, it's still difficult to get appropriately rewarded for the risk associated with investing in infrastructure.[89]

Allegations against Abraaj in 2018, a $13.6 billion emerging market specialist who was accused of improperly using funds from its Middle East and North Africa investment vehicles, which led to legal action against the manager dented investor confidence too.[90]

Increased ESG focus has changed fundraising patterns for infrastructure and natural resources with a shift to renewable energy, decarbonization, and other carbon-reducing areas, which benefits infrastructure but has hurt the fundraising prospects for natural resource funds. In 2021, for example, 69% of funds were raised for renewable energy, compared to just 14% for traditional energy. Added momentum came from the announcement of The European Green Deal, which envisaged that a substantial part of the €1.8 trillion investments from the Next Generation EU Recovery Plan and the EU's seven-year budget will go toward investment that supports the transition to renewable energy has caused a

---

[89]Wiseman (2013).
[90]Arnold (2018).

surge in funds raised that are focused on renewable energy in Europe. In 2021 capital raised for European infrastructure funds surpassed fundraising for funds focused on opportunities in the USA (Figure 10.22). Investments in renewable energy is the area where Europe also was ahead in terms of deal volume during 2010–2021.[91] But that may be about to change as renewables financing in the North American region had already trippled from 2019 to 2020.[92] This has provided momentum for renewables fundraising in the USA, were some very large funds such as the $15 billion Net Zero-Focused Impact fund closed by Brookfield in 2022 were raised.[93]

Deal-making

The global infrastructure asset class has always been dominated by transportation and energy, but the latter's importance has become even more significant since 2015. The long-term deal volume data shows how it went from about 20% in 2006 to more than 40% between 2015 and 2022 (Figure 10.23), although with regard to traditional energy there may be some double-counting with natural resource funds. Deals involving renewable energy and cleantech have mainly been responsible for the large share of energy-related investments, in particular, since 2015.[94]

The performance record of renewable energy investments is, however, mixed. While it is a sector that requires development and offers M&A opportunities to exit the investment once a plant is operational, the suspension of the feed-in tariffs in 2013 in response to the euro crisis by the Spanish government highlighted the sovereign risk that investors are taking when an investment thesis hinges on subsidies. As operators were struggling to meet debt payments on their existing investment and investors faced heavy write-downs new investment activity in the sector came to a grinding halt. However, as the prices for photovoltaic (PV) modules and battery storage have fallen sharply some of those investments have become

---

[91] Preqin (2023e).
[92] Quoted from Preqin (2023f). On November 15, 2021. President Joe Biden signed the more than $1 trillion bipartisan infrastructure bill into law. The package will put $550 billion in new funds into transportation, broadband, and utilities and could significantly boost the prospects of US infrastructure funds (Pramuk, 2021).
[93] Segal (2021).
[94] Preqin (2023e).

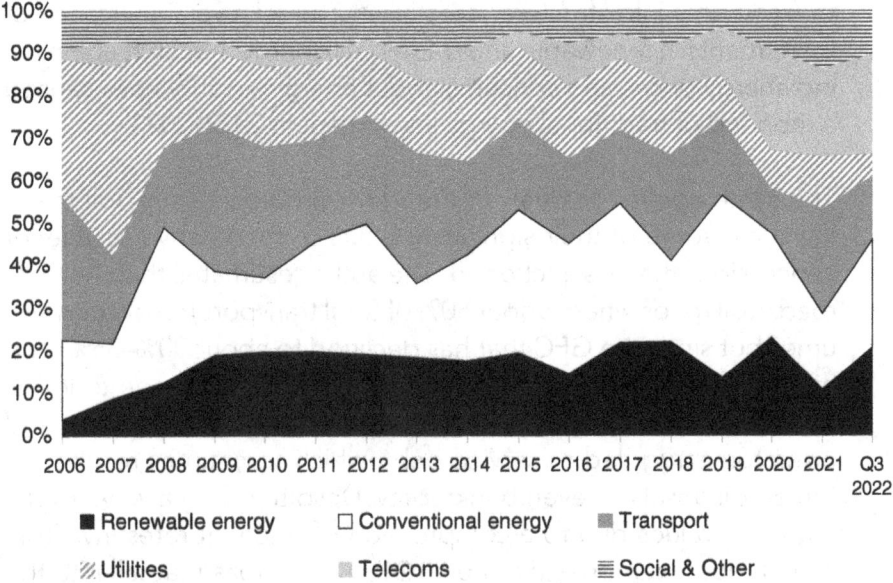

Figure 10.23   Sector share of global IS deal numbers, 2006–Q3 2022
Source: Adapted from Preqin, 2023e.

viable again or became profitable for second round investors that acquired them from distressed sellers.[95] But going forward the case for renewable energy as an infrastructure investment will change as auctioning schemes that allow "zero bids" and other adjustment mechanisms for feed-in tariffs become increasingly common and their effect is that a developer is no longer assured of a minimum electricity price. Several subsidy-free solar photovoltaic and onshore projects in Spain and offshore projects in Germany and the Netherlands have been approved. This shift in the renewables market suggests that the sector is moving into the next stage of market integration, during which governments will discontinue subsidies and developers will be completely exposed to wholesale prices.[96] this could shift investment patterns: Brookfield, for example, has taken an alternative approach to buying into the development of renewable projects by investing in the supply chain for equipment manufacturing. Owning the company that makes the "picks and shovels" gives funds broader exposure to the energy transition rather than focusing only on the build- out of assets. Such investments result in more buyout-like risk exposures compared

---

[95] Castro-Rodríguez and Miles-Touya (2019).
[96] Heiligtag, Kühn, Küster, and Schabram (2018).

to traditional infrastructure investing.[97] The relative significance of investments in renewable and traditional energy may shift again rising energy prices and concerns about energy security have caused a rebound of traditional energy investment in 2022–2023.

The same applies to deals in the transportation sector. Toll roads have lost some of their significance due to the relative scarcity of concessions that are auctioned. The author estimates that the GFC roads/toll roads where about 50% of total transport transaction volumes but since the GFC that has declined to about 30%–35%. The highly contested auctions drove valuations and leverage to levels that moved those arguably low-risk assets up the risk spectrum and operators struggled to service debt, which sometimes resulted in forced disposals or even bankruptcy. Despite riding a wave of rising asset values due to a compression of discount rates investors sometimes lost money (Figure 10.24). Other areas that fall into the transportation sector are railroads, municipal transport systems, ports and airports, where annual deal volumes can vary sharply.

Figure 10.24   In 2006, the sale of the Indiana Toll Road) for $3.8 billion to a consortium led by Macquarie and Ferrovial was the largest infrastructure privatization deal in US history. In 2015 the operating company could not service its debt anymore and filed for bankruptcy. IFM Investors bought the concession for $5.7 billion. The case illustrates that for such long-duration assets the secular decline in interest rates was a powerful driver of valuation that dominated the effect of lower than estimated (by the previous owners) revenues, which caused their insolvency.
Source: ITR Concession Co. LLC. / www.indianatollroad.org/facebook/ last accessed 8 August, 2023.

---

[97] Rosacia and Sabater (2021).

Increasingly investments in roads may not necessarily target the operation and ownership of the actual road but the investment may relate to charging networks or traffic management systems.

Another significant sector within the infrastructure is communications, which includes investment in broadband, cloud, telecom, electric vehicle (EV) charging networks, battery storage and cell tower assets. Investment in those sectors has more than doubled its share of infrastructure deal value from 11% in 2016 to 27% in 2020. These assets possess numerous attributes sought after by infrastructure investors, including tangible assets, secure market positions, and the capacity to produce consistent cash yields.[98]

Lastly, infrastructure technology or "Infratech" is the third type of infrastructure experiencing rapid expansion. Maturing network technology, combined with social changes such as the acceptance of remote working as well as the ongoing digital revolution have moved some digital assets down the risk spectrum. Modernizing existing infrastructure and building new digital infrastructure are the two primary forms of Infratech. It requires greenfield projects to roll out the required hardware. Infratech activity is already substantial: announced deals totalled $34 billion from January 2020 to July 2021.[99] These deals may not be reflected in Figure 10.23 as they often represent venture capital investments.

Investors need to be aware that there is significant overlap in infrastructure investing with other private market asset classes and vice versa. Data centers, schools, student housing, warehouses are often classified as real estate due to their bricks-and-mortar character and facility management needs. However, they are also part of the social infrastructure asset class. Mid-stream investing in pipelines or decarbonization (cleantech) investments are also example of dual asset class characteristics those deals can be found in IS or NR funds alike.

Capital Deployment and Performance Remains Challenging

Concerns about deploying capital have arisen due to the significant increase in fundraising in the private infrastructure sector in recent years. This surge has resulted in a substantial amount of

---

[98] Brinkman and Sarma (2022)
[99] Preqin (2022d). Preqin (2010b).

uninvested capital, commonly referred to as "dry powder," which reached approximately $260 billion in 2021. For funds raised between 2016 and 2021, the uninvested capital amounts to roughly 40% of the committed capital, significantly higher than the 25% seen across all private markets. The challenge of finding investment opportunities has always been a key issue, and competition for these opportunities has led to increased deal multiples and valuations over the past decade until 2021. This, in turn, has led to substantial premiums being paid for assets compared to the multiples of publicly listed infrastructure companies, which often compete for the same infrastructure assets.[100]

The concentration of fundraising suggests that significant funds must focus on substantial transactions. However, such opportunities can be challenging to come by, especially in sectors like alternative energy, communications, and infrastructure technology, where deals may not match the scale of investments that result from privatizations or auctioning of concessions. Alternatively, infrastructure funds may shift their focus toward public-to-private transactions, given the size of the listed infrastructure sector, which offers numerous opportunities. This shift raises the question for investors about how the asset class distinguishes itself from traditional buyouts or other types of private market investing and the fact that many infrastructure deals lack the typical characteristics of classic infrastructure investments, leaves investors wondering about the performance of this asset class relative to other private market strategies and compared to listed infrastructure.

Using year-end 2021 Burgiss data, the performance of infrastructure investments within the private markets exhibited relatively modest results, boasting a pooled IRR of 9.6% for funds raised in vintage 2009 to 2018, as of the end of 2021. When considering individual vintage years, the pooled IRR ranged from 5.4% to 11.6%. This result puts infrastructure fund performance at the bottom of all private market strategies (natural resources funds were not included in the data), significantly underperforming buyouts or real estate.

---

[100] Calculations of the author based on Preqin data (Preqin 2022e). (Kempler, 2020) has analyzed premiums paid by private capital compared to valuations of listed assets and found in the water and transportation sectors premiums of around 20% of EV.

While it's important to make the caveat that the performance of listed investments (ROI) is not directly comparable to the IRR, the S&P Global Infrastructure Index reported a performance of 8.8%, which suggests that the net returns of private market infrastructure funds may still be ahead of public infrastructure. In a study conducted by Australian asset manager Maple-Brown Abbott (Kempler, 2020), the FTSE Global Core Infrastructure 50/50 Index was juxtaposed with the EDHEC Global Unlisted Infrastructure Equity Infra300 Index over ten years ending on June 30, 2020. This analysis revealed an annual performance of 6.9% for listed infrastructure, compared to 10% for unlisted infrastructure. The key takeaway from this comparison is that private infrastructure investments appeared to outperform their unlisted counterparts. However, it's noteworthy that, in the broader context, infrastructure performance as an asset class remained lackluster, irrespective of whether one invested in listed or unlisted infrastructure. The study concludes that the fact that private infrastructure transactions come with higher debt levels than listed infrastructure is the main factor driving past outperformance.

A Case of Irrational Expectations?

Since 2019, each vintage year has been the lowest or second lowest performance, with median net IRRs barely reaching double digits in "good" vintage years.[101]

Investors may not mind as surveys both in the past and more recently have shown that investors expect lower risk-adjusted and absolute returns from infrastructure compared to other asset classes but believe in a high degree of inflation protection and a reliable income stream.[102]

Infrastructure investing is associated by investors with high cash flow visibility and a degree of inflation protection due to

- assets typically having high capital costs representing a significant barrier to entry

---

[101] Preqin (2022d).
[102] Preqin (2010b, 2022d), Lowe (2021).

- assets frequently operating in a regulated or contracted environment
- relatively inelastic demand
- long asset life and high replacement cost (it is also claimed to provide a hedge against inflation)
- availability of subsidies and government incentives in some sectors.

Investors regard infrastructure investments as less risky than private equity and expect their return to be a mix of capital gains and income, which is different from private equity where almost all the return is generated through capital gains.

Several studies have shown that the risk-return profile of brownfield investments can be classified between fixed income and equity investments, whereby greenfield infrastructure investments exhibit considerably larger risk-return variations than investments in classical equity.[103] The share of greenfield investments in the portfolio should therefore matter for investors as much as the allocation between core and opportunistic strategies in a real estate portfolio.

How do investors square their expectation of stable long-term returns with the fact that greenfield (new construction) investments play a significant part in their infrastructure portfolios while brownfield investments (already income-generating assets with long-term contractual cash flows) are relatively rare?[104]

Relative to rising institutional demand, there was a lack of investable, stable, income-producing assets and investments focused on infrastructure that had to be built first before it could generate income. In accepting this reality, investors often opted to invest in funds that would do greenfield projects or acquire brownfield assets that require significant investment. The strategy implied that such a fund would only generate income late in its life. Some GPs proposed longer fund lives of 12–15 years. But this comes with a trade-off. Funds with extended holding periods may lack fee reversion

[103] Beyerle, Voss, and Weber (2011), Credit Suisse Asset Management (2010).
[104] For many years infrastructure managers have described the comparative lack of deal opportunities as their biggest challenge (Preqin, 2022d).

clauses that switch from a private-equity fee structure to lower "core portfolio" fees more suitable for income-oriented investments. There is also a conflict of interest between the manager who earns carried interest upon selling an asset, while investors may prefer to keep it and receive income. As a result, investors who subscribed to these funds for their cash yields once the asset was developed realized that the private equity fee structure significantly reduces their income.[105] Even though most investors believe incentives need to be more aligned, the fact that a private equity fee structure may not be appropriate for the asset class did not deter investors.

Why do investors accept private equity-type terms (management fees, carried interest) while expecting lower risk-adjusted returns? Why would one invest through a limited life partnership if the goal is to receive long-term stable cash flows after the asset has been developed? One answer is that there was a lack of alternatives. While this is changing (see the following description of continuation funds), there simply needed to be more income-oriented infrastructure funds when demand surged in response to the low-interest rate environment post-GFC.

In a paper published in 2021, A. Andonov, of the University of Amsterdam, together with R. Kräussl and J. Rau, both at Stanford University and the Hoover Institution, analyzed the exposure that investors actually get through their participation in private IS funds.[106] According to the researchers, infrastructure funds demonstrate cash flow volatility and cyclicity that can be likened to other private equity investments. Like private equity, the primary driver of their performance is the realization of valuation gains through deal exits rather than income generation. Despite poor

---

[105] This issue has been identified for quite a long time by industry analysts and academic research (Preqin, 2010b; Birtsch, Buchner, and Kaserer, 2010).
[106] The analysis relies on Preqin data, but the authors also compare the performance of infrastructure funds reporting in Preqin with the funds reporting in Burgiss. The sample includes infrastructure investments from January 1990 until June 2020, but the vast majority of investments happened during the 2008–2020 period when infrastructure developed as an asset class. In total, the paper draws on 5,920 commitments of investors to infrastructure funds and 2,049 direct investments in assets. Directly and through funds, institutional investors gained exposure to 5,907 unique infrastructure assets (Andonov, Kräussl, and Rau, 2021).

risk-adjusted performance and a frequent inability to source transactions that match the purported characteristics of infrastructure assets, closed-end funds have gained more commitments over time, especially from public investors. The authors then attempt to shed light on investors' motivations for investing in infrastructure strategies and investment vehicles that are not fully aligned with their stated objectives and may appear to be a poor (less well performing) cousin of traditional buyouts.

Despite the somewhat unfavorable risk-return characteristics of the past, their findings suggest that demand for infrastructure funds is driven by the desire to make "green" investments, at least among public pension funds. According to their results, public investors who signed the UN Principles of Responsible Investment (UN PRI) allocated more capital to infrastructure investments than those who did not. The authors assert that the adoption of the UN PRI and voluntary ESG regulations account for between 25% and 40% of the increase in infrastructure investments made by public investors. The UN PRI principles were established on the belief that integrating ESG criteria into the investment process aligns with traditional risk and return objectives, but the reality may be more complex. When it comes to the trade-off between ESG-friendly investments and performance, investors face the challenge of finding the right balance. They must also keep an eye on the evolving interpretation of fiduciary duties. But there is also a performance debate and some jurisdictions have seen a backlash against ESG considerations in investments, such as Florida's ban on ESG considerations in state investments, which resulted in the state pension fund withdrawing funds from ESG-themed investments.[107]

Policy Initiatives to Boost Infrastructure Investments

Infrastructure investing has been moving up the political agenda. Regulation has enabled the increasing prominence of infrastructure in institutional portfolios.

By amending the rules on how much capital insurance companies need to hold, the European Commission aimed to unlock

---

[107] DeSantis (2023).

more institutional investments in infrastructure. In April 2016, the Solvency II Delegated Regulation provided insurers and reinsurers with better capital treatment for a new distinct asset category of "Qualified Infrastructure Investments," with the calibration of the stress factor for such an investment in equity being lowered from 49% to 30%.[108] While there is room for interpretation about how these lower capital charges will apply to private infrastructure funds, it has boosted investment in the sector and further increased demand for continuation vehicles with stable cash flow-generating assets. On November 6, 2021, the US House of Representatives passed the $1.2 trillion bipartisan Infrastructure Investment and Jobs Act that will provide funding for a broad range of infrastructure projects across the transportation, water, power, broadband, and cybersecurity sectors.[109] Further proposals that have not been passed into law would increase social infrastructure and healthcare funding.

In September 2020, the EU Commission outlined its plan to reduce CO_2 emissions by 55% by 2030 and announced at least 30% of the EU's €1 trillion long-term budget will be spent on climate-related measures.[110] There will be opportunities for private market investors, in particular, in infrastructure, a sector that has already seen a market shift toward investment strategies that focus on renewable energy. In reaction to Russia's invasion of Ukraine, the EU presented the RePowerEU policy proposal in March 2022. RePowerEU builds on the EU's July 2021 adoption of the Fit for 55 law. The idea incorporates energy efficiency-enhancing techniques that would reduce energy consumption. In addition, REPowerEU wants to accelerate the transition to green energy and encourage investment in renewables. REPowerEU will enhance the EU's renewable energy target for 2030 from 40% to 45%.[111]

---

[108] While the initial relaxation of capital requirements was focused on brownfield assets with stable cash flows (Schearer, 2016), there are further initiatives underway to relax capital requirements for a broader range of investments and security types and to include banks' capital requirements (Frost, 2022).
[109] US Congress, Public Law No: 117-58 (11/15/2021).
[110] BBC (2021).
[111] Kreke (2022).

These initiatives reflect growing political support and public money for infrastructure investments that can be expected to create additional investment opportunities going forward.

Continuation Vehicles and Open-Ended Funds

Permanent vehicles and platforms that are jointly owned by institutions address the objective of holding assets for the longer term (income motive) at moderate fees and have become the preferred route in Australia for most pension funds since the GFC. In the "Australian model," infrastructure funds like to portray themselves as "investor-friendly," as they tend to have lower fees than the closed-end, private equity–type funds that are most commonly used for infrastructure investment in Europe and the United States. Pension funds own some asset managers (e.g., Industry Funds Management (IFM)) or government agencies run investment vehicles where institutional investors can invest (e.g., Queensland Investment Corporation, QIC). Outside Australia, there are signs that the market is changing too, and the available options for investors have expanded in this area. Firms such as IFM[112] and AMP Capital[113] (both Australian) run multibillion-dollar platforms of open-ended funds that specialize in acquiring stabilized infrastructure assets. Macquarie Capital, one of the largest infrastructure asset managers, raised several of its Super Core Series open-ended funds. Another large player, Infrastructure Partners, raised a total of $22 billion for its open-ended funds in early 2022,[114] and Brookfield announced the launch of its fifth flagship core infrastructure fund with a target size of $25 billion in February 2022.[115]

Rather than selling assets to third-party investors, typically large pension funds and SWFs that make direct investments, GPs may

---

[112] IFM Investors (est. 1999) started as the Development Australia Fund (DAF Limited). It is owned by a group of pension funds and has $48 billion of infrastructure AuM (IPE, 2021). Its platform includes large open-ended infrastructure vehicles as well as SMAs. It is expanding its business globally through various offices in the USA, Europe, and Asia.

[113] AMP Capital is part of AMP Group (est. 1849) which is one of Australia's largest retail and corporate pension providers. It offers open-ended core real estate and infrastructure funds.

[114] Petersen (2022).

[115] Odeh (2022).

use continuation funds to extend the holding period. This pattern has already been seen in buyouts and is also visible in infrastructure investments.

The market for secondaries-focused infrastructure funds is expected to exceed $15 billion by 2025. Several managers are actively raising funds to invest in GP-led secondaries and their continuation vehicles or to buy stabilized assets directly out of funds that have reached the end of their fund life. For example, Pantheon Ventures was marketing its fourth flagship infrastructure fund in late 2021 after raising $2.2 billion for its third flagship fund in 2018. Furthermore, Pantheon Ventures raised £400 million ($550 million) on the London Stock Exchange in November 2021 for a continuation vehicle. Ardian, based in Paris, also marketed a pure infrastructure secondaries fund in 2021.[116] In January 2022, Stonepeak Infrastructure Partners, New York, announced that it had secured $3 billion in commitments for a continuation fund that houses Colonix, a data center platform that previously was held by one of its funds.[117]

Investors may allocate infrastructure through small stakes in infrastructure partnerships and negotiate the first right of refusal to acquire holdings from investors who do not wish to roll over into a continuation vehicle. By supplying funds to pay off exiting investors, they can accumulate considerable interests in the continuation vehicle. Stabilized assets have a smaller capital charge under Solvency II than private equity–type investments, making them more appealing to insurance companies.

Considerations When Investing in Continuation Vehicles or Open-Ended Funds

- **Valuation:** Transferring an asset into a continuation fund is treated as an exit. The valuation determines the carried interest the GP receives. Often investors demand that the GP reinvests such performance fees into the continuation vehicle to align GPs and LPs. As non-participating LPs receive cash, there is a potential conflict of interest as continuing investors, as well as any new investors, benefit from a low entry valuation. Participation

---

[116] Chong (2022).
[117] Bentley (2022).

of outside investors, such as a secondary fund, does not automatically mean that the external validation results in a "fair" valuation.

- **Fund life:** The fund life limit applies to continuation vehicles too, but it is conceivable to use generous extension rights. Typically, a continuation fund will have a liquidity period of three to four years, as opposed to ten years for the original fund. LPs must ensure that the duration of the continuation vehicle and any extensions are adequately defined.

- **Exit provisions:** For investors in open-ended funds, it is important to understand redemption rights and limit their stakes in individual funds to avoid being a significant investor and avoid liquidity issues once they decide to redeem. Generally, large capital pools are more credible in providing such redemptions, and having cornerstone investors willing to buy additional stakes helps too.

- **Tiered fee structures:** An examination of the evidence of tiered fee structures in private market funds, by looking at 218 public pension funds' reported net-of-fee returns across 2,400 fund commitments, revealed that most funds have multiple tiers of fees. The fee dispersion (either management fee or carried interest) (i) varies during the fundraising cycle (higher dispersion when fundraising is difficult as in 2003–2004 or 2008–2010) and (ii) that within-fund dispersion in management and carry is highest for infrastructure funds.[118] It is, therefore, an advantage to concentrate investments and become a significant stakeholder, which needs to be weighed against the potential exit issue that may cause.

- **Alignment of incentives:** Extending holding periods with the primary objective of receiving a cash yield necessitates lower management fees and the substitution of carried interest with incentives tied to achieving specific cash yield targets. Many investors will find that their objectives for infrastructure investment will only be met when negotiating these provisions. An understanding of how auctions for concessions work and the impact of leverage restrictions (or their absence) on valuations is essential for investors seeking to manage the risk profile of their

---

[118] Begenau and Siriwardane (2022).

infrastructure commitments. By imposing appropriate restrictions, most notably on deal-level leverage, investors can steer managers toward investments that better fit their objectives and risk appetite.

- **More extended holding periods can have a downside too:** While investors are not asked to provide rescue funding for an underperforming investment they must still consider a scenario in which such an asset encounters unforeseen difficulties or is unpopular, making it difficult to sell at the end of the expected holding period.[119]

Natural Resources

After the drop in oil prices during the GFC, prices recovered and stayed historically high, with West Texas Intermediate (WTI or NYMEX) trading above $100 from November 2009 until October 2014. This spurred investment activity. Natural resources funds were invested in approximately 300 exploration and production (E&P) companies in the United States in 2013.[120] Well-established PE firms continued to raise multibillion-dollar E&P funds. Blackstone, for example, raised a $4.5 billion energy fund in February 2015, only three years after introducing a fund of $2.4 billion, and EnCap raised Capital Fund XI above target at $7 billion, in 2017.[121] Between 2015 and 2019, US PE firms spent $64 billion, of which $44 billion was spent on unconventional E&P in the United States—fundamentally transforming the US energy landscape.[122]

When the oil price fell and remained mostly below $60 per barrel between 2014 and 2020, it was difficult for natural resource funds and their portfolio companies to meet their profitability targets. The flurry of PE-fueled E&P activity led to an oversupply of E&P companies that wanted to sell their assets to the big oil companies while they were cutting back on production and slowing their acquisition pace. The oil and gas PE model that dominated the

[119] Forestner and Young (2021).
[120] Haines (2013).
[121] EnCap (2017).
[122] Kumar et al. (2016), Field (2021). Unconventional oil and natural gas exploration refers to horizontal drilling and hydraulic fracturing technologies.

industry for over a decade completely broke down. Then, the fall in oil prices in early 2020 pushed the entire US hydrocarbon industry into a full-scale retraction, making natural resources the worst performing asset class in 2020.[123] The value adjustments on their portfolios pushed returns down, and many funds lost money.

But things changed in 2021: by the end of that year, natural resources funds were on a hot streak as energy prices worldwide rose quickly due to a faster-than-anticipated post-COVID-19 rebound and geopolitically motivated supply threats and limits. After Russia invaded Ukraine, the supply shortages entered an entirely new phase. The supply constraints for most commodities, especially energy, have grown even more severe due to waves of previously unheard-of sanctions placed on Russia by numerous nations. The USA became the largest LNG exporter in the world during the first half of 2022, overtaking other historical exporters such as Qatar and Australia. Growth was driven by LNG exports to Europe whose share doubled to 70% compared to 2021.[124]

After the war started, commodity prices rose, making natural resources the best-performing asset class among alternatives. Through March 2022, this asset class had a record-high one-year horizon IRR of 34.6%. Pure natural resources funds called $15 billion in capital for the year ending March 2022 while distributing $37 billion, resulting in a record-breaking net distribution of $22 billion. But natural resources funds only raised $3.8 billion through the first three quarters of 2022, despite the extraordinary returns and the persistent global energy crisis. Investor interest in the conventional energy sector has been low, however, 2022 was projected to be on track to be the worst year for pure natural resources fundraising in more than a decade (Figure 10.25).[125]

The opposite trend was observed in the field of renewable energy. Bound by commitments made in the Kyoto Protocol in 1997 and the Paris Agreement in 2016, a number of countries had formulated plans to expedite the development of alternative energy sources such as wind, solar, and biomass. This included guaranteed feedin

---

[123] Flowers (2019).
[124] Renshaw and Scott Disavino (2022).
[125] Preqin (2023f).

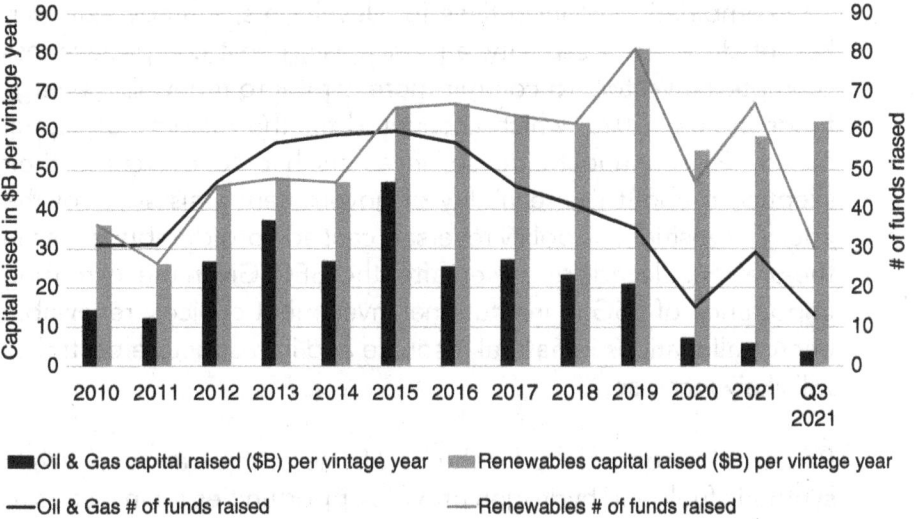

Figure 10.25   Natural resources capital and # of funds raised for traditional and renewable energy, vintage years 2010–Q3 2021, $B.

Source: Adapted from Preqin.

Note: the chart does not show fundraising for other types of natural resources such as timber or mining.

tariffs, subsidies, preferential loans, and commitments by large energy utilities to target a particular proportion of renewable energy in power generation.

As a result, electric utilities began acquiring renewable energy production plants and the companies that operate them. According to the Bain Capital Report (2022), energy transition transactions accounted for approximately 20% of all energy-sector transactions greater than $1 billion in 2021.[126]

The growing demand for renewable energy has also increased its cost competitiveness compared to traditional energy sources. The global benchmark levelized cost of electricity, or LCOE, from onshore wind was $47 per megawatt-hour in the second half of 2019, according to Bloomberg NEF analysis. This was down 49% compared to the second half of 2009. For offshore wind, the global benchmark LCOE in the second half of 2019 was $78 per MWh, 51% lower than in 2009.[127]

---

[126] Keuer, Lee, and Leroi (2022).
[127] Frankfurt School-UNEP Centre/BNEF (2020).

The combination of incentives for developers, a ready exit market for developed capacity, and increasing cost competitiveness prompted investors to commit more capital to renewable energy funds in 2019–2020, which accounted for the majority of capital raised. To continue to do so, investors had to overcome their skepticism about the reliability of government assistance for the energy transition, as policy reversals caused considerable losses in the previous decade and even after the GFC. Given the increasing importance of ESG in institutional investment choices, renewable energy allocations in natural resource and infrastructure portfolios will likely increase.

Renewables continue to be the backbone of this transition. While synthetic fuels and hydrogen provide opportunities for investors to get in early on new technology, traditional renewable energy will continue to be the central pillar of the energy transition.[128] Renewable energy and clean technology require more precious metals and minerals in their production—chiefly lithium, cobalt, nickel, and graphite—than their fossil fuel counterparts. US manufacturing will need sources for these materials to keep up with demand, many of which, particularly cobalt and lithium, will need to come from other countries, creating a potential bottleneck in its progress toward net zero.[129] This creates opportunities in the mining sector which raised only 15% of the funds compared to those that went into conventional energy funds during 2010–2021.

10.5   A POWERFUL TIDE THAT LIFTED ALL BOATS

After the GFC, investors repositioned their portfolios to include more private market exposure. As of year-end 2021, venture capital has been the best-performing strategy for vintage years 2009–2018, followed by buyouts and growth financing (Table 10.11). Abundant liquidity, low inflation, decent economic growth, and a technology boom were powerful drivers for deal-making and performance.

---

[128] Palmer (2022).
[129] IEA (2021).

Table 10.11   Fundraising for private market asset classes, 2010–2021, $B

Year of Final Close	VC	Buyouts	Growth	IS	NR	RE	Private Debt	FoFs	Secondaries FoFs
2001	46.4	59.6	6.9	0.2	2.7	16.3	13.0	10.4	4.1
2002	18.9	63.0	7.1	1.4	3.8	13.9	16.2	11.8	4.2
2003	13.6	43.8	3.3	1.1	7.7	13.7	12.3	8.0	5.8
2004	28.8	67.5	4.2	4.8	15.1	39.8	26.5	19.4	8.4
2005	36.3	143.2	16.0	9.8	24.7	69.7	26.1	29.9	6.5
2006	44.6	225.8	17.3	25.3	42.9	95.6	43.0	31.7	15.9
2007	47.7	250.0	29.2	44.5	73.7	127.4	81.1	55.0	12.8
2008	51.3	234.3	38.6	41.5	76.6	129.8	51.0	52.6	7.2
2009	27.7	113.1	36.7	16.7	34.7	42.0	30.6	25.3	22.2
2010	34.8	79.8	50.8	46.0	52.6	51.1	46.2	14.7	12.2
2011	52.3	93.4	55.9	37.0	72.1	60.4	46.6	17.0	10.3
2012	48.5	103.2	63.8	60.0	63.6	77.5	78.6	23.0	19.9
2013	46.3	191.3	70.8	89.0	68.6	92.8	77.0	19.0	22.6
2014	70.1	187.7	81.6	88.0	80.6	91.8	79.5	20.5	28.8
2015	102.8	179.4	94.3	109.0	61.4	125.5	119.3	37.6	19.9
2016	147.9	244.4	100.6	105.0	40.2	108.0	135.0	57.9	28.2
2017	170.3	308.4	165.1	110.0	52.3	103.7	145.3	57.7	47.7
2018	179.1	240.5	128.6	128.0	46.1	120.8	151.9	49.3	46.5
2019	154.9	388.9	140.5	135.0	50.4	160.8	161.0	42.7	32.8
2020	170.5	274.2	220.9	111.0	39.4	113.3	192.5	43.3	98.9
2021	221.4	333.0	233.7	129.2	49.0	150.2	230.2	68.0	63.8

Source: Preqin, PitchBook, various sources cited previously.

Private markets became more diverse as private debt and infrastructure captured a significant share of total fundraising. At the same time, venture capital made a comeback, holding the performance top spot in most vintage years during 2009–2018 (Figure 10.26). But even at the low end of the performance scale, returns were still compelling, keeping in mind that the numbers relate to average pooled IRRs and not top-quartile returns.

Private markets have seen a continued upward trend over the past four decades, with new investors and larger allocations from institutions. Despite financial crises and recessions causing temporary pauses, 2021 saw impressive milestones, including buyout deal

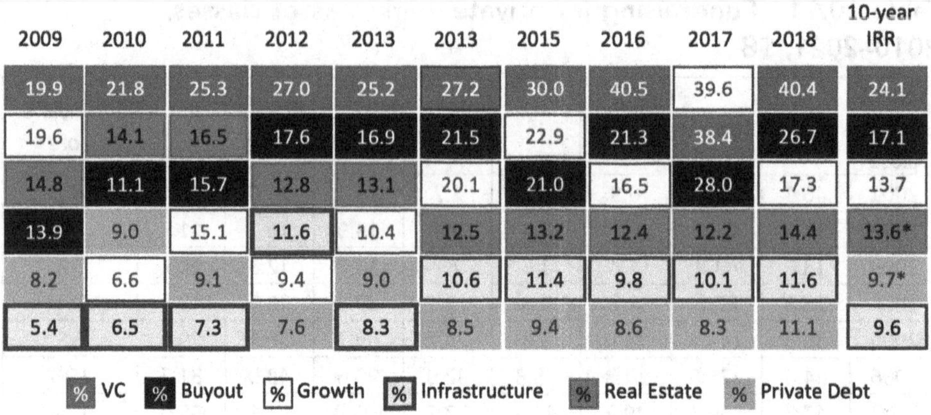

2009	2010	2011	2012	2013	2013	2015	2016	2017	2018	10-year IRR
19.9	21.8	25.3	27.0	25.2	27.2	30.0	40.5	39.6	40.4	24.1
19.6	14.1	16.5	17.6	16.9	21.5	22.9	21.3	38.4	26.7	17.1
14.8	11.1	15.7	12.8	13.1	20.1	21.0	16.5	28.0	17.3	13.7
13.9	9.0	15.1	11.6	10.4	12.5	13.2	12.4	12.2	14.4	13.6*
8.2	6.6	9.1	9.4	9.0	10.6	11.4	9.8	10.1	11.6	9.7*
5.4	6.5	7.3	7.6	8.3	8.5	9.4	8.6	8.3	11.1	9.6

% VC   % Buyout   % Growth   % Infrastructure   % Real Estate   % Private Debt

Figure 10.26   Looking back at the end of 2021: private market sub-asset class performance by vintage year, 2009–2018, and 10-year pooled IRR, as of December 2021.
Source: Adapted from McKinsey, 2022; data: Burgiss; pooled net IRR since inception as of December 2021 for 2009–2018 vintage year funds.

volume surpassing $1 trillion, the valuation of unicorns reaching $4 trillion, and SPAC mergers exceeding $300 billion. Non-traditional investors like hedge funds, sovereign wealth funds, and large pension funds also invested more than $260 billion in later funding rounds for technology companies.

Not all private market investments will yield positive returns or even return capital. Overfunding and overinvestment are common in the technology sector, and trends such as SPAC issuance may not survive a downturn. However, some changes, such as longer private ownership and increased permanent capital, may persist beyond the current cycle. Similarly, despite fluctuations in demand, efforts to provide retail investors access to private markets are expected to continue.

Similar to past cycles, the industry is not only facing pressure on valuations and an uncertain outlook for some investments but also has ample capital to deploy going forward. According to one estimate, uncalled capital exceeded $1 trillion in January 2022. Roughly half of this capital is relatively "fresh," with a vintage year of 2019 or later.[130] GPs are thus under no pressure to deploy capital quickly, and their revenues are somewhat protected by the fact that management fees are generally based on committed capital

---

[130] Alluve (2022).

during the investment period rather than NAVs, which started declining after 2H 2022. Private market funds can also keep assets during a downturn without providing liquidity or responding to redemption requests.

Many institutional investors regard private markets as well positioned to drive long-term innovation, job creation, and play a role in closing the infrastructure gap. It, therefore, seems reasonable to assume that private markets will continue to play an important role in the asset allocation of institutional portfolios. The experience of outperformance that many of those investors have had over long periods suggests that investors' demand will remain strong.

But the nimbleness and opportunistic investment behavior that are hallmarks of its ability to realize opportunities in very different economic environments also point to changing risk-return profiles that investors need to appreciate. As secondaries have increasingly provided replacement capital for continuation funds, their risk profile has changed. Co-investments and direct investments require different skills and require substantial scale to ensure exposure to a number of deals that is large enough to provide a high probability of benefiting from high-performers that drive returns. The growth of the private debt markets comes with a proliferation of deals with weak covenant protection, and this may haunt investors in the event that defaults increase and workouts become more numerous.

Investors have been sanguine about conflicts of interest that multiply as a result of the transition from one-strategy firms to multi-product providers that not only the very large firms underwent. The allocation of deals, investing in both equity and debt of a transaction, trading assets within a GP's roster of affiliated funds, or selling assets to perpetual pools of capital that have different risk-return profiles, all pose challenges that are different from the old days when GPs would invest in one fund at a time. Transparency is still an issue as investors often lack both the resources and the information to truly verify the actual interpretation and implementation of provisions in the limited partnership agreements that describe those matters. Traditionally, value-generation in private markets has always been driven by an alignment of interest that ensured that capital was invested and realized within flexible but ultimately constrained time frames, LPs have been willing to loosen that constraint and give GPs more discretion over holding periods. The hallowed "time diversification" that is often cited as a strength of the asset class has been weakened in favor of "market timing." Limited time ownership is slowly moving toward a Berkshire Hathaway model. But Warren Buffet is famous because he is an outlier in doing something so successful that has generally not worked (conglomerates).

While the future remains uncertain, one thing is clear when looking back at the development of private markets since the end of the Global Financial Crisis: investors in the asset class have experienced unprecedented levels of success after the GFC. However, the industry's biggest challenge may lie in the potential for hubris that can come with such success. It is important for GPs to remain grounded and not overestimate their ability to generate outsized returns in a rapidly evolving and increasingly competitive market.

10.6   BACK TO THE BEGINNING AND BEYOND

In early 2022, Bain & Company published its 13th annual Global Private Equity Report entitled "A Year for the Record Books." The title suggests that we had reached a peak that marked the end of an era after two decades that were turbocharged by low interest rates and abundant liquidity. It sometimes seemed as if anyone could make a healthy return from private market investing.

And then the tide went out. Rising inflation, economic slowdown fears, the war in Ukraine, and supply chain issues caused a stock market downturn led by the technology sector. Similar to the correction that followed the dotcom boom, some venture-backed listed firms witnessed 80–90% declines in their share price. The FED raised interest rates aggressively, risking a hard landing in the real economy. Sovereign debt faced stress, with Italian ten-year bond yields reaching 4.6% in December 2022.[131] China lost favor with investors even before the US Secretary of Commerce

---

[131] *The Economist* (2023b) quotes a BlackRock survey that shows that 43% of institutions were planning to substantially increase their allocation to private markets.

called the country "uninvestable."[132] MSCI China Tech 100 was
down 33% in November 2022, more than MSCI World Information
Technology, which was down 25%.[133] Private markets investing did
not escape the downturn. Economic uncertainty and the higher
cost of debt drove a wedge between buyer and seller expectations. Deal numbers and volumes declined in 2022 and were below
50% of 2021's volume. Exits are similar. In the first nine months of
2022, private equity exits fell 60% in value and 54.5% in the number of deals. The IPO market has also declined, and IPO exits had
not been this low since 2008. Some 65.5% of investors surveyed
by Preqin in September 2022 believed portfolio companies are
overvalued.[134] A growing chorus of voices warned of a more prolonged downturn. Tesla CEO Elon Musk announced a hiring freeze
and warned of a 12–18-month recession. JPMorgan Chase CEO,
Jamie Dimon said: "Brace yourself for an economic hurricane,"
and Sequoia described the combination (in mid-2022) of turbulent
financial markets, inflation, and geopolitical conflict as a "crucible moment" of uncertainty and change.[135] Investors may discover
that achieving the robust internal rates of return experienced in
recent years could prove challenging, and gains in valuation may
dissipate. It is easy to get fixated on the here and now and commentators will be busy explaining what it all means. However, it is
crucial to recognize that this is not the first downturn and will not
be the last. Just as in previous cycles, the private market industry
has the potential to adapt and capitalize on the opportunities presented by a different market environment.

These historical examples have demonstrated the categorization
of investors into two distinct groups since ancient times: active
participants, such as lead investors and entrepreneurs, and passive
investors, such as partners and stockholders. Over time, the role
of active players has transitioned to skilled professional managers, while passive investors have witnessed a shift toward greater
involvement through intermediation by asset management professionals.

---

[132] ABC News (2023).
[133] MSCI (2022).
[134] Preqin (2023a).
[135] Quoted from Reuters (2022), Son (2022), and Di Stefano, Clark and Wingfield
(2022).

As capital needs rose and capital ownership was more dispersed, collective investment vehicles emerged—with limited partnerships and joint-stock companies being the most common ones—to facilitate participation of an increasing number of investors. Intriguingly, as ownership of financial capital expanded, a simultaneous centralization of fiduciary responsibilities occurred. The driving force behind this centralization was the ascendancy of institutional investors, most notably pension funds, insurance companies, and mutual funds, which progressively asserted their influence over financial markets. This seismic shift gave birth to the modern asset management industry and private markets investing, which was effectively created in response to the institutionalization of financial markets. Private markets investing grew through the support of large investors, particularly pension funds and more recently a growing cohort of sovereign wealth funds. The distinct characteristic of this asset class, demanding significant entry investments often ranging from millions to tens of millions of dollars, inherently targets large pools of capital rather than catering to the broader landscape of private investors.

Limited partnerships introduced the concept of temporary ownership, which was matched by firm capital commitments with no redemption rights. Partnerships are designed to incorporate time diversification, safeguarding GPs and investors against overconfidence in their market-timing abilities. Market-timing and stock-picking have been the cornerstone of alpha generation (or the lack of it) by traditional active management. Blackstone and BlackRock offer contrasting yet complementary alternatives to the traditional approach. BlackRock's ascent reflects the growth in demand for passive investments in public markets, whereas Blackstone thrives on value creation through active ownership. The rise of index investing marks a departure from conventional stock-picking, with an emphasis on eliminating company-specific risk in portfolios and offering consistent liquidity at very low cost. In the realm of private markets, the focus shifts from market timing, even though it involves substantial company-specific risk, facilitated by firm capital commitments and investors' willingness to agree to an incentive structure that is aligned with the goal of substantial capital gains. Put together, the two approaches look like a barbell approach in comparison with traditional portfolio management, and their success shows that investors have been willing to follow those guides.

However, temporary ownership introduces a conflict between the need for discipline imposed by limited investment horizons and the desire to maximize investment potential. The rise of direct investments by large institutional investors, not bound by these constraints, has compelled private markets managers to respond by seeking to extend the duration of their asset ownership. However, prolonged ownership may lead to increased correlation with public markets and the momentum for value creation may decline over longer holding periods. More discretion for managers to extend holding periods may expose investors to the perils of market timing, which would all make the industry more like the traditional active managers it has come to replace.

A fascinating parallel emerges when comparing the dynamics of the private markets industry to the broader financial sector. The consolidation pattern, where a handful of dominant entities appear amidst a sea of smaller players numbering in the thousands, is not unique to private markets but rather emblematic of the financial industry's natural progression. Notably, the architects of the thriving mega-firms within the private markets domain identified and seized upon this dynamic. And it will not stop there.

Private credit is now disrupting the conventional role of banks, as their lending practices often hinge on volatile short-term deposits, causing cyclic fluctuations in lending activities. In contrast, private debt funds, backed by committed equity, have the advantage of offering loans with the assurance that their funding remains steadfast. The recurring instability within the banking realm, and the systemic risks that are tied to bank financing heavily reliant on transient deposits, underscores the growing significance of private credit and its potential as an alternative model for lending.

However, the private markets investment approach, where equity is available for a limited time and a fee structure designed for a capital gain-oriented absolute return strategy, might have been stretched too far. Investors are increasingly turning to investment models in sectors like infrastructure or private debt that align better with their investment timelines and objectives. The industry has to evolve to provide this alignment not only to maintain its investor base but also to tap new sources of capital.

As private markets investing has become widely adopted, it is approaching a saturation point with its core institutional capital providers. This suggests that future growth in funds raised will likely match those investors' overall growth of assets rather than the rapid expansion seen over the last two decades due to limited penetration and portfolio under-allocation.

The significant rise in allocations from sovereign wealth funds (SWFs) to private markets since the early 2000s is a development that will not repeat itself. Therefore, further expansion requires the introduction of fresh investment models and the cultivation of new investor bases.

Already, solutions that offer some liquidity and cater to high-net-worth individuals and sometimes retail investors have emerged and are expected to gain more prominence. Additionally, strategies that move toward lower risk and return starting points, diverging from the higher risk and return characteristics that define many private market strategies, offer a way to pursue further growth.

It remains to be seen whether private markets will evolve toward more permanent ownership or if temporary ownership will continue to prevail. Investors will decide whether to support these trends or maintain the status quo. Additionally, their responsibilities will expand in other areas as well. They must strike a balance between qualitative investment objectives while remaining focused on their fiduciary duties and the imperative to generate attractive risk-adjusted returns for their stakeholders. Investment decisions require judgment grounded in understanding value creation and acknowledging that investing involves navigating randomness and uncertainty. While the literature and media often spotlight the successes and failures of deal-makers, this book offers an empirical perspective that aims to debunk some myths surrounding the asset class.

Capital for all types of private market investments is now widely available. Private market firms currently have investments in all sectors of the economy. Given the expanding scale and scope of private markets, the increasing role of large institutions as direct and co-investors, and the dry powder of more than $1 trillion in private market funds, there is the ability to address mounting social and environmental challenges. To take up that task is becoming increasingly important. In doing so, the private markets industry will benefit from its pragmatism, the ability to help solve future challenges not simply by extrapolating our current capabilities but by powering our ability to transform new knowledge into solutions.

The reader may wonder whether the industry will not outgrow the opportunities where its capital can be profitably employed.

Looking back at centuries of private capital investing there is one reassuring trend—a steadily growing opportunity set requiring ever-increasing amounts of capital despite the cyclical ups and downs. There is one singular reason for that: the expansion of human knowledge.

Based on a catalog of technological breakthroughs and scientific discoveries that he compiled in his book, R. Buckminster Fuller concluded that not only is knowledge increasing exponentially, but its growth rate is accelerating in a way that surpasses our existing reference points. Since World War II, knowledge has experienced exponential growth and has become the primary driver of trans-formative changes in how we live, work, consume, and interact. To unlock human knowledge and create real-world impact requires capital—both human and financial. The profound magnitude of accelerating transformations does provide a steady stream of opportunities (Figure 10.27).

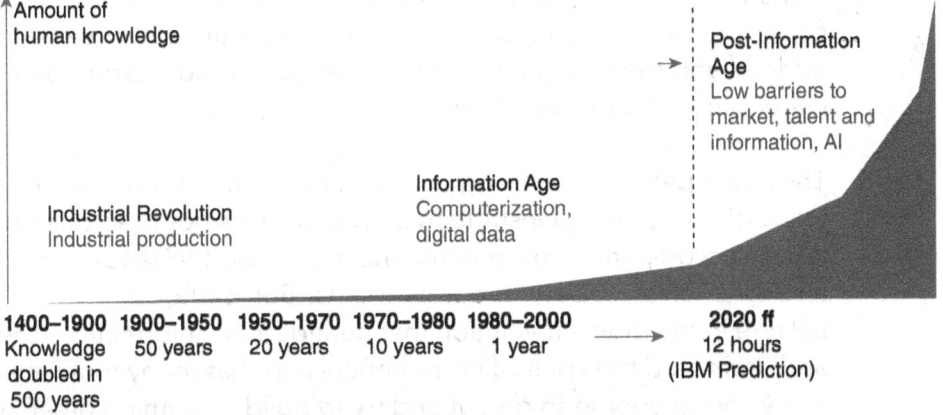

Figure 10.27   IBM and Buckminster Fuller's knowledge doubling curve.
Source: Fuller (1982); www.medium.com.
Note: The IBM forecast was added to a 1982 reprint of the book by IBM.

As new markets and new ways of doing things emerge, individuals and organizations struggle to adopt and adapt. The transformation of businesses and industries is an inescapable part of progress and a steady source of investment opportunities. And this process is ongoing.

> Companies that don't adopt AI may find it difficult to stay relevant in a rapidly changing market, as their products and services may no longer meet the needs of their customers. The integration of AI and cloud computing has the potential to greatly impact businesses as it allows businesses to access AI tools and resources on demand, without the need for large upfront investments in hardware and software. This makes it easier for businesses of all sizes to adopt AI and reap its benefits.[136]

And there is the human element. Since Frederick Terman promoted entrepreneurship, the idea of not following your ideas out of fear of failure has, for many people, become somewhat foolish. Entrepreneurship has spread worldwide, with many more people willing to accept the risk of joining a startup instead of opting for the relative safety of employment in a large enterprise.

The increasing acceptance of entrepreneurship widens the available talent pool to unlock and utilize the explosive growth of knowledge that characterizes the post–Information Age. Fuller's curve suggests that we need a vast collection of talent. And if necessity is the mother of invention, the growing awareness of ESG issues points to great and grave challenges that humanity needs to address and these require a transformation that goes beyond our current means and capabilities.

The rise of patient capital and private markets' inclusion in the portfolios of thousands of institutional investors was not preordained. It was accompanied by booms and busts, performance cycles, and an endless debate about its merits. But it played an essential role in the digital revolution that heralded the Information Age and promoted the spirit of entrepreneurship that today motivates many young people to go out and try to build something great. It

---

[136] This statement has been generated by ChatOpenAI, based on the GPT-3 language model, which is one of the largest and most advanced language models developed to date.

also helped to improve the performance of many companies, put infrastructure in place, and generated attractive returns for investors along the way.

So, as an investment model and asset class, private markets have stood the test of time. While there will be setbacks and disappointments, there is no reason to doubt—amidst accelerating change—that the deployment of patient risk capital through a variety of strategies and across the size spectrum of opportunities will continue to play an important role in institutional and increasingly private investment portfolio and thus reshape capital markets.

The book began by depicting Magellan's ships sailing into the unknown for a westward route to the East. Its final image shows the *Nao Victoria*, the expedition's only ship to return (Figure 10.28). The mission was a financial success since its cargo compensated for the lost ships and profited its investors. The expedition's success ensured the knowledge and information about faraway lands were returned home. When the ship's captain anchored at Seville, he also proved a point: there are risks worth taking.

Figure 10.28   The *Nao Victoria*—under its captain Juan Sebastián Elcano— accomplished the circumnavigation and was the only ship to return from the Magellan expedition in September 1520. The cargo carried by the *Nao Victoria* made the whole expedition profitable. Also, for mapmakers, the true size and scope of the planet had been revealed.

Source: Detail from a map by Abraham Ortelius. Created January 1590. www.helmink .com, public domain.

References

Aarts, S. and Baum, A.E. (2016). Performance persistence in real estate private equity. *Journal of Property Research*, 33: 1–16.

ABC News. (2023). US Commerce Secretary warns China will be 'uninvestable' without action on raids, fines. August 30. https://abcnews.go.com/Business/wireStory/us-commerce-secretary-warns-china-uninvestable-action-raids-102671265

Acemoglu, D., Johnson, S., and Robinson, J. (2005). The rise of Europe: Atlantic trade, institutional change, and economic growth, *American Economic Review*, 95(3).

Acharya, V.V. and Richardson, M. (2021). Causes of the financial crisis. *Critical Review*, 21(2–2): 195–210.

Achleitner, A.-K.B. (2018). Private equity group reputation and financing structures in German leveraged buyouts. *Journal of Business Economics*.

Adams Street Partners. (2021). Distribution of total gain by portfolio companies. https://www.adamsstreetpartners.com

Adams Street Partners. (2022). Our firm: history. https://www.adamsstreetpartners.com/our-firm/history/

Advent International. (2022). Our team. https://www.adventinternational.com/team/?region=andcountry=andsector=andkeywords=portfolio+support

Advisor Investments. (2021). Vanguard to offer private equity investments to individuals. https://www.adviserinvestments.com/adviser-fund-update/vanguard-private-equity-funds-for-individuals/

Agelides, P. (2011). *Financial Crisis Inquiry Report*. DIANE Publishing.

Aggrawal, D., Eldar, O., Hochberg, Y., and Litov, L.P. (2022). The rise of dual-class stock IPOs. National Bureau of Economic Research. working paper No. 28609. http://www.nber.org/papers/w28609

Aguliar, J. (2023). Sovereign wealth funds 2022. IE Center for the Governance of Change. https://docs.ie.edu/cgc/SWF%202021%20IE%20 SWR%20CGC%20-%20ICEX-Invest%20in%20Spain.pdf

Aitken, H.G.J. (1985). *The Continuous Wave: Technology and American Radio, 1900–1932.* Princeton University Press.

Akst, D. (2019). Daniel Defoe's hard-earned lessons on business and life. *Strategy and Business* – a PWC publication. Blog. May 16. https://www .strategy-business.com/blog/Daniel-Defoes-hard-earned-lessons-on-business-and-life

Alibaba. (2023). DAMO Academy. https://damo.alibaba.com/labs?spm=a 2c4g.11186623.2.9.32f7201flKYzKV

Alija, O., Kruppa, M. (2021). Wall Street's hottest investment has emerged as 'gold mine' for sector, but detractors warn it is not free money. *Financial Times* (March 11). https://www.ft.com/content/812b243b-4831-4c65-92b2-f72bfdc6eff6

Allen, J. (1991). The MIT Radiation Laboratory: RLE's microwave heritage. RLE Currents – Massachusetts Institute of Technology.

Alluve. (2022). How private equity dry powder has grown. March 14. https:// www.allvuesystems.com/resources/private-equity-dry-powder-hits-new-highs-and-brings-old-challenges/

Amadeo, K. (2020). AIG bailout: Cost, timeline, bonuses, causes, effects. November 16. https://www.thebalance.com/aig-bailout-cost-timeline-bonuses-causes-effects-3305693

American Banker. (1993). Chemical said to finance big buyout. July 26. https://www.americanbanker.com/news/chemical-said-to-finance-big-buyout

American Investment Council. (2021). Economic contribution of the US private equity sector in 2020, Report prepared by EY.

Anderson, J. (2007). Blackstone founders prepare to count their billions. *The New York Times* (June 12).

Anderson, J., and Michael, J. (2007). Kohlberg Kravis plans to go public. *The New York Times* (July 4).

Andonov, A., Kräussl, R., and Rau, J. (2021). Institutional investors and infrastructure investing. *The Review of Financial Studies*, 34(8).

Ang, A., Papanikolaou, D., and Westerfield, M. (2013). Portfolio choice with illiquid assets. NBER working paper series.

Anson, M. (2009). *CAIA Level I: An Introduction to Core Topics in Alternatives*, CAIA Association/Wiley.

Apax. (2022). Our history. https://www.apax.com/our-firm/history/

Applebaum, E. and Batt, R. (2020). Private Equity Buyouts in Healthcare: Who Wins, Who Loses? https://papers.ssrn.com/sol3/papers .cfm?abstract_id=3593887

Aramonte S., and Avalos, F. (2021). The rise of private markets. *BIS Quarterly* (December 6).

Aran, A. (2022). AWS: Powering the Internet and Amazon's profits. www.visualcapitalist.com

Arnold, T. (2018). Abraaj fund investors hire Duff and Phelps to help recover money. Reuters. November 5. https://www.reuters. com/article/us-abraaj-funds-idUSKCN1NA1JB

Ashton, T.S. (1964). *The Industrial Revolution, 1760–1830*. Oxford University Press. Originally published 1948.

Athanasia, G. (2022, Oct 10). Lessons of Silicon Valley: A world-renowned technology hub. https://www.csis.org/blogs/perspectives-innovation/lessons-silicon-valley-world-renowned-technology-hub

Auchard, E. (2007). Kleiner Perkins entering China with $360 Mn fund. Reuters, April 23. https://www.reuters.com/article/china-vc-kleiner-idUKN2338208220070424

Audren T. (2023). Private debt – an all-weather asset class. Stepstone Research Report. April 19.

Auerbach, A., and Shivanada, A. (2017). When secondaries come first. Cambridge Associates.

Avery, H. (2002). European funds' use of private equity grows. IPE. https://www.ipe.com/european-funds-use-of-private-equity-grows/6095.article

Avnimelech, G., and Teubal, M. (2006). *The Emergence of Israel's Venture Capital Industry: How Policy Can Influence High-Tech Cluster Dynamics*. Oxford University Press.

Bagli, C.W. (2013). *Other People's Money: Inside the Housing Crisis and the Demise of the Greatest Real Estate Deal Ever Made*. Penguin Group.

Bain & Company. (2020). *Bain Global Private Equity Report 2019*. Bain & Company.

Bain & Company. (2021). *Bain Global Private Equity Report 2020*. Bain & Company.

Bain & Company. (2022). *Bain Private Market Report 2021*. Bain & Company.

Bain & Company. (2023). *India Venture Capital Report 2023*. Bain & Company.

Bain Capital (2023, last accessed). Bain Capital healthcare. https://www.baincapital.com/healthcare/print-report/files/basic-html/page29.html

Baker, G.P. (1992). Beatrice: A study in the creation and destruction of value. *The Journal of Finance*, 47(3).

Baker Capital. (2004). Wine.com announces $20 million in funding led by Baker Capital. http://bakercapital.com/press/pdf/9-8-2004-Wine.pdf

Baldwin, N. (1995). *Edison: Inventing the Century*. Hyperion.

Baltimore Sun. (1992). Investors rush to snap up initial offering of Snapple. (December 16).

Banerjee, D. (2013). Schwarzman says selling BlackRock was "heroic" mistake". Bloomberg. September 30. https://www.Bloomberg.com/news/

articles/2013-09-30/schwarzman-says-selling-blackrock-was-heroic-mistake#xj4y7vzkg

Barrachi, F. (2008). Private equity 'club deals' and European competition policy: A primer. SSRN: https://ssrn.com/abstract=1137085.

Barron's (2017). These Ancient Closed-End Funds Still Deliver. https://www.barrons.com/articles/these-ancient-closed-end-funds-still-deliver-1483767180

Barton, R.E., and Ward, M.E. (2021). SPACs and speculation: the changing legal liability of forward-looking statements. Reuters. July 7. https://www.reuters.com/legal/legalindustry/spacs-speculation-changing-legal-liability-forward-looking-statements-2021-07-07/

Baruch, M. (2021). Which top PE managers have used continuation funds? Private Equity International. https://www.privateequityinternational.com/which-top-pe-managers-have-used-continuation-funds/

Bass, D. (2023). Microsoft invests $10 billion in ChatGPT maker OpenAI. Bloomberg. January 23. https://www.bloomberg.com/news/articles/2023-01-23/microsoft-makes-multibillion-dollar-investment-in-openai#xj4y7vzkg

Bassett, R.K. (2007). *To the Digital Age: Research Labs, Start-up Companies, and the Rise of MOS Technology*. Johns Hopkins University Press.

Baudel, F. (1992). The Wheels of Commerce. University of California Press. 0-520-08144-5.

Bayaz, D. (2013). Heuschrecken zwischen Rendite, Reportage und Regulierung. PhD thesis University of Hohenheim.

Bazerman, M., and Patel, P. (2021). SPACs: What you need to know. *Harvard Business Review*, July–August.

BBC. (2021). Climate change: EU to cut CO_2 emissions by 55 % by 2030. April 21, https://www.bbc.com/news/world-europe-56828383

Bedier, M. (2018). Demystification of mergers and historical overview. Elga-ronline, September 28. https://doi.org/10.4337/9781788110891.00010

Beer, S. (1959). *Cybernetics and Management*. English Universities Press.

Begenau, J., and Siriwardane, E. (2022). How do private equity fees vary across public pensions? National Bureau of Economic Research working paper No. 29887.

Bell, J., and Foote, J. (2007). Comparison of recent toll road concession transactions in the United States and France. University of Barcelona and Harvard University working paper.

Belle, J., and Leighton, M. (2000). *Grand Central: Gateway to a Million Lives*. W. W. Norton and Company.

Bellis, M. (2009). Samuel Morse and the invention of the telegraph. https://www.thoughtco.com/communication-revolution-telegraph-1991939

Bell Laboratories. (1948). The big announcement. PBS Online, June 30. https://www.pbs.org/transistor/background1/events/bigannouncement.html

Beltran, L. (2002). WorldCom files largest bankruptcy ever. CNN, July 22.

Benson, P. (2022). What Blackstone's American campus communities deal means for the student housing sector. May 6. https://www.perenews.com/what-blackstones-american-campus-communities-deal-means-for-the-student-housing-sector/?utm_source=newsletter-alertandutm_medium=emailandutm_campaign=perealertandutm_content= 09-05-2022

Bentes, L., and Costa, O. (2018). Mergers and acquisitions: The Facebook and WhatsApp case. ISCTE Business School.

Bentley, Z. (2022). Stonepeak raises $3bn continuation fund to recapitalize Colonix. January 5. https://www.secondariesinvestor.com/stonepeak-raises-3bn-continuation-fund-to-recapitalise-cologix/

Berlin, L. (2008a). Lessons of survival from the Dotcom Attik. *The New York Times* (November 21).

Berlin, L. (2008b). Draper, Gaither, and Anderson: First venture capital firm in Silicon Valley. https://thebhc.org/draper-gaither-and-anderson-first-venture-capital-firm-silicon-valley

Berlin, L.R. (2001). Robert Noyce and Fairchild Semiconductor, 1957–1968. *Business History Review*, Spring.

Berlin, M. (1998). That thing venture capitalists do. https://www.philadelphiafed.org/-/media/frbp/assets/economy/articles/business-review/1998/january-february/brjf98mb.pdf

Bernanke, B., et al. (2011). International capital flows and the returns to safe assets in the United States, 2003–2007. International Finance discussion papers, No. 1014.

Bernstein S., Lerner, J., and Schoar, A. (2013). The investment strategies of sovereign wealth funds. *Journal of Economic Perspective*, 27(2): 219–238.

Beyerle, V., Voss, O., and Weber, H. (2011). *Investitionen in Infrastruktur. Chancen durch die Energiewende in Deutschland*. IVG.

Bhagat, S. (2022). An inconvenient truth about ESG investing. *Harvard Business Review*. March 31.

Bhidé, A. (1994). *The Origin and Evolution of New Businesses*. Oxford University Press.

Bild. (2005). Interview with Franz Müntefering. *Bild am Sonntag* (April 17).

Bilo, S., Christophers, H., Degosciu, M., and Zimmermann, H. (2005). Risk, returns, and biases of listed private equity portfolios. University of Basel, Switzerland working paper.

Biography. (2022). Arthur Rock biography. https://biography.yourdictionary.com/arthur-rock

Birtsch, A., Buchner, A., and Kaserer, C. (2010). Risk, return and cash flow characteristics of infrastructure fund investments. EIB Papers.

BIS. (2010). Speech presented by Mr Deepak Mohanty, Executive Director of the Reserve Bank of India, at the international conference on "Frontiers of interface between statistics and science," Hyderabad, 30 December 2009. *BIS Quarterly Review*, February 2010.

BIS. (2019). The capital buffers in Basel III: An executive summary. https://www.bis.org/fsi/fsisummaries/b3_capital.htm

BIS. (2020). Ratio. https://www.bis.org/basel_framework/ chapter/LEV/40.htm?inforce=20230101andpublished=20200327

Biswas, S. (2020). Neiman Marcus Owners to hand over part of Mytheresa to creditors. *The Wall Street Journal* (July 31).

Black, G.J. (2018). The evolution of liquidity: Shifting exit strategies for private market investors. Preqin.

BlackRock. (2022). iShares MSCI USA SRI UCITS ETF. https://www.ishares.com/ch/privatkunden/de/produkte/283565/ishares-sustainable-msci-usa-sri-ucits-etf

Blackstone. (2006). Press release. https://www.blackstone.com/news/press/ blackstone-real-estate-partners-v-closes-on-5-25-billion/

Blackstone. (2007). Press release. https://www.blackstone.com/news/press/ blackstone-private-equity-fund-closes-on-21-7-billion/

Blackstone. (2010). Blackstone agrees to manage in excess of $2 billion of Merrill Lynch Asia real estate assets. November 23. https://www.blackstone.com/news/press/blackstone-agrees-to-manage-in-excess-of-2-billion-of-merrill-lynch-asia-real-estate-assets/

Blackstone. (2013). Blackstone announces acquisition of Credit Suisse's Strategic Partners business. April 22. www.blackstone.com/news/press/blackstone-announces-acquisition-of-credit-suisse-s-strategic-partners-business/

Blackstone. (2021). Blackstone announces $4.5 billion final close of Blackstone Growth (BXG) Fund, largest first-time growth equity vehicle in history. March 19. https://www.blackstone.com/news/press/blackstone-announces-4-5-billion-final-close-of-blackstone-growth-bxg-fund-largest-first-time-growth-equity-vehicle-in-history/

Blackstone. (2022). Portfolio operations. https://www.blackstone.com/our-businesses/portfolio-operations/

Blackstone. (2023). Blackstone strategic partners closes record private equity secondary funds at $25 billion. January 18. https://www.blackstone.com/news/press/blackstone-strategic-partners-closes-record-private-equity-secondary-funds-at-25-billion/

Blanchard, M. (1969). The railway policy of the Second Empire. In: *Essays in European Economic History 1789–1914*. F. Crouzet et al. (Eds.), St Martin's Press, pp. 98–111.

Blind, G., and von Mandach, S. (2021). Not a coincidence: sons-in-law as successors in successful Japanese family firms. MPRA, University Library of Munich.

Block, J., Jang, Y.S., Kaplan, S.N., and Schulze, A. (2023). A survey of private debt funds. National Bureau of Economic Research working paper No. w30868. http://www.nber.org/papers/w30868

Bloomberg. (2012). Singapore's GIC said to offer $700 million in buyout-fund stakes. January 20. https://www.bloomberg.com/

Bloomberg. (2021). ESG assets may hit $53 trillion by 2025, a third of global AUM. February 23. https://www.bloomberg.com/professional/blog/esg-assets-may-hit-53-trillion-by-2025-a-third-of-global-aum/

Bloomberg News. (2014). Ontario Teachers' Pension Plan scoring big after its early wager on Chinese online retailer JD.com. August 14. https://financialpost.com/news/fp-street/ontario-teachers-pension-plan-scoring-big-after-its-early-wager-on-chinese-online-retailer-jd-com

Bock, C., and Hackober, C. (2020). Unicorns—what drives multibillion-dollar valuations? https://link.springer.com/article/10.1007/s40685-020-00120-2

BoF. (2015). Hugo Boss $2.7 billion return is the biggest for Permira. March 18. https://www.businessoffashion.com/articles/finance/hugo-boss-2-7-billion-return-biggest-permira.

Bolt, J.A. (1988). Management considering buyout of RJR Nabisco: October 20. https://apnews.com/article/b96711ca688d2e5b27c331a58009e198

Bondarenko, P. (2022). Enron scandal. In: *Encyclopedia Britannica*. August 13. https://www.britannica.com/event/Enron-scandal

Bortolotti, B., and Scortecci, A. (2019). The rise of collaborative investing: sovereign wealth funds' new strategies in private markets. SIL-BCG Report. Universita Bocconi.

Bottazzi, L., Da Rin, M., van Ours, J.C., and Berglöf, E. (2002). Venture capital in Europe and the financing of innovative companies. *Economic Policy*, 17(34): 229–269.

Bradley, R.L. Jr. (2011). *Edison to Enron: Energy Markets and Political Strategies*. John Wiley & Sons.

Braggion, F., Frehen, R., and Jerphanion, E. (2020). Does credit affect stock trading? Evidence from the South Sea Bubble. CEPR discussion paper no. 14532.

Brasse, J. (2023). Korea's NPS to buy Berlin landmark from MSREV VI. Infrastructure Investor. March 23. https://www.infrastructureinvestor.com/koreas-nps-to-buy-berlin-landmark-from-msref-vi/

Braudel, F. (1992). *The Wheels of Commerce*, vol. 2. University of California Press.

Braun, R., Jenkinson, T., and Schemmerl, C. (2017). Adverse selection and the performance of private equity co-investments, Institute for Private Capital working paper, December.

Brewer, P. (2020). Analysis: Three decades of IPO deals (1990–2019). Bloomberg. January 9. https://news.bloomberglaw.com/bloomberg-law-analysis/analysis-three-decades-of-ipo-deals-1990-2019

Bridgepoint. (2022). About us. https://www.bridgepoint.eu/about-us

Brinkman, M. and Sarma, V. (2022). Infrastructure investing will never be the same. https://www.mckinsey.com/industries/private-equity-and-principal-investors/our-insights/infrastructure-investing-will-never-be-the-same

British Land. (2009). Strategic partnership for Broadgate, Presentation to shareholders. British Land Plc. www.britishland.com/

British Land. (2012). UBS pre-let and lease extensions completed at Broadgate, January 30. https://www.britishland.com/news-insights/press-releases/ubs-pre-let-and-lease-extensions-completed-broadgate

Brock, D.C. (2006). *Understanding Moore's Law: Four Decades of Innovation*. Chemical Heritage Foundation.

Brooke, D. (2019). Covenant-loose is the new norm in the private debt market. Reuters. August 15. https://www.reuters.com/article/cov-loose-idUSL2N25B0ES

Brooks, J. (1976). *Telephone: The First Hundred Years*. Harper and Row.

Brown, G., Harris, R., Hu, W., Jenkinson, T., Kaplan, S., and Robinson, D. (2020). Can investors time their exposure to private equity? NBER working paper series, no. 26755.

Brown, G., Jenkison, T., and Stoff, I. (2017). The persistence of performance. *Journal of Financial Economics*, 123(2): 273–291.

Brown, G., and Kaplan, S. (2019). Have Private Equity Returns Really Declined? https://uncipc.org/wp-content/uploads/2019/05/HavePrivate EquityReturnsDeclined_05022019.pdf

Bruene, J. (2022). The 309 fintech unicorns of the 21st century. May. https://fintechlabs.com/115-fintech-unicorns-of-the-21st-century-changes -to-the-list-october-2020/

Bryan, H. (2022). Venture capital 2021 recap: A record-breaking year. Factset, January 19. https://insight.factset.com/venture-capital-2021-recap-a-record-breaking-year

Buchner, A., Mohamed, A., and Schwienbacher, A. (2016). Does risk explain persistence in private equity performance? *Journal of Corporate Finance*, 39: 18–35.

Bunker, T., and Cooper, L. (2022). Tiger Global closes on $12.7 billion for latest growth fund. *The Wall Street Journal* (March 22).

Bureau of Economic Analysis. (2007). Bureau of Economic Analysis GDP estimate Q2 2007.

Burnard, T. (2017). *Planters, Merchants, and Slaves: Plantation Societies in British America, 1650–1820*. The University of North Carolina Press.

Burrough, B.A. (1989). *Barbarians at the Gate: The Fall of RJR Nabisco*. Harper and Row.

Bush, V. (1945). *Science, the Endless Frontier: A Report to the President on a Program for Postwar Scientific Research*. Princeton University Press. Reprinted 2021.

Business Insider. (2010). Here is why the dotcom bubble began and why it popped. December 15.

Business Week. (2004). Special report: Stars of Asia – financiers: Lip-Bu Tan. July 12. //http://www.businessweek.com/magazine/content/04_28/b3891421.htm

Businesswire. (2020). HarbourVest Partners closes HarbourVest Fund XI above $2 billion target. January 15. https://www.businesswire.com/news/home/20200115005142/en/HarbourVest-Partners-Closes-HarbourVest-Fund-XI-Above-2-Billion-Target

Butcher, M. (2011). Index ventures forth, bridging Silicon Valley with Silicon Roundabout. November 30. https://techcrunch.com/2011/11/30/index-ventures-forth-bridging-silicon-valley-with-silicon-roundabout2/?guccounter=1andguce_referrer=aHR0cHM6Ly9lbi53aWtpcGVkaWEub3JnLwandguce_referrer_sig=AQAAALVzRPsZkgJjIMzhe5Xn_6itlssJbtMRbvC0s4ZJi2qmP2bDSPdPbp73rrfQA8PES

Byte Magazine. (1978). Most important companies. http://www.byte.com/art/9509/sec7/art15.htm

CA. (2017). US Venture capital index and selected benchmark statistics. Cambridge Associates, December 31. https://www.cambridgeassociates.com/wp-content/uploads/2018/05/WEB-2017-Q4-USVC-Benchmark-Book.pdf

CAIA. (2022). Increasing smaller investor access to illiquid alternative investments: Approaches, developments and the expanding role of technology. CAIA Association.

Cain, M., McKeon, S., and Solomon, S. (2014). Do takeover laws matter? Evidence of five decades of hostile takeovers. DERA/SEC working paper. October.

Calcagnini, G., et al. (2016). The role of universities in the location of innovative startups. *The Journal of Technology Transfer,* 41(4).

Cambridge English Dictionary. (2022). Raider. https://dictionary.cambridge.org/dictionary/english/raider

Campbell, K. (2021). Speyer: China is an anchor to our global business. www.prenews.com. https://www.perenews.com/speyer-china-is-the-anchor-to-our-global-business/

CAPA. (2014). London City Airport is London's most expensive airport. CAPA, Centre for Aviation, Airport Coordination Limited.

Capital Dynamics. (2016). Introductory guide to investing in private equity secondaries. January. https://caia.org/sites/default/files/capital_dynamics_secondaries_ update.pdf

Capital Dynamics. (2022). GP-led secondaries reshaping the landscape for investors, managers, and portfolio companies. Capital Dynamics Holding.

Cardillo, Y. (2012). *Agency Information.* U.S. Department of Energy.

Cardson, B. (2021). The arms race in seed funding. September 25. https://www.protocol.com/newsletters/pipeline/greylock-a16z-sequoia-seed-funding?rebelltitem=3#rebelltitem3

Carleton, M. (2022). Samuel F.B. Morse. In: *Encyclopedia Britannica*. https://www.britannica.com/biography/Samuel-F-B-Morse.

Carlo, A., Eichholtz, P., and Kok, N. (2021). Three decades of institutional investment in real estate. Maastricht University working paper. https://ssrn.com/abstract=3802518

Carlyle. (2011). APG and PGGM agree to sell AlpInvest Partners to the Carlyle Group and AlpInvest Management. January 26. https://ir.carlyle.com/news-releases/news-release-details/apg-and-pggm-agree-sell-alpinvest-partners-carlyle-group

Carlyle, CalPERS. (2021). Private equity industry establishes first-ever LP and GP partnership to standardize ESG reporting. https://www.carlyle.com/media-room/news-release-archive/private-equity-industry-establishes-first-ever-lp-and-gp-partnership-standardize-esg-reporting

Carlyle Group. (2011). The Carlyle Group issues 2010 annual report. https://www.carlyle.com/media-room/news-release-archive/carlyle-group-issues-2010-annual-report

Carlyle Group. (2021). Audax Private Equity announces successful closing of a $1.7 billion continuation fund led by AlpInvest Partners. https://www.carlyle.com/media-room/news-release-archive/audax-private-equity-announces-successful-closing-led-by-alpinvest-partners

Carlyle Group. (2022). About the Carlyle Group. https://www.carlyle.com/sites/default/files/Mill_Digital_Media.pdf

Carosso, V. P. (1987). *The Morgans: Private International Bankers, 1854–1913*. Harvard Studies in Business History no. 38. Harvard University Press.

Casson, M. (2009). *The World's First Railway System: Enterprise, Competition, and Regulation on The Railway Network in Victorian Britain*. Oxford University Press.

Castro-Rodríguez, F. and Miles-Touya, D. (2019). Assessment of support schemes promoting renewable energy in Spain. https://www.funcas.es/wp-content/uploads/Migracion/Articulos/FUNCAS_SEFO/025art08.pdf

Cave, D. (2000). Dot.com party madness. *Salon* (April 25).

Cawley, R. (1999). Crossroads uses EDS portfolio to launch fund. *Dallas Business Journal* (September 24).

CB Insights. (2019a). From Alibaba to Zynga: 45 of the best VC bets of all time and what we can learn from them. January 4. https://www.cbinsights.com/research/best-venture-capital-investments/

CB Insights. (2019b). Capital efficiency: Do larger investments make better businesses? July 22. https://finerva.com/report/capital-efficiency/

CB Insights. (2021). From Alibaba to Zynga: 40 of the best VC bets of all time and what we can learn from them. June 9. https://www.cbinsights.com/research/ best-venture-capital-investments/

CBPP. (2018). *The Legacy of the Great Recession*. Center of Budget and Policy Priorities.

Ceruzzi, P. E. (2003). *A History of Modern Computing*. MIT Press.

CFA. (2022). What are debt covenants? Corporate Finance Institute. May17.corporatefinanceinstitute.com:https://corporatefinanceinstitute .com/resources/knowledge/finance/debt-covenants/

Chandler, A.D. (1962). *Strategy and Structure: Chapters in the History of the American Industrial Enterprise*. MIT Press.

Chandler, A.D. (1984). The emergence of managerial capitalism. *Business History Review*, Winter.

Chang, E. (2019). 10 of the most important IPOs of the 2010s. *US News* (December 3).

ChannelPartner. (1999). Biodata-Chef Siekmann setzt auf Sicherheit-slösungen. April 6, https://web.archive.org/web/20130928023017/ http://www.channelpartner.de/ index.cfm?pid=54andpk=612060

Chaplin, J.E. (2016). The origins of the 1855/6 introduction of general limited liability in England. PhD thesis, University of East Anglia.

Chapman, S.D. (1970). Fixed capital formation in the British cotton industry, 1770–1815. *The Economic History Review*, 23(2): 235–266,

Chediak, M. (2013). Energy Futures proposes pre-packed bankruptcy for some of its units. Bloomberg News. April 16.

Chemmanur, T.L. (2014). Corporate venture capital, value creation, and innovation. *Review of Financial Studies*, November 5.

Cheng, E. (2021). Investors pour money into Chinese startups despite regulatory crackdown. CNBC. October 27. https://www.cnbc.com/ 2021/10/27/investors-put-money-in-chinese-start-ups-despite-regulatory-crackdown.html

Chernow, R. (1991). *The House of Morgan: An American Banking Dynasty and the Rise of Modern Finance*. Atlantic Finance Press.

Chesbrough, H. (2000). Designing corporate ventures in the shadow of private venture capital. *California Management Review*, 42(3).

chicaelmoh. (2020). Top 10 S&P 500 companies by market cap (1980–2020). June 24. https://www.youtube.com/watch?v =kfMFDcuDKYA

China News. (2017). Mobile web. January. https://en.wikipedia.org/wiki/ Mobile_web#cite_note15

China Mobile. (2023). About China Mobile. https://www.chinamobileltd .com/en/about/overview.php

CHM. (2022a). ICs rocket to success. https://www.computerhistory.org/ revolution/digital-logic/12/278

CHM. (2022b). 1958: Silicon MESA transistors enter commercial production. https://www.computerhistory.org/siliconengine/silicon-mesa-transistors -enter-commercial-production/

CHM. (2022c). Fairchild, Fairchildren, and the family tree of Silicon Valley. https://computerhistory.org/blog/fairchild-and-the-fairchildren

Chong, F. (2022). Prime time for infrastructure secondaries. March. https:// realassets.ipe.com/infrastructure/prime-time-for-infrastructure-secondaries/10058314. article

Christensen, C. (1997). *The Innovator's Dilemma: When New Technologies Cause Great Firms to Fail*. Harper Business.

Christensen, C.M., Raynor, M.E., and McDonald, R. (2015). What is disruptive innovation? *Harvard Business Review*, 12. hbr.org/2015/12/what-is-disruptive-innovation

Christie, L. (2007). California cities fill top 10 foreclosure list. *CNN Money*. August 14.

Christofidis, C., and Debande, O. (2001). Financing innovative firms through venture capital. European Investment Bank.

Cision PR Newswire. (2018). Leading wine retailer partners with world-class capital provider to accelerate growth. November 19. https://www.prnewswire.com/news-releases/winecom-closes-32-5-million-growth-capital-investment-from-goldman-sachs-asset-management-private-credit-group-300752657.html

Cision PR Newswire. (2023). FS Investments and Portfolio Advisors to combine, creating a $73 billion alternative investment firm. February 22. https://www.prnewswire.com/ news-releases/fs-investments-and-portfolio-advisors-to-combine-creating-a-73-billion-alternative-investment-firm-301736926.html

Clark, C., and Harshad, L. (2021). ESG improvers: An alpha-enhancing factor. Rockefeller Capital Management.

Clark, R.L., Craig, L.A., and Wilson, J. (2003). History of public pensions. In: *Public Sector Pensions in the United States*. Pension Research Council, The Wharton School of the University of Pennsylvania.

Clarke, B. (2019). 'Canadian model' for approaching public pension funds must evolve. *The Globe and Mail* (February 14).

Clifford Chance. (2020). "Decoding" the secondaries market Part IV: Continuation funds. September. https://www.cliffordchance.com/content/dam/cliffordchance/briefings/2020/09/decoding-the-secondary-market-part-IV-continuation-funds.pdf

Cliffwater. (2022). Study on private fund fees and expenses for direct lending. https://cliffwater.com/

Cliffwater. (2023). 2023 Q2 Report on U.S. direct lending. https://cliffwater.com/files/cdli/docs/Cliffwater_Report_on_US_DirectLending.pdf

CNBC. (2008). Dollar fall may trigger German property sell-off. May 7. https://www.cnbc.com/2008/05/07/dollar-fall-may-trigger-german-property-selloff.html

Cohen, J. (2021). For GPs, it's time for a new perspective on ESG. https://www.sasb.org/blog/for-gps-its-time-for-a-new-perspective-on-esg/

Cohen, S.S. (1988). *Manufacturing Matters*. Basic Books.

Cohen, W. (2020). How to apply Peter Drucker's most effective management ideas. October 29. https://www.processexcellencenetwork.com/lessons_from_peter_drucker/articles/how-to-apply-peter-druckers-most-effective-management-ideas

Cole, R.J. (1985). Beatrice accepts Kravis's bid. *The New York Times* (November 14).

Colin, N. (2015). Low risk, high reward: Why venture capital thrives in the digital world. *Salon* (November 7). https://salon.thefamily.co/low-risk-high-reward-why-venture-capital-thrives-in-the-digital-world-ed56d0b14dc

Colin, N. (2016). A brief history of the world of venture capital. *Salon* (May 4). https://salon.thefamily.co/a-brief-history-of-the-world-of-venture-capital-65a8610e7dc2

Collinson, P. (2017). Revealed: The huge profits earned by big banks on overseas money transfers. *The Guardian* (April 8).

Columbia Threadneedle. (2022). 2021 high-yield market year in review. February. https://www.columbiathreadneedleus.com/binaries/content/assets/cti/public/2021_high_yield_market_year_in_review.pdf

Companiesmarketcap.com. (2022). Market capitalization of Just Eat Takeaway (TKWY.AS). August 28. https://companiesmarketcap.com/just-eat-takeaway/marketcap/

Computer History Museum Archive. (2011). *1960 – First Planar Integrated Circuit is Fabricated.*: CHM.

Congressional Budget Office. (1977). *Income Policies in the United States: Historical Review and Some Issues.* Congressional Budget Office.

Constable, O.R. (1994). *Trade and Traders in Muslim Spain: the Commercial Realignment of the Iberian Peninsula 900–1500 AD.* Cambridge University Press.

Conway, N. (2019). Sweatshops almost killed Nike in the 1990s. Now there are modern slavery laws. https://www.thefashionlaw.com/visibility-is-central-to-a-successful-supply-chain-heres-what-brands-need-to-know/

Copley, M. (2017). Schroders buys $7bn private equity firm Adveq. April 20. https://www.fnlondon.com/articles/schroders-buys-7bn-private-equity-firm-adveq-20170420

Corfmann, T.A. (2015). To Zell and back: How did financier Sam Zell plant the seeds for his late 1990s dominance of the US commercial real estate market? https://www.investmentnews.com/to-zell-and-backhow-did-financier-sam-zell-plant-the-seeds-for-his-late-1990s-dominance-of-the-u-s-commercial-real-estate-market-by-focusing-on-non-real-estate-opportunities-in-the-1980s-a-look-i-922

Cornelius, P. (2011). *International Investments in Private Equity.* Academic Press.

Correia, J.E., Vidigal, G., and Dionisio, A. (2021). Unicorns and their IPO: Are they overvalued? CEFAGE working paper. https://dspace.uevora.pt/rdpc/bitstream/10174/30310/1/CorreiaJose_Unicorns_and_their_IPO_-_Are_they_Overvalued.pdf

Credit Suisse Asset Management. (2010). An overview of PE. www.credit-suisse.com

Crittenden. (1983). Reaping the big profits from a fat cat. *The New York Times* (August 7).

CRS. (2022). President Nixon's emergency tariff. https://www.everycrsre port.com/files/20190624_IN11129_b3be8a068571a20ee193d9ff6d514 9a8a5ef247c.html

Crunchbase. (2020). Series H – DoorDash. June 18. https://www.crunch base.com/funding_round/doordash-series-h--5d9706b7

Crunchbase. (2022a). Greylock Portfolio companies. April 2. https://www .crunchbase.com/hub/greylock-portfolio-companies

Crunchbase. (2022b). Startups acquiring startups: An essential catalyst for growth. April 4. https://www.crunchbase.com

Crunchbase. (2022c). List of WhatsApp's 3 funding rounds. May 16. https://www.crunchbase.com/search/funding_rounds/field/ organizations/fundingtotal/whatsapp

Crunchbase. (2022d). HarbourVest Partners: Crunchbase Investor Profile and Investments. https://www.crunchbase.com/organization/harbourvest-partners

CSI Markets. (2022). T-Mobile US Inc.: https://csimarket.com/stocks/ compet_glance.php?code=TMUS

Csiszar, J. (2019). The best and worst decades for America's money. finance. Yahoo! March 27. https://finance.Yahoo!.com/news/best-worst-decades-america-money-090709225.html

Cumming, D.J., and MacIntosh, J.G. (2003). Venture-capital exits in Canada and the United States. *The University of Toronto Law Journal*. 53(2): 101–199.

Curry, D. (2022). DoorDash revenue and usage statistics. May 4. https:// www.businessofapps.com/data/doordash-statistics/

Da Rin, M., Hellmann, T., Puri, M., Constantinides, G., Harris, M., and Stulz, R. (2013). A survey of venture capital research. In: *Handbook of the Economics of Finance*. Elsevier.

DARPA. (2018). *DARPA 60 Years 1958–2018*. Faircount Media Group.

David, E. (1990). *Electrifying America: Social Meanings of a New Technology, 1880–1940*. MIT Press.

Davies, A., Wilkes, T. (2013). Buyout firm Apax to cut staff, shrink London. Reuters. March 22. https://www.reuters.com/article/us-apaxpartners-cuts-idUSBRE92L0XN20130322

Davies, K.G. (1952). Joint-stock investment in the later seventeenth century, *The Economic History Review*, 4(3): 283–301.

Davis, A. (2021). These 6 charts show how much VC is awash in capital in 2021. PitchBook. October 17. https://pitchbook.com/news/ articles/2021-us-vc-fundraising-exits-deal-flow-charts

Davis, M. (2008). TPG humbled by WaMu losses - investor letter. Reuters, September 26. https://www.reuters.com/article/washingtonmutual-tpg-idUSN2631351920080926

Davis, Z. (1975). The Altair 8800 computer kit. *Popular Electronics*, January.

Dawe, C. (2022). Cleantech venture capital investment trends 2021. https://www.s-ge.com/en/article/expertise/2022-e-clean-venture-capital-investment-cleantech-trends-2021

Dawson, J., and Boquist, A. (2004). US venture capital in Europe in the 1980s and the 1990s. *The Journal of Private Equity*, 8(1): 39–54.

Day, R. (2019). Stock ticker/ticker tape. June 17. https://innowiki.org/stock-ticker-ticker-tape/

Dayaramani, N., and Rocha, J. (2016). Understanding and comparing ESG terminology. April 16. https://www.ssga.com/investment-topics/environmental-social-governance/2018/10/esg-terminology.pdf

Defoe, D. (1697). An essay upon projects. The Project Gutenberg eBook. Released: August 10, 2014. eBook #4087, pp. 12–14.

Degeorge, F., Martin, J., and Phalippou, L. (2013). Is the rise of secondary buyouts good news for investors? ISEG working paper.

Degner, H. (2009). Schumpeterian German firms before and after World War I: The innovative few and the non-innovative many. *Zeitschrift für Unternehmensgeschichte*, 54(1): 50–72.

Deloitte. (2023). PAC transactions: Considerations for target-company CFOs. https://www.cooley.com/-/media/cooley/pdf/reprints/2020/cobranded-spac-transactions--considerations-for-targetcompany-cfos-secured.ashx?la=enandhash=6346947744D0F11E6E38FFD58F9532CD

Del Ponte, K. (2005). Funds of funds: A brief history. Probitas Partners.

Demaria, C., Pedergnana, M., He, R., Rissi, R., and Debrand, S. (2021). *Asset Allocation and Private Markets*. Wiley & Sons.

Dertouzos, M., Lester, R., and Solow, R. (1989). *Made in America*. The MIT Press.

DeSantis, R. (2023). Governor Ron DeSantis further prohibits Woke ESG considerations from state investments. News release. January 17. https://www.flgov.com/2023/01/17/governor-ron-desantis-further-prohibits-woke-esg-considerations-from-state-investments/

Deutsch, A.L. (2022). WhatsApp: The best Meta purchase ever? March 29. https://www.investopedia.com/articles/investing/032515/whatsapp-best-facebook-purchase-ever.asp

Deveau, S. (2021). Peltz to depart P&G Board, capping nearly four-year overhaul. Bloomberg. August 6. https://www.bloomberg.com/news/articles/2021-08-05/ peltz-to-depart-p-g-s-board-capping-nearly-four-year-overhaul

Dick, A. (2011). Anlageverhalten von Schweizer Pensionskassen im Umgang mit Immobilienanlagen. Universität Zürich.

Die Welt. (2009). Der umstrittenste Fall: Grohe. August 26. https://www.welt.de/wirtschaft/Private-Equity/article4404842/8-Der-umstrittenste-Fall-Grohe.html

Di Stefano, M., Clark, K., and Wingfield, N. (2022). Sequoia warns founders of 'crucible moment,' advises how to 'avoid the death spiral.' May 24. https://www.theinformation.com/articles/sequoia-warns-founders-of-crucible-moment-advises-how-to-avoid-the-death-spiral

Dobbs, I. (2020). How Mark Zuckerberg and his "super paranoid" inner circle spent billions snapping up rivals. *The Telegraph*, December 10.

Doenecke, J.D. (2000). Young, Owen D. In: *American National Biography*. Online. https://doi.org/10.1093/anb/9780198606697. article.0600740

Domitrovic, B. (2020). Why did people buy stocks in the 1920s? *Forbes*. January 9. https://www.forbes.com/sites/briandomitrovic/2020/01/09/why-did-people-buy-stocks-in-the-1920s/

Donaldson, D., and Hornbeck, R. (2013). Railroads and American economic growth: A "market access" approach. NBER working paper No. 19213.

Douvas, J. (2012). Twenty years of opportunistic real estate investing, *Wharton Real Estate Review*, Spring.

Drucker, P. (2007). People and performance. In: Peter Drucker quotes. https://www.goodreads.com/ author/quotes/12008. Peter F. Drucker

Drummond, D.K. (2003). Sustained British investment in overseas railways, 1830–1914: The imperial dream, engineers' assurances or an 'investment hungry' public? In: *Across the Borders: Financing the World's Railways in the 19th and 20th Centuries*. R. Roth and G. Dinhobl (Eds.). Ashgate, pp. 207–224.

Dubocage, E., and Rivaud-Danset, D. (2010). The development of venture capital in Europe. Nomura Institute.

Duhigg, C. (2012). *The Power of Habit*. Random House.

Duignan, B. (2023). Causes of the Great Depression. In: *Encyclopaedia Britannica*. https://www.britannica.com/story/causes-of-the-great-depression

Duksin, J., Van Hock, P., Schuster, D., and Jordan, C. (2021). Redefining private equity in the 2020s. Credit Suisse.

Dunkin, C. (2019). Goldman Sachs quietly unloaded some of its WeWork shares while its investment bankers were pitching the company a $60+ billion IPO. *Business Insider*. October 16. https://www.businessinsider.in/finance/news/goldman-sachs-quietly-unloaded-some-of-its-wework-shares-while-its-investment-bankers-were-pitching-the-company-a-60-billion-ipo/articleshow/71606007.cms

Dyck, A., and Virani, A. (2012). Buying into the 407: The syndication protocol as a new model for infrastructure investing. ICPM Case Study. May 29. http://www.rijpm.com/case_studie/case-study-6-buying-into-the-407-the-syndication-protocol-as-a-new-model-for-infrastructure-investing

ECB. (2012). Technical features of outright monetary transactions. European Central Bank. https://www.ecb.europa.eu/press/pr/date/2012/html/pr120906_1.en.html

ECB. (2017). Guidance on leveraged transactions. European Central Bank.

Edison Electric Institute. (1953). *Edison Electric Institute: Annual Report.*

eFront. (2019). BlackRock to acquire eFront. March 22. https://www .eFront.com/en/news-press-releases/blackrock-to-acquire-eFront-industry-leading-alternatives-investment-software-provider

EIB. (2016). The impact of EIF on the venture capital ecosystem. European Investment Bank.

Eichenwald, K. (1990). The collapse of Drexel Burnham Lambert; Drexel, Symbol of Wall St. Era, is dismantling; bankruptcy filed. *The New York Times* (February 14).

Eide, S. (2013). The deal of a lifetime. *City Journal*, May 31.

EIOPA. (2018). Failures and near misses in insurance. European Insurance and Occupational Pensions Authority.

EIOPA. (2022). Solvency II background. https://www.eiopa.europa.eu/ browse/solvency-ii/solvency-ii-background_en

Elliot, L. (2023). The AI industrial revolution puts middle-class workers under threat. *The Guardian* (February 18). https://www.theguardian .com/technology/2023/feb/18/the-ai-industrial-revolution-puts-middle-class-workers-under-threat-this-time

Elliott, J. (2010). IBM mainframes: 45+ years of evolution. IBM Canada Ltd.

Ellis, C. (2008). *The Making of Goldman Sachs.* Penguin.

Ellis, C. (2020). The (easily misunderstood) Yale Model. *Institutional Investor*, February 1.

EnCap. (2017). EnCap closes fund XI at $7.0 billion. https://www .encapinvestments.com/news/encap-closes-fund-xi-above-target-70-billion

Encyclopaedia Britannica. (2022a). East India Company. https://www .britannica.com/topic/East-India-Company

Encyclopaedia Britannica. (2022b). Mississippi Bubble. https://www .britannica.com/event/Mississippi-Bubble.

Encyclopaedia Britannica. (2023a). Western Union Corporation. https:// www.britannica.com/topic/Western-Union-Corporation

Encyclopaedia Britannica. (2023b). John D. Rockefeller. https://www .britannica.com/biography/John-D-Rockefeller

Energy Information Administration. (2011). Shale oil may mirror the shale gas boom. EIA.

European Commission. (2014). Corporate sustainability reporting. https:// ec.europa.eu/info/business-economy-euro/company-reporting-and-auditing/company-reporting/corporate-sustainability-reporting_en

European Commission. (2021). A European Green Deal. https://ec.europa .eu/info/strategy/priorities-2019-2024/european-green-deal_en

Evans, B. (2020). How to lose a monopoly. b-vans.com. January.

Evans, J. and Archer, S. (1968). Diversification and the reduction of dispersion: An empirical analysis. *Journal of Finance*, 23(5): 761–767.

Evening Standard. (2013). Broadgate Sale to net £600m profit. (August 20). www.standard.co.uk

Fama, E., and Jensen, M.C. (1983). Separation of ownership from control, *Journal of Law and Economics*, 26: 301–325.

Fan, J.S. (2022). The landscape of startup corporate governance in the founder-friendly era. *New York University Journal of Law and Business*, 18(2): 317–389. https://digitalcommons.law.uw.edu/faculty-articles/595

Fang, L., Ivashina, V., and Lerner, J. (2015). The disintermediation of financial markets: Direct investing in private equity. *Journal of Financial Economics*, 116: 160–178.

Fannin, R. (2018). Mary Meeker's exit from Kleiner Perkins sure to impact its China ventures. *Forbes* (September 15). https://www.forbes.com/sites/rebeccafannin/2018/09/15/mary-meekers-exit-from-kleiner-perkins-sure-to-impact-its-china-ventures/

Fannin, R. (2019). China venture returns outdo most US funds, new research shows. *Forbes* (March 18). https://:www.forbes.com/sites/rebeccafannin/2019/03/18/china-venture-returns-outdo-most-us-funds-new-research-shows/?sh=238a45141af7

Farr, C. (2013). Investors eager to dump Wine.com, sources say. https://venturebeat.com/2013/07/02/investors-eager-to-dump-wine-com-sources-say/

Fayol, H. (1949). *General and Industrial Management.* Sir Isaac Pitman and Sons, Ltd.

FBI. (2007). Mortgage fraud report, 2006. https://www.fbi.gov/stats-services/publications/mortgage-fraud-2006

Federal Savings and Loan Insurance Corporation. (n.d.). About us. https://en.wikipedia.org/wiki/Federal_Savings_and_Loan_Insurance_Corporation

Feld, B. (2014). Why the SBIC doesn't work for venture capital anymore. July 28. https://feld.com/archives/2014/07/sbic-doesnt-work-venture-capital-anymore/

Fernandes, N. (2020). The value killers. January 8. https://corpgov.law.harvard.edu/2020/01/08/the-value-killers/

Fetzer, T. (2014). Fracking growth. London School of Economics working paper.

Field, S. (2021). Risk and responsibility: Private equity financiers and the US shale revolution. *Economic Anthropology*, 17 August; https://anthrosource.onlinelibrary.wiley.com/doi/full/10.1002/sea2.12221

Financial Times. (2008). British Land completes Broadgate deal. (September 18). https://www.ft.com/content/62e7e098-a3d1-11de-9fed-00144feabdc0

Financial Times. (2013a). Axa spins out private equity arm. (September 29).

Financial Times. (2013b). Singapore's GIC agrees £1.7bn Broadgate deal. (December 23).

Financial Times. (2018). Amazon elbows Alphabet aside as second most valuable company. March 20.

Financial Times. (2020). Pension funds are playing a loser's game in alternative assets. (June 28).

Financial Times. (2022a). Tiger Global hit by $17bn losses in tech rout. (May 9).

Financial Times. (2022b). EU court ruling expands Brussel's powers to scrutinize tech mergers. (July 13).

Firestone, K. (2022). Op-ed: These big names propelled the SP 500 last year. Here's what's ahead for 2022. CNBC. January 13. https://www.cnbc.com/2022/01/13/op-ed-these-big-names-propelled-the-sp-500-in-2021-heres-whats-ahead-for-2022.html

Fisher Phillips. (2022). Can trade secret laws protect algorithm-based intellectual property? 6 steps for employers to consider. December 16. https://www.fisherphillips.com/news-insights/trade-secret-laws-protect-algorithm-based-intellectual-property.html

Fishman, C. (2019). How NASA gave birth to modern computing—and gets no credit for it. June 13. https://www.fastcompany.com/90362753/how-nasa-gave-birth-to-modern-computing-and-gets-no-credit-for-it

Flanders, R.E. (1945). Can private enterprise do the job? *The New York Times Magazine* (November 18).

Fletcher, L. (2022). Private loan funds struggle to find a home. *Financial Times* (March 21).

Flink, J.J. (1990). *The Automobile Age*. MIT Press.

Flowers, S. (2019). Private equity assesses its options for exiting oil and gas. *Forbes* (November 13). https://www.forbes.com/sites/woodmackenzie/2019/11/13/private-equity-assesses-its-options-for-exiting-oil-and-gas/#2b6160bd6f04

Fogelström, E., and Gustafsson, J. (2021). GP stakes in private equity. Stockholm School of Economics.

Forbes. (1967). *Forbes Magazine* 50th Anniversary Issue (September 15).

Forbes. (2022). Thomas Lee. (September 7).

Forbes. (2023a). Hans Tung GGV. https://www.forbes.com/profile/hans-tung/

Forbes. (2023b). Microsoft confirms its $10 billion investment into ChatGPT, changing how Microsoft competes with Google, Apple and other tech giants. (January 27). https://www.forbes.com/sites/qai/2023/01/27/microsoft-confirms-its-10-billion-investment-into-

Forestner, M., and Young, B. (2021). Continuation funds: Gifts that keep on giving. Mercer.

Fortier, D.L. (1989). Hostile takeovers and the market for corporate control. economic perspectives. January. Federal Reserve Bank of Chicago.

Fr-academic. (2022). Société des autoroutes du Nord et de l'Est de la France. About us. https://fr-academic.com/dic.nsf/frwiki/1550041

Frankfurt School-UNEP Centre/BNEF. (2020). Global trends in renewable energy investment 2020. https://www.fs-unep-centre.org/wp-content/uploads/2020/06/GTR_2020.pdf

Frederick J.A., and Beck, J. (2019). Venture capital in China: An overview and analysis of trends shaping Chinese VC activity. PitchBook. March 18.

Freightwaves. (2021). J. P. Morgan controlled US railroads and industry policies. FreightWaves Classics. October 21. https://www.freightwaves.com/news/freightwaves-classicsleaders-jp-morgan-greatly-influenced-us-railroads-in-the-late-19th-century

French, H.W. (2021). *Born in Blackness: Africa, Africans, and the Making of the Modern World*. Liveright Publishing Company.

Fried, V.H., and Hisrich, R.D. (1995) The venture capitalist: A relationship investor. *California Management Review* 37(2): 101–115.

Frost, L. (2022). Solvency II update could boost bond investment. www.iflr.com

Frost Brown Todd. (2020). Navigating the plan asset rules: ERISA plan investments in private equity funds. April 13. https://frostbrowntodd.com/navigating-the-plan-asset-rules-erisa-plan-investment-in-private-equity-funds-fiduciary-focus-series/

Fruchbom, P. (2007). Private equity real estate funds raise $60B in 2006. Private Equity International.

Fryer, V. (2023). The history of SaaS: From emerging technology to ubiquity. Blog. https://www.bigcommerce.com/blog/history-of-saas/

FTC. (2020). FTC to examine past acquisitions by large technology companies: Agency issues 6(b) orders to Alphabet Inc., Amazon.com, Inc., Apple Inc., Facebook, Inc., Google Inc., and Microsoft Corp. US Federal Trade Commission.

Fuller, R.B. (1981). *Critical Path*. St. Martin's Press.

Fundinguniverse. (2022). Texas Pacific Group Inc. History. http://www.fundinguniverse.com/company-histories/texas-pacific-group-inc-history/

Gabbert, J., Bowden, A., and Tarhumi, N. (2021). Exploring trends in add-on acquisitions. PitchBook Data, Inc.

Gabor, D. (1964). *Inventing the Future*. Penguin.

Gahng, M., Ritter, J.R., and Zhang, D. (2021). SPACs. University of Florida working paper, SSRN. https://ssrn.com/abstract=3775847.

Gara, A. (2020). Blackstone now more valuable than Goldman Sachs and Morgan Stanley amid the Coronavirus chaos. *Forbes* (March 5).

Garland, J. (2013). Sierra Club launches Beyond TXU campaign with Dallas ad buy. Sierra Club.

Garner, A.C. (2008). Is commercial real estate reliving the 1980s and early 1990s? Federal Reserve Bank of Kansas.

Gates, B. (1976). An open letter to hobbyists. *Homebrew Computer Club Newsletter*. January.

Gebauer, J. and Ginsburg, M. (2003). The US wine industry and the internet: an analysis of success factors for online business models, *Electronic Markets* 13(1): 59–66.

Gelderbom, O., de Jong, A., and Jonker, J. (2013). The formative years of the modern corporation: The Dutch East India Company VOC, 1602–1623. *The Journal of Economic History*, 73(4): 1050–1076.

Gerace, T.A. and Klein, L.R. (1996). Virtual vineyards, Harvard Business School Case 9-396-264. HBS Press.

German Historical Institute. (2022). Trading floor of the New York Stock Exchange 1889. www.immigrantentrepreneurship.org/images/trading-floor-of-the-new-york-stock-exchange-1889/

GLA. (2008). Credit crunch and the property market. Greater London Authority.

Glasner, J. (2023a). 2023 Crunchbase. newsletter@email.crunchbase.com. Mailed on January 18.

Glasner, J. (2023b). Series D hits lowest point in years. what does that mean? Crunchbase. May 4. https://news.crunchbase.com/venture/series-d-startup-funding-down/ 2023

Glassman, J.K. (2005). Looking back on the crash. *The Guardian* (March 10).

GlobalData. (2022). Cautious investors put brakes on unicorn boom in 2022. https://www.globaldata.com/media/disruptor/cautious-investors-put-brakes-unicorn-boom-2022-finds-globaldata/

Global Energy Monitor. (2012). Energy future holdings. June 18. https://www.gem.wiki/Energy_Future_Holdings

Global Subsidies Initiative. (2010). Fiscal deficit forces Spain to slash renewable energy subsidies. https://www.iisd.org/gsi/subsidy-watch-blog/fiscal-deficit-forces-spain-slash-renewable-energy-subsidies

Goldman Sachs. (2019). Firm's first IPO uses new earnings-based approach to valuation. https://www.goldmansachs.com/our-firm/history/moments/1906-united-cigar.html

Goldsmith, C. (1998). Blackstone to buy Savoy's Hotels, expand luxury brand overseas. *Wall Street Journal* (April 8).

Goldstein, M. (2022). SPACs were all the rage. Now, not so much. *The New York Times* (June 2). https://www.nytimes.com/2022/06/02/business/spacs-inflation-regulation.html?searchResultPosition=4

Gompers, P. (1994). The rise and fall of venture capital. *Business and Economic History*, 23(2): 1–26.

Gompers, P., and Kaplan, S. (2022). *Advanced Introduction to Private Equity*. Edward Elgar.

Gompers, P., Kaplan, S., and Mukharlyamov, V. (2015). What do private equity firms say they do? Harvard Business School working paper No. 15-081.

Gompers, P., Kaplan, S., and Mukharlyamov, V. (2016). What do private equity firms say they do? *Journal of Financial Economics*, 121(3): 449–476.

Gompers, P., and Lerner, J. (1997). Risk and reward in private equity investments: The challenge of performance assessment. *Journal of Private Equity*, 1: 5–12.

Gompers, P., and Lerner, J. (1998). Venture capital distributions: Short- and long-run relations. *Journal of Finance*, 3: 2161–2183.

Gompers, P.A., and Lerner, J. (2001). The venture capital revolution. *The Journal of Economic Perspectives*, 15(2): 145–168.

Gompers, P., Lerner, J., and Scharfstein, D. (2005). Entrepreneurial spawning: Public corporations and the genesis of new ventures, 1986 to 1999, *Journal of Finance*, 60; 577–614.

Gompers, P., Lerner, J., Scharfstein, D. and Kovner, A. (2010). Performance persistence in entrepreneurship and venture capital, *Journal of Financial Economics*, 96(1): 18–32.

Gonella, C. (2023). Stuy Town-Peter Cooper Village tenants group win lawsuit securing rent regulation for their units. January 7. https://gothamist.com/news/stuy-town-peter-cooper-village-tenants-group-win-lawsuit-securing-rent-regulation-for-their-units

Gopinath, G. (2020). The great lockdown: The worst economic downturn since the Great Depression. Blog. April 14. https://blogs.imf.org/2020/04/14/the-great-lockdown-worst-economic-downturn-since-the-great-depression/

Gordon Bell, G.C. (1978). *Computer Engineering: A DEC View of Hardware*. Digital Press.

Gorman, M., and Sahlman, W.A. (1989). What do venture capitalists do? *Journal of Business Venturing*, 4: 231–248.

Gottschalg, O., Hahn, M., and Kehoe, C. (2013). Corporate governance and value creation: Eevidence from private equity. *The Review of Financial Studies*, 26(2): 368–402.

Govindarajan, V., and Srikanth, S. (2013). When organizational memory stands in the way. *Harvard Business Review*, March 11.

Govindarajan , V., and Srivastava, A. (2021). What Zomato's $12 billion IPO says about tech companies today. *Harvard Business Review*, August.

Graham, J., Leary, M., and Roberts, M. (2014). A century of capital structure: The leveraging of corporate America. May 6. https://voxeu.org/article/century-corporate-america-leverage

Grant, E.X. (2005). TWA – Death of a Legend. *St. Louis Magazine* (October 21).

Greenhill. (2022). Global secondary market trends and outlook. Greenhill and Co.

Greenhouse, S. (1989). 5 RJR units sold for $2.5 billion. *The New York Times* (June 7).

Griffith, E. (2020). DoorDash soars on first day of trading. *The New York Times* (December 9).

Grimm, C.B. (1999). A paper print pre-history. *Film History*, 11(2): 204–216.

Gross, D. (2022). The bubbles that build America. CNN. https://money
.cnn.com/galleries/2007/news/0705/gallery.bubbles/2.html

Grove, A.S. (1996). *Only the Paranoid Survive*. Random House.

Growth Cap. (2022). The top 25 growth equity firms. February 22. https://
growthcapadvisory.com/the-top-25-growth-equity-firms-of-2021/

Groww. (2023). FAANG stocks: A look at their performance in the last
decade. Blog. November 10. https://groww.in/blog/faang-stocks-
performance-over-the-last-decade

GuruFocus. (2022). Deutsche Telecom. November 23. https://www
.gurufocus.com/stock/DTEGY/data/pe-ratio

Haagen, F. (2008). The role of smart money: What drives venture capital
support and interference within biotechnology ventures? *Zeitschrift für
Betriebswirtschaft*, 78(4): 397–422.

Haines, L. (2013). Superstars in private equity. *Oil and Gas Investor*, June.

Hall, E. (1996). *Journey to the Moon: The history of the Apollo guidance
computer*. American Institute of Aeronautics and Astronautics.

Hamblen, M. (2010). Yankee group 2009 report: One in four households
now has only mobile phones. Comuterworld.com. May 20.

Hamel, G. (2011). First, let's fire all the managers. *Harvard Business Review*,
89(12).

Hamilton Lane. (2017). Hamilton Lane acquires Real Asset Portfolio
Management. August 14. https://www.hamiltonlane.com/en-US/
News/68ba0557-b51d-4170-9a2d-45cce0ddd8eb/Hamilton-Lane-
Acquires-Real-Asset-Portfolio-Manage

Hamilton Lane. (2021). Hamilton Lane to acquire 361 Capital, further
expanding its presence in the private wealth channel. January 28.
https://www.hamiltonlane.com/en-US/News/9ff2461c-c648-4ad0-9cba-
e5808937c299/Hamilton-Lane-to-Acquire-361-Capital,-Further-Expa

Hamilton Lane. (2022). Benchmarking in the private markets: The four
minute mile. February 18. https://www.hamiltonlane.com/en-US/
Insight/2f635b48-cd33-41b0-8b85-bb4b57df78ae/Benchmarking-in-
the-Private-Markets-The-Four-Minut

Hammer, B.K. et al. (2017). Inorganic growth strategies and the evolution of the private equity business model. *Journal of Corporate
Finance*. March 31.

Hannah, A., and Sy, S. (2016). Sovereign wealth funds investing in private
equity. Preqin, June.

Hapgood, F. (1996). What makes virtual vineyards rule? June 15. https://
www.inc.com/magazine/19960615/1966.html

Haque, S. (2021). (Over-)leveraged buyouts of private equity: Myth or
reality? Board of Governors of the Federal Reserve System. https://
blogs.worldbank.org/allaboutfinance/over-leveraged-buyouts-private-
equity-myth-or-reality

Harris, R. (2009). The institutional dynamics of early modern Eurasian trade: The Commenda and the corporation. *Journal of Economic Behavior and Organization*, 71(3).

Harris, R. (2020). A new understanding of the history of limited liability: An invitation for theoretical reframing: SSRN. http://dx.doi.org/10.2139/ssrn.3441083

Harris, R., Jenkinson, T., and Kaplan, S. (2014). Private equity performance: What do we know? *The Journal of Finance*, 69(5): 1851-1882.

Harris, R., Jenkinson, T., and Kaplan, S. (2015). How do private equity investments perform compared to public equity? Darden Business School working paper, No. 2597259, SSRN. https://ssrn.com/abstract=2597259

Harris, R., Jenkinson, T., Kaplan, S. and Stucke, R. (2020). Has persistence persisted in private equity? Evidence from buyout and venture capital funds. https://papers.ssrn.com/sol3/papers.cfm?abstract_id=2304808

Harrison, M. (2004). Macquarie Bank buys National Grid's Wireless Unit for £2.5bn. *The Independent* (November 29). https://www.independent.co.uk/news/business/news/macquarie-bank-buys-national-grids-wireless-unit-for-pound25bn-5349775.html

Harvard Business School Baker Library. (2022). The South Sea Bubble Timeline. https://curiosity.lib.harvard.edu/south-sea-bubble/feature/the-bubble

Hassan, T., Bloom, N., Kalyani, A., Melo, M., and Lerner, J. (2023). The diffusion of disruptive technologies. LSE discussion paper.

Hayes, T. (2009). Realogy said to plan swap of some debt for equity. *New York Times* (June 1). https://www.nytimes.com/1984/06/23/business/financial-corp-dops-debt-equity-swap-plan.html

HBS. (1997). Arthur Rock – MBA '51. December 1. https://www.alumni.hbs.edu/stories/Pages/story-bulletin.aspx?num=5686

Heaton, C.S. (2021). Why the Yale model of investment teaches us the wrong lessons. *Money Week*, May 17.

Heaton, H. (1937). Financing the industrial revolution. *Bulletin of the Business Historical Society*, 11(1): 1–10, published by The President and Fellows of Harvard College.

Hege, U., and Nuti, A (2011). The private equity secondaries market during the financial crisis and the "valuation gap." *The Journal of Private Equity*, 14(3): 42–54.

Heiligtag, S., Kühn, F., Küster, F., and Schabram, J. (2018). Merchant risk management: The new frontier in renewables. McKinsey and Company, November 12.

Helblich, S., and Trew, A. (2017). Banking and industrialization, University of St. Andrews School of Economics and Finance, discussion paper, No. 1506.

Helwege, J., and Opler, T. (1993). Leveraged buyouts in the late eighties – how bad were they? Board of Governors of the Federal Reserve System.

Hepp, S. (2021). London City Airport: when the sky has its limits. *Schweizer Personalvorsorge*, July.

Hern, A. (2016). WhatsApp drops subscription fee to become fully free. *The Guardian* (January 18).

Heton, T. (1707). Preface. In: *Some Account of Mines, and the Advantages of Them to This Kingdom*, pp. 18–21, 33–35.

Hicks, M.E. (2017). Financing the Luso-Atlantic slave trade, 1500–1840, *Journal of Global Slavery*, 2(3): 273–309.

Higson, C., and Stucke, R. (2012). The performance of private equity. Coller Institute of Private Equity, London Business School working paper.

Hills, R.L. (1979). Hargreaves, Arkwright and Crompton. Why three inventors? *Textile History*, 10(1): 114–126.

Hinden, S. (1989). Brady view of LBOs is assailed. *The Washington Post* (February 1).

Hirsch, L. (2023a). Bank turmoil is paving the way for even bigger 'shadow banks'. *The New York Times* (June 5). https://www.nytimes.com/2023/05/06/business/dealbook/bank-crisis-shadow-banks.html

Hirsch, L. (2023b). Venture capital Giant Sequoia spins off China and India units. *The New York Times* (June 6). https://www.nytimes.com/2023/06/06/business/dealbook/sequoia-capital-split-china-india.html

History.com. (2020). Henry Ford. https://www.history.com/topics/inventions/henry-ford

Hoeffler, D. (1971). Silicon Valley. *Electronic News*.

Hoeren, T., Guadagno, F., and Wunsch, S. (2015). Breakthrough technologies - semiconductor, innovation, and intellectual property. World Intellectual Property Organization, Economic Research working paper, No. 27.

Hoffman, R., and Yeh, C. (2018). *Blitzscaling: The Lightning-Fast Path to Building Massively Valuable Companies*. Penguin Random House.

Holl, M. (1989). How to kill a company. *The Washington Post* (April 23). https://www.washingtonpost.com/archive/opinions/1989/04/23/how-to-kill-a-company/6c4ecddb-a0a6-47c7-a810-4c552f6e2205

Horsley Bridge. (2021). Horsley Bridge Partners LLC. https://aum13f.com/firm/horsley-bridge-partners-llc

Hover, G. (2018). George Eastman: The greatest technology entrepreneur in US history? American Business History Center. https://americanbusinesshistory.org/george-eastman-the-greatest-technology-entrepreneur-in-u-s-history/

Howell, S.T., Lerner, J., Nanda, R., and Townsend, R. (2020). Financial distancing: How venture capital follows the economy down and curtails innovation. NBER working paper, No. 27150.

Hsu, D.H. (2004). What do entrepreneurs pay for venture capital affiliation? *The Journal of Finance*, November 27. https://doi.org/10.1111/j.1540-6261.2004.00680

Hsu, D.H., and Kenney, M. (2005). Organizing venture capital: The rise and demise of American Research and Development Corporation, 1946–1973. *Industrial and Corporate Change*, 14(4): 579–616. http://dx.doi.org/10.1093/icc/dth064

Hu, J., Parry, J., and Rubinstein, J. (2022). 2021: A spectacular year for SPACs. February 17. https://corpgov.law.harvard.edu/2022/02/17/2021-a-spectacular-year-for-spacs/

Hu, K. (2023). ChatGPT sets record for fastest-growing user base – analyst note. Reuters. February 27. https://www.reuters.com/technology/chatgpt-sets-record-fastest-growing-user-base-analyst-note-2023-02-01/

Hubbard, G.R., and Palia, D. (1999). A re-examination of the conglomerate merger wave of the 1960s: An internal capital markets view. *Journal of Finance*, June: 1131–1152.

Huff-Eckert, V. (2022). Living in a world of unicorns, PWC. January 17.

Hughes, T.P. (1983). *Networks of Power: Electrification in Western Society, 1880–1930*. Johns Hopkins University Press, pp. 41–42.

Hunt, B.C. (1935). The Joint-Stock Company in England, 1830–1844. *Journal of Political Economy*, 43(3).

IBM. (2022). System 360: From computers to computer systems. https://www.ibm.com/ibm/history/ibm100/us/en/icons/system360/

IDG. (2023). Quan Zhou. https://en.idgcapital.com/team/quan

IEA. (2021). Minerals in clean energy. *Transitions*. https://www.iea.org/reports/the-role-of-critical-minerals-in-clean-energy-transitions

IFM. (2022). Indiana Toll Road case study. April. https://www.nga.org/wp-content/uploads/2022/05/ITR-Case-Study-4.22.pdf

IFSWF. (2022). Collaboration in private markets: Are asset owners collaborating enough?. International Forum of Sovereign Wealth Funds. May 2022. https://www.ifswf.org/sites/default/files/Collaboration%20in%20private%20markets_FINAL.pdf

Ilmanen, A., et al. (2019). Demystifying illiquid assets: Expected returns for private equity. AQR working paper.

Inderst, G. (2009). Pension fund investment in infrastructure. OECD working papers on insurance and private pensions, No. 32.

Inderst, G. (2014). Pension fund investment in infrastructure: Lessons from Australia and Canada, *Rotman International Journal*, 7.

Infrastructure Investor. (2021). Meet the world's 50 largest infra investors. June 2. https://www.infrastructureinvestor.com/gi-50-meet-the-worlds-50-largest-infra-investors/

Infrastructure Partnerships Australia. (2017). The role of superannuation in building Australia's future. http://infrastructure.org.au/wp-content/uploads/2017/06/The-Role-of-Superannuation-FINAL.pdf

Ingram, E. (2023). M7 business schools dominate in venture capital and private equity fields. Clear Admit. February 2. https://www.clearadmit.com/2023/02/m7-dominate-venture-capital-private-equity-2022-mba-graduates/

Insurance Journal. (2004). AIG forks up $126 million to SEC. November 24.

Intel. (2012). Robert Noyce: Mayor of Silicon Valley. December 13. https://newsroom.intel.com/editorials/robert-noyce-mayor-of-silicon-valley/#gs.4ocs1j

International Banker. (2021). The dotcom bubble burst. September 29. https://internationalbanker.com/history-of-financial-crises/the-dotcom-bubble-burst-2000/

Invest Europe. (2020). Private equity in CEE. https://www.investeurope.eu/media/3595/invest-europe_private-equity-in-cee_report_final.pdf

Invest Europe. (2021). Private equity backed companies create over 250,000 jobs, growing six times faster than European average. Private Equity Wire: May 27. https://www.privateequitywire.co.uk/2021/05/27/300981/private-equity-backed-companies-create-over-250000-jobs-growing-six-times-faster

Invest Europe. (2022). Investing in Europe: Private equity activity 2021. May 3. https://www.investeurope.eu/research/activity-data/

IPE. (2021). IFM investors (infrastructure): key data. https://hub.ipe.com/asset-manager/ifm-investors-infrastructure/key-data/10051463.supplierarticle

Ippolito, R. (2020). *Private Capital Investing: The Handbook of Private Debt and Private Equity.* Wiley.

Israel Ministry of Defense. (2021). Innovative strength. https://english.mod.gov.il/About/Innovative_Strength/Pages/Military_Research_and_Development.aspx

Isser, S. (2015). *Electricity Restructuring in the United States: Markets and Policy from the 1978 Energy Act to the Present.* Cambridge University Press.

Ivashina, V., and Kovner, A. (2011). The private equity advantage: Leveraged buyout firms and relationship banking. *Review of Financial Studies,* 24: 2462–2498.

Ivashina, V., and Lerner, J. (2019). *Patient Capital.* Princeton University Press.

Izelis, C. (2020). The world's dominant investors in private equity. *Institutional Investor.* November 6.

Jacks, D. (2018). The first great trade collapse: The short- and long-run effects of World War I on international trade. In: *The Economics of World War I: A Centennial Perspective,* S. Broadberry and M. Harrison (Eds.). CEPR Press, pp. 175–181.

Jacobius, A. (2007). Allocations grow a bit, but 'expect a flood of cash. *Pensions and Investments.* March 19.

Jacoby, N.H. (1970). The conglomerate corporation. *Financial Analysts Journal,* 26(3): 35–38, 40–42, 44–48.

James, F. (2010). Burger King sold for $3.26 billion to private investors. September 2. https://www.npr.org/sections/thetwo-way/2010/09/02/129604272/burger-king-sold-for-3-26-billion-to-private-investors?t=1659864617562

Janeway, W.H. (2018). *Doing Capitalism in the Innovation Economy*. 2nd edition. Cambridge University Press.

JDSupra. (2022). Venture capital set records in 2021, faces headwinds in '22. January 24. https://www.jdsupra.com/legalnews/venture-capital-set-records-in-2021-1011895/

Jefferies. (2021). Global secondary market review 2021. July. www.jefferies.com.

Jensen, M. (1989). Eclipse of the public corporation. *Harvard Business Review*, 67: 61–73.

Jensen, M., Kaplan, S., and Stiglin, L. (1989). Effects of LBOs on tax revenues of the US Treasury. *Tax Notes*, 42(6).

Jensen, M., and Meckling, W.H. (1976). The theory of the firm: Managerial behavior, agency costs, and ownership structure. *Journal of Financial Economics*, 3(4): 305–360.

Jensen, M. and Murphy, K.J. (1990). Performance pay and top-management incentives. *Journal of Political Economy*, 98: 225–264.

Jerndal, E., and Varga, V.M. (2018). Introducing REITs in Europe: The effect on housing real estate. University of Gothenburg.

Jiahui, N. (2020). What is the 'disruptive innovation' theory that pushed Intel to the top of the industry but put it in a pinch again? November 16. https://gigazine.net/gscnews/en/20201116-intel-disruptive-innovation/

Johnson, T. (2000). That's AOL, folks. CNN. January 10.

Jolly, C. (2021). Shell faces shareholder rebellion over fossil fuel production. *The Guardian* (May 18).

Jones, K. (2000). Barons of buyouts. *Texas Monthly* (December).

Jungermann, J. (2021). These are the 10 largest real estate fundraisers of the last 5 years. December 8. https://therealdeal.com/2021/12/08/these-are-the-10-largest-real-estate-fundraisers-of-the-last-5-years/

Junglescout. (2022). Amazon vs. Walmart online sales–2021 ecommerce report. Junglescout.com.

Kadzin, J., Schwaiger, K., Wendt, V., Ang, A., and Blackrock. (2021). Climate Alpha with predictors also improving company efficiency. *The Journal of Impact and ESG*, July 15.

Kandell, J. (2021). How Blackstone chose its heir apparent — without the usual hunger games. *Institutional Investor*. December 15.

Kaplan, S., Brown, G., Harris, R., Jenkinson, T., Hu, W., and Robinson, D. (2020). Private equity portfolio companies: A first look at Burgiss holdings data. https://ssrn.com/abstract=3532444.

Kaplan, S., Gompers, P., Gornall, W., and Strebulaev, I. (2016). How do venture capitalists make decisions? working paper, No. 477/2016.

Kaplan, S., Harris, R., Jenkinson, T., and Stucke, R. (2013). Has persistence persisted in private equity? Evidence from buyout and venture capital funds. University of Chicago Booth School of Business and NBER working paper.

Kaplan, S., Jenkinson, T., Harris, R., and Stucke, R. (2017). Financial intermediation in private equity: How well do funds of funds perform? National Bureau of Economic Research, working paper No. 23428.

Kaplan, S., and Schoar, A. (2005). Private equity performance: Returns, persistence, and capital flows. *Journal of Finance*, 60(4):1791–1823.

Kaplan, S., and Stein, J. (1993). The evolution of buyout pricing and financial structure in the 1980s. *Journal of Quantitative Economics*, 108(2): 313–357.

Kaplan, S., and Strömberg, P. (2000). How do venture capitalists choose investments? University of Chicago, working paper.

Kaplan, S., et al. (2015). What do different commercial data sets tell us about private equity performance? SSRN, 2701317.

Kastelberg, T. (2019). Difference in American and European equity waterfalls. CRE Foundation. https://www.bullpenre.com/insights/difference-in-american-and-european-equity-waterfall

Kaufman, A., and Englander, E. (1993). Kohlberg Kravis Roberts and Co. and the restructuring of American capitalism. *The Business History Review*, 67(1): 52–97.

Kaufman, D., and Kavanaugh, H. (2021). Key considerations for target companies in a SPAC merger. April 14. https://www.thompsoncoburn.com/insights/publications/item/2021-04-14/key-considerations-for-target-companies-in-a-spac-merger

Kavanagh, M. (2018). Macquarie acquires Arqiva for £1.6bn. *Financial Times* (July 17). https://www.ft.com/content/e829e6d0-89e2-11e8-affd-da9960227309

Kawamoto, D. (1997). Amazon.com IPO skyrockets. May 15. https://www.cnet.com/tech/tech-industry/amazon-com-ipo-skyrockets/

Kawamoto, D. (2002). TheGlobe.com's IPO one for the books. January 2. https://www.cnet.com/tech/services-and-software/theglobe-coms-ipo-one-for-the-books/

Kay, J., and King, M. (2020). *Radical Uncertainty*. The Bridge Street Press.

Kedrosky, P. (2009). Right-sizing the US venture capital industry. Ewing Marion Kauffman Foundation.

Kelley, L. (1990). Milken helped three prosper: Junk bond gains feathered nests of Paul, Osner, and Peltz. *Sun Centennial* (April 29).

Kempler, S. (2020). Listed vs unlisted infrastructure – where do you sit in the debate? https://assets-au-01.kc-usercontent.com/e7200d2a-b5a9-02cf-c52b-2a2591a4cfcd/10be6ef8-0c55-493c-a80d-7d24f103b626/Maple-Brown%20Abbott%20Global%20Listed%20Infrastructure_Research%20paper_Listed%20Vs%20Unlisted%20Infrastructure_Sept%202020.pdf

Kenney, M.A. (2019). Unicorns, Cheshire cats, and the new dilemmas of entrepreneurial finance. *Venture Capital*, 21(1): 35–50.

Kenton, W. (2022). Tulip mania. https://www.investopedia.com/terms/tulipmania.asp

Kessler, R.A. (1979). The new uniform limited partnership act: A critique. *Fordham Law Review*, 49(159).

Kester, C.W. and Luehrman, T.A. (1995). Rehabilitating the leveraged buy-out. *Harvard Business Review*, May–June.

Keuer, W., Lee, H., Arnaud Leroi, A. (2022). M&A opportunities in the energy transition. In: *Global Energy and Natural Resources Report 2022*. Bain & Company.

Keynes, J.M. (1976 [1936]). The General Theory of Employment, Interest and Money. In: *The Collected Writings of John Maynard Keynes*, vol. 7. Johnson, E. and. Moggridge, D. (Eds.). Cambridge University Press.

Khajuria, S. (2022). *Two and Twenty: How the Masters of Private Equity Always Win*. Penguin Random House

Khosla Ventures. (2021a). Khosla Ventures SPAC sponsor LLC SEC CIK #0001846071. March 8. www.sec.com

Khosla Ventures. (2021b). Archives: Edgar. February 12. https://www.sec.gov/Archives/edgar/data/1841873/000119312521041902/d32231ds1.htm

Khosla Ventures. (2021c). Filed. 425 1 d187643d425.htm 425. March 23. www.sec.com

Kimura, D. (2015). $2.7 B=billion loan announced for Stuyvesant Town Purchase. *Affordable Housing Finance*. December 7. https://www.housingfinance.com/news/2-7-billion-loan-announced-for-stuyvesant-town-purchase_of

Kirk, M. (2005). The making of the world's best pest control company. Atlanta: Rollins, Inc. www.en.Wipikedia.org

Kitching, J. (1998). Early returns on LBOs. *Harvard Business Review*, November–December.

Klausner, M., Ohlrogge, M., and Ruan, E. (2022). A sober look at SPACs. Finance working paper, No. 746/2021.

Klein, K. (2023). Could CMGI have been the Google of Boston? https://venturefizz.com/stories/boston/could-cmgi-have-been-google-boston

Klein, M. (2008). *The Power Makers: Steam, Electricity, and the Men Who Invented America*. Bloomsbury.

Klepper, S. (2010). The origin and growth of industry clusters: The making of Silicon Valley and Detroit. *Journal of Urban Economics*, 67(1): 15–32.

Kline, G. (2003). Mosaic started Web rush, Internet boom. *The News-Gazette* (April 20).

Kocis, J., Bachman, J., Long, A., and Nickels, C. (2009). *Inside Private Equity*. Wiley.

Kocka, J. (1972). Siemens und der unaufhaltsame Aufstieg der AEG. Zeitschrift für Firmengeschichte und Unternehmerbiographie. 17(3/4): 125–142.

Kofner, S. (2006). Private equity investment in housing: The case of Germany. Paper presented at European Network of Housing Research, International Housing Conference, July 2.

Kortum, S., and Lerner, J. (2000). Assessing the impact of venture capital on innovation. *Rand Journal of Economics*, 31(4): 674–692.

Kotula, T. (2020). ESG and financial returns: The academic perspective. Axa Investment Managers.

KPMG. (2019). KPMG report on startup ecosystem in India, 2019. https://assets.kpmg.com/content/dam/kpmg/in/pdf/2019/01/startup-landscape-ecosystem-growing-mature.pdf

KPMG. (2022a). The ESG journey to assurance. https://assets.kpmg.com/content/dam/kpmg/sg/pdf/2022/09/the-esg-journey-to-assurance.pdf

KPMG. (2022b). IFRS announce new ESG reporting standard. March 7. https://home.kpmg/dp/en/home/insights/2021/10/ifrs-announce-new-esg-reporting-standard.html

Kreké, E. (2022). Repowering the European Union. GIS Report. https://www.gisreportsonline.com/r/repower-eu/

Kreutzer, L. (2020). Bain Capital raises $800m for second impact investing fund. PE News, November 23. https://www.penews.com/articles/bain-capital-raises-800m-for-second-impact-investing-fund-20201123

Kreuzer, L. (2003). Landmark Partners raises $400 million, considers selling stake in holding company to AIG. *The Private Equity Analyst*, February 24.

Krishnan, C.I. (2011). Venture capital reputation, post-IPO performance, and corporate governance. *The Journal of Financial and Quantitative Analysis*, May 3.

Krupp, M. (2020). For Silicon Valley tech tycoons, angel investing is a status symbol. *Los Angeles Times* (February 25).

Kumar, R., Dayaramani, N., and Rocha, J. (2016). Understanding and comparing ESG terminology. https://www.ssga.com/investment-topics/environmental-social-governance/2018/10/esg-terminology.pdf

Kunthara, S. (2021a). These are the tech companies that went public in 2021, A record year for IPOs. Crunchbase. December 9. https://news.crunchbase.com/news/heres-whos-gone-public-in-2021-so-far/

Kunthara, S. (2021b). Here's which VC-backed companies are going public Via SPAC this year (so far). Crunchbase. December 16. https://news.crunchbase.com/news/heres-which-vc-backed-companies-are-going-public-via-spac-this-year-so-far/

Kuri, J. (2001). Biodata macht hohe Verluste. December 12. https://www.heise.de/newsticker/meldung/Biodata-macht-hohe-Verluste-52001.html

La Monica, P.R. (2019). Amazon is now the most valuable company on the planet. CNN. January 8. www.edition.cnn.com

Lamoreaux, N.R., Sokoloff, K.L., and Sutthiphisal, D. (2013). Patent alchemy: The market for technology in US history. *Business History Review*, 87(Spring): 3–38.

Landes, D.S. (1969). *The Unbound Prometheus*. Press Syndicate of the University of Cambridge.

Lang, F. (2010). Access to finance for SMEs. KFW.

Langton, J. (2022). Private credit a lurking systemic risk. *Moody's Investment Executive*. May 9.

Larson, C. (2016). Disruptive innovation theory: What it is and 4 key concepts. Harvard Business School. Online. November 15. https://online.hbs.edu/blog/post/4-keys-to-understanding-clayton-christensens-theory-of-disruptive-innovation

LaSalle. (2021). Accessing the real estate investment universe in 2021. hub.ipe.com/asset-manager/lasalle-investment

Latta, A. (2017). VC time to exit reaches 8.2 years. PitchBook, May 20. http://www.allenlatta.com/allens-blog/vc-time-to-exit-reaches-82-years-pitchbook

Lattman, P. (2008). WaMu fall crushes TPG. September 27. https://www.wsj.com/articles/SB122247093070880789

Lattman, P. (2012). A record buyout turns sour for investors. *The New York Times* (February 28).

Laws, D. (2016, Dec 20). Fairchild, Fairchildren, and the family tree of Silicon Valley. https://computerhistory.org/blog/fairchild-and-the-fairchildren/

Laws, D. (2018). 13 sextillions and counting: The long and winding road to the most frequently manufactured human artifact in history. April 2. www.computerhistory.org/blog/13-sextillion-counting.

LeBlanc, M.O. (2016). Entrepreneurship - blitzscaling. *HBR*. April. https://hbr.org/2016/04/blitzscaling

Lécuyer, C. (2006). *Making Silicon Valley: Innovation and the Growth of High Tech, 1930–1970*. MIT Press.

Lehmann-Hasemeyer, S., and Streb, J. (2016). The Berlin Stock Exchange in imperial Germany: A market for new technology? *The American Economic Review*, 106(11): 3558–3576.

Le Nadant, A., and Perdreau, F. (2006). Financial profile of leveraged buyout targets: Some French evidence. *Review of Accounting and Finance*, 5(4): 370–392.

Lenz and Staehelin. (2012). BlackRock acquires Swiss Re Private Equity Partners. September. https://www.lenzstaehelin.com/en/news-events/deals-cases/blackrock-acquires-swiss-re-private-equity-partners

Lerner, J. (1999). The government as venture capitalist: The long-run impact of the SBIR program. *The Journal of Business*, 72(3).

Lerner, J. (2007). Yale University Investments Office. Harvard Business School Case Study. August 2006.

Lerner, J. (2015). Yale University Investments Office. Harvard Business School Case Study. February 2015.

Lerner, J. (2022). Government incentives for entrepreneurship. NBER working paper series,. DOI 10.3386/w26884

Lerner, J. and Nanda, R. (2020). Venture capital's role in financing innovation: What we know and what we still need to learn. *Journal of Economic Perspectives*, 34(3): 237–261.

Lerner, M. (2018). 10 years later: How the housing market has changed since the crash. *The Washington Post* (October 4).

Levey, H.B. (2020). History of the auditing world, part I. *CPA Journal*, November.

Levitin, A.J., and Wachter, M. (2017). The commercial real estate bubble. https://realestate.wharton.upenn.edu/wp-content/uploads/2017/03/747.pdf

Levitt, T. (1983). *The Marketing Imagination*. The Free Press.

Lienemann Associates LLC. (2004). A disconnect in real estate pricing? *Wharton Real Estate Review*, VIII(1).

Lietz, N.G., and Andrade, R. (2016). *Partners Group: Ain't No Mountain High Enough*. Harvard Business Publishing.

Lione, F. (2022). Are the times ripe for "super senior" capital structures that include term loan debt? *Butterworths Journal of International Banking and Financial Law*, October: 579–581

Lipschultz, B. (2022). SPAC winter freezes out warrant holders as time runs out for merger deals. Bloomberg. February 11. https://www.bloomberg.com/news/articles/2022-02-11/-spac-winter-buries-warrants-amid-fruitless-hunt-for-takeovers

Litan, R. (2002). *The Telecommunications Crash: What to Do Now?* Brookings Institution.

Liu, B., and Leslie, R. (2022). China's tech crackdown. Blog. January 7. https://www.lawfareblog.com/chinas-tech-crackdown-year-review

Loizos, C. (2022). The biggest VC firms are managing a lot more moolah than you thought. https://techcrunch.com/2022/04/04/the-biggest-vc-firms-are-managing-a-lot-more-moolah-than-you-thought/

Lojek, B. (2007). *History of Semiconductor Engineering*. Springer.

Long, A., and Nickels, C. (1996). A private investment benchmark. Paper presented at AIMR Conference on Venture Capital Investing, The University of Texas.

Lopato, E. (2019). WeWork is not a tech company; it is a soap opera. August 15. https://www.theverge.com/2019/8/15/20806366/we-company-wework-ipo-adam-neumann

Lopez, L. (2015). A dark narrative about the stock market is starting to take hold on Wall Street. *Business Insider*. November 3. https://www.businessinsider.com/wall-street-worried-about-conglomerates-2015-11?r=USandIR=T

Lorenz-Hennig, K., and Zander, C. (2007). Dollar fall may trigger German property selloff. Bundesamt für Bauwesen. https://www.cnbc .com/2008/05/07/dollar-fall-may-trigger-german-property-selloff.html

Los Angeles Times (1989). Drexel pleads guilty, to pay record fine: $650 million accord closes Boesky chapter. (September 11).

Loutskina, E., and Strahan, P. (2009). Securitization and the declining impact of bank finance on loan supply: Evidence from mortgage acceptance rates. *Journal of Finance*, 64(2): 861–889.

Lowe, R. (2021). Infrastructure investor survey 2021: Strategies reinforced. *IPE Real Assets*. September.

Lozano, A. (2019). Cellular telephony: Just a niche market, March 25. https://www.upf.edu/web/angel-lozano/innovation/-/asset_publisher/ AZaAOTtL3c4Z/ content/id/223464268/maximized#.YsQjQy8RoRY

Lu, A., Chen, J., and Fu, F. (2018). China's venture capital (VC): Bigger than Silicon Valley's? INSEAD.

Lueck, T. (1987). High-tech glamor fades for some venture capitalists. *New York Times* (February 6).

Lump, D. (2015). A brief history of AOL. December 15. https://www .fastcompany.com/3046194/a-brief-history-of-aol

Luong, N., Zachary, A., and Murphy, B. (2021). Understanding Chinese government guidance funds. Center for Security and Emerging Technology.

Luttrel, L.B. (1965). Interest rates, 1914-1965. St. Louis Fed. https:// fraser.stlouisfed.org/files/docs/publications/frbslreview/pages/1965- 1969/62472_1965-1969.pdf

Macey, J., and McChesney, F. (1985). A theoretical analysis of corporate greenmail. *The Yale Law Journal*, November. https://openyls.law.yale .edu/handle/20.500.13051/1023

MacFraquar, L. (2012). When giants fail. *The New Yorker* (May 14).

Macintosh, P. (2022). A record pace for SPACs in 2021. January 6. https:// www.nasdaq.com/articles/a-record-pace-for-spacs-in-2021

MacLeavy, J., Springer, S., and Birch, K. (2016). *The Handbook of Neoliberalism*. Routledge,

MacMillan, I.K. (1989). Venture capitalists' involvement in their investments: Extent and performance. *Journal of Business Venturing*, 4(1): 27–47.

Macrotrends. (2023). DoorDash operating margin 2019–2022. https:// www.macrotrends.net/stocks/charts/DASH/doordash/ebitda-margin

Mader, U. (2001). *Emil und Walther Rathenau in der elektrochemischen Industrie (1888–1907). Eine historische Studie*. Berlin Trafo-Verlag Weist.

Malkin, A. (2021). China's experience in building a venture capital sector. https://www.jstor.org/stable/pdf/resrep28842.7.pdf

Mallaby, S. (2022). *The Power Law*. Penguin.

Mamgain, P. (2018). Bangalore and Delhi figure among the top 20 global cities for contribution to VC investment growth. DealStreet Asia. https://www.dealstreetasia.com/stories/bangalore-beijing-singapore-among-top-20-cities-attracting-highest-vc-capital-report-110014

Maple-Brown, A. (2015). Evaluating global listed infrastructure indices. June 1. https://www.maple-brownabbott.com.au/evaluating-global-listed-infrastructure-indices

Maple-Brown, A. (2023). Is the tide turning for listed infrastructure returns? https://www.maple-brownabbott.com.au/is-the-tide-turning-for-listed-infrastructure-returns/

Marquit, M. (2021). Here's how companies get listed on the NASDAQ. *TIME* (October 18). https://time.com/nextadvisor/investing/nasdaq-listingrequirements/

Marshall, M. (2008). Cash panic sweeping VC industry: The capital calls problem. November 7. https://venturebeat.com/2008/11/07/cash-panic-sweeping-VC-industry-the-capital-calls-problem/

Massoudi, A. (2012). Realogy sets terms for $1bn share offering. *Financial Times* (September 28). https://www.ft.com/content/2a2b87e2-5a71-11de-aea3-00144feabdc0

Matney, L. (2021). Sequoia dramatically revamps its fund structure as it looks to rethink venture capital model. Sisense. October.

Matthews, T.L. (1999). *Always Inventing: A Photobiography of Alexander Graham Bell*. National Geographic Society, pp. 19–21.

MBN. (2023). Anglo-Saxon capitalism: Definition and meaning. https://marketbusinessnews.com/financial-glossary/anglo-saxon-capitalism/

McBride, J., and Chatzky, A. (2019). Is 'Made in China 2025' a threat to global trade? Council on Foreign Relations. https://www.cfr.org/backgrounder/made-china-2025-threat-global-trade

McCullough, B. (2018a). A revealing look at the dotcom bubble of 2000 — and how it shapes our lives today. https://ideas.ted.com/an-eye-opening-look-at-the-dotcom-bubble-of-2000-and-how-it-shapes-our-lives-today/

McCullough, B. (2018b). *How the Internet Happened: From Netscape to the iPhone*. W. W. Norton and Company.

McElhaney, A. (2017). Funds of venture capital funds have edge over buy-out peers. *Institutional Investor*. May 26.

McElhaney, A. (2019). LBOs make (more) companies go bankrupt, research shows. *Forbes* (June 26).

McGrath, D. (2011). IDC cuts PC microprocessor forecast. August 2. https://www.eetimes.com/electronics-news/4218438/IDC-cuts-PC-microprocessor-forecast

McGrath, R. (2014). Management's three eras: A brief history. *Harvard Business Review*, July 30. https://hbr.org/2014/07/managements-three-eras-a-brief-history

McKinsey. (2021). *Global Private Markets Review 2020*. McKinsey and Company.

McKinsey. (2022). *Global Private Markets Review 2021*. McKinsey and Company.

McKinsey. (2023). *Global Private Markets Review 2022*. McKinsey and Company.

Macleod, C. (1986). The 1690s patents boom: Invention or stock-jobbing? *The Economic History Review*, 39(4): 549–571.

McNally, C. (2017). Nearly 1 in 4 households don't have internet—and a quarter million still use dial-up. https://www.reviews.org/internet-service/how-many-us-households-are-without-internet-connection/

McQuaig, L., and Neil, B. (2013). *Billionaires' Ball: Gluttony and Hubris in an Age of Epic Inequality*. Beacon Press.

McWilliams, G. (1991). Can Prime patch the hole where minis used to be? Bloomberg. October 21. https://www.bloomberg.com/news/articles/1991-10-20/can-prime-patch-the-hole-where-minis-used-to-be#xj4y7vzkg

McWinney, J. (2022). A brief history of the mutual fund. https://www.investopia.com/articles/mutual fund/05/mfhistory.asp

Mendoza, C. (2022). Private equity 2021 fundraising report. *Private Equity International*, January 18.

Megginson W., Malik, A. I., and Zhou, X. Y. (2023). Sovereign wealth funds in the post-pandemic era. *Journal of International Business Policy*. April 12.

Mercedes-Benz Group. (2023). History. https://group.mercedes-benz.com/unternehmen/tradition/geschichte/1885-1886.html

Mercer. (2015). Setting an appropriate liquidity budget: Making the most of a long investment horizon.

Mercer. (2021). Private market review, Mercer Alternatives AG, September 15.

Mergers and Acquisitions. (2001). Fund-raising reaches an all-time high in 2000. March 2.

Mergr. (2022). Microsoft mergers and acquisitions summary. July 21. https://mergr.com/microsoft-acquisitions

Merlin-Jones, D. (2010). The industrial and commercial finance corporation: Lessons from the past for the future. Civitas.

Messer Industry GmbH. (2005). Messer Industry acquires MEC from The Carlyle Group. https://newsroom.messergroup.com/messer-industrie-gmbh-acquires-mec-group-from-the-carlyle-group/

Metinko, C. (2022). SoftBank, Sequoia Capital China help push Asia venture funding to new heights. Crunchbase. January 14. https://news.crunchbase.com/news/SoftBank-sequoia-capital-china-asia-venture-investors/

Metrick, A., and Yasuda, A. (2010). The economics of private equity funds. *The Review of Financial Studies*, 23(6): 2303–2341.

Metrick, A., and Yasuda, A. (2021). *Venture Capital and the Finance of Innovation*. 3rd edition. Wiley.

Metzger, G. (2016). Building momentum in venture capital across Europe. KFW.

Miller, M.E. (2002). Moral hazard and the US stock market: Analysing the 'Greenspan Put.' *The Economic Journal*, 112(478): C171–C186.

Minneapolis FED. (2023). Consumer Price Index, 1800–. https://www.minneapolisfed.org/about-us/monetary-policy/inflation-calculator/consumer-price-index-1800-

Minsky, H.P. (1981). The United States' economy in the 1980s: The financial past and present as a guide to the future. *Giornale degli Economisti e Annali di Economia*, 40(5/6): 301–317.

Mistry, S., and Ripka, T. (2017). Private debt in an institutional portfolio. Mercer.

Mitchell, A. (2000). *Great Train Race: Railways and the Franco-German Rivalry, 1815–1914*. Berghahn Books.

Mitchell, O., and Hustead, E. (2021). *Pensions in the Public Sector*. The Pension Research Council of the Wharton School of the University of Pennsylvania.

Moazed, A., and Johnson, N. (2016). Why Clayton Christensen is wrong about Uber and disruptive innovation. TechCrunch. February 27. https://techcrunch.com/2016/02/27/why-clayton-christensen-is-wrong-about-uber-and-disruptive-innovation/

Mobelli, A. (2018). The day UBS, the biggest Swiss bank, was saved. October 16. https://www.swissinfo.ch/eng/2008-crisis_the-day-ubs-the-biggest-swiss-bank-was-saved/44474630

Monegro. (2018). Information technology market cycles (a brief history). February 20. https://monegro.org/work/2018/2/20/information-technology-market-cycles-a-brief-history

Monfared, S. (2022a). Persistency in alternative asset strategies: Private equity buyouts. August 9. https://www.preqin.com/insights/research/reports/persistency-in-alternative-asset-strategies-private-equity-buyouts

Monfared, S. (2022b). Persistency in alternative asset strategies: Venture capital. Prequin. September 22. https://www.preqin.com/insights/research/reports/persistency-in-alternative-asset-strategies-venture-capital

Monfared, S. (2022c). Persistency in alternative asset strategies: Real estate value added funds. December 1. https://www.preqin.com/insights/research/reports/persistency-in-alternative-asset-strategies-real-estate-value-added

Montgomery, S., and Iodice, S. (2022). Lending and secured finance 2021. ICLG.com.

Moody's Analytics. (2011). Regulation guide: An introduction. Moody's.

Moore, G. (1965). Cramming more components onto integrated circuits. *Electronics Magazine.*

Moore, G. (1975). Progress in digital integrated electronics. *IEEE Technical Digest.* Intel.

Moore, G., and Noyce, R. (1959). (Filed). USA Patent No. 3,108,359. June 30.

Moore, R. (2016). *Slow Burn City: London in the Twenty-First Century.* Pan Macmillan.

Mordor. (2022). Online advertising market: Growth, trends, COVID-19 impact and forecasts (2022–2027). https://www.mordorintelligence.com/industry-reports/online-advertising-market

Morgan, C.F., and Thomas, W.A. (1971). *The London Stock Exchange.* St. Martin's Press.

Morgan, V.E. (1940). Railway investment, Bank of England policy and interest rates, 1844–48. *Economic History*, 4(15): 329–340.

Morgan Stanley Research. (2009). *The Mobile Internet Report.* Morgan Stanley, Inc.

Morris, R., and Penido, M. (2014). How did Silicon Valley become Silicon Valley? Three surprising lessons for other cities and regions. https://endeavor.org.tr/wp-content/uploads/2016/01/How-SV-became-SV.pdf

Mouawad, J. (2006). Kinder Morgan agrees to an improved buyout offer led by its chairman. *The New York Times* (August 29).

MSCI. (2022). MSCI China Tech 100 Index (USD). https://www.msci.com/documents/10199/03c81af0-4969-aa52-ed11-f18e70c04d2e

Mulcany, D. (2013). Six myths about venture capitalists. *Harvard Business Review.* https://hbr.org/2013/05/six-myths-about-venture-capitalists

Multiplicity. (2018). Private equity secondary market – pricing and volume. Multiplicity Partners.

Munn, C.W. (2022). History of Scottish banks and bank notes. http://www.rampantscotland.com/SCM/story.htm

Müntefering, F. (2005). Rede auf der Tagung der Friedrich Ebert Stiftung. SPD Konferenz Tradition und Fortschritt. Friedrich Ebert Stiftung.

Murphy, A.L. (2009). *The Origins of English Financial Markets: Investment and Speculation before the South Sea Bubble.* Cambridge University Press.

Mustafa, M. (2019). Overview of venture capital landscape in India. *The Journal of Private Equity*, 23(1): 63–89.

Mustafina, D., and Nacksten, V. (2020). Private equity fund managers going public: A study of the characteristics of seven listed private equity fund managers. Stockholm School of Economics.

NASDAQ. (2018). Marsh and McLennan's (MMC) Unit closes Pavilion acquisition: December 5. https://www.nasdaq.com/articles/marsh-mclennans-mmc-unit-closes-pavilion-acquisition-2018-12-05

NASDAQ. (2022a). 5200. General procedures and prerequisites for new and continued listing on the NASDAQ Stock Market. March 21. https://listingcenter.nasdaq.com/rulebook/nasdaq /rules/NASDAQ%205200%20Series

NASDAQ. (2022b). Initial Listing Guide. January 6–7. https://listingcenter.nasdaq.com/assets/initialguide.pdf

Natarajan, S. (2022). Goldman is pulling out of most SPACs over threat of liability. Bloomberg. May 9. https://www.bloomberg.com/news/articles/2022-05-09/goldman-is-pulling-out-of-most-spacs-over-threat-of-liability?sref=GUP2BhaG

National Geographic. (2022). Effects of transportation on the economy. https://education.nationalgeographic.org/resource/effects-transportation-economy

NBER. (2023). Business cycle expansions and contractions (list of NBER Recessions). https://www.nber.org/research/business-cycle-dating

Neal, L. (1971). Trust companies and financial innovation, 1897–1914. *The Business History Review,* 45(1): 35–51.

Nesbitt, S. (2022). Cliffwater 2022 Study on private fund fees and expenses for direct lending. December 3. https://caia.org/blog/2022/12/03/cliffwater-2022-study-private-fund-fees-expenses-direct-lending

Neuman, J. (2015). Heat death: Venture capital in the 1980s. January 15. https://reactionwheel.net/2015/01/80s-vc.html

Newcomer, E. (2022). Tiger Global and SoftBank bet the farm. May 12. https://www.newcomer.co/p/tiger-global-and-SoftBank-betthe?s=r

New England Historical Society (2014). William Phips finds sunken treasure, named Massachusetts governor. https://newenglandhistoricalsociety.com/william-phips-goes-sea-making-colonial-sheriff/

New York Times. (1989). Microchips make dinosaurs of mainframes (April 10).

New York Times. (1992). T. H. Lee in Snapple deal (April 3).

New York Times. (1997a). Blackstone raises $4 billion for fund (October 10).

New York Times. (1997b). Red-hot revival in real estate: Overheating is feared with surge in vulture investing (November 6).

New York Times. (2008). Two views of innovation, colliding in Washington (January 13).

Nicholas, T., and Akins, J. (2012). *Whaling Ventures.* HBS.

Nicodemus, A. (2022). Investment advisers fret over SEC's proposed ESG disclosure rule. https://www.complianceweek.com/regulatory-policy/investment-advisers-fret-over-secs-proposed-esg-disclosure-rule/31740

Nietzel, M.T. (2023). College endowments took a big hit in fiscal year 2022. *Forbes* (February 18). https://www.forbes.com/sites/michaeltnietzel/2023/02/18/college-endowments-hit-the-skids-in-fiscal-year-2022/?sh=7dfa29ac1986

Norman, J. (2011). Gordon Moore promulgates "Moore's Law." November 19. https://www.historyofinformation.com/detail.php?id=835

Norris, F. (2000). The year in the markets: Extraordinary winners and more losers. *The New York Times* (January 3).

Norris, F. (2004). Fund books loss on RJR after 15 years: A long chapter ends for KKR. *The New York Times* (July 9).

Nussey, S. (2022). SoftBank Vision Fund posts $26 bln loss. Reuters. May 12. https://www.reuters.com/business/finance/SoftBank-reports-13-bln-fy-net-loss-2022-05-12/

NVCA. (2004). *NVCA Yearbook 2004*. NVCA.

NVCA. (2011). *NVCA Yearbook 2011*. https://www.slideshare.net/nikhilkal/nvca-yearbook-2011

NVCA. (2022). *NVCA Yearbook 2020*. https://nvca.org/wp-content/uploads/2020/03/NVCA-2020-Yearbook.pdf

NYC. (2015). Mayor, local elected officials and tenant leaders announce 20-year agreement with Blackstone and Ivanhoé Cambridge to protect middle class housing at Stuyvesant Town and Peter Cooper Village, Office of the Mayor of NYC. October 20. https://www.nyc.gov/office-of-the-mayor/news/736-15/mayor-local-elected-officials-tenant-leaders-20-year-agreement-blackstone-and#/0

Odeh, L. (2022). Brookfield to target $25 billion for biggest infrastructure fund: Bloomberg. February 18. https://www.bloomberg.com/news/articles/2022-02-18/brookfield-to-target-25-billion-for-biggest-infrastructure-fund#xj4y7vzkg

Odlyzko, A. (2010). *Collective Hallucinations and Inefficient Markets: The British Railway Mania of the 1840s*. School of Mathematics and Digital Technology Center University of Minnesota.

OECD. (1999). Germany's Phase 4 Monitoring Report. OECD. https://www.oecd.org/daf/anti-bribery/anti-briberyconvention/2386529.pdf

OECD. (2005). Pension markets in focus. Newsletter, June 2005, Issue 1. https://www.oecd.org/finance/private-pensions/35063476.pdf

OECD. (2023): OECD Convention on Combating Bribery of Foreign Public Officials in International Business Transactions. https://www.oecd.org/corruption/oecdantibriberyconvention.htm

Officer, M., Oguzhan, O., and Sensoy, B. (2010). Club deals in leveraged buyouts. *Journal of Financial Economics*, November.

Official Inflation Data. (2023). "$1 in 1914 → 1920 | Inflation Calculator." Alioth Finance, January 23, 2023, https://www.officialdata.org/us/inflation/1914?endYear=1920&amount=1

Ogabo, B., Godspower, O., and Tasha, N. (2021). Ownership structure and firm performance: The role of managerial and institutional ownership-evidence from the UK. *American Journal of Industrial and Business Management*, 11(07): 859–886.

O'Gorman, P. (2015). So, what after the mobile era? (Mobile in Focus #3). May 6. https://patoguru.medium.com/so-what-after-the-mobile-era-mobile-in-focus-3-a8f0e1d20dcf

Oguh, C. (2019). Blackstone raises $20.5 billion for largest ever real estate fund. Reuters, September 12. https://www.reuters.com/article/us-blackstone-group-real-esate-fund-idUSKCN1VX00B

Oguh, C. (2020). Blackstone's Schwarzman says cannot buy Bloomberg while owning Refinitiv. Reuters. February 27. https://www.reuters.com/article/us-blackstone-m-a-bloomberg-idUSKCN20L19Y

Olson, P. (2018). Exclusive: WhatsApp cofounder Brian Acton gives the inside story on #DeleteFacebook and why he left $850 million behind. *Forbes* (September 26). https://www.forbes.com/sites/parmyolson/2018/09/26/exclusive-whatsapp-cofounder-brian-acton-gives-the-inside-story-on-deletefacebook-and-why-he-left-850-million-behind/

OpenAI. (2021). ChatGPT: OpenAI's Large Language Model [computer software]. https://www.openai.com

Orlitzky, M. (2013). Corporate social responsibility, noise, and stock market volatility. *Academy of Management Perspectives*, 27(3): 238–254.

Orr, L. (2019). David Swensen is great for Yale. Is he horrible for investing? *Institutional Investor* (July 31).

Ortmans, J. (2016). The rise of angel investing. E. M. Kauffman Foundation. https://www.kauffman.org/currents/the-rise-of-angel-investing/

Pagliari, J.L. (2013). In commercial real estate, less risk could mean higher returns. Capital Idea #14. https://www.chicagobooth.edu/review/cbr-briefing-14

Paik, Y., and Woo, H. (2017). The effects of corporate venture capital, founder incumbency, and their interaction on entrepreneurial firms' R&D investment strategies. *Organization Science*, 28(4).

Palmer, I. (2022). The surging hydrogen economy that oil and gas are tiptoeing into. *Forbes* (September 29). https://www.forbes.com/sites/ianpalmer/2022/09/29/the-surging-hydrogen-economy-that-oiland-gas-companies-are-tiptoeing-into/?sh=5d54389f6341

Partners Group. (2007). Annual Report 2006. Partners Group AG.

Partners Group. (2008). Annual Report 2007. September 2. https://www.partnersgroup.com/fileadmin/user_upload/Files/Financial_PDFs/Annual_report_2007.pdf

Partners Group. (2014). Pearl Holding Ltd. Monthly Report 08.14. August 31. https://pgdatahotel.net/pdf/pearl_mnl_2014_8_en.pdf

Partners Group. (2022). Partners Group Shareholders. Partners Group. March 23. https://www.partnersgroup.com/en/shareholders/

Paul, H.J. (2011). *The South Sea Bubble: An Economic History of Its Origins and Consequences*. Routledge.

Paulson, H.M. (2010). *On the Brink*. Hachette.

PBS. (1999). On Shockley Semiconductor. https://www.pbs.org/transistor/background1/corgs/shocksemi.html

PE Online. (2008). MAC uncertainty grips sellers in secondary market. November 3. www.private equityonline.com

PE Online. (2012). Secondary market set to break records. February 1. www.privateequityonline.com

PEI. (2005). CapDyn buys Westport. Private Equity International.

PEI. (2008). Special Report: RJR Nabisco 20th anniversary. Private Equity International.

PEI. (2010). Partners lures German capital duo for Munich office. Private Equity International.

PEI. (2011). Carlyle acquires AlpInvest. Private Equity International.

Penell, A. (2008). Facebook to move to Stanford Research Park. *Palo Alto Online News*. August 18. https://www.paloaltoonline.com/news//08/18/facebook-to-move-to-stanford-research-park

Pennington C. (2023). Generative AI: The new frontier for VC. *Forbes* (January 17). https://www.forbes.com/sites/columbiabusinessschool/2023/01/17/generative-ai-the-new-frontier-for-vc-investment/?sh=2169b879519c

Pensions Investment Research Consultants. (2007). Private equity: A guide for pension fund trustees. www.pirc.co.uk

PERE News. (2021). PERE 100 largest real estate fundraisers. https://www.privatedebtinvestor.com/pdi-100/

Perry, K., and Taggart Jr, R. (1988). The growing role of junk bonds in corporate finance. *Journal of Applied Corporate Finance*, 1(1): 37–45.

Peters, L. (2022). Top online stores in the wine and liquor segment in the US in 2020 by e-commerce net sales. Statista. April 22. https://www.statista.com/forecasts/1218281/top-online-stores-wine-liquor-united-states-ecommercedb

Petersen, J. (2022). Blackstone's open-ended infrastructure fund got an additional $7B. *IPE Real Assets*. January 1.

Pew Trust. (2014). State public pension investments shift over past 30 years. Pew Charitable Trusts and the Laura and John Arnold Foundation.

PGIM. (2021). PGIM in agreement to acquire Montana Capital Partners. July 13, https://www.pgim.com/de/press-release/pgim-strengthens-alternatives-offering-agreement-acquire-montana-capital-partners

Phalippou, L., and Gottschalg, O. (2009). The performance of private equity funds. *The Review of Financial Studies*, 22(4): 1747–1776.

Phalippou, L., Gottschalg, O., and de Silanes, L. (2009). Giants at the gate: On the cross-section of private equity investment returns. Tinbergen Institute discussion paper. https://www.econstor.eu/bitstream/10419/87057/1/11-035.pdf

Phyllis, E. (1995). Colonial Triangular Trade: An Economy Based on human Misery. *Discovery Enterprises Ltd*.

Phipps, M. (2021). The history of pension plans in the US. *The Balance*. https://www.thebalancemoney.com/the-history-of-the-pension-plan-2894374

Pickens, T. Boone (1987). *Boone*. Houghton Mifflin.

Piketty, T. (2014). *Capital in the Twenty-First Century*. The Belknap Press of Harvard University Press.

Piscione, D.P. (2013). *What Everybody Else Can Learn from the Innovation Capital of the World*. Palgrave Macmillan.

PitchBook. (2022). Six charts that show 2021's record year for US venture capital. *Venture Monitor*. January 19. https://pitchbook.com/ news/ articles/2021-record-year-us-venture-capital-six-charts

PitchBook. (2023a). PitchBook Indices. https://pitchbook.com/news/ articles/pitchbook-private-market-indexes

PitchBook. (2023b). Vertical snapshot: Generative AI. March 21. https:// pitchbook.com/news/reports/2023-vertical-snapshot-generative-ai

Platt, E. (2023). Private credit edges out banks to offer Carlyle largest direct loan of its kind. *Financial Times* (March 6).

Pohl, M. (1988). *Emil Rathenau and the AEG*. Hase and Koehler.

Pollack, A. (1989). Venture capital loses its vigor. *New York Times* (October 8).

Ponciano, J. (2020). DoorDash IPO: Shares surge 80% at start of trading. *Forbes* (December 9).

Popper, B. (2012). Can Facebook live up to its $104 billion valuation? *The Verge*, May 18. https://www.theverge.com/2012/5/18/3028293/ facebook-ipo-peaked-over-priced-stock

Portfolio Advisors. (2007). Presentation to Fresno County Employees' Retirement Association. July 18. http://www2.co.fresno.ca.us/9200/ attachments/agendas/2007/071807/Item%2022.e.%20071807%20 Portfolio%20 Advisors.pdf

Potter, S.B. (2020). US IPOs raised more money in 2019. January 9. https:// insight.factset.com/US-ipos-raised-more-money-in-2019-despite-a-decline-in-ipo-volume

Potts, M. (1983). Esmark pursues Norton Simon. *The Washington Post* (June 25).

Powell, B. (2001). 25 rising stars. *Fortune Magazine* (May 14).

Prado, T.S., and Bauer, J.M. (2022). Big Tech platform acquisitions of start-ups and venture capital funding for innovation. *Information Economics and Policy*. http://creativecommons.org/licenses/by/4.0/

Pramuk, J. (2021). Biden signs $1 trillion bipartisan infrastructure bill into law, unlocking funds for transportation, broadband, utilities. November 15. https://www.cnbc.com/2021/11/15/biden-signing-1-trillion-bipartisan-infrastructure-bill-into-law.html

Preeti, S. (2022). CalPERS gains more control of private-equity investments. February 2. https://www.wsj.com/articles/calpers-gains-more-control-of-private-equity-investments-11645099203

Preqin. (2009). Sovereign Wealth Funds Review 2008. https://docs.preqin .com/ samples/Sample_SWF.pdf

Preqin. (2010a). Preqin alternatives investment consultants. November. https://docs.preqin.com

Preqin. (2010b). Preqin Research Report: Infrastructure investor survey. https://docs.preqin.com

Preqin. (2011). The 2011 Preqin Infrastructure Review. https://docs.preqin .com

Preqin. (2014). Billion-dollar question: Are public-to-private transactions on the way out? https://docs.preqin.com

Preqin. (2015a). LP survey: Co-Investments. https://docs.preqin.com

Preqin. (2015b). Preqin Special Report: Public market equivalent (PME) benchmarking. https://docs.preqin.com

Preqin. (2015c). Interests aligned? Infrastructure fund terms and conditions. https://docs.preqin.com/newsletters/inf/Preqin-INFSL-Nov-15-Interests-Aligned-Fund-Terms-and-Conditions.pdf

Preqin. (2017a). Preqin Special Report: The natural resources top 100. https://docs.preqin.com/reports/Preqin-Special-Report-Natural-Resources-Top-100-August-2017.pdf

Preqin. (2017b). Are Co-investments here to stay? https://docs.preqin.com

Preqin. (2017c). Preqin Special Report: Private equity funds of funds. https://docs.preqin.com

Preqin. (2018). Preqin Special Report: Sovereign wealth funds. https://www .pwc.co.uk/industries/assets/prequin-special-report-august-2018.pdf

Preqin. (2019). Preqin markets in focus: Private equity and venture capital in India. https://docs.preqin.com

Preqin. (2020). Preqin Special Report, Future of alternatives 2025. https:// docs.preqin.com

Preqin. (2021a). Funds of funds market evolution factsheet. https://docs .preqin.com

Preqin. (2021b). Global Private Equity and Venture Capital Report, 2021. https://docs.preqin.com

Preqin. (2021c). Global Real Estate Report, 2021. https://docs.preqin.com

Preqin. (2022a). Preqin private capital breakdown, 2022. March 30. https:// pro.preqin.com/analysis/privateCapitalBreakDown/%age

Preqin. (2022b). Global Private Equity Report, 2022. https://docs.preqin .com

Preqin. (2022c). Global Venture Capital Report, 2022. https://docs.preqin .com

Preqin. (2022d). Preqin Global Infrastructure Report, 2022. https://docs .preqin.com

Preqin. (2022e). Global Private Debt Report, 2021. https://docs.preqin .com

Preqin. (2022f). What is infrastructure? Preqin Academy. www.preqin .com/academy/lesson-4-asset-class-101s/infrastructure

Preqin. (2022g). Fund Size and Performance: Real Estate. Preqin Ltd. November 3.

Preqin. (2023a). Preqin Global Report. 2023: Private equity, https://docs .preqin.com

Preqin. (2023b). Preqin Global Report, 2023: Venture capital. https://docs .preqin.com

Preqin. (2023c). Preqin Global Report, 2023: Private debt, https://docs .preqin.com

Preqin. (2023d). Preqin Global Report 2023: Real Estate, https://docs .preqin.com

Preqin. (2023e). Preqin Global Report 2023: Infrastructure, https://docs .preqin.com

Preqin. (2023f). Preqin Global Report 2023: Natural Resources, https:// docs.preqin.com

Preqin Insights+. (2021a). Preqin global real estate data pack 2020. https://docs.preqin.com

Preqin Insights+. (2021b). Preqin Investor Outlook: Alternative Assets, H1 2021. https://docs.preqin.com

Preqin Insights+. (2023). Data pack (license required). Preqin Global Reports 2023. https://docs.preqin.com

Prete, R. (2021). Private equity's mega-funds are making big moves in 2021. PitchBook. July 27. https://pitchbook.com/news/articles/mega-funds-private-equity-investing

Primack, D. (2011). How much did Bain Really make on HCA? https:// fortune.com/2011/03/11/how-much-did-bain-really-make-on-hca/

Private Banker International. (2013). Blackstone closes acquisition of Strategic Partners from Credit Suisse. August 7. https://www .privatebankerinternational.com/news/blackstone-closes-acquisition-of-strategic-partners-from-credit-suisse/

Private Equity News. (2012). Goldman, Cerberus exit GSW Immobilien. https://www.penews.com/articles/goldman-cerberus-gsw-20120117

Private Equity News. (2019). Europe's 50 most influential in private equity. https://www.penews.com

Private Equity Wire. (2022). Mercer closes Mercer Private Investment Partners VI at over $4.8bn. www.privateequity wire.co.uk/ 2022/01/31/ 311716/mercer-closes-mercer-private-investment-partners-vi-over-usd48bn

Probitas Partners. (2004). Private equity market environment Spring 2004.

Putzier, K. (2015a). How Stuy Town was won. The Real Deal, October 29. https://therealdeal.com/2015/10/29/how-stuy-town-was-won/

Putzier, K. (2015b). Sweet deal: Blackstone won't have to pay back city's $144M Stuy Town "loan." The Real Deal. November 05. https:// therealdeal.com/2015/11/05/sweet-deal-blackstone-wont-have-to-pay-back-citys-144m-stuy-town-loan/

PWC. (2022a). How special purpose acquisition companies (SPACs) work. https://www.pwc.com/us/en/services/trust-solutions/accounting-advisory/spac-merger.html

PWC. (2022b). France – Corporate deductions. https://taxsummaries .pwc.com/france/corporate/deductions

Qian, Y., Ritter, J.R. and Shao, X. (2022). Initial public offerings Chinese style. *Journal of Financial and Quantitative Analysis*. November. DOI:10.1017/S002210902200134X

Qint, M. (1988). Nikko acquires 20 percent of Blackstone. *New York Times* (December 13).

Raade, K., and Machado, C. (2008). Recent developments in the European private equity markets. https://ec.europa.eu/economy_finance/publications/pages/publication12419_en.pdf.

Raff, D.M. (1991). Robert Campeau and innovation in the internal and industrial organization of department store retailing: are the '80s and "90s the '20s and '30s all over again (and why does it matter)? *The Journal of the Business History Conference*, 52–61.

Rahnama, M. (2022a). Fund size and performance: Venture capital. Preqin. March 31. https://www.preqin.com/insights/research/reports/fund-size-and-performance-venture-capital

Rahnama, M. (2022b). Fund size and performance: Private equity. Preqin. May 6. https://www.preqin.com/insights/research/reports/fund-size-and-performance-private-equity

Rahnama, M. (2022c). Fund size and performance: Private debt. Preqin. June 30. https://www.preqin.com/insights/research/reports/fund-size-and-performance-private-debt

Rahnama, M. (2022d). Fund size and performance: Infrastructure. Preqin. August 1. https://www.preqin.com/insights/research/reports/fund-size-and-performance-infrastructure

Rajiv, R. (2017). Horses, cars, and the disruptive decade. Medium. October 22. https://medium.com/@alearningaday/horses-cars-and-the-disruptive-decade-358b3fd6fdb9

Ramadan, A.L. (2014). Behind Uber's soaring value. *Fortune* (November 12). https://fortune.com/2014/12/11/behind-ubers-soaring-value/

Randolph, S. (2021). From Silicon Valley to Silicon Wadi: California's economic ties with Israel. Bay Area Council Economic Institute. October.

Ranko, J. (2011). Staying power of UK buyouts. *Journal of Business Finance & Accounting*, 38(7): 945–986.

Ravenscraft, D., and Scherer, F. (1986). Mergers and managerial performance. Federal Trade Commission of America working paper, No. 137.

Ray, A. (2015). The history and evolution of cell phones. January 22. https://www.artinstitutes.edu/about/blog/the-history-and-evolution-of-cell-phones

RealAssets. (2021). CDPQ takes stake in IFM-owned Indiana toll road. April 20. https://realassets.ipe.com/news/cdpq-takes-stake-in-ifm-owned-indiana-toll-road/10052262.article

Renshaw, J., and Scott Disavino, S. (2022). Analysis: US LNG exports to Europe on track to surpass Biden promise. Reuters. July 26. https://www.reuters.com/business/energy/us-lng-exports-europe-track-surpass-biden-promise-2022-07-26/

Responsible Investor. (2022). ESG round-up NASDAQ pushes back against sec climate rule proposal. June 17. https://www.responsible-investor.com/esg-round-up-nasdaq-pushes-back-against-sec-climate-rule-proposal/

Reuters. (2012). Dresden, Gagfah settle billion-euro lawsuit. March 16. https://www.reuters.com/article/gagfah-idUSL5E8EG1GJ20120316

Reuters. (2013a). Venture capital kingpin Kleiner Perkins acknowledges weak results. March 5. https://www.reuters.com/article/usa-venture-kleiner-meetings-idINL1N0BT00520130305

Reuters. (2013b). Timeline: Verizon and Vodafone's long relationship. April 25. https://www.reuters.com/article/us-verizon-vodafone-history-idUSBRE93O 19Z20130425

Reuters. (2022). Factbox: Elon Musk hints at an impending recession. June 3. https://www.reuters.com/markets/us/elon-musk-hints-an-impending-recession-2022-06-03/ .

Richardson, G., Komai. A., Gou, M., and Park, D. (2023). Stock market crash of 1929. https://www.federalreservehistory.org/essays/stock-market-crash-of-1929

Richmond Vale Academy. (2022). The Second Industrial Revolution: The Technological Revolution. Global issues. Blog. https://richmondvale.org/blog/second-industrial-revolution/

Richter, P. (1989). In decade of the big deals, rules were rewritten: take overs. *Los Angeles Times* (December 17).

Ricketts, D. (2021). Fidelity takes minority stake in alternatives platform Moonfare. *Private Equity News*. March 12.

Riddiough, T.J. (2021). Pension funds and private equity real estate: History, performance, pathologies, risks. University of Wisconsin-Madison, working paper.

Ritter, J.R. (2022). Initial public offerings: VC-backed IPO statistics through 2021. University of Florida working paper.

Robinson, D., Kaplan, S.N., Lerner, J., and Sensoy, B. (2011). Manager compensation, ownership, and the cash flow performance of private equity funds Unpublished working paper.: https://www.researchgate.net/publication/228760163_Manager_compensation_ownership_and_the_cash_flow_performance_of_private_equity_funds/link/02bfe50e2d757ad9db000000/download

Robinson, D.T., and Sensoy, B. (2016). Cyclicality, performance measurement and cash flow liquidity in private equity. *Journal of Financial Economics*, 122(3): 512–543.

Robinson, F. (2010). EU's bailout bond three times oversubscribed. *The Wall Street Journal* (December 21).

Rodrigez-Valladares, M. (2020). Over half of rated company defaulters are owned by private equity firms. *Forbes* (July 16).

Rodriguez, D.H. (2022). Secondaries fundraising report 2021. *Secondaries Investor*.

Romburgh, M. von., and Teare, G. (2023). Chinese startup investors are stepping up with capital as American VCs retreat. Crunchbase News. https://news.crunchbase.com/venture/china-us-vc-startup-investment-biden-order-data/?utm_source=cb_dailyandutm_medium=emailandutm_campaign=20230811andutm_content=introandutm_term=contentandutm_source=cb_dailyandutm_medium=emailandutm_campaign=20230703

Romo, V. (2021). Elon Musk is *Time*'s 2021 Person of the Year. December 13. https://www.npr.org/2021/12/13/1063792887/elon-musk-time-person-of-the-year

Rosacia, P. and Sabater, A. (2021). As construction, engineering rebuilds momentum, PE firms buy in. https://www.spglobal.com/marketintelligence/en/news-insights/latest-news-headlines/asconstruction-engineering-rebuilds-momentum-pe-firms-buy-in-64492616

Rosenblatt, R. (1989). Brady uneasy about over-leveraged buyouts but has no answers. *Los Angeles Times* (January 25).

Roser, M., and Ritchie, H. (2020). Transistor count over time. November. https://ourworldindata.org/uploads/2020/11/Transistor-Count-over-time.png

Roumeliotis, G. (2019). Blackstone to switch from a partnership to a corporation. Reuters. April 18. https://www.reuters.com/article/us-blackstone-group-results-idUSKCN1RU196

RSCM. (2010). Historical size of the US angel market. Right Side Capital Management. http://www.rightsidecapital.com/assets/documents/HistoricalAngelSize.pdf

Rubinstein, M. (2021). Blackstone's Moment. *Net Interest*. July 30. https://www.netinterest.co/p/blackstones-moment?s=r

Rubio, J. (2022). Charting how the unicorn baby boom turned bust. PitchBook. December 14. https://pitchbook.com/news/articles/2022-unicorns-year-in-review

Rüdiger, A. (2012). Die Geschichte der Deutschen Telekom. *PC Welt*, Germany.

Russel, M. (2020). Sequoia Capital has 3 funds that have hauled in returns of 8X to 11X. *Business Insider*. December 7. https://www.businessinsider.com/sequoia-capital-recent-fund-returns-2020-12?r=USandIR=T

Russell, G. (2014). *The Boom: How Fracking Ignited the American Energy Revolution and Changed the World.* Simon & Schuster.

S&P Global. (2012). Just the facts: Private equity, corporate defaults. February 6. https://www.spglobal.com/marketintelligence/en/news-insights/latest-news-headlines/leveraged-loan-news/just-the-facts-private-equity-corporate-defaults-and-mitt-romney

Saccone, M. (2020). Decoding private equity performance. Blog. February 13. https://blogs.cfainstitute.org/investor/2020/02/13/decoding-private-equity-performance/

Sahling, L. (1991). Real estate markets in the 1990s. *Challenge*, 34(4): 43–52.

Sakelaris, N. (2014). Paulson: Why I bailed out the banks, and what would have happened if I had not? *Dallas Business Journal.* February 5.

Saket, P. (2021). Understanding PME benchmarking. December 2. https://www.allvuesystems.com/resources/understanding-pme-benchmarking/

Sandberg, E. (1985). Making the laptop commonplace. *The New York Times* (December 8).

Sandelin, J. (2004). *The Story of the Stanford Industrial/Research Park.* Stanford University Press.

Satkowiak, L. (2013). How AT&T became a monopoly. https://www.cablefax.com/archives/how-at-amp-t-became-a-monopoly

Schearer, D. (2016). Solvency II recalibration. April 16. https://www.nortonrosefulbright.com/en/knowledge/resources-and-tools/capital-markets-union/investing/solvency-ii-recalibration

Schmalensee, R. (1990). *The History of Electric Power in the United States.* National Bureau of Economic Research.

Schnurman, M. (2013). Debt bomb ticking at Energy Future Holdings. *Fort Worth Star-Telegram.*

Schoenherr, E. (2004). The digital revolution. May 5. https://web.archive.org/web/20081007132355/http://history.sandiego.edu/gen/recording/notes.html

Scholes, M., and Wolfson, M. (1990). The effects of changes in tax laws on corporate reorganization activity. *The Journal of Business*, 63(1): 141–164.

Schroeder, P. (2019). Fannie, Freddie, and the government: It's complicated. Reuters. September 5. https://www.reuters.com/article/us-fannie-freddie-hurdles-factbox-idUSKCN1VQ2Q4

Schroeder, S., Masuda, B., and Schindler, B. (2022). Private company board compensation and governance in the USA. Compensation Advisory Partners. https://corpgov.law.harvard.edu/2022/10/11/private-company-board-compensation-and-governance/

Schroff, S. (2021). Presentation on private debt. CFA Forum Switzerland. Allianz Global Investors.

Schubarth, C. (2012). Three generations of Drapers surprise, succeed in venture capital. *Silicon Valley Business Journal*. October 10.

Schuyten, P. (1978). Technology; The computer entering home. *The New York Times* (December 6).

Schwab, K., and Kroos, H. (1971). *Moderne Unternehmensführung im Maschinenenbau*. VDMA.

Schwab, K., and Vandam, P. (2021). What is stakeholder capitalism? https://www.weforum.org/agenda/2021/01/klaus-schwab-on-what-is-stakeholder- capitalism-history-relevance/

Schwartz, E.S., and Tebaldi, C. (2006). Illiquid assets and optimal portfolio choice. NBER working paper.

Schwarz, G., Fouad, M., Hansen, T., and Verdier, G. (2020). Well spent: How strong infrastructure governance can end waste in public investment. International Monetary Fund.

Schwarzman, S.A. (2019). *What It Takes: Lessons in the Pursuit of Excellence*. Avid Reader Press.

Scott, G. (2022). Timeline of US stock market crashes. September 9. https://www.investopedia.com/timeline-of-stock-market-crashes-5217820

Science Business. (2007). Al Gore's cleantech fund joins forces with Silicon Valley's leading VC. November 14. https://sciencebusiness.net/news/71437/Al-Gore's-cleantech-fund-joins-forces-with-Silicon-Valley's-leading-VC

SEC. (2005). SEC rules. File number 265-23. August 3. https://www.sec.gov/rules/other/265-23/2652364.pdf

SEC. (2020). Form S-1 Registration Statements DoorDash, Inc. November 13. https://www.sec.gov/Archives/edgar/data/1792789/000119312520 292381/d752207ds1.htm#rom752207_14

SEC. (2022a). SEC proposes to enhance disclosures by certain investment advisers and investment companies about ESG investment practices. May 25. https://www.sec.gov/news/press-release/2022-92

SEC. (2022b). Recommendation of the investor advocate: Memorandum to Adena T. Friedman, President and Chief Executive Officer and John Zecca, EVP and Global Chief Legal and Regulatory Officer NASDAQ, Inc. April 21. https://www.sec.gov/about/offices/investorad/recommendation-of-the-investor-advocate-nasdaq-spac-listing-standards-042122.pdf

Secondary Investor. (James, R.). (2022). Deal volume topped $130bn last year, say Jefferies Greenhill. January 20. https://www.secondariesinvestor.com/deal-volume-topped-130bn-last-year-say-jefferies-greenhill/

Segal, M. (2021). Brookfield raised $7 billion for inaugural global impact fund. https://www.esgtoday.com/brookfield-raises-7-billion-for-inaugural-net-zero-focused-impact-fund/

Sen, A., Prentice, C., and Hu, K. (2021). US SEC cracks down a second time on SPAC equity accounting treatment. Reuters. September 28.

https://www.reuters.com/business/finance/exclusive-us-sec-cracks-down-second-time-spac-equity-accounting-treatment-2021-09-28/

Sender, H., and Crooks, E. (2014). Pain of private equity's TXU disaster fades amid renewed interest. *Financial Times* (May 15).

Sequoia. (2023). Writing a business plan. Sequoia Capital. https://articles.sequoiacap.com/writing-a-business-plan

Severns, M.E. (2022). Elon Musk hates government subsidies. His companies love them. April 20. https://www.grid.news/story/technology/2022/04/30/elon-musk-hates-the-government-his-companies-love-it/

Seymor, D. (2007). In a first, Hedge Fund launches on NYSE. *The Washington Post* (February 9).

Shamay, N. (2020). Israel funding ecosystem. Cardumen Capital. https://cardumencapital.medium.com/israel-funding-ecosystem-44878280bf00

Shares. (2022). Just Eat Takeaway plunges to record low as analyst casts doubt on Grubhub sale. *Shares Magazine*. June 29. https://www.sharesmagazine.co.uk/news/shares/just-eat-takeaway-plunges-to-record-low-as-analyst-casts-doubt-on-grubhub-sale

Sharma, D. (2020). *Financial History of Asian Private Equity, 1990–2020*. Independently published.

Sharpe, W. (1964). Capital asset prices: A theory of market equilibrium under conditions of risk. *Journal of Finance*, 19(3): 425–442.

Shell Technology Ventures. (2007). COMP/M.4609 – Shell/Coller Capital/STV. https://ec.europa.eu/competition/mergers/cases/additional_data/531154.pdf

Shen, H. (2019). China's tech giants: Baidu, Alibaba, Tencent. *Digital Asia*. https://www.kas.de/documents/288143/4843367/panorama_digital_asia_v3b _HongShen.pdf

Shi, M. (2022). Continuation funds drive GP-led secondaries wave. Pitch-Book. February 1. https://pitchbook.com/news/articles/continuation-funds-GPs-secondaries-private-equity

Shiller, R. (2021). Looking back at the first Roaring Twenties. *The New York Times* (April 16). https://www.nytimes.com/2021/04/16/business/roaring-twenties-stocks.html

Shiller, R. (2007). Understanding recent trends in house prices. Brookings Panel on Economic Activity, pp. 89–122.

Shleifer, A., and Vishny, R. (1990). The takeover wave of the 1980s. *Science*, August 17, pp. 745–749.

Shortform. (2021). Blitzscaling. www.shortform.com/summary/blitzscaling-summary-reid-hoffman?gclid=CjwKCAjw7IeUBhBbEiwAdhiEMcFk03-77WYUkMCP3klyfCq4azweGCG8z7frZYUiTu5n4e2GQGXaUhoC3u8QAvD_BwE

Siemens Historical Institute. (2018). *Shaping the Future: The Siemens Entrepreneurs 1847–2018*. Siemens Historical Institute.

Silverstein, J. (2018). A brief history of the battle between Thomas Edison and George Westinghouse over the future of electrical power. CBS News. https://www.cbsnews.com/news/a-brief-history-of-the-battle-between-thomas-edison-and-george

Similarweb. (2022). Most popular messaging apps around the globe. May. https://www.similarweb.com/corp/blog/research/market-research/worldwide-messaging-apps/

Sirri, E.R., and Tuffano, P. (2002). Costly search and mutual fund flows. *Journal of Finance*, 53(5): 1589–1622.

Sloane, A.P. (1964). *My Years with General Motors*. Doubleday.

Smiley, G. (2023). The US economy in the 1920s. Economic History Association. https://eh.net/encyclopedia/the-u-s-economy-in-the-1920s/

Smith, A. (2012). *Totally Wired: On the Trail of the Great Dotcom Swindle*. Bloomsbury Books.

Smith, J. (2022). The rise of AI accelerators: Specialized hardware for faster and more efficient AI processing. *Tech Trends*, 13(1): 23–28.

Snowberg, E., and Henderson, R. M. (2019). TXU (A): Powering the largest leveraged buyout in history. Harvard Business School Case 320-064.

Sociétés de Vinci Autoroutes. (2022). Presentation. June 13. https://corporate.vinci-autoroutes.com/fr/presentation/societes-vinci-autoroutes/asf/asf-comite-direction

Söffge, F. (2016). Private equity sponsored leveraged buyout transactions in the German-speaking region: An analysis of value drivers, determinants of performance and the impact on stakeholders. Dissertation, Technische Universität München.

SoftBank. (2022). SoftBank Group Report 2022. SoftBank Vision Funds. https://group.SoftBank/en/ir/financials/annual_reports/2022/message/misra

Solomon, G. (2015). To burn or not to burn—going long. Blog. https://goinglongblog.com/to-burn-or-not-to-burn/

Solomon, R. (1982). *The International Monetary System, 1945–1981*. Harper and Row.

Son, H. (2022). Jamie Dimon says "brace yourself" for an economic hurricane caused by the Fed and Ukraine war: CNBC. June 1. https://www.cnbc.com/2022/06/01/jamie-dimon-says-brace-yourself-for-an-economic-hurricane-caused-by-the-fed-and-ukraine-war.html

Sorkin, A.R. (2007). Carlyle to sell stakes to a Mideast government. *The New York Times* (September 21).

Sorkin, A.R. (2008). California pension fund expected to take big stake in Silverlake. *The New York Times* (January 9).

Sorkin, A.R. (2013). McKinsey and Co isn't all roses. *The New York Times* (September 3).

Sousa, M. (2010). Why do private equity firms sell to each other? SSRN *Electronic Journal*.

SPAC Research. (2022). Underwriter League. https://www.spacresearch .com/underwriter?year=2020andyear=2019andyear=2021andsector= technologyandgeography=US %2FCanada

SPD. (2005). Programmdebatte. Wohlstand heute und morgen. Berlin. German Social Democratic Party Parliamentary Group discussion paper.

Stackhouse, J.L. (2017). Why didn't bank regulators prevent the financial crisis? St. Louis Fed. May 22. https://www.stlouisfed.org/on-the-economy/ 2017/may/why-didnt-bank-regulators-prevent-financial-crisis

Staley, W. (2010). Stuy-Town: Worst real estate deal since 1626! February 2. https://nextcity.org/urbanist-news/stuy-town-worst-real-estate-deal-since-1626

Stanford Daily. (2010). Skype plans to move offices to Palo Alto (July 8).

Starr, P. (2002). The great telecom implosion. *The American Prospect.*

Startupranking. (2022). Facebook funding rounds. May 16. https://www .startupranking.com/startup/facebook/funding-rounds

Statcounter. (2022a). Market share worldwide. July 16. gs.statcounter .com: https://gs.statcounter.com/browser-market-share

Statcounter. (2022b). Browser market share. July 22. https://gs.statcounter .com/search-engine-market-share

Statista Research. (2022a). Value of venture capital investment in the United States from 1995 to 2020. January 11. https://www.statista.com/

Statista Research. (2022b). Market share of leading retail e-commerce companies in the United States as of June 2022. https://www.statista .com/statistics/274255/market-share-of-the-leading-retailers-in-us-e-commerce/

Statista Research. (2022c). Worldwide desktop market share of leading search engines from January 2010 to July 2022. August 29. https:// www.statista.com/

Statman, M. (1987). How many stocks make a diversified portfolio? The *Journal of Financial and Quantitative Analysis*, 22(3) :353–363.

Steinberg, M. (2019). T. Boone Pickens, the "Oracle of Oil,2 corporate raider, and billionaire philanthropist, dies at 91. CNBC. September 16. https://www.cnbc.com/2019/09/11/t-boone-pickens-oracle-of-oil-and-corporate-raider-dies-at-91.html

Stepstone. (2021). Private debt thoughts on relative attractiveness. Stepstone Advisors.

Stevenson, A. (2014). Goldman Sachs misses out on big Alibaba payoff, dealbook. *The New York Times* (June 11). https://archive.nytimes. com/dealbook.nytimes.com/ 2014/06/11/goldman-sachs-misses-out-on-big-alibaba-payoff/

Steward, J.B. (1992). *Den of Thieves.* Simon & Schuster.

Stewart, G.C. (2004). *Fred Terman at Stanford: Building a Discipline, a University, and Silicon Valley.* Stanford University Press.

Stewart, I. (1948). *Organizing Scientific Research for War: The Administrative History of the Office of Scientific Research and Development.* Little, Brown, and Company.

Stilo, A. (2022). Semper Augustus. https://penelope.uchicago.edu/~grout/encyclopaedia_romana/aconite/semperaugustus.html

St. Louis Fed. (2023). What caused the Great Depression? Federal Reserve Bank of St. Louis. https://www.stlouisfed.org/the-great-depression/curriculum/economic-episodes-in-american-history-part-5

Stone, D.G. (1990). *April Fools: An Insider's Account of the Rise and Collapse of Drexel Burnham.* D. I. Fine.

Strömberg, P. (2008). The new demography of private equity. In: *The Global Impact of Private Equity: Report.* J. Lerner, and G. Anuradha (Eds.). World Economic Forum, pp. 13–26.

Stucke, R. (2011). Updating history. Oxford University working paper.

Subin, S. (2021). WeWork shares jump more than 13 percent in public markets debut after SPAC merger. CNBC. October 21. https://www.cnbc.com/2021/10/21/wework-goes-public-through-spac-.html

Supreme Court of the United States. (1973). 411 US 546 (1973) *United States vs. Cartwright Executor No. 71-1665.* May 7.

Swartzberg, M., Solomon, J.F,. and Berkman, M. (2000). Clicking on Wine. Salomon Smith Barney Equity Research, Beverages Division. March 17.

Swensen, D.F. (2000). *Pioneering Portfolio Management.* The Free Press.

SWF. (2021). Temasek becomes Singapore super-incubator with a suite of in-house startups. September 1. https://globalswf.com/news/temasek-becomes-singapore-super-incubator-with-a-suite-of-in-house-startups

Swisscanto. (2022). Pensionskassenstudie 2021.

SwissRe. (2013). *A History of UK Insurance.* Swiss Reinsurance Company Ltd.

Sylla, R., Tilly, R., and Tortella, G. (1999). *The State, the Financial System and Economic Modernization.* Cambridge University Press.

Symmonds, F.L. (1931). Business trusts. *Marquette Law Review,* 211. https://scholarship.law.marquette.edu/cgi/viewcontent.cgi?referer=and https redir=1andarticle=4178andcontext=mulr

Taleb, N. (2007). *The Black Swan: The Impact of the Highly Improbable.* Penguin.

Talton, J. (2018). Jeff Skilling and a reminder that white-collar crime doesn't have to pay. *Seattle Times.* (September 4).

Tan, G. (2015). Buyout firms feel pinch from lending crackdown. *The Wall Street Journal* (March 25).

Tan, G. (2023). Morgan Stanley's private credit head envisions growing into billion-dollar deals. Bloomberg. https://www.bloomberg.com/news/newsletters/2023-02-17/morgan-stanley-s-private-credit-head-envisions-growing-into-billion-dollar-deals

Tan, G., and Devau, S. (2020). Wine.com seeks funding at valuation of more than $1 billion. Bloomberg. July 31. https://www.bloomberg.com/

news/articles/2020-07-31/wine-com-seeks-funding-at-a-valuation-of-more-than-1-billion

Taylor, A.L. (1981). Boom time in venture capital. *TIME Magazine* August 10,

Taylor, B. (2017). The first billion-dollar company. Global Financial Data.: https://www.investmentoffice.com/The_Library/The_Times_Room/The_First_Billion-Dollar_Company.html

Teare, G. (2020). Running the numbers on Y Combinator's best year yet. Crunchbase News. December 14. https://news.crunchbase.com/startups/y-combinator-biggest-startups-gone-public-airbnb-doordash/

Teare, G. (2022a). Europe's unicorn herd multiplies as VC investment more than doubled in 2021. Crunchbase. January 12. https://news.crunchbase.com/venture/europe-vc-funding-unicorns-2021-monthly-recap/

Teare, G. (2022b). The Crunchbase Unicorn Board: Value of world's biggest startups doubles in a year to $4 trillion. Crunchbase. February 22. https://news.crunchbase.com/news/crunchbase-unicorn-board-4-trillion-value/

Teare, G. (2022c). Global VC pullback is dramatic in Q3 2022. Crunchbase. October 6. https://news.crunchbase.com/venture/global-vc-funding-pullback-q3-2022-monthly-recap/

Teare, G. (2022d). Global venture funding and unicorn creation in 2021 shattered all records. Crunchbase. https://news.crunchbase.com/business/global-vc-funding-unicorns-2021-monthly-recap/

Teeter, P.A. (2017). Cracking the enigma of asset bubbles with narratives. *Strategic Organization*, 15(1): 91–99.

Tegtmeier, L. (2021). Testing the efficiency of globally listed private equity markets. *Journal of Risk and Financial Management*, 14(7): 313.

Temkin, M. (2023). VC Sarah Guo buys AI startups, but not the hype. Pitch-Book. February 17. https://pitchbook.com/news/articles/conviction-generative-AI-VC-SarahGuo

Temple-West, P., and Masters, B. (2023). Wall Street titans confront ESG backlash as new financial risk. *Financial Times* (March 1).

Tencent. (2023). "Digital Ark" Program. https://www.tencent.com/en-us/business/digital-ark-desc.html

Thackray, J. (1986). Leveraged buyouts: The LBO craze flourishes amid warnings of disaster. *Euromoney* (January 2).

The Economist. (1991). The ebb tide. October 8.

The Economist. (1999a). Cutting the cord: Mobile phones are everywhere, thanks to falling prices, rising quality and clever marketing. October 7.

The Economist. (1999b). The key to industrial capitalism: limited liability. December 25.

The Economist. (2002a). Victor Posner, master of the hostile takeover. March 7.

The Economist. (2002b). The great telecoms crash. July 20.

The Economist. (2008). Cracks in the crust. December 11.

The Economist. (2010). A Netscape Moment? February 10.

The Economist. (2012). Maple revolutionaries. March 3.

The Economist. (2016). The barbarian establishment. October 22.

The Economist. (2019). Tech's new stars have it all—except a path to high profits. April 20. https://www.economist.com/leaders/2019/04/17/techs-new-stars-have-it-all-except-a-path-to-high-profits

The Economist. (2020a). Technology startups are headed for a fall. April 4.

The Economist. (2020b). Life is getting harder for foreign VCs in China. September 1.

The Economist. (2021a). The Chinese state is pumping funds into private equity. June 3.

The Economist. (2021b). Hard truths about SoftBank. June 19.

The Economist. (2021c). Cloning DARPA. July 5.

The Economist. (2021d). The flywheel delusion. November 9.

The Economist. (2021e). China's communist authorities are tightening their grip on the private sector. November 18.

The Economist. (2021f). The bright new age of venture capital. November 25.

The Economist. (2022a). Pensions in Germany: Aversion therapy. January 15.

The Economist. (2022b). Some lessons on inventing the future in Britain. February 12.

The Economist. (2022c). Alternative fund managers are increasingly mainstream. February 23.

The Economist. (2022d). More borrowers turn to private markets for credit. February 23.

The Economist. (2022e). Can Silicon Valley still dominate global innovation? April 16.

The Economist. (2022f). Toddlers, not titans. June 25.

The Economist. (2022g). The great Silicon Valley shake-out. July 2.

The Economist. (2022h). Venture capital's reckoning. July 28.

The Economist. (2022i). The VC-industrial complex. July 2.

The Economist. (2022j). Mothering invention. October 13.

The Economist. (2023a). China's startup boom: A new breed of unicorn. April 19.

The Economist. (2023b). Private's progress. April 29.

The Harvard Crimson. (2009). Harvard sells $1.5B of private equity portfolio. November 5. https://www.thecrimson.com/article/2008/11/5/harvard-sells-15b-of-private-equity/

The Journal Record. (1998). Blackstone buys Watergate Hotel (June 26).

The Planetary Society. (2022). Cost of Apollo. https://www.planetary.org/space-policy/cost-of-apollo

The Royal Bank of Scotland. (2000). The Royal Bank of Scotland asset sale.: May 25. https://web.archive.org/web/20080506142308/http://www.collercapital.com/assets/html/pressrelease.html ?ID=2

The White House (2023). FACT SHEET: Biden-Harris Administration Announces 31 Regional Tech Hubs to Spur American Innovation, Strengthen Manufacturing, and Create Good-Paying Jobs in Every Region of the Country. Oct 23, 2023. https://www.whitehouse.gov/briefing-room/statements-releases/2023/10/23/fact-sheet-biden-harris-administration-announces-31-regional-tech-hubs-to-spur-american-innovation-strengthen-manufacturing-and-create-good-paying-jobs-in-every-region-of-the-country/

Thiel, P., and Masters, B. (2014). *Zero to One: Notes on Startups, or How to Build the Future*. Crown Business.

Thinking Ahead Institute. (2022). Global top 300 pension funds. https://www.thinkingaheadinstitute.org/content/uploads/2022/09/PI-300-2022.pdf

Thorndike Jr., W.N. (2012). *The Outsiders*. Harvard Business Review Press.

Thorne, J. (2022). China's tech crackdown did little to deter foreign VCs. PitchBook.

Thrasyvoulou, X. (2014). Understanding the innovator's dilemma. December. https://www.wired.com/insights/2014/12/understanding-the-innovators-dilemma/

TIME. (1956). Corporations: Retreat. (June 25). https://content.time.com/time/subscriber/article/0,33009/824463,00.html

TIME. (1967). Corporations, double the profits, double the pride. (September 8), pp. 86–87.

TIME. (1979). The oil squeeze. (February 5).

TIME. (1985). The takeover game – T. Boone Pickens (cover). (March 4).

Tirole, J. (2011). Illiquidity and all its friends. *Journal of Economic Literature*, 49(2): 287–325.

Tomayko, J.E. (1988). Computers in spaceflight: The NASA experience. NASA. https://history.nasa.gov/computers/Ch2-5.html

TPG. (2022). Rise. https://therisefund.com

Traxcn. (2023). Acquisitions by Delivery Hero. https://tracxn.com/d/acquisitions/acquisitionsbyDelivery-Hero

Trehan, R. (2006). The history of leveraged buyout. *4Hoteliers*, December 4.

Tricostar. (2023). Software and technology since the 1980s. https://www.tricostar.com/tricostar-news/news-feed/industry-news/software-technology-market-since-1980s

Troutman Pepper. (2022). The co-investment landscape review. Troutman Pepper.

Tuovila, A. (2020). Loss carry-forward: definition, example, and tax rules. Investopedia. https://www.investopedia.com/terms/l/ losscarryforward .asp

Tykvová, T. (2018). Venture capital and private equity financing: An overview of recent literature and an agenda for future research. *Journal of Business Economics*, 88: 325–362.

Tykvová, T., and Borell, M. (2012). Do private equity owners increase risk of financial distress and bankruptcy? *Journal of Corporate Finance*, 18(1): 138–150.

Tykvová, T., and Kolb, J. (2016). Going public via special purpose acquisition companies: Frogs do not turn into princes. *Journal of Corporate Finance*, 40: 80–96.

Ubeda, F., et al. (2019). Do firms located in science and technology parks enhance innovation performance? *The Journal of Technology Transfer*, 44: 21–48.

Ulrich, H. (1968). *Die Unternehmung als produktives soziales System: Grundlagen der allgemeinen Unternehmungslehre.* Haupt.

Ulrich, H., and Krieg, W. (1972). *Das St. Galler Managementmodell.* Haupt.

United States. (1906). Hepburn Act, 59th Congress, Sess. 1, ch. 3591, 34 Stat. 584, enacted 1906-06-29.

Unquote (2005). Deal Analysis Tool – Private equity database. quoted in: Private Equity – A UK Success Story. BVCA. https://www.bvca .co.uk/Portals/0/library/Files/News/2006/2006_0007_.._PE_successuk .pdf?ver=2013-06-14-154053-837

U.S. Census Bureau. (2017). Computer and internet use in the United States: 2016. https://www.census.gov/library/publications/2017/acs/ acs-37.htmlUSCongress.

US Department of Labor. (1999). Issues in Labor Statistics. www.dol.gov

US Department of Transportation's Bureau of Transportation Statistics (BTS). (various years). Historical mileage statistics: US railroads. https:// www.bts.gov/content/historical-mileage-statistics-us-railroads

US Energy Information Administration. (2010). Annual Energy Outlook 2011. EIA.

Usselmann, S.W. (2013). Research and development in the USA: An interpretive history. Yale University. Economic History workshop. November.

Vandevelde, M. (2021). Michael Rees: How a private equity chief turned the tables on his peers. *Financial Times* (July 22).

Van Schie, P. (2021). Global CLO market hits $1 trillion milestone. Neuberger Berman. https://www.nb.com/en/global/insights/nb-blog-global-clo-market-hits-$1-trillion-milestone

Verdun, P., and Chang, J. (2018). A primer for today's secondary private equity market. June. https://caia.org/sites/default/files/a_primer_for_ todays_secondary_pe_market.pdf

Victor, J. (2023). Google invests $300M in OpenAI rival Anthropic. https://www.theinformation.com/briefings/google-invests-300m-in-openai-rival-anthro-pic?utm_source=googleandutm_medium=cpcandutm_campaign=19751942151_andutm_content=andutm_term=andgclid=EAIaIQobChMI6uW7n7bD_gIV_SazAB1RUAJMEAAYASAAEgLq4PD_BwE

Villamarin, J.P. (2022). Semi-liquid funds: The new good looking beast in town. *Investment Strategy*. Retrieved from: https://investmentstrategyin.com/semi-liquid-funds-the-new-good-looking-beast-in-town/

Vise, D. (1986). Forstmann Little: Small firm specializes in major deals. *Los Angeles Times* (May 5).

Vise, D., and Coll, S. (1989). Drexel settles massive civil fraud charges. *The Washington Post* (April 14).

VisualizingEconomics. (2023). Long-term real growth in US GDP per capita 187–-2009. https://www.visualizingeconomics.com/blog/2011/03/08/long-term-real-growth-in-us-gdp-per-capita-1871-2009.

Vo, L. (2013). All the wealth we lost and regained since the recession started. NPR.

Wadhawa, V. (2009). The valley of my dreams: Why Silicon Valley left Boston's Route 128 in the dust. October 31. https://techcrunch.com/2009/10/31/the-valley-of-my-dreams-why-silicon-valley-left-bostons-route-128-in-the-dust/

Wagner, K. (2014). Facebook Paid $19 billion for WhatsApp, which lost $138 million last year. *Vox*. October 28. https://www.vox.com/2014/10/28/11632404/facebook-paid-19-billion-for-whatsapp-which-lost-138-million-last-year

Wall Street Journal. (2006). Apollo Nears deal to control Realogy. December 18. https://www.wsj.com/articles/SB116640629830653052

Wall Street Journal. (1976). A.J. Industries says investors group bids $25.6 million for firm, ProQuest Historical Newspapers. September 2, p. 17.

Wall Street Journal. (2022a). China notifies firms of tougher investment rules for big tech. January 19.

Wall Street Journal. (2022b). The ESG investing backlash arrives. August 15. https://www.wsj.com/articles/the-esg-backlash-arrives-blackrock-mark-brnovich-strive-asset-management-attorneys-general-11660600459WURK (2020, accessed).

Walton, G.M., and Rockoff, H. (2017). *History of the American Economy*. Cengage.

Wang, I., Cheng, T., Srivastava, V., and Yi, C. (2023). Approaches to benchmarking listed infrastructure. S&P Dow Jones Indices Research. https://www.spglobal.com/spdji/en/documents/research/research-approaches-to-benchmarking-listed-infrastructure.pdf

Ward, C., Brill, F., and Raco, M. (2022). State capitalism, capitalist statism: Sovereign wealth funds and the geopolitics of London's real estate market. *Environment and Planning A: Economy and Space.* 55(3). DOI:10.1177/0308518X221102157.

Warren, E. (2021). Warren, Baldwin, Brown, Pocan, Jayapal, colleagues reintroduce bold legislation to fundamentally reform the private equity industry. https://www.warren.senate.gov/newsroom/press-releases/warren-baldwin-brown-pocan-jayapal-colleagues-reintroduce-bold-legislation-to-fundamentally-reform-the-private-equity-industry

Washington Mutual. (2008). WaMu to strengthen capital position, raising $7 billion anchored by a TPG capital investment. April 9. https://www.sec.gov/Archives/edgar/data/933136/000095013408006239/v39678aexv99w1.htm

Waters, R. (2020). Big Tech's 'buy and kill' tactics come under scrutiny. *Financial Times* (February 20).

Waters, R., and Hook, L. (2016). Unicorns: between myth and reality. *Financial Times* (June 27).

Watts, S. (2005). *The People's Tycoon: Henry Ford and the American Century.* Knopf Doubleday Publishing Group.

WDR. (2021). 18. November 1996—Start der Telekom-Aktie an der Börse. November 10. https://www1.wdr.de/radio/wdr5/sendungen/zeitzeichen/zeitzeichen-telekom-aktie-boersenstart-100.html

Webb, T. (2011). Spain's financial crisis claims another victim: The solar power industry. *The Guardian.* (March 30). https://www.theguardian.com/world/2011/mar/30/new-europe-spain-solar-power.

Weiner, P., and Hunter-Reay, D. (2021). Tips for liability prevention for SPACs. Baker McKenzie.

Weinman, E. (1974). Venture capital for small businesses. *University of Baltimore Law Review,* 3(2): Article 2.

Weiser, M. (1991). The computer for the 21st century. *Scientific American* (September 1).

Westinghouse. (2023). History of George Westinghouse: Innovation changing the world. https://www.westinghousenuclear.com/about/history

Wetzel, W. (1987). The informal venture capital market, *Journal of Business Venturing,* 2: 299–314.

Wharton. (2008). Victimizing the borrowers: Predatory lending's role in the subprime mortgage crisis: Knowledge@Wharton, February 20. https://knowledge.wharton.upenn.edu/article/victimizing-the-borrowers-predatory-lendings-role-in-the-subprime-mortgage-crisis/

Wharton. (2009). The rise of the Renminbi fund: China's local private equity market gets a new boost. Knowledge@Wharton. October 28. https://knowledge.wharton.upenn.edu/article/the-rise-of-the-renminbi-fund-chinas-local-private-equity-market-gets-a-new-boost/

Whipps, H. (2008). How sugar changed the world, June 2. https://www .livescience.com/4949-sugar-changed-world.html

White, L.J. (2010). The credit rating agencies. *Journal of Economic Perspectives*, 24(2). 211–226.

White, R. (2011). *Railroaded: The Transcontinentals and the Making of Modern America*. W. W. Norton.

White & Case. (2023). US de-SPAC and SPAC data and statistics roundup. https://www.whitecase.com/sites/default/files/2023-02/us-spac-de-spac-data-statistics-round-up-v2.pdf

Wiggers, K. (2023a). VCs continue to pour dollars into generative AI. TechCrunch. https://techcrunch.com/2023/03/28/generative-ai-venture-capital/

Wiggers, K. (2023b). These Y combinator-backed startups are trying to build 'ChatGPT for X'. TechCrunch. : https://techcrunch.com/2023/04/04/these-y-combinator-startups-are-trying-to-build-chatgpt-for-x/

Wiggins, K. (2022). Inside private equity's race to go public. *Financial Times* (January 10).

Wiggins, K., and Gara, A. (2022). Inside private equity's race to go public. *Financial Times* (January 14).

Wigglesworth, A., and Kasumov, A. (2021). David Swensen, the Yale pioneer who reshaped investing. *Financial Times* (May 7).

Wikipedia. (2022a). Société des autoroutes du Nord et de l'Est de la France. https://fr.wikipedia.org/wiki/Société_des_autoroutes_du_Nord_ et_de_l_Est _de_la_France

Wikipedia. (2022b). Just Eat Takeaway. https://en.wikipedia.org/wiki/ Just_Eat_Takeaway.com

Wikipedia. (2022c). US Securities and Exchange Commission, : https:// en.wikipedia.org/wiki/US_Securities_and_Exchange_Commission

Wilhelm, A. (2012). Kauffman Foundation: The venture capital model is "broken". thenextweb.com: https://thenextweb.com/news/kauffman-foundation-the-venture-capital-model-is-broken.

Wilhelm, A. (2017). A look back in IPO: Facebook's trailing profit and mobile intrigue. TechCrunch. August 22. https://techcrunch.com/ 2017/08/22/a-look-back-in-ipo-facebooks-trailing-profit-and-mobile-intrigue/

Wilhelmus, J., and Lee, W. (2019). Private equity IPOs generating faster job growth and more investment. Milken Institute.

Williams, K., Brakat, N., and Braffman, P. (2011). Commercial real estate: Has the tide turned? Credit Suisse.

Williams, M. (2010). *Uncontrolled Risk*. McGraw-Hill Education.

Wilson, K. (2015). Policy lessons from financing innovative firms. OECD Science, Technology and Industry Policy Papers No. 24.

Winkler, J.K. (2017). *Five and Ten: The Fabulous Life of F. W. Woolworth*. Pickle Partners.

Whipps, H. (2008). How sugar changed the world, June 2. https://www
.livescience.com/4949-sugar-changed-world.html

Wiseman, M. (2013) Rethinking infrastructure: An investor's view. (R. Kirk-
land, Interviewer). McKinsey and Company. March 13. https://www
.mckinsey.com › mark-wiseman

Wolfe, T. (1983). The tinkerings of Robert Noyce. *Esquire Magazine.*
December. https://web.stanford.edu/class/e145/2007_fall/materials/
noyce.html

Wolmar, C.T. (2008). *Fire and Steam: A New History of the Railways in
Britain.* Atlantic Books.

Woodmann, A. (2022). Private funds might have to give up a bigger share
of their profits. PitchBook.

World Bank. (2017). The evolution of the Canadian Pension Model. International Bank for Reconstruction and Development / The World Bank.

Wright, G. (2004). NTL to sell masts in £1.3bn deal. The Guardian
(December 2). https://www.theguardian.com/business/2004/dec/02/
citynews.money

WURK. (2022). How does DoorDash make money? DoorDash funding history. https://www.wurk.cc/side-hustle/how-does-doordash-make-money

Wysocki, B. (1999). Companies chose to rethink a quaint concept: Profits.
The Wall Street Journal (May 19).

Yale Investment Office. (2022). Investment Managers. https://investments
.yale.edu/investment-managers

Yang, Y. (2018). China surpasses North America in attracting venture capital funding for first time as investors chase 1.4 billion consumers. *South
China Morning Post* (July 5). www.scmp.com/tech/article/2153798/
china-surpasses-north-america-attracting-venture-capital-funding-
first-time

Yeh, N. (2018). Case study: Blackstone's Buyout of Equity Office Properties (EOP). Wharton.

Yergin, D. (2022). Preemptive under-investment in oil/gas likely to
lead to recurrent economic crises in coming years. https://www
.drillingcontractor.org/ preemptive-under-investment-in-oil-gas-likely-
to-lead-to-recurrent-economic-crises-in-coming-years-62126

Zachary, G.P. (1997). *Endless Frontier: Vannevar Bush, Engineer of the
American Century.* The Free Press.Zacks Equity Research. (2014a). Marsh's
Mercer to add SCM, Brace Alternative Investments. November 24. https://
finance.Yahoo!.com/news/marshs-mercer-add-scm-brace-190002705.html

Zacks Equity Research. (2014b). Fortress to fully offload its stake in Gafah.
https://sg.news.Yahoo!.com/fortress-fully-offload-stake-gagfah-
214507286.html

Zak, P. (2013). Measurement myopia. https://www.drucker.institute/thedx/
measurement-myopia/

Zaman, R. (2022). Christensen's disruptive innovation and technology. *The Waves*. https://www.the-waves.org/2020/07/21/christensens-disruptive-innovation-and-technology/

Zeng., Y. (2018). Foreign developers regain shine as mainland developers seek out expertise in commercial property management. *China Morning Post* (January 31).

Zhang, J. (2007). The advantage of experienced start-up founders in venture capital acquisition: Evidence from serial entrepreneurs, IZA discussion paper No. 2964, SSRN: https://ssrn.com/abstract=1010607

Zhang, X., Zheng, H., and Wang, Y. (2019). The valuation gap between Chinese and US tech companies is shrinking. *Harvard Business Review*. March 2019. https://hbr.org/2019/03/the-valuation-gap-between-chinese-and-u-s-tech-companies-is-shrinking

Zeng., Y. (2018). Foreign developers regain shine as mainland developers seek out expertise in commercial property management. *China Morning Post*, January 31.

Zheng, J., and Zhou, W. (2022). Chinese corporate venture capital: A golden decade and a looming fall. https://technode.com/2022/02/15/chinese-corporate-venturecapital a golden decade and a looming-fall/

Zider, B. (1998). How venture capital works. *Harvard Business Review*, November–December.

Zippia. (2022a). The Carlyle Group history.. https://www.zippia.com/the-carlyle-group-careers-57355/history/

Zippia. (2022b). KKR and CO. L.P. history, https://www.zippia.com/kkr-co-careers-59845/history/

Zippia. (2022c). Blackstone history. https://www.zippia. com/blackstone-group-careers-344156/history/

Acknowledgments

What major forces are responsible for the increasing significance of private market investments within institutional portfolios? How has the funding landscape for entrepreneurial ventures transformed over time, and what are the underlying reasons for these changes? The story of private markets investing class has typically been told through the eyes of founders and deal-makers. Undoubtedly, it is important to recognize the leaders behind organizations managing trillions in investor capital due to their investment expertise. While examining the success stories of individual deal-makers is valuable, it's insufficient to comprehend the factors that have shaped private markets as an asset class. Comprehensive research is necessary to delve into the broader economic forces, capital market dynamics, and technological advances that have played a pivotal role in shaping the industry. By drawing on research from economic historians, economists, and scholars of entrepreneurship, the book takes readers on a journey to examine the economic currents as well as capital markets and the technological developments that led to the rise of this asset class and its specific investment models.

N. Colin's "A brief history of the world of venture capital" sparked my desire to create a reader for my students, and as I delved deeper into the subject, I realized there was no single comprehensive historical narrative on the evolution of financing entrepreneurial ventures and the lessons learned by investors over time. This realization led me to write this book.

More than 50 years have passed since the emergence of modern buyouts and venture capital. I felt that now was the ideal time to explore the private markets industry's challenges and opportunities. As someone with over 25 years of experience in this industry, I have gained invaluable personal experience, oral history, and contacts that have prepared me for this task.

By examining key success factors for investors and entrepreneurs, the challenges and opportunities of investing in private markets, and the role of private markets in shaping the global economy's future, this book aims to fill the gap in the literature as the first comprehensive historical narrative of the private markets industry. Throughout the writing process, Dr. Bernd-Michael Rumpf provided me with invaluable guidance. As a tech entrepreneur and senior executive in large technology firms, his experience and insights were instrumental in shaping this book. Writing a book can be a lonely process, and I am deeply grateful for Bernd's time, critical reviews, directional input, and encouragement. When you're an author, it's easy to get lost in too many stories or too much information and forget the main point. Bernd's question, "Why should people read this?" helped me stay on track while working on this big project, hopefully keeping everything together.

Throughout the writing process, I received valuable insights, suggestions or fact-checking support from numerous individuals and organizations, many of whom I cannot thank enough. I would like to express my gratitude to Jennifer Berman and Alison Mass from Goldman Sachs, Jonathan Gray, Thomas Clements and Laurie Carlson from Blackstone, and Marcel Erni and Alec Zimmermann from Partners Group, who generously provided their time to discuss the industry and their firms. Thomas Foussé from the Carlyle Group, Tai Lim Hok from GIC, Manish Kothari, who launched the Chicago Booth "Distinguished Speaker Series" that provided an opportunity to gain close-up insights from Reid Hofmann, Greylock Partners, Brooks Zug from HarbourVest Partners, Walter Kortschak from Summit Partners, Jung Son from Sequoia Capital, Shant Mardirossian from Kohlberg & Company, Arthur Rock, Ruediger Stucke from Warburg Pincus, Emilio Voli and Luke Charalambous from Apax Partners, Lukas Burkhard from Mercer Private Markets and Blair Jacobson from Ares, also provided insights, support, and encouragement throughout the writing process.

I am indebted to Nicolas Colin for The Family Papers (Colin, 2016). His essay, "A Brief History of the World of Venture Capital" inspired me to look beyond the more recent developments and look at the history of financing entrepreneurial ventures. While I did not always follow his path, his narrative provided the structure and many insights I used to tell this fascinating story.

Special thanks go to Thorsten Hens from the University of Zurich, who introduced me to my publisher, Wiley & Sons. Gemma Valler, Stacey Rivera and Sunnye Collins helped me to navigate the daunting publishing process and they played a crucial role in the final outcome of this project. Susan Dunsmore and Rene Caroline have been excellent editors and their commitment and support were crucial to get the book over the finishing line.

This book owes a great deal to the invaluable contributions made by numerous academic and business writers, accomplished individuals, and data providers. While teaching at the Booth Graduate School of Business, I had the opportunity to engage with research conducted by a distinguished faculty, notably led by Steven N. Kaplan. His extensive body of research spans a wide range of topics that have significantly influenced the discourse on private assets, unraveling their complexities. I am grateful for the research of scholars such as Gregory Brown from UNC Kenan-Flagler, Kenneth G. Davis from St. John's College, Oxford, Howard French from Columbia University, William Janeway from the Institute for New Economic Thinking, Ron Harris from Tel Aviv University, Josh Lerner and Paul Gompers from Harvard University, Sebastian Mallaby, Anne Murphy from the University of Hertfordshire, Max Rumpf from ETH Zürich and Carnegie Mellon University, and Theresa Tykvova from the University of St. Gallen. I also want to acknowledge the valuable contributions of my students in my "Private Markets from an Investor's Perspective" classes. They provided insightful comments and diligently spotted errors and inconsistencies in the manuscript. Their passion, coupled with the supportive environment at the University of Chicago Booth Graduate School of Business, greatly assisted me in completing this work. I am grateful to them for their enduring impact.

The archives of Mercedes Benz in Stuttgart and Amanda Packel at the Rock Center for Corporate Governance at Stanford University, Massimo Petrozzi at the Computer History Museum in Mountain View, CA, as well as helpful staff at Crunchbase in San Francisco, Real Deals in London, PERE in London, PitchBook Data in Seattle, Burgiss Hoboken NJ, and *The New York Times* Archive in New York provided valuable data and information. I would also like to thank Kwame Ababio from Preqin for his support in providing extensive data for this book and helping me to access the impressive resources that Preqin has built in the private markets domain.

Finally, I express my profound gratitude for the unwavering support and motivation offered by my partner, Brunno Cesar Messias. His presence and encouragement have been instrumental in making this book a reality. Additionally, I extend my heartfelt appreciation for the lifelong guidance and mentorship provided by Professor Dr. Frank Jehle, whose influence and support have shaped my journey over many decades. Although Frank Jehle will not have the opportunity to witness the book in its completed form, it is dedicated to his memory.

About the Author

Stefan's career in finance began in the late 1980s, when he worked for some of the industry's most prominent names, including Salomon Brothers, Meeschaert Rousselle, and Morgan Stanley. Later, he founded SCM Strategic Capital Management, a global private markets investment firm that managed multibillion-dollar investment programs on behalf of institutional investors. After Marsh McLennan acquired SCM in 2015, Stefan went on to lead Mercer's private markets division as a global business leader for several years.

Throughout his career, Stefan has continued to build an impressive investment track record, serving on the boards and investment committees of several leading financial institutions and pension funds. His background working for prominent financial institutions and founding his own private markets investment firm has provided him with a wealth of practical knowledge and insights into the industry. Additionally, he serves on the faculty at the Chicago Booth Graduate School of Business, where he teaches courses on institutional private capital investments. Notably, his classes are the first at a major US business school that offer a comprehensive exploration of the entire spectrum of private markets investments.

Stefan's educational background includes an MBA from the University of Chicago Booth School of Business, a PhD in Economics from the University of St. Gallen, and an MSc from the University of Birmingham. In addition, he has previously published two books and numerous articles in business journals and financial publications.

Index

Note: Page numbers with "f" and "t" refer to figures and tables, respectively.

10-year Treasury rate, 371f
1973 oil crisis, 130
3Com, 162
3i Group, 211
54 Madison Partners, 257
80/20 split of gain (carried interest),
    141, 351–352
401K plans, investment ability, 433, 445
1977 Trinity, 126f

A

Aberdeen Proving Grounds, 85
Absolute returns, 583
Abraaj (growth capital firm), 577
Abu Dhabi Investment Authority, 279,
    305, 386, 449
Accelerated cost recovery system
    (ACRS), 169, 190
Accel Partners (venture capital
    firm), 109b, 160, 162, 163,
    465, 502, 505b
Accounting rules/audits, 30–31
Active venture capital firms, number
    (increase), 227
Adams, Rick, 163
Adams Street Partners (FoFs
    manager), 205, 350
Add-on acquisitions, 523–524, 523f
Advanced Research Projects Agency
    (ARPA), 81

Advanced Project Agency for Health
    (ARPA-H), 83
Advanced Research and Invention
    Agency (ARIA), UK, 83
Advantage Partners (private equity
    firm), 302
Adveq (FoFs manager), 208, 445
Advent International (buyout firm),
    founding, 184, 206f, 207
Advisors, role, 196–197
AEG, 41
Aegos
AEW Partners, opportunistic fund, 191
Aetos, 258
Affinity Equity Partners (buyout firm),
    304
Africa Company, 22
African trade, 15
AIG, 360b–361b, 360f, 454
Airbnb, 293
Alberta Investment Management
    Corporation (AIMCo), 339
Albourne, 196
Alfa Capital (private equity firm), 322
Alibaba, 241, 241f, 392, 394, 403, 410b,
    487, 494, 498, 500, 502, 512,
Alleghany Corporation, control, 58
Allen, Paul, 67
Allianz Insurance, 366
Alphabet, 3, 240, 392, 395, 486, 487

AlpInvest, 389, 444

Altair (PC), 86

AltaVista, 211

Altius Associates, 196, 443

Amazon, 3, 240–243, 287, 392, 395,
    396, 397, 400, 415, 468, 473,
    486, 491, 494

Amelco Corporation, 100

American Bell Company, 40

Alternative Investment Management
    Program, 196

Amazon (telecom bust survivor)

Amelco Teledyne Corporation,
    creation, 100

American Campus Communities,
    Blackstone acquisition, 568

American Research & Development
    Corporation (ARD), 68–75, 146,
    210, 212, 213, 464
  creation/establishment, 75, 127
  experience, 120
  long-term capital, need, 114

American waterfall, 154b

Andonov, R., 585

Andreessen, Marc, 86, 216f

Angel investing/investors,
    290–294, 480

Anglo-Saxon capitalism, 35

Anti-competitive behavior, 500

Anti-monopoly legislation,
    implementation/
    enforcement, 63

Anti-monopoly movement, 36

Antin Infrastructure Partners, 460, 461

AOL, 215, 233

Apax Partners, 74, 109b, 113, 189,
    389, 672

Apollo Management, 180

Apollo guidance computer, 83, 84f

Apple, 113, 126f, 240

Applied Materials, 108b

Arcis, 209

Ardian, 208, 366, 455, 589

Ares (private markets firm), 389, 431,
    460, 461, 462, 546, 672

Arkwright, Richard, 27–28

Arnault, Bernard, 68

Artificial intelligence (AI), 486–492,
    501, 503, 604

Asia Alternatives (FoFs manager), 304

Asia, investment opportunities, 494

Asian Financial Crisis, 303

Asset classes, 372, 375–382, 595t, 596f
  boundaries, blurring, 581
  private debt, 543–545

Assets
  allocation, 146, 163, 385
  capital costs, 583
  life/replacement cost, 583

Asset-stripping, 168

Assets under management (AUM),
    1–2, 2f, 159, 376f, 546, 573
  dry powder, 145
  impact, 374–377, 382
  private market AUMs, 343f, 377f

Audits, 30–31

Australian Future Fund, 263, 405

Autoroute Paris-Rhone, 333f

Australia, asset privatizations, 327, 328

Autoroute du Sud (toll road), 334f

Aviation industry, growth, 60

Axa Private Equity, 208

B

Baidu (venture capital firm), 241, 487,
    494, 495, 498

Bain Capital (buyout firm), 184, 524

Bank of England, 24

Banks, feeder funds (purpose), 446f

Barbarians at the Gate (Burrough), 178

Baring Asia (buyout/growth capital
    firm), 302

Baring Vostok (buyout growth capital
    firm), 302

Bardeen, John, 41f, 87

Basel II/III, 364

BASIC interpreter, 125

Bass, Robert, 252

Battery Ventures, 160, 406

BC Partners (buyout firm),
    founding, 185

Bear Stearns, 138, 175

Beatrice Foods, LBO, 175, 177–178

Bechtolsheim, Andy, 480

Bell, Alexander Graham, 40, 52

Bell Telephone Company, establishment, 52

Benchmark Ventures, 221, 401, 483, 485

Bentley, Thomas, 27

Benz, Carl, 43

Benz & Co. Rheinische Gasmotoren-Fabrik, 42f

Berkshire Hathaway, 137

Bezos, Jeff, 67

Bharti Airtel, 303

Big Bang (UK), 253, 380

Billion-dollar companies (creation), mergers/acquisitions (impact), 51–53

Bismarck, Otto v., 38

Biodata, founding, 217

Black Monday (1929), 60

Black Monday (1987), 165

BlackRock, 314, 316b, 444, 600

Blackstone, 185, 383, 462t, 524, 571b–572b
  investments, acquisitions, 257, 298–300, 312–314, 515
  IPO, 281–282

Blackstone Real Estate Partners, funds (raising), 257

Black swan event, 372

Blank-check vehicles, funds, 425

Blank, Julius, 88, 89f

Blitzscaling (1990s), 218–220

Boeing, 60

Boesky, Ivan, 169, 174

Bonderman, David, 252

Boom-and-bust cycles, pattern, 37

Boston Consulting Group, 74, 102, 191, 206, 206f, 494

Boston, Route 128 ("America's Technology Highway"), 102–103

Bötsch, Wolfgang, 224f

Boulton, Matthew (Watt partnership), 27

Bower, Christopher, 196

Brattain, Walter H., 41f, 87

Braudel, Fernand, 17–18

Break-out deals, 271, 350, 352

Brem, Monte, 196

Brenninkmeijer family office, 68

Bridgepoint (buyout firm), 253, 269, 337, 460, 524,

Britain's Canal Mania, 26

British Airways, 340b

British East India Company, 19–20

British Land Company/Blackstone joint venture, 571b–573b

British Railway Mania, 37

Broadgate, 570, 571b–572b, 571f

Brooke, Peter, 74, 206f, 207

Brookfield Asset Management (real assets manager), 461

Brown, Greg, 269

Brownfield infrastructure, 332

Brun, Leslie, 196

Bubble Act of 1719, 32

Buffett, Warren, 137, 169

Bulk discount, obtaining, 318

Burger King, 297

Burgiss, 182, 197, 226, 266, 272, 323, 440, 451, 512, 526, 568, 582, 585

Bush, Vannevar, 79–80, 80f

Business
  digital space business models, characteristics, 399–400
  opportunities, ESG adoption (impact), 530–532
  plans, ITT system, 134
  risk, 116
  separation, 311

Business Development Companies, 146

Buttonwood Agreement, 29

Buy-and-build, 522–526

Buyer, cash flow profile, 272f

Buyouts, 296–305, 565–570
  capital structure, example (HCA 2006), 541t
  co-investments, relative performance, 452f
  deals, 273–274, 522t

Buyouts (*continued*)
  early buyout firms, establishment,
    137–142
  European LBOs
  firms, impact, 140, 183–185, 249, 302
  funds, 352f, 520t
  global buyout co-investment
    volume, 450f
  globalization, 301–307
  leveraged buyout (LBO) model,
    137–142
  mega buyouts (2003–2007), 297–299
  occurrence (1970s), 130–137
  performance, 254–255, 272–274
  post-GFC boom, 517–532
  size/ranking of managers,
    177–178, 298t
  value creation/performance,
    522–526
Byers, Brook, 113
Byte Shop, 125
ByteDance, 410, 413

C
CalPERS, 196, 269, 279, 317, 387,
    528, 562
Campbell Lutyens, 198
Campeau, Robert, 168
Canada, pension funds, 328, 335b
Canada Pension Plan Investment
    Board (CPPIB), 335, 576
Canadian Model, 328, 385
Candover (buyout firm), 140
Capital, 140, 381
  deployment, 430, 565
  efficiency, 414
  structure, 539–543, 541t
Capital at work (limited partnership
    feature), 151b
Capital Dynamics (FoFs
    manager), 208, 442
CapVis (buyout firm), 302
Carlucci, Frank, 300
Carlyle Group, The, 183, 383, 389, 461
Carnegie, Andrew, 51
Carried interest, 154b, 247

Case, Steve, 233f
Cash flows, 181, 329, 583
  condominium development project,
    timeline/cash flow pattern, 567f
  limited partnership feature, 149
  net cash flows (PE global
    pattern), 518f
  portfolio cash flows, FoFs
    (comparison), 440f
  profile, 144f, 152f
Cash reserves, increase, 372
Catch-up, 154b, 306–307
Category kings, 401
Caufield, Frank J., 113
Cayman Islands holding structure,
    447, 495
C-corporation, 339
Cecil, Lord Charles, 198
Celler-Kefauver Act (1950), 131
Central processing unit (CPU),
    91b, 99, 126
Cerberus (asset manager), 318, 320
Chan Zuckerberg Initiative, 67
Chandler, Jr., Alfred D., 166
Chan Zuckerberg Initiative, 67
Charles River Ventures (CRV), 74
ChatGPT (OpenAI), impact,
    486–487
Chartered trade companies, 17
Chicago Booth School of
    Business, 495
Chicago Skyway, toll road, 333f–,
    334–335
China, 304, 492–504, 499f
  Belt and Road Initiative, 575–576
  startups, 241–242
  state-guided model, 4
  startup tech sector weight/
    value, 497f
China Investment Corporation, 263
China Mobile, IPO, 494
China Securities Regulatory
    Commission (CSRC), 493
Christensen, Clayton, 69, 96, 96b,
    97f, 218–219
ChrysCapital (buyout firm), 303

Chrysler, 59, 180, 370

Cintra Infraestructuras, 333

Cinven (buyout firm), 140

Citigroup, 303, 454

Clayton Act (1914), 54, 58, 131

Clayton, Dubilier & Rice (buyout firm), 140

Cleantech, 122, 327, 579, 581

Cliffwater Direct Lending Index (CDLI), 548, 549f

Closed-end funds, collapse, 65

CLO managers, 536

Cloud computing, integration, 604

Club deals, 299–300

Clusters, importance/creation, 104–105

Coatue Management (hedge fund), 404

Coca-Cola

Cohen, Sir Ronald, 113

Co-investments, 448–450, 450f, 451b–452b, 452f
rights/strategies, 387, 436–437
role, growth, 441

Cold War, 80–84

Coles, John, 32

Collateralized debt obligations (CDOs), 536

Collateralized loan obligations (CLOs), 308, 383, 536, 544

Coller Capital (Secondaries FoFs manager), 209, 267, 268, 269, 454, 455

Coller, Jeremy, 454

Colony Capital, 256

Columbus, Christopher, 11, 13

Commenda (medieval partnership), 14

Commercial mortgage-backed security (CMBS), 308f, 562

Commercial property valuations, 562

Committed capital (private market term), 146

Commodore PET 2001, 126f

Compagnie des Indes, Banque Générale (merger), 23–24

Compagnie d'Occident, founding, 23

Companies
acquisition, 133, 249–250
management, ITT system (usage), 134

Companies Act of 1862, 32

Companies Registration and Regulation Act of 1844, 32

Company of Merchant Adventurers of London, founding, 17

Company of the Indies, 23

Compaq, IPO, 160

Computer-aided design (CAD), adoption, 162

Computer History Museum, 92f, 214

Condominium development project, timeline/cash flow pattern, 567f

Conglomerates, boom (legacy), 131–137, 167

Consumer price inflation (CPI), fees adjustment, 330

Continental Airlines, buyout, 252

Continuation funds/investment vehicles, 388–391, 391f, 428, 455, 585, 589

Conway, Ron, 292

Core funds, usage, 310

Cornelius, Peter, 349

Corporate raiders, 165–169

Corporate takeovers, criticism, 172

Corporate R&D, 40

Corporations, mergers (problems), 134

Costner, Charles, 54

Coulter, James, 252

Covenants, role, 533, 551, 553b–554b, 555, 597

Creative destruction, 497

Crossover funds (cross-over funds), 404–405, 511

Cullman, Lewis, 137

Current War, 45

CVC (buyout firm), founding, 184

D

Dachis, Jeff, 221f

Da Gama, Vasco, 11, 13

Daimler, Gottlieb Wilhelm, 43

Data, asset value
Database providers, impact, 198
Data General, 103
Davis & Rock (venture capital firm), 75, 118
Davis, Thomas J., 112
Davis, Tommy, 75
DDR&D - Directorate of Defense Research & Development, 106b–107b
Deal-making, 161–164, 225, 277
Debt
  covenants, 185, 551
  instruments, types, 533–539
Decacorns, 410, 428
Defense Advanced Research Projects Agency (DARPA), 80–83, 106
Defoe, Daniel, 22
Delaware Uniform Limited Partnership Act (1973), 147
Delayed draw acquisition, 541
Delivery Hero, 478
Demand, inelasticity, 584
Deregulation, M&A 1980s boom, 169–175
Dermot, Desmond, 338
De-SPACs, 417f
de Tocqueville, Alexis, 30
Deutsche Bank, 268
Deutsche Edison-Gesellschaft für angewandte Elektricität, founding, 41
Deutsche Telekom, price drop, 236, 239
Digital Equipment Corporation (DEC), 70
Digital infrastructure, overinvestment, 235
Digital Revolution (Third Industrial Revolution), 103
Digital space business models, characteristics
Dimon, Jamie, 599
Dimson, Elroy
Dintersmith, Ted, 74
Direct deals, preference, 385

Direct investments, 448–453
Directorate of Defense Research & Development (DDR&D), 106b
Discounted cash flow (DCF) approach, 467
Disorderly expansion of capital (China), 499
Distressed commercial real estate loans, 543
Disruptive innovation, 97b–98b, 97f, 218
Disruptive technologies, 87–100, 105
Distributed value, 247
Distribution channels, access (FoF manager strategic option), 442
Distributions, 146, 153b
  in-kind, 247
Distribution to paid-in (DPI) (private market term), 146
Diversification, impact, 273, 354
Dodd-Frank Wall Street Reform and Consumer Protection Act, 363
Dodge, John/Horace, 43
Doerr, John
Doing Capitalism in the Innovation Economy (Janeway), 116
DoorDash, 477–481, 479f
Doriot, Georges, 68, 69f, 73–74, 213
Dotcom boom, 193, 214–221, 240–247, 290
Dotcom bust (1990s), 225, 236, 240, 241, 242, 245, 252, 280, 290, 362, 399, 467
Double-dip recession, 162
Double Impact Fund, 527
Double-promote (real estate), 305
Double-sided network effects, 395
Doughty Hanson (buyout firm), 183, 250, 255
Douglas Aircraft, 60
Dow Jones Brookfield Infrastructure Index, 321
Dow Jones Industrial Average (DJIA), 52
Draper and Johnson Investment Company, co-founding, 74

Draper, Bill, 73–74, 75f
Draper II, William, 75f
Draper, Tim, 75f
Drexel Burnham Lambert, impact,
    170, 170b–172b, 174–175,
    184–186, 253
Dry powder, 143, 146
Dutch East India Company (VOC),
    18, 18f
Dynamics, shifts (responses), 435

E

Early buyout firms, establishment,
    137–142
Early-stage funding, decrease, 163
Early stage investing, risk-reward
    profile, 483
Earnings before interest and taxes,
    depreciation and amortization
    (EBITDA), 335b, 478,
    535, 542, 560
East Texas Railroad, 37f
Economic growth (2006–2021), 371f
Economic liberalization policies, 78
Economic market indicators, 131t, 165t
Economic Recovery Tax Act of 1981
    (ERTA), 165, 169–170, 190
Economies of scale, 399
Edison General Electric Company,
    Thomson-Houston Electric
    Company (merger), 46, 52
Edison, Thomas Alva, 39–40, 45–46, 62
eFront, 197, 444, 496
Eichner, Bruce, 191
Eisenhower, Dwight D., 80, 83
Electrical utilities, establishment, 45
Electricity, impact, 44–45
Electronic design automation (EDA),
    usage, 162
Electronics Magazine (cover), 92f
Elfers, Bill, 74
Emerging markets, 321–322
Emerging technologies, basis, 128
Employee Retirement Income Security
    Act of 1974 (ERISA), 114, 139,
    160, 166, 170, 190

EnCap (infrastructure, natural
    resources firm), 344, 591
Energy Future Holdings (TXU),
    369b–370b, 528
Energy Information Administration
    (EIA) shale gas fields map, 345f
English Patent Boom (1692-1695), 245
Enron Corporation, scandal, 237
Enterprise financing, 67
Enterprises (First Industrial
    Revolution), funding, 25–28
Entrepreneurial ventures, financing
    system (problems), 61–63
Entrepreneurship, government
    role, 78–84
Entrepreneurs, success/rise, 121,
    391–409
Entry/exit rules, 432–433
Environmental Defense Fund, 528
Environmental, Social, and
    Governance (ESG), 3, 526–532,
    573, 586, 594
Equity Office Properties (EOPs),
    312–314, 314b–316b
Equity waterfalls, tiers, 154b
Erni, Marcel, 281f
Ethernet, 162
E-Trade, 403
Etsy, 244
Euromezzanine, 302
Euronext, 217
Europa Capital (private equity
    firm), 258
Europe, 189–190, 258
    investors, catalysts, 208
    private equity investment, deal
        value basis, 254f
    private equity programs, 196
    sovereign debt crisis, 261
    venture capital (VC), 229–233,
        243–245
European AIFMD
European Commission, 529, 586
European Green Deal, The, 577
European Investment Bank (EIB),
    VC perspective, 231

European Union, venture investment/funding
European sovereign debt crisis, 362, 454
European Stability Mechanism (ESM), 362
European Venture Capital Association, 232, 285
Europe-focused PE FoFs, 439f
Euroventures, 302
Evergreen investment vehicle
Exchange-traded funds (ETFs), examination, 464
Excite, 220, 403
Exit provisions, 590
Exploration and production (E&P) companies, 346, 591

F

Facebook, 3, 86, 240, 284, 287, 394
Facebook, Amazon, Apple, Netflix, and Google (FAANG), 392, 395–398, 396f, 466, 473
Factor risk models, usage, 385
Fairchildren, 100–102, 106, 129f
Fairchild Semiconductor, 88–89, 88f–89f, 90f, 121, 129f, 498
Fake tech, 416, 477
Fang, Andy, 482
Fannie Mae, 308, 317
FBI - warning on fraudulent mortgages
Federal Agency for Disruptive Innovation, Germany, 83
Federal Deposit Insurance Corporation (FDIC), impact, 543, 561
Federal Employees Retirement Act (1920), 65
Federal Government, R&D spending
Federal Open Market Committee (FOMC), interest rates (decrease), 261
Federal Reserve Board, 164, 262f, 322, 361
Federal Savings and Loan Insurance Corporation (FSLIC), abolishment, 256

Federal Securities Acts of 1933 and 1934, enactment, 31
Federal Trade Commission (FTC), creation, 55
Feeder funds, 446f, 448t
Fee (fees), impact, 337, 433, 448t, 451b–452b, 483, 590
Fee-offset, 249
Feri Trust, 68, 196
Ferri, Paul, 74
Fiber-optic networks, tangible asset (development), 222
Fidelity, 65, 405, 444
Financial distress, experience, 182
Financial dominance, geographic shift of capital, 57
Financial engineering, usage, 320
Financial industry, growth, 60
Financial Institutions Reform, Recovery, and Enforcement Act of 1989 (FIRREA), 256
Financial sector, GFC (impact), 365–366
Financing risk, 116
Fink, Larry, 283
FIRE Capital, 322
First Industrial Revolution, enterprise funding, 25–28
First Reserve Corporation (natural resources manager), founding, 184
Fisher Brothers, 191
Fisher, Irving, 57
Five-year treasury bond rates, 164f
Flanders, Ralph, 69
Fleming, Robert/Ian, 68
Food delivery, competitors, 480f
Ford, Henry, 42
Ford Foundation, 113
Ford Motor Company, 42–44, 47f, 58
Foreign Corrupt Practices Act, of 1977
Foreign VCs, pressure, 502
Forstmann, Little & Company, 140
Fortress Investment Group, 281
"Founder-Friendly" terms, 290–294
Founders Fund, 290, 293, 406

Founders, coaching ability, 482–483
Fountainvest Partners, 304
Fourth Industrial Revolution (digital revolution), 486
Free cash flow, strength, 330
French auction terms, comparison, 333f
French railway system
French Second Empire, 38
French toll roads, buyers assumptions/ winning bids, 334f
French, T. Bondurant, 205
Friedman, Tully, 75
FRT Resolution Trust Corporation, creation, 256
Fuller, Buckminster (knowledge doubling curve), 603f
Fundraising (private market funds), 159–161, 309, 519, 545–551, 546f
    activity, 285, 565t
    IPO boom impact, 225–226
    private real estate mega-firms, role, 565
Funds
    administrators, characteristics, 199t
    co-investment funds, raising, 450f
    continuation funds, 388–389
    distributions, allocation, 153f
    key man provision, 306
    life (limited partnership feature), 149b
    life, extensions, 306
    number, raising, 255f
    performance, comparison, 227
    pooled IRRs, 294f
    secondaries, 270
    small funds/large funds, median IRR, 557f
    software/service providers, characteristics, 199t
    structure, 432
    terms and conditions, 150b, 247–248, 306–307
    venture capital managers, examples, 353t

Funds of firms, 279, 280, 377
Funds of funds (FoFs), 196, 204–210, 265–266
    appeal, reduction (reasons), 438–440
    capital, raising, 210f, 265f, 437f
    FoF-type solutions, usage, 354
    intermediaries, landscape (change), 436–448
    managers, impact, 205t, 439–440
    median IRRs, 270f
    portfolio cash flows, comparison, 440f
    value for money, determination, 440b–441b
Future, underestimation of technological progress, 223b–224b

G

Gabor, Denis, 13
GAFAH
GAGFAH, 318, 319, 321
Gantner, Alfred, 281f
Gatekeepers, 194, 197t
Gates, Bill, 214, 214f
Gatwick (LGW), revenue per passenger (GBP), 340f
Gaw Capital (real estate firm), 321
GEHAG, 319
Geneen, Harold, 134
Genentech, 113, 119, 284, 287
General Atlantic, investment firm, 515
General Electric Company (GE), 52, 59
General Motors, 59
General-purpose technology, 78
Generally accepted accounting principles (GAAP), usage, 31
General Partners (GPs), 277, 456–458, 457f, 459f
    co-investments, 148
    law firms/placement agents, usage, 199t
    management control, 149
    operational control, 143
    performance fee, 154

General-purpose technologies, drivers, 105
Generative AI (GenAI), 486
GeoCities, 211, 403
Geographical allocation, 575
Geographical diversification, improvement, 320
German Capital (buyout firm), 442
German railroad construction, 29
German property, 318–321, 319f
German V2 missile launcher, 79f
Gerstner, Lou, 300
Gibson Greetings, acquisition, 171–172
GIC, 386
   Stuyvesant Town deal
Gilde, 302
Glass-Steagall Banking Act, 64
Global buyouts, 450f, 523f
Global Financial Crisis (GFC), 312, 348, 357–368, 367f, 532
   liquidity crisis, 203
   post-GFC boom, 517
   private market brand benefit, 383–384
   stock market recovery, 395–398
Global growth equity fundraising, 514f
Global IS deal value, sector share
Global Infrastructure Partners (infrastructure firm), 337, 347
Global LPE, market capitalization, 460f
Global private market, 376f
Global private real estate, 564f, 566f
Global savings, glut, 308
Gold Coast, trading, 15
Goldman, Henry, 54f
Goldman Sachs, 54f, 225, 234, 237b, 256, 303, 320, 347, 369b, 378, 383, 405, 425, 494, 528, 546
Gompers, Paul, 122, 159, 526
   1970s VC fundraising, 115
   exit behaviour of less established VCs
   grandstanding of VCs, 161
   management equity stakes in buyouts

market risk of PE
PE recruitment
spin-outs
stock price effects and carried interest
unicorn valuation
Goodwill value, 467
Google (Alphabet), telecom bust survivor, 240
Governance, impact/weakness, 277, 482
Government incentives, availability, 584
GP Investimentos, 305
GP-led secondaries, 390, 428, 456–458, 589
Graham, Paul, 290
Gramm-Leach-Bliley Act (1999), 380
Grand Central Depot (NYC), 37f
Gray, Jonathan, 315f
Great Depression, 60–66, 174
Great financial crisis, 7, 358–368
Great Northern railroad, financing, 50
Greenberg, Hank (dismissal), 360
Greenfield infrastructure/investment, 329–332
Greenmailing, 168
Greenspan, Alan, 245, 262f, 307
   put, 261, 370
Green technologies, focus (increase)
Gregory, Dan, 74
Grinich, Victor, 88, 88f
Griswold, Merrill, 68
Gross asset yields, 552f
Groupon War, 497
Grove, Andy, 101
Growth equity, 510f, 513, 514f
Growth financing, 294–296, 294f, 435, 508–515, 509f
Growth equity funds, 520t
Growth investments, investor ranking, 511f
"Growth over profits" mentality, 219
GS Capital Partners, founding, 185
Gulf Oil, 174, 175
Gurley, Ben

H

H&Q Asia Pacific, 185
Hall, Eldon C., 83, 84f
Hamilton Lane, establishment, 196
HarbourVest/Adams Street, FoF
    model, 207
HarbourVest Partners, co-founding,
    206–207
Hard-cap, 265
Harris, R., 1432, 181
    performance of PE, 456
    persistence in VC returns, 229
    persistence of PE returns
Harriman, Edward H., 51
Harrison, Leigh
Harvard Business School, 109
Harvard Endowment
Harvard Law School Forum on
    Corporate Governance, 526
Harvard Management Company,
    454
Hayden Stone, 111
Heaton, H., 26
Hellman & Friedman, founding, 184
Helix Associates, 198
Henry Hub natural gas spot price
    (2008–2016), 369
Herding, 161, 490
Hertz
Hewlett, Bill, 67
Hewlett-Packard, 85
Hicks & Haas (buyout firm),
    founding, 184
Hicks, Mary E., 16
Hicks Muse Tate & Furst (buyout
    firm), 184
High-impact patents, drivers, 105
High Voltage Engineering Company,
    ARD investment, 70
High yield bonds (high-yield bonds),
    172b–174b, 175, 537t, 549f, 549
Hines, 191, 322
HM Capital, 184
Hoefler, Don, 106
Hoerni, Jean, 88, 88f
Hoffman, Reid, 400f

Holding periods, 246, 590–591
Homebrew Computer Club
    (HCC), 125, 125f
Home internet access, trends,
    235f
Honor of Kings, 498
Hony Capital, 304, 496
Hoover Institution, 585
Horsley Bridge, 206, 350
Hostile takeovers, 51
H&Q Asia Pacific, founding, 185

I

IBM, 94–95, 94f
    knowledge doubling curve (Fuller),
        relationship, 603f
    Standard discrete diode-transistor
        logic, 89f
    System/360, 94, 95
    world market share
Icahn, Carl, 168
ICONIQ Capital, 67
Idea Cellular, 303
IDG Capital, 494, 502
Illiquidity premium,
    harvesting, 373–375
ILPA, best practice
    guidelines, 194, 529
Incentives
    alignment, 590
    requirements
Index Ventures, founding, 244
India
    funds, focus, 321
    venture capital (VC),
        505b–508b, 506f
Indiana Toll Road, 580f
Industrial Revolution, 26
Industry Funds Management
    (IFM), 588
Inflation
    during the 1920s, 43
    impact (1970s), 130
    increase (1970s/1980s), 164f
    protection, 330
Information Age, 78, 214, 222, 604

Information & communication
  technology (ITC), capital
  investments
Infrastructure (IS), 288, 325–337
  AuM level, 573–579
  continuation funds, 428
  deals (2006–2010), 337f
  entry, barriers, 330
  ESG, 3, 383, 526–532, 573, 574, 577,
    586, 594, 604
  funds/investments, 330, 336,
    586–588
  global IS deal value, sector
    share, 578f
  investors, IPE ranking, 575t
  listed IS, 247
  managers, total capital ranking, 576t
  natural resources, relationship,
    573–594
  overinvestment, 235
  renewable energy, 341, 594
  secondaries, 428
  sectors, 326f
  telecom, 163
  toll roads, 325, 327
Infrastructure technology
  (Infratech), 581
Initial public offering (IPO), 421–422,
  473t, 475f
  boom, 215, 225–228, 235–236
  Chinese IPOs, 508
  late-cycle IPO boom, 473–477
  valuation uplift (DoorDash), 478
  VC-backed IPOs (1995–2000), 242f
Innova Capital, 302
Innovation, impact, 39–49, 105–106
"Inorganic growth" methods, 401
Input/output (I/O) operations, 91b
Insight Partners (investment firm), 514
Instalment Sales Revision Act (1980)
Institutional environment, emergence
  of mutual funds, 64–66
Institutional investors, 4, , 137, 140
  co-investments, 328
  direct investments
  growing role since 1922

growing role since the 1950s
  high-yield bonds
  ranking PE
  leveraged loan holdings
  pre-IPO investments, 398
  use of consultants
Institutional Limited Partner
  Association (ILPA),
  initiation, 194
Institutional rounds, stakes
  (reduction), 482
Integrated circuits (ICs), 90b–91b, 99
Intel Corporation, 90f, 101
Interest rates, increase, 58
Intermediaries, 435
  changes, 441–445
  function, 193–200
  landscape, changes, 436–448
Internal rate of return (IRR), 143,
  151, 255f, 266
  concept, time-weighted/
    money-weighted return
  formula/calculation/generation,
    150t, 324
  limited partnership IRR, 152b
  private market terms, 145
  return on investment (ROI), com-
    parison, 144t
  US buyout funds, relationship, 181f
  US VC one-year rolling IRRs, 471f
  vintage years, 270, 324f
Internal resources, investment
  teams, 385
Internal Revenue Act (1921), 65
International Nickel, hostile
  takeover, 142
International Monetary Fund (IMF),
  358, 362, 373
International Sustainability
  Standards Board (ISSB), IASB
  establishment, 529
International Telephone and
  Telegraph Company (ITT),
  business mergers, 134
Internet, impact, 214–221, 225,
  234–236, 235f

Interstate Commerce Commission, 52, 55
Investment (investments)
  advisors, role, 196–197
  banking, 378
  cases, economic/regulatory frictions, 485
  companies (private equity firm type), 211
  funding rounds, 484
  gains, 141
  landscape, change, 427–431
  opportunities, ESG adoption (impact), 530–532
  paradigm, venture capital, 398–402
  periods, 150b, 306
  pooling, 354
  risk, management, 385
Investment Corporation of Dubai, 263
Investment trusts, 50
Investran, 197
Investors, 413–415
  bond yields problems, options, 372
  fund managers, interests (alignment), 354
  investment approach, 351–354
  ranking, 511f
Investors, engagement characteristics, 330
IPOs on the German stock marketing the 19th century, 43
Iranian revolution, 131
IREO Real Estate
Irrational expectations, 583–586
iShares Listed Private Equity, 463
Israel, Silicon Wadi, 106b–109b
ITT system, usage, 134

J
Japan, investment opportunities, 258–259
Japanese Financial Services Agency (SFA), 259
J-curve, 152
J.H. Whitney & Company, founding, 62
JD.com, 498, 502

Jenkinson, Tim, 226, 228, 229, 349, 440
Jensen, Michael C.
  LBOs and taxes
  managerial incentives and conglomerates
Jensen, Marbleton, 318
Jerusalem Global Ventures, 109
Job losses of PE owned firms
Jobs, Steve, 125f
Johnson, Franklin "Pitch," 72, 74
Johnson, Ross, 179
Joint-stock corporation, 18–28
J.P. Morgan & Co., consolidation of industries, 378
Jumpstart Our Business Startups Act (JOBS Act), 402

K
Kalanick, Travis, 484
Kanarick, Craig, 221f
Kane, Ed, 206
Kaplan, Steven, 162, 181, 226, 273–274, 348, 526
  buyout performance during the eighties, 130
  European VC performance
  fair valuation
  FoFs
  fund size effect on performance
  growth through acquisition
  holding periods of venture-backed companies, 348
  impact of junk bonds on buyout pricing
  KS PME ratio
  LBOs and taxes
  PE alpha
  PE beta
  performance of 1980s takeovers
  persistence of PE returns
  Polsky Center, 86
  private debt GP survey
  studies on PME performance
  unicorn valuation
  venture performance during the eighties

Kauffman Foundation, 285
Kellogg's
Key man provisions (partnership
    terms), 306
Keynes, John M., 120
Khosla Ventures, 421, 482
Khosla, Vinod, 122
Kilby, Jack, 89
King Charles I of Spain, 12
King Ferdinand and Queen Isabella
    of Spain, 11
King, Mervin, 357
Kincaid Furniture Co. Forstmann,
    Little, and Company
    acquisition, 140
Kingsbury Commitment (1913), 52
KKR Private Equity Investors (KPE),
    listing, 282
Kleiner, Eugene, 88, 88f, 100–101,
    113, 120
Kleiner Perkins Caufield & Byers, 113,
    286t, 287, 502
Knowledge doubling curve
    (Fuller), 603f
Kohlberg, Jr., Jerome, 137–138, 138f
Kohlberg Kravis Roberts & Co. (KKR),
    138, 175–180, 187, 248,
    277, 389
  Beatrice Foods, 167, 177
  early years, 129
  Esmark takeover, 167
  establishment of institutional funds
  European office
  Henry Kravis, 138
  Hong Kong Office
  Houdaille Industries, 139
  impact fund
  IPO
  number of employees
  Oregon PERS, 176
  RJR Nabisco, 178–180, 187
  TXU, 179 528
Korea Investment Corporation, 263
Korean 2004 Law on Private Equity
    Capital Gains Tax and Fund
    Formation, 303

Kotak Real Estate
Kou, Jan, 466
Kramlich, Dick, 113
Kräussl, R., study on performance
    of IS, 585
Kravis, Henry, 138, 138f, 178, 179f
Kyoto Protocol (1997), 592

L

L Chatteron (LVMH), 68
Laffont, Philippe, 404
Landmark Partners (secondaries FoFs
    manager), 209
Laptop computers, 99, 126
Large funds, median IRR, 558f
Large language model (LLM)
    services, 491
Largest US companies in 1929, 57
LaSalle, 258, 562
Last, Jay, 88, 89f, 100
Late-cycle IPO boom, 473–477
Later-stage growth financing, 294
Late-stage super-rounds, DoorDash
    example, 477–481
Late-stage venture, investor
    ranking, 511f
LBO France, 302
Lee, Thomas H. (buyout firm), 140
Lehman Brothers bankruptcy/
    investigation, 359, 364f
Lenders, activities (reduction), 383
Lerner, J., 115
  long-term returns of different VC
    sectors, 106
  market risk of PE, 472
  stock price effects and carried
    interest, 1185
Leverage, 509
  assumption, 228
  growth/usage, 308, 432
  private debt, 556–560
Leveraged buyouts (LBOs), 137–142,
    164–180, 183, 534, 542
  firms, self-branding, 249–250
  industry trends, 182
  momentum (Europe), 189–190

United Kingdom LBOs, Pan-
  European approach, 253–255
Leveraged loans, 534f, 537t, 459f
Leveraged transactions, capital
  structure (factors), 539–543
Leverage, impact, 23–25
Levin, Gerald, 233f
Levitt, Theodore, 133
Lexington Partners, 444
LGT Capital (FoFs manager), 208
LIBOR, 535
Limited liability
  Delaware, 147
  impact, 31–33
  New York State, 33
  Trust companies, 32–33
Limited partners (LPs), 231–232
  competition, 384–388
  ESG policies/disclosure demand,
    increase, 529–530
  investing, trend, 40
  mega IPOs, 476f
  passive investor status, 143
  questions/answers, 483–485
  shareholder role, 149–150
Limited Partnership Agreement
  (LPA), 150b, 449
Limited partnerships, 143–149
  cash flows, 151b, 152f
  characteristics, 149b–152b
  features, 150b–151b
  fee structure, 153b–155b
  IRR, 152b
  law firms/placement agents,
    usage, 199t
  overview, 148f
  performance measurement, 151b
  waterfall, 154b–155b
Limited Partnerships Act (1907), 33
Lin, Shirley, 494
Liquidity preference, 418, 482, 483
Listed private equity (LPE), 210–213,
  459–465
  annualized returns, 464t
  global LPE, market capitalization,
    460f

investment companies, share price/
  NAV performance, 465t
manager IPO, 275–284
Litinsky, James, 134
Litton Industries, 84
Liverpool and Manchester Railroad, 36
Loan-to-value ratio (LTV),
  reduction, 570
Local stock exchanges, company
  listings, 212
Lockheed, 60
Lock-up (limited partnership
  terms), 150
London and South Western
  Railroad, 36
London City Airport, 338b–341b, 340f
London Heathrow (LHR), revenue per
  passenger (GBP), 340f
Long, Austin M., 444
Lone Star Opportunity Fund, funds
  (raising), 257
Long-term capital, need, 114
Long-Term Credit Bank, 303
Long-term liabilities, funding, 330
Lotus Development, IPO, 160
LSI Logitech, IPO, 162
Lucent Technologies, 252
LPX Composite index, 212f,
  459–460
Luton (LTN), revenue per passenger
  (GBP), 340f
Lycos, 211
Lyft, 293

M
Ma, Pony, 493
Ma, Jack, 494
Maastricht Treaty, 253
MAC clauses, 454
Mackay, Charles, 24
Macquarie (infrastructure firm), 303,
  330, 454
  Chicago Skyway acquisition, 326
  National Grid Wireless transaction,
    326
Made in China 2025, 499, 503

Magellan, Ferdinand, 11–13, 12f
Magnetic Telegraph Co.,
    establishment, 39
Mainframe computer
    industry - 1960s, 93
Maintenance budget, French
    demand, 335
Management
    agency problems, 188
    companies (private equity firm
        type), 211
    fees, 153b, 306
    teams, investments, 385
Management buy-in (MBI), 137
Management buyout (MBO),
    137, 171, 269
Management by walking around
    (MBWA), 102
Managerial capitalism, 165–169
Managers (private equity firms)
    concentration, 574
    IPO, 275–284
    IS managers, total capital
        ranking, 576t
    selection/diversification,
        importance, 353
MAN Group, 442
Manhattan Project, 85
Marconi Wireless Telegraph Company,
    GE acquisition, 52
Margins of FoFs managers,
    decline, 441–442
Maritime ventures, funding, 13–15
Martin Lake Power Plant (Tatum,
    Texas), 369f
Markowitz, Harry, 316
Marsh & McLennan Companies, 443
Matam High-Tech Park (Haifa,
    Israel), 108f
Material-adverse-change (MAC)
    clauses, usage, 454
Matrix Partners, 74, 160, 503
Maybach, Wilhelm, 43
Mayfield Partners, 113
McClure, Dave, 292
Mayo, Elton, 132

McDonnell Aircraft Corporation,
    founding, 62
McDonnell, James, 62
MCI, 302
McKinsey & Company, 223, 443
Medline Industries, 522
Median duration, determination, 273
Median IRRs, 162, 255, 270f, 557f,
    569f, 583
Mega buyouts (2003–2007),
    297–299
Mega-deals, 522
Mega-firms
    dominance, 382–384
    investments, 300–301
    private real estate role, 564–565
Mega IPOs, 476f
Meituan, IPO, 498, 500
MENA region, 576
Menlo Ventures, 160
Mercapital, 302
Merchant banking, revival, 378–382
Mergers and acquisitions (M&A), 36,
    58, 268–269, 437, 475, 507
    boom, 54, 169–171
    impact, 51–53, 62–63, 536, 538
    regulatory backlash, 54–55
    transactions, 131, 442, 468, 533
Meta, 392, 395
Metcalfe, Robert, 219
Mezzanine financing, 538, 543, 566
Michigan State Employees Retirement
    System, 176
Microchip, 90f
Micrologic ICs, usage, 99
Microsoft, 240
    acquisitions, 294
    first product, 93
    IBM contract, 95
    IPO, 120
    OpenAI investment, 392
    Windows 1.0, 127
    using Yahoo!'s search engine, 215
Middle East and North Africa (MENA),
    infrastructure investment, 576
Mid Europe Partners (buyout firm), 302

Mid-market acquisition finance, 551
Midstream infrastructure, 347
Milken, Michael, 172–175, 173f, 186, 536
Millner, Yuri, 512
Mineral and Battery Work company, 21
Mines Royal company, 21
Minicomputers, 123
Minuteman missile, 89, 96
Mississippi bubble, 23–25, 29
MIT, 80
Mobile phones, underestimations, 224f
Mobility, drivers, 105
Money-weighted return, 152f
Montana Capital Partners (secondaries FoFs manager), 445
Moonfare, 444
Moonshot, Japan, 83
Moore, Gordon, 82, 88, 89, 92b
Moore's Law, 82, 89, 92b, 93f, 101
Morgan, J.P., 49–52, 54f, 378
Morgan Stanley, 142
Moritz, Michael, 407
Morningstar, 198, 459
Morse, Samuel, 39
Mortgage-backed securities, 308, 308f, 358
Mortgage lending, growth (factors), 308
Mosaic, release, 214
MOSFET transistor, 90f
Motorola 8000X (Brick), introduction, 223
MS-DOS, usage, 127
Mubadala Development Company, 263
Multi-billion-dollar funds, performance (maintenance), 474
Multi-stage funds, early-stage focus (maintenance), 483
Multi-strategy firms, incentives (requirements), 276–277
Müntefering, Franz, 527
Muscovy Company, founding, 17
Musk, Elon, 392f, 394

Mutual funds
    ROI/cash flow profile, 151, 152f
Mytheresa, 553b–554b, 553f

N

Nao Victoria (illustration), 605f
Napoleon III, 38
NASA, 80
    Apollo mission, 82
    Fairchild Semiconductors, 75
    moon landing, 82
NASDAQ, 245
    China tech shares, 501
    companies, dominance, 395
    Composite Index (1995–2005), 217, 218f
    crash/changes, 284–286
    ESG plans, 527
    performance, 225, 238
    founding, 246
    post-2000 listing rules, 239
    tech sub-indices/performance/ capitalization, 396f
    unicorn IPOs, 409
National Aeronautics and Space Administration (NASA), 80–83, 82f, 95–100
National Broadcasting Company (NBC), co-founding, 52
Natural Resources Defense Council (NRDC), 528
National Venture Capital Association (NVCA), 422
Natural resources (NR), 341–347, 342f, 591
    capital (raising), vintage years, 342f
    fund managers, capital ranking, 344t
    infrastructure, relationship, 573–594
    Shale gas, 342, 344–347
    US pipeline network, 342. 346, 347
NatWest Equity Partners, 268
Navis Capital (buyout/growth firm), 304
Neiman Marcus, 553f
Neoliberalism, 78

Net asset value (NAV), 146, 269–272, 366–367, 448t
  operational cost, 448f
  performance, 464, 465t
  reporting/entry, 447
Net Debt/EBITDA, leverage limit, 334
Netflix, 392, 395
Net internal rate of return (net IRR), 352f, 570f, 583
Net present value, 151
Netscape, impact, 215, 287, 394
Neuberger Berman, 279
Neuer Markt, 216
Neumann, A., 412
Neuralink, 392
"New economy" invincibility, 219–220
New Enterprise Associates (NEA), 113
New World, trade, 23
New Venture Challenge, 86
New York State Common Retirement Fund, 196
New York Stock Exchange (NYSE), 29, 30f
  bank partnerships' liability, 25
  blank check companies, 420
  Buttonwood Agreement, 29
  capitalization, comparison, 412
  floor, panic, 363f
  Roaring Twenties, 57
  unicorn IPOs, 411
Nine Years' War, 21
Nixon, Richard, 130
Non-military defense R&D model (WWII), 79–80
Non-traditional asset classes, identification/addition, 373
Non-traditional investors, 294–296, 402–409
Nordic Capital (buyout firm), 253
Northern Pacific railroad, financing, 50
Northern Rock, 357, 358f
Nossa Senhora (slaving vessel), cargo (possession), 16
Nouveau Marché, 217

Noyce, Robert, 88, 89f, 101–102
NPS - National Pension Service of Korea, 264

O

Occupational pension schemes, 66
Office of Naval Research (ONR), 83
Off-balance-sheet entities, rise, 308
Office of Scientific Research and Development (OSRD), 79, 81
Offshore fundraising (venture capital), 499f
Ohio Bureau of Workers Compensation, 269
Ohio State Pension Fund (OPERS), 528
Oil embargo/price increases, 72, 114
Oil prices (1970s), 130
Oliver Wyman, 443
OMERS, the Ontario Teachers, 328
OneWeb, 404
Online advertising, competitors, 399f
Ontario Municipal Employees Retirement System (OMERS), 328
Ontario Teachers, 328, 335, 339
OpenAI, 392
Open-ended funds/investment vehicles, 65, 563, 588–591
Operating system (OS), 91b–92b
Operational improvements, 524–526
Opportunistic funds, value-creation playbook, 569
Opportunistic real estate, 324
Oracle, 108, 127, 128
OrbiMed Advisors (venture capital firm), 160
Oregon PERS, 176
Organizational complexity, VC handling, 484
Orion (private markets firm), 258
Orkin Exterminating Company, 137
Orlando, 302
Outcomes, dispersal of fund returns, 273
Outsiders, The (Thorndike), 166

Overfunding, We Company example, 413f
Overinvestment, 161, 235
  China, 377
  herding and over investment, 163
  Just Eat Takeaway, 481
  railroads, 29
Ownership, temporariness, 141
  agency problems, 486

P

Pacific Corporate Group (PCG), founding, 196
Packard, David, 67
Pagliari, J. A., 323
PAI Partners (buyout firm), 302
Paid-in capital, 144, 153
Palantir Technologies, 293
Panic of 1825, 32
Panic of 1893, 38
Panic of 1907, 55
Pantheon Ventures (FoFs manager), 207–208
Paradyne, TPG acquisition, 252
Pareto distributions, 273, 351–352
Paris Agreement (2016), 592
Partners Group (private markets firm), 212–213, 280, 382, 442, 460, 461t
Partnerships
  limited life, 141
  terms/conditions, trends, 306
Partners (managerial roles), incentives (GP organizational challenge), 276
Patria Investimentos (private markets firm), 305
Patricof & Co. (private markets firm), 74, 113, 164
Paulson, Hank, 359
Pavilion Financial Corporation, 443
Payback time, impact, 270
Payment in kind (PIK), 534, 566
PayPal, 241, 242, 291, 292, 392, 400
PDP-9 minicomputer, 123f
Pearl Harbor, Japan attack, 79

Peltz, Nelson, 168, 174
Pension Consulting Alliance, Partners Group acquisition, 442
People/ideas, drivers, 105
Performance, 140, 150b, 396f, 556–559
Perkins, Tom, 112f, 113, 119, 120
Permanent capital, increase, 384–388
Permira (buyout firm), founding, 185
Personal computers (PCs), 124–129, 224f
Petersen, Peter G., 282f
Philadelphia & Reading Railroad, reorganization, 50
Philco Ford, 96
Philip Morris, tobacco price wars, 180
Pickens, T. Boone, 174, 175f
Piketty, Thomas, 17
Pioneering Portfolio Management (Swensen), 204
Pioneer Petroleum, 174
Pitango, 109
PitchBook, 116
Placement agents, 198
Poison pills, usage, 185
Polsky Center at the University of Chicago, 86
Popular Electronics (cover), 124f
Portfolio Advisors (FoFs manager), FS Investments (merger), 442
Posner, Victor, 137
Post-dotcom era VC, 284–296
Power laws, 351–352, 351f
Preemption right, 328
Preferred return (fee/incentive structure feature), 153b
Preferred stock/shares, 34
  voting rights, 34
  convertibility into common stock, 130
  reduced voting rights, 493
  liquidation preference, 512
Preqin, 145
Pre-WWII private/public equity, 55–61
Price-earnings ratio, 53
Priceline (social networking site), 216
Primary commitments, 204

Principles of Responsible Investing
(PRI), UN launch, 529, 586
Private capital, sugar boom
(relationship), 15–18
Private debt (PD), 518, 537t,
546f, 551–560
asset class, 543–545
AuM (2010/2021), 548f
funds, 545, 559
GFC as a catalyst, 532
loss rates, attractiveness, 550f
managers, aggregate capital
(raising), 547t
post-GFC boom, 517
private equity deals (capital structure), relationship, 558t
returns, basis, 556f
US private debt issuance, 534f
Private enterprise, funding, 11
Private equity (PE), 55–61, 159,
297, 518f
actual/target allocations, 375f
deal volume, increase, 469
Europe, private equity investment
(deal value basis), 254f
fund, 144f, 272f
fundraisers/fundraising, 265f, 267f,
437f, 520t
institutional investors, ranking, 387t
investments, 266, 453
secondaries fundraising, 455f
strategies, public market performance (contrast), 367f
structure, private debt (relationship), 558t
US private equity (1960s–1970s), 111
value-added US private equity real
estate funds, 570f
Private investment in public equity
(PIPE), 424
Private investors, distribution,
433, 445–447
Private market funds
development, 598
distribution, allocation, 153f
tax implications, 434

time-and-money-weighted
performance, 145
semi-liquid funds
Private markets
alternative assets under
management, 2f
asset classes, 342f, 595t
AuM, 377f
boom, 261, 370–375
brands, GFC benefits, 383
data, lessons, 347–351
diversity, increase, 594
ecosystem, 195f
evolution, timeline, 3f
firms, 280–284, 461t, 529–530
global private markets, 376f
intermediaries, function, 193–197
investing/investments, 147, 264,
428f, 527–532
legal/regulatory matters, 433
managers, ranking, 384t
mega-firms, investments, 300–301
overview, 145–146
resources, requirements, 354
strategies, public market performance (contrast), 367f
sub-asset class performance, 596f
surge in AuM, 276
terms ("Swiss Army Knife"), 145f
valuations, GFC impact, 366–368
Private real estate, 190–192, 256–259
evolution after 2000, 304–325
funds, 310f, 312f, 323–325, 563f, 564t
global private real estate fundraising, 564f
mega-firms, role, 564
performance (IRR), vintage years
(1994–2010), 324f
US private real estate, S&L crisis
(impact), 256–258
Private wealth, 431–434
Procter & Gamble, 168
Profits, sharing (Noyce
recollection), 102
Property increase of fundamentals
after 2010, 561

Property valuations, increase until 2007, 320

Prudential Property Investment Separate Account (PRISA), 190–192

Prudent man rule, 114–115, 170

Public equity (pre-WWII), 55–61

Public equity, issuance, 68–71

Public market performance, 367f

Public markets, 44–49, 422f

Public pension funds (PPFs), 176, 427–428

Public-to-private transactions, 309–314, 521–522

Putnam III, George, 74

Q

Qatar Investment Authority, 263

Qiming Ventures, 495

Quadrant, 303

Qualcomm (social networking site), 216

Quant family (BMW), 68

Quantum Fund (Soros), 173–174

Quarterly US venture capital investments, 226f

Quasi-monopoly rents, 399

Queensland Investment Corporation (QIC), 588

R

Rabois, Keith, 292

Radio Corporation of America (RCA), 52, 59

Rad Lab, 85–86

Railroads, 36–38, 47–53

Railroad Mania (1846–1848), 36

Ramadan, Al, 401

Rathenau, Emil, 41

Raytheon, 72

RCA, 46

Reagan, Ronald, 165, 170

Real Asset Portfolio Management, Hamilton Lane acquisition, 442

Real assets, post-GFC boom, 517

Real estate, 561–570
  during the 1980s, 139
  during the 1990s, 191
  European banks' disposals, 396
  funds, median IRR, 569f
  German municipal housing privatisations, 241
  market, 322–323, 562
  public-to-private, 236, 309–314
  S&L crisis, 191

Real estate investment trusts (REITs), 310–311, 320, 383, 562

Real GDP growth, 371f

Recession, impact (1970s), 130

Rede Partners, (AU: Not found)

Reform, Recovery, and Enforcement Act of 1989 (FIRREA), 256

Regulated/contracted environment, assets operation, 584

Renewable energy, 327

Renewables financing, increase, 573–574

Renminbi (RMB) funds/fundraising, 496, 499f, 510

REPowerEU, 587

Research and development (R&D), rise of corporate R&D, 43–44, 64

Research breakthroughs, importance, 102

Research infrastructure, 105

Resolution Trust Corporation, 256–257

Resource allocation (GP organizational challenge), 278

Retailers, IPOs, 53

Return on investment (ROI), 143–144, 144t, 151

Revenue growth, overestimation, 231

Rhine capitalism, 35

Riedel, Gary, 495

Rimer, Neil/David, 244

Ripplewood Holdings, 303

Rise Impact Fund, 532

Risk-adjusted returns, 557f, 583

Risk capital (Second Industrial Revolution), 34

Risk (STD), comparison, 464t
Riverstone Holdings (real assets manager), 347
Risk, control, 202b–204b
RJR Nabisco ("Winner's Curse, The"), 178–180, 187
Robert, Joe, 257
Roberts, George R., 137, 178, 179f
Roberts, Sheldon, 88, 88f, 138f
Rock, Arthur, 74–75, 100, 111–112, 112f
Rockefeller, John D., 51
Rockefeller, Laurance (Eastern Airlines), 62
Rollover equity, 540
Roosevelt, Franklin D., 79
Routers, 222
Route 128 in Boston, 102
Royal Dutch Shell, 269
Rubenstein, David M., 184f
Russian R7 rocket, usage, 81f

S

Sacca, Chris, 292
Saint-Domingue, sugar plantations, 15
Salesforce, 108
Salomon Brothers, 175
Sand Hill Road, 256, 408
São Tomé, sugar plantations, 15
Sales Revision Act, impact, 169
Sarbanes-Oxley Act (SOX), 245, 286, 296
Satellites, tangible asset (development), 222
Saul Steinberg, 168
Savings & Loan (S&L) crisis, impact, 191, 256, 312, 321, 561
Scale-up (FoF manager strategic option), 441
Scholes, Myron S., 170
Schroders Plc, 445
Schwab, Klaus, 527
Schwarzman, Stephen A., 184f, 282f, 378, 461
Scientific Data Systems, 75

SCM Strategic Capital Management, Marsh & McLennan acquisition, 443
Sea loan, 14
Sears, 41
SEC, 64, 282, 360
    PE disclosure rules, 445
    Office of the Investor Advocate, 308
Secondaries FoFs, 209–210, 210f, 266–275, 267f, 270f, 458
Secondary buyout transactions, 299–300
Secondary fundraising/funds, 455f, 454–455
Secondary markets, 453–458
Secondary purchase, benefits, 271
Secondary transactions, 270–275, 453f
Second Industrial Revolution (Technological Revolution), risk capital, 34
Second-lien debt, issuance, 535
Secured Overnight Financing Rate (SOFR), 535
Securities and Exchange Commission (SEC), creation, 64
Selden, G. B., patent, 42
Semiconductor producers, spinoffs, 104t
Semi-liquid funds, private wealth (access), 431–434
Separate managed accounts (SMAs), segregated accounts, 438, 547–548
Sequoia Capital (venture capital firm), 113–117, 287, 405–409, 408f, 467, 476, 486, 502
Service providers, 197–198, 199t
Shale gas, 345b–347b, 345f
Shanghai Stock Exchange, 493
Shareholder value, 165–169
Shearson Lehman Hutton, 179Shell Technology Ventures, 269
Shen, Neil, Sequoia, 495
Shenzhen Stock Exchange, 493
Sherman Antitrust Act (1890), 54
Shiller, Robert, 322

Shockley Semiconductor Labs, 87, 111

Shockley, William, 41f, 87–89, 103

SICAV/SICAF, investments, 433

Siekmann, Tan, 217

Siemens & Halske, 40Siemens
     Brothers, UK, 40

Siemens, Werner von, 40, 62

Silicon Valley
   industrial cluster, 102–109
   origin/formation, 77, 160
   Shockley, move, 87–88
   technology cluster, drivers
     (overview), 78f

Silicon Wadi, 83

Silver Lake Partners (venture capital
     firm), 279

Silverstein, Larry, 191

Simon, William E., 171–172

Singleton, Henry, 111–226

Skoll, Jeff, 531

Skype, founding, 86

Slave plantation complex, 15

Sloane, Alfred P., 132

Small Business Investment Act (SBDA),
     passage, 71–72

Small Business Investment
     Corporations (SBICs), 71–73,
     127, 210, 493

Snap, 498

Snapple Beverages, Thomas H. Lee
     Partners acquisition, 251

SoftBank, 220, 295, 387, 403–406, 409,
     412, 474, 475, 494, 502, 511
   1990s investments, 295
   2000s investments, 295
   Vision Fund, 403, 404
   Yahoo! investment, 215

Software as a Service (SaaS)
     model, 491

Software, impact, 90b–91b

Solar One, 344

Solid Logic Technology (SLT), 94

Solvency II, 365

Sommer, Ron, 224f

Son, Masayoshi, 220, 404f, 483, 502

Soros Real Estate Investors, 258

Soros, George, 300

South America, funds, 3041

South Sea Bubbles, 23–25, 29

South Sea Company, monopoly, 24

South Sea scheme, emblematical
     print, 25f

Sovereign wealth funds (SWFs),
     176, 263–264, 385–388, 403,
     417–418, 601
   influence, increase, 427

Space Shuttle, 82

SpaceX, 392, 410
   government subsidies, 79

S&P 500
   comparison, 464t
   infrastructure index, 583
   listed private equity index, 339
   tech sub-indices/performance/
     capitalization, 396f

Special purpose acquisition
     companies (SPACs), 7, 419–422,
     422f, 430, 477
   DoorDash merger, 477
   mergers, 596
   number/life cycle, 420f, 423f
   US-tech focused SPACs, underwrit-
     ers (league table), 426f

Special purpose vehicle (SPV),
     creation, 269

Spinouts, impact, 87–100

S&P listed private equity index,
     concentration, 463f

Sputnik, impact, 80–83, 81f

Standard Oil, founding, 51

Stanford Industrial Park, 84, 108

Staples Corp., 119

Startups, 513
   1980s/2000s, 163f, 295f
   business model robustness,
     examples, 241f
   financing, 68–71, 127–129

Starwood Capital, 256

State Administration of Foreign
     Exchange (SAFE), 502

State Planning Commission (SPC),
     China, 493

State of Victoria, 327
Steel, trust boom, 49–53
Steinberg, Saul, 168
Stein, Jeremy, 182
Steinhardt Partners, 173
Stock markets
    crash (1929/1974), 60–65,
        130–131
    GFC recovery, 395–398
    indicators, 131t, 165t
    organization, 29–34
Stone, Hayden, 111
Stonepeak Infrastructure
        Partners, 589
Stop Wall Street Looting Act, 527
Storer Communications, hostile
        takeover, 175
Stucke, Rudiger, 348
    fair valuation, 590
    performance of PE, 454
    persistence of venture capital per-
        formance, 169
Stuyvesant Town, 316b–317b
Subprime loan purchases,
        expansion, 308
Subsidies, availability for renewable
        energy, 584
Successor fund, launch, 353–348
Sugar boom, private capital
        (relationship), 15–18
Summit Partners (venture/growth
        capital firm), 514
Sun Microsystems, 162
Supermajority voting
        requirements, 185
Super-Return conferences, 305, 305f
Super-Round (super-round),
        220–221, 415
Super senior loan (super-senior
        loan), 555
Sustainability Accounting Standards
        Board (SASB), 530
Sustainable Finance Disclosure
        Regulation (SFDR), 530
Sutter Hill Ventures, 74
Swensen, David, 200, 200f

Swiss Re
    Pearl Holding guarantee, 213
    Swiss Re Private Equity Partners, 323

T
TA Associates (venture capital
        firm), 514
Tail-end secondary, discount, 272f
Tailored listing standards, 420
Takeovers, 172b–174b, 181–190
Taleb, Nassim, 372
Tandy-Radio Shack TRS-80, 126f
Tangible assets, development, 222
Tan, Lip-Bu, 494
Target, Inc., 291
Tax shield, 539
Tax loss carry-forward and capital
        structure, 542
Tax overhaul (M&A 1980
        boom), 169–173
Tax Reform Act (TRA), passage,
        170–171, 190
Tax transparency (limited partnership
        feature), 150b
Tchénio, Maurice, 113
Tech IPO bubble, early example,
        20–23
Technology
    boom, 391–409, 465–476, 510–515
    clusters, drivers, 105–106
    cost curve, 98f
    IPOs, valuations/momentum, 466f
    risk, 116
    sector weight in VC financing
        (China), 497f
    tech-focused growth financing area,
        participants, 513–515
    underestimations, 224f
Telecom
    boom, 221–225
    bust, 233–242, 245–247
    fraud, 237–239
    sector, problems/leverage, 234–236
Teledyne, formation, 100
Telegraphen-Bauanstalt von Siemens
        & Halske, founding, 40

Telephone/cable TV networks (upgrade), tangible asset (development), 222

Temasek, 303, 386

Tencent, IPO, 495

Terman, Frederick, 80, 84–87, 85f, 108, 604

Tesla, government subsidies, 79

Textile industry, opportunities, 26

The Boring Company, 392

The Employee Retirement Income Security Act of 1974 (ERISA), 85

The European Green Deal, 577

The Internal Revenue Act of 1921, 51

The Investment Company Act of 1940, 51

The National Aeronautics and Space Administration. See NASA

The Sierra Club, 528

TheGlobe (social networking site), 215

Thiel, Peter, 290–290, 291f

Thomas H. Lee Partners, 140

Thomson-Houston Electric Company, 46, 52

Thyratron vacuum tube, 90f

Thyssen Krupp Immobilien, 319

Ticker tape machine, 22

"Tidal Wave Memo" (Gates), 214, 214f

Tiered fee structures, 590

Tiger Global Management, 511, 514

Time Warner, AOL merger, 172

Time-weighted return, 152f

Tishman Speyer, 191, 321

T-Mobile USA, 239

Toll road privatizations, outcomes, 332b–335b

Total gain, company contributions, 350f

Total liabilities/assets, US corporate balance sheets, 186f

Total private markets, FoF capital (percentage), 208f

Total value to paid-in (TVPI), 146, 227, 274–275

TPG, 252, 368, 369, 515
Continental Airlines, 252
impact fund, 532
IPO, 337
TPG Growth, 515
WaMu, 368

Transatlantic telegraph, 29

Transistors, 90b

Treynor, Jack L., 470

Triangular trade, 15

Triangle Industries, takeover, 174

Trust boom, 49–53

Trust Companies (quasi holdings), 32–33

Trustbridge, 496

Tsai, Andy, 196

Tung, Hans, 494

Twitter, 292

TXU, 179, 297

Tykvová, T., 673

U

Uber IPO, 414, 473

UBS AG, 268

UK Companies Act of 1862, 32

UK Limited Partnerships Act of 1907, 25

UK pension funds, 264

Undervalued properties, acquisition ability, 320

Unemployment, impact (1970s), 130

Unfunded capital (private market term), 146

Unicorns, 409–419, 410b–411b, 410f

Uniform Limited Partnership Act (1916), 33

Union Pacific Railroad, 51

United Kingdom
LBOs, Pan-European approach, 253–255
railroad mania, 36–38

United States Patent and Trademark Office (USPTO), founding, 39

United States, railroad mania, 36–38

United States v. IBM, 126–127

University of Chicago Booth Graduate
    School of Business, 66
Unix operating systems, 162
Unlisted IS fundraising (2000–2010),
    329f
US toll road auction terms,
    comparison, 330f
US buyout funds, 181f, 255f
US corporate leverage,
    development, 186f
US economy, 56–57, 130–131, 164–165
US Economic Recovery Tax Act of
    1981 (ERTA), 162
US-focused PE FoFs, 439f
US gas pipelines/price chart,
    map, 346f
US high yield bond, 534f
US House Financial Services
    Committee (screenshot), 364f
US leveraged loan, 548
US private debt, 534f, 544f
US private equity (1960s–1970s), 111
US private real estate, S&L crisis
    (impact), 256–258
US real estate, capital
    deployment, 561
US SPACs, number, 420f
U.S. Steel, creation, 51
US Tax Cuts and Jobs Act (TCJA),
    passage, 541
US-tech focused SPACs, underwriters
    (league table), 426t
US Telecommunications Act
    (1996), 222
US toll roads, buyers' assumptions/
    winning bids, 334f
US venture capital (US VC), 230–233,
    231f, 248
  exits, 465f
  one-year rolling IRRs, 471f
Utilities, capital raising (limitations), 49

V
Vacancy trends, 561
Vacuum tube, replacement, 123
Valentine, Don, 112f, 113, 120

Value-added US private equity real
    estate funds, top quartile/
    median/bottom quartile
    net IRR, 566f
Value-add funds (value-added
    funds), 310, 569
Value creation, 40, 122, 141, 142, 152,
    171, 176, 177, 250, 252, 259,
    300, 312, 320, 324, 522,
    525, 540
Vanguard, 444
Venrock, 62
Venture-backed public market
    exits, 422f
Venture capital (VC), 111–129,
    159–164, 225, 435
  active venture capital firms, number
    (increase), 227
  backing, IPO median age/
    fraction, 473t
  bubble, impact, 415–418
  China, 492–504
  cleantech, 510
  co-investments, relative perfor-
    mance, 452f
  deals, characteristics, 230f, 470f
  deal-by-deal carried interest, 248
  Europe, venture capital, 229–230
  firms, formation, 160
  focus on tech and biotech, 88, 92
  foreign VCs, pressure, 502
  funding, 231f
  fund managers, examples, 353t
  funds, 228, 273, 294f, 471f, 476f
  founder-friendly terms, 290
  global fundraising, 471f
  "grandstanding", 161
  implementation, time
    (necessity), 241
  investment, 231f
  Israel, 107
  non-traditional investors, 295
  offshore/RMB fundraising
    (China), 499f
  partnerships, 73–75
  post-dotcom era VC, 284–296

quarterly US venture capital investments, 226f
secondaries, transaction volume/pricing, 268f
Silicon Valley, 84
startups, IPO successes, 476f
technology boom, 465–476
terms/conditions, telecom bust (impact), 247–248
top-performing managers, 457
VC-backed IPOs (1995–2000), 242f
VC/PE investment, 161t
vintage years, pooled net IRR, 476f
Venture Capital Fund of America (private equity firm), 209
Venture capitalists (VCs), 482–484
differences, 228–229
investment risks, 492f
Venture investing, 72–73
Venture performance, IPOs (impact), 227
Ventures, risk (increase),
Verizon Communications, price drop, 239
Vesting of founders shares (venture capital), 259
Vintage year (private market term), 145
Virality, 400
Vision Brazil, 322
Vision Fund, 403
Viterra, 319
VKontakte, 512
Volcker, Paul, 164
Volksaktie, promotion, 225
von Bismarck, Otto, 38
von Siemens, Werner, 40
Voting rights, 33–34

W

Waigel, Theo, 224f
Waite, Charles, 74
Wall Street, crowd (panic), 61f
Warburg Pincus Capital Corporation (buyout firm), 148, 254
Warren, Elizabeth, 527
Washington Mutual, 265, 271

Washington State Investment Board, 174
Waterfalls, GP-LP split of returns, 153b–154b
Water-powered textile mill, energy supply, 28f
Watt, James (Boulton partnership), 27
Wealth managers, feeder funds (purpose), 446f
We Company, overfunding example, 412f
Webvan, 220
Wedgwood, Josiah, 27
Weiser, Mark, 100
Weizhong, Wang, 501
Welsh, Carson, Anderson & Stowe, 140
Westbrook Fund I, funds (raising), 257
Western Electric Company, 52
Westinghouse Electric Company, 59, 59f
Westinghouse, George, 40, 45–46
WhatsApp, Facebook acquisition, 466–468
White knight, purchases, 167
Wietlisbach, Urs, 281f
Wine.com (Internet usage), 236b–237b
"Winner's Curse, The" (RJR Nabisco), 178
"Winner takes all" logic/dynamic, 219–220, 399
Wireless systems, tangible asset (development), 222
Wiseman, Mark, 576
Wolfson, Louis E., 166–167
Wolfson, Mark A., 170
World Economic Forum (WEF), 527
WorldCom, bankruptcy, 238
World Trade Organization (WTO), establishment, 193
World War II, 603
non-military defense R&D model, 79–80
pre-WWII private/public equity, 55–61
Wozniak, Steve, 125, 125f

X

Xu, Tony, 482

Y

Yahoo!, impact, 215
Yale University, model/assets,
    200b–204b, 202f, 322
Y Combinator (YC), 290, 293, 482
Yandex, 512
Young, Owen D., 52

YouTube, 295
Yuma, 490

Z

Zell, Sam, 191, 192f, 256, 314
Zero to One (Thiel), 290
Zocco, Giuseppe, 244
Zuckerberg, Mark, 67, 393f,
    392, 512–513
Zug, Brooks D., 206f
Zynga, 287